Dictionary of Literary Biography • Volume Twenty-nine

American Newspaper Journalists, 1926-1950

Dictionary of Literary Biography

 1: *The American Renaissance in New England*, edited by Joel Myerson (1978)
 2: *American Novelists Since World War II*, edited by Jeffrey Helterman and Richard Layman (1978)
 3: *Antebellum Writers in New York and the South*, edited by Joel Myerson (1979)
 4: *American Writers in Paris, 1920-1939*, edited by Karen Lane Rood (1980)
 5: *American Poets Since World War II*, 2 parts, edited by Donald J. Greiner (1980)
 6: *American Novelists Since World War II*, Second Series, edited by James E. Kibler, Jr. (1980)
 7: *Twentieth-Century American Dramatists*, 2 parts, edited by John MacNicholas (1981)
 8: *Twentieth-Century American Science-Fiction Writers*, 2 parts, edited by David Cowart and Thomas L. Wymer (1981)
 9: *American Novelists, 1910-1945*, 3 parts, edited by James J. Martine (1981)
10: *Modern British Dramatists, 1900-1945*, 2 parts, edited by Stanley Weintraub (1982)
11: *American Humorists, 1800-1950*, 2 parts, edited by Stanley Trachtenberg (1982)
12: *American Realists and Naturalists*, edited by Donald Pizer and Earl N. Harbert (1982)
13: *British Dramatists Since World War II*, 2 parts, edited by Stanley Weintraub (1982)
14: *British Novelists Since 1960*, 2 parts, edited by Jay L. Halio (1983)
15: *British Novelists, 1930-1959*, 2 parts, edited by Bernard Oldsey (1983)
16: *The Beats: Literary Bohemians in Postwar America*, 2 parts, edited by Ann Charters (1983)
17: *Twentieth-Century American Historians*, edited by Clyde N. Wilson (1983)
18: *Victorian Novelists After 1885*, edited by Ira B. Nadel and William E. Fredeman (1983)
19: *British Poets, 1880-1914*, edited by Donald E. Stanford (1983)
20: *British Poets, 1914-1945*, edited by Donald E. Stanford (1983)
21: *Victorian Novelists Before 1885*, edited by Ira B. Nadel and William E. Fredeman (1983)
22: *American Writers for Children, 1900-1960*, edited by John Cech (1983)
23: *American Newspaper Journalists, 1873-1900*, edited by Perry J. Ashley (1983)
24: *American Colonial Writers, 1606-1734*, edited by Emory Elliott (1984)
25: *American Newspaper Journalists, 1901-1925*, edited by Perry J. Ashley (1984)
26: *American Screenwriters*, edited by Robert E. Morsberger, Stephen O. Lesser, and Randall Clark (1984)
27: *Poets of Great Britain and Ireland, 1945-1960*, edited by Vincent B. Sherry, Jr. (1984)
28: *Twentieth-Century American-Jewish Fiction Writers*, edited by Daniel Walden (1984)
29: *American Newspaper Journalists, 1926-1950*, edited by Perry J. Ashley (1984)

Documentary Series:

 1: *Sherwood Anderson, Willa Cather, John Dos Passos, Theodore Dreiser, F. Scott Fitzgerald, Ernest Hemingway, Sinclair Lewis*, edited by Margaret A. Van Antwerp (1982)
 2: *James Gould Cozzens, James T. Farrell, William Faulkner, John O'Hara, John Steinbeck, Thomas Wolfe, Richard Wright*, edited by Margaret A. Van Antwerp (1982)
 3: *Saul Bellow, Jack Kerouac, Norman Mailer, Vladimir Nabokov, John Updike, Kurt Vonnegut*, edited by Mary Bruccoli (1983)
 4: *Tennessee Williams*, edited by Margaret A. Van Antwerp and Sally Johns (1984)

Yearbooks:

1980, edited by Karen L. Rood, Jean W. Ross, and Richard Ziegfeld (1981)
1981, edited by Karen L. Rood, Jean W. Ross, and Richard Ziegfeld (1982)
1982, edited by Richard Ziegfeld; associate editors: Jean W. Ross and Lynne C. Zeigler (1983)
1983, edited by Mary Bruccoli and Jean W. Ross; associate editor: Richard Ziegfeld (1984)

Dictionary of Literary Biography • Volume Twenty-nine

American Newspaper Journalists, 1926-1950

Edited by
Perry J. Ashley
University of South Carolina

A Bruccoli Clark Book
Gale Research Company • Book Tower • Detroit, Michigan 48226

Manufactured by Edwards Brothers, Inc.
Ann Arbor, Michigan
Printed in the United States of America

Copyright © 1984
GALE RESEARCH COMPANY

Library of Congress Cataloging in Publication Data
Main entry under title:

American newspaper journalists, 1926-1950.

    (Dictionary of literary biography; v. 29)
    "A Bruccoli Clark book."
    Includes index.
    1. Journalists—United States—Biography. I. Ashley,
Perry J. II. Series.
PN4871.A52 1984   070'.92'2[B]   84-8182
ISBN 0-8103-1707-9

for

Niel Plummer

Mentor and Friend

Contents

Plan of the Series

The advisory board, the editors, and the publisher of the *Dictionary of Literary Biography* are joined in endorsing Mark Twain's declaration. The literature of a nation provides an inexhaustible resource of permanent worth. It is our expectation that this endeavor will make literature and its creators better understood and more accessible to students and the literate public, while satisfying the standards of teachers and scholars.

To meet these requirements, *literary biography* has been construed in terms of the author's achievement. The most important thing about a writer is his writing. Accordingly, the entries in *DLB* are career biographies, tracing the development of the author's canon and the evolution of his reputation.

The publication plan for *DLB* resulted from two years of preparation. The project was proposed to Bruccoli Clark by Frederick G. Ruffner, president of the Gale Research Company, in November 1975. After specimen entries were prepared and typeset, an advisory board was formed to refine the entry format and develop the series rationale. In meetings held during 1976, the publisher, series editors, and advisory board approved the scheme for a comprehensive biographical dictionary of persons who contributed to North American literature. Editorial work on the first volume began in January 1977, and it was published in 1978.

In order to make *DLB* more than a reference tool and to compile volumes that individually have claim to status as literary history, it was decided to organize volumes by topic or period or genre. Each of these freestanding volumes provides a biographical-bibliographical guide and overview for a particular area of literature. We are convinced that this organization—as opposed to a single alphabet method—constitutes a valuable innovation in the presentation of reference material. The volume plan necessarily requires many decisions for the placement and treatment of authors who might properly be included in two or three volumes. In some instances a major figure will be included in separate volumes, but with different entries emphasizing the aspect of his career appropriate to each volume. Ernest Hemingway, for example, is represented in *American Writers in Paris, 1920-1939* by an entry focusing on his expatriate apprenticeship; he is also in *American Novelists, 1910-1945* with an entry surveying his entire career. Each volume includes a cumulative index of subject authors. The final *DLB* volume will be a comprehensive index to the entire series.

With volume ten in 1982 it was decided to enlarge the scope of *DLB* beyond the literature of the United States. By the end of 1983 twelve volumes treating British literature had been published, and volumes for Commonwealth and Modern European literature were in progress. The series has been further augmented by the *DLB Yearbooks* (since 1981) which update published entries and add new entries to keep the *DLB* current with contemporary activity. There have also been occasional *DLB Documentary Series* volumes which provide biographical and critical background source materials for figures whose work is judged to have particular interest for students. One of these companion volumes is entirely devoted to Tennessee Williams.

The purpose of *DLB* is not only to provide reliable information in a convenient format but also to place the figures in the larger perspective of literary history and to offer appraisals of their accomplishments by qualified scholars.

We define literature as the *intellectual commerce of a nation*: not merely as belles lettres, but as that ample and complex process by which ideas are generated, shaped, and transmitted. *DLB* entries are not limited to "creative writers" but extend to other figures who in this time and in this way influenced the mind of a people. Thus the series encompasses historians, journalists, publishers, and screenwriters. By this means readers of *DLB* may be aided to perceive literature not as cult scripture in the keeping of cultural high priests, but as at the center of a nation's life.

DLB includes the major writers appropriate to each volume and those standing in the ranks immediately behind them. Scholarly and critical counsel has been sought in deciding which minor figures to include and how full their entries should be.

Wherever possible, useful references will be made to figures who do not warrant separate entries.

Each *DLB* volume has a volume editor responsible for planning the volume, selecting the figures for inclusion, and assigning the entries. Volume editors are also responsible for preparing, where appropriate, appendices surveying the major periodicals and literary and intellectual movements for their volumes, as well as lists of further readings. Work on the series as a whole is coordinated at the Bruccoli Clark editorial center in Columbia, South Carolina, where the editorial staff is responsible for the accuracy of the published volumes.

One feature that distinguishes *DLB* is the illustration policy—its concern with the iconography of literature. Just as an author is influenced by his surroundings, so is the reader's understanding of the author enhanced by a knowledge of his environment. Therefore *DLB* volumes include not only drawings, paintings, and photographs of authors, often depicting them at various stages in their careers, but also illustrations of their families and places where they lived. Title pages are regularly reproduced in facsimile along with dust jackets for modern authors. The dust jackets are a special fea-

ture of *DLB* because they often document better than anything else the way in which an author's work was launched in its own time. Specimens of the writers' manuscripts are included when feasible.

A supplement to *DLB*—tentatively titled *A Guide, Chronology, and Glossary for American Literature*—will outline the history of literature in North America and trace the influences that shaped it. This volume will provide a framework for the study of American literature by means of chronological tables, literary affiliation charts, glossarial entries, and concise surveys of the major movements. It has been planned to stand on its own as a vade mecum, providing a ready-reference guide to the study of American literature as well as a companion to the *DLB* volumes for American literature.

Samuel Johnson rightly decreed that "The chief glory of every people arises from its authors." The purpose of the *Dictionary of Literary Biography* is to compile literary history in the surest way available to us—by accurate and comprehensive treatment of the lives and work of those who contributed to it.

The *DLB* Advisory Board

Foreword

Never in history have the channels of communication expanded as rapidly as they did during the second quarter of the twentieth century. Mass-circulation magazines, which had originated during the 1890s, more than doubled their circulation from 153 million copies in 1925 to 385 million in 1947, thereby bringing information, opinions, and entertainment into millions of new American homes. Radio, which went commercial in 1920 when KDKA in Pittsburgh broadcast its first regularly scheduled programs, had almost 3,000 stations on the air by 1950 and was being heard in 96 percent of American homes. In the early years radio was basically an entertainment medium, and regaled its audiences with such characters as Amos 'n Andy, Edgar Bergen and Charlie McCarthy, and Jack Benny. However, after Franklin D. Roosevelt won his first term in the White House in 1932 and began his broadcast "fireside chats," newspaper publishers realized that radio had become serious competition for news delivery. In 1933 they formed the Press-Radio Bureau in an effort to eliminate the competition: the wire services promised to provide radio stations with two five-minute news programs each day, provided that the new networks would refrain from gathering their own news; but, when H. V. Kaltenborn and Edward R. Murrow began broadcasting live war news from Europe in 1936, a new era of news competition began. Radio came of age as a news medium during World War II, when some stations devoted as much as 25 percent of their time to news. Television, still in an experimental state during most of this period, began broadcasting in 1939 when President Roosevelt cut the ribbon to open the New York World's Fair and thereby became the first American president to appear on television. The medium advanced from nine stations and 8,000 receivers in 1945 to ninety-seven stations and 6 million receivers by 1950; even so, in 1950 only 13 percent of American homes had television sets. Two years later, the Federal Communications Commission lifted the freeze on new stations and television boomed during the 1950s, as radio had during the 1920s, reaching 156 stations and 55 million sets by 1960.

Due both to competition from the new media and to economic hard times, the number of newspapers published, which had reached a peak of about 2,600 in 1915, declined to 1,760 by 1954, resulting in less than 10 percent of American cities having competing publishing companies. However, in spite of the reduction in numbers of newspapers, circulation rose from approximately 30 million daily in 1925 to more than 50 million in 1950. Chain ownership continued to increase during the second quarter of the century, from thirty-four groups with 158 newspapers and 31 percent of the total daily circulation in 1923 to ninety-five groups controlling 485 newspapers and 45 percent of the total circulation in 1954.

The decline in the number of newspapers being published and the acquisition of many of the remaining newspapers by chains led to several major criticisms of the press, including George Seldes's *Lords of the Press* (1938) and Harold Ickes's *American House of Lords* (1939). Journalism historians Edwin and Michael Emery point out that the "favorite target of the critics were those publishers dubbed 'the press lords'—notably William Randolph Hearst, Robert R. McCormick, and Roy Howard. Their prominence kept them at the center of an upsurge of criticism that affected newspapers generally, in a time when America was engaged in a searching reexamination of its social, political, and economical institutions." The Emerys note that criticism of the press had existed since the beginning of newspapers, but became "particularly pointed during the liberal resurgence of the 1930s known as the New Deal—but while much of the earlier criticism had dealt with the cultural and social values of the press, the emphasis in the 1930s was on its political power."

Noting the marked reduction in the number of units of the press relative to the total population, the Commission on Freedom of the Press, a group of thirteen scholars from various disciplines outside journalism, said in 1947: "Although in small communities we can still see a newspaper plant and product that resemble their Colonial prototype, these are no longer the most characteristic or the most influential agencies of communication. The right of free public expression has therefore lost its earlier reality . . . the owners and managers of the press determine which persons, which facts, which versions of the facts, and which ideas shall reach the public." The commission observed that the press had "been transformed into an enormous and complicated piece of machinery" and, by necessity, had "become big business." The commission concluded that if modern society "requires great agencies of mass communication" and "if these concentrations become so powerful that they are a threat to democracy," then these agencies must either "control themselves or be controlled by government." However, if they are controlled by government, "we lose our chief safeguard against totalitarianism—and at the same time take a long step toward it." In arguing against government control of the press, the commission suggested that the public must be more demanding of the press and that the remaining newspapers should be more diligent in presenting a balance of news so that all segments of society would still have a forum for the expression of opinions and ideas.

For the newspaper press of America, the greatest changes were in the expanded coverage of government, the beginning of interpretative reporting, and the invention of the political column. All of these developments were interrelated. Calder Pickett suggests "that never before had government seemed so important a force, for beginning with the stock market crash, news of government was a standard feature on the front pages of the land."

With the increased complexity of national and world affairs following the worldwide social and political crises of the 1930s, newspapers and news services began to turn to interpretative journalism. Editors grew concerned that giving the readers facts alone was insufficient and, consequently, they began to turn their efforts to giving the background information in order to place news reports in their proper context. In 1933, the American Society of Newspaper Editors noted that "the procession of national and international events, significant, complete and colorful, is moving more rapidly than at any other period in the recent history of the world" and that "men and women in every walk of life are taking a deeper interest in public affairs." The society adopted a resolution which encouraged editors to "devote a larger amount of attention and space to explanatory and interpretative news and to presenting a background of information which will enable the average reader more adequately to understand the movement and the significance of events."

The most important sign of journalism's adaptation to the growing complexity of the world was the invention of the syndicated political column. Signed columns had appeared as early as the 1890s but had tended to focus on humor, literature, or local color reporting; columns primarily devoted to appraising political and economic affairs did not appear until the 1920s with the work of David Lawrence, Mark Sullivan, and Frank Kent. By the late 1930s columnists such as Heywood Broun, Walter Lippmann, and Raymond Clapper were being syndicated in hundreds of newspapers. Noting this trend, the *New Republic* said in 1937 that much of the influence once "attached to the editorial page has passed to the columnists." In the political columns, at least, there seemed to be a return to the subjective journalism of the nineteenth century.

Even though the political "pundits" were the most prominent, other writers and columnists were also widely read and enjoyed. Red Smith and Grantland Rice were expounding on the great and the near great in sports, Walter Winchell was creating the show-business gossip column, and Marie Manning (Beatrice Fairfax) and Elizabeth Gilmer (Dorothy Dix) were setting the pattern for advice columnists who were to follow.

The coverage of World War II was probably American journalism's greatest achievement during these years. The *New York Times,* the *New York Herald Tribune,* the *Christian Science Monitor,* the *Chicago Tribune,* the *Chicago Daily News,* and the Scripps-Howard Newspaper Alliance are usually cited for their extensive coverage through the excellent work of correspondents such as Webb Miller, Edgar Ansel Mowrer, Paul Scott Mowrer, Anne O'Hare McCormick, and the GIs' friend, Ernie Pyle.

By the 1930s, the pattern of American newspaper journalism seems to have been established for the rest of the twentieth century. The extended use of political columnists and news analysis, the one-newspaper city, and the growth of group ownership have certainly continued into the last quarter of the century. However, concern over the "lack of community voices" may have subsided through the rapid expansion of radio, television, and magazines. The American people now have more information available to them than ever before—and probably feel overwhelmed by the deluge.

–Perry J. Ashley

Acknowledgments

This book was produced by BC Research. Karen L. Rood is senior editor for the *Dictionary of Literary Biography* series. Philip B. Dematteis was the in-house editor.

Art supervisor is Claudia Ericson. Copyediting supervisor is Joycelyn R. Smith. Typesetting supervisor is Laura Ingram. The production staff includes Mary Betts, Rowena Betts, Kimberly Casey, Patricia Coate, Mary Page Elliott, Lynn Felder, Kathleen M. Flanagan, Joyce Fowler, Patricia C. Sharpe, and Meredith Walker. Jean W. Ross is permissions editor. Joseph Caldwell, photography editor, did the photographic copy work for the volume.

Walter W. Ross did the library research with the assistance of the staff at the Thomas Cooper Library of the University of South Carolina: Lynn Barron, Daniel Boice, Sue Collins, Michael Freeman, Gary Geer, Alexander M. Gilchrist, Jens Holley, David Lincove, Marcia Martin, Roger Mortimer, Harriet B. Oglesbee, Jean Rhyne, Karen Rissling, Paula Swope, and Ellen Tillett.

Dictionary of Literary Biography • Volume Twenty-nine

American Newspaper Journalists, 1926-1950

Dictionary of Literary Biography

Willis J. Abbot

(16 March 1863-19 May 1934)

Stuart James Bullion
Southern Illinois University

MAJOR POSITIONS HELD: Managing editor, *Chicago Times* (1892-1893); editor in chief, *New York Journal* (1895-1898); editor/member of editorial board, *Christian Science Monitor* (1921-1934).

SELECTED BOOKS: *Blue Jackets of '61: A History of the Navy in the War of Secession* (New York: Dodd, Mead, 1886);

Blue Jackets of 1812: A History of the Naval Battles of the Second War with Great Britain (New York: Dodd, Mead, 1887);

Blue Jackets of '76: A History of the Naval Battles of the American Revolution (New York: Dodd, Mead, 1888);

Battle-fields of '61: A Narrative of the Military Operations of the War for the Union up to the End of the Peninsular Campaign (New York: Dodd, Mead, 1889);

Battle Fields and Camp Fires: A Narrative of the Principal Military Operations of the Civil War from the Removal of McClellan to the Accession of Grant (New York: Dodd, Mead, 1890);

Battle-fields and Victory: A Narrative of the Principal Military Operations of the Civil War, from the Accession of Grant to the Command of the Union Armies to the End of the War (New York: Dodd, Mead, 1891);

Midshipman Davy (Chicago: Searle & Gorton, 1891);

Carter Henry Harrison: A Memoir (New York: Dodd, Mead, 1895);

The Naval History of the United States (New York: Dodd, Mead, 1896);

Blue Jackets of '98: A History of the Spanish-American War (New York: Dodd, Mead, 1899);

Willis J. Abbot

The Battle of 1900; An Official Hand-Book for Every American Citizen, by Abbot, L. White Busbey, Oliver W. Stewart, and Howard S. Taylor (Chicago: Monarch, 1900);

American Merchant Ships and Sailors (New York: Dodd, Mead, 1902);

The Story of Our Navy for Young Americans, from Colonial Days to the Present Time (New York: Dodd, Mead, 1910);

Notable Women in History; also published as *Women of History* (Philadelphia: Winston, 1913);

Panama and the Canal in Picture and Prose (New York: Syndicate, 1913);

Panama and the Canal: The Story of Its Achievement, Its Problems and Its Prospects (New York: Dodd, Mead,. 1914);

The Story of Our Army for Young Americans, from Colonial Days to the Present Time (New York: Dodd, Mead, 1914);

The Nations at War: A Current History (New York & London: Syndicate, 1914);

Aircraft and Submarines: The Story of the Invention, Development, and Present-Day Uses of the War's Newest Weapons (New York & London: Putnam's, 1918);

Soldiers of the Sea: The Story of the United States Marine Corps (New York: Dodd, Mead, 1918);

The Story of Our Merchant Marine: Its Period of Glory, Its Prolonged Decadence and Its Vigorous Revival as the Result of the World War (New York: Dodd, Mead, 1919);

Pictorial History of the World War (New York: Leslie-Judge, 1919);

The United States in the Great War (New York: Leslie-Judge, 1919);

Blue Jackets of 1918 (New York: Dodd, Mead, 1921);

Philip Derby, Reporter (New York: Dodd, Mead, 1922);

Headlining Happiness (Boston: Christian Science Publishing Society, 1925);

Mussolini Tells Why He Prefers Fascism to Parliamentarism for Italy (New York: Italian Historical Society, 1928);

Watching the World Go By (Boston: Little, Brown, 1933).

OTHER: *The Press: Its Responsibility in International Relations, Discussed by Willis J. Abbot, Silas Bent and Moses Koenigsberg* (New York: Foreign Policy Association, 1928).

PERIODICAL PUBLICATIONS: "William Jennings Bryan: A Character Sketch," *Review of Reviews*, 14 (August 1896): 160-173;

"Academic Freedom," *Arena*, 22 (October 1899): 472-481;

"Harrison Dynasty in Chicago," *Munsey's*, 29 (September 1903): 809-815;

"Melville E. Stone's Own Story," *Collier's* (7 February 1920): 16, 51;

"Dragon's Teeth: The Press and International Misunderstandings," *Virginia Quarterly Review*, 4 (July 1928): 3-14;

"A.S.N.E. and Its Ethical Code," *New Republic*, 59 (22 May 1929): 15-16.

Willis J. Abbot recalled his half-century newspaper career in an autobiography entitled *Watching the World Go By* (1933), but his legacy amounts to far more than an impartial reminiscence of the passing scene. His life was one of total commitment—to journalism, to citizenship, and above all to the ethical principles that marked his deeds as well as his words. His instinct for decency and truth belies the seeming paradox of a career that moved successfully from service in Hearst's "yellow" press to leadership of the idealistic and "clean" *Christian Science Monitor*.

The only child of Waldo and Julia Holmes Abbot, Willis John Abbot was born 16 March 1863 in New Haven, Connecticut. Literary and journalistic expression was a family tradition: Abbot's grandfather, the Reverend John S. C. Abbott, was honored by Napoleon III for his "Life of Napoleon Bonaparte," serialized in *Harper's Monthly*; with his brother Jacob, John Abbott (both had added a "t" to their patronymic) coauthored a series of *Pioneers and Patriots* popular biographies. In his memoirs, Willis Abbot recounted as a lad cheerfully spending long winter afternoons as his grandfather's research assistant in the family library. A cousin, Dr. Lyman Abbott, was editor of the weekly *Christian Union*, later retitled *Outlook*.

"It was perhaps not unnatural," Abbot wrote, "that with a writing ancestry I should not have rested entirely content with journalistic expression." In addition to *Watching the World Go By*, Abbot authored more than twenty volumes between 1886 and 1922 detailing military history, travel, politics, and the lives of notable women.

Julia Abbot, a practicing physician, was widowed before Abbot was one year old, when her husband, collector at the port of Key West, Florida, died of yellow fever. She eventually married Sabin Smith, and the family moved to Chicago, where Abbot's adolescent interest in politics and social problems matured into a lifelong fascination. Young Abbot heard street-corner anarchist orators and observed radical labor groups holding paramilitary drills. In 1880, as a page, he attended the first of the twenty-one national political conventions in which he would participate.

*Abbot as a young man (courtesy of The First Church
of Christ, Scientist)*

In 1881 Abbot entered the University of
Michigan to study literature and emerged in 1884
with a bachelor of laws degree. He never really
began a law career, however. While living in New
Orleans for health reasons shortly after graduating,
Abbot took up a half-jesting offer from a family
friend, the editor of the *Times-Democrat*, to join the
paper. He cut his teeth as a "cub" in a city of romantic Gallic charm, where journalistic rivalries not uncommonly were settled at gunpoint. His first day on
the job was made unforgettable by the shooting of a
local political boss, who burst into the *Times-
Democrat* nursing an amputated trigger finger,
which made him, as Abbot recalled, "a pacifist for
life." In counterpoint to this atmosphere of ven-
detta, Abbot enjoyed the companionship of *Times-
Democrat* colleague Lafcadio Hearn, whose literary
columns added a poetic and intellectual grace to the
paper, qualities Abbot found sadly lacking in
twentieth-century journalism.

As New Orleans correspondent for the *New
York World*, Abbot was assigned to interview former
Confederate president Jefferson Davis, to gather
the latter's impressions of Gen. Ulysses S. Grant,
who lay dying in 1885. Abbot came away from the
encounter without the story he had hoped for but
having met a man who, he later said, impressed him

more favorably than any of the other statesmen and
dignitaries he knew over the years.

Within a year, Abbot took his second and final
reporting post, writing for the *New York Tribune.*
Here he was introduced to "the most instructive
class in journalism the profession has ever
known"—not in the newsroom, but at Perry's
Pharmacy, where New York reporters gathered
after midnight for serious, if bibulous, critiques of
the day's news coverage.

From "Doc" Perry's seminars, Abbot moved
on to what he later termed "probably the most expensive journalism school in the country," when he
and several partners "undertook to establish an
evening newspaper in Kansas City, in opposition to
the *Star* and its forceful editor, Colonel William R.
Nelson." The paper, launched in 1886, was the
Evening News. In 1887 Abbot married Marie
Amanda Mack in Ann Arbor, Michigan. By the end
of the 1880s, Kansas City's economic boom had
collapsed, and with it the *News.*

In 1889 Abbot followed his fortunes to his
boyhood home, Chicago, and began writing editorials for the *Chicago Evening Mail,* a paper "perishing of senile debility," as he recalled. In 1891 the
Mail and its morning edition, the *Chicago Times,* got
a new lease on life when the company was purchased by the ill-fated Carter Henry Harrison, the
four-term mayor who was planning a reelection bid
in time to preside over the 1893 World's Fair. During his five years in Chicago, Abbot honed his editorial talents, developed his political interests, and still
found time to savor the city's diverse cultural and
social scene.

He described Chicago journalism in the Gay
Nineties as "an entertaining, an engrossing and not
particularly profitable pursuit." Chicago was, however, "just the right size" for a young and ambitious
newsman. "If at all clever," Abbot wrote, "he knew
and was known by everyone worth knowing in the
city."

Harrison promoted Abbot to managing editor
in 1892, and Abbot marshaled the *Times* behind his
chief's reelection the next year. Harrison was returned to office, and proudly opened the Chicago
World's Fair in early October. By the end of the
month, he had been shot dead by a demented young
man whose strange postcards to the *Times* Abbot
had often read during the campaign. Such was Abbot's admiration for Harrison that in 1895 he
memorialized him in *Carter Henry Harrison: A
Memoir.*

During these Chicago years, Abbot also met
and came to revere John P. Altgeld, elected Illinois

governor in 1892. Like Harrison, Altgeld was a "people's candidate," and Abbot's own sympathies for the poor and dispossessed resonated to such ideals. Abbot's assessment of Altgeld reflects the equanimity Abbot himself practiced in his editorial judgment of political and social conflicts: "An intimate friend during the years of his sorest trial, when all the forces of capital in Chicago seemed to be united in the effort to beggar him, I never heard him repay slander, hatred and denunciation in their own coin. His nature appealed particularly to the more thoughtful people of his time."

The 1890s witnessed the rise of the populist movement, which Abbot enthusiastically remembered as "the beginning of the most gorgeous political fight the United States has ever known." Silver, tariffs, taxes, and peace were to preoccupy him for the balance of his political and journalistic careers.

Harrison's sons sold the *Times* to a barkeeper turned lawyer. Abbot and his brother-in-law soon purchased the paper and merged it with the *Herald,* with themselves as minority shareholders. With the majority owner's untimely death, Abbot and his relative were unable to assume the outstanding interest, and the *Times-Herald* was acquired by H. H. Kholsaat. The paper's fortunes continued to ebb; it changed hands again, and a series of mergers ultimately combined the *Chicago Times-Herald, Record,* and *Inter Ocean.* Abbot confessed that he was not proud of his role in this "malign process." However, it marked the end of his journalistic apprenticeship and the beginning of almost two decades of association with the then expanding press empire of William Randolph Hearst.

Hearst interviewed Abbot in New York City one day in 1895. An hour later, Abbot was appointed editor in chief of the *New York Journal,* nominally responsible for producing the editorial page. But Hearst had neglected to inform the *Journal* staff of Abbot's status, and his first days at the paper were a frustrating introduction to Hearst's unconventional newspapering style. He was also soon to learn that Hearst was in fact the editor in chief of all his papers. Abbot wrote a Chicago friend that he had secured "very remunerative employment in a lunatic asylum." He stayed at the *Journal* (renamed the *American* in 1897) until 1898, later returning for briefer stints.

It is not surprising, in view of his charitable personality, that Abbot recorded very little in the way of direct criticism of Hearst the man or his journalistic methods. Abbot's comments on the evils of press sensationalism and jingoism while serving at the *Monitor* years later, however, leave little doubt

as to his personal standards as a journalist. Hearst, he remembered as a "puzzle," brazen in print, shy in society, and erratic as a policymaker, especially in personnel matters. A friend of Abbot's who had served under both James Gordon Bennett and Joseph Pulitzer told of an incident in which the aging Pulitzer was nearly thrown from his horse: he prepared to strike the animal with his crop, hesitated, then petted the animal. Abbot quoted his friend: "I said to myself that if it had been Bennett, he would have beaten the horse cruelly. Had it been Hearst—and I was lost in conjecture. No one could tell what the reaction of that enigmatic mind would have been." Yet Abbot remembered Hearst as magnanimously loyal to employees whose work and unquestioning devotion he appreciated, and always supportive of religion in his papers.

From the 1890s on, Abbot was a prolific contributor of magazine articles covering domestic and world affairs, travel, and distinguished personalities. His by-line appeared in the *Review of Reviews, Literary Digest, New Republic, Outlook, Collier's, Forum, Munsey's,* and *Harper's Weekly,* among others.

For Abbot the most memorable news event he covered was doubtless the 1896 Democratic National Convention, where he fell under the spell of the eloquent and starry-eyed William Jennings Bryan. The Chicago convention also marked a transition in Abbot's career priorities, and for several years thereafter, he devoted as much time to political pursuits as to journalism. The unexpected strength of the prosilver, populist camp, galvanized by Bryan at the convention, was a revelation to Abbot, who saw many of his personal political convictions vindicated. This was the finest hour of what he termed the nation's "most gorgeous political fight," which was to remain a major factor in Democratic policies until the nomination of Woodrow Wilson in 1912.

Having met Bryan some years before 1896, Abbot later remembered him as "just one more of those hayseed Congressmen, never for a moment visioning what the future had in store for him." After Chicago, Abbot's assessment of this "sincerest of men" bordered on adulation: "He was tall, slender, obviously a very model of physical vigor. But his face! Pale and crested with black hair, a nose like the beak of an eagle, a chin which in later years the blind Joseph Pulitzer first tested with a hovering hand, then described it as 'likely to make trouble,' the mouth of an orator and eyes that burned deep with conviction and radiated perfect sincerity. . . . He convinced himself of the righteousness of every cause before he became its prophet. Once convinced of its worth, he would brush aside the protestations of his closest friends and fling himself into what he thought a contest for truth. He may not have been—few of us are—master of his fate, but emphatically from that day when he confronted a yelling, cursing, howling mob in the Chicago convention, until the summer evening thirty years after, when in a little Tennessee town he laid down his life for the religious convictions he held dear, he was always and in every contingency the captain of his soul." Assigned to report the convention for the progold Hearst, Abbot was amazed at Bryan's calm assurance of nomination. Abbot's skepticism vanished as he stood at the foot of the speaker's platform and heard Bryan—invited to the dais only because the scheduled orator had succumbed to "the temptations of a pre-prohibition era"—deliver his electrifying "Cross of Gold" speech.

So moved was Abbot by the "spiritual exhaltation" of the oration that he undertook to swing Hearst behind Bryan and silver, despite Hearst's personal convictions and his investments in gold mining. Shortly after Bryan's nomination, he and Abbot repaired to the candidate's hotel bathroom, where they drafted a comprehensive telegram to Hearst. The latter had already decided to endorse Bryan, but Abbot's plea surely reinforced his stand. According to one source, Abbot argued with shrewd journalistic insight that "since most, if not all, important New York and Eastern papers would oppose silver, the *Journal,* if it supported the cause, might in one jump become the leading Democratic paper of the east, with the joyous prospect of a swift rise in circulation." Hearst instructed his editors to press for the silver cause and the man Abbot dubbed "The Great Commoner."

Still associated with the Hearst organization, Abbot spent the next several years as a Democratic activist. In 1897 he chaired the New York mayoral campaign of Henry George, who died before election day. The experience of fighting the Tammany machine further distilled Abbot's revulsion at the abuses of political power.

Abbot admitted he had played a part, albeit with reservations, in helping the *Journal* and *American* fan the sparks of war with Spain in the late 1890s. Without detailing his role, his memoirs describe the hoaxes, exaggerations, and hysterical misrepresentations that were daily fare before and after war was declared. His account casts no new light on what Hearst called "our war," but it does recreate some of the opéra-bouffe atmosphere in the New York press: "*Cuba libre!* became the password in the *American* offices, and our editorial

rooms were haunted by dark, undersized men who spoke in whispers and revealed to the very cub reporters secrets which should have made thrones topple." Looking back on the belligerent climate that prevailed nationwide, Abbot concluded that Hearst was not solely to blame for inciting it but was "only the most sensational of its advocates."

Following this brief stint back at the *Journal,* Abbot managed the Democratic national press bureau during the 1900 presidential campaign in which Republican incumbent William McKinley again defeated the ever-hopeful Bryan. But Abbot could not ignore his journalistic calling. After the 1900 election, he edited the *Pilgrim,* a monthly magazine "for the home," in Battle Creek, Michigan. In Detroit he managed a free-distribution "trading stamp" newspaper, the *United States Daily,* but was unable to counter pressures from the *Free Press* and *Evening News* exerted on major advertisers. Marie Abbot died in 1903, leaving Abbot a son, Waldo Mack. Two years later, Abbot married a Detroit banker's daughter, Elsie Maples. From 1905 to 1907, he was chief editorial writer at the *New York American.*

Abbot again ran Democratic party press activities during Bryan's final vain presidential bid in 1908. He also wrote a pro-Democratic column for the Republican *Chicago Tribune*; so successful was this venture that large numbers of Democratic voters began to take the *Tribune,* and Republican organizers expressed concerns over his influence on their party's faithful.

Following William Howard Taft's defeat of Bryan, Abbot spent one of several sojourns in Europe. He only halfheartedly (and in vain) tried to comply with a stateside editor's cabled request to "interview King of England, President of France, Emperor of Germany and King of Italy concerning life and services of Theodore Roosevelt particularly upon his example set youth in good citizenship." For the next four years, he alternated between Chicago and Washington, D.C., where he produced syndicated political analysis.

At the end of this period, he was commissioned to write a book on the Panama Canal and spent several weeks gathering impressions in the isthmus. He was favorably impressed by the benevolent despotism by which the Canal Zone was administered, less so by the rigid social stratification of its expatriate colony. *Panama and the Canal in Picture and Prose* (1913) was marketed by newspaper mail order and sold more than one million copies at ninety-eight cents apiece. Abbot credited his publisher with the enormous sale. An initial pressrun of

300,000 copies permitted the low sales price, and the books were printed in New York, Chicago, and San Francisco and shipped in carload lots for additional economy.

An author of more than twenty books, Abbot said little about these writings in his memoirs. Most were children's or popular "drum and trumpet" titles chronicling military history from the American Revolution through the Great War. Abbot wrote few books after he joined the *Monitor* in 1921; in this phase of his career he increasingly devoted his energies to promoting world peace. He wrote in 1933 that "one of the best steps toward eradicating the war spirit in youth might . . . be the prohibition of books eulogizing, as mine did, the purely military virtues." It is probably no exaggeration to say that Abbot was as well known by American youngsters for his war stories as he was by their parents for his political commentary.

By the end of 1913, Abbot had returned to the *New York American*. In July of the next year, he took leave for a pleasure trip to Europe, where the assassination of Archduke Francis Ferdinand had failed to alert *American* editors to ask Abbot to report back on rising tensions. August brought war. For nearly two months, Abbot endured the frustrations of life in wartime Paris, where, he later remembered, both taxis and money had disappeared. Above all, he later recalled his admiration for the fortitude and fatalism of the French in facing disaster.

At the *American*, Abbot grew increasingly ill at ease with Hearst's pro-German sympathies. After Hearst concluded that the 1915 sinking of the *Lusitania* had been a legitimate act of war, Abbot was relieved to accept Frank Munsey's offer to write editorials for the *New York Sun*. As a cub at the *New York Tribune* in the 1880s, Abbot had "put in an hour after midnight almost nightly studying this paper." While short-lived, Abbot's move to the *Sun* at the age of fifty-three was a young man's dream come true.

At the *Sun*, Abbot worked for "the ablest man I had met in my profession," the seventy-year-old Edward P. Mitchell. Abbot remembered the open, creative atmosphere Mitchell fostered for his editorialists, and his aversion to the "timely" editorial because of its tendency to be commonplace. The ideal of the broader perspective, especially, Abbot later perfected in his tenure at the *Monitor*.

Abbot worked briefly at the *Chicago American* in 1917, then returned to Washington, where he again wrote as a syndicated columnist and correspondent for *Collier's Weekly* and the *Times* of London. He also worked for a newspaper editor whom he later admired more as a politician than as a journalist. Of Herbert Hoover, then co-owner of the *Washington Herald*, Abbot wrote, "As an editor he was a great mining engineer." Despite Hoover's Republican credentials, Abbot (and the *Monitor*) would later support him in the face of adversity, much as he had done for Bryan in 1896, 1900, and 1908.

In 1921, much to Abbot's "amazement and joy," the Christian Science Board of Directors invited him to become the third editor of the *Christian Science Monitor*. Thus began the last and most distinguished phase of his career.

Abbot had become a believer in Christian Science in his late forties, after years of "nervous prostration and insomnia" had begun to impede his work. At the suggestion of his wife, he had consulted a Christian Science practitioner in Detroit. In 1933 he noted that his complaint had never recurred. When he assumed the editorship of the *Monitor*, Abbot had to draw on his wealth of journalistic experience as well as his natural optimism to effect the "healing" of a newspaper then at a low ebb.

Mary Baker Eddy had founded the *Monitor* in 1908 "to injure no man, but to bless all mankind." Its first editor, Archibald McClelland, had vowed to produce "an absolutely clean and unsensational newspaper" that would appeal to people in all walks of life around the world. It is ironic that Abbot, a former Hearst executive, was tapped to lead a paper dedicated to the very antithesis of yellow journalism. (Possibly the church's leaders favorably recalled a 1906 article Arthur Brisbane had written for Hearst, rebutting muckraking attacks on Mrs. Eddy that had appeared in the *New York World* and *McClure's* magazine. Abbot himself was aware of Hearst's positive attitude toward religion in general.)

The *Monitor* had prospered until 1919, when an internecine struggle over control of the paper erupted between the church's board of directors and its publishing society's board. While the case was being arbitrated by the courts, circulation fell from more than 120,000 to less than 18,000. The courts having found for the Christian Science Board of Directors, Abbot set about rebuilding the paper in early 1922, concentrating on revitalizing the staff, strengthening overseas bureaus, and molding an editorial policy in keeping with the *Monitor*'s constituent ideals of decency and constructiveness. Within five years, circulation was approaching 130,000.

The groups of which he was a member or

officer reflect the two related causes he tirelessly promoted in the last part of his career: responsible journalism and the pursuit of world peace. He was a member of the League to Enforce Peace, the Institute of Pacific Relations, the World Peace Foundation, the Foreign Policy Association, the International Chamber of Commerce, the English Speaking Union, the American Economic Association, and the Japan Society of Boston. A founder of the American Society of Newspaper Editors, of which he was a director and vice-president, he also belonged to the Pan-American Congress of Journalists and was a charter member of the National Press Club in Washington, D.C. In addition to membership in the University Club of Boston and the Century Club of New York, he was a thirty-second degree Mason.

In 1923 Abbot married his passions for responsible journalism and harmony among nations in drafting the *Monitor*'s "Peace Plan," proposing a constitutional amendment that would remove the profit motive from warmongering by legalizing the conscription of labor and capital in the service of a national war effort. Inspired perhaps by his earlier impressions of the Panama Canal administration, and certainly by his horror of World War I, his plan amounted to a form of socialism: "Capital equally with labor would be subject to the imperative demand of the state. The revolting theory that the state might command the lives of its youths, but that the money of the prosperous should be sacred, would be repudiated. Nor would the farmer or the miner be immune from the call to service. Food would be raised, but taken by the state at a price which would eliminate all profit; neither the digger of iron, the smelter, the puddler, nor the millionaire magnate who controlled the operation of all, should be allowed as the fruit of his labor during the continuance of the war more than what the boy in the trenches would be getting—namely, a bare livelihood." The plan was given serious consideration for a time in Congress, and it certainly foreshadowed some aspects of the 1930s' New Deal and wartime policies of the 1940s.

Abbot served as *Monitor* chief until mid-1927, when church directors vested editorial responsibility in a four-member editorial board, to which Abbot was appointed as "contributing editor." Active on the board until his death, Abbot continued to write editorials and his signed column, "Watching the World Go By." He informed *Monitor* policy, traveled extensively, and served as *Monitor* goodwill ambassador as a lecturer and member of numerous public service groups.

In foreign as in domestic affairs, Abbot preferred to be a firsthand observer, ever advocating practical experience over secondhand acquaintance. During one trip to Europe in 1928, he managed to interview Benito Mussolini, President Thomas Masaryk and Foreign Minister Edward Benes of Czechoslovakia, England's Viscount Cecil, Dr. Gustav Stresemann of Germany, French industrialist Andre Citroen, and several other Continental leaders. So pleased was he with Abbot's impartial analysis of Italian fascism that the Duce ordered 100,000 reprints of the article distributed. Yet despite his admiration for the director's personal charm and his system's seeming efficiency, Abbot still wondered in his interview whether "the sense of liberty which once led Italian children to sing its beauties in the streets . . . had been blunted."

Thirty years later, as a mature editor, Abbot observed the early storm clouds of World War II brewing in Europe. Recalling the press's impact on public opinion in the war with Spain and World War I, he spoke out on "the press and international misunderstandings" in a scholarly article entitled "Dragon's Teeth." In it he deplored the manipulation of the news media by government propagandists, the poor training of foreign correspondents, and the sensationalistic nationalism of foreign news coverage. In calling for a "higher sense of responsibility" among newspaper executives at home and abroad, he concluded: "Sensationalism in domestic news contributes to a certain extent to the spread of crime, and to the blunting of the public consciousness by its effects on the minds of individuals. Sensationalism in international news reacts immediately upon the attitudes of governments, and antagonisms created between states logically lead to war." By 1928 any vestige of yellow journalism in Abbot's journalistic soul had been laid to rest.

In his *Monitor* editorials and columns, in other writings, and in speeches such as the Yale University Paul Block lecture of 14 March 1934, Abbot reiterated his conviction that the press could turn from a "provocative" role in international relations to serving the causes of peace. At Yale he advocated freeing journalism from manipulation by government, opening international conferences to the press, and heightened responsibility on the part of news executives. His assessments of international news flow adumbrated problems and principles still hotly contested fifty years after his passing.

Not content to have helped draft the American Society of Newspaper Editors' 1923 Canons of Journalism Ethics, he fought tenaciously to give them sanction power over journalistic misconduct by member papers. Quietly yet forcefully, Abbot was a reformer in journalism as in politics. More than a decade before the (Hutchins) Commission on Freedom of the Press aired its recommendations in 1947, Abbot had formulated a philosophy of journalistic social responsibility grounded in his firm belief that the press could indeed "bless all mankind" while avoiding injury to individuals and groups. In his speeches and writings he held up the *Monitor* as a worthy example of journalistic completeness, decency, and constructive analysis. Yet the *Monitor* under Abbot's influence was far from effete. Despite strong pressures from German Christian Scientists in the early 1930s, Abbot counseled keeping a non-German correspondent in Berlin to weed out Nazi propaganda. An unyielding prohibitionist, he was a major force behind the *Monitor*'s "dry" stand and its unprecedented endorsement of a presidential candidate in 1928 and again in 1932—Herbert Hoover, a foe of repeal.

Abbot's personal code as a journalist is as enduring as his insights into national politics and foreign affairs. Shortly before the *Monitor* editorship was consolidated in a board, he drafted a memorandum on the duties and functions of an editor, which included the following:

> The primary and principal function of the editor of a daily newspaper is to furnish the intellectual stimulus for the paper;
>
> An editor ought to be able to write well—better as a rule than any of his staff, and he ought to be a practical judge of the writing of others;
>
> It is quite possible for an editor to write too much himself. Pride of authorship not infrequently causes such a one to make his editorial page reflect a single individual rather than the well-rounded and considered work of an editorial organization;
>
> The editor must understand the mechanism of the paper from press room to copy desk, and should have the knowledge and acquaintance to enable him to judge what other papers are doing, and what his organization is capable of doing;
>
> An editor must know the history of his country and its present politics;
>
> Proper equipment for an editor implies a life-time of apprenticeship in the various departments of editorial work. The experience

cannot be improvised, nor the knowledge gained from books.

In reviewing his own career, Abbot had a keen appreciation for his youthful trials and errors, and he remained a lifelong advocate of hard experience as the novice journalist's best teacher. For an editor, especially, he recognized the value of hands-on exposure to every phase of the newspaper enterprise—production, business, advertising, and circulation as well as news processing. An aspiring editor could even learn from a disaster such as his own in Kansas City, Abbot believed:

> Given a small interest in a paper in not too large a town, all these things will be forced upon him, and as his monetary capital wanes his professional capital will increase. He may end his apprenticeship broken financially, but thoroughly equipped to serve a paper of a more ambitious sort in any of its departments.

Yet to Abbot, the core of journalism training was reporting; and even as an internationally acclaimed editor, he regretted not having spent more time on the beat. "Don't let anybody fool you," he once told a cub at the *Monitor*. "There's only one

New headquarters of the Christian Science Publishing Society, Boston, in 1933

title a man would want on any newspaper, and that's the title of reporter."

Formal journalism education was in its infancy during Abbot's career, and he took a wait-and-see attitude toward the value of a journalism diploma compared with what he described as "gruelling, but formative, experience of years as a reporter under hard-boiled city editors." He had, however, no doubt as to the value of solid liberal schooling to a reporter's success on the job. His sights set on a reporting job at the *Monitor*, the young Joseph C. Harsch asked Abbot if he should pursue two years of postgraduate journalism study in the United States or attend Cambridge University in England. "Cambridge, by all means," Abbot told Harsch, destined to become a respected *Monitor* columnist. "I can make a journalist out of an intelligent man, but can't make an intelligent man out of a journalist."

Abbot the editor inspired even his most junior colleagues by his very appearance and demeanor, as Erwin D. Canham, later head of the *Monitor* newsroom, recalled: "The gleam in his eyes, the neat little goatee on his chin, his tweeds, his easy kindness and sophistication composed a personality which charmed and inspired the eager young cubs. And, if one of the cubs may add a personal note, the sight of Mr. Abbot's gracious wife and handsome collie dog waiting in the car in which they would all drive home, composed a picture of just what the cub thought an editor should be!" Sixty years after Abbot joined the *Monitor*, he was fondly remembered by the former cubs who had become deans of their profession. "He was genial and friendly," wrote Richard L. Strout, veteran Washington analyst, "but I was just a beginner and watched him as head of the *Monitor* with awe." Senior columnist Joseph C. Harsch remembered Abbot as "always friendly" and generous with sound advice.

Abbot was honored by Greece and Romania for international service. His alma mater conferred on him an honorary doctorate of laws. In 1943 a Liberty ship was named for him.

Abbot died of undiagnosed causes on 19 May 1934, active until the end. His ashes were interred at Mount Auburn Cemetery, Cambridge, Mas-

sachusetts. Survivors included his wife of twenty-nine years and his son, Waldo.

The *Monitor* of 21 May devoted two news articles, a column, and an editorial to the passing of its former helmsman. Tributes were noted from distinguished journalists, statesmen, and business leaders from around the world. One of the most glowing memories of Abbot came from his old friend from Kansas City days, William Allen White, in a profile for the *Atlantic Monthly* shortly before Abbot died: "Mr. Abbot's career recalls a well-born youth with average American college education setting forth in the newspaper profession to find his Holy Grail: this being, first, distinction through services; second, security in his person; third, a modicum of honor; and finally, but above all, well-grounded self-respect. He begins as a reporter in New Orleans, tries his hand at establishing an evening paper in Kansas City and fails like a gentleman, turns up in Chicago, capitalizes his experience, becomes managing editor and editor in chief of a number of journals in the interior metropolis, moves up and on until he finds himself seated in the editorial chair of the *Christian Science Monitor*." With a subtle wit Abbot would have appreciated, White concluded that "his career exemplifies a typical American journalist of, let us say for euphony, the best type."

References:

E. D. Canham, *Commitment to Freedom: The Story of the Christian Science Monitor* (Boston: Houghton Mifflin, 1958);

S. Huddleston, *In My Time: An Observer's Record of War and Peace* (London: Cape, 1938);

C. E. Pellisier, "Romances in American Journalism; Stories of Success Won by Leaders of the Press," *Editor & Publisher* (17 January 1931): 14, 44;

W. A. White, "Good Newspapers and Bad," *Atlantic Monthly*, 153 (May 1934): 581-586.

Papers:

Willis J. Abbot's unpublished papers and correspondence are in the archives and library of the First Church of Christ, Scientist, Boston.

Robert S. Abbott

(28 November 1868-29 February 1940)

Jean Lange Folkerts
University of Texas at Austin

MAJOR POSITIONS HELD: Editor and publisher, *Chicago Defender* (1905-1940); publisher, *Abbott's Monthly* (1929-1933).

PERIODICAL PUBLICATION: "Making Good," *Southern Workman* (February 1919).

Suppressed at first by poverty, then later by vigilante groups in the South which sought to halt distribution of his *Chicago Defender*, Robert Sengstacke Abbott nevertheless continued to publish his newspaper from 1905, when he was thirty-seven years old, until his death in 1940. In establishing the *Defender*, Abbott changed the character of the black press. The *Defender* abandoned a strictly rhetorical political style, adopted the sensational makeup and headlines of Hearst and Pulitzer fame, and imitated the old motto of the *New York Sun*, "If you see it in the *Defender*, it's so!" Abbott encouraged pride in being black. He wanted blacks to demand economic and political rights, and he beckoned to Southern blacks to come out of the land of oppression and to seek the pure light of freedom in the North. For many blacks in the early 1900s, the *Defender* was the sole link to a black world that transcended neighborhood boundaries. "I feel so sad in heart," a girl from Georgia wrote to a friend, "my definder [*sic*] diden [*sic*] come yesterday."

Robert Abbott, who achieved nationwide distribution for his newspaper and a national reputation for himself, came from a small town not unlike that of the girl who looked forward so eagerly to receiving her *Defender*. Born on St. Simons Island, off the coast of Georgia, Abbott was the son of former slaves, Tom and Flora Butler Abbott. Abbott's father's family, who had been house slaves, had objected to the marriage of his parents, arguing that Flora's social status as a field hand was unacceptable; nevertheless, the marriage had taken place. When Tom Abbott died, his family began legal proceedings to take the fourteen-month-old Robert from his mother so he could be raised by the Abbotts. The mother moved to Savannah, where she sought help from John Hermann Henry Sengstacke, a half-black immigrant from Germany,

Robert Sengstacke Abbott

who retained a white lawyer to help Flora keep her son. In 1874, Sengstacke married Flora Abbott.

Sengstacke had been born in Savannah, the son of a white German and a black slave his father had purchased out of sympathy for her plight and then married. When his mother died giving birth to a younger sister, Sengstacke's father decided to send the one-year-old child to Germany to be raised outside the world of black slavery. He was, to all appearances, white. Living in Germany with an aunt and uncle, Sengstacke received his education at a Latin academy and was graduated from the Friederichsdorf Institute. He traveled on the Continent, spoke five languages, and played the piano and organ. After immigrating to the United States in 1869, he was amazed at the problems he encountered because of racial discrimination.

Sengstacke had a profound influence on his stepson, Robert Abbott, who was five when Sengstacke and Flora Abbott were married. In 1876 Sengstacke, after several business ventures, was ordained a minister by the Congregational church and appointed as a missionary in a church in Woodville, a rural black community outside Savannah. He was also hired as a teacher by the Savannah public-school system and for the next twenty-five years he preached and taught in that poor community. Sengstacke quickly learned the meaning of being black in America, and had he returned to Germany he would have been able to escape the labeling that characterized his life in Georgia. But he chose to identify himself with the black race, and this lesson no doubt spurred Abbott to champion the black and to create a sense of identification for all blacks through their reading of the *Defender*.

Abbott's career as a newspaperman began when, as a child, he worked on one of Savannah's oldest newspapers, the *Echo*. "I worked there," he said, "until a misunderstanding with the foreman made it imperative that I 'hot foot' it home to my mother. My ambition one day overpowered me and I set out to perform a more complicated assignment than was my duty. As a result I scratched up the imposing stone on which the printer made up type, and dug holes in it with an awl. The foreman started after me, when he saw my handiwork, intending to 'give me the works,' but I beat it and took the nearest exit and the shortest cut home." Abbott first attended his father's school in Woodville, then Beach Institute in Savannah in preparation for college. Sengstacke was determined that his stepson and his and Flora's seven other children would be educated.

His biographer, Roi Ottley, suggests that Beach was difficult for Abbott because the student body "was composed primarily of the fair-skinned offspring of Savannah's first families" and Abbott was undeniably black. Abbott left Beach before finishing his studies there and went to Claflin College in Orangeburg, South Carolina. After six months at Claflin, Abbott returned home with "his visions considerably expanded, and determined to learn a trade." He went back to work at the *Echo* and assisted his stepfather in publishing a new newspaper, the *Woodville Times*. Abbott then went to Hampton Institute in Virginia to learn the printer's trade, and when he finished his work there in 1896, he returned to Woodville to help his stepfather and to teach school.

When he was rejected in his bid to marry

Catherine Scarborough, the daughter of the richest mulatto in Savannah, Abbott left for Chicago, where he entered the Kent College of Law in 1897. Until this time he had used his stepfather's name as his own last name, but when registering in Chicago he relegated Sengstacke to a middle name and resumed his own last name of Abbott. "He graduated in ceremonies held at the LaSalle Street Association's Auditorium, May 20, 1899, the lone Negro, with no wellwishers, in a class of seventy, and was awarded a Bachelor of Laws degree," according to his biographer.

Abbott never was admitted to the Illinois bar. Another black lawyer, who was fair-skinned, told Abbott he was "a little too dark to make any impression on the courts in Chicago." After searching for work in Kansas and Indiana, Abbott returned to Chicago, accepting a job as a piecework printer setting railroad timetables. He began talking to anyone who would listen about his desire to start a newspaper, "an organ that would mirror the needs, opinions and the aspirations of my race." He began publishing the *Defender* on 15 May 1905. It was largely a one-person operation, although many of Abbott's friends donated time and energy to writing, printing, and distributing the paper.

As one of the first mass-produced black newspapers, the *Defender* attempted to serve as a community paper for blacks in the nation, chronicling accomplishments, social gatherings, and other activities. This newspaper's importance to the national black community was reflected in several works of fiction. In his autobiography Malcolm X wrote, "And every time Joe Louis won a fight against a white opponent, big front-page pictures in the Negro newspapers such as the *Chicago Defender*, the *Pittsburgh Courier* and the *Afro-American* showed a sea of Harlem Negros cheering and waving and the Brown Bomber waving back at them from the balcony of Harlem's Theresa Hotel." Although the black press was well established when the *Defender* was begun, most newspapers had been vehicles for personal journalism. But, as Abbott's biographer claimed, "they prepared the stage for Abbott by cleaving close to the line of race rights and originating the idea of 'race loyalty.' "

Helping the *Defender* move into the modern journalistic world was managing editor J. Hockley Smiley. He copied the front pages of the Chicago dailies, treating the news sensationally and adopting banner headlines, some of them printed in red ink. Smiley's copy matched his makeup, until women in the shop refused to handle his stories. Together he and Abbott departmentalized the paper, anticipating a development of the metropolitan press that would become popular in the 1970s. Departments included sports, editorials, women's news, and state news. Smiley was also responsible for disregarding the terms *Negro* and *Afro-American* in the newspaper and simply used the term *Race*: black issues were referred to as "Race issues," and blacks were called "people of the Race." This term was used partially in response to Abbott's dislike of *Negro*. Abbott later explained the use of the term *Race*: "We use that as a bridge, as you might say, which we intend to blow up pretty soon. We are leading the people away from the word 'Negro,' especially in our paper. And in cases where white men are well known in the country we never put 'white' after their names. We never put 'colored' after a colored man's name in this city." Smiley, instrumental in bringing the newspaper into the modern age, died of pneumonia in 1915.

But Abbott never relinquished the title of editor, and he exercised continual control over the newspaper.

Searching for a racial philosophy, Abbott tried not to choose sides between Booker T. Washington and W. E. B. DuBois, who during the early years of the century were the primary political spokesmen for blacks. Washington had emphasized education, with his primary goal being the conversion of blacks into efficient workers; he had advocated that blacks establish businesses and learn trades. He became a conciliator between white and black, urging separatism combined with equality of opportunity. DuBois, on the other hand, argued that the race would be saved by its exceptional men and wanted the best men to be educated in the best schools of the land. He attacked Washington as a compromiser and claimed that Washington wanted blacks to abandon their struggle for political, civil, and educational rights.

Abbott identified with the masses of blacks who were searching for economic opportunity and political rights. He designed a platform which he printed in every issue of the *Defender*:

1. American race prejudice must be destroyed.
2. The opening up of all trade-unions to blacks as well as whites.
3. Representation in the President's Cabinet.
4. Engineers, firemen and conductors on all American railroads.
5. Representation in all departments of the police forces over the entire United States.
6. Government schools open to ALL American citizens in preference to foreigners.
7. Motormen and conductors on surface, elevated and motor bus lines throughout America.
8. Federal legislation to abolish lynching.
9. Full enfranchisement of all American citizens.

The influence of the *Defender* became apparent after the Arkansas riots of 1918, as the nation moved into a period of post-World War I fear. Carl Sandburg, writing in the *Chicago Daily News*, said that "a colored man caught with a copy in his possession was suspected of 'Northern fever' and other so-called disloyal ties." Those who sought to control the blacks in society sought also to control distribution of the *Defender*. More than twelve agent-correspondents for the *Defender* were driven from their homes, and two were actually killed while distributing the newspaper. In the twenty-fifth anniversary issue of 10 May 1930, Abbott wrote that to "bring about a medium of communication whereby people in the different states would know what was going on and being accomplished in their businesses," it was necessary to establish "methods of communication through agents and writers in the various states of the Union." People in the South, according to Abbott, had started writing to the *Defender*, seeking information about family members who had been separated from them for years; "through the *Defender* they were able to learn of each other's whereabouts."

Abbott's personal life was overshadowed by his work. After his initial attempt to marry Catherine Scarborough, he plunged into his career and, according to his biographer, was never even casually involved with women until 1918 when, after asking Catherine Scarborough a second time to marry him, she agreed. However, a few months later she changed her mind. During the same year he married Helen Thornton Morrison, a widow from Athens, Georgia. Abbott was almost fifty and his bride was thirty years younger. Like Catherine Scarborough, she was extremely fair-skinned. After his marriage, Abbott seemed more concerned with his social status and often entertained the black upper class of Chicago; however, his marriage did not make him popular. One letter writer said, "The South has lost faith and admiration for you since you married a white face." His family was also unhappy about the marriage; one cousin said, "We tried to show him that he would be much better off with a black woman. But he was 'color struck.'"

In 1919 an incident in Chicago in which a young boy was killed by a rock thrown at his head was the impetus for a full-scale riot. The city's news-

Abbott's home in Chicago

papers covered the riots sensationally, and the *Defender* was no exception. While the *Daily News* falsely claimed that black men had attacked and killed white women, the *Defender* erroneously informed its readers: "The homes of blacks isolated in white neighborhoods were burned to the ground and the owners and occupants beaten and thrown unconscious into the smoldering embers." But as the riots continued, Abbott altered his position and urged blacks to end the rioting. In an extra edition, he urged blacks to "do your part to restore quiet and order. . . . Every day of rioting and disorder means loss of life, destruction of property, loss of money for you and your families, and for some of us these losses will be large and irredeemable."

When the rioting stopped, Gov. Frank O. Lowden appointed a Commission of Race Relations, and Robert Abbott was one of the six blacks appointed to the twelve-member commission. In its report, the commission noted that editorials in the *Defender* generally were more thoughtful than its news coverage, but urged the Negro press to use "greater care and accuracy in reporting incidents involving whites and Negroes, the abandonment of sensational headlines and articles on racial ques-

tions, and more attention to educating Negro readers as to the available means and opportunities of adjusting themselves and their fellows into more harmonious relations with their white neighbors and fellow citizens."

The causes of the riots were many, but one major factor in Chicago had been the massive migration of Southern blacks to the city. Historian William Tuttle reports that Chicago's black population nearly doubled in the years of 1916 to 1920. In 1916, according to Tuttle, the *Defender* had not encouraged blacks to come to Chicago, "questioning the wisdom of a black's trying to live in that city, where 'conditions make it practically impossible . . . to secure a flat or a house in a desirable neighborhood at anything like a moderate rental, if, in fact, they can be had at all.' " But by 1917 the *Defender* was contributing to the popular conception that the North, particularly Chicago, was a place where Southern blacks would find jobs and education for their children. In April 1917 the *Defender* pictured a single-room "Jim Crow School" contrasted with an "expansive, stone-columned building housing Chicago's Robert Lindblom High School, 'where no color line is drawn' and 'one of the many reasons why members of the Race are leaving the south.' " Tuttle says that perhaps "the most effective institution in stimulating the migration was the *Defender*, which prompted thousands to venture North. It was the *Defender*'s emphatic denunciation of the Southern treatment of blacks and its emphasis on pride in the race that increased its circulation tenfold between 1916 and 1918. The Oct. 7, 1916, issue of the *Defender* said, 'Turn a deaf ear to everybody. You see they are not lifting their laws to help you. Are they? Have they stopped their Jim Crow cars? Can you buy a Pullman sleeper where you wish? Will they give you a square deal in court yet?' The *Defender*'s answer was no. So to the North we have said, as the song goes, 'I hear you calling me,' and have boarded the train singing, 'Good-bye, Dixie Land.' "

During the 1920s Abbott achieved financial security. He maintained his stand on racial integration, but wavered on other issues. He continued to ask for black participation in "everything from the President's cabinet to baseball teams," wrote Metz Lochard, Abbott's foreign editor, in a 1947 article in *Phylon* magazine. "His stand on racial integration was as uncompromising twenty years ago as the most radical advocates of equality today."

Abbott's position on labor varied during the years. During World War I he encouraged black workers not "to be made a tool or strike breaker for any corporation or firm," and he warned them

Office of the Chicago Defender *in a former synagogue. The newspaper moved into the building in 1921.*

against being put into a separate union. In 1927, however, when the Pullman porters attempted to organize, Abbott's general manager, Nathan Magill, assumed an antiunion position. When another black newspaper attacked the *Defender* and urged blacks to boycott it, subscriptions declined and Abbott reversed the *Defender*'s position on labor unions.

The *Defender* always had been job printed until the riots of 1919, but because of difficulty getting access to printers during that time, Abbott decided to install a full-fledged printing shop. For the dedication of the plant he brought his mother from Georgia to Chicago to push the button that started the presses rolling. The establishment of the printing plant was considered a major accomplishment, and one of his employees wrote to Hampton, Abbott's alma mater, that the *Defender* had "moved into a three-story, modern building with four linotype machines, a four-deck Goss straight-line press, and a print shop the like of which no colored man ever saw before or dreamed of owning."

Abbott was proud of his financial success and wanted to be accepted into a social class that recognized his achievements. He contributed $500 to be-

come a member of the Chicago Natural History Museum and he paid $100 to become a life member of the Art Institute of Chicago. He contributed money to the Chicago Urban League, joined a variety of clubs, sent money to his family, and bought a Rolls Royce. Abbott also was being publicly recognized by the black community he sought to help. He received honorary doctorate degrees from Morris Brown College at Atlanta and Wilberforce University of Xenia, Ohio. Hampton's alumni association elected him president and the Columbus Business Association of Ohio gave him an award for his "labors and achievements" as an "advocate of justice and equal rights." In 1923 Abbott and his wife traveled abroad for the first time, touring South America; he was particularly impressed with Brazil, believing that prejudice was much more limited there than in the United States.

Personal tragedy soon struck. Shortly after Abbott's return from South America, economic shortages began to appear at the *Defender*. Four of his trusted employees were dipping into the paper's coffers, and although Abbott dismissed them, he refused to press charges. In his thirtieth anniversary edition, he described the action as a conspiracy against him. More likely, the irregularity of finances simply reflected Abbott's longtime avoidance of creating a good financial system and his absolute trust of employees who were given large sums to handle.

The financial problems did not permanently impair Abbott or the publication of the *Defender*, and in 1929 he and his wife traveled to Europe. While the Abbotts received what he considered to be fair treatment in France, and Abbott was invited to place a wreath on the tomb of an unknown soldier at the Arc de Triomphe, England was another matter: nowhere in all of London could the Abbotts find a hotel that would admit them. When he returned he wrote a series of articles for the *Defender*, focusing on freedom for blacks in France. He concluded the series with the statement: "I have returned with a stronger determination to plunge into the fight and never to rest until our people shall receive the same treatment that I, a foreigner, received in the white man's country—that treatment a white foreigner receives in America, the land of my birth."

Shortly before the stock market crash of 1929, Abbott published the first issue of a magazine, *Abbott's Monthly*. The monthly was edited by Lucius C. Harper, who worked for Abbott on the *Defender*, and carried features, stories, verse, and a short biographical sketch of the publisher. One of Abbott's employees told the *Chicago Daily News* that the magazine was circulating worldwide. Indeed, 50,000 copies of the first issue sold rapidly. "Besides providing a market which did not exist before for the work of talented Negro writers and artists we intend to create a medium which will tell white and Negro people of the United States what we are doing." The magazine achieved a circulation of 100,000, but died in 1933 after rapidly dropping in circulation. Massive unemployment among black workers meant they could not afford to buy such a publication.

During the Depression the *Defender* lost money for the first time. Abbott lost his savings and was forced to borrow money, while circulation dropped from 200,000 in 1925 to 60,000 in 1935. Along with the financial decline came a decline in the quality of the *Defender*. Illness kept Abbott away from direct control of the paper, but he constantly wrote memoranda to his city editor, hoping to reverse trends of editorial wordiness and erratic makeup.

Further complicating the situation was Nathan Magill. Late in 1934 Abbott discovered that the general manager was attempting to deposit a *Defender* check in his own account. Further investigation revealed other irregularities in finances, and Abbott dismissed Magill. Magill subsequently sued Abbott for back wages; Abbott countersued and was awarded $17,000, which Magill never paid, having declared bankruptcy. The *Defender* survived, but at great personal cost to Abbott. Despite his ill health, Abbott resumed direction of the newspaper. He rehired many staff members whom Magill had fired in previous months and eventually appointed his nephew and heir, John H. Sengstacke, a recent graduate of Hampton Institute, as vice-president and treasurer of the Robert S. Abbott Publishing Company.

Meanwhile, Abbott had grown disillusioned with his marriage and finally moved out of the house; he and Helen were divorced in 1933. Abbott was concerned that the court would consider his wife to be white and the judgment would be difficult for him. The court awarded her $50,000, $5,000 for lawyer's fees, a Pierce Arrow, and the furniture. In spite of the court order, he later told a cousin, "I didn't have to give her a dime. But she bore the name of Robert S. Abbott, which made it my duty to see that she lived in the style she had become accustomed to." Abbott did not attempt to influence coverage of the divorce in the *Defender*, and when the decree was granted the story was on page one.

Abbott remarried in 1934. His new wife, Edna Rose Brown Denison, had been married to the late Col. Franklin Denison, a distinguished army officer and a friend of Abbott's. Like Catherine Scarborough and Helen Morrison, Edna Denison was very fair-skinned. Abbott and his wife were married only six years before Abbott died in February 1940 at the age of seventy-one.

The 9 March 1940 issue of the *Defender* devoted much of its space to Abbott's death. Lucius Harper, who had edited the short-lived *Abbott's Monthly*, announced, "The Dean of Negro journalism is dead. Even his contemporaries who often doubted the wisdom of his course in life will not deny him that honorable title in death." The *Defender* reported that 10,000 persons attended the funeral at the Metropolitan Community Church, the National Airmen's Association flew over the gravesite and dropped roses onto the grave, and dignitaries such as Chicago Mayor Edward J. Kelley paid tribute to Abbott. Kelley called Abbott a "close friend and one whose achievements and ideals must place him among immortals of the Race." The National Conference of Negro Publishers, which was meeting in Chicago at the time of Abbott's death, adjourned the opening session and passed a resolution honoring Abbott's contributions to the black press.

But despite Abbott's accomplishments, despite his advances in breaking down discrimination toward the members of his race, he did not break through the color line, even in his own field of journalism. For at his death, the city's major daily, the *Chicago Tribune*, carried no special tribute to Robert Abbott. An obituary, about four paragraphs long, appeared on the paper's standard obituary page, at the back of the newspaper.

Biography:
Roi Ottley, *The Lonely Warrior* (Chicago: Regnery, 1955).

References:
Henry G. La Brie III, *Perspectives of the Black Press: 1974* (Kennebunkport, Maine, 1974);

Metz Lochard, "Robert S. Abbott—Race Leader," *Phylon*, 8 (Second Quarter, 1947): 124-132;

William M. Tuttle, Jr., *Race Riot: Chicago in the Red Summer of 1919* (New York: Atheneum, 1970).

Franklin P. Adams
(15 November 1881-23 March 1960)

Nancy L. Roberts
University of Minnesota

MAJOR POSITIONS HELD: Columnist, *Chicago Journal* (1903-1904), *New York Evening Mail* (1904-1913), *New York Tribune* (1914-1921), *New York World* (1922-1931), *New York Herald Tribune* (1931-1937), *New York Post* (1938-1941).

BOOKS: *In Cupid's Court* (Evanston, Ill.: Lord, 1902);

Tobogganing on Parnassus (Garden City: Doubleday, Page, 1911);

In Other Words (Garden City: Doubleday, Page, 1912);

By and Large (Garden City: Doubleday, Page, 1914);

Weights and Measures (Garden City: Doubleday, Page, 1917);

Among Us Mortals (Boston & New York: Houghton Mifflin, 1917);

Something Else Again (Garden City: Doubleday, Page, 1920);

Overset (Garden City: Doubleday, Page, 1922);

Women I'm Not Married To, by Adams, and *Men I'm Not Married To*, by Dorothy Parker (Garden City: Doubleday, Page, 1922);

So There! (Garden City: Doubleday, Page, 1923);

So Much Velvet (Garden City: Doubleday, Page, 1924);

Half a Loaf (Garden City: Doubleday, Page, 1927);

The Column Book of F.P.A. (Garden City: Doubleday, Doran, 1928);

Christopher Columbus and Other Patriotic Verses (New York: Viking, 1931);

The Diary of Our Own Samuel Pepys, 1911-1934, 2 volumes (New York: Simon & Schuster, 1935);

The Melancholy Lute: Selected Songs of Thirty Years (New York: Viking, 1936);

Percy Hammond: A Symposium in Tribute, by Adams, John Anderson, Brooks Atkinson, and others (Garden City: Doubleday, Doran, 1936);

Heywood Broun as He Seemed to Us, by Adams, John L. Lewis, Herbert Bayard Swope, and others (New York: Random House, 1940);

Nods and Becks (London & New York: McGraw-Hill, 1944).

OTHER: C. L. Edson, *The Gentle Art of Columning: A Treatise on Comic Journalism*, introductory essay by Adams (New York: Brentano, 1920);

The Book of Diversion, compiled by Adams, Deems Taylor, Jack Bechdolt, Helen Rowland, and Mabel Claire (New York: Greenberg, 1925); revised and enlarged as *The Weekend Companion*, compiled by Adams, Taylor, Rowland, and Percival Wilde (Cleveland & New York: World, 1941);

The Conning Tower Book, edited by Adams (New York: Macy-Masius, 1926);

The Second Conning Tower Book, edited by Adams (Garden City: Doubleday, Page, 1927);

Answer This One: Questions for Everybody, compiled by Adams and Harry Hansen (New York: Clode, 1927);

John T. Winterich, ed., *Squads Write! (A Selection of*

Franklin P. Adams (Underwood and Underwood)

the Best Things in Prose, Verse and Cartoon from *"The Stars and Stripes"*), contributions by Adams (New York: Harper, 1931);

Berenice Dewey, *Poems*, edited by Adams (New York: Galleon Press, 1933);

Finley Peter Dunne, *Mr. Dooley at His Best*, edited by Elmer Ellis, foreword by Adams (New York: Scribners, 1938);

William Congreve, *Love for Love*, introduction by Adams (New York: Scribners, 1940);

Innocent Merriment: An Anthology of Light Verse, edited by Adams (New York & London: McGraw-Hill, 1942);

The F.P.A. Book of Quotations, compiled by Adams (New York: Funk & Wagnalls, 1952);

John K. Hutchens and George Oppenheimer, eds., *The Best in the World*, contributions by Adams (New York: Viking, 1973).

SELECTED PERIODICAL PUBLICATIONS: "If I Owned a Newspaper," *New Republic*, 92 (3 November 1937): 365-367;

"Button, Button, Who's Got the Button?," *Nation's Business*, 27 (July 1939): 27, 28, 52, 53;

"Inside 'Information, Please!,'" *Harper's,* 184 (February 1942): 252-257;

"I Know Almost Everything," *Atlantic Monthly*, 170 (August 1942): 29-31;

"Literary Memories," *Atlantic Monthly*, 181 (January 1948): 114-116.

For nearly thirty years, Franklin P. Adams pounded out a daily column of wit and erudition, "The Conning Tower," which successively enriched the op-ed pages of the *New York Tribune*, the *New York World*, the *New York Herald Tribune*, and the *New York Post*. As he scrutinized news events, reviewed plays and books, and generally opined on the American scene in satirical light verse and prose, Adams—or F.P.A., as he always signed his work— gained an enormous following.

Born in Chicago on 15 November 1881 to Moses and Clara Schlossberg Adams, Franklin Pierce Adams graduated from the Armour Scientific Academy there in 1899. He then attended the University of Michigan in Ann Arbor for less than a year before setting out to earn a living. In June 1900, Adams started as an insurance supply clerk with Adolph Loeb and Sons in Chicago. When he became an insurance solicitor about six months later, one of his first customers was the humorist George Ade. It was the frozen February of 1901, and, Adams later wrote, as he observed Ade enjoying strawberries for breakfast at noon, "I resolved then to abandon trade for belles-lettres, that I too might lie long and have strawberries in February."

In 1903 he started a column of verse and miscellany called "A Little about Everything" in the *Chicago Journal*; Adams also produced a daily weather story, all for a weekly salary of twenty-five dollars. His only other published writings at the time were his contributions to Bert Leston Taylor's *Chicago Tribune* column, "A Line o' Type or Two." His education had been mainly mathematical and scientific, with scant attention to English; but Adams had learned to venerate truth and clarity of expression from Victor Clifton Alderson, his mathematics professor at the Armour Scientific Academy, and he had learned to respect forthright and fearless expression from Rabbi Emil G. Hirsch of Chicago. From childhood, Adams had been an eager reader, raiding the well-stocked family bookshelves for Dickens, Thackeray, Balzac, Hawthorne, Bret Harte, George Eliot, Horatio Alger, history, and classics; Eugene Field sparked his interest in verse. Before long Adams's salary at the *Journal* was raised to thirty dollars a week and he was allowed to sign his initials, which were soon recognized everywhere.

In 1904 Adams married Minna Schwartze and moved to New York, where he wrote a column called "Always in Good Humor" for the *Evening Mail* until the end of 1913. The column's title was created by the newspaper's publisher, Henry L. Stoddard, and he insisted that it be lived up to. Adams occasionally balked, once shouting to his coworkers in an agonized voice, "My God! I can't write about anything except the weather and Rockefeller's wig!"

In January 1914, Adams began to conduct a column—"The Conning Tower"—for the *New York Tribune*. Adams's farewell to the *Evening Mail* was a Horatian ode which, read acrostically, said "Read the *Tribune*." His readers followed en masse, for by now his wit was well known. That year the University of Michigan awarded Adams an honorary master of arts degree. Writers, artists, and the general public pondered over his clever epigrams, while professors shared his versified slang translations of Horace, Propertius, and other Latin poets with their classes. The columnist was also addicted to punning, and readers everywhere repeated F.P.A.-isms such as "He [Walter Lippmann] appears to think that Roosevelt is putting the Court before the horse."

During World War I Adams left the *Tribune* to serve as a captain in the United States Intelligence Service in France. His wit found a continuing outlet in an occasional column, "The Listening Post," for the Allied Expeditionary Forces magazine *Stars and Stripes*. (Edited by Harold Ross, that lively publication was the first cradle of the *New Yorker*.) Characteristically forthright about his own experiences, Adams wrote of his wartime service: "I didn't fight and I didn't shoot/But General, how I did salute!"

After the war, Adams returned to the *Tribune*, but in 1922 he moved his column to the *World*. In 1925, having divorced his first wife, he married Esther Sayles Root. When the *World* expired in 1931, he returned to the *Tribune*, which had become the *Herald Tribune* in 1924. He was paid $25,000 a year for his "Conning Tower" column, which was syndicated in six other newspapers; but he left in March 1937, laconically explaining: "They just wanted me to work for less money, whereas I wanted to work for more." Adams's break from the *Herald Tribune* made headlines in the New York papers, *Time*, *Newsweek*, and many other publications. In her column "My Day," Eleanor Roosevelt

Adams working on "The Conning Tower" at the Chicago Tribune *(Culver Pictures)*

lamented, "I wish very much that F.P.A. and the New York *Herald Tribune* had not parted company so suddenly. . . . If this could have been done in a more leisurely fashion we might have been able to find his column in another paper."

Adams's column surfaced in the *New York Post* in 1938, but he left in 1941 when management decided that his poetry and prose were too sophisticated for the subway reader. The *Post* declared the parting amicable, but Adams remarked: "Amicable my eye. . . . There is nothing amicable in being fired." In an article in *Harper's* in February 1942, Adams said that he "never understood why so many persons—advertising executives and newspaper and magazine publishers—assume that the public is illiterate, or at any rate impervious to literacy.

Still, Adams could not claim that his editorial freedom had been fettered during his years as a New York columnist. "I could say, and did say, what I liked about anything or everybody, as much or as little . . . no owner or editor ever asked me to write this or not to write that, or to devote more space to this or less to that," he had written in 1937. In 1921, for example, P. F. Collier and Son had run a full-page Sunday advertisement in the *Tribune* for the "Five-Foot Shelf," a set of classical works selected by Charles W. Eliot. The ad showed two men trying to impress a young woman, pointed out that the well-read man was much more successful, and concluded that Beauty would beam on him who would burrow for fifteen minutes a day in his Five-Foot Shelf. In his column, Adams recalled, he had "kidded the priggishness of it; the notion that the bookworm was a fascinator." The next day, the advertising manager wrote him: "I want to thank you for 'The Art of Fascinating,' which you ran in yesterday's column. It has only cost us about $12,000 in the first 24 hours. My congratulations on your effective work." But even then F.P.A. was not asked to lay off advertising.

Such forthright and fearless expression increased F.P.A.'s audience appeal. For his "Conning Tower" in the *Herald Tribune*, syndicated in six newspapers, F.P.A. started at $25,000 a year. Wherever it appeared, the column won many readers. Sprinkled with verses, epigrams, puns, and paragraphs, the column also incorporated early contributions from the day's celebrated writers, who eagerly vied for Adams's annual prize, the Conning Tower watch. The list of those who contributed gratis to the column is a who's who of journalism and literature, including Edna St. Vincent Millay, Christopher Morley, Sarah Cleghorn, Ring Lardner, George Kaufman, Edna Ferber, Arthur

Guiterman, Sinclair Lewis, George Jester, Elinor Wylie, William Rose Benét, William Allen White, John Erskine, Moss Hart, Deems Taylor, and Groucho Marx. It was said that Adams raised Dorothy Parker "from a couplet"—an accurate appraisal, for the columnist disdained unrhymed free verse, describing it as "prose masquerading as poetry." Writers produced it, he explained, because

> The editors
> Buy it
> At
> So much
> A
> Line

Adams's notes of acceptance or witty, gentle rejection to contributors were always penned in green ink, and often parodied the style of the contribution.

Quick to recognize and encourage new talent, Adams would often rush to the city desk to discover and congratulate the author of an unsigned article. Friends knew him as a man devoted to his family, and partial to good cigars, poker, pool, tennis, good reporters, obscure writers, and loud neckties. Adams was "a pioneer who has done more for the crimson cravat than any other man living," Frank Sullivan once remarked.

Adams's own "sane and salty" verse was the mainstay of "The Conning Tower"; the *New York Times* once called him "the direct intellectual descendant of Charles Stuart Calverly and Sir William Gilbert." Adams was a good-humored connoisseur of grammatical and typographical errors; he spent a lifetime gently chiding people who mispronounced and misused the English language. "I developed a passion for accuracy, mostly because I always have hated sloppiness," he confessed in the August 1942 *Atlantic Monthly*. "You may be ignorant of most facts, and careless, and wise; you may have great knowledge and accuracy and no wisdom," he continued. "but oftener knowledge and wisdom, in varying degree, are in the same person." In "Vain Words," Adams confessed one of his great ambitions as a conservator of the language:

> Humble, surely, mine ambition;
>   It is merely to construct
> Some occasion or condition
>   When I may say "usufruct."
>
> Earnest am I and assiduous;
>   Yet I'm certain that I shan't amount

To a lot till I use "vidious,"
    "Indiscerptible," and "tantamount."

The conductor of "The Conning Tower" had hilarious words of wisdom for all. "To the Just Graduated" he wrote:

Youth of the bounding ambition,
    Out in the strenuous mob,
Shall you Accept a Position?
    Or will you Hunt for a Job?

Impudent and sardonic, his verse used honest rhyme to deflate presidents, prohibitionists, and any others who merited comment. In "Why the Socialist Party is Growing (Dedicated to the School of Journalism)," Adams good-naturedly criticized newsroom ethics:

"A story," the reporter said, "about commercial
                                        crime.
A merchant's been convicted of selling phony stuff.
The sentence is a thousand meg and seven years of
                                        time—"
"A hundred words," the city Ed. replied, "will be
                                        enough."

"A story," the reporter said, "about crimson dame
Just landed from the steamer, wearing slippers that
                                        are red,
She used to be the Dearest Friend of Emperor
                                        Wotsisname—"
"Three columns and a layout!" cried the eager city
                                        Ed.

Adams spared neither literary masters nor himself, as in "Us Poets":

Wordsworth wrote some tawdry stuff;
    Much of Moore I have forgotten;
Parts of Tennyson are guff;
    Bits of Byron, too, are rotten.

All of Browning isn't great;
    There are slipshod lines in Shelley;
Everyone knows Homer's fate;
    Some of Keats is vermicelli.

Sometimes Shakespeare hit the slide,
    Not to mention Pope or Milton;
Some of Southey's stuff is snide.
    Some of Spenser's simply Stilton.

When one has to boil the pot,
    One can't always watch the kittle.

You may credit it or not—
    Now and then *I* slump a little!

Perhaps Adams's most widely quoted poem is "Baseball's Sad Lexicon," his eulogy for the immortal Chicago Cubs infield:

These are the saddest of possible words:
    "Tinker to Evers to Chance."
Trio of bear cubs, and fleeter than birds,
    Tinker and Evers and Chance.
Ruthlessly pricking our gonfalon bubble,
    Making a Giant hit into a double—
Words that are heavy with nothing but
    trouble:
"Tinker to Evers to Chance."

Many of Adams's poems were collected in book form. Beginning with *In Cupid's Court* (1902), his verse proceeds through more than ten books, including *The Melancholy Lute* (1936), his selection of the outpourings of thirty years. *The Conning Tower Book* (1926) and *The Second Conning Tower Book* (1927) anthologize selections from that column, while *Nods and Becks* (1944) collects prose and verse gleanings from "The Conning Tower" along with a selection of Adams's occasional articles from the *Atlantic Monthly, Harper's*, the *Saturday Review of Literature*, and other magazines.

Each Saturday, Adams turned his column into a personal diary in the manner of Samuel Pepys, indeed calling his version "The Diary of Our Own Samuel Pepys." Adams was recognized as a powerful influence in popularizing Pepys's *Diary* among modern readers. He confessed that he started the Saturday diary column "solely to get a day off," but it soon became a popular feature. In 1935, critic Clifton Fadiman observed in the *New Yorker* that "for decades," the columnist "has been hugging to his breast, with primitive glee, the pitiful delusion that his diary was just a shrewd device enabling him to save one column's worth of work every week"; instead, the feature was the frank revelation of "an amusing, intelligent, unpretentious personality." Adams's molehills of casual comment on everyday occurrences added up to a mountain of insight. In a rather seventeenth-century style, he advised readers of where he went during the week, the dinners he ate, the books he read, the tennis and poker he played, the clothes he wore, the teeth he had had repaired, the plays he viewed, the literary affectations he denounced, the slang he was amused by, the social injustices he deplored, the politicians he distrusted, and especially, the comings and goings

The Conning Tower

THE DIARY OF OUR OWN SAMUEL PEPYS

Saturday, October 7

A DULLISH gray day, and read hard in the day's journals, in this one what a fine man is Mr. Smith and what a sorry fellow is Mr. Miller, and that one what a fine man is Mr. Miller and what a churl is Mr. Smith, but it did not confuse me at all, forasmuch as I know them both to be good men, and far better than most of those who are going to vote for them and against them. Read this day the worst parody of a thing ever I read, called "If Winter Don't," by Barry Pain, maladroit and without skill or humour, and utterly without any sense of the Hutchinsonian style. Yet very pretentious.

So to the courts, but it come on to rain, so stopped there all afternoon, like a zany, waiting for it to stop, and indulging in footless chatter with M. Wheeler and L. Howard and G. Moran, and so home and with my wife to G. Kaufman's for dinner, which I had too much of, and felt ill,

but not till past midnight, and thence home and lay awake all the night till nine Sunday morning, in great pain and in greater rage at myself for having it.

Sunday, October 8

UP BY eleven, and was in poor fettle, but went to the courts and met there Dr. Coburn and asked him whether it would harm me to play, and he said it would be good for me but bad for my game, and so it turned out, for even M. Wheeler beat me a match, and so home, and felt weak, but H. Ross and Jane come in for supper and my wife cooked me some soup and some chicken and I had some, and was much cheered at the tayles H. Ross tells of the troubles he is having with his new house, what with carpenters and plumbers and plasterers and carpenters' helpers and plumbers' helpers and plasterers' helpers, and so early to bed, but I was stunned to think of the time and pains that are expended by all of us in obtaining food, shelter, and raiment; and the time we put in on all else is much too little, which thought kept me awake, and my vigilance fretted me, forasmuch as I cannot do fair work save I am well rested.

Adams's "The Conning Tower," which on Saturdays was a diary written in an archaic style (Culver Pictures)

and sayings of his friends. Since those friends included most of Manhattan's writers and artists, a typical sentence might read: "And in the evening Rosemary Benét and Stephen come to dinner, and we talked of the days the Benéts spent in Paris, and of his studies of the Civil War"; or "later to George and Beatrice Kaufman's where I sat with Mrs. Dorothy Parker who is deeply cherished by me; then on to an evening with H. Swope, M. Van Doren. . . ."

Adams's Saturday morning columns provide a firsthand look at many events and trends of the day. On 18 June 1927, he commented: "Early up, and saw an airplane in the sky at 8 o'clock, and wondered whether it were Lindbergh, and found later it was, on his way to St. Louis. . . . My amazement at the conspicuous sanity of Lindbergh grows daily, for those who introduce him and praise him become wordier all the time, and in his place I should be screaming with boredom."

As war clouds gathered in Europe during the 1930s, Adams was ready with analysis and comment. In Germany on 9-13 November 1938, during successive nights of terror that collectively came to

be called *Kristallnacht* ("Night of Broken Glass"), Jews were beaten and killed, their stores looted and burned. In his 12 November column, Adams called the news from Berlin "so cruel as to be incredible in any age; but there is this about Hitler and his followers: that daily it seems that human indecency and savagery can go no further, and daily it seems that yesterday all of us were in error."

"The Diary of Our Own Samuel Pepys" was also an arena for Adams's sharp critical abilities. Though he often wrote of seemingly minor events in his diary column, he had nearly impeccable taste. He was one of the first to recognize merit in the writings of D. H. Lawrence, Somerset Maugham, Ring Lardner, Sinclair Lewis, and many others. As early as 1915, he observed that "Mistress Wharton will never, I fear, do so good a story again as 'Ethan Frome.'" Of then-youthful Spanish guitarist Andrés Segovia, F.P.A. noted on 4 February 1928: "I enjoyed his playing mighty much, in especiall his playing of Bach and Haydn, which I liked better even than his playing of the Spanish musique."

Adams also used his weekday column for literary and dramatic criticism. On 3 March 1924 he evaluated burgeoning playwright Eugene O'Neill's latest work, *All God's Chillun Got Wings*. The columnist denounced objections to the play because of a scene in which a Negro kissed the hand of a white woman: "I deem such objection foolish. Lord, if it be a good play, let it run free; whereas if it be not, and when I read it it seemed dull to me, it will make no great stir. What would the Klan and such people have done about 'Othello'?" By 22 April 1925, Adams had seen O'Neill's *Desire Under the Elms*, which he ranked as the best the playwright had written to date—until October 1931 when he saw *Mourning Becomes Electra*. But though Adams criticized the play for being too long, he also praised O'Neill's singular "humourlessness . . . which hath carried him toward the stars." Ever ready with a couplet, Adams advised:

> Stick close to your desk with a heart of steel
> And you all may be playwrights like Eugene
>   O'Neill!

In six additional lines, Adams summed up O'Neill's aesthetic:

> When I was a lad on the Provincetown staff
> I was never guilty of a smile or a laugh;
> I wrote of the human race's fall,
> And I never thought of laughing at myself at all,
> I wrote of that fall so incessantly
> That now I am the author of a trilogy.

Adams's talents were not confined to the newspaper column. In 1909 he coauthored with O. Henry a musical comedy called *Lo*. With Montague Glass, George Kaufman, Ring Lardner, and others, he wrote *The '49ers*, produced at New York's Punch and Judy Theatre in 1922. In 1947 he wrote a new version of George M. Cohan's *Forty-Five Minutes from Broadway*, which had been a 1906 musical comedy success. He compiled a book of quotations in 1952.

Adams's interest in quizzes and questionnaires had been manifested as early as 1927, when he and Harry Hansen published a book of questions and answers called *Answer This One*. In his later years, Adams combined his wit, erudition, and remarkably precise memory to win yet another enormous following among radio audiences, starting in 1938 as a panelist on the program "Information, Please!" Contributing his esoteric knowledge on subjects as diverse as Gilbert and Sullivan, baseball, and barbershop singing, Adams joined experts such as Clifton Fadiman and John Kieran in answering obscure questions. "Now this game was old stuff to

Adams on the popular radio program "Information, Please!," which went on the air in 1938 (Culver Pictures)

me," Adams wrote in the February 1942 *Harper's* magazine. "For years we had played this, or variations of it, at Herbert Bayard Swope's house parties—the host, Alexander Woollcott, Laurence Stallings, Arthur Krock, and I." Still, he confessed to being "frightened" when "Information, Please!" was awarded the *Saturday Review of Literature*'s 1940 award for "Distinguished Service to Literature." To Adams, it seemed "pretentious . . . we were men who were having a good time, and by a miracle, paid for having it." Some of the "Information, Please!" programs were made into movie shorts, and the program moved to television in 1952.

Adams died in New York on 23 March 1960 at the age of seventy-eight. He had suffered from arteriosclerosis for five years and had been confined to the Lynwood Nursing Home on West 102nd Street for most of that time. He left his widow, their four children—Anthony, Timothy, Jonathan, and Persephone—and thousands of readers who would not easily forget the wit and wisdom he had pounded out almost daily for so many decades.

References:

James Boylan, ed., *The World and the Twenties* (New York: Dial, 1973);

" 'Conning Tower' Down," *Time*, 29 (15 March 1937): 52-55;

Clifton Fadiman, "The Education of Franklin P. Adams," *New Yorker*, 11 (9 November 1935): 81-82;

"F.P.A. of the *New York Tribune*," *Everybody's*, 34 (May 1916): 598-599;

"F.P.A. Surfaces Again," *Time*, 47 (11 February 1946): 65;

"F.P.A.: Veteran Pilot Calm as 'Conning Tower' Submerges," *Newsweek*, 9 (13 March 1937): 32;

Rupert Hughes, "F.P.A.," *Everybody's*, 42 (April 1920): 52-53;

Thomas L. Masson, "Franklin P. Adams," in his *Our American Humorists* (New York: Moffat, Yard, 1922), pp. 21-25;

"Post-Script and F.P.A.," *Newsweek*, 27 (11 February 1946): 78;

Clarke Robinson, "Radio I.Q. Gets a Boost," *Christian Science Monitor Magazine*, 21 December 1938, p. 4;

Bert L. Taylor, "F.P.A.," *American Magazine*, 77 (April 1914): 66-68;

Carl Van Doren, "Day In and Day Out," *Century*, 107 (December 1923): 308-315;

John Wheelwright, "Poet as Funny Man," *Poetry*, 50 (July 1937): 210-215;

"Wit Fired," *Time*, 38 (25 August 1941): 51.

Paul Y. Anderson

(29 August 1893– 6 December 1938)

Edmund B. Lambeth
University of Kentucky

MAJOR POSITIONS HELD: General assignment reporter and Washington correspondent, *St. Louis Post-Dispatch* (1914-1938).

Although he allowed himself only forty-five years of life, twenty-seven in the craft he loved, Paul Y. Anderson, at his death in 1938, had helped reinvigorate muckraking, nudged forward a fledgling movement toward press criticism, and lent his unique charisma to a newspaper that served as a pioneer setter of standards of daily journalism. Anderson's reporting and writing were honored by a 1929 Pulitzer Prize and a 1937 Headliners' Club award and have been collected in treasuries of the craft and in textbooks. They are distinguished for their accuracy, conciseness, flair, and courage. His role in exposing the Teapot Dome scandal in the 1920s did much to reawaken the press's image of itself as a watchdog of government.

Born in Knoxville to William Holston and Elizabeth Dill Haynes Anderson, Paul Anderson was the only son among the three of their six children who survived infancy. When Anderson was three years old, his father, a stonecutter, was killed when a faulty derrick fell on him in a quarry. In the opinion of members of his family, this loss angered and embittered the future journalist, generating much of the energy that was later to be channeled into long hours of investigative reporting. To make ends meet, Anderson's mother returned to teaching school, a vocation that had a significant impact on her son's knowledgeability and his use of language. To help the family, Anderson delivered telegrams and newspapers. In 1911, through family friends, the eighteen-year-old Anderson found a reporting job on the *Knoxville Journal*.

In 1912 he moved to the *St. Louis Times*, in 1913 to the *St. Louis Star*, and in 1914 to the *St. Louis Post-Dispatch*, which published his stories for the next twenty-three years. Also in 1914, Anderson married Beatrice Wright of East St. Louis, by whom he had two sons, Paul Webster and Kenneth Paine.

Anderson arrived at just the time his energy, intrepid spirit, and facile pen could be of most use to the *Post-Dispatch*'s great managing editor, O. K. Bovard, who helped build it into a crusading newspaper with an international reputation for honest and adroit reporting. His supervision of the young Anderson has been recognized as a fortuitous match of ideal reporter and editor.

Anderson first came to national attention when a congressional committee investigated the East St. Louis, Illinois, race riots of 1917. As a reporter covering East St. Louis for the *Post-Dispatch*, Anderson was one of many newspapermen called to testify. In its report to the House of Representatives, the committee singled out Anderson's reporting for high commendation. Anderson, the committee said, "reported what he saw without fear of consequences; defied the indignant officials whom he charged with criminal neglect of duty; ran a daily risk of assassination, and rendered an invaluable public service by his exposures." The committee's report made front-page news in the *Post-Dispatch*, and the young reporter's reputation soared. His personal life, however, was not as successful: he was divorced from his wife in 1919.

Anderson did the spadework for the *Post-Dispatch*'s first successful crusade—to free political prisoners unjustly incarcerated during and after World War I. In 1923, after two years as an editorial writer, Anderson was unable to persuade the *Post-Dispatch* to send him to Washington; so he quit his job to go on his own. In the move to Washington, Anderson was following the suggestion of Sen. Robert La Follette, Sr., whom he had met when the Wisconsin lawmaker visited St. Louis.

La Follette had predicted that Anderson's detective talents would find a fertile outlet in Washington; as a free lance, whose earliest stories appeared in such newspapers as the *Omaha World-Herald* and the *Raleigh News and Observer* as well as in the *Post-Dispatch*, Anderson fulfilled La Follette's expectations. Helped by La Follette, then in his twilight years, Anderson saw more clearly than most the significance of the emerging controversy over the leasing of oil lands under federal government ownership in Teapot Dome, Wyoming, and Elk Hills, California. In the first phase of the investigation, it was disclosed that Interior Secretary Albert Fall had corruptly leased land and had been paid off in the form of $230,000 in Liberty Bonds. Anderson's stories on the scandal and its investigation by La Follette and others helped the Progressives in the Senate do battle with the Harding and Coolidge administrations. Impressed with Anderson's Washington performance, Bovard rehired him. In 1924 Anderson reported wryly on the heresy trial of Cleveland's Episcopal Bishop William Montgomery Brown. In that same year the *Post-Dispatch* sent him to Chicago to cover the bizarre and grotesque trial of Nathan F. Leopold, Jr., and Richard A. Loeb, both nineteen, for the abduction and murder of fourteen-year-old Bobby Franks. The next year brought the nation a legal confrontation less gruesome but intellectually more significant, the famous "Scopes monkey trial" in Dayton, Tennessee. In these two assignments Anderson mixed with the elite of daily journalism and became known to them

Paul Y. Anderson

as a master of observation, fact gathering, and reportage.

In 1925 Anderson contributed materially to an investigation which resulted in the resignation of Federal Judge George W. English in the face of impeachment on corruption charges. Another *Post-Dispatch* reporter who also played a major role in the investigation, John T. Rogers, won the 1925 Pulitzer Prize. In 1926, when the socialist government of Mexico became a lightning rod for the wrath of Washington, Anderson called into question an Associated Press story which, without attribution, asserted that the Mexican government, by means of a propaganda campaign, was attempting to establish a "Bolshevik hegemony" between the United States and the Panama Canal. Anderson decided to investigate what evidence there was for the charge and, finding little, wrote a story identifying the source of the report, a top State Department official. In typically acerbic tone, Anderson said the AP had behaved "in the fashion of the 'reptile' press of Europe," carrying out the wishes of the government. Discussing his exposure, Anderson recalled: "The effect upon the conduct of affairs at the State Department was prompt and salutary."

Anderson remarried in 1928; his second wife was Anna Alberta Fritschle of St. Louis, whom he married on 19 March. Also in 1928—four years after Anderson's initial coverage of the Teapot Dome episode—Bovard suggested that he look into what had happened to the more than $2,770,000 in remaining bonds which had been acquired by the Continental Trading Company, the implicated instrument of corruption. If a portion had been used for bribery, why not the rest? Anderson took it upon himself to find a way to reopen the investigation.

Owen Roberts, the special United States counsel who had headed the government's investigation of the oil scandal, told Anderson that he, Roberts, lacked authority to open a new inquiry. The Secret Service likewise declined. Attorney General John G. Sargent gave Anderson the brush-off. Democratic Senator Thomas J. Walsh of Montana, who had conducted the initial hearing, was weary and anxious to avoid further accusations that he was playing politics with the oil scandal. Not giving up, Anderson turned to his old friend Republican Senator George Norris of Nebraska. Norris agreed on the need for a Senate investigation, but he wanted to give President Coolidge an opportunity to act first. When Coolidge did not act, Norris introduced, and the senate passed unanimously, a resolution calling for a new hearing.

As a result of the ensuing congressional investigation and government prosecutions, Robert W. Stewart, head of the Standard Oil Company of Indiana, was indicted for contempt of the Senate and perjury. Although acquitted in both cases, he later was ousted from his job. Oil magnate Harry Sinclair was jailed. Stewart and James O'Neil, another principal in the scandal, made restitution, and eventually the government regained $6,000,000. For his work resulting in the reopening of the investigation, Anderson won the Pulitzer Prize.

Anderson's prizewinning Teapot Dome series, calling attention to loose ends in the investigation that could not be officially ignored, are the most celebrated newspaper articles of his career. But his standing in the history of reporting in the first third of the century rests on his work on other stories as well. On stories of national significance, he was frequently the reporter of choice at the *Post-Dispatch*. In 1930, after the Al Capone mob killed

Jake Lingle, a reporter later shown to be in the employ of gangsters, the *Post-Dispatch* sent Anderson to Chicago, where he put together a massive account of the rise of gang influence in Chicago's public life. With a Pulitzer Prize to his credit and with a reputation for vivid and penetrating reportage, Anderson had become an influence in his own right. With a salary of $16,000 in the 1930s (the equivalent of $100,000 in the 1980s), Anderson was a Horatio Alger of the Fourth Estate.

When arriving in Washington at the age of thirty, Anderson had shared the optimistic, idealistic perspective of the elder La Follette. But within his first decade in the capital, he became disillusioned. His favorites, the Progressives, not only did not always "win," but they, too, were revealed to have feet of clay. Moreover, the growing complexities of modern life did not always yield with ease to the model solutions of the earlier Progressive era. With Conservatives holding sway in the White House of the 1920s, it was not easy, at least from a Progressive's point of view, to have an abiding faith in the wisdom of the American electorate.

As a journalist with deep feelings about the events he covered, Anderson found a purgative for his skepticism as a columnist in the liberal magazine the *Nation*, starting in 1929. There, he gave free rein to sentiments which could not be wholly vented even in the *Post-Dispatch*, considered among the most liberal of newspapers. He dissected the machinations of the chemical and power industries' attempt to stop government development of electric power at Muscle Shoals, Alabama. Mercilessly he critiqued the Herbert Hoover administration, whose leader he dubbed "The Great White Feather." He documented and bemoaned the underdevelopment of the emerging technology of radio. He monitored and wrung hands over corruption in the Reconstruction Finance Corporation. He cheered labor's militancy and criticized the captains of industry he deemed blameworthy: "Tardily but inexorably the sharp hook of justice is sinking into the tough gullet of the boldest industrial outlaw of our times [Henry Ford]." In embracing the ill-fated National Recovery Act against criticism that it was undemocratic, Anderson wrote that "there is a very serious question about whether we can end this depression before revolution breaks out," adding: "When ten million men have been without jobs for three years and are asking themselves whether they will ever work again, when they have seen their women fade and their babies wither and die, when they have seen their boys turn to thievery and their girls to prostitution, it strikes me as a poor time to play dilettante over the classical ideas of Jeffersonian democracy."

In his *Nation* column these critical progressive and muckraking perspectives also were focused on the press. He deplored the attitude of publishers toward the N.R.A. and its efforts to regulate the economic aspects of the newspaper industry. He helped organize the American Newspaper Guild and applauded its progress. Despite, and perhaps even because of their stature, he poked holes in what he deemed to be the pretensions of such standout journalists as Walter Lippmann, William Allen White, Arthur Krock, and the young Marquis Childs, his colleague on the *Post-Dispatch*. On the occasions when he believed that editorial writers had maligned the institutions of the Congress, he sprang to its defense, particularly that of the Senate. He critiqued his colleagues' performances in covering Congress, Hoover's presidency, and the New Deal. He denounced as "cowardly and pusillanimous" the American Society of Newspaper Editors' rejection of an amendment to its constitution which would allow it to censure, suspend, or expel members for gross misconduct or violation of ethics. To encourage and applaud what he judged to be good journalism, he published a "Washington Honor Roll," listing the stories and their authors.

When the demands of his occupation pressed in upon him, Anderson began to drink heavily. Attempts by the *Post-Dispatch* to help him and his own attempts to help himself were evident in the 1930s. In a *Nation* column on 7 March 1934 entitled "Amenities from a hospital pallet," he wrote: "Well, here I am in the Johns Hopkins Hospital again, a living testament to the fact that no one with a nervous system like mine can long survive on a steady diet of hard work and moral indignation." In that year he surrendered his column in the *Nation*. In 1936 he divorced his second wife.

Further deterioration followed a period in which many believed he had regained his old resilience and form. In 1937 he won the Headliners' Club award for his initiative and thoroughness in exposing the suppressed Paramount newsreel film which depicted the massacre of ten workers by police patrolling the struck Republic Steel Company plant near Chicago. On 30 August he married Katherine Lane, a New York actress and radio personality; their marriage was celebrated in a second ceremony on 3 September but soon ended in separation. In January 1938 Anderson was dismissed from the *Post-Dispatch* for prolonged absences from and inattention to his job; he was quickly hired by

the *St. Louis Star-Times* for its Washington bureau. On 31 October 1938, although he knew it would subject him to charges of ideological partisanship, Anderson took to the radio in a critical description of the methods of Rep. Martin Dies, chairman of the notorious Un-American Activities Committee. Anderson became increasingly despondent and depressed. On 6 December 1938 he took an overdose of sleeping pills, leaving behind a note saying his "usefulness was at an end."

Testimony to Anderson's achievements and influence is ample. Marquis Childs described him as a "brilliant reporter and writer." Samuel Tait, Jr., writing at the peak of Anderson's career, said that Anderson "deserved almost as much credit for the present fame of the *Post-Dispatch*" as did the paper's celebrated editor: "If Bovard charted the new course of the *Post-Dispatch*, Anderson has so far done more than anyone else to steer it over that course." Looking back to the 1920s and 1930s from the perspective of 1973, Carey McWilliams, editor of the *Nation*, wrote: "If the *Nation* had done nothing more than publish Paul Y. Anderson in these years it would have made a significant contribution to the continuance of the muckraking tradition."

Anderson's personal and professional faults have also been amply identified. Fred Freed quotes a contemporary describing Anderson as "an egoist and intellectual bully." *New York Times* reporter Cabell Phillips, in a study of Washington correspondents, called him "brilliant" but also "erratic." Richard Strout, the *Christian Science Monitor*'s longtime Washington correspondent and *New Republic* columnist, admired him but criticized his "prosecutorial complex." William Allen White likewise admired Anderson's work, but he said Anderson's bitterness limited his effectiveness.

Perhaps the most moving tribute came from Heywood Broun, who, in a column on his colleague's life, took umbrage at a *Time* article calling attention to Anderson's drinking. Anderson, Broun wrote, had worked "constantly under punishing tension" and had worn "a hair shirt of complete dedication to the things in which he believed," adding: "But just about the last person in the world with any right to mention the matter is some little snip sitting with scissors and paste pot in the office of *Time* piecing out the curious sign language in which that magazine is written for the delectation of commuters and clubwomen. Paul Y. Anderson, drunk or sober, was by so much the finest journalist of his day that it is not fitting for any moist-eared chit even to touch the hem of his weakness. . . . It is not necessary for anybody to make apologies for

Paul Y. Anderson. Taken in his entirety he stands up as a man deserving of love and homage from every working newspaperman and woman in the United States. We will carry on."

References:

Leslie Erhardt, "Anderson of the *Post-Dispatch*," *Quill* (April 1935): 8-10;

Fred Freed, "Paul Y. Anderson," *Esquire*, 29 (March 1948): 101-105;

Freda Kirchwey, Oswald Garrison Villard, and Marguerite Young, *Where is There Another? A Memorial to Paul Y. Anderson* (Norman, Okla.: Cooperative Books, 1939);

Samuel Tait, Jr., "The St. Louis *Post-Dispatch*," *American Mercury*, 22 (April 1931): 403-406.

Hugh Baillie
(23 October 1890-1 March 1966)

Richard A. Schwarzlose
Northwestern University

MAJOR POSITIONS HELD: President and general manager, United Press (1935-1955).

BOOKS: *Two Battlefronts* (New York: United Press Associations, 1943);
High Tension: The Recollections of Hugh Baillie (New York: Harper, 1959).

OTHER: "Open Channels for News," in *Treasury for the Free World*, edited by Ben Raeburn (New York: Arco, 1946), pp. 264-268.

PERIODICAL PUBLICATION: "Two European Highlights: Mrs. Simpson; Peace vs. War," *Vital Speeches of the Day*, 3 (1 February 1937): 236-238.

"During the years, I have held a lot of jobs in the United Press—from chairman down—but I was a REPORTER all the way," was the way Hugh Baillie summed up his forty-two-year career with the wire service in 1959. After a meteoric eight-year rise to general news manager and twelve years in various UP executive positions, Baillie emerged as president of the news agency and presided during two decades over a tripling of UP's clientele, including a historic move into the radio news business and a vast post-World War II expansion in the foreign news market. A fiercely competitive newshound and a writer of burly, image-laden news copy, Baillie frequently left his executive duties to subordinates while he took to the field to direct his staff and report news events.

There were journalists on both sides of his

family when Baillie was born 23 October 1890 in Brooklyn, New York, to David Gemmell and Fannie Mead Hays Baillie. His father, born in Scotland and a writer for newspapers in Dumfries and Birmingham, had set off in 1887 for Australia in search of new worlds to conquer. Stopping en route in New York City, he decided to stay, getting a reporter's job with the *New York Tribune* and a second job as literary secretary for Andrew Carnegie. He later wrote for the *New York World* and the *New York Press*. Baillie's grandfather on his mother's side was John B. Hays, political writer for the *New York Tribune* and dean and president of the New York City Hall Reporters' Association. Young Hugh was permitted to accompany his father and grandfather on assignments, meeting such personalities as Grover Cleveland, Theodore Roosevelt, Chauncey Depew, Mark Twain, Adm. George Dewey, and Thomas A. Edison. As a lad of six Baillie accompanied his father aboard President William McKinley's inaugural train from Canton, Ohio, to Washington, D.C.

When Baillie was thirteen, the family moved to California, where his father found work on the editorial-page staff of the *Los Angeles Herald*. Baillie served as campus correspondent for the *Herald* while attending the University of Southern California from 1907-1910. Itching to break into the newspaper business and have the kinds of experiences his father had, Baillie cut short his education and took a job for twelve dollars per week on the *Los Angeles Record*, owned by E. W. Scripps. The *Record* was the town's "razzle-dazzle paper," Baillie later said, "more likely than any other to carry a screaming headline across all eight columns of the front

Hugh Baillie (UPI)

page." After a short stint as a sportswriter, Baillie moved to police reporting, where he was attracted to the human drama and violence of crime news. He carried a revolver (a privilege granted Los Angeles police reporters then), joined police on raids, rode the paddy wagons to crime scenes, invented sinister nicknames for notorious criminals, and interviewed dying murder victims. The exhilaration and feeling of self-importance derived from such experiences captivated young Baillie and extracted from him lurid, raffish stories that caught his editors' and the public's eyes. His lifelong love affair with violence and its news potential had begun.

In 1912, Baillie was asked by United Press, then only five years old and also owned by the Scripps organization, to cover the Los Angeles trial of famed lawyer Clarence Darrow on charges of trying to bribe a juror. The assignment was the twenty-one-year-old reporter's first wire-service work. For twelve weeks Baillie's by-line, which drew national attention and the approval of his superiors, topped UP coverage of the trial. He wound up his trial coverage by beating all competitors with the "not guilty" verdict. Baillie joined UP's San Francisco bureau in 1915, writing and filing the news report for the wire's West Coast clients. It was his first chance to see individual stories in the perspective of a full news report.

The summer of 1916 found him in Portland, Oregon, in charge of a two-man UP bureau. He was accompanied by a new bride, Constance Scott, who had formerly been with the *Oakland Tribune*. Good fortune again smiled on Baillie: UP, only nine years old and hungry for clients, held a nationwide contest among bureau chiefs with a prize for the one signing up the most new clients; Baillie won with eight or nine (his later recollection was unclear as to the exact number). In March 1917 UP moved Baillie to its Chicago bureau, where he dictated an abbreviated news report over the phone to small newspapers in the region.

His stay in Chicago was cut short after three weeks by a call to join the New York City bureau. The gathering war clouds in Europe had caused UP to redistribute its reporters, and Baillie was needed for reporting and rewrite duties in the wire's headquarters. He was on hand when the New York bureau relayed to American clients UP's famous false armistice bulletin on 7 November 1918. Although UP struggled for years to free itself from the stigma of ending World War I four days too soon and setting off premature victory celebrations across the country, the experience did not dampen Baillie's lifelong drive to do anything to beat competing wire services on breaking news events.

Two years of staff work in New York led in 1919 to a major stride in Baillie's career: he was made Washington, D.C., bureau manager—"one of the most important posts in the organization," Baillie later observed. At twenty-eight years of age Baillie was "the youngest man in the bureau which was staffed . . . by great reporters," he wrote in 1959. "One of my first acts as manager was to appoint an assistant manager who could handle the inside job while I went out and covered stories." This strategy allowed him "to assign myself to what was—both in significance and in human interest—one of the great stories of this century," President Woodrow Wilson taking his case for the League of Nations to the people. Throughout the twenty-two days of Wilson's ill-fated eight-thousand-mile whistle-stop campaign, UP's coverage was headed by Baillie's by-line. He had found a way to satisfy his desire to be where the action is and to climb UP's corporate ladder at the same time.

Heading UP's contingent of reporters at the Republican national convention in Chicago in 1920, Baillie briefly became part of the news. With the convention deadlocked over a presidential nominee, Baillie spied several party leaders huddling on the platform. Sensing a story brewing, Baillie joined the huddle, and soon other reporters were attempting to do the same. The convention chairman, Sen. Henry Cabot Lodge, became aware of the intrusion and ordered Baillie off the platform. Baillie

Baillie (in shirt sleeves) in the New York United Press newsroom in 1920

refused to leave, and in an ensuing scuffle his right fist grazed the chin of the sergeant at arms. Baillie found himself mentioned in other reporters' convention coverage.

Personnel changes in UP's hierarchy soon brought Baillie into the executive pipeline that eventually led him to the agency's presidency. UP's second president, Roy W. Howard, moved from the wire service to the Scripps newspaper publishing division in 1920. His successor, William W. Hawkins, led UP for only two and a half years before following Howard into the newspaper end of the parent organization and turning over the presidency to Karl A. Bickel in 1923. Amid these shifts, Baillie after the 1920 national election was made manager of the New York bureau. He was soon promoted to assistant general news manager, then to general news manager of the United Press. The wire's historian, Joe Alex Morris, later described Baillie's rapid movement through the organization as "several lightning shifts." At thirty-three years of age, after having been a UP staffer for only eight years, Baillie was in 1923 "responsible personally for what went out on the UP wires," as he later explained.

"There was no secret about the fact that I was ambitious," Baillie wrote in 1959, "thought I could run the UP someday, and wanted the chance." Realizing this, Bickel told Baillie to get some experience on the business side of the wire and assigned him to the business department in 1924. "I stepped down from the top spot on the news-gathering end of the UP and went out as a salesman. I felt terrible," Baillie later recalled. "I was as welcome in the business department as a case of smallpox. I had a reputation: I was a competitor. I was such a goddamn competitor a lot of people didn't want me around." They assigned him to the Old South, a tough assignment because the region was dominated by the Associated Press. Noting that UP's circuit terminated in Atlanta, Baillie figured he could open up Florida and south Georgia to UP by convincing the *Miami Herald* to subscribe to the service. He succeeded, added twelve new clients, and within nine months was UP sales manager.

In 1927 Baillie moved a step closer to the presidency by being named vice-president and general business manager. Although still officially separated from his beloved news report, Baillie would be able to report on news events which he happened upon while on the road or in New York. He also kept his eye on the news report because its by-lines, scoops, and special features were strong UP selling points. And sell it he did: while he was responsible for UP's business side, the wire added about 200 clients and pulled even with AP's 1,300 members. In the spring of 1931, when UP moved out of offices in the old *New York World* building and into the new *Daily News* building on Forty-second Street, Baillie had just been named executive vice-president and general manager. As second in command and heir apparent to Bickel, Baillie once again had active responsibility for the news department.

While in Europe in the summer of 1932, touring UP's facilities and assessing the likelihood of war, Baillie conducted an interview with German chancellor Franz von Papen, who declared that "Germany must have her place in the sun" and predicted that his country would "battle relentlessly to wipe out the discriminations imposed on her" by the Versailles Treaty. Although the interview was widely published in the United States, the Depression and the coming presidential election overshadowed von Papen's predictions of war.

At home, United Press was caught in the throes of a different kind of "treaty": the so-called Biltmore Agreement of 1933 by which UP, AP, International News Service, the Columbia Broadcasting System, and the National Broadcasting Company set up the Press-Radio Bureau to funnel harmless droplets of news to radio clients and thus not threaten the many newspaper publishers who feared radio's news potential. Many at UP, including Bickel and Baillie, feared that attempts to limit the flow of news to radio stations would prompt the development of independent news agencies which would not only serve radio but could expand into the newspaper field as well. Efforts to sell the Scripps company on abandoning the agreement and offering a radio service proved taxing to Bickel, whose health had been deteriorating for several years. Finally, in April 1935 UP's board approved a radio service, accepted Bickel's retirement, and named the forty-four-year-old Baillie as the company's fifth president and general manager.

"There had been no doubt in Baillie's mind for years—perhaps never—that he could run a news agency better than anybody else," Morris comments. Baillie "had the thorough knowledge of operations, the inexhaustible energy, the dramatic showmanship in news coverage, and the self-confidence that would be so vital to success in perhaps the most frenzied and difficult twenty-year period ever to face a press association."

"Showmanship" became a Baillie trademark. While Kent Cooper, his counterpart at AP, operated as a corporate executive, generally sticking close to the office, regularly playing golf with other business executives, and writing thoughtful articles and speeches on freedom of the press, Baillie seemed to be traveling all the time both to oversee UP's news-gathering and business interests and to cover headline news. "Baillie was no armchair brass hat," Morris says. "He had the experience, the craftsmanship and the drive of a good reporter and . . . demonstrated a remarkable ability to turn up at the scene of action." Assertive, demonstrative, always pushing his reporting troops to be first with the brightest copy, Baillie peppered his bureaus with telegrams demanding better coverage—scattering "a few red ants," as he put it.

But his special strength was getting into the field to inspire his staffers, to create the "mystique" of the UP which urged staffers to outdo themselves and to feel an intense loyalty to the organization. This is the way Baillie described his attitude in 1959: "It's part of the job of the president of the United Press to travel around the world, carrying an evangelical fervor, and leaving some of that fervor behind him when he departs. Meanwhile, of course, he also picks up a firsthand knowledge of how events are going in all parts of the world. . . . Soon he begins to *feel* the news that's coming up. . . . That's what you need more than anything else when you're president of a news agency—a kind of second sense . . . which smells tomorrow's news."

Baillie's first major outing as UP president was to return to Europe for interviews with Adolf Hitler, Benito Mussolini (whose troops were engaged in Ethiopia), and various Russian officials. On 7 January 1937, when he addressed the New York State Chamber of Commerce, he spoke of "the dreaded Big War which hangs over us," and characterized the Spanish Civil War as a "strange . . . experimental war laboratory" in which Europe's powers tested their own military machines and each other's desire to enter the inevitable "general European conflagration."

In November 1936 Baillie arrived in London while the British papers were still suppressing the news of King Edward VIII's romance with American divorcée Wallis Simpson, even though the rest of the world knew about the love affair. After surveying the situation, Baillie ordered his London bureau to step up coverage. He traveled to Europe many times in the late 1930s, at times accompanied by his wife, and was in London in the fall of 1939 when Hitler's invasion of Poland brought England into the war. He ordered his staff to "shoot the works," argued with the British about heavy-handed censorship, and interviewed Prime Minister Neville Chamberlain (although the story was scrubbed when Baillie and Chamberlain could not agree on a text).

Many times in the next six years Baillie escaped the confines of New York headquarters to see the action firsthand and to interview world leaders. His most famous sojourn was between mid-June and early August 1943 when he visited London, Sicily, and the North African front, filing dispatches as he traveled. "My trip was a business trip, although somewhat more exciting than most," Baillie told *Editor and Publisher* upon his return. "I wanted to live in the field with our men covering this phase of the war, get acquainted with the conditions under which they are working both at the front lines and in the big relay bureaus such as Algiers and London and see if I had any ideas for improving the coverage and preparing for the next big developments."

His dispatches reflect the "brutal realism" he demanded of his war correspondents. In one wartime directive Baillie ordered his foreign news manager to "tell those guys out there to get the smell

Baillie in war correspondent's uniform, covering the Allied invasion of Sicily in 1943

of warm blood into their copy. Tell them to quit writing like retired generals and military analysts, and to write about people killing each other." To make his point, he collected his 1943 dispatches from London, Sicily, and Algiers in a book called *Two Battlefronts*, published in 1943 by UP to serve as a model for its correspondents. A Baillie dispatch from Catania on Sicily, where British and German armies were fighting over every acre of countryside, illustrates his style:

> The sharp crack-crack of artillery comes intermittently, followed by the abrupt yell of shells arching overhead. There are pauses. Then sometimes many shots in rapid succession. You see smoke drifting where the shells hit. It looks like a smudge from grass fires.
>
> The bridge you stroll over is an occasional target for German guns. There are shell holes around here and there. The farm houses in the vicinity are smashed as if by earthquakes.
>
> That is the look of the battlefield—peaceful and rural except for the smashed houses. You get used to the noise. The banging behind you and the screaming shells overhead seem impersonal. The armies are invisible.
>
> But there is plenty of the stink of battle. One sharp bend in the road nearby is called, most appropriately, Dead Horse Corner and you know why when you whiff the breeze. There was sharp fighting here recently and the evidences remain. Graves are here and there, and rough crosses, some with helmets stuck on them. Several very dead Germans lie in attitudes utterly relaxed, like men deep in sleep. One has his right arm over his head in a macabre caricature of Heil Hitler. It was the way he fell. Rifles, ammunition and iron helmets are strewn everywhere but you don't touch anything. Remember booby traps.

Referring to his 1943 dispatches, Baillie later explained, "I am naturally dramatic, and that is why I write such damned dramatic copy." But he demanded the same drama of his correspondents, instructing them that "we want our readers to see, hear, feel, even smell the war!" Despite such goading, Baillie had traveled among his correspondents and appreciated their efforts. "My hat is off to . . . [the] small army of correspondents who endure the same hardships and face many of the same perils as the actual combat troops whose activities they are reporting," Baillie told *Editor and Publisher*.

Baillie was back in Europe in 1944, interviewing Generals Eisenhower and Bradley and Field Marshal Montgomery, among others, but this time he had more on his mind than dramatic war dispatches. In January, while addressing the Michigan Press Association, Baillie had outlined a four-point postwar plan for international press freedom: (1) news sources "competitively open to all," (2) transmission facilities "competitively available to all," (3) "minimum official regulation of news content," and (4) "equal access to all news sources" for newspapers throughout the world. While in Europe Baillie contacted and secured approval from several Western government leaders for his plan.

Baillie's campaign for "international reciprocity in the gathering and selling of news" was a reassertion of UP's thirty-year stance as an independent international wire service. By 1925 UP was serving clients in thirty-six foreign countries; and in 1934, when Associated Press finally broke its cartel agreement with the Reuters news agency of England (which had confined AP to delivering a news report to the United States and a handful of Latin American countries), UP had clients in nearly fifty foreign nations. Freed of the cartel, Baillie's counterpart at AP, Kent Cooper, had begun a campaign for international press freedom in 1942. Baillie wryly cabled Cooper: "As you know, [UP has] always favored and fought in the cause of having all news fields competitively open to all with no government restrictions . . . and we welcome you most heartily as a great associate at long last in this high cause." But despite the efforts of the United Nations and continued attention by newspeople such as Baillie and Cooper, Baillie would lament in 1959 that little progress had been made since the war, adding: "But the fight goes on. The crusade continues." Meanwhile, even in the face of postwar governmental censorship and propaganda, by 1952 UP had clients in seventy-seven foreign countries and AP in sixty-nine.

The postwar period for Baillie continued to be a series of big stories, usually interviews with famous persons. The autumn of 1945 found him in the Pacific interviewing Generalissimo Chiang Kai-shek of China; Emperor Hirohito of Japan; and General Douglas MacArthur, whom he persuaded with much difficulty to grant an interview to explain his Japanese occupation policy, which was being criticized at home. Baillie fought for and secured a change in military orders to permit newsmen to witness executions of those convicted during the Nuremberg war crimes trials; and in October 1946 he received a telegram from Joseph Stalin answering thirty-one questions which Baillie had telegraphed to him a few days earlier. The *New York Times* called Baillie's Stalin interview "the most important and most hopeful statement of Russian policy made since the war."

Baillie was back in war correspondent's garb during the Korean War, first in the Pusan area where U.N. forces clung desperately to a beachhead on the peninsula and later aboard MacArthur's plane flying to the recaptured capital city, Seoul. Baillie's account of MacArthur's entry into the city and "procession" to the remnants of South Korea's capitol building received good play in American newspapers. The dispatch read in part:

> The war air was tainted with smoke and death. The route of the "triumphal procession" had been past smashed and burning buildings, through dense clouds of the infamous Korean dust, past columns of refugees now heading for home. . . . In the seated crowd before MacArthur squeezed into benches where the legislators used to sit, were many wearing camouflaged helmets or caps, and most were keeping them on their heads because shards of glass tinkled down from the wrecked dome of the hall at intervals.
>
> Then MacArthur said: "In humble and devout manifestation of gratitude, I ask that all present rise and join me in reciting the Lord's Prayer."
>
> There was the rumbling shuffle of many feet. Off came the camouflaged helmets, the canvas caps, the snappy blue Air Force hat, the Navy caps. Every head was bowed and, as from the rear I looked over the assembly, many carbines were sticking up. The man directly in front of me wore two pistols and had a knife dangling at his back. . . . MacArthur's voice uttered the words which have come down the ages, slowly and with great feeling.

UP's general news manager, Earl Johnson, cabled congratulations to Baillie the day after the Seoul story had been a big hit in the American press, commenting, "This is first time any correspondent ever scored front page play with Lord's Prayer." But Korea was not World War II and American newspapers were not inclined to use as much news-service copy on the Korean War as Baillie thought they should. A memo to UP's Far Eastern headquarters in the summer of 1952 read in part: "Baillie suggests 'Let's revive Korean War. Bring it back to life now it's merely another bore war. American troops who are out there and their people here deserve better treatment than this. Let's have first person stories from troops under fire [for] first time. Suggest scenes [of] dressing stations, military funerals, evacuation [of] wounded by helicopter, bringing up supplies, just as if it were all brand new. . . . All this battlefield stuff should be vivid and raw because otherwise it won't get printed. . . .' "

Seven years later Baillie recalled: "Our push helped for a while, but not for long. Hard as it was to believe, the American people simply did not want to think about their own boys . . . in the stinking Korean mud." The American people had acquired new tastes in news and new distastes for wars like Korea. Even Baillie's revival of Korea's "brutal realism" in UP's news report could not attract a press and public weary of conflict and dispirited by a postwar era that had brought neither peace nor universal freedom. The reporter's lust for violence and blood, which for Baillie had stretched from the Los Angeles police beat in 1910 to the hills of Sicily in 1943, was an anachronism in many sectors of journalism in the early 1950s.

On 6 April 1955 Baillie turned over the presidency of UP to Frank H. Bartholomew, ending a twenty-year occupancy of that post, the longest in UP's history. Morris calls Baillie's two decades as president "a momentous, history-making period in world affairs and in news-agency affairs" during which UP entered the radio news field, increased the number of both domestic and foreign clients, and pioneered in facsimile delivery of photos and Teletypesetter delivery of copy. But much of this innovativeness swirled around Baillie, who always saw himself primarily as a reporter. His autobiography fails to mention that he served as chairman of UP's board between 1955 and 1957; that position paled for him beside the years of chasing ambulances, touring battlefields, and interviewing world leaders.

Morris describes Baillie as "a tall, square-shouldered man who had an erect military bearing and, despite his Scots ancestry, rather resembled the Hollywood version of a Prussian officer. His hair was closely trimmed in a bristling pompadour, his voice was strong and penetrating even above the chatter of a room full of printer machines, and his bearing was deliberately aggressive." Writer Jack Alexander in a *Saturday Evening Post* biography called Baillie "a simon-pure extrovert" who "took the godlike view of himself," dubbing him "Rip-roaring Baillie." Despite his high-energy aggressiveness, ill health had begun to overtake Baillie in

the years preceding his retirement as UP president. On 1 March 1966, at the age of seventy-five, Baillie died of a heart ailment in Scripps Memorial Hospital in La Jolla, California. He and his wife, who had died in 1962, had one son, Hugh Scott Baillie, who was a sportswriter for United Press International in San Francisco when his father died. Memorial services for Baillie were held in St. James-by-the-Sea Episcopal Church in La Jolla and at Christ Episcopal Church in Guilford, Connecticut, where he was buried in Alderbrook Cemetery.

Reviewing Baillie's 1959 autobiography, *High Tension*, CBS news commentator Ned Calmer asserts that "Much of this book—too much of it, in one opinion—is little more than repetition of the main outlines of national and international events known to every person of Baillie's generation. . . . It is not a profound or searching analysis he gives us, but rather the day-to-day recital, as from a diary or reporter's notebook, of how the stories broke seen by the man covering them." But that, after all, was Baillie's perspective of his job—to be on the front lines or at the desks of world leaders so that the people of his generation would know the events of the day. Growing postwar complexity in the wire-service business called for a new kind of executive, one who, despite yearnings to travel and write "two-fisted" stories of "brutal realism," would act the part of a corporate president. By 1955 the world and journalism had left Hugh Baillie behind, a dramatic and hard-driving reporter of the old school who coincidentally was also UP's president longer than any other man.

References:

Jack Alexander, "Rip-roaring Baillie," in *More Post Biographies*, edited by John E. Drewry (Athens: University of Georgia Press, 1947), pp. 1-34;

"Crusade for Truth," *Fortune*, 31 (April 1945): 146-149, 185-186, 188, 191;

Joe Alex Morris, *Deadline Every Minute: The Story of the United Press* (Garden City: Doubleday, 1957);

"The New Boss Walks Like a Prize Fighter," *Newsweek*, 5 (20 April 1935): 16;

"UP," *Newsweek*, 22 (6 September 1943): 100.

Papers:

Hugh Baillie's papers, covering the years 1913 to 1940, are in the University of Oregon Library at Eugene.

Meyer Berger

(1 September 1898-8 February 1959)

James S. Featherston
Louisiana State University

MAJOR POSITIONS HELD: Reporter and columnist, *New York Times* (1928-1937, 1938-1959).

BOOKS: *The Eight Million: Journal of a New York Correspondent* (New York: Simon & Schuster, 1942);
The Men of Maryknoll, by Berger and James Keller (New York: Scribners, 1943);
Growth of an Ideal, 1850-1950: The Story of the Manhattan Savings Bank (Philadelphia: Beck Engraving Co., 1950);
The Story of the New York Times, 1851-1951 (New York: Simon & Schuster, 1951);
New York: City on Many Waters (New York: Arts, 1956);
The Library (New York: New York Public Library, 1956);
Meyer Berger's New York (New York: Random House, 1960).

For three decades Meyer Berger was perhaps the finest reporter and writer on America's most prestigious newspaper, the *New York Times*. That he was regarded as such by the management of the *Times* was evident in the fact he was chosen to write the "official" history of the first 100 years of the newspaper. Berger was also a columnist, and, in addition, he wrote several other books along with numerous articles for the nation's leading magazines. He was widely respected and liked throughout the profession and elsewhere, and it was said that he had hundreds of friends and no known enemies. When he died, there was wide resentment among his fellow employees when the *New York Times* did not print his obituary on the front page.

After his death, his colleague, the famed drama critic Brooks Atkinson, wrote: "Although his name was Meyer Berger, he was 'Mike' to his colleagues on the *New York Times* and his many hundreds of friends. For a man who was accessible to everyone, 'Meyer' seemed too formal. It lacks the quiet intimacy that his nickname expresses. In his professional life he was a brilliant, tireless, probing reporter who assembled and wrote some of the most

Meyer Berger (New York Times)

memorable stories the *Times* had published. In 1950 he won a Pulitzer Prize for one of his greatest. It was an inspired police reporter's chronicle of the shooting of thirteen persons by an insane war veteran in Camden, New Jersey. No one else could have collected and observed so closely all the facts and details of a multiple crime and then told them so swiftly in four thousand concise words that put a grisly news event into human perspective. Since Mike was a great reporter, no one would have blamed him if he had been cocky, callous and omniscient. But nothing coarsened in any way the innate gentleness of a shy, kindly, humorous man whose sympathies reached out in all directions. . . .

He could not bear to see a moth killed; if it was in the house it had to be liberated through a window. Nothing alive was outside his range of sympathy."

Meyer Berger was born on New York's Lower East Side on 1 September 1898. One of eleven children, he was reared in poverty in a slum in Brooklyn. His father, Ignace Berger, was a tailor who had emigrated from what is now Czechoslovakia, and his mother, Sarah Waldman Berger, operated a candy store. He began selling newspapers at the age of eight. His formal education was cut short when the poverty of his family forced him to leave the Eastern District High School in the Williamsburg section of Brooklyn after only two terms.

Berger was only eleven when he was hired as a night messenger for the *New York World* at $1.50 a week, running copy between Park Row and the newspaper's downtown Brooklyn office. He later became the head office boy. During those early years, Berger later said, he began learning newspaper work almost by "osmosis." He recalled: "When there was no copy I ran hot coffee and hot bean sandwiches from Dirty Smith's, or, sometimes, cold pints from Dixon's. On winter nights I'd hold the sandwiches against my chest so the heat would come through the paper and warm me. On hot nights I'd linger outside the office door the longer to cool my hands on the tin growler. Best of all, when the copy was in, I could stand near the long copy table in the cavernous old *World* office and watch the poker games. Here I absorbed all the legends of the craft, ancient and contemporary. I contracted newsprint fever in this way, by a kind of osmosis. Here I learned, I think, a sounder journalism than is taught in graver halls of learning. The men from whom I caught this fever have, for the greater part, long since died of it. They didn't know, but they were my faculty. I was their sole student."

He continued to work for the *World* until the outbreak of World War I, when he enlisted in the army. According to one story, he was at first rejected because of his defective eyesight, but managed to enlist after memorizing the eye chart. Another tale is that he posed as a musician to win acceptance in the regimental band. At any rate, he turned up in France as a sergeant in the 106th Infantry, 27th Division, and he won a Silver Star for carrying wounded men back to the American lines under heavy fire. He also won the Purple Heart and the Conspicuous Service Cross.

After the war, Berger became a police reporter for the *World* in Brooklyn, and then the top rewrite man for the Standard News Association, also in Brooklyn. He married Mae Gamsu on 27 August 1926. In March 1928, when the *New York Times* started a Brooklyn-Queens news section, Berger was hired as chief rewrite man for that section. In time he became a principal rewrite man and general reporter. Except for one year, he was to remain on the staff of the *New York Times* the rest of his life.

His first stories to attract wide attention were about a series of murders among Brooklyn waterfront gangsters; he went on to write many stories about racketeer shootings and trials during Prohibition. His sixteen stories on the trial of gangster Al Capone for income tax evasion were nominated for a Pulitzer Prize in 1932. In his book about the *Times, The Kingdom and the Power* (1969), Gay Talese writes: "There had practically been a work stoppage in the newsroom in 1932 when Berger's stories on the Al Capone tax trial in Chicago began to arrive, page by page, on the telegraph machines; copyboys would grab the pages, reading them as they slowly walked to the copy desk; then the copy readers would re-read every word of the courtroom drama and the dialogue of Al Capone; finally the editors would take their turn, being as absorbed as the others before sending the story up to the printers on the floor above."

Talese recounts another incident from the gangster era that became part of the legend of the *Times*: "When Berger wrote similar pieces about the tax trial of Dutch Schultz, even Schultz read them with grudging admiration, although he was offended that Berger had quoted one source as saying Schultz was a 'pushover for a blonde.' When the gangster next saw Berger, he called him over and complained about that line. 'But it's the truth, isn't it?' Berger asked. 'Yes,' Schultz said. 'But what kind of language is that to use in the *New York Times*?' "

Berger was perhaps the most admired and honored member of the *Times* staff. Even after becoming a star reporter and columnist, he continued to work at a desk in the city room, ceaselessly interrupted by telephone calls, colleagues, and a stream of visitors—policemen, thieves, street people, bankers, all sorts of persons. He seemed constitutionally unable to dismiss anyone, no matter how busy he might be. Talese describes Berger at work in the city room as a "tall, thin, shy, gentle man with a long nose and soft inquiring eyes who sat in the front row and talked to the copyboys, clerks, and reporters who usually stood around his desk; he would regale them with humorous stories, would advise them on *Magazine* or 'Topics of the Times' pieces they were trying to write, and he would listen patiently while they spoke of personal problems. And then, as his deadline approached, he would turn to his typewriter and, within a half-hour, he would produce a dramatic 1,000-word article about a gangland murder he had covered earlier in the day, or a poignant sidewalk scene he had observed while coming to work; or he might produce a prose poem to New York."

The year away from the *Times* was spent at the *New Yorker* magazine. Since his knowledge of New York was extensive, the *New Yorker* felt it needed him and persuaded him to join its staff in 1937. Berger, however, was not happy at the *New Yorker*, and apparently the magazine's irascible editor, Harold Ross, was not happy with Berger. Longtime *New Yorker* writer A. J. Liebling later recalled: "Meyer Berger had once written a *New Yorker* profile of a man who fished for lost coins through subway gratings, and Ross had been trying for months to disinfect the magazine by running pieces about the Supreme Court and the Persian Room of the Plaza." Berger returned to the *Times* in 1938, discovering that he worked best surrounded by noise, distractions, and the constant pressure of a newsroom and a daily deadline. Brooks Atkinson remembered Berger's return: "After he had remained for one year in an alien pasture his colleagues on the *Times* were delighted and gratified to receive him back, for it was not only pleasant but reassuring to have Mike back in the city room."

Berger first began to write his column, "About New York," in 1939, but it was discontinued in 1940 when the supply of newsprint was curtailed. The column was reinstated in 1953 and continued until he died. In these columns, Berger wrote about the city he knew so well and loved so much. He had this to say about the sounds of the metropolis: "New York's voice speaks mystery, too. It has a soft, weird music, a symphony of winds at high altitudes, of muted traffic in endless serpentine twisting over city hills and grades; of jet hiss and propeller thrum, of the hoarse call of tugs on many waters, of great liners standing in from the broad sea, or moving out. You hear another voice when you stand on the Brooklyn Bridge in early morning; the sigh of great smokestacks, the raspy breathing of tugs, the gull flocks, sighing wind in the bridge cables, the quivering complaint of the whole span under its moving freight." Some of these columns appeared in his book *The Eight Million* (1942).

Berger, who for years suffered from ulcers, went to London as a war correspondent during World War II, but returned home after only two months because of his health. He was emotionally involved in the ordeal of his country, and was unhappy being away from the action.

Meanwhile, his reputation as a great reporter continued to grow. In the field of human interest, Berger was a master. His keenly felt stories and columns on blind children, wounded soldiers, and the old and destitute were classics of journalism. He also wrote humorous stories, typically about queer old codgers he found in his beloved city, with a gentle raillery that hurt no one and delighted everybody. He was a master of the color story—the descriptive narrative of sights and sounds. His heart-tugging account in 1947 of the first dead soldiers to be brought back from Europe is considered a journalistic masterpiece.

"The first war dead from Europe came home yesterday," Berger wrote. "The harbor was steeped in Sabbath stillness as they came in on the morning tide—6,248 coffins in the hold of the transport John V. Connolly. Then came the long march up Fifth Avenue's pavement. The crowds at the curb were moved. Some let tears run freely. Some wiped them away. Some made the sign of the cross as the caissons rolled past them. In the Metropolitan Tower, bells tolled and the pealing echoes hung over the marchers. In Fifth Avenue's canyons muted brass played 'Onward, Christian Soldiers.' . . . A woman started up. She stretched out her arms and screamed the name 'Johnny.' Then in a brief space of silence, she screamed out again: 'There's my boy; there's my boy,' and other women, beside her, put comforting arms on her shoulders." In 1945, toward the end of the war, Berger managed to tour North Africa, Europe, and other war areas, but this was only a sort of a consolation tour for this man who believed in sharing the worst aspects of the war with other Americans.

In 1949 an insane war veteran named Howard Unruh went berserk in the streets of Camden, New Jersey, and killed thirteen people before surrendering to police. Berger's superb reporting of this tragedy won him a Pulitzer Prize for local reporting. Berger spent six hours retracing Unruh's steps, interviewing fifty people who had seen parts of the rampage, and then sat down and reconstructed the whole scene in a four-thousand word article written in two and a half hours. "Men and women dodged into open shops, the women with panic, men hoarse with fear," Berger wrote. "No one could quite understand for a time what had been loosed in the block. Unruh first walked into John Pilarchik's shoe repair shop near the north end of his own side of the street. The cobbler, a 27-year-old man who lives in Pennsauken Township, looked up open-mouthed

[Heywood Broun's] great gifts of heart and mind were ever directed toward his purposes. Neither slander nor calumny nor thought of personal consequences ever deterred him once he had entered a fight in the cause of right and justice as he saw it. He was a hard fighter but always a fair adversary and no matter for whom he worked he wore no man's collar.

--President Franklin D. Roosevelt

Heywood Broun was a man who earned accolades from presidents and inspired loyalty in his friends. He commanded respect from those who knew him only in print and who had difficulty both pronouncing and spelling his name, which Broun considered changing to Broon to eliminate the problem. He achieved this renown despite a diffident manner and a rumpled appearance that was legendary. His shoes did not always match, and he sometimes wore neither shoelaces nor socks. His suits lost their shape on first wearing, due in part to his narrow, sloping shoulders and ample midsection, and in part to his habit of stuffing his coat pockets with food and other objects. He carried perhaps 250 pounds on a six-foot, four-inch frame, and sometimes an interval of flesh was exposed between his trousers and his shirt. A military officer once inspected Broun in his ill-fitting war correspondent's uniform and asked, "Did you fall down?"

Broun was a mass of contradictions. Margaret Case Harriman described him as "gently bred, slovenly of person, softhearted, steel-minded, evasive and direct, brave and terrified, considerate and tough, gregarious and solitary." He was a confirmed hypochondriac who sometimes displayed to friends his latest set of electrocardiograms, prompting Alexander Woollcott to suggest that he "hold a one-man show of those things some time." Claustrophobia led him to give up his role as drama critic because he could not bear to remain for long in a darkened theater, and he was so terrified of trains that he hired taxis to ferry him from New York to his home in Stamford, Connecticut.

Despite all this, Broun was a founder and the first president of the American Newspaper Guild and was widely regarded as a champion of the underprivileged. He was the author of thirteen books, including a best-selling biography, a scholarly analysis of prejudice, two books describing American troops at war, three novels, and several collections of daily journalism. He was perhaps the most highly respected newspaper essayist of his era, a facile writer able to turn out a daily column in thirty

Heywood Broun (Culver Pictures)

or forty minutes. That column, "It Seems to Me," was said to be worth 50,000 readers to the newspaper which carried it.

These distinctions could not have been predicted from his childhood and academic life. Heywood Campbell Broun was born 7 December 1888 in Brooklyn, New York, to Henrietta Brosé and Heywood Cox Broun. The Brouns were fairly well-to-do: the elder Broun had risen through the ranks to become the owner of a printing firm, sold it, and begun a second career as a wine merchant. Heywood was sent to Horace Mann, a private school, for his elementary and secondary education. He did reasonably well in school—better in composition than in languages—and he was named editor of the school newspaper. He was also voted "the best all around" by his senior classmates, and he went on to Harvard.

His Harvard career was undistinguished. Although he already had expressed interest in journalism as an occupation, he was thrice turned down in his bid to become a member of the *Harvard Crimson* staff. He did enjoy one literary triumph while at Harvard; in 1909 he had a short story entitled "And the Greatest of These" published in the *Harvard Advocate*. In the summer following his sophomore year he managed to find work on the *New York Morning Telegraph*, where his first published piece was, typically, a lighthearted sports story. Back at Harvard, he cut a few too many classes in order to watch Tris Speaker and the Boston Red Sox. As a result of his truancy—and also, perhaps, as a result of his general ineptitude at foreign languages—he left Harvard in 1910 a few credits short of a degree. But the lack of a diploma did not prevent him from joining the staff of the *Morning Telegraph* on a full-time basis. The *Telegraph* was located on Fiftieth Street and Eighth Avenue in what had been the carbarn of an adjacent streetcar railway. It was, Broun later said only half facetiously, "a publication devoted chiefly to horses and vaudeville actors." He was assigned general duties—sports stories, entertainment interviews, and occasional editorials. There was a nightly poker game, and the night editor, Shep Friedman, sometimes assigned Broun to that, too. Years later, in an article for the *Nation*, Broun nostalgically recalled the atmosphere at the *Telegraph*: "The city room was always cluttered up with all sorts of people who didn't seem to have any business there. Very often you couldn't get to your desk because there would be a couple of chorus girls sitting there waiting for a friend who was finishing an editorial. . . . Everybody wrote editorials. Generally at the last minute somebody would remember that we didn't have any editorials. Then Bide Dudley and I would each write one. The editorials were not regarded as very important because the *Telegraph* had no policy about anything except that it was against reformers. Vaudeville reviews were very important because the actors advertised." The *Morning Telegraph* might not have been a distinguished newspaper, but Broun was never sorry that he went to a "car barn instead of a school of journalism."

Broun's regard for the *Telegraph* apparently was not entirely reciprocated. He had been there less than a year as a full-time reporter when he asked for a two-dollar raise to thirty dollars weekly. This was rejected, and Broun went job hunting. Fortunately for him, in 1911 there was no dearth of newspapers in New York: besides the *Telegraph* there were Pulitzer's *World*, Hearst's *Journal*, the *Herald*, the *Telegram*, the *Sun*, the *Times*, the *Tribune*, and many others as well. Even so, it took him six months to find work on the *Tribune* as a copyreader at twenty-five dollars weekly—three dollars less than he had made at the *Telegraph*.

After a stint on the copydesk Broun moved to the sports department, where he seemed to specialize in puffing the exploits of Christy Mathewson, Babe Ruth, and other stars. This formula worked well: Broun earned his first by-line and received a raise to thirty-five dollars a week. Broun's ability to adapt the Bible to his sportswriting prose is evident in this piece on "Southpaws":

> Our text today is from the fifteenth verse of the third chapter of the Book of Judges, in which it is written: "And afterwards they cried out to the Lord, who raised them up a saviour called Aod, the son of Gera, the son of Jemini, who used the left hand as well as the right."
>
> . . . .
>
> But the complete triumph of the left-hander comes in baseball. Tris Speaker, greatest of outfielders and manager of the world's champion Cleveland Indians, is left-handed. So is Babe Ruth, the home-run king, and George Sisler, who led the American League in batting. Ty Cobb, like the Roman emperor before whom Paul appeared, is almost persuaded. He bats left-handed. Almost half the players in both leagues adopt this practice since it gives them an advantage of about six feet in running to first base. And yet, in spite of this fact, thousands of meddling mothers all over the country are breaking prospective left-handers into dull, plodding, conventional right-handedness. Babe Ruth was fortunate. He received his education in a protectory where the good brothers were much too busy to observe which hand he used. His spirit was not broken nor his natural proclivities bent. Accordingly he made fifty-four home runs last season and earned over one hundred thousand dollars. The world has sneered at us all too long. Even a left-hander will turn in time.

The mythopoeic quality of his prose was duly noted by the *Tribune*'s higher echelon, and in 1915 Broun became the paper's drama critic. (His elevation may have also resulted in part from his status as a Harvard near-graduate and from his having survived Prof. George Pierce Baker's famed English 47 Workshop in playwriting.)

Broun distinguished himself as the paper's fledgling drama critic in his first season, when he was sued for libel by actor Geoffrey Steyne, one of whose performances Broun had labeled the worst to be seen in contemporary theater. The suit was still pending when Broun reviewed another play in which Steyne appeared. Broun wrote that Steyne's latest performance was not up to his usual standard. The actor's suit was dismissed, reportedly on the grounds that a critic's opinion did not have to be accurate or intelligent.

Broun's first season as a drama critic was a dubious success in other ways as well. He fell in love with and became engaged to Lydia Lopokova, a lithe Russian ballerina whose performance he gushed over in print. Lopokova accepted his attentions but in a short while switched her affections to a Russian dancer; she later married the economist John Maynard Keynes.

Broun was not devastated by his loss. Waiting to console him was Ruth Hale, whom he had met several months earlier. Her profession was press agent for a theatrical producer, but her preoccupation was feminism. Broun admired her intellectual vigor; she was a contentious advocate of women's rights, and she stimulated his sense of justice. Despite her rancorous nature, he was attracted to her, and their friendship matured into an uneasy courtship. They agreed to marry—on her terms: she was to retain the name Hale; they were to be coequal heads of the household; they were to be free to live private lives, without the right to make demands upon each other. She recognized her obligation to produce a child, but only one. Having come to terms, they were joined together on 7 June 1917.

World War I had begun in Europe, and both Broun and Hale had negotiated assignments to France—she on the Paris staff of the *Chicago Tribune*, and he with the Allied Expeditionary Force under Gen. John J. Pershing. They sailed for France aboard a passenger liner which was part of the Allied convoy. For Broun it was an opportunity to become a war correspondent—perhaps not as dashing as Richard Harding Davis, but a correspondent nonetheless. For Hale it was simply an occasion to rage at her biological inequality, for she became pregnant and was forced to return to New York within six months in order to simplify the matter of their son's citizenship. Broun followed shortly thereafter.

In his short tenure as the *New York Tribune*'s war correspondent Broun had amassed enough material for two books, both copyrighted in 1918. Always a facile writer, he outdid himself to complete *The A.E.F.: With General Pershing and the American Forces* and *Our Army at the Front*. The first includes attempts to describe for his American readers the local color of France in anecdotal style; the second is a collection of chapters describing the progress of the American forces in Europe and includes, in his typical mode of whimsical irony, tales of American courage in battle.

Ruth Hale, whom Broun married in 1917 (Maurice Goldberg)

Safely back at the *Tribune* in New York, Broun could justly express some satisfaction with his life: he had published two books, had served as a war correspondent and as sports editor for a major newspaper, had established a fair reputation as a drama critic, and was married with a young son. Heywood Hale Broun had been born on 10 March 1918 and was very much on his father's mind as Broun tried his hand at a new challenge: as literary editor he was appointed to write a thrice-weekly column of book reviews. Occasionally the columnist ignored the books and wrote instead about his son, whom he called "H. 3rd." Those moments of whim-

It Seems to Me
By Heywood Broun

We want to add "Tramping on Life," by Harry Kemp (Boni & Liveright), to the list of current books which seem to us worth reading. This is an autobiographical novel by an adventurous person who is happily devoid of self-consciousness.

Nor does Mr. Kemp go in very much for reticence. He manages to be frank without seeming either abject or boastful. The early portion of the book, which deals with a boy's encounters with what are known as "the facts of life," seems to us to be exceptionally good. This should be prescribed reading for all radical young authors who plan to write a novel about sex. Kemp shows that it can be done without either whispering or shouting.

Another book which has interested us is "Shouts and Murmurs," by Alexander Woollcott. This is a collection of essays on plays and players, written originally in the Sunday columns of the Times and in various magazines. Of all American reviewers, Woollcott has undoubtedly the greatest passion for the theatre. He remains a barrier against the argument that no man can go to the theatre three or four times a week throughout a year and fail to become blasé and jaded. With him the magic of the playhouse has persisted. We are informed on reliable authority that during a busy season he saw one particular play which he happened to like no less than fifteen times.

Since our own temperament is much more crabbed we often find the judgments of Mr. Woollcott in violent disagreement with our own. To be sure, he has hates but he is moved to anger more slowly. Moreover, he has a distinct interest in acting as a thing apart from a play itself. A thoroughly bad play leaves us inconsolable, but Mr. Woollcott often manages to cheer himself up with the memory of some particular person in the cast who was not so evil as all the rest. "Shouts and Murmurs" deals chiefly with things which he has enjoyed and it is a zestful book full of grace and humor.

Broun's column in the New York World *in 1922 (Culver Pictures)*

sical homeliness represented the beginning of another stage in his journalistic career: Broun as light essayist.

As Broun's reputation grew, so also did his circle of friends. One day he received an invitation to join a number of them for lunch at the Hotel Algonquin. Among the others invited were Alexander Woollcott, George S. Kaufman, Franklin P. Adams, Robert Benchley, Harold Ross, Dorothy Parker, and Robert Sherwood: the elite of the New York literary crowd. The group became known as the Algonquin Round Table and began meeting regularly. Some of the same people met again at the Algonquin on Saturday nights for a running poker game; they called themselves the Thanatopsis Literary and Inside Straight Poker Club, and besides Broun and other members of the Round Table their numbers included Marc Connelly, Herbert Bayard Swope, Westbrook Pegler, Quentin Reynolds, and Harpo Marx.

Broun was moving in fast company, but his friendships were not entirely social: he was picking up ideas for his column and testing those ideas in conversations with thoughtful and creative people. Occasionally, during meetings of the Thanatopsis Club, he would sit out a hand or two, find a type-writer, and bang out his column in twenty minutes or so—enlarging upon an idea that had been bandied about the table.

As he moved further into personal journalism—the expression of his ideas and reflections—he came to feel that the conservative *Tribune* was not the proper vehicle for his column; for example, he ran contrary to the *Tribune*'s views when he expressed sympathy for imprisoned Socialist Eugene Debs. In the summer of 1921 he called Swope, who was editor of the *New York World*, and suggested that he would like to come over to the *World*, where he expected to find greater freedom of expression. "It Seems to Me" began running in the *World* on 7 September 1921. Other luminaries on the *World* during Broun's tenure included Walter Lippmann, Frank I. Cobb, Alexander Woollcott, Franklin P. Adams, Laurence Stallings, Maxwell Anderson, Allan Nevins, James M. Cain, and Arthur Krock.

Broun's third book, *Seeing Things at Night*, appeared the year he moved to the *World*. It was, as Broun described its contents in his introduction, a collection of "newspaper articles of any sort done more or less on the spur of the moment for the next day's consumption." The collection contains pieces that had originally appeared in the *New York Tribune, Vanity Fair, McCall's, Collier's Weekly,* and the *Nation.* They vary from fantasy to religious allegory to commentary to simple whimsy—though the whimsy is rarely as simple as it may at first appear.

Broun's years with the *New York World*—1921 to 1928—were his most productive. That period saw the publication of two collections of light essays, three novels, and a biography. *Pieces of Hate* (1922), a collection of articles first appearing in the *World,* the *Tribune, Vanity Fair, Collier's Weekly,* the *Bookman,* and *Judge,* reveals the flaws which might be expected in any such collection: unevenness in subject, treatment, and length. The book contains theater criticism as well as boxing reportage, essays on censorship as well as on Prohibition. Broun himself "reviewed" the book in its preface, noting in his self-deprecating way that "All the vices of haste are in this book of stories, critical essays and what not." In the same year Broun's first novel, *The Boy Grew Older,* was published. Ever since his classes under Prof. Charles Townsend Copeland at Harvard, Broun had wanted to write novels; in his first attempt, he achieved mild success: 10,000 copies of the book were sold. It is transparently autobiographical, describing the life of a sportswriter who becomes a father. In its introspective way, tinged with low-key humor, it resembles the style of Broun's newspaper work. *The Sun Field,* his second novel, was published in 1923. It, too, is autobiographical: the narrator is a sportswriter with a heart condition (Broun's palpitations were diagnosed by one doctor as "hysterical"); the heroine is a militant feminist; and there are characters resembling Babe Ruth, Walter Lippmann, and other people Broun knew. Another collection of articles and columns appeared in 1924 under the title *Sitting on the World.* A subtle shift in Broun's attention from casual topics to more serious matters can be traced in this book. Here he finds meaning in the ability of a caught fish to cling to life, seeks to define God, and demonstrates concern for politics and politicians.

In 1926 Broun had a short story, *A Shepherd,* privately printed in an edition of 250 copies. The same year his third novel, *Gandle Follows His Nose,* was published. He was proud of this allegorical fairy tale in which Bunny Gandle faces great odds—evil spirits, giants, and armies—while completing the circle of life. It was not a critical success, but it was popular among his friends, and one of them— Deems Taylor—adapted it into an opera. If the allegory is a bit enigmatic, the prose does reveal that Broun had moved beyond mere clarity into the use of words for poetic effect.

With Margaret Leech as coauthor, Broun produced his most successful book, a biography of Anthony Comstock, in 1927. *Anthony Comstock: Roundsman of the Lord* describes the career of the noted crusader against pornography, the man whose war against obscenity resulted in a federal law forbidding the mailing of publications of indecent character. Although Broun was constitutionally opposed to censorship, this biography is a fair and scholarly treatment of the man for whom the Comstock Law was named. The book sold well and was named a Literary Guild selection.

Despite the fact that in 1927 Broun's column was the "brightest star in Manhattan journalism," that he was earning perhaps $25,000 annually, and that seven of his books had been published in six years, his days at the *World* were numbered. Always liberal, Broun had become increasingly political, and his positions were generally to the left of the moderate editorial policy of the *World.* But the issue which drove a wedge between the paper and its prize columnist was the Sacco-Vanzetti case. The two Italian anarchists had been sentenced to die for murder, and Broun argued that their deaths were politically motivated. In a famous column published in the *World* on 5 August 1927, Broun wrote: "The men in Charlestown Prison are shining spirits, and Vanzetti has spoken with an eloquence not known elsewhere within our time. They are too bright, we shield our eyes and kill them. We are the dead, and in us there is no feeling nor imagination nor the terrible torment of lust for justice. And in the city where we sleep smug gardeners walk to keep the grass above our little houses sleek and cut whatever blade thrusts up a head above its fellows." The *World's* publisher, Ralph Pulitzer, asked Broun to write no more on this issue, but Broun had another column published and submitted two more which the *World* refused to print. Instead, the paper printed a note from Pulitzer which referred to Broun's opinions as "utmost extravagance" and indicated that it was exercising its right of final decision in omitting further articles by Broun.

The columnist thereupon took a "sabbatical" for four and a half months, during which time he contributed regularly to magazines. One notable article—a third-person profile of himself—seeks to assess his career in apologetic fashion. He describes himself as "exceptionally timorous" and a "confirmed hypochondriac." He acknowledges that he has "occasional fits of recklessness" at the rate of "one rash act every seven years." He maintains that the "recent row with the *World* was inevitable" be-

Broun carrying a picket sign during a strike against the Wisconsin News *(Wide World Photos)*

cause his "planetary course of quietude had passed," and to his own surprise, "he bit the hand that fed him." He describes himself as "Hamletish" and concludes that "in the secret places of his heart he is a crusader riding out to do battle even though he dreads it." It was an extraordinary piece of introspection, designed in part, it would seem, to ameliorate his difficulties with the *World*; and in January 1928 he was back in his old spot on the op ed page. But only briefly. In May an article was published in the *Nation* in which he deplored the lack of a liberal newspaper in New York. The *World* was not liberal, he argued; it switched its point of view frequently and lacked both courage and tenacity. On 3 May the *World* announced that Broun had been fired.

It was not long before Roy Howard made an offer Broun could not refuse: $30,000 annually and syndication in the Scripps-Howard newspapers, plus freedom of expression. The chain had recently purchased the *New York Telegram*, and Broun made

his headquarters there. For a while he and his new employer got along very well: Broun continued to lambaste conservative impulses in politicians and clerics, and Howard remained silent. But in 1930, as Broun watched the bread lines grow, he decided he could do more good in Congress than in a column and announced his candidacy on the Socialist ticket. Howard immediately published his views that it was inappropriate for a journalist to become politically involved. Broun offered a rebuttal in his column and continued his campaign, but he was defeated rather handily by the Republican candidate. In fact, he was defeated almost as handily by the Democrat, finishing third with 6,662 votes out of nearly 46,000 cast.

In 1931, with George Britt as coauthor, Broun's eleventh book was published. *Christians Only: A Study in Prejudice* consists of 333 pages of arguments against racial and religious prejudice—particularly prejudice against Jews—in education, employment, personal relations, and general attitudes. It was characteristic of Broun to speak for the Jews, although he was not Jewish. In fact Broun embraced no faith, although as a child he had attended Episcopal Sunday School. He could be described as a religious man, inclined to find the person of God in the objects about him.

Also characteristic of Broun was his attempt, through his column, to find jobs for the jobless. He called his campaign "Give a Job Till June" and by this means was able to place perhaps 1,000 unemployed persons in positions created in response to his call. He was widely regarded as a spokesman for the underdog, despite his considerable salary as columnist for the *World-Telegram*. (The Scripps-Howard chain had acquired the *World* from the Pulitzer family in 1931 and had merged it with the *Telegram*.)

In addition to his campaign for the jobless common man, Broun threw himself into a project to create jobs for his unemployed theater friends. He became the producer of a revue entitled *Shoot the Works*; he raised money for it, coaxed his talented Round Table friends into writing sketches and music, persuaded them to perform on the stage, and even auditioned girls for the chorus line. Broun himself had a role in the show. *Shoot the Works* opened on 21 July 1931 and ran for eighty-nine performances, closing when Broun became ill and no longer could take part. It was an exhausting task for him because he continued his column writing as he was producing and performing in the show. But it was also rewarding: not only did he find work for his old friends, he also made new ones—in particular Maria Incoronata Fruscella Dooley, who, using the stage name Connie Madison, joined the chorus line. Widow of the dancer Johnny Dooley and mother of a daughter, Patricia, Connie had returned to the theater to eke out a living. After *Shoot the Works* closed, Connie Madison and Heywood Broun were seen frequently making the rounds of the night spots.

Broun and Ruth Hale were still married and maintained a close relationship, but they had not lived together as man and wife for several years. She had sought a divorce, but he always had been able to dissuade her. Finally he acquiesced, and on 17 November 1933, she obtained a divorce in Mexico. The following summer she became ill but refused to see a doctor. In September she lapsed into a coma, and on 18 September 1934, she died. Broun was distraught, but he assuaged his pain by putting his thoughts on paper. "My best friend died yesterday," he wrote in his column. "Ruth Hale gave me out of

the very best she had to equip me for the understanding of human problems. She gave this under protest, with many reservations, and a vast rancor. But she gave." Broun said that for seventeen years practically every word he wrote had been written with the feeling that she was looking over his shoulder. He concluded: "It would be a desperately lonely world if I did not feel that personality is of such tough fiber that in some manner it must survive and does survive. I still feel that she is looking over my shoulder."

Broun's feeling of loss was sincere, but he had fallen in love with Connie Madison. In January 1935 they were married in a civil ceremony, followed by a church wedding to satisfy Connie, who was Catholic.

Broun was already deeply involved with what was, in many respects, his most important project on behalf of the underdog: the formation of a journalists' union. In his column of 7 August 1933, he responded to a letter he had received from an unemployed reporter. The reporter argued that printers were making thirty percent more than reporters because they were unionized, whereas reporters were too proud to join unions because they had been gulled by publishers into thinking they were "professionals." Broun agreed and volunteered to form a newspaper writers' union. "Beginning at nine o'clock on the morning of October 1 I am going to do the best I can to help in getting one up. I think I could die happy on the opening day of the general strike if I had the privilege of watching Walter Lippmann heave half a brick through a *Tribune* window at a non-union operative. . . ." Broun did hold a meeting on that date to discuss what steps might be taken to form a union. It took many such meetings before the American Newspaper Guild was formed on 15 December. At its founding convention in Washington, Broun became president by acclamation. He was reelected six times by unanimous votes, holding the office until his death.

Initially the guild limited its membership to editorial department employees, but extended membership to employees in advertising, business office, and circulation departments after affiliating with the AFL in 1936 and with the CIO in 1937. In 1971 the word *American* was removed from the guild's name in recognition of its multinational membership. Today the Newspaper Guild annually awards a $1,000 prize, the Heywood Broun Award, to the news organization which, "in the spirit of Heywood Broun," exhibits an abiding concern for the underdog and the underprivileged.

Broun and his second wife, Connie, with Broun's son from his first marriage, Heywood Hale Broun (Wide World Photos)

While Broun regarded his founding role in the union as perhaps his most important contribution to the newspaper industry, he had other contributions to make. In 1935 his twelfth book, *It Seems to Me: 1925-1935*, was published. The collection included a couple of magazine pieces from the *Nation* but consisted mostly of columns from the *World*, the *Telegram*, and the *World-Telegram*.

In 1938 he founded, with the assistance of a number of his journalistic friends, a weekly tabloid called the *Connecticut Nutmeg*. For a number of years he had spent much of his time on Ruth Hale's acreage near Stamford, Connecticut, where he painted, fished, entertained, and sometimes wrote his column. Many of his friends had acquired property in the vicinity, and they decided to collaborate on a weekly newspaper. Their enthusiasm did not last out the year, however, and the little newspaper became *Broun's Nutmeg*.

On Christmas Eve 1938, Broun received one of his greatest honors: the president of the United States was going to read one of Broun's newspaper pieces over the air. When he learned, on the day of the broadcast, what Roosevelt planned to do, he gathered Connie, her daughter, and his son around the radio. At 5:30 the president read one of Broun's occasional parables, this one about a priest who was having difficulty finding a text for his Christmas sermon. The priest opened the Bible at random and found the passage which describes how Jesus forgave Judas. At that the priest was exultant, for he would preach that even to the betrayer the wine of life was given. When Broun heard the president read that Christmas column, he wept.

Although Broun had never professed any creed, his religious sensibilities were evident in this story of Judas Iscariot and in similar stories he had written over the years. In January 1939 he began looking into the prospect of conversion to Catholicism, and on 23 May he was baptized by Archbishop Francis Spellman, following instruction in the faith by Monsignor Fulton Sheen.

Later that year, Roy Howard informed Broun that his $49,000-a-year contract would not be renewed. The columnist had suspected for some time that this might happen, as Howard was reportedly unhappy with Broun's guild activities, but it saddened him to be fired for the third time in his career. He was able to find a new employer without too much difficulty: the *New York Post* wanted his by-line, albeit at about one-fourth the wages he had commanded at the *World-Telegram*.

On Friday, 15 December, his first column appeared in the *Post*. But it had been written by a sick man: Broun had contracted a cold and had been unable to shake it. Suddenly it developed into pneumonia. Monsignor Sheen arrived at the hospital where Broun had been taken and administered the last sacraments of the Catholic church. Broun remained in stable condition Sunday, but on Monday morning, 18 December, his temperature rose, and at ten minutes to ten he died.

In his memoir of the Broun family, Heywood Hale Broun sums up his father in these words:

> Almost from the beginning Heywood was a vast success in the newspaper business. In his day he was straight reporter, war correspondent, sports writer, drama critic, book critic, and general columnist. If some people did one of those things better than he did, no one could match him at all of them. And yet at the peak of his career he risked the anger of his employers, an anger that eventually destroyed that career, in order to be among the principal founders of the American Newspaper Guild, and its first president, a job he held while he lived.
>
> He was philanthropical, incorruptible, and colorful. Ten thousand people went to his funeral.

Without pretense, and seemingly without effort, Heywood Broun managed in a brief lifetime of only fifty-one years to accumulate more friends and acquire more readers than any journalist has a right to expect.

Biographies:

Dale Kramer, *Heywood Broun: A Biographical Portrait* (New York: Wyn, 1949);

Richard O'Connor, *Heywood Broun: A Biography* (New York: Putnam's, 1975).

References:

Heywood Hale Broun, *Whose Little Boy Are You? A Memoir of the Broun Family* (New York: St. Martin's/Marek, 1983);

Bennett Cerf, "Heywood Broun," in *The Saturday Review Gallery*, edited by Jerome Beatty, Jr. (New York: Simon & Schuster, 1959);

Morris L. Ernst, *The Best Is Yet . . .* (New York: Harper, 1945);

James R. Gaines, *Wit's End: Days and Nights of the Algonquin Round Table* (New York: Harcourt Brace Jovanovich, 1977);

Margaret Case Harriman, *The Vicious Circle: The Story of the Algonquin Round Table* (New York: Rinehart, 1951);

Dale E. Larson, "The Newspaperman Who Founded a Union," *Guild Reporter* (25 December 1964), special supplement;

John L. Lewis, et al., *Heywood Broun as He Seemed to Us* (New York: Random House, 1940);

M. B. Schnapper, *Heywood Broun* (Washington, D.C.: American Council On Public Affairs, 1940).

Papers:

Some of Heywood Broun's papers are in the Library of Congress.

William Henry Chamberlin

(17 February 1897-12 September 1969)

Rosemarian V. Staudacher
Marquette University

MAJOR POSITIONS HELD: Reporter, *Philadelphia Public Ledger* (1917); assistant magazine editor, *Philadelphia Press* (1918); foreign correspondent, *Christian Science Monitor* (1922-1940); editorial correspondent, book reviewer, *Wall Street Journal* (1945).

BOOKS: *Soviet Russia: A Living Record and a History* (Boston: Little, Brown, 1930; revised, 1931);
The Soviet Planned Economic Order (Boston: World Peace Foundation, 1931);
Russia's Iron Age (Boston: Little, Brown, 1934; London: Duckworth, 1935);
The Russian Revolution, 1917-1921, 2 volumes (New York & London: Macmillan, 1935);
Japan Over Asia (Boston: Little, Brown, 1937; London: Duckworth, 1938; revised and enlarged, Boston: Little, Brown, 1939);
Collectivism—A False Utopia (New York: Macmillan, 1937); republished as *A False Utopia: Collectivism in Theory and Practice* (London: Duckworth, 1937);
Japan in China (London: Duckworth, 1940);
The Confessions of an Individualist (London: Duckworth, 1940; New York: Macmillan, 1942);
The World's Iron Age (New York: Macmillan, 1941);
Modern Japan, edited by Maxwell S. Stuart (St. Louis & Dallas: Webster, 1942);
Canada, Today and Tomorrow (Boston: Little, Brown, 1942; London: Hale, 1944);
The Russian Enigma: An Interpretation (New York: Scribners, 1943);
A Durable Peace in Europe (New York: Commission on a Just and Durable Peace, 1944);
The Ukraine: A Submerged Nation (New York: Macmillan, 1944);
America: Partner in World Rule (New York: Vanguard Press, 1945); republished as *World Order or Chaos* (London: Duckworth, 1946);
The European Cockpit (New York: Macmillan, 1947);
America's Second Crusade (Chicago: Regnery, 1950);
Beyond Containment (Chicago: Regnery, 1953);
The Evolution of a Conservative (Chicago: Regnery, 1959);
Appeasement: Road to War (New York: Rolton House, 1962);
The German Phoenix (New York: Duell, Sloan & Pearce, 1963).

William Henry Chamberlin was one of the most respected foreign correspondents of his day, especially esteemed by both colleagues and critics for his thoroughness and scholarly approach. His writing on conditions in the Soviet Union, Japan, China, the Allied countries of Europe during and immediately after World War II, and Canada, are based upon the firsthand observation and research of a man who lived for years in the areas about which he wrote and who experienced many of the events and conditions he described.

Chamberlin was born 17 February 1897 in Brooklyn, New York, the only child of Ernest and May E. McClintock Chamberlin. His father was a newspaperman of modest means. From childhood, Chamberlin kept a diary which reflected his tastes, ideas, and interests. In his autobiography, *The Confessions of an Individualist* (1940), Chamberlin describes the family as never knowing "downright want" but being unable to afford "many superfluities." His paternal grandfather, William, was for a number of years head of the Associated Press bureau in Cincinnati, Ohio. Chamberlin remembered him as a "singularly sweet-tempered old gentleman, placid and modest and unruffled." He had risen to the rank of major in the Eighty-first Ohio Regiment during the Civil War and spent four years serving with the armies of Grant and Sherman. Chamberlin noted that his father "lacked the inner peace of my grandfather. He was a man, I think, for whom the pace of American urban life was too hectic and violent. . . . There was a musical streak in the family; my father's sister had studied singing under Lilli Lehmann in Berlin and my father had practiced piano for many years under a stern and exacting German music master. He lacked confidence to undertake a musical career and drifted into the hard grind and long night hours of routine newspaper inside work, with the sensitive and easily jangled nerves of an artist."

Chamberlin remembered happy hours listening to his father play Liszt, Schumann, Beethoven, and Chopin. His mother he recalled as always good-humored, a woman with many friends, a warm and loving parent. Later, when he was in Moscow as a correspondent, she acted as his publishing agent for books and magazine articles.

Chamberlin developed an early interest in reading and quickly progressed from childhood favorites by Samuel Clemens and Harriet Beecher Stowe to Gibbon's *Decline and Fall of the Roman Empire*, the novels of Sir Walter Scott, and other heavier fare. His preferences ran to history. At an early age, he became interested in German medieval history, particularly that of the House of Hohenstaufen. There were few books about the Hohenstaufens in English, but that did not daunt young Chamberlin: he discovered that there was a standard work on the period in German by Friedrich von Raumer and ordered the set of books from Leipzig. At the age of eleven, with no knowledge of German, he began to write down a translation into English; his only help was a ponderous German-English dictionary. Though the results were clumsy, Chamberlin began to acquire a feeling for the structure of the language. Eventually he became proficient in reading it but acknowledged: "My spoken German was halting and imperfect...." Later, he acquired some proficiency in Russian.

To his extraordinary love for books, Chamberlin added a love for music, particularly Wagner and Chopin, Beethoven and Paderewski. A typical Saturday for the young man included a "browsing visit" to the Philadelphia Public Library, where he discovered Flaubert, Balzac, Montaigne, Byron, Schopenhauer, Kant, Matthew Arnold, and countless others. His reading excursions were punctuated with an occasional break for hot chocolate at Whitman's and a modest supper that cost thirty-five cents at a nearby restaurant. In the evenings he attended concerts by the Philadelphia Orchestra with free tickets obtained through his father's newspaper connections. He also played tennis and was an avid baseball fan.

After Chamberlin had suffered the indignities of manual training for two years at Camden High School—and had recurring nightmares about being sentenced to remain there indefinitely because he could not master the subject—his mother learned through her pastor of a scholarship to the Quaker Penn Charter School in Philadelphia. Chamberlin enrolled there and spent the next six years in profitable study in a classical program. From Penn Charter he proceeded to Haverford, a

William Henry Chamberlin

Friends' College of about 200 students in Philadelphia. There, he remarked in his autobiography, the traditional forms of Quaker address, "thee" and "thou," were used and "the silly sides of American collegiate life were reduced to a minimum. There were no fraternities, and there was little snobbishness." Chamberlin wrote prolifically and with great energy throughout his college career. The class record at graduation said: "Chamberlin's contributions to the *Haverfordian* have edified those of us who could understand them."

Chamberlin admitted that he was graduated from college with a reasonably good preparation for life as he wished to live it, but without much foundation for making a living. His mother hoped he would become a lawyer as her father had been, but Chamberlin had no fondness for the law; lacking scientific aptitude, he ruled out medicine and engineering. Teaching piqued his imagination, but he did not regard the American student as fertile soil for the subjects he would prefer to teach. "By process of elimination, I drifted into newspaper work. My ambition was to become an editorial writer or a book and music critic. He became a cub reporter on the staff of the *Philadelphia Public Ledger* in 1917; the following year he moved to the *Philadelphia Press*, where he was assistant editor of the weekly magazine section.

The outbreak of World War I while he was in college had roused vigorous pro-Ally sentiments in Chamberlin which he later assessed as extravagant and "as silly as anything said or written . . . by Theodore Roosevelt and other advocates of war at any price." He came to feel that World War I never had the popular approval or enthusiastic backing of the American people that marked the Revolutionary War or Civil War. By 1918, Chamberlin had acquired a deep-seated aversion to the war. In the latter part of the year, he was drafted and whisked off to a training camp at State College in Bellefonte, Pennsylvania, but the war ended before he could be sent into active service abroad.

At that time, Chamberlin became decidedly pro-Bolshevik. He had watched events in Russia with avid interest, although much of the reporting seemed contradictory. He saw capitalism as the root cause of the war; now, he felt, the Soviet Union was striking back successfully at that evil. Chamberlin admitted later that his antipathy to the war probably accounted for most of his pro-Bolshevik sympathies; at the time, he actually had little knowledge of socialist theory, and did not acquire it until later when he lived in Russia.

Discharged from military service, Chamberlin went to New York, where his parents had moved, and settled in Greenwich Village. He began a round of visits to publishing houses in search of employment, and eventually was offered a job with the *New York Tribune*.

In 1919 he met Sonya Trosten, a high-school French teacher. She had been born in Elizavetgrad, southern Russia, and had immigrated to the United States with her family as a child. They were married in 1920 and remained together until she died almost fifty years later, sharing nearly all interests and activities. Meanwhile, on the *Tribune* staff, Chamberlin wrote headlines and handled cable reports from overseas. To his great joy he was soon shifted to the post of assistant book editor under Heywood Broun, whom he described as "a veritable twentieth century Dr. Johnson in girth and rolling gait if not in ideology. . . ."

During this time Chamberlin produced some pieces for the *New York Call*, a Socialist daily paper, under the pseudonym of A. C. Freeman. Chamberlin's pseudonym was convenient also for contribu-

tions to *Soviet Russia* magazine, in which he assumed the pose of a revolutionary expert on affairs abroad. He sought out persons whose interests and opinions paralleled his own, attending the gatherings of Soviet sympathizers at the Union Square apartment of Alex Gumberg, a Russian Jew who had personally known some revolutionary leaders before they rose to fame. Kenneth Durant, Albert Rhys Williams, Floyd Dell, and William Hard were among those Chamberlin met there.

In 1921 the *Tribune*, probably in an economy move, dismissed Chamberlin. Broun had left the paper previously after differences of opinion with his bosses. Later, Chamberlin viewed his dismissal as rescue from hack book reviews and surreptitious contributions to the left-wing press.

Lacking steady employment, he made plans to go to Russia to learn about the country firsthand. He had only several small commissions from ill-paying radical publications when a stroke of luck descended upon him: the *Christian Science Monitor* commissioned him to submit mail articles from time to time. On 4 July 1922, the Chamberlins boarded the *Latvia*, bound for Libau, Latvia, financing the trip out of their savings. He later admitted that the adventure was somewhat foolhardy since he had not the slightest notion what he would do in Moscow and no plans for a book or series of articles, while Sonya was putting her tenure as a teacher in jeopardy by going on a lengthy trip to a less-than-respectable country. At Riga, they were delayed for weeks until Soviet authorities decided to grant them entry to Russia.

In Moscow, disillusionment began. Housing was extremely scarce and there was only one already-filled hotel for foreigners. Befriended by a representative of the United States Communist Party, they obtained a room with two cots that had just been abandoned by the last occupant, who was dying of tuberculosis. The room was full of lice. From then on, through the twelve years he spent in Russia, Chamberlin's disillusionment grew until his youthful enthusiasm for all things Soviet had reversed itself entirely.

At the time of Chamberlin's arrival, Vladimir Ilyich Lenin and Leon Trotsky were the chief leaders of the revolution. Chamberlin first became acquainted with them through attending their public speeches. He described Lenin as remarkable for his unconcern for theatrical tricks in speaking and for his candidness in admitting mistakes. The latter, Chamberlin felt, could be attributed to Lenin's absolute faith in Marxism: as long as he clung to the infallible doctrine of Marx, Lenin had no need to claim personal infallibility as did Hitler, Stalin, and other dictators. In Trotsky, Chamberlin saw a man less stable: Trotsky was quick of wit, handy with language, and original in his ideas, but highly temperamental. Stalin was already something of a legend: "Lenin trusts Stalin; Stalin trusts no one," was a common saying at the time.

During his years in Russia, Chamberlin had wide acquaintance with other foreigners residing and working there. He noted that "nine out of ten became more negative in their attitude after having lived a reasonable length of time in the country." In 1934, Chamberlin's book *Russia's Iron Age* described and evaluated Russia as it existed when he was ready to leave. It presented a gloomy picture of the deprivations, suffering, and enslavement of the people. Five years later, he expressed his opinions in even stronger terms: "Nothing that has occurred in so-called capitalist countries can remotely compare in horror and brutality and degradation of mind and body with what I have seen and experienced under the Genghis Khan socialism of the Soviet Union." By the time Chamberlin decided to leave Russia, his journalistic work had become increasingly difficult and burdensome because of restrictions, censorship, and subtle restraints.

In 1935, the Chamberlins, who by then had a daughter, Elizabeth, sailed for Japan aboard the *Asama Maru* by way of the United States. Housing for foreigners in Tokyo was difficult to acquire, but they eventually found a house in a pleasant residential area. Chamberlin found Japanese press control rather strict: it was a negative type of jurisdiction, wherein editors were told by the police what they could not print but were not told what they could print. Japanese editors were not notably reliable, Chamberlin found. Libel laws were either nonexistent or ineffective; consequently, some newspapers regularly printed malicious gossip, sometimes involving high officials. Information for foreign consumption was mostly doled out by the Foreign Office several times a week in a question-and-answer session with a government spokesman.

Out of his experiences and observations Chamberlin produced *Japan Over Asia* (1937), in which he declared: "My purpose has been to write neither an indictment nor a vindication of Japan's expansionism, but to set forth as objectively as possible the main events and causes of the forward drive in Asia, the obstacles which it has encountered and the favorable and unfavorable auguries for Japan's imperial career in the future." Trips to China, Malaya, the Philippines, and French Indochina helped Chamberlin gain a perspective on affairs in Japan. Meanwhile, war clouds were gathering in Europe.

In March 1939, the Chamberlins returned to the United States because Sonya needed an operation. While Sonya was recovering, Chamberlin produced numerous magazine articles and revised *Japan Over Asia* for publication. There were reunions with old friends he had known in Russia and Japan and numerous discussions about world crises and the war. Chamberlin had come to the conclusion that "there is no higher responsibility for a government than to keep its people out of unnecessary wars. And my definition of an unnecessary war, for the United States, is one unprovoked by hostile aggression against the American continent."

The Chamberlins sailed from New York for Paris in April 1939. They found trenches being dug in the Champs Elysées and air raid shelters being established everywhere. The people were calm but a subtle tension pervaded the city. Sure that war was inevitable, Chamberlin and Sonya took a brief vacation in southeastern Switzerland; they felt certain that it would be their last vacation for some time to come. Elizabeth went to Northern Ireland to visit a friend from the days in Tokyo. Scarcely had Chamberlin and Sonya returned to Paris when war broke out. Chamberlin regarded the war as "the last act in the decline and fall of European civilization"; yet he did not accept the theory held by some of his acquaintances that Hitler's victory in Europe would be a prelude to an invasion of North America. On the contrary, he had the firm conviction that he must do whatever he could to help keep the United States out of the war because Americans were in no way responsible for it. The United States had not ratified the Treaty of Versailles, which had humiliated the Germans after World War I and helped bring the Nazis to power; nor was it responsible for the failure to stop Hitler in 1935, when it could have been accomplished. The United States was not associated with guarantees by the French and British to Poland. Americans should not be expected to pay for the mistakes of foreign governments, Chamberlin believed.

The Confessions of an Individualist was completed in early 1940, before the United States was drawn into World War II. Chamberlin included a personal credo in his last chapter. Its basic points were a belief in the individual's right to freedom of action and expression; in the validity of human reason; that power is the world's greatest evil; that civil liberties are essential to civilization; that individually, men are creative, while collectively, their instinct is for destruction; that the worth of individuals takes precedence over that of corporate groups. This frank declaration of personal beliefs reveals a complete turnabout from his youthful passion for Soviet principles.

The Chamberlins returned to the United States in 1940 and settled in Cambridge, Massachusetts. Between 1940 and 1945, he lectured at Yale University, Harvard University, and Haverford College. He also served as a book reviewer and editorial correspondent for the *Wall Street Journal* and was a contributing editor of the *New Leader*.

Chamberlin was highly critical of Franklin D. Roosevelt, whom he called a dictator. In *America's Second Crusade* (1950), he said he believed Roosevelt had three principle motives for involving the United States in World War II: personal ambition; the desire to bring the American economy out of the Depression; and the feeling that a move against the Axis powers was necessary. Chamberlin viewed the Japanese attack on Pearl Harbor as a result of Roosevelt's inflexible China policy. In *Beyond Containment* (1953) he attempted to analyze the historical basis for U.S./Soviet relations. His twelve years in Russia, viewed from the distance of later assignments, gave him a unique insight into the issue. Between 1946 and 1962, he made ten trips to Germany. *The German Phoenix* (1963) came out of these trips, during which he talked with German citizens and visited universities, schools, factories, and military establishments. The book attempts to analyze postwar Germany and to determine the vital forces of a renewed Europe.

Chamberlin favored the rearming of the German Federated Republic according to the guidelines of the Western alliance and favored stimulating discontent in the Soviet block countries by means of Radio Free Europe and, in the USSR itself, by means of Radio Liberty. It was his conviction that the Russian people would eventually overthrow their oppressors.

Awards and honors Chamberlin received during his life included a Guggenheim Fellowship for the writing of *The Russian Revolution, 1917-1921* (1935), honorary degrees of doctor of letters by Haverford College in 1944 and doctor of laws by Middlebury College in 1949, two Freedom Foundation awards, and two Vigilant Patriot awards.

Articles by Chamberlin on European affairs and current events in the United States appeared in *Harper's*, the *Atlantic Monthly, National Review, Foreign Affairs, Russian Review, Time, Saturday Review*, and the *Saturday Review Post*. "The Great Nonproliferation Hoax," which *National Review* claimed as "his best piece," appeared in that

magazine on 11 March 1969, six months before his death.

Chamberlin died while visiting in Samaden, near St. Moritz, Switzerland. He had suffered a stroke three weeks earlier while engaging in one of his favorite pastimes, walking on a mountain trail. He was seventy-two years old. Sonya Chamberlin had died nine months previously, and friends said Chamberlin had never recovered from the loss. Their daughter, Mrs. Klaus Epstein, and three grandchildren survived them.

Chamberlin's contemporaries generally regarded him and his work with respect. Reviewing one of his books, *The World's Iron Age* (1941), in the *Saturday Review of Literature*, Oswald Garrison Villard said that "there is no foreign correspondent, of the large number of journalists who have represented us abroad during the last ten years, more respected and trusted than Mr. Chamberlin. . . ." George S. Counts, reviewing Chamberlin's *The Russian Enigma: An Interpretation* (1943) in the *Saturday Review of Literature*, called the work "solid and scholarly" and said it had been written by one who knows the Soviet Union as only a half dozen Americans know it. . . ."

Although the *Russian Review* praised Chamberlin's contributions to its pages and lauded him for his "intellectual honesty and integrity," it also noted that Chamberlin was nearly always "swimming against the tide of popular opinion and was completely out of tune with the predominant trends of this technological, collectivist age." The *Russian Review* labeled Chamberlin "a lonely man, out of tune with his time. . . ."

James M. Minifie, reviewing *America's Second Crusade*, accused the author of "ladling out the same dish" of propaganda as Virgilio Gayda or Dr. Goebbels in his handling of Franklin Roosevelt's wartime policies.

Howard P. Whidden, reviewing *Canada, Today and Tomorrow* (1942) found the book "on the whole, an excellent account of present-day Canada." He did point out, however, that Chamberlin is "reluctant to face certain disagreeable facts about Canada. He is much too gentle with the tiny but dangerous minority of pro-fascists in Quebec and also with the die-hard Orangemen in Ontario." But Whidden ended by saying that the book is good journalism.

In the light of present-day journalistic standards, Chamberlin continues to rate highly. He was insatiably curious, thorough in research, eager for personal experiences and true knowledge, well grounded in the classics and history, careful in his writing, and scrupulously honest. Though not as colorful as some of his contemporaries, Chamberlin has contributed much to journalism and journalists through his high professional standards. His work is as readable as it is dependable.

References:

George S. Counts, review of *The Russian Enigma, Saturday Review of Literature*, 26 (4 December 1943): 27;

James Minifie, review of *America's Second Crusade, Saturday Review of Literature*, 33 (18 November 1950): 20;

Oswald Garrison Villard, review of *The World's Iron*

Age, Saturday Review of Literature, 24 (29 November 1941): 5;

Howard P. Whidden, Jr., review of *Canada Today and Tomorrow, Saturday Review of Literature*, 35 (31 October 1942): 8;

"William Henry Chamberlin," *New York Times*, 15 September 1969, p. 47;

"William Henry Chamberlin, RIP," *National Review*, 21 (7 October 1969): 1000.

Papers:

Providence College Library, Providence, Rhode Island, has William Henry Chamberlin's papers from 1912 to 1969 on microfilm.

Harry Chandler

(17 May 1864-23 September 1944)

Stephen D. Bray

MAJOR POSITION HELD: President and publisher, *Los Angeles Times* (1917-1941).

Harry Chandler was the driving force behind the emergence of the *Los Angeles Times* as one of the most influential newspapers in the United States; he was also responsible for the rapid rise of Los Angeles as one of the major cities in the country. Chandler's conservative philosophy was reflected not only in the pages of the *Times*, which was a notorious right-wing paper, but in the distinctive social character of southern California.

Chandler regarded the *Times* as an instrument of his commercial interests. Through his private investments, he largely shaped the physical expansion and commercial development of the region. One of the area's leading entrepreneurs and real estate developers, he acquired the reputation of "California's landlord." His vast personal wealth derived primarily from his extensive land speculations.

As president and publisher of the *Times*, Chandler actively promoted the enormous economic and population growth which turned Los Angeles into a sprawling, prosperous community, and which established the *Times* as a dominant political power. Under his influence the *Times* was a staunchly partisan Republican paper which was recognized as the leading conservative organ in the

state. In the 1920s, the peak of Chandler's career, he was a close friend of President Herbert Hoover. After Chandler's death, the *Times*, still under the control of the Chandler family, helped launch the political career of another Republican president, Richard M. Nixon.

Harry Chandler was born on 17 May 1864 in Landaff, New Hampshire, the eldest of four children of Moses Knight and Emma Jane Little Chandler, New England farmers. He was a descendant of William Chandler, an English immigrant who settled in Massachusetts about 1637. After attending local schools, Chandler planned to enter Dartmouth College in the fall of 1882; but before classes began, he contracted an almost fatal case of pneumonia when he dove on a dare into an ice-covered vat of starch at a nearby factory.

Doctors recommended that he move for his health to a warmer climate, so his parents sent him to California, where he found a home with a doctor who was also suffering from a lung illness. Living in a tent on the doctor's farm in the San Fernando Valley north of Los Angeles, he broke horses and picked fruit in exchange for a share of the crop. He then sold his share to the threshing crew of a nearby ranch, part of the huge Van Nuys property. Within a year he had accumulated over three thousand dollars. He went back to New Hampshire, but an immediate recurrence of his symptoms forced him

Harry Chandler in 1935

to return to California for good.

In 1885 Chandler found a job as a clerk in the circulation department of the *Los Angeles Times*, which had been founded in late 1881. He was soon supervising a delivery route of 1,400 subscribers. Realizing that newspaper circulation was handled primarily by independent contractors, he went into business for himself. He operated routes for the *Herald* and the *Express* as well as the *Times*, and was soon making more money than the owner of the *Times*, Harrison Gray Otis.

Otis had started in journalism at the age of fourteen as a printer's apprentice in Ohio and later worked for the *Louisville Journal*. In 1860 he attended the Republican National Convention as a delegate, and when the Civil War broke out he enlisted in the Union army and rose to the rank of captain. After the war he moved from job to job until he arrived in California in 1876. Six years later he settled in Los Angeles, where he became an editor of the *Daily Times*. In 1882, the city was still a small community of only 5,000 inhabitants, but the following year the Southern Pacific Railroad com-

pleted its southern route to the west coast and the migration of people to southern California began. In 1884 the population of Los Angeles stood at 12,000, and by 1886, when Otis bought out his partner, Henry Boyce, for $18,000, the number of residents had reached 100,000.

Using his position as circulation distributor, Chandler proposed to Otis a scheme to help Otis undermine the rival paper started by Boyce, the *Morning Tribune*. The plan worked, and when the *Tribune* folded, Chandler quietly purchased its entire operation, including the plant, machinery, and subscription lists. When Otis sought Chandler's help in locating the new owner of the *Tribune*, he presented himself. Otis quickly hired him as his circulation manager.

Shortly after Chandler joined ranks with Otis, the first boom period in the growth of Los Angeles had passed its peak and the city faced gloomy economic conditions. In order to ensure the city's, and, therefore, the paper's prosperity, they pushed the Chamber of Commerce to begin an organized campaign of selling the region to the rest of the country. In 1888, Chandler helped implement the first of many promotional "Midwinter" editions of the *Times*, which were sent to persons in the central

Harrison Gray Otis, owner of the Los Angeles Times *when Chandler went to work for the paper in 1885*
(Sherman Foundation)

Chandler during his early years with the Los Angeles Times
(Sherman Foundation)

states and glorified the climate and economic opportunities in California. As a result, thousands of Midwesterners resolved to make Los Angeles their future home. Also in 1888, Chandler married Magdalena Schlador; they had two daughters.

While the *Times* was interested in attracting new settlers to Los Angeles, it also wanted to protect the interests of the city's business community from the demands of labor. Its antiunion stance was directed first against its own employees. In 1890, in the midst of an economic depression, typographers went out on strike at all the papers in Los Angeles. Although formerly a union printer, Otis was the most resistant publisher to their demands and hired scab workers. To continue the struggle to make Los Angeles an open-shop city, Otis and Chandler organized a group of business leaders into the Merchants and Manufacturers Association, which for thirty years determined the economic and political policies of the business community. *Time* magazine would later say that Otis made the *Los Angeles Times* "the most rabid Labor-baiting, Red-hating paper in the United States."

Chandler gradually assumed greater authority in running the paper. In a short time he

cemented his personal as well as his business ties to Otis. After his first wife died in 1892, he married Otis's daughter, Marion, in 1894. Shortly thereafter, he was named business manager of the *Times*. In 1898 he was appointed assistant manager, and when Otis, now a general, returned to active service in the Spanish-American War, Chandler ran the paper in his absence.

In 1910, mounting tension between the *Los Angeles Times* and the unions reached a violent climax when a dynamite bomb blasted the *Times* printing plant, killing twenty employees. Each side placed responsibility on the other. After a long investigation, an official of the International Structural Iron Workers Union, John McNamara, and his brother James were indicted for the plot. Their trial attracted worldwide attention and drew the presence of nationally recognized figures: the well-known defense attorney Clarence Darrow came to represent the brothers; muckraking journalist Lincoln Steffens arrived to assume the role of independent mediator. A critical aspect of the case was that another defense attorney, Job Harriman, was the Socialist candidate for mayor in the upcoming election and was considered likely to win. Working with Darrow and Steffens, Chandler arranged a deal whereby the defendants confessed in order to save their lives. Chandler's solution, accepted by Otis despite his initial outrage, helped prevent the McNamaras from becoming labor martyrs, and, more importantly from the standpoint of the *Times*, helped defeat Harriman in the election four days later. The confession was interpreted as a victory for the *Los Angeles Times* and effectively killed the labor movement in the city.

The outcome was also seen as a personal victory for Chandler, and it represented the end of an era in the style of the *Times*. Otis, who had opposed compromising with the defendants and wanted to see them executed, was polemical and combative by nature, and attracted a lot of animosity for his bellicose rhetoric. (Two years earlier, during a bitterly contested campaign for governor and for control of the Republican party in California, Hiram Johnson, the Progressive candidate and eventual winner, had responded to one of Otis's charges by saying, "He is the one thing all Californians look at when, in looking at Southern California, they see anything that is disgraceful, depraved, corrupt, crooked and putrescent.") While Otis ran the paper as an extension of his personality, Chandler regarded it as an extension of his financial interests. In the case of the McNamaras, he was more interested in securing a business-oriented city administration than in ex-

The Los Angeles Times *Building after it was dynamited in a labor dispute in 1910 (Title Insurance and Trust)*

acting personal retribution. Chandler regarded the *Times* as an investment and as a means to exercise influence rather than as a way of informing the public. As media historian David Halberstam has written, Chandler "sought empire, he wanted above all to extend his reach and economic power."

For several years, Chandler had been using his newspaper contacts to invest in speculative real estate ventures. With street-railway developer Moses Sherman, Chandler helped finance and develop in 1903 the area which became the site of Hollywood. In his early business career he preferred to invest through syndicates; through one of these, in the early 1900s, he helped form two corporations, the California-Mexico Land and Cattle Company and its subsidiary, the Colorado River Land Company. Together they managed land in California's Imperial Valley and a huge estate across the Mexican border in northern Baja California, which in fourteen years grew to more than 800,000 acres. The company had interests in banks and canals, but most of the land was leased to tenant farmers for the production of cotton. In 1906, the company managed the largest cotton-growing enterprise under a single ownership in the world. When Mexico was in

the throes of revolution, the *Times*'s editorial policy defended Chandler's interests. The *Times* expressed its displeasure in 1911 when President Díaz was forced to resign: it wrote, "If he has been a despot, he has been a wise and benevolent despot." The *Times* proceeded to call for United States intervention to protect American business interests. By 1919, the enterprise was producing $18 million worth of cotton. In the late 1930s the land was expropriated by the Mexican government. Ultimately, however, after an appeal to the courts, the Chandlers received over $5 million plus extensive Los Angeles property.

Chandler was part of another syndicate which purchased in 1912 the 286,000-acre Tejon ranch in Los Angeles and Kern counties, on which 20,000 cattle and horses were raised. On his own he bought a 340,000-acre hunting preserve in Colorado and an interest in another of 500,000 acres in New Mexico.

His most important land speculation, however, centered on the San Fernando Valley. He began acquiring land in the Valley as early as 1905. But, as part of yet another syndicate, he purchased in 1909 over 47,000 acres from the Van Nuys estate for $2.5 million. At the same time, he used the power of the *Times* and his personal connections to lead a campaign to bring water from the Sierra Nevadas to Los Angeles. On the eve of a vote on a bond measure to finance the project, the *Times* editorialized that anyone who rejected the plan was "an enemy of the city and will be opposing its progress and prosperity." The aqueduct to carry the water 233 miles from the Owens Valley to the San Fernando Valley was completed in 1913. The new supply of water serviced the 60,000 subdivided acres of residential and commercial property which sold for an estimated $17 million to $100 million. The syndicate also arranged for the construction of a twenty-two-mile paved boulevard connecting the development with Los Angeles; the highway alone earned them an immediate $5 million profit from the sale of adjoining land. Most of the San Fernando Valley was annexed to the city in 1915. By World War I, Chandler had acquired the largest real estate network in the state, and a reputation and influence to match.

When Chandler succeeded Otis as publisher of the *Times* on Otis's death in 1917, he already had established himself as a successful manager of the paper and as one of the most powerful business tycoons in the state. He expanded the paper while preserving Otis's motto for the *Times*: "Stand Fast, Stand Firm, Stand Sure, Stand True." He added a pictorial section, a Sunday magazine, and a farm and garden supplement which evolved into a general home magazine. Of special concern to Chandler was the classified advertising: in 1921, 1922, and 1923 the *Times* led all other American newspapers in volume of want ads. The *Times* was also the first major paper to report Hollywood news and the first to hire a gossip columnist.

Chandler, though, was primarily interested in expanding the commercial base of the city and his own economic interests. In 1919 he arranged for the Goodyear Tire and Rubber company to locate in Los Angeles. In 1922 he helped negotiate the arrival of Douglas Aircraft, which initiated the extensive aerospace industry in southern California. Another of his syndicates created a local air transport company, Western Air Express. He had close ties with the development of the oil industry in the region, was involved with the construction of a major port in Los Angeles, and was connected with the shipping industry.

Chandler was seemingly involved with every aspect of Los Angeles commercial life. He was instrumental in obtaining the financial backing for the development of the California Institute of Technology, of which he served as trustee from 1919 to 1943. He owned the area's first commercial radio station, KHJ, which he sold in 1929 because of a labor dispute. He was also active in the development of the downtown area. He campaigned for the establishment of the Union railway station and organized the investment corporation which built the prestigious Biltmore Hotel. In the 1930s, when the *Times* constructed a new downtown building, he managed to get the city council to pay him over $1 million for his old building and land. Such accomplishments led *Time* magazine to describe him as "not only a capable newspaper manager, but also an inspired capitalist." *Newsweek* called him "Southern California's modern Midas."

Chandler used the *Times* to protect his personal business interests and the business environment of Los Angeles. After World War I, the *Times* actively led an anti-Red campaign. Chandler defended the raids on alleged subversives by U.S. Attorney General Alexander Palmer: the raids demonstrated, according to the *Times*, "evidence of a widespread plot to sovietize the government and industries of the country." Chandler believed that Los Angeles was "freer from the menace of Bolshevism than any other city of equal population in the United States," but he was worried about the leaders of the Industrial Workers of the World (IWW) who were coming to the city to organize the

laborers in southern California's orange groves. They were repulsed by hastily organized vigilantes, but the *Times* led an effort to prevent future organizing attempts. It promoted the passage of the repressive California Criminal Syndicalist Act, which was aimed specifically at the IWW.

While keeping the IWW away from the city, Chandler spearheaded a drive to attract more tourists and settlers to Los Angeles. In 1921 he organized the All-Year Club of Southern California to promote summer tourism. The efforts of boosters like Chandler led to a massive influx of new residents to Los Angeles during the 1920s. Los Angeles County recorded a gain of 1,272,037 inhabitants, the largest internal migration in the history of the country. For his leadership, the city's realty board bestowed on Chandler the title of "Los Angeles's Most Useful Citizen."

Under Chandler, the *Los Angeles Times* loudly proclaimed its highly partisan character. Throughout the 1920s Chandler was the acknowledged leader of southern California's conservative Republicans and exerted tremendous influence over local and state elections. Political candidates were often selected in Chandler's office, and he was dubbed the "Governor of Southern California." In its coverage of political campaigns, the *Times* virtually ignored the Democrats. Reporter Kyle Palmer once told a visiting New York correspondent, "We don't bother with them. We don't go in for that kind of crap you have back in New York of being obliged to print both sides." Palmer, who started working for Chandler in 1918, was later known as the state's Republican boss and the man responsible for bringing Richard Nixon into politics.

The conservative business spirit nationwide and local prosperity made the 1920s the happiest period of Chandler's life. He personally abstained from alcohol and was a vigorous supporter of Prohibition. He was an acquaintance of Presidents Harding and Coolidge, and later a close friend of Herbert Hoover, whom the *Times* endorsed enthusiastically. Chandler turned down several federal appointments, but in late 1929 he accepted Hoover's nomination to the National Business Survey Conference to study the economic conditions precipitated by the stock market crash.

As much as he had liked the mood of the 1920s, Chandler despised the new atmosphere of the 1930s. The *Times* editorialized that "much of the depression is psychological." Chandler was a constant critic of President Roosevelt's New Deal and found plenty of opportunity for political opposition right in California, starting with Upton Sinclair's campaign for governor in 1934.

Chandler and Sinclair were political enemies of long standing. Sinclair, the radical journalist best known for his 1906 novel *The Jungle,* had called the *Times* the "fountainhead of so much unloveliness in California." Chandler, during his anti-Red campaign after World War I, had led an effort to send Sinclair to jail. In the early 1930s, Sinclair changed his registration from Socialist to Democrat and created the End Poverty in California (EPIC) movement, which attracted thousands and became a major social force in the state. In 1934 he ran for governor. After Sinclair captured the Democratic nomination, Chandler orchestrated a business assault to stop him. The conservative business community raised an enormous sum of money and for the first time in a political campaign hired an advertising agency to mount a vigorous and vicious attack on EPIC. As part of their Red-baiting campaign, Chandler lent his top political reporter, Kyle Palmer, to Hollywood to assist with the production of inflammatory films undermining Sinclair's appeal. They willfully distorted his views and generated a powerful media blitz which led to Sinclair's defeat.

Chandler and the *Times* expressed their conservative views throughout the Depression. In 1934, they referred to the general strike in San Francisco led by Harry Bridges, president of the longshoremen's union, "as a Communist-inspired and led revolt against organized government." In 1936, the *Times* praised Los Angeles police for turning away unemployed migrants at the California border. Chandler was opposed to the Wagner Act and was especially critical of the Newspaper Guild. When a *Times* reporter made the mistake of covering a strike story impartially he was rebuked by an editor who told him, "There's only one way to cover a union story and that's the *Times*' way."

The *Times*'s partisan views attracted a number of critics. George Seldes wrote in *Lords of the Press* (1938) that "no one has ever heard Chandler say anything which could be interpreted even vaguely as humanitarian, altruistic, liberal or progressively intelligent." A poll among Washington correspondents taken in 1937 rated the *Times* as the third worst paper in the country in terms of fairness and reliability.

Ironically, the one time Chandler's prejudices aligned him in a court case with Harry Bridges it led to a coveted journalistic honor. In 1938, while praising a judge's injunction against Bridges's longshoremen's union, the *Times* printed an angry telegram Bridges had written attacking the judge.

For printing the telegram and other material concerning court cases still in process, the *Times*, along with Bridges, was cited for contempt and found guilty on two counts. When the conviction was overturned by the United States Supreme Court in 1941, the decision was heralded as a major victory for freedom of the press. For their role in the case, Chandler and the *Times* received their first Pulitzer Prize.

In 1930-1931 Chandler served as president of the American Newspaper Publishers Association. In 1936 the *Times* streamlined its makeup and won the Ayer Cup for excellence for its new typography. Chandler, despite his antilabor views, was regarded as a good employer. The *Times* was the first paper to establish a personnel department and one of the first to adopt a forty-hour week. In the early 1920s the paper had established a group insurance plan for employees paid for by the company. Chandler paid higher than going union rates and was known to reward seniority.

By the early 1940s, Chandler began turning over responsibility for the paper to three of his eight children. His eldest son, Norman, succeeded him as president and publisher in 1941, but Chandler remained as chairman of the board of the Times-Mirror Company. In 1944, at the age of eighty, he died of a coronary thrombosis, and was buried in Hollywood cemetery. He left an estate valued at an estimated $500 million. He did not want any discussion of his life or extensive holdings, so on his deathbed he ordered the destruction of all his papers.

During his life with the *Times* its daily circulation rose from 1,400 in 1885 to 325,000; at his death the Sunday circulation was over 600,000 copies. In the same period, Los Angeles had grown from a town of 12,000 to a metropolis of over 3 million people. Under Chandler, the historian of the paper wrote, "the *Times* became a classic example of the newspaper as servant of its publisher's interests, with both editorial writers and news reporters reflecting the publisher's viewpoint in their writings." In its obituary, *Time* magazine commented that Chandler "was more responsible than any other man for the growth of both the *Times* and its city." A more recent observer, David Halberstam, stated succinctly that Chandler "did not so much foster the growth of Southern California as, more simply, invent it."

References:
"An Effectively Transplanted New Englander," *Saturday Evening Post,* 198 (5 June 1926): 52;

"Death of Chandler," *Time,* 44 (2 October 1944): 58;

Robert Gottlieb and Irene Wolt, *Thinking Big: The Story of the Los Angeles Times Its Publishers and Their Influence on Southern California* (New York: Putnam's, 1977);

David Halberstam, *The Powers That Be* (New York: Knopf, 1979);

Carey McWilliams, *Southern California: An Island on the Land* (Salt Lake City: Peregrine Smith, 1946);

"Midas of California," *Newsweek,* 24 (2 October 1944): 80;

George Seldes, *Lords of the Press* (New York: Messner, 1938);

"Third Perch," *Time,* 26 (15 July 1935): 32.

Raymond Clapper
(30 May 1892-1 February 1944)

John De Mott
Memphis State University

MAJOR POSITIONS HELD: Political writer and chief of the Washington bureau, United Press Associations (1929-1933); political columnist and chief of the national bureau, *Washington Post* (1934-1935); political commentator, Scripps-Howard Newspapers and United Features Syndicate (1936-1944).

BOOKS: *Racketeering in Washington* (Boston: Page, 1933);

Watching the World, edited by Olive Ewing Clapper (London & New York: McGraw-Hill, 1944).

PERIODICAL PUBLICATIONS: "Is Ghost Writing Dishonest?," *Forum,* 101 (February 1939): 67-69;

"Social Work and the Press," *Survey Graphic,* 75 (December 1939): 365-366;

"Ten Most Powerful People in Washington," *Reader's Digest,* 38 (May 1941): 45-48;

"F. D. R.'s Unofficial Cabinet," *Reader's Digest,* 39 (October 1941): 87-97;

"Why Can't Americans Believe in America?," *Life,* 11 (27 October 1941): 52-54;

"President," *Yale Review,* 31 (March 1942): 601-606;

"Watch Out for Dictatorship, Period," *Reader's Digest,* 41 (November 1942): 117-118.

Born on a farm near La Cygne, Kansas, in the horse-and-buggy age of the 1890s, he died in an airplane crash in the far-off Marshall Islands of the South Pacific. In the eventful fifty-one years that ended in 1944, Raymond Clapper served as one of America's most perceptive and widely read interpreters of politics and national affairs. In honor of that achievement, the Raymond Clapper Memorial Association presents an annual award to the national capital press correspondent whose writings in the previous year best embody the ideals of "fair and painstaking reporting and sound craftsmanship that marked Mr. Clapper's work, and have contributed most to public enlightenment and a sound democracy."

One of the few books that Clapper was able to complete before he became a battle casualty in World War II was an explanation of political corruption in the nation's capital. *Racketeering in Washington* (1933) reveals Clapper's outrage at corruption in government. Clapper's career as a news reporter and later a national affairs commentator for the *Kansas City Star,* United Press, the *Washington Post,* the Scripps-Howard newspapers, United Features Syndicate, the Mutual Broadcasting Network, and other media of mass communication reflected his deep concern. His widow, Olive Ewing Clapper, recalled asking repeatedly, when they were beginning their life together: "Ray, can the world be filled with clean, free people?" "Well," Clapper would answer, "I suppose it is a long evolutionary haul. But if it ever happens it will start here in the good old United States. The only chance is here. The only form of government that can do it is a democracy." Such feelings about democracy and its potential for accomplishment perhaps explain Clapper's lifelong preoccupation with public affairs and their interpretation. "Democracy was an instinct with him," Mrs. Clapper observed. "He knew without thinking what would be good or bad for his

Raymond Clapper

White, the famous editor of the *Emporia Gazette* in the Flint Hills of Kansas, and read everything he could find about White. At the age of seventeen, Clapper made a pilgrimage to Emporia, more than 100 miles from Kansas City, to see and talk with his hero. Inspired by White to someday own a small-town newspaper, Clapper found employment as a printer's devil. In that apprentice role, and later as a journeyman printer, he worked evenings while attending high school in Kansas City, Kansas.

Because Clapper's former employer disapproved of his daughter "going steady" with Clapper to church and school activities, Olive Ewing and Clapper eloped on 31 March 1913 and dropped out of school. Having obtained full-time employment as a printer, Clapper managed to pay $450 down on a small house. "We never lived in that house," however, Mrs. Clapper recalled later. "Ray came home one night seemingly very angry. I wondered, as I often did over the years, what I could have done to make him so angry. But he wasn't mad at me. Pacing the floor, he finally announced, 'We are going back to school. We can never get any place without an education.' "

September found the couple hiking, knapsacks on their backs, forty miles up the Kansas river

country. He lived long enough to know that freedom's victory was sure. If only he might have participated in what we hope to make out of that victory."

Descended from a "Pennsylvania Dutch" German immigrant family, Raymond Lewis Clapper was born on Memorial Day 1892 on a small farm in Linn County, Kansas, to John William and Julia Crowe Clapper. Unable to make a satisfactory living, the family moved to Kansas City, where John Clapper obtained employment in one of the soap factories in the Armourdale packinghouse district. There young Clapper was reared, working before and after school and on weekends delivering newspapers, running errands, and doing assorted jobs at a grocery operated by a merchant who eventually became his father-in-law. Although there were no books in Clapper's "plain people" home, he became a brilliant student in history, geography, and English. He created and maintained an extensive newspaper "morgue"-type system of clippings from the Sunday supplement of the *Kansas City Star* that provided all the neighborhood's students with material for "themes" throughout high school.

During his high-school days, Clapper developed an intense admiration for William Allen

Clapper and his wife, Olive, shortly after their marriage in 1913 (photograph by D. P. Thomson, Kansas City, Mo.)

to Lawrence, home of Kansas University, where they were able to obtain admission after making up the deficiencies resulting from their failure to finish high school. The chairman of the university's department of journalism in those days was Merle Thorpe, later a famous editor of *Nation's Business*. Clapper's potential for journalism made itself apparent early, and he became the regular Kansas University correspondent for the *Kansas City Star*, and later managing editor of the university's newspaper, the *Daily Kansan*.

In 1916, Clapper obtained a full-time job on the *Star*. By autumn, he had been hired by the United Press, which sent him to Chicago. From Chicago, Clapper went to Milwaukee, and from there to St. Paul. "After a year," Mrs. Clapper related, "he begged to be sent East. When they refused he wangled a job promoting a Christmas seal campaign in New York state for the sole purpose of getting within geographical range of his ambition's goal—the nation's capital. The autumn of 1917 found him in Washington, the political reporter's heaven."

Throughout the period from World War I to World War II, Clapper was an integral part of the Washington scene. His first big news "scoop" occurred at the 1920 convention of the Republican party. A fellow Kansan, Sen. Charles Curtis, walked out of the party's famous "smoke-filled room" and disclosed to Clapper that the GOP's national leaders hoped to swing the presidential nomination to Warren G. Harding. During those early years, Clapper mainly covered Congress and the presidency, but in 1925 he went to Tennessee to cover the famous Scopes "Monkey" trial. In 1929, he became manager of UP's capital staff. In 1930, he covered the international conference of naval powers in London. In 1933, Clapper's book *Racketeering in Washington* exposed a variety of corrupt practices in the federal government's administration and its relationship with business interests.

In 1933, Clapper left UP to join the staff of the *Washington Post*, for which he was to serve as head of the national bureau and create a column of political commentary. While preparing to start the column, Clapper continued to report national news and do political analysis and interpretation. In an introduction to Clapper's column, the *Post*, in its issue of 28 September 1934, gave this explanation: "What causes news? What peculiar circumstances— outside influences—personal motives, make up the forces which create headlines yet never appear in the conventional news story? In an authoritative and absorbing new daily feature called 'Between

Clapper dictating copy to a telegraph operator at the 1932 Democratic Convention in Chicago

You and Me' Raymond Clapper takes readers backstage in the day's news. He reveals how and why things happen as they do."

Because the newspaper editorial page historically was seen as the exclusive domain of editors or publishers rather than news reporters, Clapper expressed reservations concerning his column's chances of success. However, "I want to try it," he told his wife. "In a straight news story you have to leave out so much background, so much meat, or else bury it at the end of the story. I want a chance to feature it so that people will see and understand what really goes on in the government. . . . it's a temptation to try to write lots of the kind of things you and I talk about that other people might like to read too. I'd make it a news story right on the nose of the news but put into it what I'd like someone to tell me if I was living out in Kansas about day-to-day background in Washington." The subsequent development and growth of news "analysis" and "interpretative reporting" that Clapper's own pioneering inspired and helped to foster make his reservations a bit difficult to comprehend in retrospect, but such were the times in the journalism establishment of the mid-1930s.

Clapper's column in the *Post* proved successful beyond his expectations, but in December he returned to the Scripps-Howard organization, which offered him the opportunity to write a similar column, "Watching the World Go By," for its newspapers throughout the country. Additional newspapers published Clapper's column regularly after it was syndicated nationally by United Features. Informed that his column was being printed in more than 175 newspapers having ten million readers, Clapper remarked that the column's success "is due to the patience of the editors of this country who were willing to string along printing my heavy serious stuff, plugging it when more exciting gossip columns might have brought more readers. They deserve the credit, not me."

In addition to his newspaper reportage and columns, Clapper contributed articles to periodicals that included *Life, Look, Liberty, Cosmopolitan, McCall's,* the *Reader's Digest,* the *Forum,* the *Yale Review,* the *Review of Reviews, Current History, Survey Graphic,* and the *Congressional Digest.*

During his career, Clapper interviewed and observed the activities of virtually everyone prominent on the national scene. Theodore Roosevelt, Woodrow Wilson, Warren Harding, Calvin Coolidge, Herbert Hoover, Franklin and Eleanor Roosevelt, Alf Landon, Wendell Willkie, John "Cactus Jack" Garner, Thomas Dewey, Cordell Hull, Henry Wallace, Harold Ickes, Frances Perkins, and John L. Lewis were all sources from which he obtained the precious material for creating his first rough draft of the nation's history, and his interpretations of it. Many were personal friends, for Clapper's work attracted the politically powerful, as well as other members of society's "fourth estate," to him and his family. An admirer of Franklin Roosevelt, as he had been of Woodrow Wilson, Clapper nevertheless criticized FDR frequently, in print and in his radio commentaries for the Mutual Broadcasting Network.

Clapper's efforts to remain nonpartisan were symbolized by a unique set of andirons that graced the fireplace in the library of the Clappers' "dream house" on Chain Bridge Road in Washington: one was in the shape of an elephant, the other in that of a donkey. Although his columns stressed the need for involvement in democracy's political process, Clapper refused to exercise his own suffrage. Recounting one of the couple's moves, Mrs. Clapper recalled that "I registered as a Democrat and became an active participant in state and national politics. I wanted Ray to become a voter. I believed every citizen ought to vote. Ray believed it too, but he refused to register ... fearful that he might be tempted to write as a vindication of his own vote." He explained his position: "I feel free to criticize either party without having the precinct chairman call and ask me why I was being disloyal to my party. Once some time ago I was told by a Republican friend of mine that it had been found that I had registered as a Republican in Kansas back in 1920. I had completely forgotten the matter and still do not remember it although I am inclined to take my friend's word for it. I have never bothered to check up on it. To some this may seem like indifference about my responsibilities as a citizen and perhaps there is some basis for that complaint. If so I'll just let it stand. To me it seems more important to keep free from entangling alliances in this particular kind of work—somewhat as a judge retires from active politics when he goes on the bench. I have followed the same rule with regard to propaganda organizations and have refused to join any of the numerous committees. I make the same reply to all of them. Often I am in complete accord with the purposes but I do not wish to become affiliated and be bound by a policy that might interfere with freedom of comment in my column. I have no objection to crusading by those who wish to do it. I am not the crusading type and prefer to be free to criticize or praise, to analyze and interpret as the day's news seems to require without having to sustain a position or policy of my own." "What is it that makes Ray tick?," Ernie Pyle once asked Mrs. Clapper. "What makes him slam or praise first one side, then the other?"

Despite his criticism of politicians and others who did not share his concern over the rise of Hitler—isolationist activists once accused him of being a British agent—and the outrage he had expressed toward corruption in public office, Clapper enjoyed the respect and affection of a large number of influential leaders representing a broad range of political outlook. Typical of the regard in which he was held is a comment by Henry Ford: "Mr. Clapper knows this nation. He has constantly traveled its length and breadth, observing its trends, studying its methods, familiarizing himself with the wide variety of mind and motive which marks its citizens, and reporting these with the efficiency and high impartiality which characterizes our best journalism."

For many years, as a reporter for the United Press, Clapper steadfastly avoided overseas assignments, preferring to remain in the nation's capital, close to the sources of his journalistic expertise. As the clouds that brought World War II began to gather, however, Clapper traveled to Germany, Russia, and other European countries. Olive Clapper recalled a 1937 visit: "We wined and dined in gay, irresponsible Paris; we lingered in Geneva watching the dying League of Nations; we tramped through Moscow's rubble-strewn streets sensing that Russia was staggering into a mechanical age amid purges of her people. We felt at home in London where the only worries were Wally Simpson and the Spanish civil war. In Germany we shuddered at the efficient iron thumb of the Gestapo and the factory chimneys belching smoke day and night to manufacture the instruments of war. We idled in Austria where an aged flower girl grotesquely symbolized Vienna's romantic past. I can never forget the peasants of Poland digging barefoot in the potato fields nor the Hungarians forever drinking coffee on the open terraces, dreaming dreams of their wars, mouthing words about freedom but eyeing the Nazis with ill-conceived envy." In those circumstances, Mrs. Clapper remembered, "Anyone with half an eye could see that war was inevitable. We were scared to death. When Ray returned to report in his columns and in speaking trips how certain war was, people eyed us with sad shaking of the head as though to say, 'the poor Clappers are seeing things under the bed.' "

As Clapper's perceptiveness concerning Hitler's Germany and its meaning became more clear, Clapper's reputation as a political analyst grew. Sigma Delta Chi, the society of professional journalists, elected him its honorary national president for 1938. In 1939, Clapper served as president of Washington's prestigious Gridiron Club. In addition, he was a member of the National Press Club and the Overseas Writers Club. In 1940, in a poll conducted among members of Washington's press corps, Clapper's column was voted the most significant, fair, and reliable. That same year, the *London Daily Mail* described Clapper as "America's No. 1 columnist," and stated that "his articles carry more weight than those of any other writer in the United States." *Time* magazine described him in 1940 in these terms: "Ray Clapper is a middle-sized man with wise eyes, stooped shoulders, and a burning conviction that journalism is the most important profession in the world. In themselves, these attributes would not make him unique. The quality that long ago lifted Scripps-Howard's Clapper out of the ruck of columnists is his knack of translating some event into sound sense on the very day that people want to hear about it. Somehow he manages to move a half step faster than the mass mind." Calling

Clapper "one of the ablest of U.S. political commentators," *Time* observed that although he was "rated a New Deal sympathizer, his particular passion is Republican progressivism."

Like many reporters and columnists of his generation, Clapper admired the progressive Republican character of Kansas governor Alfred Landon, and had taken a friendly attitude toward Landon's nomination for the presidency in 1936. In the 1940 campaign, Clapper actually took a stand for the GOP's standard-bearer, Wendell L. Willkie, because he was opposed in principle to President Roosevelt's bid for an unprecedented third term.

When the 7 December 1941 attack on Pearl Harbor brought war to the United States, Clapper curtailed his activities as a radio commentator and lecturer to concentrate on his column and travel needed to explain the nation's war effort. As a war correspondent, he traveled to the Near East, India, China, Sweden, and England in 1942. In 1943, he toured the battlefields of North Africa and Sicily and covered the bombing of Rome. He was covering the U.S. invasion of the Japanese-held Marshall Islands in the South Pacific when he became the sixteenth U.S. journalist killed in World War II.

Clapper was well aware of the danger. In one of the last columns before his death, datelined "Somewhere in New Guinea, Jan. 26, 1944," he wrote: "Just about every individual has some religious charm or other good-luck token. I'm not a religious man but I find myself frequently taking out a tiny brown bear which my daughter gave me as I was leaving last year for the European theatre. Over here seven war correspondents have been killed, most in the last few months, and I never get in a plane any more without checking with the little brown bear."

On 3 February, the *New York Times* and other news media carried an announcement by a spokesman for the U.S. Navy: "The Commander in Chief of the Pacific Fleet has reported that a plane, in which Raymond Clapper was a passenger, engaged in covering the Marshall invasions, collided with another plane while forming up. Mr. Clapper was in the plane with the squadron commander. Both planes crashed in the lagoon. There were no survivors."

Notified of Clapper's death immediately after it occurred, President Roosevelt sent Mrs. Clapper and the Clappers' two children, Janet Ewing and William Raymond ("Peter"), a letter of condolence that included these comments: "It was characteristic of Ray's fidelity to the great traditions of reporting that the day's work should find him at the scene of

Clapper (third from left) eating with crew of the aircraft carrier Bunker Hill *the night before his death*

action for first-hand facts in the thick of the fight." Cordell Hull, FDR's Secretary of State, said: "I was privileged to know Mr. Clapper as a friend over a long period of years and held him in the highest esteem. He was one of our most eminent and distinguished journalists who earned the confidence and respect of the American people." In a resolution, the Association of Radio News Analysts stated that Clapper "represented the best traditions of his profession. He was always fair, scrupulously honest and invariably generous in evaluating the motives of those with whom he disagreed." In its report of his death, the *New York Times* observed that Clapper "contributed in his widely syndicated column what were generally accepted as among the most objective, tolerant and understanding views on national and foreign affairs of any of the political writers." Even though he had "alternately characterized himself politically as a 'seventy-five per cent New Dealer' and a 'progressive Republican,' and even though he frequently expressed strong views on many subjects," the *Times* recalled, "political bias never tainted his objectivity." And, the *Times* added,

"he was known to members of his profession as a 'newspaperman's newspaperman.'"

As a result of Clapper's journalistic diligence, his clients were able to print his columns each day for fifteen days following his death. In an editorial, the Scripps-Howard management explained that although

some of us might have considered the arduous journey to Australia and the South Pacific islands job enough in itself, he managed not only to keep his column coming daily, but to build up a "cushion" of advance copy against the day when he would go to sea with a task force and be unable because of radio silence to send us anything for days or perhaps weeks.

And when the task force did set out, and he could no longer deliver his copy to us, he kept turning out columns so that he would be ready when transmission was available. After his death, the Navy delivered these articles to us.

When Clapper's well-worn briefcase was returned to his widow, it contained hundreds of notes taken during conversations with soldiers, sailors, and other sources. Practically all of the notes were illegible. "Curiously, however," Mrs. Clapper recalled, there was one quite legible note, written in the past tense, concerning the bombing mission that caused Clapper's death. It read: "Went out in torpedo bomber plane to see finish of Eniwetak. Went with squadron commander. Purpose to burn island, strategy could be used other islands. Contrast this bombing with that of bombing of Rome. Squadron called Bunker Hill Hotfoot. Back in time for lunch." "It seemed uncanny and slightly eerie," Mrs. Clapper observed, "but he was only preparing ahead of time to write for the folks back home his description of the flight that ended his life. . . . Unto death he worked, always the reporter."

In an introduction to the collection of Clapper's later work, *Watching the World* (1944), Ernie Pyle observed:

> There was nothing flashy nor eccentric nor glittering about Ray. He was a sound man who worked like a dog, was intelligent and honest, and used for the foundation of his writings two things—vast experience and good common sense.
>
> I had known Ray Clapper in his home at Washington and known him bunking down at night under an olive tree in Sicily; known him in London and in the flat spaces of the Middle West. There was something in him so normal, so like other people who live in houses and have families and dogs and fireplaces, that when he came to the wars somehow it always seemed impossible that anything could ever happen to him.
>
> He was in no sense an adventurer. When he flew over the hump to China, went along on the Rome raid, took a close look at the fighting in Sicily or made himself a part of the Marshalls invasion, it wasn't because he yearned for exciting things. He did it because he thought it his duty to inform himself about world events and the viewpoint of our men in the actual combat areas. I know that to be true, because he told me so more than once.
>
> Ray Clapper was blessed with the good things that come to people who are successful. He was accepted by the great; courted by the near-great. And yet he kept on working at terrific tempo, stayed personally just as he always was, and remained cognizant of the little things.
>
> Ray believed in himself, and he avoided

that state of mind which might have made it impossible for him to understand the views of others. Over the years he changed from one political viewpoint to another. Occasionally he would state bluntly in print that he had been wrong. But his work was so fully based on hard, factual reporting, and so little on ivory-tower dreaming, that it was bound to be almost always right. His mind was pliable, but his integrity was unshakable. I doubt that he ever wrote a line out of opportunism; I am sure he never wrote a line he didn't believe.

> More than anything else he was a crusader for the right of people to think things out for themselves and make their own decisions, and he spent his life giving them information that would help them. People believed what he said because they could sense the honesty in his writing.

Not long after writing those words from Italy, Ernie Pyle, the first recipient of the Clapper Award, also became a casualty of World War II.

References:

"Average Man Lost His Columnist When Raymond Clapper Was Killed," *Newsweek,* 23 (14 February 1944): 68;

"Clapper Era," *Time,* 47 (18 February 1946): 94;

"Clapper is Killed in Pacific Crash," *New York Times,* 4 February 1944, p. 3;

Olive Ewing Clapper, *One Lucky Woman* (Garden City: Doubleday, 1961);

Clapper, *Washington Tapestry* (New York: McGraw-Hill, 1946);

"Everyman's Columnist," *Time,* 40 (6 July 1942): 40-42;

Otto Fuerbinger, "Average Man's Columnist," in *More Post Biographies,* edited by John E. Drewry (Athens: University of Georgia Press, 1947), pp. 75-87;

J. K. Hutchens, "Something About People Who Read and Write," *New York Times Book Review,* 3 February 1946, p. 28;

E. K. Lindley, "Clapper and White: a Personal Tribute," *Newsweek,* 23 (14 February 1944): 52;

"Toe to Toe," *Time,* 35 (18 March 1940);

"Two Commentators," *Newsweek,* 20 (5 October 1942): 78-79.

Papers:

Raymond Clapper's papers are in the Library of Congress.

Kent Cooper

(22 March 1880-31 January 1965)

Richard A. Schwarzlose
Northwestern University

MAJOR POSITIONS HELD: General manager, Associated Press (1925-1948); executive director, Associated Press (1943-1951).

BOOKS: *Barriers Down* (New York: Farrar & Rinehart, 1942);
Anna Zenger, Mother of Freedom (New York: Farrar, Straus, 1946);
The Right to Know: An Exposition of the Evils of News Suppression and Propaganda (New York: Farrar, Straus & Cudahy, 1956);
Kent Cooper and The Associated Press: An Autobiography (New York: Random House, 1959).

OTHER: "Free News: First Step in Peace," in *Treasury for the Free World,* edited by Ben Raeburn (New York: Arco, 1946), pp. 268-274;
Houston Harte, ed., *In Our Image, Character Studies from the Old Testament,* foreword by Cooper (New York: Oxford University Press, 1949).

PERIODICAL PUBLICATIONS: "What Do You Want in the News?," *Collier's,* 75 (13 June 1925): 23;
"The Language of Friendship," *American Review of Reviews* (February 1928): 147;
"Corporation Publicity," *Century,* 117 (December 1928): 177-183;
"Whence the News?," *Saturday Evening Post,* 203 (16 August 1930): 34, 36, 145-146;
"Freedom of Information," *Life,* 17 (13 November 1944): 55-58, 60, 62;
"A Free Press in a Free World," *Vital Speeches of the Day,* 11 (1944-1945): 209-211;
"To Prevent War—No News Blackout," *New York Times Magazine,* 11 March 1945, pp. 12, 33, 35.

Kent Cooper at the time of his appointment as general manager of the Associated Press in 1925

Aggressive and confident of his own visionary ideas, Kent Cooper inaugurated the Associated Press's twentieth-century transformation from a stodgy, lean, domestic wire service to a brighter news, feature, and photo service on the international stage. A frequent critic of government news suppression and propaganda, Cooper is credited with introducing the phrase "the right to know" to the journalist's lexicon, the phrase meaning that the citizen is entitled to have access to news as a necessary condition for political freedom. As AP's chief administrative officer for a quarter of a century, Cooper diplomatically guided the news service during some of the organization's most crucial challenges: the modernizing of the news report, the news cooperative's internal conflicts over members' voting and franchise rights and service to radio stations, the breakup of the international news cartel, a court battle over AP's monopoly practices, and the beginnings of a post-World War II global expansion.

Born 22 March 1880 in Columbus, Indiana, then a town of 4,000 people fifty miles south of Indianapolis, Cooper was one of an army of young Midwestern reporters who stormed Eastern news organizations, early in the twentieth century—some, like Cooper, rising to the nation's major news positions between the two world wars. The son of George William and Sina Green Cooper, and the only brother of three older sisters, Maud, Bertha, and Beryl, Cooper was introduced to public life at an early age by his father, a lawyer and Democratic politician who was elected mayor of Columbus in 1877, city attorney in 1879, and congressman for three terms between 1889 and 1895. The family spent two of the six winters of his congressional terms living in Washington. During the elder Cooper's third successful campaign for Congress, twelve-year-old Kent organized his young friends into a Cooper Club which paraded and campaigned on his father's behalf.

The previous year Cooper had begun acquiring a "smell for printer's ink" by delivering the four-page *Columbus Republican*. During summer vacations from high school Cooper set type and eventually reported for Columbus newspapers. While setting other writers' words into type in the then politically charged atmosphere of Hoosier journalism, Cooper disapprovingly noted the ceaseless political wrangling and vituperation getting into print. Believing that the people wanted news and not partisanship, Cooper viewed political journalism as "a useless soiling of white paper with expensive ink," according to a 1926 article by Bruce Barton. This rejection of an old journalistic style foretold Cooper's attraction to the news service business, which emphasizes politically impartial reporting.

After one year at Indiana University Cooper was forced into the working world in 1899 by the death of his father. One of his father's last acts was to write the letter which secured for Cooper a reporting position on the new *Indianapolis Press* at twelve dollars per week. Although the *Press* lasted only eighteen months, Cooper's aggressiveness had been noticed by the editor of the *Indianapolis Sun,* who gave Cooper a job as a police reporter. The *Sun* received its nonlocal news from the Scripps-McRae Press Association, a Midwestern forerunner of the present United Press International. Sensing opportunity in the larger journalistic world, Cooper volunteered to be Scripps-McRae's Indianapolis correspondent in 1901. Within six months he was promoted to full-time manager of the Indianapolis bureau, filing an abbreviated 500-word news report

to a network of small Indiana newspapers he had organized.

When his request for a pay raise was denied in January 1905, Cooper quit Scripps-McRae, formed his own United Press News Association, and began delivering a state news report to eighteen Indiana papers which had followed him out of Scripps-McRae. Within a year, however, he sold his enterprise to Scripps-McRae and was back on the payroll at thirty-five dollars per week, bubbling over the revolutionary idea of delivering the wire's news report in shortened form to smaller newspapers via telephone circuits rather than by telegraph. A year later this "pony" telephone network in Indiana had increased from eighteen to twenty-seven newspapers, and Cooper was transferred to the New York City headquarters of the new United Press, which had just combined Scripps-McRae and two other regional wires to form a national wire service. On assignment from UP's first president, Hamilton B. Clark, Cooper traveled the Midwest, enticing some newspapers away from Associated Press membership, convincing others to supplement their AP service with UP's report, and establishing various local

Cooper at about the time he became Indianapolis correspondent for the Scripps-McRae Press Association in 1901

"pony" telephone networks for delivery of UP's news.

By 1910, exhausted from continuous traveling, Cooper developed a plan to leave UP and organize an independent transmission company to telephone the news reports of UP, AP, and Hearst's recently organized International News Service to their respective subscribers. He discussed his plan with American Telephone and Telegraph Company general manager Charles H. Wilson, who persuaded Cooper to present his scheme to Melville E. Stone, AP's general manager and one of journalism's respected elder statesmen. Half a century later Cooper recalled that AP's offices at 195 Broadway "reeked with old age" and that Stone was a "tired man, old beyond his [sixty-two] years," whose "position had lost its glamor for him." Stone, impressed with Cooper's grasp of news delivery problems and at the moment facing the prospect of raising assessments to AP subscribers to meet increasing transmission costs, offered Cooper a job as AP's first traveling inspector, finding and correcting costly transmission practices. Assessing his situation, Cooper noted that the upstart United Press was full of eager young men, some of whom had met and ingratiated themselves with owner E. W. Scripps; one such dynamo was Roy W. Howard, who, although one of Cooper's contemporaries in Indianapolis journalism, had risen rapidly in New York until in 1907 he was one of UP's three incorporators and the wire's first general manager. At AP Cooper found elderly men and a "moribund" organization. As Cooper put it, "I thought I might have less rivalry at The AP."

Scrapping his independent transmission company notion, Cooper reported for work at AP on 5 December 1910, immediately surveyed AP's books, and found that the wire service spent three-fourths of its revenue on telegraphic tolls and that monthly deficits averaging $4,000 would shortly require an increase in assessments to AP members. Within three months Cooper submitted a transmission plan which projected a savings of $100,000 a year and proposed the radical (to the AP's management) idea of awarding transmission contracts to telegraph companies on a competitive basis. Stone rejected the plan, but a chance meeting with AP director Valentine S. McClatchy, publisher of the *Sacramento Bee,* and the intervention of McClatchy and another director, *New York Times* publisher Adolph S. Ochs, cleared the way for Cooper to make good on his promised savings instead of resigning from the AP in frustration. His

cost-cutting plan led to the creation in 1912 of the AP's traffic department, of which Cooper was named the first chief.

With war declared by European belligerents and with propaganda beginning to seep into the reports of Europe's major wire services—Reuters in England, Havas in France, and Wolff in Germany—the *Buenos Aires La Nación* cabled AP on 8 September 1914 requesting AP's news reports as a substitute for its current Havas service. By chance Cooper noticed the cable at AP headquarters, and when he offered to arrange for the service, Stone explained that an 1893 cartel contract among the three major European wire services prohibited AP from delivering news to South American papers. The contract had continued the "Ring Combination" dating from January 1870 by which the European wires divided the globe into three mutually exclusive territories, each wire responsible to the other two for news coverage in its own territory and having exclusive rights to distribute the combined news of all three in its own area. Under the contract AP was merely an appendage of Reuters, limited to U.S. coverage and distribution and receiving the foreign news reports of the three European wires over Reuters lines. Although it greatly limited AP's operations, Stone and several AP directors would neither change nor violate this contract, which in 1893 had provided the leverage by which Stone and sixty-three maverick publishers had established the modern Associated Press and had overthrown two old and corrupt wire services.

United Press, unaffected by the cartel agreement, moved into South America in 1914—much to the frustration of AP's young traffic department chief, who resolved to free AP from the cartel's fetters if he ever had the chance. (Cooper did not realize his dream of bringing the cartel's barriers down until 1934.) Meanwhile, near the end of World War I, after applying continuous pressure, Cooper was permitted to tour South America to survey newspapers' interest in receiving AP news. Finally, late in 1918 Cooper convinced Havas to permit AP to enter the continent, and although UP had a four-year head start, AP had subscribers in ten Latin American countries by 1920.

Cooper moved a step closer to his goal of directing AP in 1920 when he was named assistant general manager, joining Frederick Roy Martin, who had been at that rank since 1912. Martin had spent less than a year on AP's board representing the *Providence Journal* when his fellow directors persuaded him to leave the board to assist Stone, who was becoming increasingly conservative and intractable. In 1921 Stone yielded his position to Martin and was designated "counselor," and Jackson S. Elliott, from AP's news operation, joined Cooper as an assistant general manager. Stone had handpicked Martin, passing over Cooper, whose news judgment, according to a 1937 *Fortune* magazine article, was "too flashy" for Stone's tastes; in the nine years before he succeeded Stone, Martin had assimilated many of Stone's biases toward a conservative news report.

Martin's appointment to AP's throne at the age of fifty shattered Cooper's hopes of ascending to the top and getting control of the news report, which he increasingly felt was the key to rejuvenating AP. (At the time, UP's code word for AP was "Grandma"; INS's was "Apathy.") Only at the urging of director Ochs and AP president Frank B. Noyes of the *Washington Star* did Cooper remain at AP, spending most of Martin's tenure on "several prolonged trips in the United States," as Cooper later put it, attempting to understand and smooth over AP members' reactions to radio's growing involvement in news. Finally, early in 1925, publishing opportunities and other continuing outside interests caused Martin to resign, and on 20 April the board unanimously approved Cooper's appointment as general manager. Cooper was nominated by Noyes, who later said: "No chronicle of my connection with The Associated Press would be complete without a record of the fact of . . . bringing forward and encouraging the energies of Cooper through a long series of years . . . and of my profound satisfaction at his subsequent fulfillment of my every hope."

The news service whose helm the forty-five-year-old Cooper finally grasped in 1925 was dull and stagnant. Since World War I AP had added only about 75 new members to its rolls, while the UP had gained 300 new clients (and was less than 200 subscribers behind AP in 1925) and INS had grown by about 150 clients. Unlike UP's and INS's flexible private corporate status, AP's cooperative membership structure, supervised by an elected fifteen-director board, slowed the wire's decision-making apparatus to an agonizing crawl—especially when facing complex issues (such as offering news service to radio stations, tampering with the international news cartel, or extending service to members' local competitors) over which members' views might greatly diverge. Officially a servant of the board, Cooper could only patiently nudge the news agency toward his personal goals by diplomatic behind-the-scenes coaxing, cautiously suggesting revisions of impeding bylaws and periodically urging the board to give him a freer hand in building the agency.

But AP's general manager was not without his options, and chief among them was effecting changes in the daily news report and projecting a positive public image of the AP—and himself. Within two months of his appointment, Cooper wrote a half-page commentary for *Collier's*, asserting that the AP had resisted the sensational and reckless tendencies of journalism in the mid-1920s and pointing out the value of accurate and decent journalism. It was the first of several articles in popular magazines over the next five years promoting AP and lending stature to Cooper. Golfing companion, writer, and publicist Bruce Barton sketched Cooper favorably in the August 1926 *American Magazine,* observing that a "great organization consists not of plants and offices but of men, and that is peculiarly true of the A.P."

The following February a one-page Cooper plea for greater understanding in the Western Hemisphere through the teaching of Spanish in U.S. schools appeared in the *American Review of Reviews,* the magazine's editors commenting: "Mr. Cooper is known throughout the world as the efficient and highly trusted executive head of the Associated Press, greatest of all news-gathering agencies." In December 1928 *Century* magazine carried a seven-page article by Cooper on corporate publicity, subtitled "The Press-Agent and the Associated Press," reviewing several cases of publicity fakery and serving notice on press agents (and comforting the reader) that "the Associated Press applies to [press agents'] offerings the acid test of: 'Is It News?' " Cooper had become AP's best press agent. Again in August 1930 he was in print, this time in the *Saturday Evening Post* with "Whence the News?," a stirring recounting of several AP correspondents' experiences with world leaders or with danger, concluding that each reporter "contributes to human happiness and education much more than is realized." The following January, in an interview in the *American Magazine,* Cooper listed his ten top news stories of 1930, the interviewer saying he had gone to Cooper "because he is an acknowledged authority on everything that has to do with the news. Keen and alert, . . . he has a notable reputation . . . for his unerring 'sixth sense' in detecting news values."

While he aimed this publicity blitz at the public, Cooper executed a frontal assault on AP's news report, in his first year introducing regular staff by-lines, news features, a livelier writing style, and a human-interest emphasis. His aim was to report "the true day-by-day story of humanity, . . . a picture of the lives of the people, their varied activities and interests, their joys and their sorrows, their amusements and their devotions, their work and their play," Cooper told gatherings of AP publishers. Ultimately, he believed, his news report improvements would make members proud enough of AP's service to pay for other improvements Cooper planned, which in turn would allow for increased salaries to attract competent staffers who could produce an even better news report, which in turn would increase membership loyalty. These news report changes became a permanent and successful AP fixture, prompting former AP director Oswald Garrison Villard, equally a critic of AP's conservatism under Stone and its "distinct lowering in . . . character" under Cooper, to write in 1944 that AP's news report "has followed the general trend of the American press in the direction of amusement and entertainment features, including many light and 'spicy' items of dubious value, intended to offset the criticism that the Associated Press dispatches are always heavy and deadly factual." Some saw Cooper as copying his sprightlier, more rambunctious former colleagues at United Press. Silas Bent, writing in *Independent* magazine in 1927, observed that "the disquieting truth is that the AP has succumbed to what I may call United Pressure. It has bobbed its hair and got out its lipstick in order to keep up with a flapper."

News photos were Cooper's next goal, but while it was relatively easy to modernize the news report gradually, a photo service would have to be developed from the ground up—an undertaking AP had avoided up to 1928 for many reasons, not the least of which was that three of its largest members (the *New York Times,* the *Chicago Tribune,* and the *New York Daily News*) operated national photo services. Cooper paved the way for news photos soon after he took over by introducing illustrations to the feature service delivered by mail. He next launched a major sales campaign on his board, focusing not on his next step—mailed spot news photos—but on his third step—delivery of news photos by telephone wires. The wire photograph proposal, although unbelievably visionary at that time, intrigued enough directors to give Cooper board approval for both steps. AP commenced mailing news photos in 1928, but many tests and failures followed before AT&T technicians developed Wirephoto, which AP inaugurated on 1 January 1935. Cooper later proclaimed that Wirephoto "brought a new era to American journalism and The Associated Press was elevated to a new summit of achievement."

To gain feedback on his news report changes and to stimulate AP loyalty within members' news rooms, Cooper proposed the creation of the AP Managing Editors Association, which held its first meeting in 1933. The organization aimed at getting managing editors "in co-operation with The AP management, [to] share responsibility for the betterment of . . . news service, a membership obligation in which few publishers interest themselves," Cooper wrote in 1959.

Meanwhile, Cooper's grand plan of expansion and improvement benefited indirectly from two waves of bylaw revisions which democraticized AP's membership structure. The first, in 1928, had redistributed voting power among the members, putting older and newer, larger and smaller newspapers on a more equitable footing and gradually resulted in the election of younger and more progressive directors from communities of various sizes. In 1937 the board was expanded from fifteen to eighteen directors, the additional seats earmarked for publishers from towns of less that 50,000 in population. At the same time, directors were limited to three three-year terms, insuring a more rapid turnover.

A persistent thorn in Cooper's side, however, was the franchise, or "protest," right, by which members could deny AP service to local competitors, thus limiting AP's opportunities for domestic growth. Begun in the 1890s as a protection for some of AP's largest loyal members, the franchise extended in some cases to a radius of up to 160 miles. As a counterbalance to the 1928 redistribution of voting strength, all members were granted a franchise right. On the positive side, the effective radius by 1928 was generally only up to ten miles, and more members were waiving their protest right for the good of the organization as the years passed. Nonetheless, the right was a time bomb ticking away in the bylaws, and Cooper believed that AP stood the best chance of surviving its blast by shifting members' basis for loyalty to AP from such bylaw protections to an appreciation for a superior news report.

Indeed, the issue did finally explode during World War II, when the federal government filed an antitrust suit against AP because Marshall Field III's *Chicago Sun* was denied AP service by the *Chicago Tribune*'s refusal to waive its franchise right. The U.S. Supreme Court on 18 June 1945 upheld a lower court order forcing AP to eliminate the right from its bylaws. In the aftermath, while some old-line members predicted AP's disintegration, Cooper found himself in the happy position of being ordered by the Court to seek new domestic members wherever he could find them. "It pleases me to believe that the reason the Supreme Court decision did not weaken The Associated Press," Cooper wrote in 1959, "was because of the defense [in the form of an improved news report] I built up during thirty years against the day the Government might attack and gain annulment of the 'franchise' rights."

In his first decade as general manager Cooper saw only 150 new members join AP while UP and INS each added more than twice that number. Franchise rights accounted for some of AP's sluggish growth between 1925 and World War II, but two additional factors, neither of which affected UP or INS, were AP members' inability to reach a consensus until 1939 on supplying news to radio stations, and the international news cartel's restrictions on AP's global growth. For twenty years after he helplessly watched Stone abide by AP's contract with Reuters and ignore *La Nación*'s request for service in 1914, Cooper squirmed and tugged to free himself and his news agency from the cartel. Not until after Stone's death in 1929 did Cooper receive board permission to visit London in search of cartel changes. Reuters, however, would not negotiate then, nor in 1930. Finally, during a third attempt in 1932, Reuters general manager Roderick Jones, as a conciliatory gesture, permitted AP to establish a service for papers in Japan and China, which had been exclusively Reuters territory. What happened next doomed the cartel and created Cooper's most significant contribution to AP. Cooper hastened to Tokyo and in May 1933 signed a nonexclusive news-exchange contract with Japan's Rengo news agency. Jones, stunned by the swiftness and, as he viewed it, the secrecy of AP-Rengo negotiations, denounced the new pact and disciplined its signatories, informing AP that reinstatement of the Reuters-AP portion of the cartel was possible only by payment of a large cash differential by AP. AP's board responded that such a demand violated the forty-year-old cartel agreement and that AP considered the contract broken. Jones, described by Reuters historian Graham Storey as having "been brought up under the old system: his ambition was to maintain the *status quo*," had underestimated AP's and Cooper's resolve to reorganize international news gathering. Jones rushed to New York City and, after a round of negotiations, found himself signing a nonexclusive news-exchange contract with Cooper on 12 February 1934. The cartel was dead.

Cooper's 1942 book, *Barriers Down*, details his long campaign to "emancipate" AP from the cartel, indicating that Jones acceded to Cooper's demands on all points during negotiations and commenting, "I was glad that I was present at the dawn of a new era not only in the relations between Reuters and The Associated Press but of all news agencies." While Cooper's book casts these affairs as a one-man moral crusade to free information flow for the world's people and thereby establish world peace, it is difficult to imagine the cartel surviving World War II. Oswald Garrison Villard's review of *Barriers Down* sums up the matter appropriately: "Though it may seem a somewhat egotistical narrative to some, it was well worth recording at length, for there is no more important chapter in the history of news-gathering in America, if not the world."

In addition to telling the cartel story, *Barriers Down* proposed a five-point postwar program for international free expression: (1) guarantee freedom of the press throughout the world, (2) guarantee that "at least one news agency in each country be owned and controlled mutually by the newspapers it serves," (3) guarantee that agencies may make such international news exchange arrangements as they choose, (4) guarantee "equality to all in the . . . availability of all official news and transmission facilities," and (5) prohibit "the intentional covert inclusion in any news service of biased international propaganda." Officials at UP and INS had for many years quietly worked for international freedom of information as independent global news brokers operating outside the cartel. The publication of *Barriers Down*, however, momentarily projected Cooper as American journalism's leading crusader for worldwide press freedom, a role he eagerly assumed in speeches and articles in popular magazines. At a 1943 "Journalism in War-Time" symposium, as reported by *Time* magazine, Cooper hypothesized that "one cause of war [is] perverted presentation of international news," adding that "it is the truth that makes men free." UP president Hugh Baillie, not to be upstaged in what he saw as his long-standing leading role, announced a four-point postwar program for international freedom at a meeting of the Michigan Press Association in January 1944. An amicable rivalry between these two news executives developed, and while it is pointless to ask whether one or the other won the contest for public attention, together they garnered support from leaders of several Western nations,

Reuters, the United States Congress, Secretary of State Edward R. Stettinius, Jr., and the 1944 platforms of both the Democratic and Republican parties.

Cooper sought, with modest success, a commitment favoring international press freedom from Franklin D. Roosevelt during a meeting with the president in October 1944. The next month Cooper wrote of the necessity for global "freedom of information" in *Life* magazine. In December he addressed a war and conversion congress of the National Association of Manufacturers, observing that no postwar association of nations to maintain the peace can succeed "unless it includes a method of news dissemination that will bring understanding to the whole world community." On 21 January 1945, speaking at New York City's Temple Emanu-El, Cooper, according to the *New York Times,* originated the concept of the citizen's "right to know," the *Times* defining it as the citizen being "entitled to have access to news, fully and accurately presented." (The phrase became the title of a book written by Cooper in 1956.) In the *New York Times Magazine* for 11 March 1945 Cooper wrote, "The history of the European press in the years preceding the present war reveals clearly how large a part poisoned news played in bringing on the war."

No one could quarrel with his lofty goals of international understanding and peace, but skeptics began to question the motives behind Cooper's protracted crusade. "Emancipation" in 1934 from Reuters had clearly choked off a flow of presumed foreign propaganda into the AP system, but it had also cleared the way for AP to open foreign news bureaus and begin signing up foreign subscribers. London's *Economist* judged Cooper's "ode to liberty" as meaning that "huge financial resources of the American [news] agencies might enable them to dominate the world." Cooper, "like most big business executives, experiences a peculiar moral glow in finding that his idea of freedom coincides with his commercial advantage. . . . Democracy does not necessarily mean making the whole world safe for the AP," said the *Economist.* Some at home also questioned his motives: *Fortune* considered the possibility that "in the postwar world there may be great possibilities for the A.P. to expand its activities— particularly if the way is cleared by an international free-press doctrine," but concluded that the matter of Cooper's "mixed motives is irrelevant" because "his campaign has had a success equaled by few other war aims and . . . if there is any progress in the achievement of worldwide press freedom, a large share of the credit must go to Kent Cooper."

Another element of Cooper's campaign was his second book, *Anna Zenger, Mother of Freedom* (1946). It was a novelized biography of John Peter Zenger's wife, "the unrecognized genius" who established press freedom "because she bravely continued to help publish the [*New York Journal*] during the whole period of her husband's imprisonment . . . and because during all that time she contributed what she could to establish the right of the press to be free." But Cooper's campaign was by no means successful, as the postwar world proved, and a decade later Cooper's third book, *The Right to Know,* was still beating the drum with such ringing phrases as: "If peace really is the goal, let truthful mutual news exchange bring acquaintance and understanding, peoples to peoples." Although Cooper's plan was more utopian than practical, the death of the cartel and decisive Allied military victories permitted AP to move into the international market as a rising new world news power. AP's foreign subscriber list shot from little more than 200 papers (all in the Western Hemisphere and the Far East) before World War II to 1,200 in 1949 and 2,705 in 1951, the year Cooper retired from AP.

The board had added "executive director" to Cooper's title in 1943, both as an honor and to facilitate his dealings with foreign news agencies and governments. In 1948, at the age of sixty-eight Cooper handed over the general manager's post to Frank J. Starzel, an AP staffer and executive of nineteen years, but at the board's request Cooper remained executive director until 1951, helping oversee AP's rapid expansion. By his own assessment Cooper's last fifteen years of AP service, from 1936 to 1951, "gave me an opportunity to observe what the fulfillment of my plans had done for The Associated Press and gave me the feeling of satisfaction for which I hoped." Having broken the cartel, introduced Wirephoto, and reshaped and expanded the news report, Cooper assumed an elder statesman's role in AP, replacing a desk with several overstuffed chairs and a small table for buzzers and telephones, thus preventing people from "dumping" problems and papers on his desk. Some AP staffers in later years referred to his office in Rockefeller Center, where AP had moved in 1940, as "the throne room," its occupant remote and unapproachable.

An ardent golfer throughout his life, Cooper enjoyed the companionship of many golf partners who were also leaders in a variety of business fields. He played almost every Saturday and Sunday during the season, either on Long Island or more frequently at St. Andrew's, Irvington-on-Hudson. An active musician from the time his father gave him a secondhand violin when he was twelve, Cooper composed many songs, beginning with "My Village Girl" when he was sixteen, and including "The Associated Press March." In 1943 he wrote an operetta, "About the Girl," set on the Alaska Highway and featuring a woman-hating construction engineer and a beautiful Chicago nightclub singer. Portions of the operetta were performed on the Mutual Broadcasting System's "Theatre of the Air" on 11 September with Henry Weber, a friend of Cooper's, conducting the orchestra.

Cooper was married three times, first to Daisy McBride of Indianapolis from 1905 to her death in 1920, second to Marian Rothwell of New York City from 1921 to their divorce in 1940, and third to Sarah A. Gibbs, who had been his executive secretary, from 1942 until his death. He had one daughter, Jane, by his first marriage.

Cooper entered Good Samaritan Hospital, West Palm Beach, Florida, on 22 January 1965 after a heart seizure; he died early Sunday, 31 January, at the age of eighty-four. Several hundred persons, including executives of many leading journalism companies, attended the funeral three days later at the Park Avenue Christian Church at Eighty-fifth

Cooper in 1958

Street in New York City. As the funeral began, the AP's news wires went silent in a one-minute tribute to the man who had guided the news agency to a position of domestic and global power during a quarter of a century. Burial was in Sleepy Hollow Cemetery, Tarrytown, New York.

In his autobiography, published in 1959, Cooper looked back to the time when he joined AP and said, "I saw opportunity ahead that aroused my ambition to try to scale the heights in the work I had chosen. I seized that opportunity and hopefully proceeded to plan some radical departures for The Associated Press." One can measure his "ambition" by reading AP copy in newspapers of the late 1920s and the 1930s. He brought an overdue life and diversity to AP's copy, weathering the protests of a dwindling number of reactionary publishers and currying the favor of managing editors who had a street-level sense of what sells papers. As with any growing business, however, he could "scale the heights" only with the help of many others, notably a cooperative board of directors and an approving membership. Cooper credits his publisher-comrades with assistance but permits himself to be AP's guiding spirit; his public image, shaped through his many articles, speeches, and books, was the personification of AP in his day. In some respects, that impression will inevitably be accurate when one is considering an organization's chief executive officer; but even more than his counterparts at UP and INS, Cooper derived his stature and success from the cooperative organization he served.

The first general manager drawn from the technical rather than the news side of the organization, Cooper foreshadowed AP's subsequent innovative leadership with new technology, including the recent introduction of computers and satellite communication. Unlike many leaders at UP and INS, Cooper preferred the company of business executives and the challenge of moral crusades to getting into the field and covering major news stories. Cooper left to subsequent AP administrations his detachment from AP's daily work and his calculating sense of product and expansion. It was under Cooper's tutelage that AP started its journey to becoming the far-flung, hierarchical, and powerful journalistic enterprise it is today.

Interview:
M. K. Wisehart, "The Ten Great News Stories of 1930," *American Magazine*, 102 (January 1931): 46-51, 74, 76.

References:

"AP's Tilt at Monopolies," *Newsweek*, 22 (14 December 1942): 102-104;

Bruce Barton, "How Did *That* Get in the Paper?," *American Magazine*, 102 (August 1926): 34-35, 68, 70, 72, 74;

"Cooper: The AP's Self-Made, Hard-Boiled General Manager," *Newsweek*, 5 (20 April 1935): 15;

"Crusade for Truth," *Fortune*, 31 (April 1945): 146-149, 185-186, 188, 191;

"GM of AP," *Newsweek*, 29 (5 May 1947): 65-66;

Oliver Gramling, *AP: The Story of News* (New York: Farrar & Rinehart, 1940);

[Richard Edes Harrison], "(AP)," *Fortune*, 15 (February 1937): 88-93, 148, 151-152, 154, 156, 158, 162;

"Kent Cooper, Composer," *Newsweek*, 17 (26 May 1941): 74;

"100 for the A.P.," *Time*, 51 (17 May 1948): 63-65;

Graham Storey, *Reuters' Century, 1851-1951* (London: Max Parrish, 1951);

"Storm Warning," *Time*, 44 (11 December 1944): 55-56;

Oswald Garrison Villard, "The Associated Press," in his *The Disappearing Daily: Chapters in American Newspaper Evolution* (New York: Knopf, 1944), pp. 40-59;

"Young Man with a Mission," *Time*, 47 (11 February 1946): 65-66.

Papers:

The Lilly Library, Indiana University, Bloomington, has a collection of Kent Cooper's papers, including some 2,000 items. Cooper memorabilia are displayed at the Kent Cooper Room of the Indiana University Main Library.

Gardner Cowles
(28 February 1861-28 February 1946)

Jean C. Chance
University of Florida

and

Marianne Salcetti
University of Iowa

NEWSPAPERS OWNED: *Algona* (Iowa) *Republican* (1883-1884); *Des Moines Register and Leader*, renamed *Register* in 1916 (1903-1946); *Des Moines Evening Tribune*, briefly renamed *Tribune-Capital* in 1927 (1908-1946); *Des Moines Daily News*, immediately absorbed into *Tribune* (1924); *Des Moines Capital*, immediately absorbed into *Tribune* (1927); *Minneapolis Star*, merged to form *Star-Journal* in 1939 (1935-1946); *Minneapolis Tribune* (1941-1946); *Minneapolis Times* (1941-1946).

Gardner Cowles, Sr., practiced his favorite slogan of "things don't just happen. Somebody makes 'em happen" when he not only cultivated a Midwestern tradition of quality journalism but also established one of America's more distinctive publishing and communication empires. Cowles (pronounced "Coles") balked at the label "empire builder," but his corporate holdings included the *Des Moines* (Iowa) *Register and Leader*, the *Des Moines Evening Tribune*, the *Minneapolis Star-Journal*, the *Minneapolis Times* and *Tribune*, *Look* magazine, the Register and Tribune Syndicate, and several radio and television stations.

While Cowles's family roots were not journalistic ones, it was from his parents, Maria Elizabeth LaMonte Cowles and the Reverend William Fletcher Cowles, that Gardner Cowles apparently derived his business acumen and a later emphasis on newspaper circulation as both a source of profit and a maximum opportunity to educate and inform readers.

Gardner Cowles was born on 28 February 1861 in Oskaloosa, Iowa. His father, a Methodist minister, frequently preached against slavery, sometimes to his parishioners' consternation. The elder Cowles was later appointed by President Lincoln to serve two terms as the internal revenue col-

Gardner Cowles

lector for the Iowa Fourth District. Education was a particularly valued activity in the Cowles household because of Maria LaMonte Cowles's background as a schoolteacher. She died when Gardner Cowles was twelve, and, with the later addition of a stepmother, the household lived the life of a transient minister's family. Cowles received an early exposure to the small towns that dot Iowa's landscape; these experiences undoubtedly influenced his later creation of a statewide newspaper, the *Des Moines Register,* which carries on its nameplate, "The Newspaper Iowa Depends Upon."

After attending Penn College in Oskaloosa for a year and Grinnell College for two years, Cowles received a bachelor's degree from Iowa Wesleyan College in 1882 and a master's degree from the same college in 1885. During his college career, he taught school and served as school superintendent for two years in Algona, Iowa. In 1884, he married Florence Maud Call, who was also a teacher. Two of their six children—Russell, John, Gardner (Mike), Jr., Helen, Florence, and Bertha—later played key roles in the expansion and operation of the Cowles family communications enterprises.

His first journalistic foray occurred in 1883, when he purchased a half interest in the weekly *Algona Republican*, an event that prompted charges of job conflict by competitor Harvey Ingham, then editor-owner of the weekly *Upper Des Moines.* Ingham accused Cowles of "threatening to neglect the pupils of the town to make a few dollars on a second-rate newspaper." Cowles and Ingham soon became close friends. Cowles sold his interest in the *Republican* after eighteen months. He also briefly edited another weekly, the *Algona Advance.* For the next twenty years, Cowles pursued other career avenues, including banking, real estate, and a rural mail delivery route; he was also a Republican member of the Iowa House of Representatives from 1899 to 1903. Many of these experiences were later drawn on by Cowles in building his publishing business.

By 1903 Harvey Ingham had become editor of the *Des Moines Register and Leader* and pursuaded Cowles to purchase a majority interest in the company. This venture would test Cowles's business skills: the morning *Register and Leader*'s 14,000 circulation was dwindling in the state capital's competitive market. Three years after Cowles's arrival at the newspaper, circulation had risen to 25,000. *Leader* was dropped from the paper's name in 1916. In 1908, Cowles launched the Register and Tribune Company by purchasing the *Des Moines Evening Tribune*, and assumed the titles of president and treasurer of the new firm. Cowles was disappointed when his oldest son, Russell, rejected a career in journalism after graduating from Dartmouth University in 1909 and became an artist; but John joined the Register and Tribune Company in 1920 after his graduation from Harvard. The family was firmly established as an American publishing dynasty when Mike joined his father and brother in the business on his graduation from Harvard in 1925.

Despite the nation's declining economy during this period, the company continued to expand with the 1924 purchase of the *Des Moines Daily News* from the Scripps-Howard newspaper group and the 1927 acquisition of the *Des Moines Capital*; both papers were combined with the *Tribune.* In 1927 Cowles assumed the chairmanship of the Register and Tribune Company's board of directors while his son Mike succeeded him as president. By 1930, the Iowa market was dominated by Cowles newspapers.

During these formative years, policies of the growing newspaper company reflected Gardner Cowles's philosophy that "the more honestly a

Cowles's sons Mike (Gardner, Jr.) and John in the mid-1930s

paper is conducted, the more successful it will be." Cowles pioneered the practice of deriving more revenue from circulation than from advertising. His newspapers were forbidden to accept liquor advertisements, and bureaus were established to screen ads for false claims or harmful products. Cowles implemented a "vigorous editorial viewpoint" and encouraged readers to express their opinions in letters to the editor.

Innovation and exploration were evident as the Cowles newspaper group expanded. In 1925, the Cowleses recruited George Gallup to teach at Drake University and also hired him to survey *Register* and *Tribune* readers. This survey became the first of the now-famous Gallup opinion polls. Gallup reported reader preference for more photographs in the newspapers; this led to experiments such as publishing more sequence photographs and improving sports photography. This new treatment of photography increased Sunday circulation for the Cowles papers. In 1928, the Cowles Broadcasting Company was founded to operate KRNT radio in Des Moines, WNAX in Yankton, South Dakota, and WOL in Washington, D.C. Gardner Cowles was

an early advocate of broadcast news. In 1930, the Cowles group introduced picture transmission by airplane, which not only reflected the growing interest in pictures for newspapers but led in 1937 to the formation of Cowles Magazines Inc. for publication of the national picture periodical *Look*.

Cowles's commitment to public service continued during his publishing career. His close friend and fellow Iowan Herbert Hoover appointed him to the Federal Commission on Conservation and Administration of the Public Domain in 1929. During the 1932 bank disaster, he was a director of the Reconstruction Finance Corporation. In 1934, Gardner and Florence Cowles created the Gardner Cowles Foundation to aid twenty-eight private colleges and hospitals in Iowa. During this time, Cowles introduced company benefits for his employees, such as group insurance, retirement, and stock purchase plans.

The 1930s were a busy time for Gardner, Mike, and John Cowles. The Register and Tribune Syndicate was started, and in 1935 the family purchased the evening *Minneapolis Star,* merging the paper with the *Minneapolis Journal* in 1939. In

Cowles's longtime friend and editor, Harvey Ingham, in 1942

1941, the purchase of the morning *Minneapolis Tribune* and its evening edition, the *Times,* resulted in the Cowles family controlling Minneapolis's newspaper market in a similar fashion as they controlled the Des Moines market.

Advancing age and failing eyesight forced Gardner Cowles to withdraw from active publishing in the 1930s, although he continued to visit the Des Moines office and attend stockholders' and board of directors' meetings. As his vision declined, Florence Cowles read aloud to him as he played solitaire. Cowles died on his eighty-fifth birthday, 28 February 1946, and was buried in Glendale Cemetery in Des Moines. His estate was valued at just under $700,000. The largest portion—about $155,000—established cash payments for employees of the *Register,* the *Tribune,* and KRNT radio. A total of thirty-three bequests were given to friends and relatives, with one-fifth of the estate earmarked for the Gardner Cowles Foundation.

Gardner Cowles's journalistic legacy flourished as company holdings continued to expand through the efforts of his children and grandchildren. While *Look* magazine ceased publication in 1971, by the early 1980s, corporate holdings of Cowles Communications included the *Des Moines Register* and *Tribune,* the *Minneapolis Star-Journal,* and *Tribune* (the *Times* was discontinued in 1948), the *Buffalo* (New York) *Courier-Express,* the *Jackson* (Tennessee) *Sun,* the *Waukesha* (Wisconsin) *Freeman,* the *Rapid City* (South Dakota) *Journal,* the *Great Falls* (Montana) *Tribune,* the *Burley South Idaho Press,* weekly newspapers in Baltimore and Denver, KCCI-TV in Des Moines, WFSH-TV in Daytona Beach, Florida, a cable television franchise, an engraving company, and thirty-one percent ownership of Harper and Row Publishing Company. Revenues reported for the first three quarters of 1981 totaled $12.8 million, with a net income of $4.4 million.

Gardner Cowles, Sr.'s successes in journalism can be measured in other ways besides the corporate ledger. As of 1979 the *Des Moines Register* had garnered twelve Pulitzer Prizes—second only to the *New York Times.*

Biographies:
Des Moines Register, Gardner Cowles, 1861-1946: Pub-

lisher of the Des Moines Register and Tribune, 1903-1946 (Des Moines, Iowa: Register and Tribune Co., 1947);

George Mills, *Harvey Ingham and Gardner Cowles, Sr.: Things Don't Just Happen* (Ames: Iowa State

University Press, 1977).

Reference:
Kenneth Stewart and John Tebbel, *Makers of Modern Journalism* (New York: Prentice-Hall, 1952), pp. 310-324.

Josephus Daniels
(18 May 1862-15 January 1948)

Elizabeth Brown Dickey
University of South Carolina

MAJOR POSITIONS HELD: Editor and Publisher, *Raleigh State Chronicle* (1885-1892), *Raleigh News and Observer* (1894-1948).

SELECTED BOOKS: *The First Fallen Hero: A Biographical Sketch of Worth Bagley, Ensign, U.S.N.* (Norfolk, Va.: S. W. Bowman, 1898);

Making the Navy a Real Training School (Washington, D.C.: Navy Department, 1913);

The Mastery of Self: Address Delivered before the Graduating Class of the United States Naval Academy at Annapolis, Md., on June 14, 1915 (Washington, D.C.: Government Printing Office, 1916);

Men Must Live Straight If They Would Shoot Straight (Washington, D.C.: Navy Department, 1917);

Development of Naval Strength: Address Delivered to the Graduating Class of 1918 at the Naval Academy on June 6, 1918 (Washington, D.C.: Government Printing Office, 1918);

The Navy and the Nation: War-Time Addresses by Josephus Daniels (New York: Doran, 1919);

Our Navy at War (Washington, D.C.: Pictorial Bureau, 1922);

The Life of Woodrow Wilson, 1856-1924 (Philadelphia & Chicago: Winston, 1924);

Tar Heel Editor (Chapel Hill: University of North Carolina Press, 1939);

Editor in Politics (Chapel Hill: University of North Carolina Press, 1941);

The Wilson Era: Years of Peace, 1910-1917 (Chapel Hill: University of North Carolina Press, 1944);

The Wilson Era: Years of War and After, 1917-1923 (Chapel Hill: University of North Carolina Press, 1946);

Shirt-Sleeve Diplomat (Chapel Hill: University of North Carolina Press, 1947);

The Cabinet Diaries of Josephus Daniels, 1913-1921, edited by E. David Cronon (Lincoln: University of Nebraska Press, 1963).

Josephus Daniels, editor and publisher of the *Raleigh News and Observer* for fifty-four years, devoted more than fifteen years of his life to serving his country in two major capacities: he was secretary of the navy from 1913 to 1921 and ambassador to Mexico from 1933 to 1941. He managed to have some type of presidential appointment in every Democratic administration from Grover Cleveland to Harry Truman, but he always returned to his first love: the newspaper. While Daniels worked for the government, he gave himself newspaper titles: managing editor of the navy, foreign correspondent in Mexico, and Washington columnist. He brought to these jobs the same integrity and principles he used on his newspaper. Daniels was a crusader who believed that "a paper must always be for something and against something. The editorial page has got to make folks mad and glad." Through the years he fought to improve the state of North Carolina, calling for such things as a hospital in every county, free public schools, child-labor laws, and better roads. He once encouraged the legislature to pass a $100-million-bond offering to improve the highways; when told he was sending everybody in North Carolina to the poorhouse, he replied, "That may be so, but we'll go there riding on good roads." He fought against the railroads, prompting one company to spend $250,000 on a rival newspaper to try to put Daniels out of business. Once a federal judge had him placed in custody

(Courtesy of Dr. Worth B. Daniels)

because Daniels had criticized a "court decree in connection with the fight to enable the people of the state to maintain control of the railroad, which had been built by the state for the promotion of industry and agriculture." He was prounion and for the rights of the working man; he became an honorary member of the pressman's union and held honorary membership in the International Typographical Union for fifty years. He was against alcohol and in favor of women's suffrage.

For many years the *News and Observer* was North Carolina's foremost newspaper. Daniels insisted on printing the news regardless of who or what the newspaper attacked, and it has been said that many politicians were "singed, scorched, or burned." One North Carolina governor told his appointees, "Don't ever do anything you wouldn't want to read about in the *News and Observer* the next day." Daniels filled his paper with the latest, most interesting news of the day. Page one was usually

made up of international and national news accounts. In 1911, a country doctor won a fifty-dollar prize from *Collier's Weekly* for an article on the *News and Observer*. "Ask any of the enemies," the article began, "why they read *The News and Observer* and the answer is always the same: 'It publishes the news.' That is literally the truth; nothing of real interest is suppressed. By 'news' I do not mean the sickening stories of crime and domestic infelicity that fill the columns of most daily newspapers. I mean news of political importance or of significance to society in general. In other words, its news matter is clean and healthy. In its editorials it reflects the best thought of the soundest thinkers in the country and especially in the South." At one time the *News and Observer* was said to be the "only newspaper in the world with more subscribers than the population of the city it is printed in."

Daniels believed that "a newspaper should be like a preacher—always upholding righteousness." He considered church news big news and said, "Anything to make folks better goes on page one-A." He published all the news regardless of the cost to him personally, and once said, "I'll put everything in the paper that God Almighty allows to happen in his world." When a congressman stole some county funds, Daniels ran the story in his first daily newspaper, the *State Chronicle*. This meant losing the friendship of the man's brother, who wrote, "*The State Chronicle* was the only paper in the state to print my brother's trouble." In 1901 Daniels wrote in an editorial: "Men who pay their good money for newspapers do so to get the news, and if they find there is a 'back-door' to the newspaper office through which large advertisers or stockholders can enter to suppress the news, they rightly feel that they are not getting the worth of their money. They trust to an editor's judgement not to prematurely print what is not legitimate news, not to print gossip or suspicion that would work injury, and not to print what ought not to be printed. But they demand the news when it is fresh and to suppress a legitimate item about an individual because he is influential they truly regard as a piece of toadyism unworthy of a public journal."

Daniels believed in being easily accessible. A sign on his office door read, "Office hours 9 a.m.- 1 a.m.; If I'm not in you can find me at my home from 1 a.m.-9 a.m." When plans were drawn for a new newspaper building, Daniels's office was supposed to be "in a quiet, secluded spot in the back of the building, suitable for editorial meditation, with a secretary outside." But Daniels insisted his office be on the ground floor, near the street, with the

Four newspapers owned by Daniels: he quit school at eighteen to edit the Wilson Advance, *and bought the paper two years later; he published the* State Chronicle *from 1885 to 1892; the* North Carolinian *was a weekly he published briefly after losing the* State Chronicle; *he published the* Raleigh News and Observer *for fifty-four years, beginning in 1894.*

door always open. "I'm not like the editors of big city newspapers who remain anonymous and who are holed up in offices way up on the 15th and 16th floors of skyscrapers where no one can find them," he said.

This "people's" editor was born 18 May 1862 in Washington, North Carolina, during a bombardment by Union gunboats. His father, Josephus Daniels, Sr., a shipbuilder, worked in the Wilmington navy yards during the Civil War. A Union sympathizer who refused to join the Confederate forces, he was killed in an ambush in 1865. Mary Cleaves Seabrook Daniels, left with three young sons, opened a millinery and dressmaking shop in Wilson, North Carolina. Later she became the town's postmistress (a job she held until she was fired because of her son's anti-Republican editorials). During the early years of Daniels's life, the family had some unbelievably hard luck: fire destroyed three of their homes in six years.

Daniels came to love journalism as a teenager and printed an amateur newspaper, the *Cornucopia*, with the help of his brother Charles. During school he was a correspondent and sold subscriptions for the *Charlotte Observer* and *Hale's Weekly*. Daniels attended Wilson Collegiate Institute and became a first-team baseball player, but he quit school at age eighteen to edit the weekly *Wilson Advance*. Two years later he bought the paper, secured by a mortgage on his mother's home. His goal in life was to go to Raleigh and publish a newspaper with statewide influence. In 1885, Daniels was elected president of the North Carolina Press Association; he also bought from Walter H. Page a controlling interest in the *Raleigh State Chronicle*, a weekly newspaper which he began publishing daily in 1889. But the economy weakened, and Daniels was forced to sell his newspaper in 1892.

His position as state printer helped him pay the bills from 1887 to 1893. Daniels studied law for one summer at the University of North Carolina at Chapel Hill, and passed the bar exam in October 1885; he never intended to practice law but thought the training would help in his newspaper career. He also published small newspapers in Rocky Mount and Kingston, North Carolina, during this period.

Daniels married Addie Worth Bagley on 2 May 1888 in a ceremony which attracted "the crème de la crème of Raleigh society." Many years later Daniels dedicated a book "To my wife, Addie Worth Bagley Daniels, the truest and tenderest and purest wife ever a man was blessed with. To have such a love is the one blessing, in comparison of which all earthly joy is of no value; and to think of her is to

praise God." The couple had four sons; a daughter died in childhood. Three sons, Jonathan, Frank, and Josephus, Jr., joined the newspaper; Worth Daniels studied medicine and became a physician in Washington, D.C. Long a proponent of education, Daniels joined the Watauga Club, which was made up of progressive young men who "visioned an industrial North Carolina and believed that before it could become a great industrial state it must train young men in mechanical trades, laying emphasis on practical knowledge of the textile industry." Daniels and his contemporaries envisioned a school modeled after the Massachusetts Institute of Technology. The North Carolina legislature authorized this land grant school in 1885, and North Carolina State University at Raleigh became a reality two years later. The Watauga Club also pushed for federal aid to education and schooling for blacks and women. Today the Watauga medal is North Carolina State's highest nonacademic honor, a living memorial to such men as Page, who edited *Atlantic Monthly*, established Doubleday and Company, and served as ambassador to Great Britain;

Daniels at the time he purchased the Raleigh News and Observer *in 1894*

One of the 100 letters Daniels wrote to prominent North Carolina Democrats to raise money for the purchase of the News and Observer.
Eighty-eight of those solicited each bought one $100 share.

Charles W. Dabney, who became president of both the Universities of Tennessee and Cincinnati; and Josephus Daniels.

In 1893 Daniels took his first federal job: chief of the appointments division in the Department of the Interior in Washington. A year later his love for newspapers brought him back to Raleigh. Thomas R. Jernigan, who had bought the *State Chronicle* and merged it with the *News and Observer*, had to sell out. The paper was sold at auction for $6,800 to J. N. Holding, who had been bidding secretly for Daniels. In order to raise the money, Daniels then wrote 100 letters to North Carolina Democrats inviting them to buy one $100 share each. The response was generous, and eighty-eight bought stock; many years later Daniels bought back these shares.

The *News and Observer* became "an aggressive exponent of Democracy, free from factions and favoritism." Daniels promised his readers, "The publication of *The News and Observer* will be continued as a sterling Democratic paper upon the same general policy as heretofore."

Daniels, while "vigorously combative in print," was said to be "sweet-tempered and affectionate at home." He had no vices and was called a perfect family man who attended the Methodist church regularly. Although his enemies called him "little," he was of medium height, with "snapping gray eyes and a lower lip that could protrude in stubbornness." According to a 1947 article in the *Atlanta Journal*, he wore the same style of clothing for sixty years—"semi-pleated, stiff-bosomed white shirts with stiff cuffs and collars and gold studs that had to be specially made. His shoes were high-topped, shiny, black that laced part way and then hooked the rest of the way in a bow-knot." He wore white socks pinned to the bottoms of long handmade drawers all year. A pocket watch hung at the end of a long black ribbon, and he wore a seven-eighths-inch tie. He carried a gold-banded cane and wore a broad-brimmed black felt hat. He told reporters he chose the fashions of 1875 "because I have four boys and want to be absolutely sure they won't always be borrowing my clothes." He was also somewhat skeptical about the modern equipment reporters now take for granted. "A man can't think on a typewriter," he said. Daniels handwrote editorials with a heavy, black lead pencil; supposedly only one linotype operator in the composing room could read his boss's writing. "You've got to go after the news," he told reporters. "See the people you're writing about. The telephone is the greatest enemy of good reporting." (Ironically, Daniels made the

Daniels's wife, Addie Worth Bagley Daniels, and their four sons in 1912: (left to right) Worth, Jonathan, Josephus, Jr., and Frank

first long distance call over a private line from Raleigh in 1898, talking to his brother in Goldsboro, North Carolina.)

Politics was one of Daniels's main interests. Biographer Joseph L. Morrison says: "Josephus Daniels became the dominant political editor of North Carolina, probably a more authentic spokesman for the New South than either [Henry] Grady or [Henry] Watterson." He was Democratic national committeeman from North Carolina for twenty years and chairman of the publicity department of Democratic headquarters during the presidential campaign of Woodrow Wilson. He admired William Jennings Bryan, "the most eloquent man the world ever produced," and supported Bryan in three unsuccessful attempts for the presidency. Two men who did become president served as his assistants: Theodore Roosevelt was Daniels's assistant at the Department of the Interior, and Franklin D. Roosevelt worked for Daniels during the latter's tenure as secretary of the navy.

Perhaps he delved into politics because of his strong belief in democracy. "Our only danger in discussing what is wrong with the world today is in failing to make democracy work," he said. "It can't work with party machines, county unit systems, men taking orders from Wall Street, labor unions, or monopolies running the country. The people themselves must be interested: democracy depends on the eternal vigilance of the common man." He supported Woodrow Wilson for president in 1912 and as a reward was named secretary of the navy. A controversial appointee, Daniels was the last of Wilson's cabinet to vote to go to war in 1917; but once he committed himself, this "Country Editor from Rolly" sought to reform the navy in the interests of the common man. He abolished the terms *port* and *starboard*, set up training schools for enlisted men, insisted that 100 sailors be admitted to the Naval Academy each year, fought the seniority system, and signed the unpopular order in 1914 that banned beer, wine, and liquor aboard navy ships. Daniels is given credit for engineering the "Bridge of Ships" in World War I: some two million doughboys sailed to Europe through submarine-infested water without the loss of a single life to enemy torpedoes. He supported the League of Nations and never forgave the Republican party for blocking United States participation; he felt this obstructionist tactic caused the Second World War. He kept no souvenirs from his cabinet job, and after he returned to Raleigh in 1921, he asked his successor for a war memento. Since government property cannot be given away, the navy made his lawn a base

Daniels during his term as Secretary of the Navy from 1913 until 1921 (Library of Congress)

and installed a Krupp gun there—to be returned when the navy wanted it.

His service record as ambassador to Mexico, beginning in 1933, is equally outstanding. Franklin Roosevelt named his old "Chief" spokesman for the "Good Neighbor Policy" and hoped Daniels would improve Latin American relations. At first, however, the Mexicans resented his presence; in his review of Daniels's *Shirt-Sleeve Diplomat* (1947), Henry Ladd Smith explains: "He would appear to have been about the worst possible choice as emissary to one of the most important countries in the hemisphere. As secretary of the navy he had ordered the United States occupation of Vera Cruz during the Mexican crisis of 1914—a humiliation that our neighbors have never forgotten. The man who banned the serving of grog in the navy and who never drank anything stronger than tea was asked to hold open house in a country where liquor is more common than drinking water. His record as a devout churchman made him suspect in a country that was openly at war with the church at that time. Finally, this Tar Heel editor with the small town manner, had to face some of the wiliest politicos, toughest hombres, and slipperiest freebooters ever assembled in one small area. He should have been listed as a failure before he had even crossed the Rio Grande on his way to his new post. Instead, he confounded all the skeptics." Indeed, Daniels became "a great servant of the cause of justice and freedom, one of the foremost champions of Interamerican solidarity." President Roosevelt called him "the most eminent Ambassador of the United States in America." A former Mexican minister of foreign affairs said Daniels showed that "it is possible to govern relations between the peoples by democratic inspiration and to substitute feelings of mutual respect, friendship, and the rule of law for the impulse of brute force."

Daniels's autobiography, *Tar Heel Editor*, was published in 1939; it is a five-volume work, 2,700 pages long. Son Jonathan, also a writer and editor, complained, "Father, your books are too big." His father responded, "You don't understand. I write for quantity, not quality. I want mine to be big enough to be useful as a deadly weapon." In the

foreword to his first volume, Daniels wrote: "It is believed that the pen pictures of the men of that period and the semi-biographical accounts of everyday events and the unfolding of how people lived and what they thought in Eastern North Carolina in his youth and manhood are typical of what went on in most communities in the South during the years after Reconstruction. The book, therefore, has more than local significance." Reviewers agreed. Raymond B. Nixon of Emory University wrote, "When it is considered that what people did and thought in the Tar Heel State during the years of reconstruction probably has been paralleled throughout the South, much in the book that appears to be of purely local interest takes on wider significance."

Daniels returned to the United States in 1941 after his wife's health failed; she died in 1943. For many years, Mexican students lived with Daniels at his home, Wakefield, while attending colleges in North Carolina. During the Second World War all three sons at the *News and Observer* became involved in the war effort. Their eighty-year-old father took over their duties. "I thought it would be quite a chore to do three men's work. The boys had me

Ambassador Daniels at a party in Mexico circa 1940 (Library of Congress)

fooled. I do not have any trouble at all doing all the work they were doing," he remarked. Daniels also related the following story: "When I got back from Mexico and the boys got back from their part in the war they all began telling me what to do, so I had three sons ordering me around. So I told them, 'Boys, you're exactly right. When a man gets over 70, he ought to listen to his sons and do anything they say. And that's what I'm going to do—as soon as you all agree on what it is I ought to do.' They haven't agreed yet. It's the only way I keep my liberty." Family ties meant a great deal to Daniels, and "Daniels Day," started in 1933 on Roanoke Island by Josephus and Melvin R. Daniels, former register of deeds in Dare County, has become one of the nation's largest family reunions.

Daniels remained active into his eighty-fifth year, when he died at his home from a cold that developed into pneumonia. State and national flags flew at half staff over the capitol in Raleigh, and tributes poured in from throughout the nation. Former first lady Eleanor Roosevelt attended the funeral; President Truman expressed "very profound grief on the news of the death of a great American." The *Washington Post* said, "Josephus Daniels' general fruitful and happy life was not without an element of tragedy. The tragedy was that he belonged to an agrarian America that no longer exists." The *Norfolk Ledger-Star* commented, "As William Allen White and others have also proved, the greatness of the American press lies not merely in vast circulation figures and huge bulk in content, but chiefly in character." The *Winston-Salem Journal* said, "But North Carolina is the most progressive state in the South today largely because of Josephus Daniels and a few others who possessed similar vision and courage and all America has felt in some degree the impact of his personality."

Daniels received a number of honors during his lifetime, including honorary doctorates from the University of North Carolina and Washington and Lee University. When Presidential Arts Medal, Inc. created a set of medals depicting one important person from each state in 1973, Daniels joined such luminaries as Henry Ford from Michigan, Mark Twain from Missouri, Robert E. Lee from Virginia, and the Wright Brothers from Ohio. The honors have continued since his death: in 1981 he was among the first five inductees into the North Carolina Journalism Hall of Fame, along with Charles Kuralt, CBS news correspondent; A. "Pete" McKnight, former editor of the *Charlotte Observer*; Vermont C. Royster, editor emeritus of the *Wall Street Journal*; and Tom Wicker, associate editor of the *New York Times*.

According to his will, Daniels intended to keep the *News and Observer* in the family. "It is my earnest desire and hope that *The News and Observer* shall be edited and directed by my descendants, though I do not believe that the dead hand should attempt to control the living spirit. . . . I have never regarded the stock I owned in the *News and Observer* as property, but as certificates of a trust to be administered for the common good of North Carolina." Also included in the will were two incidents from Daniels's life:

When I went to Washington as Secretary of the Navy in 1913 my brother-in-law was in charge of the business of the paper. Some time later he came to see me in Washington with a proposition from a newspaper broker to buy *The News and Observer*. I declared that the paper was not for sale, saying it was part of the family. . . . He advised accepting the offer, saying a price would be paid that would make me and my family rich.

During the World War another party wished to buy *The News and Observer*. I told him it was not for sale. He asked, "Will you not name a price I can take to my clients?" He was persistent. I complied saying, "Certainly you can tell your principal he can get the paper if he will pay me in gold the aggregate sum of all the bonds to carry on the War received by the Secretary of the Treasury, plus the cash value of my wife and sons."

These two incidents show that I have never regarded *The News and Observer* as property, but having an unpurchasable soul.

References:

E. David Cronon, *Josephus Daniels in Mexico* (Madison: University of Wisconsin Press, 1960);

Jonathan Daniels, *The End of Innocence* (Philadelphia: Lippincott, 1954);

"Josephus Daniels—Fighting Editor," *Atlanta Journal Magazine*, 9 November 1947;

Carroll Kilpatrick, ed., *Roosevelt and Daniels: A Friendship in Politics* (Chapel Hill: University of North Carolina Press, 1952);

Joseph L. Morrison, *Josephus Daniels: The Small-d Democrat* (Chapel Hill: University of North Carolina Press, 1966);

Morrison, *Josephus Daniels Says: An Editor's Political*

Odyssey from Bryan to Wilson and F.D.R., 1894-1913 (Chapel Hill: University of North Carolina Press, 1962);

Raymond B. Nixon, review of *Tar Heel Editor, Journalism Quarterly*, 17 (March 1940): 50.

Papers:
Josephus Daniels's papers are in the Library of Congress, the University of North Carolina Historical Collection, and the files of the *Raleigh News and Observer*.

Dorothy Day

(8 November 1897-29 November 1980)

Mel Piehl
Valparaiso University

MAJOR POSITION HELD: Editor, *Catholic Worker* (1933-1980).

BOOKS: *The Eleventh Virgin* (New York: Boni, 1924);

From Union Square to Rome (Silver Spring, Md.: Preservation of the Faith Press, 1938);

House of Hospitality (New York & London: Sheed & Ward, 1939);

On Pilgrimage (New York: Catholic Worker Books, 1948);

The Long Loneliness: The Autobiography of Dorothy Day (New York: Harper, 1952);

I Remember Peter Maurin (Cambridge, Mass.: American Friends Service Committee, 1958);

Thérèse (Notre Dame, Ind.: Fides Publishing Association, 1960);

Loaves and Fishes (New York: Harper & Row, 1963; London: Gollancz, 1963);

Meditations (New York: Newman Press, 1970);

On Pilgrimage: The Sixties (New York: Curtis, 1972).

OTHER: Thomas C. Cornell and James H. Forest, eds., *A Penny a Copy: Readings from the* Catholic Worker, contributions by Day (New York: Macmillan, 1968).

PERIODICAL PUBLICATIONS: "Peter Maurin, Agitator," *Blackfriars*, 30 (September 1949): 409-415;

"Traveling by Bus," *Commonweal*, 51 (10 March 1950): 577-579;

"Conscience and Civil Defense," *New Republic*, 133 (22 August 1955): 6.

Dorothy Day (Photograph by Ed Lettau)

Dorothy Day was a radical journalist and social activist who has had a great influence on modern American Catholicism, and on many people outside the church as well. As the cofounder of the Catholic Worker movement and, for forty-seven years, the editor of its monthly paper, she created an original and sturdy synthesis of social radicalism and orthodox Catholic religion. Through the *Catholic Worker* and her other activities Day significantly raised the level of social thought and concern in American Catholicism, trained three generations of writers and social activists who passed through her movement, and evoked the admiration of many intellectuals, religious leaders, and public figures, as well as the ordinary poor folk to whom she devoted her life's work.

Day was born 8 November 1897 in Brooklyn, New York. She was the third of five children, three boys and two girls, born to John and Grace Satterlee Day. Her father was a sportswriter, and his job changes kept the family on the move—from Brooklyn to San Francisco in 1903; then, in 1906, to Chicago, where John Day took a position on the *Inter Ocean.* The frequent moves and a paternally enforced isolation from companions reinforced young Dorothy's seriousness and sense of loneliness. At an early age she developed an intense interest in religion and was drawn to whatever manifestations of piety she witnessed in friends and neighbors. This religious interest was baffling to her parents, who were largely indifferent to such matters. Day attended an Episcopal Church in Chicago and was eventually baptized and confirmed there.

Reading provided practically the only amusement and outlet for Day, and she became early on an avid and precocious student of fine literature, a habit she retained throughout her life. For Day producing the written word went along with consuming it. As a child she kept extensive diaries and journals, and in school she wrote numerous stories and poems, including "a tale of the martyrdom of Russian revolutionaries which must have surprised the staid little woman who taught us English." By the time she graduated from Waller High School at age sixteen and went to the University of Illinois in Urbana on a scholarship provided by the Hearst newspaper in Chicago, she was already widely read in current social controversies as well as more metaphysical matters.

At the University of Illinois Day found ordinary classwork unexciting and began cutting classes, keeping odd hours, and spending all her money on books. To earn money for more books she took poorly paid housekeeping and babysitting jobs. Soon she was turning her experiences into journalism and social criticism, writing articles for the local paper attacking the exploitation of the poorer students. She also wrote for the Scribblers, a campus literary club. As she developed more so-

cially radical views at the university, Day abandoned her childhood interest in religion, which now seemed to her part of the smug and oppressive world of the comfortable classes. "Jesus said, 'Blessed are the meek,' " she said, "but I could not be meek at the thought of injustice. For me Christ no longer walked the streets of this world. He was two thousand years dead and new prophets had risen up in his place."

In 1916, after her second year, Day left college and went to New York City, where she joined many other discontented young people in what historian Henry May has called "the great rebellion." In Greenwich Village, the home of pre-World War I artistic and intellectual radicalism, Day immersed herself in the daring and unconventional movements that were trying to change American culture.

Day's own contribution to the radical movement was to be in journalism. Through some aggressive self-promotion she got her first job with the socialist *New York Call.* Day's work with the *Call* became an education in contemporary American dissent: she covered the birth-control movement, rent strikes, the peace movement, and the Wobblies, and interviewed subjects ranging from Leon Trotsky to Mrs. Vincent Astor's butler. She quickly became a skilled practitioner of the techniques of partisan, participatory journalism, excelling in emotional descriptions of the poverty she saw all around her in the immigrant slum neighborhoods. But she also chafed at the sometimes misleading propaganda expected by the editors. She quit the *Call* in April 1917, after she had helped distort the facts about a hunger strike by birth-control advocate Ethel Byrne.

After working for a short time with the Anti-Conscription League, Day became an assistant editor of *The Masses,* the sophisticated and influential little magazine that was the embodiment of Greenwich Village radicalism. When the principal editors, Floyd Dell and Max Eastman, left for a time during the summer of 1917, twenty-year-old Day found herself in charge of the journal. Although the experience was brief, it gave her valuable credentials as a radical journalist after *The Masses* passed into legend. Although Day thoroughly enjoyed *The Masses*, her career there was cut short by World War I. Because the magazine opposed the war, the Post Office refused to mail it after August 1917, and the Justice Department finally suppressed it altogether in November. For Day and her radical friends, the kind of high-spirited rebellion represented by *The Masses* was no longer possible.

The next decade of Day's life was a period of

uncertainty and struggle. After a brief job with Max and Crystal Eastman's *Liberator,* the successor to *The Masses,* she decided to give up journalism and the bohemian life of Greenwich Village and begin training as a nurse in a Brooklyn hospital. A love affair with Lionel Moise, a newspaperman she met in the hospital, ended in tragedy with an abortion; this was followed by a brief, unhappy marriage to Barkeley Tober, a literary promoter. She and Tober sailed to Europe in 1920, intending to join the American expatriate colony in Paris. After they separated Day stayed on in Italy for a year, emotionally recovering from her experiences and writing an autobiographical novel. When she returned to the United States she moved to Chicago, where she lived from 1921 to 1923. There she did various odd jobs and free-lance work for, among others, the *Chicago Post* and the *Liberator,* which had moved to Chicago under the editorship of Robert Minor. In the fall of 1923 she moved to New Orleans and went to work for the *New Orleans Item.* While she was in New Orleans her autobiographical novel, *The Eleventh Virgin* (1924), was published. Although it was not very good as literature, the novel did successfully raise the issue of the conflict between social action and personal life that especially affected many female radicals like Day. *The Eleventh Virgin* also brought Day economic security when the movie rights were purchased by a Hollywood studio for $5,000. Day quit her job in early 1924 and bought a cottage on Staten Island. She kept up her friendships with such New York intellectuals as Malcolm Cowley, Kenneth Burke, and Allen and Caroline Gordon Tate. She also wrote serials for the Bell newspaper syndicate and occasional pieces for *The New Masses,* the Communist journal. In March 1927 Day had a daughter, Tamar Teresa, by Forster Batterham, a Southern-born biologist and anarchist with whom she was living on Staten Island. When Day decided to have the child baptized, Batterham left her. In December 1927 Day herself was also baptized into the Roman Catholic church.

The decision ended what Day saw as her spiritual quest, but she still had difficulty finding a proper vocation. Although she retained her radical commitment, her new faith cut her off from her old left-wing associates and their ideas. Again she held various jobs, including a brief stint as a scriptwriter for the Pathé movie studio in Hollywood in 1929. After a stay in Mexico she returned to New York in 1931. With the Great Depression settling over the country, she witnessed a poverty nearly as severe as Mexico's: "On the fringes by the rivers, on almost every vacant lot there was a Hooverville, where the homeless huddled in front of their fires," she wrote. The Catholic journals *Commonweal* and *America* were interested in the upsurge of social agitation in the country, and Day took assignments covering strikes, Communist meetings, intellectuals' conferences, and unemployment marches. In December 1932 she was in Washington covering a Communist hunger march. Moved by the sight of the poor and unemployed marchers, she went to the national shrine at Catholic University and prayed "that some way would open up for me to use what talents I possessed for my fellow workers, for the poor."

When she returned to New York she found on her doorstep Peter Maurin, an itinerant French immigrant agitator and exponent of Catholic social thought who had been referred to her by George Shuster, the editor of *Commonweal.* Although it took her some time to understand Maurin's proposal that she start a Catholic paper for the unemployed, she eventually concluded that he had come in answer to her prayer and agreed to attempt the venture. From friends and her own earnings she put together the fifty-seven dollars needed to publish 2,500 copies of an eight-page tabloid that she called the *Catholic Worker.* Maurin, who objected to the proletarian title and content of the paper, stayed away when it was first sold in Union Square on May Day 1933 for a penny a copy. But he soon returned and assumed his place as the honored cofounder of the movement and author of the little "Easy Essays" that defined the movement's principles.

The *Catholic Worker* was an immediate success. Besides the street sales, Day sent copies of the paper to editors, bishops, and academics, who replied with encouragement and sufficient funds for a second issue. In November 1933, 20,000 copies were printed and sold. By March 1935 circulation was up to 65,000. The increase continued throughout the 1930s: circulation was 100,000 by the end of 1936; 150,000 in 1938; and 185,000 by 1940. These figures include copies sent in bulk to Catholic parishes and organizations, but the *Catholic Worker* was frequently passed from hand to hand, so the numbers are probably a rough index of actual readership. The *Catholic Worker*'s format and content reflected its intention of engaging the Catholic religious tradition with the urgent problems of the day. Day cleverly designed the paper to appeal to a diverse constituency that included the alienated poor and unemployed, religious leaders, and lay Catholics concerned about the social implications of their faith. Much about the paper suggested its distinctively working-class appeal: its name (after the Communist *Daily Worker*), the tabloid size, and the

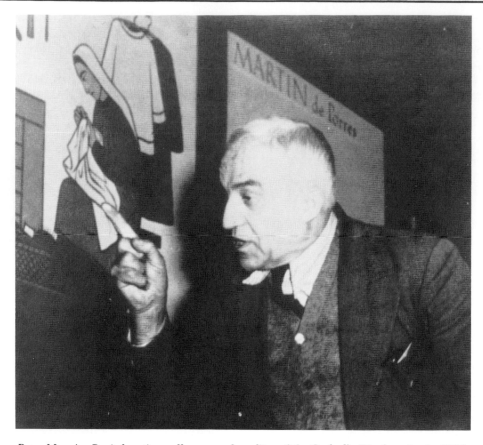

Peter Maurin, Day's longtime colleague and coeditor of the Catholic Worker, *in the 1930s*

two brawny workmen on the flag (one black, one white, at the suggestion of a reader). At the same time the book reviews, the high quality of writing, and the frequent references to church history and teaching reflected the *Catholic Worker*'s intellectual aspirations. The goal, in Maurin's phrase, was to "bring the workers to the scholars and the scholars to the workers."

Day's use of the penny price as an effective promotional device and trademark indicates her talent for a kind of ingenuous public relations: establishing a price meant that the *Catholic Worker* was sold like a normal publication, but the nominal cost and the fact that the editors received no compensation and lived in poverty underscored the paper's hostility to the capitalist profit motive. The *Catholic Worker* has retained its price of a penny a copy (twenty-five cents a year by subscription) throughout its fifty-year history, making it one of the stable landmarks of American journalism.

In its first years the *Catholic Worker* was given over to current events. The paper reported on wage reductions, strikes, evictions, racial incidents, and the like. A typical early issue (May 1935) included

reports on efforts to organize food relief for displaced sharecroppers, poor mothers in need of child care, the Scottsboro case, a farm-labor strike, and the conditions of life for slum children. But news always took second place to analysis and advocacy—Maurin's "clarification of thought." Although the paper looked like a tabloid throwaway, it was really a journal of opinion. Especially after the late thirties, most of the news that appeared concerned social problems or ideas of direct concern to Catholic workers or Catholicism in general. It was the other features that came to dominate the paper and convey its message: book reviews (which gradually grew longer); quotations from church fathers, saints, popes, theologians, and contemporary Catholic writers; editorials and commentary from Day and other movement writers and fellow travelers; and Maurin's Easy Essays. Some articles swelled to 3,000 words or more, but since the paper carried no advertising (all income came from donations), it regularly crammed several such lengthy pieces into its eight, or sometimes twelve, tabloid pages. The *Catholic Worker* also carried original artwork depicting saints and scenes

Day (right) and two other members of the Catholic Worker movement, Bill Callahan and Margaret Polk, outside the movement's headquarters at 115 Mott Street, New York City, in 1936

from the movement by Ade de Bethune and Fritz Eichenberg.

The *Catholic Worker* began as simply a paper for the unemployed, but it quickly developed into the organ of an important social movement. Day believed that the *Catholic Worker* could not advocate social change without acting to bring it about. Soon the paper's "editorial offices" (originally a barbershop below Day's apartment) were transformed into a "house of hospitality" which provided meals and lodging to the unemployed. By 1938 St. Joseph's House of Hospitality on Mott Street was feeding an estimated 1,200 persons mornings and evenings. Readers of the paper came from everywhere to participate in "the work," which included a wide range of radical social activities. "Never was there such a paper as the *Catholic Worker*," Day observed. "Do the readers of *Commonweal, America, Nation,* the *New Republic* come to spend weeks, and by the hun-

dreds at that?" The New York house of hospitality was soon imitated by *Catholic Worker* readers in other cities. By 1940 there were over thirty Catholic Worker houses and farms across the country, all loosely connected by the *Catholic Worker* and the anarchist leadership of Dorothy Day.

Although many other individuals contributed significantly to the Catholic Worker through the years, Day's organizational, journalistic, and religious talents remained crucial to the movement. As Dwight Macdonald said, "The only recent American institutions that fit Emerson's generalization [that 'an institution is the lengthened shadow of one man'] are J. Edgar Hoover's FBI and Dorothy Day's Catholic Workers." As with Hoover, Day's longevity accounts in part for her singular influence; but more important was her steadfast adherence to a single vision of what the movement should stand for: "the primacy of the spiritual" in social change. Although extremely radical on social questions, the Catholic Worker remained theologically orthodox and loyal to the Catholic hierarchy. "If Cardinal Spellman ordered me to shut down the Catholic Worker tomorrow, I would," Day once stated.

Besides her personal and religious leadership, Day was important to the *Catholic Worker* as a journalist and editor. The radical intentions and skidrow environment of the paper never interfered with her professional commitment to making it a first-rate journalistic product. Much as she disdained bourgeois values of the social or commercial sort, Day's enormous capacity for hard work and single-minded dedication to the success of her enterprise paid off in the high quality of writing and editing that consistently marked the *Catholic Worker,* especially after its early days. During the thirties Day edited the paper herself, except when she was away on her frequent speaking trips. After 1940 she relied on a succession of managing editors for normal editorial tasks, but she still kept abreast of editorial policy and intervened to block anything that contradicted her understanding of what the *Catholic Worker* stood for. Day also contributed to the *Catholic Worker* as a reporter and columnist. Her old talent for descriptive and partisan journalism was put to good use, especially in the thirties, when she covered some of the dramatic conflicts of the Depression as well as the unspectacular daily lives and struggles of the people she met in the slums and elsewhere. In 1936, for instance, her series of reports on evicted Arkansas sharecroppers showed that she had lost none of her touch as a muckraker:

It wasn't until late afternoon that we reached

St. Joseph's House in New York City, the first of the Catholic Worker houses of hospitality where the unemployed are fed and housed (Photograph by Ed Lettau)

the worst place of all, just outside Parkin, Arkansas. There drawn up along the road was a tent colony which houses 108 people, four infants among them, God knows how many children.

The little girls giggled and laughed with their arms around each other while we talked to this evicted crowd of sharecroppers. It was seventeen above. Only one of them had a sweater, and the heels and toes of all of them were coming out of their shoes. Their giggles started them coughing and woke one of the babies who cried fretfully, weakly. . . .

So while surveys are being made and written the Southern Tenant Farmers Union carries on, organizing the sharecroppers. They have had a hard struggle in the past, and the future looks dark. But combined with faith and charity they have hope, and the terror that walks by day and by night in Arkansas does not daunt them.

These reports, which appeared in both the *Catholic Worker* and *America*, drew the attention of Eleanor

Roosevelt; it also drew the attention of local landowners and the governor of the state who denounced "this Catholic woman who makes fat salaries off the misery of the people." Day also gave *Catholic Worker* readers some of the decade's best coverage of the labor movement. She knew many national labor figures, and interviewed union heads such as Philip Murray, John L. Lewis, John Brophy, Harry Bridges, and Joseph Curran.

In later years Day gave up most of her straight reporting in favor of her personal column, originally called "Day by Day" and changed to "On Pilgrimage" in 1946. There she could give free rein to her intimate style, which Dwight Macdonald called "an odd composite of Pascal's *Pensées* and Eleanor Roosevelt's 'My Day.'" The column's informality appealed to readers who might not care for the more abstract writing elsewhere in the paper. Bus rides, speeches, meals, visitors, wars, books, saints, deaths, weather, noises, smells, children—all appeared jumbled together in the chatty paragraphs of "On Pilgrimage." Sometimes this led to an engaging blend of domesticity and propaganda:

The children of the house were bending engrossed over a toy catalogue the other day figuring up what they would like to have for Christmas. "It's no use looking at it," one of them was saying. "It is only for rich children, this catalogue. A toy train costs fifteen dollars."

"When I grow up I'm going to be rich," five year old Freddy said. "Rich!" said seven year old Teresa. "Don't you know it's bourgeois to be rich?"

I would have liked to tell her that it· is also bourgeois to have the acquisitive spirit and to want so much for Christmas, but I didn't have the heart, so I sat down with them to look at the catalogue.

Day was not, however, just a good-natured maternal figure; anyone who mistook her disarming simplicity and earthiness for naiveté was likely to be quickly disabused. Beneath her unassuming demeanor stood a strong-willed woman whose varied life had left her no stranger to sharp personal and ideological conflict. To a writer who complained about her lack of concern for "the poor kids in Korea" during the Korean War, she replied, "If it refers to our soldiers the phrase is maudlin, and I don't think it means the children being killed by our bombs." Her column on the dropping of the atomic bomb was equally passionate. "Mr. Truman was jubilant. True Man. What a strange name, come to think of it. . . . He went from table to table on the cruiser which was bringing him home from the Big Three Conference, telling the great news. *Jubilate Deo*. We have killed 318,000 Japanese."

Besides her regular writing for the *Catholic Worker* Day contributed frequently throughout her career to many magazines and journals, including the *New Republic, Commonweal, America, Sign, Catholic Mind, Jubilee, Worship,* and *Ave Maria*. During her *Catholic Worker* career she also published six books, as well as several shorter pieces that were distributed as booklets by the Catholic Worker. *From Union Square to Rome* (1938), her first autobiography, is a convert's work, explaining her turn to Rome and the founding of the Catholic Worker movement. It is reticent about the details of her past, and much less reflective than her second autobiography, *The Long Loneliness* (1952). Although marred by the stylistic flaws that always afflicted her longer writings, *The Long Loneliness* conveys the more mature Day's perceptive interpretation of her life and work. Called a "spiritual classic" by many critics, it has been twice reprinted in paperback in the United States, published in a British edition, and translated into German, Dutch, and Portuguese. *House of Hospitality* (1939) and *Loaves and Fishes* (1963) are accounts of life in the movement. *Thérèse* (1960) is a hagiography of a nineteenth-century French saint who was an important personal model for Day, especially because she was so beloved by ordinary people. *On Pilgrimage: The Sixties* (1972) is a collection of the *Catholic Worker* columns from that decade.

After its great successes of the thirties, Day's antiwar stand sent the movement into decline for a time. The paper had briefly lost circulation when it refused to join the general American Catholic support for Franco in Spain, maintaining a neutralist and pacifist stand throughout the Civil War. With the coming of World War II the Catholic Worker experienced its greatest crisis. Day had been a longtime pacifist, but others in the movement objected strongly to her stand. With the approach of the war in 1940 Day insisted that all houses of hospitality distribute the pacifist *Catholic Worker*. The movement split over the issue, and only a handful of houses continued operation during the war; the *Catholic Worker*'s circulation declined to 45,000.

But both the paper and the movement survived the crisis. During the late forties and fifties the Catholic Worker formed the core of the small but hardy Catholic radical and pacifist movement. Day opposed the Cold War, the Korean War, and McCarthyism, and the Catholic Worker attracted such new recruits as Michael Harrington, who later used his experiences in the movement as part of the basis for his book *The Other America* (1962). Beginning in 1955 Catholic Workers also led campaigns of civil disobedience against compulsory air-raid drills in New York City; Day and other *Catholic Worker* editors were annually imprisoned for refusing to take shelter.

Such well-publicized actions and the changing political climate began to attract new readers and activists to the movement in the late fifties and sixties. The *Catholic Worker*'s circulation climbed steadily, to 65,000 in 1960 and 85,000 by 1965. New houses of hospitality began to open, with over fifty in operation by 1970, and seventy in 1980. The Catholic Worker, which had already trained many influential Catholic writers and activists such as John Cogley, Ed Marciniak, John Cort, and Harrington, began to have the same impact on many young Catholics in the 1960s. Day and the movement also received increasing recognition and praise from religious leaders and from many non-Catholic intellectuals such as Dwight Macdonald, T. S. Eliot, Hannah Arendt, and W. H. Auden. Articles on Day and the movement appeared in a wide variety of scholarly and popular publications. In the 1960s Day and the Catholic Worker were at the heart of the domestic turmoil over Vietnam. *Catholic Worker* editors led many of the early campaigns against the draft and the war. Day herself encouraged civil disobedience against the draft and against paying taxes for the war, and the Catholic Worker contributed substantially to the growth of the larger "Catholic Left" while adhering to its own distinctive witness. Day traveled extensively during the decade: to Communist Cuba, to Rome for Vatican Council II, to Britain, Australia, India, Africa, and the Soviet Union. She was widely recognized abroad as a pioneer in the contemporary lay religious movements for social justice and peace.

Day's health declined in the 1970s. She traveled and spoke less often, but continued her monthly column until her death in November 1980. At her funeral were prominent secular and religious leaders such as Terence Cardinal Cooke of New York, as well as hundreds of the Bowery men and "bag ladies" among whom she had spent her life in "voluntary poverty."

Dorothy Day was a journalist who created her own best story in the Catholic Worker, turning it into a unique phenomenon of American journalism and American history. She was also a distinguished religious and social leader who consistently challenged American society in the name of her ancient faith. When she died the *New York Times* obituary reported that she had been considered for the Nobel Peace Prize but was rejected by the Swedish committee because she was too radical. Day would have liked that, for she was an influential person who disdained worldly prestige and pursued instead her vision of a renewed Christianity in a transformed world.

Biography:
William D. Miller, *Dorothy Day: A Biography* (San Francisco: Harper & Row, 1982).

References:
Robert Coles, *A Spectacle Unto the World* (New York: Viking, 1973);

Dwight Macdonald, *Politics Past* (New York: Viking, 1970);

William D. Miller, *A Harsh and Dreadful Love: Dorothy Day and the Catholic Worker Movement* (New York: Liveright, 1973);

Mel Piehl, *Breaking Bread: The Catholic Worker and the Origin of Catholic Radicalism in America* (Philadelphia: Temple University Press, 1982).

Papers:
Dorothy Day's papers are at Marquette University.

Walter Duranty

(25 May 1884-3 October 1957)

Sally Taylor
Temple University

MAJOR POSITION HELD: Moscow correspondent, *New York Times* (1921-1941).

BOOKS: *The Curious Lottery and Other Tales of Russian Justice* (New York: Coward-McCann, 1929);

Red Economics, by Duranty, W. H. Chamberlin, H. R. Knickerbocker, and others (New York: Houghton Mifflin, 1932);

Duranty Reports Russia, edited by Gustavus Tucker-man, Jr. (New York: Viking, 1934); republished as *Russia Reported* (London: Gollancz, 1934);

Europe: War or Peace (New York: Foreign Policy Association/Boston: World Peace Foundation, 1935; London: Hamish Hamilton, 1935);

I Write as I Please (New York: Simon & Schuster, 1935; London: Hamish Hamilton, 1935);

Babies Without Tails (New York: Modern Age Books, 1937);

One Life, One Kopeck: A Novel (New York: Simon &

Walter Duranty (New York Times)

Schuster, 1937; London: Hamish Hamilton, 1937);

Solomons Cat (Grand Rapids, Mich.: Mayhew, 1937);

The Kremlin and the People (New York: Reynal & Hitchcock, 1941; London: Hamish Hamilton, 1942);

Search for a Key (New York: Simon & Schuster, 1943);

USSR: The Story of Soviet Russia (New York: Lippincott, 1944; London: Hamish Hamilton, 1944);

Return to the Vineyard, by Duranty and Mary Loos (Garden City: Doubleday, Doran, 1945);

Stalin & Co.: The Politburo, the Men Who Run Russia (New York: Sloane, 1949; London: Secker & Warburg, 1949).

PERIODICAL PUBLICATIONS: "The Turning Point of the Battle," *Current History*, 8 (July 1918): 28-30;

"How Foch Out-Generaled the Germans," *Current History*, 8 (September 1918): 416-422;

"Internal Strife Among Soviet Leaders," *Current History*, 25 (February 1927): 708-713;

"The Riddle of Russia," *New Republic*, 91 (14 July 1937): 270-272;

"The Russo-German Partnership," *Atlantic Monthly*, 165 (March 1940): 401-406.

As Moscow correspondent for the *New York Times* during the 1920s and 1930s, Walter Duranty enjoyed a virtual monopoly on news from the USSR. His dramatic and highly distinctive style of reporting made him a celebrity among the foreign correspondents of his day. In 1932 he won the Pulitzer Prize for his dispatches on the Soviet Union's first Five Year Plan, and his work was praised for its "scholarship, profundity, impartiality, sound judgment, and exceptional clarity." He became known during his twenty-year term in Moscow as the most knowledgeable source of information on the USSR and was quoted frequently by both the American right and left. A symbol of the antagonism between the United States and the Soviet Union, Duranty became the focal point of the polemic between extremist viewpoints. He welcomed the controversy and was fond of saying to younger reporters, "If a foreign correspondent is looking for a bed of roses, he would do well to go into floriculture."

Duranty was born and raised in Great Britain, where he was taught to suppress his emotions and to accept the white man's burden. He took on all the trappings of a British liberal—an advocate for the laboring man—but there was no escape for Duranty from his rigid Victorian upbringing and public-school education. Even his later complete rejection of the values of his youth would not save him from investing his own pronouncements with more importance than they were worth, leading to his flawed reportage of the great Soviet famine of 1933-1934 and the Stalinist purges of the latter half of the decade.

Duranty's father, William Steel Duranty, was a merchant, principally of cotton, in the industrial city of Liverpool. He had married Emmeline Hutchins in 1881, and the couple had moved into 10 Falkner Square, where Walter was born in 1884. The house was located in Mount Pleasant, a suburb which held a growing middle class of nouveaux riches. Liverpool's importance as a port and industrial center brought it an influx of immigrants who often fell victim to the excesses which accompanied the Industrial Revolution. From these problems, Duranty was in large part sheltered; nevertheless, his early experiences in the "Cradle of Socialism" must have had some effect upon his later assessment of the brutality of Soviet modernization in the late 1920s and early 1930s.

When Duranty was fifteen, his family moved further from the city into a more gracious suburb. As the son of a Protestant merchant, Duranty scorned both the landed gentry and the aristocracy, but no basis exists for his claim that he came from the lower middle class. There is some evidence that his father suffered a serious business reversal during Duranty's teenage years; Duranty, however, enjoyed the education of a gentleman. He had three terms at Harrow before completing his secondary-school education at Bedford. He demonstrated "impressive academic achievements" at the latter, leading to his matriculation at Emmanuel College, Cambridge, on 21 October 1903. A distinguished student, he received his honors degree in classics in 1906. George Seldes later remarked that among foreign correspondents Duranty stood out as the most erudite and the best educated, with the possible exception of Duranty's close friend William Bolitho, a South African. Duranty had an uncanny facility for learning languages, and by maturity he could translate any newspaper he happened to be reading into "flawless French, Russian, Latin, or Greek."

Duranty never discussed his upbringing or his family. Whether this was a result of his British reserve or a personal tendency toward secrecy cannot be determined; but in his fictionalized autobiography, *Search for a Key* (1943), he kills off both of his parents in a railway accident occurring when he was ten, although records show his father, at least, lived until 1933. Duranty was cynical about his education, and later in life he would disparage the British public-school system. In his apologia for his controversial treatment of the news from Moscow, *I Write as I Please* (1935), he said that both his upbringing and his schooling had marked his mind "with error and prejudice" about Russia.

Upon graduation from Cambridge Duranty left England, and during the next few years he lived a bohemian existence. He turned up in New York City and Marseilles; 1913 found him living in the Latin Quarter in Paris. Sometimes writer, sometimes tutor, he was known for his sophisticated wit and harebrained schemes. Wythe Williams, the head of the *New York Times*'s Paris bureau, was sitting in his office one afternoon that year when two young men came in and excitedly sputtered that a Frenchman intended to fly upside down in an airplane someplace over Paris the next morning.

The younger of the pair seemed the more enthusiastic, and in spite of Williams's discouragement, the unimpressively dressed little Englishman turned in a manuscript the next day. The flyer was Pegoud and the young writer was Walter Duranty. Williams corrected the pitiful example of journalism in front of Duranty, and from that day forward, he was plagued by the young man, who said he wanted to become a reporter. Williams finally relented, and Duranty began his journalistic career.

Duranty's work for the Paris bureau became important with the advent of World War I. Using the new telegraph relay system begun by *Times* managing editor Carr Van Anda, Duranty filed his first major story—a report of the zeppelin raid over Paris in 1916. It began: "A Zeppelin was heard over Paris at 9:30 o'clock, and soon after about a dozen bombs were dropped, killing ten persons and injuring thirty." This story was followed the next day by an eyewitness account which carried no by-line but was unmistakably Duranty's: "At 7 o'clock last night I saw Lloyd George and Bonar Law with a party of English officials enter the Hotel Crillon, and my companion remarked, 'The Zeppelins could have a good bag if they could drop a bomb now.'" The use of the first person, the highly dramatic presentation underlined with irony, and the unusual embroidering of detail marked Duranty's style; it was an approach he would use throughout his writing career. In addition to a flair for the dramatic, Duranty demonstrated a literary bent in his reportage on the French army. Bombed-out ammunition trucks became "fire twisted skeletons"; the red German eagle was symbolically "clotted and stained from beak to claw with the crimson of countless slaughters."

Duranty's work on the Western Front was upstaged by events on the Eastern Front when the October Revolution put the Bolsheviks in power in Russia. On 3 March 1918 the new Soviet government had signed with Germany the Treaty of Brest-Litovsk, withdrawing Russia from the war and engendering the fury of the Western Allies. The tumultuous events following in the fledgling state contributed to the *Times*'s decision to send a correspondent to Riga, Latvia, "the gateway to the East," in 1919. Duranty seized the opportunity: "I was nothing loathe [to go] because I found work as a 'second' man in the Paris office dreary after the excitement and independence of my job as correspondent."

In the early 1920s Duranty was calling Bolshevism "one of the most damnable tyrannies in history. It is a compound of force, terror and espionage, utterly ruthless in its conception and in execution." The tone of his observations very nearly kept him out of the Soviet Union in 1921, when the Volga famine forced the Soviet leaders to admit reporters under a codicil of the American Relief Administration's agreement to give aid to the starving millions. Duranty later reflected that his training had prepared him to witness the appalling conditions of the stricken regions: "The war in France had taught me a measure of indifference to blood and squalor, and fear and pity. Sudden death had become commonplace, and vermin a joke."

The thirty-seven-year-old Duranty, along with most of those admitted in 1921, spent his first few weeks in the Soviet Union fighting the bureaucracy. Meanwhile, Floyd Gibbons, the famous Hearst correspondent, scooped all of them, having gained entrance into the famine regions by the crafty and innovative methods for which he was known. When Duranty did see his first famine victims, he was quick to notice that starvation was not the cause of death in the vast majority of cases; instead, the diseases which inevitably accompany starvation took the larger toll. What struck him most was the patience of the Russian peasants, who waited for death without protest or violence.

Duranty's slant as Moscow correspondent gave rise to an investigative method of reporting. He interpreted events for his Western readers because he believed they could not comprehend what was happening, so incredible was the upheaval he was witnessing. Censorship, moreover, was an enormous burden to all the reporters in the Soviet capital. (It was termed "uncensoring" by the Soviet Foreign Office.) One of Duranty's colleagues, the German Paul Scheffer, wrote: "The journalist in Moscow had to become a master of a new art: the art of telling three quarters, a half, still smaller fractions of the truth; the art of not telling the truth in such a way that the truth would be made apparent to a thoughtful reader: or conversely, the art of telling the whole truth up to the point where its negative or positive significance would become apparent." Duranty had several advantages over most of the others in this regard. First, the *Times* accepted dispatches of 1,000 words; thus, Duranty was able to ramble within his alloted space and get a good deal of his material past the censors, who did not recognize his technique. Second, his education aided him: he grew into the habit of using classical allusions with which his ill-educated censors were unfamiliar; he threw in a little praise for the regime, interpreted the meaning of the event critically, then perhaps clouded all with a grandiose figure of

speech. Later this style would lay him open to charges of equivocation by critics. Third, his facility with languages put him ahead of his competitors, for he quickly learned enough Russian to dispense with the State-provided interpreter.

In his early years in Moscow, Duranty's economic reportage of the Bolshevik New Economic Policy and the runaway inflation was marked by his ability to simplify highly complex events. He also wrote short stories, much in the manner of Saki, which demonstrated the effects of the Bolshevik policies. Some of these were tolerably good, but Duranty never achieved his dream of becoming a first-class, or even a second-class, fiction writer.

Duranty became an advocate of the personality profile, and many of his predictions were based upon his shrewd reading of character. As early as 1923 Duranty wrote that "Stalin is one of the most remarkable men in Russia and perhaps the most influential here today." Although Duranty credited Ernestine Evans with the original insight that Stalin would eventually be the successor to Lenin, his early recognition of Stalin's power base illustrated Duranty's own discernment. Duranty's propensity to emphasize personality, coupled with his natural penchant for the literary, led him to build Lenin's image into almost mythological proportions. He was fond of recounting a story about the Bolshevik leader: "It is said that once, at the beginning of the revolution, Lenin, faced by general opposition, wrapped his head in his cloak, saying: 'All right! Argue it out for yourselves; but when you've reached the conclusion that my plan is the only possible one, wake me up and say so. I'm going to sleep.' An hour or two later they waked him and said: 'We don't like your plan much more than we did, but we agree that it's the only way. You are right.'" Duranty prided himself on his ability to size up others and believed he was able to predict the actions of the men about whom he wrote by putting himself in their place and asking himself what he would do.

The death of Lenin on 21 January 1924 gave Duranty the opportunity to do some of his finest and most dramatic reporting. The terse lead of Duranty's first dispatch emphasized the importance of the event: "Premiere Lenin died last night at 6:50 o'clock. The immediate cause of death was paralysis of the respiratory centers due to a cerebral hemorrhage." He ended the story with a poignant exchange between Lenin and a member of the proletariat—a stenographer—when Lenin first assumed power. He had greeted his secretary with these words: " 'Little Comrade,' he said, smiling, 'here I am. We must shake hands because we are going to work together.' " The following day, Duranty filed one of his most impressive mood pieces:

> Two unforgettable pictures stand out from this day of Russia's sorrow. First, Lenin lying in state—such simple state amid such grandeur—in the columned hall of the former Nobles' Club; second, the face and shoulders of Kalinin helping to bear Lenin's coffin from the station, when two steps down from the platform its weight was suddenly thrown on him in front.
>
> Kalinin was a typical Russian peasant driven by misery like millions of his fellows to work whole or part time in a city factory. During these moments of strain he symbolized the struggle of Russia's 140,000,000 peasants against the blind enmity of nature and human oppression. For two nights he had not slept, and as the level ground relieved part of the burden, he staggered from sheer exhaustion. But on he went like an old peasant plowing the stubborn earth, with sweat pouring down his cheeks in an icy snow-flecked gale, until he reached a gun caisson with six white horses waiting in the station yard to carry the coffin to the Nobles' Club.

In later stories, Duranty turned his attention to the proletariat and their open display of mourning for their lost leader. Duranty believed that the telegrams and tributes published in the official papers showed Lenin's importance to the Russian populace less than did the "human river, shorter in the grim darkness of the early morning when the north wind made the icy air well-nigh intolerable, but lengthening again to three, four, and five miles this evening when the day's work was over. . . ." Duranty's coverage of the ensuing factional struggles for power, however, was less perceptive, as he later admitted; in retrospect, he called it "a lot of sentimental twaddle." His cheerful reports of the leaders "burying the hatchet" were soon disproved by the events that eventually saw Trotsky expelled and Stalin firmly seated in power.

Later that year, Duranty made a trip to Western Europe. Between Paris and Havre the train wrecked in a tunnel. The first diagnosis of Duranty's splintered left leg bone was cautiously optimistic, but a gangrene infection required amputation. To relieve the unbearable pain, Duranty was given opium; his resulting addiction brought him more unhappiness than the loss of the leg. Rumors of Duranty's use of the drug were confirmed when

he wrote of the difficulties he encountered in breaking the habit.

It was typical of Duranty to turn a disability into an advantage. He was saved from sinking into self-pity over the loss of his leg by a friend who advised him to become a flamboyant cripple. Henceforth, Duranty, who in fact could walk without a cane, used one as a kind of identifying symbol. Whenever he wished to make a point in conversation, he would beat his cane against a chair or sofa, thus emphasizing his remark. American periodicals came to refer to him as "the Englishman with the cane."

Americans visiting the Soviet capital inevitably came to Duranty for a briefing, and this often became the basis for lifelong friendships. The young John Gunther, then a novice foreign correspondent for the *Chicago Daily News,* met Duranty in Moscow in 1928, and their friendship lasted until Duranty's death; other writers, such as Sinclair Lewis, Dorothy Thompson, and Alexander Woollcott, visited Duranty and came to know him well. He knew Isadora Duncan, who spent several years in Moscow teaching dance to the young Bolsheviks; Averell Harriman and other businessmen went to Duranty for information on Russian matters. As the years passed, Duranty became the unofficial social host for Americans in Moscow, a role he relished. His first lodging had been a cottage, which he maintained for three years rent free under an early Bolshevik decree holding that anyone who repaired a building could inhabit it. Later, his apartment, lavish by Soviet standards but typical of the flats held by foreign correspondents, became a gathering place for American intellectuals, usually of liberal leanings.

Duranty received the 1929 O. Henry Short Story Award for "The Parrot," but the circumstances proved embarrassing to him. Early in his career, he had become friends with another correspondent, H. R. Knickerbocker, and the two collaborated on short stories. They agreed to write a series, with the first six to be submitted under Duranty's name; one of these won the award. Duranty failed to inform the committee of the dual authorship, thus taking credit for work not entirely his own. When Knickerbocker won the Pulitzer Prize in 1931 for a series entitled "The Red Trade Menace," Duranty wired his congratulations, saying this in part compensated for "the other business."

By the fall of 1929 Stalin was firmly in control of the Soviet Union, having emerged victoriously from the factional intrigues following Lenin's death. He soon announced his intention of forcing the peasants onto large collectively owned farms. News of this momentous decision was eclipsed in the United States by the fall of the stock market; the West plunged into the Great World Depression, creating a vacuum between the ideals of Western democracy and harsh economic realities, which worsened year after year. American intellectuals such as Clifton B. Fadiman, Granville Hicks, Sherwood Anderson, Edmund Wilson, and Waldo Frank began viewing events in the Soviet Union with more interest, and the institution of the first Five Year Plan by Stalin became a focus for those who believed that capitalism had betrayed its followers. Duranty believed that any plan was better than no plan at all, and his incisive reportage of the execution of the Five Year Plan made him the "darling" of the left. Perhaps as a result of his newly gained prestige, Duranty seemed to welcome collectivization of the prosperous, independent peasants, or "kulaks," and although he documented with integrity their deportation to Siberia and other distant areas of the Soviet expanse, citing the excesses, he placed a good deal of faith in the regime's procedure.

He is famous among his critics for a maxim which first appeared in his 1932 poem "Red Square" in the *New York Times*: "You can't make an omelette without breaking eggs." Duranty felt no emotional involvement with the events he reported, and he admitted that the progression of history was, to his way of thinking, a theatrical production. He in no way cared about the result, except in terms of his job as a reporter. His cynicism, amusing to many, outraged early advocates of the socialist cause. William Henry Chamberlin, Eugene Lyons, and Malcolm Muggeridge—idealistic reporters with leftist leanings—found his attitude disquieting. Later, as each leaned more and more to the right, they were still bothered by Duranty's indifference. His winning of the Pulitzer Prize in 1932 rankled them, and their later writings contributed in large part to a recent assessment of Duranty as the prototype of "the dishonest journalist." As late as 1974, syndicated columnist Joseph Alsop wrote: "Duranty . . . covered up the horrors and deluded an entire generation by prettifying Soviet realities. . . . He was given a Pulitzer Prize. He lived uncommonly comfortably in Moscow, too, by courtesy of the KGB."

The basis for these accusations lies in the events surrounding collectivization, also called "the liquidation of the kulaks as a class." The deportation of the kulaks involved an estimated seven million people; even Soviet sources admit to some five million uprooted and sent to live in primitive conditions. Exact documentation as to the numbers who did not survive this debacle is lacking, but the famine which followed has been estimated as having taken the lives of as many as ten million Russian peasants. The kulaks, faced with requisitions year after year by the government, refused to replant their fields and in many cases slaughtered their livestock rather than see them sold at huge losses to the government. The result was a famine even more serious than that of 1921. But unlike the earlier famine, there was no publicity about the massive starvation in the grain-growing districts of the Soviet Union; very little word of the famine escaped the USSR. The United States was on the eve of recognizing the Soviets diplomatically; Duranty had been instrumental in bringing the two nations together. As rumors began to surface concerning the famine, Duranty's reaction was precipitant denial: on 31 March 1933, in an article in the *New York Times* headlined "Russians Hungry But Not Starving," Duranty said there was no famine. "It is all too true," he admitted, "that the novelty and mismanagement of collective farming . . . have made a mess of Soviet food production. . . . [T]o put it brutally—you can't make an omelette without breaking eggs, and the Bolshevik leaders are just as indifferent to the casualties that may be involved in their drive toward Socialism as any General during the World War who ordered a costly attack in order to show his superiors that he and his division possessed the proper soldierly spirit. In fact, the Bolsheviki are more indifferent because they are animated by fanatical conviction." But on the subject of famine, he was vehement: there were no deaths from actual starvation, yet it was possible that widespread mortality was occurring from diseases related to malnutrition. The areas particularly suffering were the Ukraine, the North Caucasus, and the Lower Volga. As late as June 1933, Duranty wired Knickerbocker, "The famine is mostly bunk as I told you. . . ." News was scarce, and even today estimates are difficult to gather because no censuses were taken during those years, but the evidence indicates that the famine was one of the most serious in the history of Russia.

Duranty traveled into the stricken areas later that September, and his dispatches in part compensated for his earlier error. By employing his usual ambiguous methods, he estimated between three million and ten million dead. The reading of his stories is highly difficult, however, since they are a patchwork of intricate mathematical propositions.

In order fully to understand his figures, the reader must be aware of his previous estimates. It is only by placing the stories side by side and using arithmetic that one can come to the three-to-ten-million estimate. Duranty's coverage was sadly inadequate, but it is unlikely that he was the linchpin in a conspiracy with Soviet authorities. And in 1941 he admitted he had made an error about "the extent and gravity of the 'man-made famine' in Russia during the fight to collectivise the farms in 1930-1933." His critics, Lyons and Chamberlin, made a record little better than Duranty's. Lyons did not go into the district, and Chamberlin's reports to the *Christian Science Monitor* refer only to desolation and "acute food shortages." Only Muggeridge, reporting for the *Manchester Guardian,* turned in exemplary reports.

Duranty's coverage of the famine had been poor; his reportage of the Stalin purges which followed was worse. Duranty evolved a "Fifth column" thesis in *The Kremlin and the People* (1941): he believed that the Soviets had succeeded in ridding themselves of Nazi sympathizers on the eve of World War II; although he did not approve, he claimed that the purges had served this purpose. Like many intellectuals during the notorious purge trials, he believed that Stalin was not the instigator, and he thought that history would ultimately vindicate Stalin. It has been estimated that by August 1937, 75 percent of the governing class of the USSR was gone, the same percentage of the intelligentsia, and one-half of the officer corps of the Red Army. Duranty's thesis excused burning down the house to roast the pig.

How Duranty's judgment could have slipped so badly can be explained by a number of factors. Soon after winning the Pulitzer, he wrote his best-selling *I Write as I Please.* His finances thus secured for a time, Duranty spent less and less time in the cold Soviet capital. His celebrity status seemed to go to his head: he began socializing and drinking more, and working less. He had become, moreover, a father by his common-law wife, a Russian girl named Katya, and far from relishing the role, the fifty-two-year-old Duranty had increased his time away from his family. Duranty, in devoting himself less to his work in Moscow, began to lose touch with the realities of Russia.

In hopes of riding his success into the world of literature, Duranty produced a novel, *One Life, One Kopeck* (1937)—a sweeping romance in which a young Communist hero dies carrying out orders of the party. His efforts would have been better placed elsewhere. Not only was the novel an economic failure, it was a critical flop. His later semiautobiog-

raphy cost him a good deal of time, and it likewise failed to please either critics or the public. From time to time, in his forays away from the capital of the USSR, Duranty reported for the North American Newspaper Alliance (N.A.N.A.), and occasionally he tried a brief appearance on some of the new broadcast news programs. His hopes for a radio career were dashed, however, by the quality of his voice, which had a high pitch that did not transmit well.

The bohemianism of Duranty's early years in Paris resurfaced during the late 1930s, and his ability to analyze events continued to decrease. In the spring of 1940 he emerged in Bucharest, not really working but amusing other correspondents with his tales of womanizing. He was well liked and admired, but he was doing very little valuable newspaper work.

In 1941, Duranty was still a celebrity, a hero to young correspondents just breaking into the trade, and an authority on Russia to the general public, but his editors at the *New York Times* had been aware for some time that his work was inadequate. Whether he was fired or whether he disassociated himself from the *Times,* Duranty left the staff that year. He continued to report for the N.A.N.A. from Japan.

His last story filed to the N.A.N.A. from Tokyo catalogued all of the sources who believed that war between Germany and the USSR was imminent. He even included part of a letter from an inside source in Moscow who insisted that very soon the two countries would be at war. Duranty said that it was possible and that his source was a good one, but it all still seemed "improbable" to him. Duranty went on record as saying, "In short, it looks as though there were some rift in the lute, but I shall be surprised if the clash occurs now." The date of the dispatch was 17 June 1941. Hitler invaded Russia on 22 June.

Lost among the various voices reporting the war, Duranty soon went to the United States, tired and ill, but still rapaciously involved in living. He wrote a respectable political analysis, *USSR: The Story of Soviet Russia* (1944), reiterating his past theses. But the book suffered from Duranty's long absence from the Soviet Union. If the newspaper business had played out, he reasoned, he still had his wit, his gift of repartee, to support him; and he believed that a career as a novelist still lay just around the corner. Always a seeker of glamour, Duranty "went Hollywood," and for a time supported himself rather meagerly by collaborating with Mary Loos, the young niece of Anita Loos. The pair produced a number of stories for slick magazines and made a fair amount of money. Their work culminated in a poorly received novel, *Return to the Vineyard* (1945). The collaboration ended when Loos quit to write screenplays.

Duranty's last successful venture was going on the lecture circuit with his old friend Knickerbocker. The pair were informative and entertaining, each having a lively sense of humor and a good deal of knowledge about the Soviet Union. Legend has it that the two would toss a coin before each appearance to see which would take the "pro-Soviet" stance. But sickness plagued Duranty, who by that time was in his sixties; then, on 13 July 1949, Knickerbocker was killed in a plane crash. Duranty suffered the loss not only of a friend but also of a partner in his new livelihood. He continued on the circuit, but the work was too demanding, and he was not as successful working alone. There is no doubt Duranty would have gone back into reporting, but no one particularly wanted to hire him unless he could get into the Soviet Union; it was believed that this was the only area he knew well. He was denied a visa, however, with no explanation from Soviet authorities. At last, poor health and a desire for a warmer climate took him to Florida.

Duranty's last years were hard. He plugged away at article after article and tried his hand at numerous short stories, but his lack of current information and his retention of an outdated grandiose style prevented his being able to support himself gracefully. After he settled in Orlando, his spirits often low, he became close friends with Anna Enwright, the widow of a judge. He continued to lecture, but the trips became more and more difficult for him to make. He wrote to John Gunther with a variety of schemes for books, which Gunther dutifully carried to publishers, but each was rejected. In 1952 Duranty wrote Gunther that he believed his lack of success might be a result of the blacklisting then proceeding in high order at the instigation of Sen. Joseph McCarthy. Alas, it was not true, Gunther wrote back: Duranty was no longer suffi-

ciently important to be blacklisted.

Duranty and Anna Enwright were married in 1957, while he was in the hospital with an illness. He was thought to be recovering, but on 3 October, the morning of the day he was to be released, he died.

Duranty never subscribed to extremist points of view, and his position and ambitions laid him open to accusations from both the left and the right. Whatever his failings in judgment, however, his integrity was rarely questioned.

Duranty was never able to adjust to the new, sparser techniques of journalism of the post-World War II era. During the war, he had criticized the work of Ernie Pyle as too personal, insufficiently objective. But Duranty's classical allusions and literary and historical parallels were unacceptable in modern newspaper writing. Duranty was never able to relinquish the grand and the sweeping for the individual and the intimate. He nevertheless remains an early example of the investigative reporter, and he was one of the forerunners of this trend in the early decades of the twentieth century. He demonstrated a keen capacity for distilling information out of a rarified atmosphere, whether by hard research or by shrewd evaluation.

His definition of news is worth remembering: "News," Duranty once told Walter Kerr, "is anything that interests a good reporter and that a good reporter thinks will interest his readers."

References:

Meyer Berger, *The Story of the New York Times* (New York: Simon & Schuster, 1951);

Michael Charles Emery, "The American Mass Media and the Coverage of Five Major Foreign Events, 1900-1950," Ph.D. dissertation, University of Minnesota, 1969;

Peter G. Filene, *Americans and the Soviet Experiment, 1917-1933* (Cambridge: Harvard University Press, 1967);

Paul Scheffer, *Seven Years in Soviet Russia* (New York: Macmillan, 1932).

Doris Fleeson
(20 May 1901-1 August 1970)

Terry Hynes
California State University, Fullerton

MAJOR POSITIONS HELD: Political reporter, *New York Daily News* (1927-1943); war correspondent, *Woman's Home Companion* (1943-1944); political columnist, Bell Syndicate (1945-1954), United Features Syndicate (1954-1969).

BOOK: *An Art to Be Practiced: The Eleventh Annual Memorial Lecture Sponsored by the Twin Cities Local, American Newspaper Guild, AFL-CIO, and the School of Journalism, University of Minnesota, Minneapolis, October 24, 1957* (N.p., 1957 or 1958).

SELECTED PERIODICAL PUBLICATIONS: "To Keep Us Out of War," *Independent Woman*, 18 (July 1939): 200, 218-219;

"Washington Views Our Vital Interests," *Independent Woman*, 19 (June 1940): 162, 188-189;

"Washington Windows," *Independent Woman*, 20 (April 1941): 101-102;

"650 WACS Defy the Subs," *Woman's Home Companion*, 70 (October 1943): 20;

"I Keep a Rendezvous with Heroes," *Woman's Home Companion*, 70 (November 1943): 4;

"Within Sound of the Guns," *Woman's Home Companion*, 71 (January 1944): 4;

"100,000 Men and a Girl," *Woman's Home Companion*, 71 (February 1944): 4;

"That Feminine Touch," *Woman's Home Companion*, 71 (March 1944): 4;

"Men With a Date," *Woman's Home Companion*, 71 (June 1944): 4;

"Catherine the Great," *Woman's Home Companion*, 71 (July 1944): 4;

"We're On Our Way!," *Woman's Home Companion*, 71 (August 1944): 4;

"Same Old Bombs, Dearie!," *Woman's Home Companion*, 71 (September 1944): 4;

"Into the Heart of France," *Woman's Home Companion*, 71 (October 1944): 4;

"Diagnosis: Political Schizophrenia," *New York Times Magazine*, 24 August 1958, p. 11.

Doris Fleeson covered the world of politics for forty years, first as a reporter for the *New York Daily News*, then, after World War II, as a columnist

Doris Fleeson

whose views were syndicated, at her peak, in nearly 100 newspapers throughout the United States. Her writing combined wit with an acerbic, straightforward presentation of information and interpretation. She was especially well known for her extensive network of federal contacts within the government, which provided her with the raw material for her scoops and examinations of political intrigue.

Fleeson was born in Sterling, Kansas, on 20 May 1901 to William Fleeson, the owner of a clothing store, and Helen Tebbe Fleeson. She attended the University of Kansas in Lawrence, where she decided to become a reporter: she thought William Allen White and Ed Howe led exciting lives and saw no reason why she should not do the same. At Kansas, too, she exchanged the Republican views of her family for the liberal political stance that marked the rest of her life.

After graduation in 1923, Fleeson worked first as a reporter for the *Pittsburg* (Kansas) *Sun*; then as society editor for the *Evanston*(Illinois) *News-Index*, while trying to break into the Chicago newspaper world. Unsuccessful in her efforts to gain a job on one of the big-city newspapers, Fleeson went to New York, where she was hired as city editor on the *Great Neck* (Long Island) *News*. Finally, in 1927, she won a job on the city staff of the *New York Daily News*.

Fleeson spent over fifteen years with the *Daily News*. She commented later in her typically direct style: "There we learned to hit 'em in the eye. We belonged to the who-the-hell-reads-the-second-paragraph school." For the first few years Fleeson was a general assignment reporter in New York City; then she was assigned to the newspaper's bureau in Albany as a political reporter. She married another *Daily News* political reporter, John O'Donnell, on 28 September 1930. They had a daughter, Doris, who was born in 1932 during Fleeson's coverage of the Seabury investigation of corruption in the state that resulted in the resignation of New York City mayor Jimmy Walker.

Fleeson and O'Donnell were sent to the *Daily News*'s newly opened Washington bureau early in 1933. Together they started the "Capitol Stuff" column, which continued to appear in the *Daily News* long after Fleeson had left the paper.

In October, at the meeting that established the Guild of New York Newspaper Men and Women, Fleeson was selected as a member of a committee charged with going to the nation's capital to urge the National Recovery Administration to mandate a thirty-five-dollar-per-week minimum wage for reporters. In pleading the reporters' case before the NRA, Fleeson protested policy provisions which labeled reporters as professionals, claiming that the label was being used to deprive journalists of the benefits of the NRA. In December, she was a delegate to the founding convention of the American Newspaper Guild in Washington and was elected to the guild's national executive committee.

As Fleeson became closer to the New Deal— she was the only woman reporter permanently assigned to accompany President Roosevelt on his campaign trips—her liberal beliefs grew firmer. As the threat of war developed in Europe, Fleeson found herself more and more at odds with her husband's conservative views and with the editorial positions of the *Daily News*. In 1942, the couple were divorced. Fleeson went to Europe to report on wartime conditions in Germany. On her return to the United States, she was assigned to desk editing, radio news, and once again to the Albany bureau.

In May 1943, Fleeson resigned from the paper and became a war correspondent for the *Woman's Home Companion*. Before leaving the magazine in 1944, Fleeson wrote ten articles from the Italian and French fronts, including "650 WACS Defy the Subs," "I Keep a Rendezvous with Heroes," "Within Sound of the Guns," "Same Old Bombs, Dearie!," and "Into the Heart of France."

In 1945, Fleeson returned to Washington and began a political-affairs column which was published initially in the *Washington Evening Star* and the *Boston Globe*. The network of sources she had developed and maintained in Washington sometimes yielded information which became front-page news. In May 1946, she revealed a feud between two Supreme Court justices. The feud began when Justice Robert H. Jackson had included in his dissent to a 1945 decision the suggestion that Justice Hugo Black should have disqualified himself from the case, in which Black's former law partner had represented the winning side. Fleeson reported that Black regarded the statement "as an open and gratuitous insult" and "a slur upon his personal and judicial honor." In 1952, a Fleeson column generated headlines when she reported that Gen. Dwight D. Eisenhower's resignation was on President Truman's desk. A day later the White House confirmed her story. In January 1953, Fleeson quoted President Truman as saying that 49,000 desertions from the armed forces during the Korean conflict could be ascribed to media influences such as the *Chicago Tribune* and the Scripps-Howard newspapers and to General of the Army Douglas MacArthur, who had been dismissed by Truman in 1951 as U.S. commander in the Far East.

Fleeson developed her network of sources in accordance with her belief that it was critical to "know the bureaucrats. They offer continuity and perspective." On the other hand, she saw press agents and other public-relations personnel as among the greatest deterrents to good reporting, and she did not attend any off-the-record briefings. In her view, "reporters need to use their legs always, and see the people and talk with the people" as the most reliable method of gaining information. She felt that the best way to influence an administration was through full disclosure of the facts rather than through preaching.

An aggressive political reporter who seldom pulled punches in her stories, Fleeson was "on the job" nearly all the time. She mined every conversation, every luncheon and dinner engagement, for material for her column. Although she considered herself a nonpartisan liberal, critics accused her of favoring the Democrats. Her defense was that she was evenhanded in her outspoken and sometimes acidly expressed criticism: "I hit people hard sometimes," she said, but they seemed to take it because "I do that to everyone." In confirmation of her claim, *Newsweek* magazine noted in 1957 that "there is, in fact, almost no Washington figure, Republican or Democrat, who has not felt the sharp edge of her typewriter. . . ." When industrialist and financier Bernard Goldfine arrived in Washington for the 1958 Congressional hearings regarding his gifts to Eisenhower presidential assistant Sherman Adams, for example, Fleeson remarked of his entourage, "Goldfine seems to have more lawyers than Carter has pills." Fleeson said that Lewis Strauss, one of Eisenhower's politically ambitious appointees, "has Potomac fever in its most virulent form." She referred to Senate Democratic leader Lyndon B. Johnson and his tactics as "Old Doctor Johnson and his snake oil" and complained of Johnson's method of packing key Senate committees: "It would be hard to figure out how the Democratic policy and steering [committee members] could be chosen so they would represent a smaller fraction of [Democratic] voters." One who did escape her critical wit, however, was Adlai Stevenson, and her admiration for him almost blinded her to his slim chance for election when she covered his 1956 presidential campaign.

Fleeson's ability to tap sources generated so much interest in her column that in 1945 it was distributed through the Bell Syndicate; in 1954 it was picked up by United Features Syndicate, with which she remained associated until her retirement. By the early 1950s her five-day-a-week "interpretive articles," as she called them, were being published in approximately 70 newspapers throughout the United States; by the early 1960s nearly 100 papers were carrying her column.

Some measure of her influence may be determined from the attention given to her by two of the major weekly news magazines. In an article on the Washington press corps in *Time* in 1951, Fleeson was listed as one of "the best Washington newspaper reporters." Fleeson was the only woman among the thirteen reporters mentioned, including Walter Lippmann, Arthur Krock, James Reston, Stewart and Joseph Alsop, and Drew Pearson. Ten years later, in an article titled "Hundreds of Washington Bylines Daily . . . And Here Are Some Big Ones,"

Newsweek featured brief sketches of five Washington correspondents. Again Fleeson was the only woman; the others discussed were Pearson, Krock, Marquis Childs, and David Lawrence.

Fleeson received many awards from other professional journalists in recognition of her accomplishments. In 1937, the New York Newspaper Women's Club gave her its first annual award for outstanding reporting for her coverage of the 1936 Republican National Convention. The club gave her a second award in 1943 for a story about Wendell L. Willkie's world trip. In 1950, Fleeson received one of four Headliner Awards for "distinguished service in the field of journalism" from Theta Sigma Phi (which changed its name in the 1970s to Women in Communications, Inc.). The University of Missouri School of Journalism gave her a medal of honor in 1953. At the 1954 convention of the American Society of Newspaper Editors, she received the Raymond Clapper Award of $500 for "exceptionally meritorious work."

Outside the profession, too, Fleeson received recognition for her achievements as a journalist. In 1951 she was honored by the ladies' auxiliary of the Veterans of Foreign Wars. In 1954 she received a distinguished alumna citation from the University of Kansas. In addition, she was awarded honorary doctorates of humane letters from Culver-Stockton College and Russell Sage College.

Fleeson was active in professional organizations. In addition to her involvement in the American Newspaper Guild and its New York predecessor, she was a member of the Women's National Press Club and was its president in 1937; she opposed the National Press Club because of its policy of not admitting women as members.

Fleeson was married on 1 August 1958 to Dan A. Kimball, a former secretary of the navy and president of the Aerojet-General Corporation of Sacramento, California. Fleeson went into semiretirement in 1967, writing only two columns a week. Early in 1969 she was incapacitated by a stroke. She died of a heart attack at her home on 1 August 1970, just thirty-six hours after the death of her husband, on what would have been their twelfth wedding anniversary. She was buried with her husband in Arlington National Cemetery.

References:

"Core of the Corps," *Time*, 58 (9 July 1951): 55;

"Hundreds of Washington Bylines Daily . . . And Here Are Some Big Ones," *Newsweek*, 54 (18 December 1961): 68-69;

"Lady about Town," *Time*, 59 (21 April 1952): 57-59;

"Mad over Politics," *Newsweek*, 50 (7 October 1957): 72.

Papers:
Doris Fleeson's papers are at the Spencer Research Library, University of Kansas.

Frank E. Gannett
(15 September 1876-3 December 1957)

Wanda A. Arceneaux
Louisiana State University

NEWSPAPERS OWNED: *Elmira* (New York) *Gazette*, merged to form *Star-Gazette* in 1907, merged to form *Star-Telegram* in 1923 (1906-1957); *Ithaca* (New York) *Journal* (1912-1957); *Rochester* (New York) *Times-Union* (1918-1957); *Utica* (New York) *Observer-Dispatch* (1921-1957); *Elmira Advertiser* (1923-1957); *Elmira Sunday Telegram* (1923-1957); *Newburgh* (New York) *News* (1925-1957); *Beacon* (New York) *News* (1927-1957); *Plainfield* (New Jersey) *Courier-News* (1927-1957); *Rochester* (New York) *Democrat and Chronicle* (1928-1957); *Hartford* (Connecticut) *Times* (1928-1957); *Albany* (New York) *Knickerbocker News* (1928-1957); *Ogdensburg* (New York) *Journal* (1928-1957); *Ogdensburg Advance-News* (1928-1957); *Brooklyn* (New York) *Eagle* (1929-1931); *Malone* (New York) *Evening Telegram* (1929-1957); *Danville* (Illinois) *Commercial News* (1934-1957); *Saratoga Springs* (New York) *Saratogian* (1934-1957); *Utica* (New York) *Daily Press* (1935-1957); *Massena* (New York) *Observer* (1937-1957); *Binghamton* (New York) *Press* (1943-1957); *Niagara Falls* (New York) *Gazette* (1954-1957).

BOOKS: *Britain Sees It Through* (Rochester, N.Y.: Gannett Newspapers, 1944);

The Fuse Sputters in Europe (Rochester, N.Y.: Gannett Newspapers, 1946);

Winging Round the World (Rochester, N.Y.: Gannett Newspapers, 1947).

OTHER: José Rizal, *Friars and Filipinos*, translated and abridged by Gannett (New York: St. James Press, 1900);

Industrial and Labour Relations in Great Britain: A Symposium, edited by Gannett and B. F. Catherwood (New York, 1939).

Frank E. Gannett, a newspaper editor and publisher for more than fifty years, is probably best remembered for his promotion of freedom of the press through the ownership of a group of twenty-two newspapers, mostly in medium-sized cities in New York. Although the number of newspapers and their total circulation figures have been impressive since the Gannett Company's inception in 1924, perhaps more notable is the fact that Gannett made an effort to insure, even after his death, that the papers would retain editorial autonomy and would fulfill their journalistic responsibilities to their local communities.

Born to Joseph Charles and Maria Brooks Gannett on 15 September 1876, Frank Ernest Gannett (pronounced Gan-*nett*) entered the world in a farmhouse in western New York's Finger Lakes district, some forty miles from Rochester, a city where he would spend much of his adult life. Perhaps because of poor health resulting from a Civil War injury and due to the poor agricultural quality of his land, Joseph Charles Gannett was never a prosperous farmer. His wife and five children were forced to help with the farm chores and find outside employment to maintain an adequate livelihood. Frank Gannett began supplementing the family income at the age of nine, when he took a job delivering Rochester newspapers to subscribers in the town of Blood's Depot, where the Gannetts then resided. After his father gave up farming and turned to the hotel business, the family moved during the next few years to various small towns in the region. No matter where he went, the boy always managed to keep himself gainfully employed, usually by selling newspapers.

When he had sold all the newspapers the population of the town of Wallace could support, he expanded his income with other business ventures. There were few subscribers in the town's northern section, Gannett discovered, because many of the inhabitants understood very little, if any, English. He noticed that when they wrote to their relatives in Italy, they had difficulty in printing the names and addresses on the envelopes. Gannett had a Rochester company make up rubber stamps bearing those names and addresses. The workers eagerly purchased the rubber stamps, and young Gannett's income increased. By the time he was twelve, Gannett had entered into another profitable enterprise, involving the collection of animal skeletons that littered the town. After finding a company that would pay fifty cents for every 100 pounds of bones shipped, Gannett hired several other boys to help him with the gathering and hauling; the employees were paid with candy and nickels. Thus went Gannett's first experience as an employer. Other of his business undertakings included gathering and selling berries to Rochester markets, and peddling a book about a broken dam that had resulted in the loss of over 2,000 lives in a nearby town. While carrying on all these business schemes, Gannett was a cornet player in and leader of a boys' band, played catcher on a baseball team, and kept up his studies with an eye toward becoming a newspaper reporter.

When his family moved to another town during his high school years, Gannett took up lodging at the Bolivar high school principal's house so as not to disrupt his education. To help pay his room and board, he performed odd jobs at a local hotel. As a temporary bartender, Gannett saw firsthand the evils of alcoholic beverages consumed to excess, and he vowed to do whatever he could to oppose them. "I saw liquor make a lot of good men bad, but I never saw it make any bad man better," he said later. "After watching booze ruin men, I made up my mind that if I ever got a chance I would fight it." The opportunity presented itself years later, and he kept his promise.

As his newspaper route grew, he was required to spend more time making the rounds. To save time, he spent some of his hard-earned money on a new "safety" bicycle—that is, one with wheels of equal size, as opposed to the era's standard variety with a large front wheel and small back wheel. This penchant for new and efficient inventions later made Gannett one of the first in his business to adopt new typesetting and photoengraving techniques.

At the principal's urging, prior to graduation Gannett took the New York State Board of Regents

Frank Gannett

annual examination and earned the highest score ever recorded for a high school student up to that time. After graduation, he worked as bookkeeper for two local firms in order to save money for further education. When a congressman he knew offered Gannett an appointment to the West Point military academy, he was tempted to accept. However, because his mother, as the wife of a permanently disabled war veteran, disliked the military, he opted instead to compete for a scholarship to Cornell University in Ithaca, New York. His efforts on the examination earned him a scholarship worth $200 each year for four years. Prior to setting out for Ithaca in the fall of 1894, Gannett mastered typing and shorthand to aid him in his quest to be a newspaperman. At Cornell, freshman Gannett landed five jobs to provide for his room, board, and spending money. Since Cornell had no school of journalism, he concentrated on a liberal arts curriculum. Again he was able to find time for sports and music, and he was also elected campus correspondent for his class on the college newspaper, his first actual reporting job. Later he became a paid campus correspondent for the *Ithaca Journal*, a newspaper he would later own. The job taught him what it was like to be without complete journalistic independence: the *Journal*, he discovered, had a list of persons whose names could not appear in the newspaper, even if they were involved in newsworthy events. Most of those blacklisted were businessmen who did not advertise in the paper, while advertisers received preferential mention. Gannett resented the policy bitterly.

Throughout his college days, Gannett was involved in newspaper reporting. His stories were carried by papers in cities as far away as Boston, Philadelphia, and Chicago as a result of his use of queries to generate interest in Cornell events. So successful was he that he had to hire some fellow students to help handle the workload. In the summer he again peddled books; he also wrote articles, at first without pay, for the *Herald* in Syracuse, the city where his parents had finally moved. At school, he was business manager for two college magazines. By the end of his fourth year, Gannett had earned not only a bachelor's degree but also savings of $1,000.

After working as a reporter for the *Herald* during the summer of 1898, Gannett decided to return to Cornell in the fall for a master's degree. Once there, he became so busy in supplying campus news to the newspapers he had served as an undergraduate that he was unable to register for or attend classes. The following semester brought another postponement of his studies in the form of an offer from Cornell president Jacob Gould Schurman. Schurman was chairman of a commission appointed by President William McKinley to make recommendations on how the Philippine Islands should be governed, and he wanted Gannett to serve as secretary to the group. Gannett accepted the position and learned Spanish to aid him in performing his duties. At the completion of the commission's study, Gannett was offered the same position on a second Philippines Commission headed by William Howard Taft, who was then an Ohio judge. On Schurman's advice he turned it down to pursue his newspaper ambitions. He may also have turned down the post because he had become intensely anti-imperialist after coming to know the Filipinos, and believed that they should not be governed by outsiders. His knowledge of Spanish enabled him to translate into English, at Schurman's request, the 1896 novel *Noli Me Tangere* by José Rizal. The novel exposed Spanish oppression and misrule in the Philippines and served as a catalyst in the indepen-

dence movement. The translation was published in the United States as *Friars and Filipinos* (1900) and earned Gannett a note of congratulations from Theodore Roosevelt. On his return from Manila in 1900 Gannett was offered the post of city editor on the *Ithaca News* by a Cornell professor who had just purchased that newspaper. He accepted, and discovered that the *News*, like the *Journal*, had strong political ties and catered to its advertisers. He bent every effort to make the *News* independent politically and financially, because he felt that this was the only way it could fulfill its obligation to expose corruption and other ills in the community. This philosophy earned him enemies among local advertisers but strong supporters among the readers.

Once he had gotten the editorial side of the newspaper on the right track, Gannett turned his energies to the business end. He developed an accounting method that enabled him to determine, on a daily basis, whether the newspaper was making or losing money. He became more and more convinced that in order to have independence, a newspaper must be healthy financially, and he made the *News* financially strong. The owner, however, wanted even more financial success, and prepared to increase the newspaper's printing facilities in anticipation of receiving government printing contracts that had been promised him by a politician. Gannett felt that conducting business on the basis of politics and preferential treatment was unethical and could jeopardize the newspaper's independence. Unable to work out a compromise between their philosophies, in 1905 Gannett and the *News* ended their five-year alliance, during which time Gannett had not only strengthened the newspaper editorially and financially, but had advanced to the positions of managing editor and business manager through his dedication and hard work.

Gannett worked briefly in New York as a subeditor for *Leslie's Weekly*, a pictorial magazine that was losing its once phenomenal popularity. When a friend of the magazine's publisher began searching for someone to edit a similar publication he intended to establish in Pittsburgh, Gannett's name was mentioned, and he was offered the position. The magazine, the *Pittsburgh Index*, was expensive to publish, and realizing that this might cause it an early death, Gannett looked for a way to get back into the newspaper field. The opportunity came in May 1906 when, on his way to visit his family in Ithaca, Gannett was asked if he would like to buy a half interest in the *Elmira* (New York) *Gazette* for $20,000. Gannett had only $3,000 in his savings, but he obtained bank loans solely on his good reputation for an additional $7,000. He presented the cash and a note for the remaining $10,000 to the owner, who accepted the offer. Thus, at the age of twenty-nine, Gannett became part-owner of a newspaper. Gannett was in charge of the editorial functions while his new partner, Erwin Davenport, handled advertising and circulation.

Not long after Gannett took over, his veteran reporter, Frank Tripp, was enticed away by Elmira's other evening daily, the *Star*. The *Star*'s editor was a young doctor named Woodford J. Copeland after the two owners of the *Star*: his father, Seymour Copeland, and James F. Woodford. Gannett and the younger Copeland agreed that the town could not support both of their papers, and since they shared the same philosophy of political independence, they decided to merge the two. The result was the establishment in 1907 of the *Star-Gazette*, with four owners—Gannett, Davenport, Woodford, and the senior Copeland—each with one-fourth of the stock. Gannett and young Copeland handled news and editorials as joint managing editors.

Gannett soon developed the editorial policy he would later advocate for all his newspapers: editing of stories down to the bare essentials in order to pack as much news as possible into the allotted space. He did this because he felt readers wanted more news, and with the high cost of newsprint, this was the most economical way to serve them. The newspaper did not stay out of politics, although it owed allegiance to no party: when a candidate was supported editorially by the *Star-Gazette*, it was because of his stand on the issues and not because he was a Democrat or a Republican. The *Star-Gazette* did not accept liquor advertisements, not only because of Gannett's personal feelings but primarily because of the establishment of the *Elmira Herald*, which was backed financially by liquor interests and politicians. It became the rival of the *Star-Gazette*, whose owners saw in the *Herald* the kind of biased reporting that could be caused when a newspaper is controlled by special interests. The *Herald* even offered two of Gannett's star reporters, Tripp and Francis W. Ross, the opportunity to buy a half interest in and run the rival paper. Tripp, ultimately one of Gannett's most trusted friends and business associates, declined the offer. Ross, however, accepted but returned to work for Gannett fifteen years later. The rivalry lasted some seven years before the *Herald* folded and left the *Star-Gazette* the only evening daily in Elmira.

About this time, Gannett heard that the *Ithaca Journal*, for which he had been a reporter during his college days, was for sale. Again he obtained bank loans to make the purchase, but this time he became the sole owner. Although he remained in Elmira, he made his presence known to the editorial staff in Ithaca by doing away with the blacklist he had so disliked during his prior affiliation with the *Journal*.

The *Star-Gazette* prospered so much that Gannett, Davenport, and Copeland decided to expand their operation. Two Rochester newspapers, the *Union and Advertiser* and the *Times*, competing evening dailies, were purchased and merged in 1918 to become the politically independent *Times-Union*. Gannett and Davenport moved to Rochester, where Gannett took over the editorial duties and Davenport became the business manager of the *Times-Union*. In 1920, Gannett married Caroline Werner, the daughter of a New York court of appeals judge. She gave birth to a baby girl in 1922, and several years later the couple adopted a son.

Three years after the *Times-Union* purchase by Gannett and his partners, the paper had become prosperous. Again they decided to expand their operations, this time in Utica, where they purchased the Democratic *Observer* and the Republican *Herald-Dispatch*, merging them to form the independent *Observer-Dispatch*.

In 1921 Rochester was invaded by William Randolph Hearst, who established the *Journal* in competition with the *Times-Union*. While Hearst tried to lure readers with flashy journalism and expensive giveaways, Gannett and company stuck to their hometown style of reporting and managed to keep up a good fight. This exposure to the Hearst papers, which were completely controlled by a central office, taught Gannett the limitations of such an operation. He realized more than ever the importance of knowing the local community and having someone actually on the spot to make decisions. In the meantime, the Gannett partners bought two morning papers in Elmira, the daily *Advertiser* and the Sunday *Telegram*; this left them owning all of that city's newspapers in 1923. At this point they decided to name their newspapers the Empire State Group. About the same time, Hearst tried to buy the *Times-Union*. Since Copeland and Davenport were nearing retirement, they were tempted to sell out; but first they allowed Gannett the chance to buy their stock, which he did. Thus, in 1924, Gannett became the sole owner of six newspapers. To finance the deal, he formed the Gannett Company, Inc., and sold bonds, which were later converted to preferred stock. Gannett insisted that his newspapers be called the Gannett Group—not "chain"—and he did much to insure that they did not operate in the same manner as most newspapers belonging to a chain. Gannett's newspapers neither looked alike nor read alike; he insured this with his policy of local autonomy and his edict that "a newspaper will serve its city if its publisher and its editor and all its employees are home folks who understand the city and its people."

Gannett continued to increase his newspaper holdings: between 1925 and 1929 he bought ten papers in the New York cities of Newburgh, Beacon, Ogdensburg, Malone, Rochester, Albany, and Brooklyn (he sold the *Brooklyn Eagle* in 1931), as well as in Plainfield, New Jersey, and Hartford, Connecticut.

Gannett wanted to insure that the Gannett Group maintained a spotless reputation. His actions demonstrated this conviction when it was alleged in 1929 that the International Paper Company, a subsidiary of the International Paper and Power Company, had lent him money to purchase several newspapers on the condition that the Gannett papers would support private ownership of electrical power companies. In fact, no such condition (nor any other) had ever been stipulated, and Gannett actually held the opposing view on ownership of power companies. Although his actions had been entirely legitimate, even the slightest doubt of his good intentions was reason enough for Gannett to quickly repay the International Paper loan. He made the arrangements while en route to Washington, D.C., where the Federal Trade Commission was conducting hearings on public utilities. He got off the train in Philadelphia, phoned the paper company for an appointment, returned to New York, and obtained permission to repay the loan. Then he procured a four-month loan from a New York bank for the entire amount and remitted a check to International Paper for the balance owed before resuming his trip. In Washington Gannett voluntarily allowed himself to be questioned, and he left the hearings completely exonerated. His employees greatly helped him accomplish the timely and expensive transfer of debt by purchasing more than a million dollars' worth of preferred stock to repay the bank loan within the short payback period.

As demonstrated by his employees' willingness to help him out of a tight spot, Gannett was a responsible employer who was deeply concerned about the welfare of those who worked for his newspapers. He felt that they should share in the success of the corporation, and so he set up a profit-sharing wage dividend.

Between 1934 and 1937 Gannett added four more newspapers to his group; all of these except the *Danville* (Illinois) *Commercial-News* were located in New York State. As he made new acquisitions he freed the editorial staffs of any political or financial dependence they may have had prior to his takeover. He insisted on their journalistic freedom, including freedom from being organs for his own views. Although Gannett was a Republican, some of the newspapers he owned would generally support Democrats. Gannett felt that they were within their rights to do so, and he made it clear that this was his policy. In 1932 his *Hartford Times* supported the Democrat Roosevelt for president, while Gannett and his *Rochester Times-Union* supported the Republican Hoover. When questioned about this, he issued the following statement:

> The staff of the *Times* knows that I have never dictated its editorial policy. I have said that if I wanted to make a statement I would do so in the news columns or over my signature. Frequently the editorial policy of the *Times* has been directly contrary to my own personal views.
>
> I believe that this is a wholesome situation. It would be a sad day for America if all our newspapers expressed only one view, or if they were owned by one person who insisted on expressing only his opinions or used the papers to promote his personal advantage.
>
> I regard the *Times* not as a personal possession to use as I may see fit; I regard it as a great institution whose first object is to serve its community. By our efforts to give it good management, to develop it and promote it as a great newspaper, we have accomplished much in making its position even more secure.

To insure that his papers would continue his policies after his death, Gannett in 1935 established the Frank E. Gannett Newspaper Foundation, Incorporated (renamed the Gannett Foundation in 1981), which would become the controlling owner of common stock upon his death. Any surplus earnings were to be used for public, educational, charitable, and philanthropic purposes.

Gannett also became personally involved in politics on several occasions. He disagreed with Roosevelt's New Deal and helped to defeat some of its measures. He agreed to be the running mate of Idaho senator William E. Borah in 1936 in Borah's unsuccessful bid for the Republican presidential nomination; soon after, he was an unsuccessful nominee for governor of New York.

Gannett viewed Roosevelt's attempt to expand the Supreme Court and pack it with his supporters as a threat to the separation of powers, and in 1937 he formed the National Committee to Uphold Constitutional Government. The committee conducted a massive mail campaign, the first on such a large scale, to obtain support to defeat the bill. The committee's efforts paid off, but the Senate investigated its lobbying activities and sought to prove that illegal Republican contributions had supported it. No such proof was found, because the committee was in fact legally supported by small contributions from thousands of concerned citizens of varying party affiliations. Thus Gannett was again unjustly accused of having disreputable associations, and he was again found innocent.

Although Gannett's papers were only involved in a few strikes, he felt there were too many such actions among American wage earners, especially when compared with their counterparts in Great Britain, where there were relatively few strikes. He decided to find out the reasons for himself, so he spent the summer of 1938 in England studying British labor practices and relations. When he completed his research, he coedited with Dr. Benjamin F. Catherwood a symposium of the opinions of prominent Englishmen on labor relations.

In 1939 Gannett resigned as chairman of the National Committee to Uphold Constitutional Government, but remained as a board member. Later renamed the Committee for Constitutional Government, the committee again generated much publicity when it took up the fight for passage of a Constitutional amendment which would limit taxes on incomes, estates, or gifts to twenty-five percent. Also in 1939 he lost in his try for the Republican presidential nomination, although he received thirty-three votes on the first ballot.

Often a contributor to his newspapers, Gannett collected his articles in three books: *Britain Sees It Through* (1944), *The Fuse Sputters in Europe* (1946), and *Winging Round the World* (1947). In 1952, at Gannett's suggestion, the Gannett Newspaper Foundation created the Gannett Newspaper Carrier Scholarships, Incorporated, to aid deserving newspaper boys.

Gannett held honorary degrees from Wesleyan University (M.A., 1929), Alfred University (LL.D., 1935), Hobart College (LL.D., 1937), Oglethorpe University (Ph.D., 1939), Keuka College (Litt.D., 1939), Hartwick College (LL.D., 1941), the University of Brunswick (LL.D., 1951), and Syracuse University (LL.D., 1953). The National Council of Veterans of Foreign Wars

awarded Gannett a gold citizenship medal in 1940. In 1951 the American College Public Relations Association awarded him and Mrs. Gannett the Fairbanks Award for "their outstanding service to higher education." In the same year, they were jointly awarded the Civic Medal of the Rochester Museum of Arts and Sciences, the Museum Association, and its Allied Councils. Gannett also received the Founder's Award from the Rochester Institute of Technology in 1952. Gannett served as president of the New York Associated Dailies in 1916 and 1917 and of the New York State Press Association in 1917 and 1918. He helped organize in 1919 the New York State Publishers Association and served as its president for seven years. He was instrumental in 1922 in establishing the Empire State School of Printing, an institution supported by the state's publishers. He served as a director of the Associated Press from 1935 to 1940. Other positions he held include member of the board of directors of the Rochester Institute of Technology, trustee of Keuka College, trustee of Cornell University, president of the Cornellian Council from 1925 to 1926, member of the Finger Lakes State Park Commission, and vice-chairman of the Republican National Committee in 1942.

Although he had discovered in 1924 that he was a diabetic, Gannett managed to conquer the handicap through adherence to a strict diet and exercise routine. He suffered a stroke in 1948 but recovered sufficiently to run his newspaper business until 1955, when he received a compressive spinal fracture in a fall on a stairway in his home. Bedridden most of the time after the fall, Gannett retired as president of Gannett Company, Inc. in April 1957. The Gannett Group then included twenty-one newspapers in sixteen cities in four states—thirteen of them in New York and one each in Connecticut, Illinois, and New Jersey. In fifteen of the cities, the Gannett papers had no competing paper. The total also included four radio stations and four television stations in five cities in three states.

When he died on 3 December 1957 at the age of eighty-one, Frank E. Gannett had never actually established a newspaper of his own. However, he will be remembered among journalists for the improvements he made in so many existing publications and for his championing of a free and responsible press, a policy best summed up in his own words: "First, a newspaper, to suit me, must be clean, one that I would be willing to have my mother, my own sister or my daughter read, and one that I myself need never apologize for. It must be honest in its news columns; it must be fair to all; it must stand for justice to all and fight injustice always; it must stand for progress and reform; it must oppose with all its power special privilege and expose corruption. It should never be afraid, no matter what may be the consequences, of attacking wrong wherever it may appear, remaining devoted at all times to the public welfare."

Biography:
Samuel T. Williamson, *Frank Gannett* (New York: Duell, Sloan & Pearce, 1940); revised as *Imprint of a Publisher: The Story of Frank Gannett and His Independent Newspapers* (New York: McBride, 1948).

References:
"Ambitious Publisher," *Scholastic*, 36 (11 March 1940): 10;

"Frank E. Gannett: He Accumulated Newspapers to Make Them Strong," *Editor & Publisher*, 90 (7 December 1957): 11, 66, 68, 70;

"Frank Gannett Estate Set at $5.6 Million," *Editor & Publisher*, 93 (8 October 1960): 57;

"Gannett Cited for Work in Education," *Editor & Publisher*, 84 (1 September 1951): 16;

"Gannett for Gannett," *Time*, 35 (22 January 1940): 22;

"Gannett Restates in Will Principles to Guide Group," *Editor & Publisher*, 90 (14 December 1957): 12;

"Gannett's Forty Years," *Newsweek*, 27 (17 June 1946): 69-70;

"Gannett Will Lists Individual Bequests," *Editor & Publisher*, 90 (14 December 1957): 90;

Harry Gray, "What Kind of President Would Gannett Make?," *Liberty*, 17 (27 April 1940): 39-42;

"Publisher Insures Future of His Newspaper Chain," *Newsweek*, 6 (5 October 1935): 34-35.

Elizabeth Meriwether Gilmer
(Dorothy Dix)

(18 November 1861-16 December 1951)

Whitney R. Mundt
Louisiana State University

MAJOR POSITIONS HELD: Reporter and columnist, *New Orleans Picayune* (1894-1901), *New York Journal* (1901-1916); syndicated columnist, Wheeler Syndicate (1916-1923), Ledger Syndicate (1923-1942), Bell Syndicate (1942-1949).

BOOKS: *Fables of the Elite*, as Dorothy Dix (New York: Fenno, 1902);

Mirandy, as Dorothy Dix (New York: Hearst's International Library, 1914; London: Low, 1914);

Hearts à la Mode, as Dorothy Dix (New York: Hearst's International Library, 1915);

My Joy-Ride round the World, as Dorothy Dix (London: Mills & Boon, 1922); republished as *My Trip round the World* (Philadelphia: Penn, 1924);

Mirandy Exhorts, as Dorothy Dix (Philadelphia: Penn, 1925);

Dorothy Dix–Her Book: Every-day Help for Every-day

People (New York & London: Funk & Wagnalls, 1926);

Mexico, as Dorothy Dix (Gulfport, Miss.: C. Rand, 1934);

How to Win and Hold a Husband, as Dorothy Dix (New York: Doubleday, Doran, 1939).

PERIODICAL PUBLICATION: "Mother Confessor to Millions," *Times-Picayune New Orleans States Magazine*, 5 May 1946, pp. 6-7.

Sister to all the world: that is how Dorothy Dix wished to be known. But more properly speaking she was a mother confessor—one to whom the troubled fled for advice and consolation. She was the archetypal Mary Worth, the progenitor of Abigail Van Buren and Ann Landers, the standard by which the advisors of today's lovelorn generation may be judged. She was said to have had the largest following of any newspaper columnist in her day.

But it was a difficult road by which she gained this pinnacle.

Elizabeth Meriwether was born 18 November 1861 in Montgomery County, Tennessee, on a farm whose land crossed over into Todd County, Kentucky. She was the firstborn of three children of William Douglas and Maria Winston Meriwether; Mary was the middle child and Charles Edward was the youngest. The three children were cared for by the black house servant, Mammy.

Elizabeth's education was her voracious reading in the Meriwether library, assisted by a tutor who arrived at the Woodstock farm intending to remain a day or two but prolonged his stay for several years. He was kin to the Meriwethers, but more important for young Elizabeth, he was an educated man who shared with her his knowledge of history and literature. Before she was twelve, she later recalled, she had read Shakespeare and Dickens and had made the acquaintance of other great English poets and novelists. Reading was not her sole activity; she was something of a tomboy and enjoyed riding horses and tracking animals in the woods.

When Will Douglas Meriwether left Woodstock with his family, settling in Clarksville, Tennessee, during Elizabeth's adolescence, she lost her tutor but found a school—the Female Academy of Clarksville—where she developed a fluency in writing "compositions." This talent and her early introduction to the masters of literature equipped her for a life of enforced self-employment which, as yet, she did not anticipate.

Following graduation she was sent to Hollins Institute in Botetourt Springs, Virginia, for six months of higher education. It was six months of humiliation for the little farm girl whom the upper-class girls liked to call "Lizzie" in their deprecating way. Elizabeth stayed long enough to win that year's composition medal before returning to Clarksville, her formal schooling ended.

Maria Meriwether, always sickly, had died when the children were young, and Will Meriwether had taken a new wife, Martha Gilmer Chase, a widow related distantly to the Meriwether clan. On a trip to Illinois to visit the Gilmer family, Elizabeth met her stepmother's brother, George. He was ten years older than Elizabeth and must have impressed her with his worldly ways; at any rate, when he proposed marriage some time later, she accepted, and they were married in 1882. It was not a romantic match: as she reported, somewhat flippantly, "Having finished school, I tucked up my hair and got married, as was the tribal custom

Elizabeth Merriwether Gilmer (Dorothy Dix)

among my people." Nor was it a happy match: George Gilmer was emotionally unstable—unable to hold either his temper or a job. But Elizabeth Meriwether Gilmer conceived it to be her wifely duty to bear up under the stress and to follow her husband whither he went. She managed to tolerate a rather nomadic existence at a near-poverty level, accepting also his abusive behavior, until in 1893 she suffered what today would probably be called a nervous breakdown.

She returned to her family, and at a doctor's suggestion they took her to the Mississippi Gulf Coast, where the white sand and the warm breeze and the melodious lap of the waters might soothe her troubled mind. They took a cottage at Bay St. Louis, near New Orleans. It was the most propitious choice they could have made: next door resided the owner of the *New Orleans Picayune*, and as a result of that chance circumstance Elizabeth Meriwether Gilmer was metamorphosed into Dorothy Dix. As she told the story: "Ill health had sent me down to the Mississippi Gulf Coast to recuperate and my good angel directed my aimless footsteps to a cottage in Bay St. Louis next to that in which Mrs. E. J. Nicholson, the owner and manager of the *Picayune*, lived. Naturally, we became acquainted and in time I showed her hesitatingly a little story that I had written but had never dreamed of offering for publication because I then held the artless belief that only those who could write like Dickens or Thackeray could ever break into print. She read this story and said: 'Why, child, you can write!' and she bought it, paying me three whole round silver dollars for it, which I still believe is the largest sum ever paid for a piece of fiction, no matter what the publishers of 'Anthony Adverse' and 'Gone with the Wind' may say to the contrary."

Encouraged, Gilmer sat on Mrs. Nicholson's doorstep and described a passionate yen to be a newspaperwoman. Mrs. Nicholson instructed her in the elimination of grand and flowery adjectives, then took her to the "big, rambling, dingy old *Picayune* building," where she was introduced to the managing editor, Major Nathaniel Burbank.

"Major," said Mrs. Nicholson, "I've brought you a girl to help you with your work." He replied that he did not require a canary to help him. However, he consented to let her sit at a little desk on the other side of the room and "constituted himself a one-man school of journalism," pouring out all the wealth of his knowledge and experience to his pupil. She was paid five dollars weekly, and she began by collecting vital statistics "and wept when my rivals had one more death or birth than I had reported. I learned to write headlines and edit syndicate stuff, then just beginning to be used. I reported women's meeting[s], and church conventions, and was literally a wow at funerals at which I made a great hit because I was always so dissolved in tears I was thought to be a member of the family and placed at the head of the coffin. I did all the odd jobs of reporting that nobody else wanted to do and I started writing for the Sunday paper the articles about men and women and husbands and wives and love and children that are now known as the Dorothy Dix Talks." She adopted the pseudonym "Dix" in memory of "Mr. Dicks," a Negro who had once helped the Meriwether family; "Dorothy" was selected for alliterative purposes. After a while, Major Burbank decided that she should have a regular column, which he named "Sunday Salad."

Her columns and stories began to be reprinted here and there—with or without credit—and soon there were inquiries about whether the *Picayune* might permit its Miss Dix to publish in the pages of other papers as well. It would, and Dorothy Dix took a step into syndication on a small scale.

In 1900, Rudolph Block of Hearst's *New York Journal* wrote for permission to use some of her articles, which were to appear on the editorial page next to those of such journalistic lions as Ambrose Bierce. She granted the request with some trepidation, but she need not have worried: her work was highly enough thought of to prompt a telegraphed offer of employment on the *Journal*. She rejected the offer, partly out of anxiety, partly out of loyalty to Major Burbank, and partly, no doubt, out of consideration for her unstable husband, who had joined her in New Orleans and had established a reasonably successful business in the distillation of turpentine products. The *Journal* was not to be deterred, however. Soon another telegram arrived, asking if Dorothy Dix could track down the notorious temperance crusader Carry Nation, then smashing saloons in Kansas, and spend a week or two drawing a word portrait of the hatchet heroine. With the blessing of the *Picayune*, she went. The stories she sent to the *Journal* were precisely what the editors wanted: dramatic accounts tersely written in a personal style; they were played up in graphic fashion, with bold headlines and profuse artwork. Then the *Journal* made Gilmer another offer, which she felt at greater liberty to accept because Nathaniel Burbank had died of a heart attack. In 1901 she became another star in Hearst's galaxy of writers and reporters.

Her tenure with the *Journal* was a lucrative one: William Randolph Hearst was not one to skimp on salaries or expenses when there was someone or something he wanted. But he received his money's worth from Dorothy Dix. She produced, besides her column, short stories, beast fables, homely philosophy in the Negro dialect she had learned at the knee of her Mammy, and serious reportage of the nation's most sensational murders and trials. Her output was so prodigious, according to her biographer, Harnett T. Kane, that in one sevente-day period she wrote fifty-two articles totaling some ninety thousand words. For this she was well compensated, Kane writes: initially the *Journal* paid her an annual salary of $5,000—more than the governor of Louisiana was making. Ultimately, as a syndicated writer, she earned over $90,000 yearly—more, according to Kane, than any other contributor, man or woman.

During Gilmer's first year with the *Journal* she was asked to cover a murder in New Jersey. Denied permission by the authorities to see the defendant, a stepmother charged with beating to death her husband's three-year-old child, Gilmer sought out the woman's family and again was frustrated. Returning to her one-horse carriage, she asked the driver to ride around a bit while she debated what to do, but he volunteered the information that he had known the woman and could introduce Gilmer to others who were familiar with the circumstances of the case. He also proposed to her on the spot, but she responded gently that she was wedded to her work. Gilmer's stroke of good luck was transposed into a story replete with fact and insight. Her editors were delighted, and her career as the *Journal*'s female crime reporter was launched. Among the stories she covered was the sensational love-triangle murder case involving architect Stanford White, playboy Harry K. Thaw, and showgirl Evelyn Nesbit. Gilmer's coverage of the trial went beyond mere reportage of fact; it was analytical, interpretive, almost sociological. Her reporting of the trial won for Gilmer a new contract calling for $13,000 a year—the most money paid to any woman in the United States.

Simultaneously she was producing the beast fables published in the *Journal* during her first year there and later collected in her first book, *Fables of the Elite* (1902). These pieces are allegories in which animal characters act out domestic incidents, at the conclusion of which the omniscient narrator draws a moral. For example, "The Bear Who Loved the Tigress" describes a courtship in which the bear promises a life of ease without want to the tigress if she will become his mate. She recognizes a good thing when she hears it, and so they are wed. Once they are married, the bear's ardor flags, leading the tigress to observe that what had promised to be a picnic had turned out to be a funeral. And so she finds means to amuse herself. "Moral: This Fable teaches that When a Man Ceases to Make Love to His Wife, Some Other Man Begins."

Gilmer was also writing articles under her real name, Elizabeth Meriwether Gilmer, and was being published regularly in Hearst's magazines, chiefly *Good Housekeeping* and *Cosmopolitan*. *Good Housekeeping* was the medium for her "Mirandy" series, which was published between 1910 and 1920. Although their brand of folk wisdom expressed in Negro dialect might be seen today as demeaning to blacks, in their day the "Mirandy" stories were popular enough to be a regular feature in *Good Housekeeping* and salable enough to be collected in two volumes in 1914 and in 1925. These were under the by-line of Dorothy Dix, although they purported to be conversations of Mirandy with other persons of her race.

The year after her first "Mirandy" book appeared, her first collection of advice columns was published under the inspired title *Hearts à la Mode*. All of the chapters dispense advice on domestic

relations in the guise of recipe instructions. Thus: "To Preserve Husbands" ("make a syrup of home comforts of three hundred and sixty-five good dinners a year. . . ."); "Deviled Mother-in-Law" ("the taste for Mother-in-Law is an acquired taste, like the taste for ripe olives. . . ."); "Minced Neighbor" ("the principal utensil that is needed is a sharp tongue, whetted to a razor edge, and a pair of curious and spying eyes"). In manner, these resemble the earlier fables, with their trenchant and satiric wit. But the setting has been moved from the yard to the kitchen.

In 1916 she signed a lucrative contract with the Wheeler Syndicate which permitted her to write three columns a week instead of six, and to quit writing the tales of murder and mayhem that had been her steady task for sixteen years with the *Journal*. Signing with Wheeler also made it possible for her to realize a long-held dream of traveling in the Orient, and in 1917 she took her husband, whose mental health was becoming more precarious, on a trip to Japan, China, and Java. For her the trip was a blissful relief, but it aggravated George Gilmer's condition. She supported him through alternating bouts of melancholia and anger until he left their New York apartment for Florida and an extended separation. Soon afterward, she moved back to New Orleans, where she was able to work at home for the rest of her career.

Gilmer remained with the Wheeler Syndicate

Gilmer in Japan on her trip around the world in 1923

until 1923, when she signed with the Ledger Syndicate. Her shift in loyalties coincided with another trip across the Pacific. She began in Hawaii, crossed over to Japan, and then went to Korea, Manchuria, and China. She visited Hong Kong, Singapore, Java, and Burma and completed her tour with a trek across India. She recorded these travels in *My Trip round the World*, published the following year. Her tourist essays are models of astute observation and piquant humor. Now sixty years old, they still can be read as guides to the traveler.

In 1924 Gilmer had reached the apex of her profession: as Dorothy Dix she had achieved recognition in both crime reporting and in advice to the lovelorn; now she was a world traveler whose observations were worthy of being expensively bound and illustrated in a full-length volume. In 1925 her second volume of "Mirandy" essays was published under the title *Mirandy Exhorts*. The following year her most important book appeared—a collection of advice essays in her own person, without the artificial devices of Negro wisdom, allegorical beast fables or "recipes."

Dorothy Dix—Her Book: Every-day Help for Every-day People (1926) sold well enough to go into three editions, but its importance is, in part at least, the result of her introduction, "My Philosophy of Life":

> I have had what people call a hard life. I have been through the depths of poverty and sickness. I have known want and struggle and anxiety and despair. I have always had to work beyond the limit of my strength. . . .
>
> Yet I have no pity for myself; no tears to shed over the past and gone sorrows; no envy for the women who have been spared all that I have gone through.
>
> For I have lived. They have only existed. I have drunk the cup of life down to the very dregs. They have only sipped at the bubbles on the top of it.
>
> I know things they will never know. I see things to which they are blind. It is only the women whose eyes have been washed clear with tears who get the broad vision that makes them little sisters to all the world.
>
> This of itself is a compensation for many sorrows, but I have more. I have proved myself to myself. I know that I have the strength to endure and the courage to carry on, and that I will not be craven enough to run up the white flag, no matter what other difficulties I may be called upon to meet. . . .
>
> *I am not afraid of poverty* because I have been poor and I know that poverty has its

consolations and brings you pleasures that money cannot buy. Nor am I afraid to support myself. I have earned my bread and butter for many years. I know the joy of work and I know that to a woman, just the satisfaction of knowing that she is self-supporting turns her crust into angel's food. . . .

> I have learned in the great University of Hard Knocks a philosophy that no woman who has had an easy life ever acquires. I have learned to live each day as it comes, and not to borrow trouble by dreading to-morrow. It is the dark menace of the future that makes cowards of us. I put that dread from me because experience has taught me that when the time comes that I so fear, the strength and wisdom to meet it will be given me. . . .
>
> I have learned not to expect too much of people and so I can still get happiness out of the friend who isn't quite true to me, or the acquaintance who gossips about me, and I can even find pleasure in the society of those whose motives I see through.
>
> Above all I have acquired a sense of humor, because there were so many things over which I had either to laugh or cry. And when a woman can joke over her troubles instead of having hysterics, nothing can ever hurt her much again.
>
> So I do not regret the hardships I have known because through them I have touched life at every point. I have lived. And it was worth the price I had to pay.

When she wrote those words, Gilmer was nearly sixty-five; no doubt she believed her career was coming to a close. But she had before her nearly twenty-five productive years of journalistic work.

In the fall of 1926 she was lured back into crime reporting by her syndicate, which asked her to cover the trial of Frances Hall, widow of the Reverend Dr. Edward W. Hall, pastor of an Episcopal church in New Brunswick, New Jersey. He had been found, shot to death, beside the body of Eleanor Mills, under an apple tree in a lovers' lane. Her body had been mutilated, and both bodies had been covered with their love letters to one another. It was a sensational story to which only Dorothy Dix could do justice. Headlines promoted her reporting on the Hall-Mills case, and she responded with personalized, analytical stories which predicted that Mrs. Hall would not be found guilty. Gilmer based her expectations on her knowledge of human nature, as she read the faces of the witnesses and the jurors, and she was right. The murders remain unsolved.

Gilmer had reached a stage of her life when honors were beginning to come her way—but painful moments were coming as well. She was chosen a member of the board of directors of the *Times-Picayune*, but as she was beginning to enjoy that distinction she received word that her estranged husband was heading to New Orleans in anger. His relatives met his train and took him to an asylum, where he could be cared for without danger to his wife. In June 1927 she received the doctor of letters degree from Tulane University in recognition of her contributions to the quality of life in the United States. The following year New Orleans celebrated "Dorothy Dix Day"—a means by which the ordinary folk of the city could honor her. In January 1929 she received word that George had died at the asylum; she had not seen him since his abrupt departure from their home in New York over ten years earlier. In 1930 her father, who had made his home with her at least part of the time for several years, died at the age of ninety-three. The next year Oglethorpe University granted her an honorary degree. Thus, within six years two of the persons most closely connected with her had died, she had received two honorary degrees, and she had been recognized both by her peers and by her readers. For a woman of her age, the swift pace of events must have been exhausting.

Nevertheless, she continued to write with her customary swiftness and fecundity, and in 1939 Doubleday, Doran brought out her seventh and last book, *How to Win and Hold a Husband*, a collection of essays advising the lovelorn. Many of the essays were written in response to letters she had received from readers of her column, and the problems her readers asked her to solve shared enough common themes that she was able to compile "ten rules for happiness" which she offered as medicine for almost any kind of heartache. Frequently, upon request, she reprinted those rules, or some version of them, in her column.

First: HAVE A WILL TO HAPPINESS. Seek happiness as intelligently and energetically as you would any other definitely good thing you desire. . . .
Second: LAUGH THINGS OFF. There are so many things in life over which we must either laugh or weep, so many things that are either tragedies or jokes, according to what we make of them. . . .
Third: ENJOY WHAT YOU HAVE NOW. Most people miss all pleasure in what they have because their whole attention is focused on wanting something they haven't got, and so they lose even the happiness they could have. . . .
Fourth: DON'T EXPECT TOO MUCH. Don't think you have the right to the whole earth with a blue ribbon tied around it. . . .
Fifth: DON'T ASK TOO MUCH. Don't be greedy. Don't expect to get more than your fair share. . . .
Sixth: DON'T BORROW TROUBLE. Don't spoil the sunshine of today by dreading the storm that may come next week or next month or next year. . . .
Seventh: THINK OF OTHERS. Someone has said that we all find it easy to bear the sorrows of our friends. That may be cynically true, but it is also altruistically true. . . .
Eighth: CULTIVATE THE HUMAN RELATIONSHIP. When all is said happiness does not consist in any particular environment or condition of life or any one big thing that happens to us. It lies in the little everyday things that the poorest and the humblest may have as well as the rich and great. . . .
Ninth: KEEP BUSY. Work. An idle brain is the devil's workshop in which he manufactures all of the thirty-seven varieties of misery, plain and fancy. . . .
Tenth: REMEMBER THAT YOU GET OUT OF LIFE JUST EXACTLY WHAT YOU PUT INTO IT. If you put envy and spite and bitterness into life you will get out of it only a bitter brew. But if you even put a modest amount of cheer and optimism and courage and faith into your life you will get out of it the wine of happiness.

This advice was derived from a lifetime of acquired wisdom, based on thousands of letters imploring her advice. It is said that toward the end of her career her column was carried in 215 newspapers on three continents and read by 30 million people. Many of the letters were poignant, and some were desperate. But the ones she saved to share with friends were generally funny, though not meant to be so. Excerpts from some of these letters have been collected by Ella Bentley Arthur, Gilmer's confidential secretary for many years, and published under the title *My Husband Keeps Telling Me to Go to Hell* (1954). For example:

My husband keeps telling me to go to Hell. Have I a legal right to take the children?
*   *   *
I have been an adolescent for the past six or seven years. When will I grow up to be an adultress?
*   *   *

Gilmer in her New Orleans home circa *1940 (Charles F. Bennett)*

He asked me to marry him Saturday night and I was all ready to do so but he didn't come so my evening was spoiled.

* * *

Will you please tell me all the facts of life and send me the addresses of some soldiers and sailors.

* * *

I stutter very badly. Should I tell my fiance?

* * *

My husband beats me, bloodies my nose, bruises my arms, slaps me hard enough to leave prints on my face, kicks my legs and leaves me alone at night. I know this doesn't sound like much, Miss Dix, but you can't imagine how I dislike it.

* * *

Should I tell my husband the baby I am expecting is not his? Please answer before Labor Day.

* * *

I have been a decent girl, as far as I remember.

* * *

I read the other day that every 7th child born into the world was Chinese. Oh, please help me, Miss Dix; I am about to have my 7th child!

* * *

Should we have our marriage consummated by a photographer?

* * *

I have six children by my present husband, who is of a cold and frigid nature.

* * *

We just got married on the spree of the moment.

* * *

When I returned home I found my girl in a house of prostitution, and, of course, Miss Dix, in your profession you know what that means.

* * *

I don't want to date him, but he is continually coming over and rapeing at my door.

* * *

I had a date with my boy friend and on the way home he said let's get married or something. But I read your column, Miss Dix, and I said, let's get married or nothing.

Gilmer continued to dispense her sage advice well past the time of life when most folks are content to retreat into themselves. In 1949, after over a half-century of column writing, she conceded that she was unable to continue. A year later she suffered a stroke, and for the last twenty-one months of her life she was hospitalized.

In the lead obituary of 17 December 1951, the *New York Times* recorded the passing of Dorothy Dix:

> NEW ORLEANS, Dec. 16—Mrs. Elizabeth Meriwether Gilmer, known as Dorothy Dix to millions of readers of her newspaper column, died of a heart ailment here this afternoon in Touro Infirmary. Her age was 90. She had been in the hospital for more than a year. . . .
>
> Probably more women sought advice from Dorothy Dix than from any other woman of her day. For more than fifty-five years her name appeared over the column in which she gave advice to the lovelorn and which was noted for its sympathy, common sense and realism.
>
> Her mail exceeded 2,000 letters a week at the height of her popularity, and it was her pride for many years that she herself attended to as much of this correspondence as possible. . . .
>
> Her long career as a newspaper writer included twenty years as one of the most widely known woman reporters of her time. But it was as a columnist giving advice to men and women beset with problems of the heart that she gained her greatest fame.

For the *New York Times* the obituary was appropriately dispassionate. But to her readers the dispassionate tone was ironically inappropriate, for Dorothy Dix, counselor to the lovelorn, was the most compassionate of women.

Biography:
Harnett T. Kane and Ella Bentley Arthur, *Dear Dorothy Dix: The Story of a Compassionate Woman* (Garden City: Doubleday, 1952).

References:
Ella Bentley Arthur, ed., *My Husband Keeps Telling Me to Go to Hell* (Garden City: Hanover House, 1954);
Herman B. Deutsch, "Dorothy Dix Talks," in *Saturday Evening Post. Post Biographies of Famous Journalists*, edited by John E. Drewry (Athens: University of Georgia Press, 1942), pp. 29-47;
Hildegarde Dolson, "Dear Miss Dix—This Is My Problem," 46, *Reader's Digest* (February 1945): 39-42;
Ishbel Ross, *Ladies of the Press* (New York: Harper, 1936).

Harry J. Grant
(15 September 1881-12 July 1963)

Richard M. Brown

MAJOR POSITIONS HELD: Publisher, *Milwaukee Journal* (1919-1937); director, Associated Press (1940-1941).

Harry J. Grant combined business acumen with editorial vision to make the *Milwaukee Journal* one of the outstanding twentieth-century newspapers. Although Grant took no direct part in the handling of news, he set the standards in that area and required that they be met. He cherished editorial excellence and freedom above all other newspaper virtues. "We don't trade with politicians," he once said. "We don't make commitments. We must have freedom, freedom, freedom—not to be willful or bigoted or swell headed or to give us delusions of grandeur, but so the *Journal* can act entirely as it sees best for the community." His statement reflecting similar sentiments, "Go for the truth and to hell with right or left," remains the core of the paper's editorial policy. A shrewd businessman, Grant made the *Journal* the largest newspaper in Wisconsin both in content and circulation, and for several years it carried more advertising than any publication in the world. He rejected the opportunity to acquire sole

Harry J. Grant (Milwaukee Journal)

ownership of his creation and was one of the pioneers of employee ownership of newspapers.

Harry Johnston Grant was born 15 September 1881 in Chillicothe, Missouri, to Benjamin T. and Ida Belle Johnston Grant. His father was a horse dealer and a widely known horseman in northern Missouri, and the family was moderately prosperous until his death. Ida Grant tried to support the family by teaching dancing in St. Louis, but after his freshman year in high school, Grant went to work for the Vandalia Railroad at five dollars per week, first as a messenger and then as a clerk. He spent six years at railroading and working as an invoice clerk in the East St. Louis, Illinois, stockyards.

Tutoring himself at night, he was able to enter Harvard as a special student in 1903. Although lack of funds forced him to quit after a year, he managed to return in 1905. He got his introduction to publishing as an advertising salesman for student publications before dropping out to try to set up an export-import business in New York. Failing at that, he went to work with N. W. Ayers, an advertising firm and publisher of business directories. He was hired away from Ayers by one of his early accounts, the Rubberset Brush Company, and became their

representative in London. There he met Dorothy Glide Cook of Pittsburgh, and they were married in 1910; Dorothy Grant died in 1923. They had one daughter.

Also in 1910, Grant returned to the United States, where he became involved in the establishment of the rayon industry as manager of the American Viscose Company's first plant. The business prospered and he was able to retire in 1912. He found the life of a gentleman of leisure unattractive, however, and a year later joined O'Mara and Ormsbee, a national advertising firm handling newspaper placement. As vice-president in charge of their Chicago office, he became acquainted with Lucius W. Nieman and got to know his *Milwaukee Journal* well. When the *Journal*'s advertising manager retired in 1916, Nieman offered the position to Grant.

At thirty-five, Grant began his journalistic career on a newspaper that was in trouble: Nieman, who had built the paper from a three-week-old partisan political organ to a substantial afternoon daily, was aging and ailing; and the *Journal*'s editorial stand favoring intervention on the side of the Allies in World War I had earned it a Pulitzer Prize but had shattered its popularity in strongly German Milwaukee. Grant brought to the paper not only fresh business acumen but, surprisingly when one considers his background, a kind of editorial vision that complemented and extended the principles Nieman espoused. Grant was firmly committed to the idea of newspaper independence: when one advertiser sought special treatment in the news section because of his $50,000 advertising contract, Grant canceled the contract. Within three years he became vice-president and treasurer of the Journal Company and a stockholder, and then became one of the company's three directors and publishers.

Under Grant, the *Journal* became a model of thoroughness with detailed local coverage and comprehensive national and world news, employing the wire services, the *New York Times* news service, and its own correspondents in New York and Washington. The *Journal* ran 100 pages on weekdays and up to 400 pages on Sunday. When important news came in after edition time, a peach-colored supplement called the "peach sheet" was given to the readers free of charge. The *Journal* pioneered new methods of photography and printing to set high standards in run-of-the-press color. Cash was paid for improvements in plant and equipment to forestall charges that a lender could influence the paper. A lively entertainment package, the daily four-page Green Sheet, was instituted with comics, pictures, features, columns, and puzzles. Although the *Journal* had a monopoly in the afternoon field and could offer advertisers run-of-the-press color and sophisticated services, its advertising rates were kept very low as the paper expanded. The Journal Company also entered the broadcasting field with WTMJ radio, a top money-maker, and later, with the arrival of commercial television, instituted WTMJ-TV.

There was an aggressive agility about Grant. Standing 5 feet 8¾ inches, he carried over 200 pounds on his chunky figure and moved with an unrepressed vitality and force. When he walked with others, invariably he was half a step ahead. A skilled mimic, he could recount a conversation among several people, reproducing speech mannerisms, inflections, and gestures in a way that would set his companions roaring. His charisma, pugnacious vitality, and confident management were inspiring to those who worked on the *Journal*, but even more, their confidence in Grant was based on the totality of his dedication to the *Journal*, its employees, and the community it served.

One of his greatest contributions lay in achieving a plan for employee ownership. Although he backed the concept of employees owning interest in the newspaper as early as 1919, he was unable to bring his ideas to fruition until after the death of Nieman in 1935. At that time, Grant held 400 of the 2,000 shares, the Nieman estate held 1,100, and the heirs of Lloyd T. Boyd, the paper's first business manager, held 500. Nieman's will provided for sale of the stock not necessarily to the highest bidder but to the buyer who, in the judgment of the trustee, would best carry out Nieman's ideals. Moses L. Annenberg, owner of the *Philadelphia Inquirer* and a racing wire service, made a firm cash offer of $4,250 per share. Although Grant had financial backing that would have permitted him to buy the Nieman stock on his own account, he refused the offer, stating that he would resign and leave if employee participation could not be achieved. The negotiations were complicated by Mrs. Nieman's death, which left the bulk of her estate, including her return from sale of the stock to Harvard University. In the court battles that followed, Miss Faye McBeath, Nieman's niece and an heiress to her uncle's estate, backed Grant's plan of employee ownership. The Journal Company bid $3,500 per share and, following a lengthy hearing which brought out that Grant would make no personal gain in the transaction, Harvard acceded to the lower purchase price.

Transfer of control of the multimillion-dollar corporation to employees who had few assets was a complex matter that took more than ten years. Grant began by having the Journal Company buy and retire 800 shares of its own stock. Next, each share was split a hundredfold to bring its price to $35. Each of the major stockholders—Grant, McBeath, and the Boyd estate—provided 10,000 shares for the employee pool. One of the early worries was that individual employees might sell their shares, creating an opportunity for an outside speculator to gain control. To avoid this risk, Grant had the shares held in trust by the Journal Company and the employees bought units of beneficial interest which allowed them all benefits of the stock except the right to sell to anyone other than the company. The first twenty-five percent interest was made available in 1937. Purchase by employees was assisted by bonuses and dividends. By the tenth anniversary of the unit shareholders plan, the employees had bought forty percent of the company; at the celebration, Grant announced the release to them of an additional fifteen percent to give them majority control. On that occasion he said, "We know that employee stock ownership serves the best interests of the company and will secure to the community the benefits of a locally owned newspaper. Actual stock ownership is something greater than profit sharing, annual bonuses or work guarantee plans which can be dissolved at the discretion of management."

Grant gave up the day-to-day control of the *Journal* in 1937, fearing that age would eventually make him hard and stubborn, but he remained chairman of the board. Grant enjoyed the almost unbounded confidence of the *Journal*'s employees. When the American Newspaper Guild first sought to organize the paper's workers, Grant said, "The time has come for you to choose between my management or the Guild—you can't have both." The guild was rejected.

Although Grant belonged to many organizations and clubs, he rarely took an active part in them, always fearing that such activities might cloud his vision of the course the *Journal* should follow. However, he found it impossible to avoid the many honors his career brought him both from within and without the newspaper industry. The University of Wisconsin and Marquette University awarded him honorary doctorates, and the universities of Missouri and Minnesota awarded him medals for his distinguished journalistic achievement; he also received numerous civic honors. But it was characteristic of Grant that the two most treasured honors came from the rank and file of the *Journal* employees. One was a lifetime membership in the International Printing Pressmen and Assistants' Union of North America (AFL), awarded at the fiftieth anniversary dinner of Milwaukee Local 7. The union's citation read, in part, that The Milwaukee Journal's employees' pension fund "contemplates the continuation of good will, which is so important to the life of any industry. It is a further recognition of the principle that there is a community of interest between management and labor through their association in producing newspapers." The other was a portrait of Grant to be hung in the lobby of the Journal Building. This was a 1937 project that originated with the employees, and of which no executive was aware until pledges for payment had been collected. When an employee committee called on Grant to ask him to sit for the portrait, he was visibly delighted but said he did not want them to spend their money on it; either he would pay or the directors would authorize the funds. A linotype operator promptly put him in his place: "Mr. Grant, this is to be our portrait. This is one time you are not running the show."

Grant's later years were divided between his Milwaukee apartment and winters in Florida, where he owned a home on Miami Beach's Rivo Alto Island and a seventy-one-foot yacht, *High Tide*. Death came quietly for the eighty-one-year-old Grant at his Milwaukee apartment on 12 July 1963. Although in ill health for months with the infirmities of age, he was bedridden for only a week. His son-in-law, Donald B. Abert, succeeded him as chairman of the board.

Reference:

Sidney Kobre, *Development of American Journalism* (Dubuque, Iowa: Brown, 1969), pp. 654-656.

Roy W. Howard

Alfred Lawrence Lorenz
Loyola University of New Orleans

BIRTH: Gano, Ohio, 1 January 1883, to William A. and Elizabeth Wilson Howard.

MARRIAGE: 14 June 1909 to Margaret Rohe; children: Jack Rohe, Jane.

MAJOR POSITIONS HELD: Reporter, *Indianapolis News* (1902); sports editor, *Indianapolis Star* (1902-1905); assistant telegraph editor, *St. Louis Post-Dispatch* (1905-1906); news editor, *Cincinnati Post* (1906); general manager, Publishers Press Association (1906-1907); New York manager, San Francisco manager, general manager, president and general manager, chairman of the board, United Press (1907-1920); business manager, Scripps-McRae League (1920-1922); chairman of the board, Scripps-Howard Newspapers (1922-1936); president, Scripps-Howard Newspapers (1936-1953); editor/publisher, *New York Telegram* (1927-1931), *New York World-Telegram* (1931-1950), *New York World-Telegram and Sun* (1950-1960).

DEATH: New York City, 20 November 1964.

It was said of Roy W. Howard, president of Scripps-Howard newspapers, that "to see him stride through a city room on one of his best days is to see an army with banners." Short, with a large round head that made him seem even shorter, he dressed in plaid or striped suits with hand-tailored checked shirts of bright yellow, green, or even purple, with a bow tie of the same material, and a fresh boutonniere in his lapel. Until the 1940s he carried a walking stick, and pince-nez hung from his vest.

He was also a one-man army of journalistic talent. Even as president of Scripps-Howard at the company's acme he could and did roll up his shirtsleeves and plunge into a breaking story. "I have never been one of those birds who could sit back and say, 'All right boys, go get them,' " he once said. "I have to say, 'All right boys, let's go get 'em.' "

Roy Wilson Howard was born on New Year's Day 1883 in Gano, Ohio, a village near Cincinnati, where his grandmother operated a tollhouse. His father was a brakeman for the Big Four Railroad. When the boy was seven his family moved to Indianapolis, and there he grew to manhood. As he

Roy W. Howard

matured he acquired a dry, Hoosier twang, a vocabulary of profanity, and a sharp tongue always ready with an insult. He also developed habits of hard work and thrift.

While Howard was a student at Manual Training High School in Indianapolis, his father suffered from tuberculosis; he died during Howard's senior year. Much of the family's income went to pay for medical care, and to help out, young Howard rose early every morning to deliver the *Indianapolis Star;* in the afternoons he threw the *Indianapolis News.* He also acted as school correspondent for the *News,* and working at space rates he could make up to thirty-five dollars each week. Later Howard would acquire a reputation as a man tight with a dollar, and some traced his penuriousness to these youthful experiences. On his graduation in 1902, the *News* found it more economical to hire him as a full-time reporter for eight dollars a week, but within a short time the ambitious Howard

had jumped to the *Star* as sports editor at a salary of twenty dollars a week.

Many newspaper journalists at the turn of the century regarded Joseph Pulitzer's *New York World* as the paramount newspaper in the country, and Howard agreed with that assessment. It had matured out of its "yellow" adolescence, and in both news columns and editorial pages it was an intelligent, brightly written, vigorously edited newspaper—a newspaper for everyone. Howard wanted to work for the *World,* and at twenty-two, still little more than a cub reporter, he went to New York to apply for a job with the newspaper. He was turned down.

When the direct method failed, Howard thought he might have better luck approaching the *World* indirectly, and in 1905 he became assistant telegraph editor of Pulitzer's *St. Louis Post-Dispatch.* When the editor's job opened a short time after he started, Howard thought he deserved the position, but he was passed over in favor of a man he called "an old crock" of thirty. He quit and left St. Louis for Cincinnati, where he was hired as news editor of the *Post,* owned by E. W. Scripps. The move began a lifelong relationship with the Scripps organization.

If Howard had a problem as an editor it was that he was too much the reporter. He preferred the rough-and-tumble excitement of gathering news to the more sedate business of making assignments and editing what others had gathered and written, and he was soon out reporting again. He persuaded John Vandercook, the editor of the *Post,* to transfer him to New York as a special correspondent for the Scripps-McRae League of newspapers, and in 1906, when Scripps bought the Publishers Press Association, a cooperative news-gathering organization with headquarters in New York, Howard was named general manager.

Publishers Press Association became one of the three news-gathering combines servicing the Scripps-McRae League. While its reporters ranged the East, reporters for the Scripps-McRae Press Association and the Scripps News Association, both established in 1897, covered the Midwest and the Pacific coast, respectively. In 1907 Scripps combined the three into the United Press Associations, with Vandercook as president. Vandercook named the dapper and energetic young Howard as New York manager.

Howard was the perfect choice to spur the fledgling organization. He was everywhere and doing everything in those first days. He hired reporters, developed story ideas, made assignments, and filed the news. He went on the road to organize new United Press bureaus. He sold the service to new clients.

Early in 1908, Vandercook had Howard temporarily exchange assignments with his counterpart on the West Coast, Max Balthasar, so that each could see the operations in the other's territory. Howard headed across the country with his first stop at San Diego, where he was to meet Scripps, who lived near there on his Miramar ranch.

Edward Willis Scripps was a formidable man, as Howard undoubtedly knew. When Howard met him, Scripps was fifty-four, a self-styled "damned old crank" who had taken up residence at Miramar eighteen years earlier. From there he directed his chain of newspapers, most of them evening papers aimed at the workingman.

Scripps had gotten into newspapering at the age of nineteen when his half brother James E. Scripps established the *Detroit Evening News* and enlisted him as both reporter and circulation manager. Finding newspaper work to his liking, the younger Scripps went to Cleveland in 1878 and, operating out of a back-alley shack, began publishing the *Penny Press* in competition with the town's three well-established newspapers. The *Penny Press,*

Howard's eccentric employer, E. W. Scripps, aboard his yacht

an unlikely survivor in that field, nevertheless flourished. Five years later Scripps took control of the *Cincinnati Post,* which the family had started in 1880, and soon began increasing circulation as he had done in Cleveland. The *Penny Press* and the *Post* became the flagship newspapers for a chain of "people's newspapers," low in price and having a mass appeal, which Scripps went on to establish in the growing industrial cities of the Midwest.

The big, burly Scripps lived a "man's man" existence at Miramar. He drank perpetually—at one time, he claimed, a gallon of whiskey a day—much of it consumed at a poker table under a cloud of cigar smoke. Before he was fifty he was half blind; his limbs had shrunk; his hands shook so badly he could hardly write. But he kept a close watch on his empire, and it was customary for employees to pay a visit to the ranch when they were on the West Coast. First, however, they ordinarily stopped at a San Diego dry goods store to outfit themselves like Scripps in khaki shirt and trousers and Western boots.

Howard did not observe this custom: when he showed up at Miramar he was outfitted in his usual fashion—a shirt with a bold stripe, a gaudy necktie, spats, and a derby cocked jauntily on his head. Scripps had been meeting with a group of other men not long before, all of them much shorter than he, and when the five feet, seven inches tall Howard was introduced he muttered, "My God! Another little one?" "Perhaps another little one, but this time a good one," Howard replied in his retelling of the story in later years. Scripps remembered Howard at that first meeting as "a striking individual, very small of stature with a large head and striking countenance, and eyes that appeared to be windows for a rather unusual intellect. His manner was forceful, and the reverse from modest. Gall was written all over his face. It was in every tone and every word he voiced. There were ambition, self-respect, and forcefulness oozing out of every pore in his body." Brash though Howard might have been, Scripps liked him. The publisher found him "so completely and exuberantly frank . . . that it was impossible for me to feel any resentment on account of his cheek." He also liked the impression he received that "that young man will never get indigestion from licking my boots."

Howard went north to San Francisco after his visit with Scripps, and through the spring of 1908 he showed that his self-confidence was not misplaced. He worked the editorial desk, overseeing the rewriting of stories coming into the newsroom from the West Coast bureaus. The stories were, for the most part, simply rehashed accounts from morning newspapers in cities in which bureaus were located—yesterday's news. Howard demanded that his rewrite men comb the stories carefully for any "today angle" that would make the news fresh. Howard also ordered that the flow of information from the Midwest be stepped up. At the turn of the century, with the country still little populated between the Mississippi River and the Pacific coast, the United Press did not have enough client newspapers to justify the cost of a leased wire from the East to the West, so stories had to be sent out from Chicago in the form of abbreviated telegrams. The system could not have been particularly satisfying to the clients; it certainly did not satisfy Howard. He ordered the skimpy telegraph service augmented with more substantial material—whatever could be put together in advance of planned events—mailed out from Chicago. The packets, delivered to the office each day, allowed the rewrite men to flesh out the skeletonized telegrams and, thus, to greatly expand the service. Ever the admirer of the *World*, Howard also encouraged his staff members to turn out brightly written news stories and features. He required every bureau to file at least one "human interest" story every day.

While Howard was in California, Vandercook, on a visit to the Chicago bureau, suffered a ruptured appendix. Howard was called back to New York; by the time he arrived Vandercook had died. Scripps installed Howard as general manager of the United Press.

Howard took firm control immediately. He insisted that Unipressers, as his employees came to be known, stand firm against the well-established Associated Press and compete with the older service, not imitate it. "We've got to do things that have never been done before," he told them. "Study the way Pulitzer and Hearst humanize the news in their papers. Get interviews with people in the news. People are usually more interesting than the things they are doing. Dramatize them." The approach paid off. United Press began to compete, and it began to make money.

In 1909, Howard married a fellow journalist, Margaret Rohe. She had been a feature writer for the *New York Morning Telegraph* and the *World* and had published some light verse, but she had tired of newspapering and had gone on the stage. Howard had met her in New York, and when he was in Europe developing the fledgling overseas service for UP she was in London in the cast of *The Chorus Lady*. They renewed their acquaintance and were married there. They had two children, Jack and Jane.

In January 1912, Howard was named president and general manager of the United Press. One of his first efforts as president was to continue to expand the organization as a worldwide news agency. The Associated Press had broad coverage overseas through links with various quasi-official news services, including Reuters, the British news agency. But Howard considered that arrangement a weakness, not a strength. When Baron Reuter approached him in 1912 with an offer to drop the AP in favor of the United Press, Howard turned Reuter down. The United Press would cover the news itself, wherever the news occurred. To that end, he traveled to Europe in the years preceding World War I to recruit young Americans living there to serve as correspondents, and when the war came, the United Press was prepared to cover it.

Howard was no desk-bound news general during the war but personally headed overseas in 1914 to supervise the United Press staff buildup. He went back two years later as a reporter, and he was everywhere. In the trenches, in government offices, wherever anything of importance was happening, there was Howard, "three jumps ahead of the news." He scored a clear beat on every other reporter by winning a rare interview with the crown prince of Germany and another with David Lloyd George, the British prime minister, in which Lloyd George announced that Britain intended to prosecute the war to the finish. The exclusive interviews won Howard a good measure of celebrity.

Another episode won him a good measure of notoriety. It began as he was making preparations to sail from France to America on 7 November 1918. He was lunching at Brest with Adm. Henry B. Wilson, commander of American naval forces in France, who told him that an armistice agreement ending the war had just been signed and showed him a dispatch to that effect which had been sent out by Capt. R. H. Jackson, United States naval attaché at the American embassy in Paris. Wilson made arrangements for Howard to get to a telegraph office, and from there Howard sent the news back to United Press headquarters in New York:

URGENT ARMISTICE ALLIES GER-
MANY SIGNED ELEVEN SMORNING
HOSTILITIES CEASED TWO SAFTER-
NOON SEDAN TAKEN SMORNING BY
AMERICANS HOWARD SIMMS

In the meantime, word of the armistice had filtered

through Wilson's officers to sailors, and then to the people of Brest, and all gathered in the streets to celebrate. Among the merrymakers were the censors who should have read Howard's dispatch. Wrongly assuming that they had, the telegraph operator clicked out the message. In accordance with a company rule that all United Press messages from France had to bear the name of William Philip Simms, the United Press manager in Paris, Howard had signed the two names. Because the manager's name was on the dispatch, the United Press cable desk in New York wrongly assumed that the message came from Paris via Brest, not directly from Brest, and that gave it greater credibility. The desk editor put a "flash" priority on the story and sent it out over the wires to client newspapers across the country. As the wonderful news spread throughout the United States and the other Allied nations, millions joined the people of Brest in pouring into the streets to celebrate. But wonderful though the news may have been, it was premature; or, as the United Press State Department correspondent at the time put it, the exclusive was "too damned exclusive." The real Armistice was still four days away, on 11 November.

Howard may have been too eager to get the story on the wire; some critics have said that he should have checked it further. But Admiral Wilson would have to have been considered a reliable source of official information, and he later stated publicly that he had believed the information to be official and that Howard had sent it in good faith. President Woodrow Wilson's aide Col. Edward House, who was in Paris at the time, cabled Secretary of State Robert Lansing on 8 November that "most of the officials in Paris and practically every non-official person here believed yesterday that the armistice had been signed." House exonerated Howard of any wrongdoing, telling Lansing that it was "perfectly clear that the United Press was not at fault in this matter, and that the fault, if any, lies with Jackson or the French official who started the rumor."

The incident soiled United Press's reputation for accuracy, and for a time readers in the United States were hard put to find any United Press dispatches in their newspapers. Even today the successor news service, United Press International, bears a slight reputation for inaccuracy. Howard himself shrugged off the incident. "In my opinion, no real reporter would have done otherwise in the circumstances," he said. When the matter came up in later years, Howard simply joked it out of the conversation.

That the incident had no serious detrimental effects is attested to by the fact that the United Press enjoyed another period of expansion in the postwar era. In the early years of the war it had secured some clients in South and Central America who had been dissatisfied with the self-serving war reportage of the European news services; following the armistice it was able to build on that core. Howard also planned the development of a service for European clients. In the period between the wars the United Press expanded from 21 bureaus with 267 clients to 104 bureaus with 1,350 clients.

Although he laid the groundwork for it, Howard was not to be directly involved in the major expansion. Scripps had other plans for him. He tapped Howard to join his son Robert P. Scripps in running the Scripps-McRae League of newspapers. In June 1920, Howard resigned as president of United Press to take up duties as general business manager of the league. Within two years, Robert Scripps gave him equal power in both editorial and business matters, and in 1922 the name of the organization was changed to Scripps-Howard Newspapers, with Howard as chairman of the board of directors.

By the time Howard made the shift, E. W. Scripps and his partner Milton A. McRae had built one of the largest chains of the day. It was made up of more than thirty newspapers in cities across the country, including Cincinnati, Cleveland, Akron, and Columbus, Ohio; Terre Haute and Evansville, Indiana; Memphis, Knoxville, and Nashville, Tennessee; and Pueblo, Colorado.

Howard and the younger Scripps set about consolidating the business arrangements of the organization. Over the next decade they closed out newspapers in Des Moines, Sacramento, Terre Haute, and Baltimore. They established other newspapers in Washington, Fort Worth, Birmingham, and Norfolk. In a departure from the Scripps tradition of founding, rather than buying, newspapers, the pair bought papers in Youngstown, Albuquerque, Buffalo, Pittsburgh, and Indianapolis. In the following ten years they eliminated newspapers in Toledo, Oklahoma City, San Diego, and Buffalo. They merged other properties: in Akron, for example, they pulled together the *Press* and the *Times* in 1925; the following year they joined two Knoxville newspapers, the *News* and the *Sentinel;* and they merged still others in Birmingham, Memphis, Denver, Columbus (Ohio), and El Paso. In 1929, Scripps-Howard published twenty-four newspapers, but the number had dropped to nineteen by 1940; at the time of Howard's death in 1964 the chain consisted of twenty-nine newspapers.

Howard led the company into other ventures, as well. Scripps-Howard bought the Newspaper Enterprise Association in 1921 and began to build it into the nation's largest news and feature syndicate. Two years later Scripps-Howard acquired United Features Syndicate, another feature service. In 1924 Acme Newspictures was set up as a subsidiary of UP and NEA; through Acme Howard became one of the pioneer promoters of radio transmission of news photos.

Howard was said to be a hard bargainer in making purchases. In 1925, negotiations with Ross Walker for the *Akron Times* were snagged over a difference of $10,000. Howard took out a quarter, gave it to Walker, and told him to flip it, with the winner getting the $10,000. Walker tossed the coin, won, and put the quarter in his pocket. Later Howard said he did not mind losing the $10,000 but complained that "the cheapskate took my quarter."

Howard was considered a cheapskate by many of his employees. He was said to be a string and paper saver, and reporters told of seeing him pick up a discarded piece of carbon paper from the floor and put it on a desk. Scripps-Howard was known for paying among the lowest salaries in the newspaper business.

Howard was not one to shrink from any confrontation. He dropped the Associated Press membership of the *Memphis News-Scimitar* when he acquired that newspaper in 1926. The AP retaliated: when Scripps-Howard bought the *Rocky Mountain News, Denver Times,* and *Knoxville Sentinel* later in the same year, the AP directors cancelled their memberships. Howard would not bend. He was unwilling, he said, "to accept a so-called membership in an organization collecting and selling a basic journalistic commodity—news—in a highly competitive field, if acceptance of that membership must be at a price of our own right of disposal of our own property."

The most controversial of all of Howard's dealings came about in 1931. While E. W. Scripps lived, he resisted entering any city larger than Cleveland or Cincinnati, while Howard believed that the chain ought to be represented in New York. In 1927, the year following Scripps's death, Howard bought the *New York Telegram;* four years later, he jumped at the chance to buy Pulitzer's *World.* Pulitzer's will assigned his heirs "the duty of preserving, perfecting, and perpetuating the *World* newspaper, in the same spirit in which I have striven to create and conduct it, as a public institution, from motives higher than mere gain." The heirs did not

perpetuate it in the same manner; on the contrary, they fast depleted its resources. When Howard showed up with an offer of $5 million, they sold, and the courts upheld their breaking of the elder Pulitzer's will. In the meantime, a group of *World* employees scraped together $1 million and made a desperate bid for the newspaper, but Howard won out—at the same time winning the animosity of many of those employees, who harbored bitterness toward him for years. Howard killed the Sunday and morning editions of the *World* and merged the evening edition with the *Telegram* to form the *New York World-Telegram.* (In 1950, with the acquisition of the *Sun,* the paper became the *World-Telegram and Sun.*)

Howard took charge of the *World-Telegram* as editor, and he prided himself on his journalistic capabilities. Even as head of Scripps-Howard he thought of himself as "a thirty-eight dollar a week reporter, in there daily, pitching hay with the rest of the hands," albeit at a somewhat lofty level. While other Scripps-Howard reporters might have been out interviewing mayors and police chiefs, Howard in 1933 won the first interview with Japan's Emperor Hirohito ever granted an American journalist. In 1936, Howard gained access to the Kremlin and an interview with Premier Joseph Stalin of the U.S.S.R. Reporting on the latter achievement, *Literary Digest* headed its story "Super Reporter." The magazine judged Howard to have "the most highly trained and natural news sense of any man alive today."

Others were more critical. Howard had a galaxy of journalistic stars on the *World-Telegram,* including cartoonist Rollin Kirby and columnists Heywood Broun, Westbrook Pegler, Raymond Clapper, Hugh Johnson, and even Eleanor Roosevelt, whose famed "My Day" column was syndicated by Scripps-Howard's United Features Syndicate. But Howard proved to be a heavy-handed editor, and Broun, Pegler, and Kirby all ultimately left the newspaper in disagreements with Howard over the views they expressed in their work. Broun, perhaps the most celebrated of Howard's "op ed" page columnists, broke with Howard in 1939. An outspoken liberal while Howard was becoming increasingly conservative, Broun was told that his columns would be edited when they were "unsatisfactory." Kirby, who had won three Pulitzer Prizes for the *World* before Scripps-Howard acquired it, left the fold the same year after his cartoons were tampered with. Pegler, in 1944, went over to the Hearst newspapers in a disagreement over editing of his columns, even though Howard generally agreed

Front page of Howard's New York World-Telegram, *which he formed by merging the Pulitzers'* Evening World *with the Scripps-Howard* Telegram *in 1931.*

with Pegler's antilabor and anti-Roosevelt stance.

Robert Scripps died at the age of forty-two in 1938, and under the terms of E. W. Scripps's will, Howard, William W. Hawkins (vice chairman of the board of Scripps-Howard), and George B. Parker (editor in chief of the newspapers) were to serve as trustees until the sons of Robert Scripps were twenty-five. There was no question that Howard was in charge.

E. W. Scripps had considered himself "the advocate of that large majority of people who are not so rich in worldly goods and native intelligence as to make them equal, man for man, in the struggle with the wealthier and more intellectual class." With Howard at the helm, however, there was a noticeable shift in the chain's editorial positions. While Scripps had supported Theodore Roosevelt's reforms and his newspapers had come out for Robert M. La Follette and the Progressives in the 1924 presidential campaign, in 1928 the Scripps-Howard newspapers supported Herbert Hoover, although it was reported that a majority of the editors favored the Democrat Al Smith.

Howard and his editors supported Franklin D. Roosevelt in 1932 and 1936, but broke with him in 1937 over FDR's plan to enlarge the Supreme Court. In 1940, Howard became one of the prime movers behind the Republican candidacy of Wendell Willkie. Before the election, the president asked Howard to go to South America to talk to influential persons he knew there to try to find out what could be done about fifth column activities in Latin countries. Howard refused, saying that he did not have the sort of contacts Roosevelt imagined him to have. At a news conference Roosevelt publicly attacked Howard as the only person who had refused to help him in his program for national defense. In the fall of 1940, when Howard was on a trip to the Far East, the U.S. minister to Thailand, Hugh G. Grant, reported that Howard complained that the president had put him into an impossible situation, since he was a supporter of Willkie. Howard also charged, according to the diplomat, that the president was "down and out physically and mentally." As a result, the president considered ways to discredit Howard. The following year, when Howard was ill with a heart ailment, Roosevelt sent him a letter in which he said, "There couldn't be anything wrong with your heart. That always has been in the right place. It has just been your head, Roy." Howard's subsequent relations with Roosevelt soured to the point that the president ordered that Howard was not to be issued a passport or allowed to go overseas as a foreign correspon-

dent. After 1940, Howard supported only Republican candidates for president.

More damning in the eyes of Howard's critics than his support of the "wrong" presidential candidates was what they saw as the opposition of the Scripps-Howard newspapers, formerly friends of the workingman, to union activities. The newspapers editorially fought the American Newspaper Guild and the Wagner Act; they published a series exposing alleged Communist activities within the Congress of Industrial Organizations, a series labeled "Red-baiting" by some. The chain also attacked the New Deal's Works Progress Administration. The liberal *Nation* charged that "the chain had become in effect a Republican institution, subject to occasional moments of liberal heresy."

Some traced Howard's rightward shift to his shift from the news to the business side of journalism. In a profile of the publisher in the *New Yorker* in 1941, A. J. Liebling pointed out that the advertising contracts of the three *World* editions were based on a circulation of less than 300,000 when Scripps-Howard bought them, but that when the *World* was merged with the *Telegram* the combined circulation was about 500,000. Howard had to raise the advertising rates to reflect the new circulation, and many advertisers left the newspaper. To woo them back, Howard moderated the paper's traditional liberalism.

Howard condemned himself in the eyes of his critics when, in a speech in Denver, he said, "we come here simply as news merchants. We are here to sell advertising and sell it at a rate profitable to those who buy it. But first we must produce a newspaper with news appeal that will result in a circulation to make that advertising effective. We shall run no lottery." The result was not only a change in political philosophy but, in the view of some, a watering down of the journalistic product. Robert Bendiner and James Wechsler wrote in the *Nation* in 1939 that "Scripps published newspapers which were as journalistically colorful as they were editorially pugnacious, which viewed the world from the lowly side of the railroad tracks. Today the same newspapers are increasingly drab, spiritless, reconciled to the perspective of Park Avenue."

By the time those words were written, Howard was no longer chairman of Scripps-Howard; he had given up the chairmanship in 1936 but remained as president of the organization until 1953, when, at age seventy, he relinquished that post to his son, Jack. He remained active, however, as a director of the company and as chairman of its executive committee. He stepped down as editor of the *New York*

World-Telegram and Sun in 1960 and resigned the presidency of the newspaper in 1962. But he remained a major influence in the direction of Scripps-Howard's Newspapers, and he was at his desk in his office in Scripps-Howard headquarters at 200 Park Avenue on 20 November 1964, when he suffered a fatal heart attack.

The Scripps-Howard organization lost something of its vitality after Howard's death. In 1966, two years after his passing, the *World-Telegram and Sun* merged with two of its rivals, the Hearst Corporation's *New York Journal-American* and John Hay Whitney's *Herald Tribune,* to form the *World Journal Tribune.* The amalgamated newspaper lasted less than a year: it was shut down in May 1967. Other Scripps-Howard properties, most of them evening newspapers, also succumbed, primarily due to changing reading habits. By 1984, the chain held only fifteen daily newspapers. United Press International (UP had merged with Hearst's International News Service in 1958), after suffering economically for many years, was sold to private interests in June 1982, seventy-five years after its founding.

As the driving force behind the development of United Press and as the strong-willed director of the fortunes of the Scripps-Howard chain, Howard had exercised a broad influence on American readers. Some argued that while the Scripps newspapers had supported the cause of the American workingman, Howard's positions, especially his views on labor and social reform, were detrimental to the public welfare. On the other hand, he did not force-feed his ideas to his editors, who were free to cope with local issues as they saw fit. Neither was his chain doctrinaire on national and international matters; individual newspapers were allowed to endorse or oppose any idea or any candidate. Most important, perhaps, United Press and the newspapers had thrived under his leadership to provide the public with varied voices in the news and information marketplace, and that, in the long run, had been his aim.

References:

"Armistice: Documents Give True Story of Nov. 7 'Peace,' " *Newsweek,* 1 (8 July 1933): 26;

Robert Bendiner and James Wechsler, "From Scripps to Howard," *Nation,* 143 (13 May 1939): 553-556; (20 May 1939): 580-584;

Heywood Broun, "Roy Howard and the Guild," *Nation,* 143 (8 August 1936): 158;

Negley D. Cochran, *E. W. Scripps* (New York: Harcourt, Brace, 1933);

Gilson Gardner, *Lusty Scripps: The Life of E. W. Scripps* (New York: Vanguard, 1932);

"Journalistic Dynasty: Scripps-Howard Chain," *Time,* 27 (14 March 1936): 44-46;

A. J. Liebling, "Publisher," *New Yorker,* 17 (2 August 1941): 19-26; (9 August 1941): 20-29; (16 August 1941): 20-27; (23 August 1941): 23-30;

"Roy Howard: Super Reporter," *Literary Digest,* 121 (14 March 1936): 38-39;

E. W. Scripps, *Damned Old Crank: A Self-Portrait of E. W. Scripps Drawn from his Unpublished Writings,* edited by Charles R. McCabe (New York: Harper, 1951);

Scripps, *I Protest: Selected Disquisitions of E. W. Scripps,* edited by Oliver Knight (Madison: University of Wisconsin Press, 1966);

George Seldes, "Roy Howard and His Papers," *New Republic,* 95 (27 July 1938): 322-325;

Oswald Garrison Villard, "Scripps-Howard and the United Press," in his *The Disappearing Daily* (New York: Knopf, 1940), pp. 167-174.

Gerald W. Johnson

(6 August 1890-22 March 1980)

Michael Kirkhorn
University of Kentucky

MAJOR POSITION HELD: Editorial writer, *Baltimore Sunpapers* (1926-1943).

BOOKS: *The Story of Man's Work*, by Johnson and W. R. Hayward (New York: Minton, Balch, 1925);

What Is News? A Tentative Outline (New York: Knopf, 1926);

The Undefeated (New York: Minton, Balch, 1927);

Andrew Jackson: An Epic in Homespun (New York: Minton, Balch, 1927);

Randolph of Roanoke: A Political Fantastic (New York: Minton, Balch, 1929);

By Reason of Strength (New York: Minton, Balch, 1930);

Number Thirty-Six: A Novel (New York: Minton, Balch, 1933; London: Lovat Dickson, 1933);

The Secession of the Southern States (New York: Putnam's, 1933);

A Little Night Music: Discoveries in the Exploitation of an Art (New York: Harper, 1937);

The Sunpapers of Baltimore: 1837-1937, by Johnson, Frank R. Kent, H. L. Mencken, and Hamilton Owens (New York: Knopf, 1937);

The Wasted Land (Chapel Hill: University of North Carolina Press, 1937);

America's Silver Age: The Statecraft of Clay-Webster-Calhoun (New York: Harper, 1939);

Roosevelt: Dictator or Democrat? (New York: Harper, 1941); republished as *Roosevelt: An American Study* (London: H. Hamilton, 1942);

American Heroes and Hero-Worship (New York: Harper, 1943);

Woodrow Wilson: The Unforgettable Figure Who Has Returned to Haunt Us (New York: Harper, 1944);

An Honorable Titan: A Biographical Study of Adolph S. Ochs (New York: Harper, 1946);

The First Captain: The Story of John Paul Jones (New York: Coward-McCann, 1947);

Look at America: The Central Northeast (Boston: Houghton Mifflin, 1948);

A Liberal's Progress: Edward A. Filene, Shopkeeper to Social Statesman (New York: Coward-McCann, 1948);

Gerald W. Johnson

The Maryland Act of Religious Toleration: An Interpretation (Baltimore, Md.: Committee for the 300th Anniversary of the Maryland Act of Religious Toleration, 1949);

Our English Heritage (Philadelphia: Lippincott, 1949);

Incredible Tale: The Odyssey of the Average American in the Last Half-Century (New York: Harper, 1950);

This American People (New York: Harper, 1951);

Pattern for Liberty: The Story of Old Philadelphia (New York: McGraw-Hill, 1952);

The Making of a Southern Industrialist: A Biographical Study of Simpson Bobo Tanner (Chapel Hill:

University of North Carolina Press, 1952);

Mount Vernon: The Story of a Shrine (New York: Random House, 1953);

Andrew Jackson (New York: Bantam, 1956);

The Lunatic Fringe (Philadelphia: Lippincott, 1957);

Peril and Promise: An Inquiry into Freedom of the Press (New York: Harper, 1958);

Personality in Journalism (Minneapolis: University of Minnesota Press, 1958);

The Lines Are Drawn: American Life since the First World War as Reflected in the Pulitzer Prize Cartoons (Philadelphia: Lippincott, 1958);

America: A History for Peter: America Is Born, America Grows Up, America Moves Forward, 3 volumes, (New York: Morrow, 1959-1960);

De Senectute: A Paper Presented to the 14 West Hamilton Street Club, December 8th 1960 (Baltimore, Md.: Privately printed, 1961);

The Man Who Feels Left Behind (New York: Morrow, 1961);

The Government: The Presidency, The Supreme Court, The Congress, The Cabinet, 4 volumes (New York: Morrow, 1962-1966);

Hod-Carrier: Notes of a Laborer on an Unfinished Cathedral (New York: Morrow, 1964);

Communism: An American's View (New York: Morrow, 1964);

Franklin D. Roosevelt: Portrait of a Great Man (New York: Morrow, 1969);

The British Empire: An American View of its History from 1776 to 1945 (New York: Morrow, 1969);

The Imperial Republic: Speculation on the Future of Any of the Third United States of America (New York: Liveright, 1972);

America-Watching: Perspectives in the Course of an Incredible Century (Owings Mills, Md.: Stemmer House, 1976).

In *What Is News?* (1926), the second of his many books, Gerald W. Johnson defended the art of popularizing, which he considered to be one of the more important obligations of the daily press. Only because it usually is done badly do scholars regard popularization with "holy horror," Johnson wrote; popularization undertaken with suitable seriousness is "as rare as first-rate newspapermen":

> What often passes for popularization is the muddle-headed work of incompetent journalists which, so far from clarifying an obscure subject, renders it unrecognizable even to the expert.
>
> Genuine popularization is principally clarification. Its difficulty lies in the fact that

no man is capable of clarifying a subject until he understands it himself.

The journalist who possesses "genuine learning" will excel at clarification, and his reports to the general public will provide important contributions to the advancement of knowledge.

Johnson was a master clarifier. His industry and intellect were formidable; his sense of responsibility for the enlightenment of the public never flagged; his style became more fluent as he grew older. The century which he closely observed saw no consistently more intelligent, lively, and comprehensive reporter than this writer of history, biography, and, of course, journalism. Personally gracious, an agent of civility in rude and disturbing times, Johnson could be pungent and audacious in his prose. Throughout his long career his writing, which at times recalls the invective of his friend and associate at the *Baltimore Sunpapers,* H. L. Mencken, was rippled with an indignant dislike for falseness and hypocrisy. But Johnson possessed an intellectual elegance, an aptness of reference, superior at least in historical references to Mencken's. At the age of eighty-four he wrote an essay on the American presidency, a subject about which he worried continually, which included this observation: "The frightening truth is that within the past 25 years the Sovereign American Citizen has acquired much of the intellectual and moral coloration of the late Merovingian kings of France, the *rois faineants,* 'nothing kings,' who couldn't be bothered with ruling and were content to let power drift into the hands of the mayor of the palace."

Almost from his birth on 6 August 1890 at Riverton, North Carolina, Gerald White Johnson learned to combine journalistic skill with moral principle: his father, Archibald Johnson, edited a Baptist church publication. Johnson's mother was Flora Carolina McNeill Johnson. While still a student at Wake Forest College in Winston-Salem, North Carolina, Johnson established his own newspaper, the *Thomasville Davidsonian.* After graduating from Wake Forest in 1901 Johnson worked as a reporter on the *Lexington* (North Carolina) *Dispatch* and then as the music critic on the *Greensboro* (North Carolina) *News.*

After serving with the Twenty-first Infantry in France during World War I he returned to the *News.* In 1922 he married Kathryn Dulsinea Hayward; they had two daughters. In 1924 he refused an offer from the *Baltimore Sunpapers* and became professor of journalism at the University of North Carolina. There, with W. R. Hayward, he wrote his first book, *The Story of Man's Work* (1925).

From 1926 to 1943 he wrote editorials, first for the *Baltimore Evening Sun* and then for the *Baltimore Sun*. Clement G. Vitek, chief librarian for the *Sun*, was a copyboy in the late 1930s and recalled later that Johnson "would write quickly with great clarity and . . . in contrast to most editorial writers, his copy was incredibly clean, which endeared him to the linotype operators."

Throughout his career Johnson's impressive seriousness was balanced by a playfulness which added unpredictability to his writing. In "The Third Republic—and After," an essay published in 1928, this political observer who would become one of the more compelling advocates of liberal democracy nevertheless urged his fellow citizens to consider the virtues of the plutocrat. "It is foolish," he wrote, "to rail at plutocracy on account of what it does, for it is giving us, and may be expected to continue to give us, what is in many respects the best government we have ever had. If he is the least inspired, the plutocrat is also the least dizzy of all our rulers, not excluding those in the prerepublican era or theocracy and autocracy. The foundation of his statecraft indeed may be described in two words—No Nonsense. Since the average man has always suffered much more from the nonsense than from the rascality of his rulers, that is, from his standpoint, an excellent foundation for any polity."

Johnson's ironic article on lynching, "Note on Race Prejudice," in a 1932 issue of the *North American Review*, cites the "magnificent consciousness of superiority" of the French, which dismisses as inferior all other races and nationalities, and proposes that "the race prejudice of the poor white trash" be elevated "to a level somewhat closer to that of the French." This means that Southern whites need economic superiority, Johnson said:

> The most powerful forces working against lynching in the South are not interracial commissions composed of learned doctors of both races . . . but the unromantic, unconsidered Babbitts who are slowly, but surely, erecting an economic structure that will withstand the strain even of a modern depression.
>
> Sermons and soda-water are all well enough, in their way; but the Negro's best assurance of a chance to die in bed, or at least to be hanged by the warden, rather than by the mob, is a pass-book in every white man's pocket. For only when he has money in his pocket is the white man's race prejudice so

inflated that he can, with tolerant scorn, leave the Negro criminal to the police.

Johnson's tolerance could not include the terror of Hitlerism, but he saw Nazism as a perversion of ideas and not as an exercise of unadulterated power. In a 1941 issue of the *Atlantic Monthly*, he said: "It is important to eliminate Hitler's armed forces as menaces to our peace and safety; it is vastly more important to eliminate Hitler's ideas if we are to enjoy peace for any considerable length of time. But an idea is impervious to bayonets and bullets. It can be killed only by another idea. Now Roosevelt has given a majority of the American people the idea that democracy can be made to work to the satisfaction of the average man, and this idea, whether true or false, is a powerful prophylaxis against infection with the idea that the only hope for common people is embodied in the 'leadership principle,' or 'master race,' the 'protection of the blood,' and all the other fantasies of which Germany has been so fearfully productive in recent years."

In 1943, by then author of fourteen published books, Johnson left newspaper work to free-lance, but his observations on journalism were always astute, and the topic seemed, as it did with Mencken, to incite in Johnson exceptionally vivid phrasing. One outrage he never committed during his brief period as a journalism professor, he said, was to tell students "that personal journalism is a thing of the past. . . . The idea is a false one; it is applesauce, it is hooey, it is the sublime and ineffable baloney. . . . For we still have journalism, and as long as we have it at all we must have personal journalism, because there is no other kind. That is, there is no other kind that is worthy of the name."

In daily journalism, as in all other human enterprise, "dreadful incompetents" will be found, Johnson wrote.

> But every good newspaper indicates the existence of at least one good journalist; it is the personality of a competent man that makes a newspaper good—that, and nothing else under heaven.
>
> Newspaper work is not a science, but a craft, and its practitioners are craftsmen, that is to say, artisans or artificers. They fall naturally into the three grades of apprentice, journeyman and master-craftsman.

Superb journalistic competence enhanced by "a touch of genius" produced "not a professional man, but an artist." Johnson conceded the existence of a kind of journalism "that is almost completely impersonal." Hundreds of newspapers are "as mechanical as the presses they are printed on," but "it is not by the dull, machine-minded, uninspired hacks that journalism deserves to be judged, but by the best it can produce." That high standard is met not by corporations or committees "but by individual men who stamp their personalities upon their papers."

Among those powerful, individualistic innovators was Adolph S. Ochs, owner of the *New York Times* and member of the board of directors of the Associated Press. In Johnson's biography of Ochs, *An Honorable Titan: A Biographical Study of Adolph S. Ochs* (1946), the newspaper owner exemplifies the powerful financial figures of the late nineteenth century who, Johnson said, may have been at times unscrupulous but were led by men who "always recognized that power cannot rightfully be exercised unless the responsibility to which it is linked is assumed. It was Adolph Ochs's distinction among the Titans that he made this conspicuously clear. Freedom of the press represents power; but no man may exercise that power rightfully unless he accepts the responsibility that goes with it—the responsibility to tell the truth as far as it is humanly possible to know the truth, without deviation for his own benefit, or that of his party, his sect or his friends."

From 1952 to 1954 Johnson was a news commentator for a Baltimore television station, winning the Du Pont Commentators Award, the Sidney Hillman Foundation Award, and the George Foster Peabody Award.

The witty and erudite Johnson admired another learned wit, Adlai E. Stevenson, and wrote speeches for his presidential campaigns in 1952 and 1956. When Johnson was given a surprise party on his seventieth birthday in 1960 (columnist James H. Bready called it the best Baltimore party of the century, bringing "utter joy" to Johnson's face), Stevenson said of Johnson: "He is the critic and conscience of our time. Every friend and reader of Gerald Johnson is in debt for a thousand rescues from boredom in an age when humor is suspect and conformity a virtue." On the day of Stevenson's death in 1965, Johnson wrote a tribute for the *New Republic*, quoting from Stevenson's last speech: "This must be the context of our thinking—the context of human interdependence in the face of the vast new dimensions of our science and our discovery. . . . we can never again be a squabbling band of nations before the awful majesty of outer space." Of Stevenson's "reduction to absurdity of the ideologies, the dogmas, the so-called immortal principles which men use as excuses for cutting one

another's throats and ravaging with fire and steel the planet on which all must live," Johnson said:

> To attain such a view a man must be either a supreme cynic or imbued with a faith that escapes the comprehension of men of more modest capacity. Cynicism, however, is not impressed by "the vast dimensions of our science and our discovery." This leaves faith as the only explanation of the power of Adlai Stevenson.
>
> This explanation of him is extraordinary, certainly, but not unprecedented in the experience of Americans. On the contrary, every great leader in our history has possessed faith in a principle of moral and intellectual development analogous to the biological process of growth, not as the endowment of an elite, but as a potential of all mankind. . . . Without this faith Washington, Jefferson, Lincoln would be inexplicable; with it, the obscure and humble have faced life and death steadily and undismayed.

The dreadful realities of the twentieth century must have tested the convictions of this realist, who valued above all a consistently sane and clear outlook. Toward the end of *The Lines Are Drawn* (1958), his commentary on Pulitzer Prize-winning editorial cartoons between 1922 and 1958, Johnson had criticized the earnest idealism and "mellow American humor" which permeated these cartoons. "All of which is praiseworthy," he said. But "if American life in those years was composed entirely, or mainly, of humor, wit, morality and idealism then we who survived can have little faith in our own sanity, for not many of us were fortunate enough to see it that way. . . . Fury, terror, hatred and agony seared their brand upon [this period] far more conspicuously than the gentler emotions. It can be plausibly argued that for long-continued, unremitting stress, intellectual, moral and physical, these years have no parallel in the history of the republic." After recounting a few scandals and reminding his readers of the unceasing violence of the period, Johnson observed that "we learned through the rough stuff. . . . The American people came through all this by dint of courage, first of all, but powerfully aided by wrath and fear; and they came out stronger than they were at the beginning. So deprecation of the rough stuff, pushing it into the background as something that may have to be acknowledged but that is never to be emphasized, is a distortion of history."

These frequent crises had summoned

Johnson's idealism and eloquence, and the crises of the 1960s and 1970s continued to do so. The murders in 1964 of civil rights workers Michael Schwerner, Andrew Goodman, and James E. Chaney provoked in Johnson an outrage which replaced the irony of his 1932 article on bigotry. With obvious agony over the revival of racial violence he wrote of this "hideous crime" that it was an "assault upon civilization." "What force could conceivably propel any man into commission of a crime more hideous than plain murder?," he asked. "The answer is not far to seek. It is the policy, pursued for generations by the proper gentlemen of Mississippi, of controlling and manipulating the wool-hat boys, the rednecks, the lintheads, by stuffing them with lies that blind their eyes to the real world.... So now we have Philadelphia [Mississippi, where the murders occurred] and twenty-one men [arrested by the FBI, and released] walking at large, but not in the familiar ways of men, walking still in the shadow of death, possibly at the hands of the law, but probably under the claws of the fiend that has been conjured up, the terrorism from which America has been almost free for many years. . . ."

The confidence in the integrity of the powerful that Johnson had expressed in his biography of Adolph Ochs was severely challenged as the United States ventured and then plunged into the ruinous war in Vietnam. As early as 1962, declaring that "Hell-gate is ajar in Vietnam and is plainly swinging open," Johnson had demanded that President Kennedy speak candidly to the American people about the United States' military intentions in Southeast Asia. He was asking, however, only for information. "Whatever is really necessary to do, we will do," he wrote, "and with right good will even though the cost runs high in both blood and money."

Johnson's gradually growing, increasingly troubled, judiciously expressed reservations about the war were later described by some obituary writers as "opposition" to American involvement. That he should have been seen as an opponent rather than a careful questioner is one measure of the estranging effect of a conflict in which critics were regarded at best as nuisances, at worst as traitors. Johnson sought sanity. Beneath the vivid simplifying of his journalistic prose his measured if somewhat disturbed inquiry continued. In an essay published in 1967 he scornfully dismissed three image-tending presidents as specimens of Mencken's "*Boobus americanus*"—"the sawdust-stuffed father image that we called Eisenhower, the

fake Prince Charming that passed as Kennedy, and the television cowboy furiously applying quirt and spur to his bucking swivel chair we designate as Johnson." But his criticism of the war in the same essay retained a note of injured patriotism: "The current situation is that we are dribbling away a great army and a magnificent air force in a war 9,000 miles from our borders against an enemy less than a third as numerous as our field forces—ill fed, ill clad, and ill armed, but, so far, indomitable." Again, in 1968, he pleaded for rational judgment: "The tragedy of Vietnam showed that pious aspirations not guided by realistic intelligence can land us in hellish situations." His castigations continued. He expected the government of the people to be honest and reasonable. He avoided excessive blaming, and remained hopeful. Of Watergate he said: "The realistic American should pinch his nostrils long enough to give consideration to what this implies with respect to the theory that democracy is a viable form of government."

So toward the end of his career Johnson's realism evolved into a radical skepticism. Yet in one of his last writings, published when he was eighty-five years old, he sounded cautiously hopeful: A civilization which produces "successive responses each more energetic than the challenge" can afford to regard a time of troubles as prelude to

> some masterwork greater than anything that we have done hitherto or that we can now imagine.
> That is the choice that appeals to the mentality of the freeman. It involves labor and danger, both great, but what of that? Freedom has never been easy or safe, and democracy is the most difficult of all forms of government. But a certain number of Americans are committed to it and they have some of the qualifications necessary to preserve it. The question is, are they numerous enough, and skillful enough? And the only answer to that is, God only knows.

In 1964 Johnson won the Gold Medal of the state of North Carolina; in 1969 he received the Andrew White medal from Loyola College. He was also awarded honorary doctoral degrees by Goucher College, Towson State University, and Johns Hopkins University.

Visiting journalists knew that an interview with Johnson would elicit provocative comments. A reporter for the magazine *Railway Age* interviewed Johnson in 1975 about the rapid transit system in

Baltimore—a matter of concern to Johnson, who saw no sense in automobile commuting—and came away with this description of Johnson's setting: "From floor to ceiling, the shelves in Johnson's study are stuffed with books, with the overflow piled neatly in stacks on the floor and less neatly in mounds on his desk. On a metal reading stand next to his rocking chair hangs a green eyeshade, the kind worn by editors and gamblers. Rocking slowly back and forth, one hand on the reading stand, he talked about another chronic Baltimore problem—its politicians, whom Johnson called collectively, 'the damned fool city.' " Johnson complained of the "inertia" of politicians. "They have to be pitchforked into doing anything," he told the reporter:

> I am convinced that about one-third of the people run this country—always have and always will. They are the people who see what is necessary to be done, and do it, or try to do it. They still can sweep along the less active.
>
> But the trouble is, when they clean up a mess, they get things started again—and they *quit*. The human being just hates to think, and by the time he's attended to his private business he isn't going to pay much attention to public affairs—until something happens, and then he gets mad. And for a while, oh, boy, the way things happen. . . . It takes intelligence to guide our country, but it takes emotion to start it. Wrath is one of the most powerful movers.

Henry Steele Commager's introduction to Johnson's last book, the collection of essays called *America-Watching* (1976), observed that while Johnson's life had been represented by a continual outpouring of reporting, criticism, history, and biography, what was impressive was not the quantity but the quality—"a quality unfailingly Johnsonian." For fifty years, Commager wrote, Johnson had been "a most perspicacious reporter of the passing scene, a thoughtful interpreter of politics and morals, a re-creator of the American past, and, for good measure, a prophet of the American future. One of Henry L. Mencken's aptest disciples, he possesses a style unfailingly lively, pungent and witty, and often eloquent; and it has one quality that Mencken conspicuously lacked—at least in his journalistic forays; it is balanced and judicious."

Baltimore Sun columnist Peter Kumpa visited the "Sage of Bolton Hill" (Johnson disliked the nickname) in his ninetieth year and found him im-

paired by partial blindness and deafness, but willing to answer a few questions. Johnson and his wife, Kathryn, then eighty years old, shared their town house with three female toy poodles, Wiffles, Smidgeon, and Pup-pup (the latter deficient in canine character, therefore unnamed). In his later years, Johnson's favorite reading was detective fiction, Kumpa reported—the novels of writers such as Nero Wolfe, Agatha Christie, and Dorothy Sayers. A neighbor kept him informed about Baltimore's progress toward renovation of its downtown district and the Inner Harbor. Johnson told Kumpa that old Baltimore money had left the city and contributed little to its renewal. "Old habits still rule," Kumpa observed. "Mr. Johnson runs through a daily critique of the day's editorials. Not a bad one on that British woman, [Prime Minister Margaret] Thatcher, he says. And he quips that the daily grist of the *Sun*'s editors is 'better than Baltimore deserves.' "

At the time of his death on 22 March 1980, Johnson was firmly established as a resident not only of Baltimore, which he called "a genuine shellback . . . the greatest harker back . . . a mighty tolerant and livable city," but in that city rich with neighborhoods, of Bolton Hill, the district near the Lyric Theatre and the University of Baltimore, where he and his wife spent their mature years. In their last years the couple had moved to a modern town house, which nevertheless retained the adornments of Baltimore life. "You can't be a Baltimorean without white marble steps and red brick," he had once told a visitor.

"A Southerner and a Democrat," the *Baltimore Sun*'s obituary said of Johnson, "he was known as a liberal, but once described himself simply as a realist." The obituary quoted Hamilton Owens, who as editor in chief of the *Sunpapers* had hired Johnson, the first of a distinguished line of North Carolinians to serve on the papers: "At first sight you would think him benign, but when you saw his eyes flash you knew there was something of the avenging angel in him." Johnson, the obituary writer observed, "was a man who never seemed flustered or hurried. He was almost always seen with his cigar or pipe. . . . In manner he was graciousness itself, gentle and soft-spoken, and it was hard to imagine that in his personal relations he could have offended anyone. His writings were another matter. He never hesitated to espouse strong positions. He was, for example, one of the first figures prominent on the national scene to attack U.S. involvement in Vietnam. And his ideas often made readers irate."

Johnson's legacy consists of more than forty volumes and countless articles. His output was continuous; he flourished in old age and was undaunted by the grim uncertainties of his time. His first book was published when he was thirty-five years old, during a period of bulging and illusory prosperity. He proceeded with his running commentary through economic depression, wars hot and cold, scandal and national disgrace. Twenty of his books were published after his sixtieth year, ten of those after his seventieth birthday. The century's turmoil was the stuff of his maturity, but he never seemed, as some journalists do, to feed parasitically on unhappy events. If anything, his careful attention dignified the object exposed to journalistic scrutiny. He cared about history, and he had arrived at his own understanding of the sources of disorder and conflict; sometimes irately, now and then venomously, most often calmly and with great intelligence, he wrote of events, always insisting on

the immediate and ultimate desirability of rationally arrived-at decisions and consistent and humane action.

The editorials which appeared in the *Sunpapers* after Johnson's death expressed an appreciation for the unusual dimensions of his journalism. Johnson, one editorial writer observed, "examined this country's growing pains almost one by one. . . . When Gerald Johnson spoke out against the expansion of American influence clear across the Pacific, his point had collective experience behind it, not just individual logic; when he warned against policies transforming this country from a republic into an empire, which he felt it urgently necessary to do throughout the 1960s, lesser men had no answer. . . . Those who knew him, those who read him, felt they were in the presence of something that was old-fashioned after all: a gentleman. Those who would carry onward something of Gerald W. Johnson need only be of gentlemanly mind and heart themselves, if they can."

Frank R. Kent
(1 May 1877-14 April 1958)

Elizabeth Brown Dickey
University of South Carolina

MAJOR POSITIONS HELD: Managing editor, *Baltimore Sun* (1911-1921); vice-president, A. S. Abell Company, publishers of the *Baltimore Sunpapers* (1921-1958); syndicated columnist (1934-1958).

BOOKS: *The Story of Maryland Politics* (Baltimore, Md.: Thomas & Evans, 1911);
The Great Game of Politics (Garden City: Doubleday, Page, 1923; London: Heinemann, 1923; revised and enlarged, Garden City: Doubleday, Doran, 1930);
The Story of Alexander Brown & Sons (Baltimore, Md.: Privately printed, 1925; revised, Baltimore, Md., 1950);
The Democratic Party: A History (New York & London: Century, 1928);
Political Behavior (New York: Morrow, 1928);
Without Gloves (New York: Morrow, 1934);
Without Grease (New York: Morrow, 1936);

The Sunpapers of Baltimore, 1837-1937, by Kent, Gerald W. Johnson, H. L. Mencken, and Hamilton Owens (New York: Knopf, 1937).

Frank R. Kent is recognized by journalism historians as one of the first daily political columnists in America (along with David Lawrence and Mark Sullivan). Kent's influence reached its peak during the first half of the twentieth century. His front-page commentary on politics, politicians, and controversial issues angered many who disagreed with his positions, and earned praise from those who shared his beliefs. He attracted the attention of nearly every politician on Capitol Hill. Presidents Woodrow Wilson and Herbert Hoover became his close friends; Dwight Eisenhower considered Kent a great journalist.

Kent's boundless energy amazed his associates. Often he would complete a morning's work in Baltimore, then rush off to Washington to gather more information. He had a keen wit and could quickly analyze almost any political situation. He was of a rather slight build, wore smartly tailored clothes, and walked with a brisk step. Friends knew him as a conversationalist who excelled in telling anecdotes.

A son of Thomas Marine and Mary Richardson Kent, Francis Richardson Kent was born into a newspaper family in Baltimore. His grandfather Beale H. Richardson owned the *Baltimore Republican*, which was shut down during the Civil War because of its bias toward the South. Kent was named for an uncle, Francis A. Richardson, Washington correspondent for the *Sun* from 1898 to 1901.

Kent began his newspaper career in the late 1890s as a sports reporter for the *Columbus* (Georgia) *Enquirer Sun*; his experiences on this beat made him a lifelong sports fan. After a short time in Georgia, he returned to Baltimore to report for the *American*. On 15 January 1900 he joined the *Baltimore Sun*, one of the first three-penny papers in the United States (the others were the *Philadelphia Public Ledger* and the *New York Sun*), and like countless other cub reporters, he started out covering the police beat.

He quickly won promotion to city hall, where he often encountered his future colleague on the *Sun*, H. L. Mencken; at that time, Mencken was working for the *Baltimore Morning Herald*. By 1906, Kent was recognized as Maryland's top political reporter. During that year he married Minnie Whitman, who was a member of an old Baltimore family: they had a son, Frank, Jr., who grew up to work for the *Sunpapers*.

Kent left the *Sun* for a year in 1909 to serve as secretary and treasurer of the Maryland Agricultural College (now the University of Maryland). In 1910 he returned to the *Sun* as Washington correspondent, but was called back to Baltimore later in the year to become managing editor. His wife died that year. In 1911 Kent took on additional duties as managing editor of the newly established *Evening Sun*. In 1916 he married Elizabeth Thomas.

For a decade, Kent worked hard to improve the variety and amount of news published in the two papers. Near the end of World War I he became irritated by censored and unrealistic news from Europe and went abroad to cover the closing days of the war himself. His article "Paris Seethes with International Jealousy and Suspicion" caused an uproar when it was published on 28 November 1918. An editor's note beneath the headline called the piece "the first uncensored account of actual condi-

tions in Paris to be printed in this country or abroad. The writer was in Paris at the time the terms of the Armistice were determined and returned to this country on the first ship after it had been signed. It was not possible to have got this article to America by mail or cable." Other newspapers in the country were saying that the Allies had no differences of opinion; Kent wrote: "For weeks past, under the surface, Paris has been simply seething with international jealousies, friction and feeling, and between us and our noble allies at this time there is a tension and a strain that does not appear on the top but that is very real none the less. The truth is, and everybody in Paris knows it, that in government and political circles they do not love us over there, neither the English nor the French." These statements infuriated readers, and some suggested that Kent be arrested for treason. As conditions abroad worsened, people gradually began to believe him, and Mencken thought that Kent's revelations had a great deal to do with the growth of Americans' suspicions about the Versailles Conference.

In 1921 Kent became the first London correspondent for the *Sun*. At the same time, he was elected vice-president of the A. S. Abell Company, publishers of the *Sunpapers*. He held this position until he was seventy years old.

Kent's political commentary began in 1922 under news headlines on the front page of the *Sun*; it attracted national attention. On 4 February 1923, Kent adopted the title "The Great Game of Politics" for the column. A series of the columns were collected under the title *The Great Game of Politics* (1923). This book, which has been used in college political science classes, explains the intricacies of politics and emphasizes the importance of primary elections to America's political bosses. In the preface, Kent wrote that the book was "written wholly with the idea of presenting the human facts about practical politics and the people who engage in it as a profession, so simply and clearly that they can be easily understood by the average man and woman." Kent described how politicians get power and how they use it. "Primaries are the key to politics," he wrote. "So long as the primaries are controlled by machines, the general election voter, no matter how independent he may be, 99 per cent of the time, is limited in his choices of two machine selections." Kent noted that it is rare for more than twenty percent of the voters to take part in primaries; this permits the party machine to select the candidates who run for office. "Then at the general election, when perhaps 60 and 70 per-cent of the voters come out to the polls, one set or the other of the boss-picked candidates is elected to office. That is the simple story of elections all over the country—the bosses pick the candidates in the primaries because the voters, other than machine men, do not come out in sufficient numbers to bother them, and the people are compelled to choose between one or the other machine ticket in the general election." Although he frequently criticized politicians and their tactics, Kent felt that "political organizations are absolutely essential to the conduct of the government—city, state or national. This is a government by parties. Parties can no more be held together and made to function without organization than any great business can be run without organization. Without organization, there would be no parties. Without parties, there would be no government."

Kent observed, "There isn't one politician anywhere who doesn't wince from newspaper criticism. And the higher they climb, the more they wince. What they don't want is for a newspaper man to go behind the front and tell what sort of man he really is without his false whiskers, what sort of game he is really playing and why. But what they resent more than anything else is humor. Make a little fun of one of these and he goes all to pieces."

Kent's column was syndicated starting in 1934 and went to 140 newspapers across the United States. In the 1940s the title was dropped and the column appeared under Kent's name. In *The Columnists* (1944), Charles Fisher calls Kent "the most fastidious of the ax-men who have observed the outlandish doings in Washington with such splendid single-mindedness in recent years. He keeps his little finger crooked elegantly in the air, so to speak, as he takes his carefully considered swipes at each new demonstration of untidy humanity getting its feet tangled gracelessly in politics."

Kent himself was a Democrat from 1900 until the Franklin Roosevelt era. Then he voted for Republican candidates nationally but supported Democrats in city and state elections. An outspoken critic of Roosevelt, he believed that the New Deal deviated from the Democratic philosophy of the Wilson era. According to Fisher,

> In Roosevelt he [Kent] long ago discovered a subject who could be pressed into universal service. He probably owes more to the President than any man in America.
>
> In the unhappy event that a tidal wave should sweep far inland and, let us say, exterminate the village of Ong's Hat, New Jersey, Mr. Kent would almost certainly point out next day that such a thing would not have

happened had Mr. Roosevelt concentrated on domestic affairs instead of the war. And if, a fortnight later, a falling meteor should destroy three acres of standing corn in Iowa, Mr. Kent would declare with calm weariness that such a tragedy could occur only in a country where the President was so interested in matters at home that he ignored the world outside.

Kent attended every political convention from 1900 to 1952 except for 1920, when he was in Europe. It was on the national scene that he achieved status as a journalist. A popular speaker, known for his wit, Kent liked to tell audiences about his profession as a columnist, "I am free as a bird and should like to say it seems to me the best job in the world."

Kent officially retired as a daily columnist in 1947. On that occasion, Arthur Krock of the *New York Times* said:

> This is a loss to his large reading public that no other journalist can repair. Mr. Kent has certain qualities as a reporter and analyst of news which are unique in a profession where there are many others of distinction.
>
> I think he is not only the best craftsman of us all who attempt this type of newspaper work, but he is also an accurate observer whose eyes and ears and brain have grown steadily more competent in his long career.
>
> Moreover Mr. Kent has the high degree of courage and integrity which newspaper readers have a right to expect. And he always practices journalism as the trade of a gentleman.

Kent continued to write a weekly column. He went to his office at the *Sun* every day and was the oldest active member of the editorial staff, both in age and service. His final column appeared in the *Sun* on 5 January 1958; he died on the following 14 April, two weeks before his eighty-first birthday.

Kent received several awards during his lifetime, including an honorary master of arts degree from the University of Maryland, a Phi Beta Kappa key from William and Mary College, and an honorary doctorate from Oglethorpe University. He served on the Columbia University Pulitzer Prize selection committee.

At Kent's death, former President Herbert Hoover said, "Frank Kent's . . . brilliant mind, his sterling honesty and his moral courage were the background of his every action. America has been a better place for his having been here." President Eisenhower's press secretary, James C. Hagerty, said, "The President asked me on his behalf to express his sadness at the news of the passing of Mr. Kent. Mr. Kent was one of the President's favorite columnists, he read him frequently and had a great deal of respect for his writings. . . ." Vice-President Richard Nixon said, "The death of Frank Kent Sr. is a great loss not only to his family and the newspaper he served so ably for so long but also to the whole nation. His keen and penetrating columns have helped millions of Americans to gain a better understanding of national issues." Senator Harry F.

Byrd, a senior Democratic member of the United States Senate from Virginia, commented: "Frank Kent was a notable political writer of his day, always objective, fair-minded and forceful in his opinions. He wielded great influence among his readers. As his close personal friend for many years, I am deeply grieved. He was one of the most lovable men it has ever been my privilege to know."

Reference:
Charles Fisher, *The Columnists* (New York: Howell, Soskin, 1944).

John S. Knight

(26 October 1894-16 June 1981)

James L. Baughman
University of Wisconsin, Madison

NEWSPAPERS OWNED: *Akron* (Ohio) *Beacon-Journal* (1933-1981), *Massillon* (Ohio) *Independent* (1933-1937), *Miami Herald* (1937-1981), *Detroit Free Press* (1940-1981), *Chicago Daily News* (1944-1959), *Charlotte* (North Carolina) *Observer* (1955-1981), *Charlotte News* (1959-1981), *Tallahassee* (Florida) *Democrat* (1965-1981), *Macon* (Georgia) *Telegraph* (1969-1981), *Macon News* (1969-1981), *Milledgeville* (Georgia) *Union-Recorder* (1969-1981), *Boca Raton* (Florida) *News* (1969-1981), *Philadelphia Inquirer* (1969-1981), *Philadelphia Daily News* (1969-1981), *Columbus* (Georgia) *Ledger* (1973-1981), *Columbus Enquirer* (1973-1981), *Bradenton* (Florida) *Herald* (1973-1981), *Lexington* (Kentucky) *Herald* (1973-1981), *Lexington Leader* (1973-1981), *New York Staats-Zeitung* (1974-1981), *St. Paul* (Minnesota) *Pioneer Press* (1974-1981), *St. Paul Dispatch* (1974-1981), *Aberdeen* (South Dakota) *American News* (1974-1981), *Grand Forks* (North Dakota) *Herald* (1974-1981), *Duluth* (Minnesota) *News-Tribune* (1974-1981), *Duluth Herald* (1974-1981), *San Jose* (California) *Mercury & News* (1974-1981), *Long Beach* (California) *Independent* (1974-1981), *Long Beach Press-Telegram* (1974-1981), *Pasadena* (California) *Star-News* (1974-1981), *Gary* (Indiana) *Post-Tribune* (1974-1981), *Boulder* (Colorado) *Daily Camera* (1974-1981), *Wichita* (Kansas) *Eagle* (1974-1981), *Wichita Beacon* (1974-1981), *Centre Daily Times* (State College, Pennsylvania) (1979-1981), *Fort Wayne* (Indiana) *News-Sentinel* (1980-1981).

John S. Knight began assembling what ultimately became one of the largest newspaper groups in the United States at a time when chain newspaper companies were both losing money and being criticized by prominent liberal opinion leaders. Yet Knight managed to create in Knight Newspapers a journalistic enterprise that consistently made profits while granting to each newspaper an editorial autonomy that virtually silenced the chain newspapers' traditional adversaries. In the process, Knight helped to usher in a new phase of newspaper management, one in which rising production costs and competition from newer news media compelled publishers to pay stricter attention to operating expenses and to the possibilities of changes in format. Knight himself was less a great editorial writer than a very shrewd entrepreneur. In a fiercely competitive environment, his papers not only survived but flourished.

John Shively Knight was the son of a prominent Akron, Ohio, editor, Charles Landon Knight, and Clara Irene Sheifley Knight. The first Knight came to America in 1662, a Cromwellian refugee from the Restoration. Charles Knight, a Southerner with a degree from Columbia University, practiced law prior to taking a series of newspaper jobs in Pennsylvania and Ohio. In the early 1900s— sources conflict as to the exact date—C. L. Knight began to work at the *Akron Beacon-Journal* as advertising manager. By 1915 he controlled the paper. As editor of the *Beacon-Journal*, Knight strode a middle path between the party leader-as-editor tradition and the "new journalism" that eschewed partisanship. Armed with fierce metaphors, Knight wrote stinging front-page editorials decrying Cleveland and Cincinnati Republican party bosses, ridiculing the budding temperance movement, and attacking the Ku Klux Klan. He paid little attention to the paper itself or to changes in journalism nationwide (he wrote his editorials in pencil); nevertheless, his editorials gained him something of a national reputation. Knight tried to stand clear of the regular organizations in Ohio, but in 1912 he became a supporter of Theodore Roosevelt's Progressive party candidacy and in two years was serving on the state Republican committee. In 1920, Knight won election to Congress; two years later, he ran well but lost in the Republican gubernatorial primary. The defeat left him bitter for the remainder of his life.

John S. Knight inherited some of his father's qualities. Like his father, he distrusted political organizations; but he also enrolled as a Republican. Unlike his father, he endeavored to control his temper at all times, to the point of having to apologize to employees for seeming aloof. Much of the younger Knight's newspaper career may be explained by his wish to remove his own personality from his papers, to separate himself as his father had been unable to do. Knight also determined, on the basis of his father's experience, never to run for public office, even though friends suggested in the late 1930s and early 1940s that he seek elective office in Ohio or Florida or run for president.

Next to his father, the greatest influence on Knight was his army service in World War I. After a relatively protected childhood during which he attended the Akron public schools and Tome Preparatory School in Maryland, and three years at Cornell University, Knight enlisted in the army in 1917. For the first time in his life, Knight mixed with a variety of people—most notably, perhaps, some former taxi drivers in the Motor Transport Corps who bilked him at dice. Knight learned their tricks, memorized the odds at dice, and became something of a gambling aficionado. Knight was commissioned a second lieutenant in the infantry and saw action in Alsace-Lorraine and the Argonne; later he became a gunner-observer in the air corps.

John S. Knight

After demobilization, Knight returned to Akron. His father wanted him to go to work at the paper, but Knight first tried his hand at ranching in California, where he married Katherine McLain in 1920. That spring, Knight did join his father's newspaper. Not a naturally gifted writer, Knight so disliked his early copy that he used the pen name "Walker." His father kept encouraging him, however, and named him managing editor of the *Beacon-Journal* in 1925.

Between 1925 and 1933, Knight's editorship of the *Beacon-Journal* was beset by two challenges. The first concerned competition: Knight succeeded his father as editor just as the Scripps-Howard chain combined Akron's other two papers, the *Times* and *Press*, into the evening *Times-Press*. The Knights' morning paper now faced a rival who operated papers throughout the nation. The second challenge was that C. L. Knight's health declined, forcing the younger Knight to act as publisher. Unlike his father, Knight studied newspapers across the country to look for innovations in layout, syndicated features, and production equipment. When C. L. Knight would travel to Florida to recuperate from an illness, his son would alter the paper, then greet his angry father on his return to Akron and patiently explain the change. Perhaps the son's greatest move came when the *Times-Press* voluntarily surrendered its Associated Press franchise. Knight took up the AP service and with its many bulletins was able to put out a late-afternoon paper in direct competition with the *Times-Press*. During this period the Knights acquired small newspapers in two other Ohio cities: the *Springfield Sun* in 1925 and the *Massillon Independent* in 1927.

In 1933 Knight confronted another round of problems. His father died, leaving him in charge just as the paper was suffering with Akron's hard fate during the Great Depression. Akron had become America's tire manufacturing center during the 1920s; the smell of burning rubber greeted the city's visitors. Yet compared to such other large Ohio cities as Cleveland, Dayton, Columbus, and Toledo, Akron had few consumer goods or service-sector industries, and was severely affected by the long drop in demand for new automobiles and rubber products. The Depression hurt the local newspaper business. At the time of C. L. Knight's death, the *Beacon-Journal* had so little cash on hand that employees were being paid in scrip. John Knight had to borrow money to pay his inheritance tax.

With C. L. Knight gone, the editors of the *Times-Press* confidently set out to eliminate the *Beacon-Journal*. Like much of Akron's business establishment, the *Times-Press* managers regarded C. L.'s son as spoiled and soft, a poor substitute for the old man. Such reports got back to Knight and made him all the more determined to save the *Beacon-Journal* from receivership. He kept the paper operating and was able to expand its features while the *Times-Press* had to follow a formula dictated by the Scripps-Howard chain's New York executives. As he acquired papers in other cities, Knight never forgot how he undercut the *Times-Press* because its owners had failed to give the editors the flexibility to compete in a specific environment.

Although many newspapers had championed "objectivity" prior to the Depression decade, many editors so disliked Franklin Roosevelt, the New Deal, and the advent of union organization in basic industries like rubber that they could not rise above their prejudices when selecting and editing news stories. As Akron's thousands of rubber workers began to join the Committee for Industrial Organization (CIO) in 1936, Knight determined to be evenhanded in his treatment of the labor issue, even though his fellow Republicans and fellow members

of the exclusive Portage Country Club disdained the union. When an assistant wrote an editorial, "No Room for Vigilantes," criticizing an antiunion group's formation, Knight ordered that the commentary be placed on page one. Knight's operation of the *Beacon-Journal* during Akron's 1936 labor troubles won him and his paper national attention. Even the *Times-Press* touted Knight for governor in 1938.

Knight's stand on the CIO in Akron made good economic sense. Many more of his readers were rubber workers than members of the local country club. In respecting that working-class constituency, Knight followed a policy similar to those of editors of papers in Youngstown, Canton, and Warren; a year later, when the CIO invaded Ohio steel valley, the Republican papers there, too, endeavored not to offend their working-class readers. Personally, Knight never became overly sympathetic to mass unionism; he remained a Republican critical of the New Deal.

In October 1937, Smith Davis, a Cleveland broker who specialized in newspaper sales, persuaded Knight to purchase the morning *Miami Herald*, one of the Florida city's three dailies, for $2 million. Knight had been reluctant to buy the paper because one of his rivals in Miami would be Moses Annenberg. The millionaire publisher of the *Racing Form* was channeling vast sums into the tabloid *Miami Tribune*; but within a year Knight bought the *Tribune* from Annenberg in exchange for cash and his profitable Massillon, Ohio, paper.

In 1938, Knight's Akron paper scored a complete victory over the *Times-Press*. The *Beacon-Journal*'s survival had been costly to the Scripps-Howard daily. In August, representatives of the chain offered to buy the *Beacon-Journal* from Knight; when Knight refused, they offered him the *Times-Press*. Knight promptly bought out his rival. The *Times-Press*'s assets included a plant which had been built in 1930 and was far superior to the *Beacon-Journal*'s.

With Knight's acquisition of the *Times-Press*, Akron with its 300,000 population became the largest American city served by a single newspaper. Knight refused to gloat over the development and offered to sell the *Beacon-Journal*'s older plant to anyone wishing to establish a new daily in the rubber city. There were no takers.

At Miami, Knight instituted major changes. The *Herald* had been owned and operated by the eighty-one-year-old Col. Frank B. Shutts, who patterned his daily after the staid *New York Times*; he encouraged little investigative or police reporting and had been less than ready to adopt new technologies for his operation — the *Herald's* roof still housed carrier pigeons. Knight had the pigeons removed and without ruffling the feathers of too many long-time employees, he altered the paper's format. More concise, readable writing was emphasized. The women's section was expanded while the social page began to include the activities of Miami's affluent Jewish population, which had previously been virtually excluded from the paper. Investigative reporting—which had been the forte of Annenberg's *Tribune*—was taken up with enthusiasm: in 1938, the *Herald* helped to expose city officials' efforts to obtain bribes from the electric company. In 1939, Knight's paper fought for pasteurized milk, then a rarity in south Florida. The *Herald* soon launched an edition for air delivery in Latin America. Although the *Herald's* reputation and circulation improved, it remained in a hard circulation war with the evening *News*, owned by former Ohio governor James M. Cox.

On 30 April 1940, Knight again expanded his operations by securing the morning *Detroit Free Press*. As in the case of the *Herald*, the *Free Press* had been the property of an elderly gentleman, Edward D. Stair, who had been relatively inattentive to developments in newspaper management. The *Free Press* in 1940, writes the paper's historian, "still came across as a tired institution in its coverage and presentation of news." Moreover, Stair, by baiting New Dealers and the CIO's auto union, had antagonized Detroit's huge working-class readership. Tipped off by Davis, Knight secured the *Free Press* for $100,000 in cash and $3.2 million in notes. He immediately toured the city and entertained CIO officials. As in Akron, Knight insisted that his reporters and editorial writers treat unions fairly, and CIO leaders were soon praising Knight for his disinterested approach to labor relations.

Knight could never satisfy his more liberal readers, however: he remained a generally faithful Republican. An Eastern rival later remarked that Knight was "fairly liberal much of the time, but when a national election rolls around and the chips are really down, you will always find him on the conservative side." In 1940, an old friend and former Akron resident, Wendell Willkie, received the Republican presidential nomination and earned Knight's ardent support. Into 1941, the publisher remained a firm isolationist, convinced that Roosevelt sought American involvement abroad only to help Great Britain. In a 1 June 1941 editorial Knight did embrace Roosevelt's interventionist foreign policies, but only after the president had

announced that America was in an undeclared war with Germany as a result of incidents involving German submarines and the American navy, and that the national interest demanded unity.

Knight's support for Roosevelt's foreign policy may have led to his being recruited by the Roosevelt administration in 1943 to serve in London as a liaison to the British censorship office. On his return, Knight became president of the American Society of Newspaper Editors.

In 1944 Knight was approached about buying the evening *Chicago Daily News*. The *Daily News* had been published by Frank Knox, a Republican who had served as Roosevelt's secretary of the navy until his death in April of that year. The Knox family wished to sell the paper to any Chicago-based group that would maintain its great reputation. In the early 1940s, the *Daily News* was commonly dubbed "the *New York Times* of the Middle West," mainly for its extensive foreign-affairs coverage. Several groups, including one headed by Adlai Stevenson, who had been a Knox aide at the Navy Department, bid for the *Daily News*. But Knight outbid the Stevenson party's offer and matched those of operators of whom the Knox family did not approve. The Knight papers' performance in Akron, Miami, and Detroit had apparently impressed Knox's heirs: even though Knight flatly stated that he would not move to Chicago to operate the paper but would retain his Akron residence, the Knox family accepted his bid of $2.2 million. Knight now owned dailies in three of America's largest cities.

Again, Knight's acquisition of a major newspaper brought forth changes in its operation. As he had elsewhere, Knight insisted that news copy be tightened, an edict that offended some of the *Daily News's* more verbose foreign correspondents, a few of whom quit the paper. The *Daily News* under Knight sacrificed some of its overseas coverage for more local news, especially feature stories. While the rival evening daily, Hearst's *Herald American*, stuck to an older formula—what *Time* magazine in 1950 termed "canned crusades" and "sex, sensation, anti-vivisection and MacArthur-for-President"—the *Daily News's* layout and coverage were deliberately designed for postwar American readers, especially the young veteran with a family. By 1950, the *Daily News* was cutting deeply into the *Herald-American's* circulation and advertising sales. In 1956, the Hearst Corporation sold the *Herald-Examiner* to the *Chicago Tribune*. The *Daily News* meanwhile enjoyed profits averaging $1.25 million a year after taxes and was able to retire a debt of $12 million left by Knox.

To some critics of American journalism, Knight had paid too high a price for success in Chicago. The *Daily News*, once edited by Wilbur Storey and Victor Lawson, had long been regarded as one of Chicago's great newspapers. Knight, detractors complained, had sacrificed the paper's old emphasis on national and international reportage to increase circulation. "He has put bobby socks on the Madonna," moaned one *Daily News* veteran in 1945. Knight perhaps took such criticisms into account when he commented on the *New York Sun*'s demise in January 1950. After the death of editor Charles Henry Dana in 1897, he wrote, "the *Sun* became just another good newspaper with dull factual reporting and complete market coverage, but wholly lacking in sparkle, imagination and impact."

Knight's papers did win Pulitzer Prizes for investigative reporting. The *Miami Herald*'s exposé of gambling rackets (despite Knight's enthusiasm for games of chance) in 1949 was a precursor to the Senate's organized crime investigation of 1950-1951. In Detroit, the *Free Press* revealed lobbying payoffs in the Michigan legislature, while the *Daily News* attacked filth at Chicago's stockyards and problems on Skid Row.

The real success of the Knight papers, however, was based on certain general principles by which Knight oversaw his "empire." First, Knight believed—in contrast to William Randolph Hearst or Roy W. Howard—that no paper in his chain should lose money. "Knight has a passion for solvency," one writer observed in 1945; indeed, "his insistence that each paper pay its way is a fairly radical concept in multiple newspaper operation." Thus, he purchased papers with one eye firmly fixed on their future profitability. "I'm not interested in acquiring papers simply to say we have a lot of papers," he told the liberal New York newspaper *PM* in October 1944. Second, he consistently ran his "group" (he disliked the value-laden term *chain*) in a decentralized fashion. Each paper's editor decided which stories merited coverage, which features to include, and which candidates to endorse. In 1944, for example, Knight's papers endorsed Democrats in some states and Republicans in others; the *Herald* even endorsed a New Deal Democrat, Sen. Claude Pepper, in 1938 and 1944. Knight's experience in fighting the Scripps-Howard *Times-Press* had taught him that a less centralized operation could best assess and meet the needs of a specific community and best respond to a threat from an individual competitor. "I don't like chains," Knight told *PM*. "We try to maintain each paper's individuality, to present a cross-section of the region in which it is published. Editorials are written locally and I think you get better ones that way than when they are handed out from Washington or Park Avenue." In this regard, Knight's management can be likened to the successful, decentralized corporate structure that Alfred Sloan developed at General Motors in the 1940s and 1950s.

The Knight managerial philosophy had implications for the postwar American newspaper. In the late 1930s, such prominent critics of the news media as George Seldes and Harold Ickes had decried the tendency toward chain newspapers. Their unhappiness in part flowed from the erratic and egocentric behavior of such press magnates as Hearst and Col. Robert R. McCormick. In the postwar world, however, Knight and other chain newspaper managers such as S. I. Newhouse did not treat newspapers as extensions of their egos or forums for their political views. Knight's performance, in fact, may partly explain why fewer and less severe criticisms of chain ownership were issued in the 1950s and 1960s. Knight belied the image of the press "lord" dictating each paper's news policies from some distant Xanadu. In a complimentary piece on Knight in May 1968, *Time* magazine referred to the Knight Newspapers as "the chain that doesn't bind."

The one exception to Knight's design for local autonomy was a front-page commentary he wrote for his papers' Sunday editions beginning in December 1936. Knight's editorials were relatively inoffensive ramblings, best known for conveying his occasional independence from the Republican party or from commonly accepted beliefs; they pale when compared to the diatribes his father and his own colorful contemporaries regularly provided readers. Under the heading "Editor's Notebook," Knight criticized wartime extravagance and later punctured some of the more dubious assumptions concerning the Cold War. He criticized foreign aid and antiunion "right-to-work" bills. He was also one of the few early critics of American involvement in Vietnam. Many of his political endorsements were lukewarm, as when he picked Richard Nixon over John F. Kennedy in 1960 (Knight was a personal friend of Senator Kennedy's father, Joseph P. Kennedy). In 1972, Knight refused to endorse either Nixon or his Democratic opponent, George McGovern.

Knight's success rested more with his management than his editorial writing. In the 1950s, the Knight papers continued to engage in investigative reporting, increased and improved their features, and were among the first newspapers to employ behavioral scientists to survey the readability of news copy and the story preferences of readers.

Although he was honored for his fairness toward organized labor, Knight, like many publishers in postwar America, found newspaper unions exasperating. The *Detroit Free Press* between 1956 and 1968 was hit by several long and costly work stoppages. Knight accepted unionization on his larger papers, but he found the International Typographical Union's demands at the *Herald* so outrageous that he condoned strikebreaking in 1949. Thereafter unorganized, the *Herald* proved to be Knight's most profitable property, earning $22 million in 1972 to the *Free Press*'s $6.5 million, even though the Miami paper had fifty percent less circulation than the *Free Press*.

In January 1959, after long negotiations, Knight appeared to be beginning to dismember his newspaper fiefdom with the sale of the *Chicago Daily News*. The *Daily News* had become the leading afternoon newspaper in Chicago, but annual earnings had begun to decline from a high point of $1.5 million in 1955 to $784,000 in 1957. In addition, Knight faced new capital expenses in printing facilities. He also had an eager prospective buyer, Marshall Field IV, who published the morning *Sun-Times* and other publications without Knight's eye for the balance sheet. Field had recently failed to acquire the *Herald-American* from Hearst and yet had a new plant capable of printing all day. After raising capital through the sale of Simon and Schuster Pocket Books, Field offered Knight $18 million for the *Daily News*; Field's offer amounted to three times the listed value of *Daily News* stock a year earlier. Knight accepted. Instead of selling off other properties, however, Knight bought papers in Florida and North Carolina.

A year and a half after the sale of the *Daily News*, the Knight chain faced a different crisis. In the wake of the 1959 Cuban revolution, the Central Intelligence Agency planned an invasion by exiled Cubans of their homeland; several *Miami Herald* reporters began piecing the plot together through garrulous Cubans in Miami. Before running the resulting 1,500-word exposé of the plan, however, two Knight lieutenants met with CIA director Allen Dulles, who dissuaded them from printing the story. President Kennedy, who permitted the disastrous invasion at the Bay of Pigs to take place in April 1961, later said he wished that such papers as the *Herald* had informed readers of the CIA's intentions; the exposure might have forced abandonment of the plan and averted the fiasco.

The Bay of Pigs episode offered one indication of the Knight papers' style of journalism. Although Knight himself might periodically challenge a cardinal tenet of the Cold War, his editors and reporters tended to reflect the consensus of American Cold War liberalism. The Knight group tended to take up causes that had already been fought elsewhere or only when they could no longer be avoided. Despite the *Herald*'s proximity to Cuba, the Miami paper had barely covered the Cuban revolution and Castro's rise to power. In 1967, Detroit suffered the worst riot in its racially troubled history and one of the most deadly of the many that happened throughout America in the 1960s. The *Free Press* had run one story about ghetto grocery stores just prior to the rioting. But the paper won a Pulitzer for stories done *after* the disastrous summer, not for exposing ghetto life to readers prior to the explosion. The Knight papers, a former editor told *Business Week* in August 1970, practiced "safe, formula journalism" with "the Knight news level high, though not superior."

By the late 1960s Knight was sharing the management of the company with his younger brother James L. Knight, Lee Hills, and Alvah Chapman. The three proposed an extraordinary purchase: two Philadelphia papers, the morning *Inquirer* and evening *Daily News*, both owned by Moses Annenberg's son, Walter. John Knight opposed the acquisition: neither of Annenberg's papers ranked ahead of the evening *Bulletin* in circulation; indeed, both had suffered losses in readers and ad linage. Annenberg's hot-type printing plant was outdated and the price was high: $55 million, or twenty times earnings. But Knight was talked into making the transaction. By paying for the papers with cash and notes, Knight Newspapers increased its total revenues fifty percent without issuing new stock. Once debts were retired and new equipment purchased, the two Philadelphia units could become major profit centers.

Knight's company took over the *Inquirer* and *Daily News* in January 1970. Almost immediately, Knight-trained editors moved in to change Philadelphia journalism, which had been wallowing in parochialism. An "Action Line," first tried with enormous success at the *Free Press*, in which readers sent in consumer questions and complaints, was instituted. The editorial page's tone shifted from conservative Republican to moderate Democratic. National and international coverage expanded, as did the comic section. In perhaps the most significant development, the *Inquirer* took on Police Chief Frank Rizzo, whom it had, under Annenberg, been cheering on for his department's hardline policies toward the black community.

In July 1974, the Knight papers acquired the Ridder group of nineteen newspapers, most based in western states, and Knight Newspapers became Knight-Ridder. Two years later, Knight stepped down as executive officer to become editorial chairman of Knight-Ridder. By the late 1970s, Knight-Ridder consisted of thirty-five dailies in seventeen states with a total circulation of 25 million. Revenues for 1980 were just over $1 billion.

Many honors came to Knight and his papers. In 1968 he won the Pulitzer Prize for political commentary; the same year, both his Charlotte and Detroit papers won Pulitzers. In 1974, a survey conducted by *Time* ranked the *Miami Herald* as one of America's ten best daily newspapers. Knight also received the Cabot Gold Medal, the University of Missouri School of Journalism Citation, the John Peter Zenger Award, the Elijah Parish Lovejoy Award, and the Citation of Merit from the Poor Richard Club; he was awarded honorary degrees by the Ohio State University, the University of Akron, and Northwestern University.

In the deadly game of big-city competition, Knight had proved as skilled a gambler as any of his buddies in the army. He had bested the Hearst *Herald-American* for evening readers in Chicago and then sold out to an owner who eventually had to close the *Daily News*. In Detroit, Hearst's *Times* had died in November 1960. Six years later, the *Miami News* had closed down its own plant and rented presses and office space from the triumphant *Herald*. By the end of the 1970s, the *Philadelphia Inquirer* had driven the *Bulletin* to desperation; the *Bulletin* ceased operations in February 1982. Although the *Detroit News* still enjoyed a slender circulation lead over the *Free Press* at the beginning of the 1980s, its hold was by no means assured.

Ironically, Knight had never intended to see so many rivals suffer for his entrance into chain newspaper management. After his victory over the *Akron Times-Press*, Knight had become reluctant to destroy a rival daily. He shared the fears of those who disapproved of "one-newspaper towns." Although a tough-minded investor, he refused to follow the Gannett Company's model and only seek newspapers lacking intracity rivals, even though Wall Street analysts preferred such acquisitions. (Gannett spokesmen had derided Knight's acquisition of the *Inquirer* and *Daily News* in Philadelphia.) But Knight's papers have probably been superior to those of other chains, especially in their local cover-

age, precisely because they have had to operate in competitive environments.

Knight's personal life contrasted tragically with his public success. His first wife died in 1929 of a brain tumor; a son, Frank, died from the same cause in 1958; his eldest son and namesake died in World War II. A third son was paralyzed from polio. Knight married Beryl Zoller Comstock in 1932; she died in 1974. His grandson, John S. Knight III, who was generally considered to have been designated to succeed Knight, was murdered in 1975 in Philadelphia, where he had been working for the family's papers.

Knight ended his "Editor's Notebook" column in 1975, but retained an active interest in his holdings. His brother James assumed a greater control of the papers, as did Lee Hills and Chapman. Knight maintained his mansions in Akron and Miami and in 1976, in his last effort at irreverence, spoke to the National Press Club in Washington. When a concerned questioner asked about reporters' rights and imprisonment if they failed to indicate a confidential source, Knight replied, "What's wrong with going to jail?"

Knight married Frances Elizabeth Augustus in 1976, and outlived her by about six months. He died of a heart attack at the home of an Akron friend on 16 June 1981. His twenty percent share of Knight-Ridder stock was placed in a trust.

References:

Jack Alexander, "Up from Akron," *Saturday Evening Post*, 218 (18 August 1945): 10-11;

Frank Angelo, *On Guard: A History of the Detroit Free Press* (Detroit: Free Press, 1981), pp. 1-20, 169-267;

Edwin A. Lahey, "John S. Knight," *New York Herald-Tribune Sunday Forum*, 13 November 1960, II: 3;

Eugene L. Meyer, "The Knights Invade Philadelphia," *Columbia Journalism Review*, 10 (May/June 1971): 44-49;

Nixon Smiley, *Knights of the Fourth Estate: The Story of the Miami Herald* (Miami: Seeman, 1974), pp. 141-332;

Kenneth Stewart, "The Man Who Bought the Chicago Daily News," *PM*, 29 October 1944, pp. 6-9; 5 November 1944, pp. 6-8.

Papers:
John S. Knight's papers are at the University of Akron.

Frank Knox
(1 January 1874-28 April 1944)

Mark Fackler
Wheaton College

MAJOR POSITIONS HELD: Publisher, *Sault Sainte Marie Evening Journal,* renamed the *Evening News* in 1903 (1902-1912); founder and publisher, *Manchester Leader* (1912-1944); publisher, *Manchester Union* (1913-1944), *Boston American, Sunday American,* and *Advertiser* (1927); general manager, Hearst Newspapers (1928-1930); publisher, *Chicago Daily News* (1931-1944).

BOOKS: *The Price of a Managed Economy* (Chicago: *Chicago Daily News,* 1934);
Labor under Dictatorships and Democracies (Chicago: *Chicago Daily News,* 1937);
"We Planned It That Way" (New York & Toronto: Longmans, Green, 1938);
The United States Navy in National Defense (Washington, D.C.: American Council on Public Affairs, 1941).

From the battle of Santiago to the Argonne to Pearl Harbor, publisher Frank Knox combined a career of letters with active political and military service. Knox always considered himself a Republican, but he was free enough from party loyalty that his positions could shift with the changes of a crisis-laden half-century.

William Franklin Knox was born in Boston on New Year's Day 1874, the eldest of five surviving children of William Edwin and Sarah Barnard Knox. His parents were Presbyterians, the father from Scottish roots and the mother from English. Both had been born in Canada and had come to the United States during childhood. Sarah was thrifty and religious, while William Knox was a merchant whose small businesses tended to flounder as customers buying on credit failed to pay. Frank Knox's later political posture reflected these domestic differences: he campaigned as a progressive but called the New Deal "madness."

In 1881 William Knox settled his family in Grand Rapids, Michigan, where he opened a grocery store. The business could barely support the seven Knoxes, so Frank dropped out of high school before his senior year and took a job as a clerk's helper at a book and stationery store. He earned

Frank Knox (The Granger Collection)

five dollars a week, and his industry was rewarded with a promotion to route salesman. But a promising business career was cut short by the panic of 1893; as the only bachelor on the sales team, Knox was the first to be laid off.

With jobs scarce, Knox was convinced by the family's minister to enroll at Alma College, a Presbyterian school that pushed Knox through a classical curriculum while it tested his mettle at the new intercollegiate game, football, and gave him a wife. He was only five feet, nine inches tall and weighed 160 pounds, but his vigor and optimistic self-confidence made him a leader on the field. He was also active in the campus YMCA and the Zeta Sigma literary club. When Alma constructed a gymnasium in 1895, Knox offered his services as recreation director. Among his gym students during that two-year assignment was Annie Reid, the daughter of a local farmer. Love bloomed, but world events intervened.

War fever was growing in late 1897 and early 1898. The sinking of the *Maine* in Havana harbor, the revelation of a Spanish official's letter calling President McKinley a weakling, and finally a joint congressional resolution giving McKinley authority to drive Spain out of Cuba brought calls for enlistment. Knox organized a group of volunteers at Alma, taught them military drill as best he could, and marched them off to join a Michigan regiment which, much to his chagrin, filled up while he was absent from camp attending the funeral of Annie Reid's father. Determined to enter the fray, he accompanied the Michigan troops to Tampa and there, in a stroke of boldness and fortunate timing, presented himself to Lt. Col. Theodore Roosevelt as a volunteer for the elite Rough Riders. Four days later, while the Michigan regiment fought mosquitoes and campsite boredom, Knox followed Roosevelt and 560 horsemen of the First U.S. Volunteer Cavalry aboard a commandeered ferry—the Rough Riders were bound for Cuba.

Knox saw two months of bloody fighting, including the 1 July assault on San Juan Hill. Stricken with malaria and dysentery, he returned home on convalescent furlough. Knox had been one of only two Michigan sons to wear the Rough Riders' floppy campaign hat, a political asset which the publisher of the *Grand Rapids Herald*, E. D. Conger, was quick to exploit. He brought Knox into the 1898 congressional race of Republican William Alden Smith; Knox traveled with Smith, warming up the crowds with stories about his Rough Rider adventures before Smith's speeches. After Smith won the election, Knox hired on as a reporter for Conger's paper. On 28 December 1898 he married Annie Reid.

Energetic and restless, Knox scooped the entire state with a story on the Michigan quartermaster general, who was accused of mishandling the sale of surplus war material. In late 1899 Knox was promoted to city editor and a year later to circulation manager, despite his protestations that he knew little about the business side of newspapers. He learned fast: on a trip to Chicago and Minneapolis to scout circulation techniques, he picked up the idea of free metal boxes for rural subscribers. Circulation in Grand Rapids grew by 50 percent during his year on the job.

In late 1901 Knox was ready for a paper of his own. Sault Sainte Marie in Michigan's Upper Peninsula was a rough lumber and shipping town at cen-

tury's turn, and its *Lake Superior Journal*, a trifling paper with no linotype and only a gas-driven press, was for sale. Knox offered a partnership to John A. Muehling, a Grand Rapids printer, and together they raised $3,000 for the purchase. The venture was not without risk. The "Soo" had another paper, the *News-Record*, and owned a reputation as a brawling port town where saloons and brothels enjoyed the benefits of a cooperative police force. Nevertheless, Knox turned down a raise in salary in Grand Rapids, invested all his savings in the *Journal*, and faced aggressive competition in the market he entered.

But his timing was right. Knox brought out the first issue of his paper, renamed the *Sault Sainte Marie Evening Journal*, on 7 April 1902, promising "a Republican newspaper but the organ of no faction." The reform element in the Soo was ready to support it. Gradually Knox increased circulation, first by training newsboys to yell the headlines, then with tough editorials against lawlessness, and finally by tougher copy attacking the *News-Record*. Put to the test by a saloonkeeper who, irate over an editorial, stormed into the *Journal* offices intent on revenge, Knox set the matter straight with a decisive first punch—language respected by merchant mariners and reformers alike. Only a year after his first issue, Knox announced to the *Journal* staff that the owner of the *News-Record* had offered to sell. He combined the two papers and his *Journal* became the *Evening News*.

In 1901 Knox had met Chase S. Osborn, an Upper Peninsula journalist who shared his bent for rugged outdoorsmanship and progressive politics. Osborn had encouraged the young editor in his new venture at the Soo, often purchasing ten-year subscriptions for distant relatives to help Knox meet his payroll. Knox had responded with editorials calling Osborn Michigan's best candidate for governor. In 1910 Knox managed Osborn's successful gubernatorial race and was rewarded with the chair of the Republican State Central Committee.

In many ways, however, Knox was a misfit among old-guard Michigan Republicans. Against the party line, his paper had supported the local plumbers' union in its effort to have a union plumber inspect the Soo's water mains. The *News* led progressives in calling child labor an "unnatural and infamous wrong." Then, in 1912, Knox threw full support to Teddy Roosevelt's campaign, first in an unsuccessful try to put TR on the Republican ballot, then in an equally frustrating effort to unify the splintered Michigan progressives after Taft captured the GOP convention.

But Knox's undoing as a force in Michigan politics came as an indirect result of Osborn's effort to remove state tax commissioner Robert Shields, whom Osborn accused of favoring liquor interests. Apparently to embarrass the governor, Shields made public a letter written to him by Knox in 1909 urging the commissioner to pressure mining companies for contributions to Osborn's 1910 campaign. Knox's enemies seized upon the disclosure, demanding his resignation from the state central committee. After months of controversy, Knox wrote to state senator Otto Fowle: "My letter to Shields was so inexcusably, thoughtlessly and carelessly written and is . . . readily capable of misconstruction and distortion. . . . Life has its lessons. I have learned a valuable one from this transaction." Though Osborn apparently received no illegal contributions, the damage had been done. With his influence on the wane, Knox sold the *Evening News* to his city editor, and with Muehling moved to Manchester, New Hampshire, to found a progressive paper there.

The move to New England was no less a risk than his previous venture in Sault Sainte Marie. Manchester had two papers, both Republican, and neither was for sale. Yet Knox's friend and Progressive party ally, Republican governor Robert Bass, urged him to start a state newspaper to carry on the political program he had championed in Michigan. Knox and Muehling brought out a new six-day evening paper, the *Leader*, on 9 October 1912. They had 10,000 readers, still 4,000 under the *Union*, when the worried *Union* owner, Roscrans Pillsbury, offered to buy them out for $100,000. Instead, less than nine months after breaking into the market, Knox bought the *Union*, making it the state paper and the *Leader* a city paper. He also made the *Union* politically independent, lest two Progressive party sheets render a circulation advantage to the remaining Republican *Mirror*.

Progressives were beaten at the polls in 1914; the heyday of the third party was past. In 1915 Knox realigned with the GOP, explaining his move in a personal letter to Roosevelt. Vainly Knox worked to get TR on the Republican ballot in 1916, but the Chicago convention went to Charles Evans Hughes. Roosevelt himself followed Knox's example, urging Progressives to support the GOP ticket rather than draft him as their favorite. When Wilson was reelected in November, Knox was crushed and promised to help reform the New Hampshire Republican party around progressive principles. Before he could engage in that battle, however, he was on his way to the hot one already raging in Europe.

Less than a week after Wilson delivered his war message to Congress in April 1917, Knox volunteered for military duty. At age forty-three, he passed the physical tests for Officer's Training Camp, but was informed by the army bureaucracy that he would have to wait until younger volunteers had completed the course. Unaccustomed to such delays, Knox joined the First New Hampshire Infantry Regiment as a private, was promoted immediately to regimental sergeant-major, and a day later drew an assignment to officers' training under the quota alloted to the National Guard. By the time his division sailed in January 1918, Major Knox was in command of a horse-drawn ammunition train. He took part in campaigns at St. Mihiel and the Meuse-Argonne, and was en route to Verdun when the Armistice was declared. For several weeks he bided his time in Europe; then, impatient to resume his newspaper duties, he made a personal visit to army headquarters and was relieved of command. He returned to New Hampshire in February 1919.

Again his roles of publisher and politician coalesced. He was elected first state commander of the New Hampshire American Legion, a post which heightened his stature among state Republicans. With renewed political energy, Knox rallied to Gen. Leonard Wood's campaign for the 1920 Republican presidential nomination. As chairman of the state delegation at the party's convention, Knox managed Wood's floor fight, holding on until the tenth ballot, when Harding pulled ahead as a conciliatory candidate. Knox returned to Manchester and endorsed his party's nominee, but did little else. When scandal later ripped the administration, Knox's editorials were heated and critical.

Knox had traveled to Denmark in 1920 to study Danish cooperatives, and in 1921 he helped found the first farm cooperative in New England, a successful effort for four years. His wartime commission, his editorial fights against state income taxes and government extravagance, and his efforts on behalf of New England agriculture set the stage for his first political campaign on his own behalf. He announced his candidacy for governor in November 1923. Farmers rallied around him and small businessmen supported his stand against increased taxation. But the irony of the campaign for Knox was his opposition to the progressive platform of his younger opponent, John G. Winant, who spent a great deal of money to win the primary. Knox spent little, campaigned for fiscal conservatism, and after he lost he abandoned the last progressive plank he had championed in Michigan: the direct primary was, after all, a "rich man's plaything," he wrote to his wife. At last Knox had become an orthodox Republican, appreciative of President Calvin Coolidge and later a friend and supporter of Herbert Hoover.

The Knoxes seemed content to spend their mature years in Manchester. In January 1927, however, William Randolph Hearst invited Knox to New York to discuss joining his enterprise, so much bigger and more flamboyant than any of Knox's past newspaper associations. The high salary demand that Knox thought would discourage Hearst did not, and Knox first became publisher of the three Hearst papers in Boston; then director of all New England activities for the Hearst oganization; then, in February 1928, general manager of all Hearst papers. Knox instituted a tight budget policy and made efforts to give the Hearst papers a boost in respectability. He directed the managing editor of the *Boston Advertiser* "to eliminate all salaciousness and make crime and criminals always abhorrent."

Knox was guaranteed a free hand by the eccentric Hearst, but as the Depression began to reduce profits, Hearst could not so easily keep away. Twice he sent directives to publishers, bypassing Knox. In the fall of 1930 Hearst began to criticize Hoover, a personal friend of Knox's. Finally, in December, Hearst ordered all his publishers to reduce their accounting staffs, which Knox had built up to monitor cash flow. Twice previously Knox had sent resignation letters to Hearst; this time, to assure its acceptance, he released the letter to the wire services as he sent it to the boss. On 1 January 1931, Knox left the Hearst employ and its annual salary of over $100,000.

Victor F. Lawson had purchased the *Chicago Daily News* six months after its start in 1875 and had built it into a prosperous paper, barring ads for liquor and untested medicinal cures, refusing to publish on Sunday, developing a foreign bureau, and fiercely supporting civic reforms. When he had died in 1925, the *News*'s business manager, Walter A. Strong, had become publisher and had followed the same progressive tradition his boss of twenty years had built. But the youthful Strong had had only six years at the helm. At his death in 1931, the directors and executors sought a rare person to save the paper: a businessman (the *News* had never paid a dividend on its common stock, gross revenues were down $3 million from the previous year, and indebtedness stood at $17.5 million), a wealthy person (Strong's 58 percent of the common stock, a controlling interest, was worth more than $2 million), and an experienced journalist who could meet the competition (Chicago had six metropolitan dailies at the time). Into their search came the name of Frank Knox, largely unknown to the Chicago

business community, but given highest recommendations from Charles Gates Dawes, United States ambassador to Great Britain. In August 1931 Knox became president of the Daily News Corporation and publisher of the paper. New England financier Theodore Ellis helped supply the money Knox needed to buy into the *Daily News*.

The company soon felt the effects of Knox's business sense. He retained the domestic editorial staff, a generous decision in days of declining profits, choosing to trim $1 million in costs by other means. Rather quickly he sold to NBC a half interest in the corporation's radio station, WMAQ, and ordered that preferred stock dividends be withheld for the first time. He abandoned branch pressrooms, and made plans to cut the number of foreign correspondents. When his economy expert put fifteen-watt bulbs in the hallways, however, Knox overruled him. The results were impressive. In 1932 the company paid its first common dividend, and preferred dividends were bought up to date. Despite gross annual revenues of only about $10 million—two-thirds of the annual gross of the late 1920s—during the Depression years, the *News* consistently showed profits.

Knox was hastily adopted by the Chicago business elite. Within a year he became a trustee of the Century of Progress Exposition and of the Armour Institute of Technology, and a director of City National Bank and Trust Company; later he was elected a full member of the exclusive Commercial Club.

Six months after Knox's arrival in Chicago, President Hoover asked him to head the administration's antihoarding drive. The Colonel (so called after his move to Chicago—he had been promoted to lieutenant colonel in the reserves in 1925) took charge of the Citizens' Reconstruction Organization, which he built into a network of 2,300 local committees with headquarters in the News Building. On 6 March 1932, Knox launched the campaign by introducing Hoover over a two-network national radio hookup. The president urged people to bring their money out of hiding, to invest, to buy. The campaign was not a success (only an estimated $200 million came back into circulation), but Knox had moved into the national spotlight for the first time.

Knox supported Hoover for reelection, and took a wait-and-see attitude when the Democrats moved to Washington in 1933. At first supportive of the new president (Franklin D. Roosevelt was, after all, distantly related to Knox's quintessential leader, Teddy), the *News* became increasingly critical of the "recent and numerous manifestations of bureaucratic tyranny in Washington." In 1933 Knox traveled abroad to inspect the *News*'s foreign bureaus, and caught a first glimpse of the economic and political volatility of Europe. When he returned, the National Recovery Administration was in place, and Knox was alarmed at the prospects of centralized government control chipping away at the freedoms of his homeland.

Beginning in August 1933, the *News* lashed out at NRA codes and federal power. When NRA chief Hugh Johnson warned that code violators would go to prison, Knox saw ominous days ahead for the press. In a front-page editorial, Knox called Johnson's pronouncement a threat to freedom of the press if codes were adopted for the newspaper business—as Knox believed they would be. Freedom to speak was fundamental, in the public forum of the press and in the academy. During the Communist witch-hunt at the University of Chicago in 1935, Knox wrote: "Even if some individual teacher is guilty of unlawful activity . . . it would be unjust and contrary to public interest to impose shackles upon teaching and inquiry. It would be a permanent setback to this community if, in a moment of hysteria, the cardinal principles of academic freedom and the perennial quest of truth should be circumscribed."

The managed economies of Europe were to Knox the antithesis of the American ideal. In Italy and Germany he had seen "the negation of everything that we understand as a popular democracy." The Soviet Union, he wrote, had merely seen "a change of exploiters." The same could happen in the United States, he warned his readers, with an eye on the Wagner Bill and the growing federal debt. "Upon what food does this our Caesar [FDR] feed? What madness has seized upon him? Does he not see how dangerously close [The New Deal] comes to conspiracy to break down our institutions of government?" Later in 1935 Knox claimed that New Dealers intended to "seize private property on the Marxian philosophy of government ownership." Especially onerous to Knox were attempts to fix the price of newsprint and to regulate advertising. Believing laissez faire economics an unquestionable virtue, Knox condemned the AAA, the Social Security Act, and the Wagner Act, and suggested "fewer and better Roosevelts."

As his editorials grew more critical after FDR's first three months, so did Knox's political speeches. Knox's remarks in Des Moines and Grand Rapids in 1934 impressed Republican leaders. Upon his return from Europe later that year, he had a private meeting with FDR, neither party effecting a change

in the other's ideas. In July Knox spoke on a network radio broadcast for the Republican National Committee. "Roosevelt versus Roosevelt" was his title; disparity between the European-like regimentation of FDR and the stalwart Americanism of Teddy was his theme. Knox stumped the Midwest for the GOP during the summer and fall, but Republicans lost heavily in that year's Congressional races.

In late 1934, Knox began to be mentioned as a possible presidential candidate. Apparently Knox disregarded the overtures, even a forceful one from William Allen White, until a meeting in April 1935 during which Hoover assured Knox that he would never run for office again. With Hoover to the side, Knox felt free to test his strength. For the next year his speeches railed against the New Deal, though to attract Midwestern votes he came out in favor of bonuses to farmers who took land out of production. With an eye to the American Legion, he supported a veterans' bonus to be paid from funds already designated for relief, not from new tax revenues.

Knox was a declared presidential candidate by November 1935. In the Illinois Republican primary, Knox beat his chief opponent, Sen. William E. Borah of Idaho, by a solid margin, Chicago going to Knox two to one. But FDR, running unopposed in the Democratic primary, polled more votes than Knox and Borah combined.

In the weeks that followed, Borah's star dimmed and Knox failed to win Hoover's endorsement. Into the heat came Alfred Landon, governor of Kansas, who arrived at the convention assured of 470 votes to Knox's 100. With GOP leaders seemingly skittish over a frontal assault on the New Deal, Knox gave up his bid before the balloting began, rallied behind the party's choice, and even gave a seconding speech for Landon. On his return to Chicago, Knox heard a radio broadcast announcing the party's selection for vice-president: himself. With typical verve, Knox campaigned earnestly and forthrightly, opening his race by proclaiming: "I preach to you the doctrine, not of the soft and spineless kept citizen of a regimented state, but of the self-respecting and self-reliant men who made America."

All the intensity of a national campaign paid Knox few dividends, however; the Landon ticket was overwhelmed. Knox cooled his editorial attacks against Roosevelt until a 1938 tour of Europe, during which Knox interviewed Mussolini and observed the new German Reich. Thereafter he revived talk of FDR as an ambitious would-be dictator.

To the 1938 campaign Knox contributed a collection of articles entitled *"We Planned It That Way."* The New Deal, his book explained, was a conspiracy worked out in Roosevelt's mind in 1932. Parallels to Europe's dictators were obvious. In speeches Knox assaulted the administration for "destroying the currency system of America and in so doing destroying the currency system of the whole world." He urged that relief be the job of state and local governments to end this "saturnalia of waste which has been bleeding the country for years." Democrats lost ground at the polls that year, and Knox was hopeful of a Republican resurgence in 1940. But by decade's turn the rush of world events would overshadow partisan differences—at least for Knox.

Though he was Roosevelt's adversary on domestic matters, Knox supported FDR's foreign policy. Armed isolationism with material support to the Western powers was the wisest course, Knox maintained. The inevitable war would be short, he predicted, with Poland, Britain, and France overpowering Hitler's surrounded regime. Knox was shocked when, twenty days after he had published those views, the Blitzkrieg had reduced Poland, leaving only one front for the Nazi armies to press.

To unify the country against the threat, the British cabinet reorganized itself in September 1939 to include opposition party members. Soon thereafter, FDR spoke with Secretary of the Interior Harold Ickes about doing the same, and the latter suggested Knox and Landon as possible cabinet members. In December Roosevelt called Knox to the White House to request his services as secretary of the navy. The Republican publisher declined, as did Landon, and talk of a coalition cabinet subsided.

By April 1940, however, Hitler had swept into Denmark and Norway, and in May he moved into the Netherlands, Belgium, and Luxembourg, with the British army narrowly escaping at Dunkirk. Once more Roosevelt appealed to Knox, whose Rough Rider patriotism had by then overcome his fear of being called a party traitor. Knox agreed to join the Democratic cabinet if another Republican was also brought on board, and if he was not required to stump against his party in the 1940 races. Both conditions met (Henry L. Stimson was nominated as secretary of war), FDR presented Knox in June 1940 to the Senate, which confirmed his nomination sixty-six to sixteen.

Knox believed that a strong navy and air force were the country's best defenses. His plan required only a small standing army, but he urged that troops be concentrated on the coasts, abandoning the string of inland posts that since the end of the Indian wars had served little purpose. In his own departmental planning, travel to naval bases was a top priority; in September Knox surveyed Pearl Harbor, later writing that if war came to the Pacific, it might start there. In dealing with the press, the secretary faced a new ambivalence. He urged editors to voluntarily censor war information, and himself came under the press's blast when he criticized editors who printed names of British ships docked in New York Harbor.

Japan's attack on Pearl Harbor caught Knox by surprise. He flew at once to survey the damage and to do his part to revive morale. During his tenure as secretary, Knox traveled 200,000 miles, from Guadalcanal to Italy. Fully supportive of FDR's wartime policies, Knox drew on the president's support to restrain admirals from increasing their authority at the expense of civilian control. Knox is generally credited with building one of the most successful administrative teams in naval history. He was not slow to make changes in command as he saw the need; the commander at Pearl Harbor was quickly replaced after the surprise Japanese attack. He built a strong civilian team—including Adlai E. Stevenson, who left a Chicago law practice to join Knox's staff—and worked for maximum coordination among the military services.

In January 1944, Knox caught influenza; in April he suffered a heart attack. He died on 28 April at age seventy in Washington, D.C., and was buried with full military honors at Arlington National Cemetery.

Knox was respected for his energy, shrewdness, and lack of pretentiousness in the face of honors and responsibilities. Political losses took a toll on his native buoyant optimism, but he maintained a resilient sense of duty, prizing rugged activism over sedentary editorial philosophizing. His gifts at management were not, on the whole, matched by versatility with ideas, but he did not fear to make his ideas public.

Of Knox's three principal newspaper interests, two continue publishing. Annie Reid Knox sold her control in the New Hampshire papers to William Loeb in 1946. The *Chicago Daily News* was sold to John S. Knight, who in turn sold it to Marshall Field IV in 1959. The paper printed its last edition on 4 March 1978.

Biographies:
Norman Beasley, *Frank Knox: American* (New York: Doubleday, 1936);

George H. Lobdell, Jr., "A Biography of Frank Knox," Ph.D. dissertation, University of Illinois, 1954.

References:
Jack Alexander, "Secretary Knox," *Life,* 10 (10 March 1941): 56-72;
"Who is Frank Knox?," *Fortune,* 12 (November 1935): 109-122.

Papers:
Frank Knox's papers are at the Library of Congress.

Arthur Krock
(16 November 1886-12 April 1974)

Ronald T. Farrar
University of Kentucky

MAJOR POSITIONS HELD: Editor in chief, *Louisville Times* (1919-1923); assistant to the publisher, *New York World* (1923-1927); reporter, Washington bureau chief, columnist, *New York Times* (1927-1966).

BOOKS: *In the Nation, 1932-1966* (New York: McGraw-Hill, 1966);
Memoirs: Sixty Years on the Firing Line (New York: Funk & Wagnalls, 1968); republished as *Memoirs: Intimate Recollections of Twelve American Presidents from Theodore Roosevelt to Richard Nixon* (London: Cassell, 1970);
The Consent of the Governed and Other Deceits (Boston: Little, Brown, 1971);
Myself When Young: Growing Up in the 1890's (Boston: Little, Brown, 1973).

OTHER: *The Editorials of Henry Watterson*, edited by Krock (New York: Doran, 1923).

Arthur Krock

During a career that spanned more than sixty years, Arthur Krock came to symbolize journalistic enterprise and integrity. As a Washington correspondent, he broke more news exclusives, perhaps, than any other journalist of his time. As a news analyst, he—along with Walter Lippmann and David Lawrence—helped perfect the form of the modern political column. As an administrator he developed the Washington bureau of the *New York Times* into a formidable reporting force that commanded unparalleled access to the corridors of power in the nation's capital. He was honored by the Pulitzer Prize committee four times—more than any other journalist in history—receiving two Pulitzer Prizes, a special commendation, and a spe-

cial citation. Though his generally conservative views frequently contrasted with the *Times*'s political liberalism, Krock retained the respect of journalistic professionals for his energy, historical perspective, and a rigid ethical standard that held fast throughout a long and distinguished lifetime in newspaper work.

Of Prussian Jewish stock, Krock was born and raised in Glasgow, Kentucky, to Joseph and

Caroline Morris Krock. His father, a bookkeeper, was of modest means, but his maternal grandfather, "Squire" Morris, a prosperous local merchant, had enough money—and a big enough house—for both families. As a result, Krock grew up in comfortable circumstances. Encouraged by his grandfather's keen interest in books, the child developed a love for reading that sustained him throughout his life. His boyhood in rural Kentucky was a happy time for him—"without pain or sorrow," as he described it later—but his teenage years brought a harsh change; his father found work in Chicago, and Arthur finished high school in the city under less idyllic circumstances. In 1904 he enrolled at Princeton; but after only one semester his family's worsened financial situation obliged him to return to Chicago, where he attended Lewis Institute, a small but respected college. In 1906, he was graduated with an associate in arts diploma, having paid his own expenses by assisting professors and working on the college yearbook. Then, in his own words, "I took the first train I could get to Louisville with a newspaper job as my objective."

Krock's first newspaper work was as a general assignment reporter on the *Louisville Herald*. He did not always perform well on spot news assignments—years later he claimed that a four-alarm fire provided more challenges to a reporter than a peace conference ever could—but his city editor shrewdly sensed Krock's abilities to size up political stories: in 1908 he assigned the cub to cover the Democratic national convention. Krock met the challenge by reporting an exclusive account of a split within a key state's delegation. It was a major scoop, and the young correspondent was rewarded by being assigned to the paper's prestigious political beat. He seemed clearly on his way, but financial difficulties—this time, those of the paper—again forced a change in his plans. The *Herald* went through a retrenchment; Krock gave up his job so that a colleague who had a family might stay on. For a short time Krock found work in the local sheriff's department, then spent two years as a night editor in the Louisville bureau of the Associated Press.

In 1910, Gen. W. B. Haldeman, the editor and part owner (with Henry Watterson) of the *Louisville Times*, offered Krock a job as the paper's Washington correspondent because of what he had heard about Krock's reporting performance at the Democratic convention two years earlier. Krock leaped at the chance. The next year he was named correspondent for the *Times*'s sister paper, the *Louisville Courier-Journal*, also. That was also the year he married Marguerita Polleys of Minneapolis.

Krock headed the combined Washington bureau of both papers until 1915. Then, still in his late twenties, he was summoned back to Louisville to become, first, managing editor for both papers, then editor in chief of the *Times*.

In 1918 Krock accompanied President Woodrow Wilson to the Versailles peace conference in France. While there, he obtained an exclusive interview with the supreme Allied commander, Marshal Foch, and impressed a number of other prominent figures on the scene—notably Herbert Bayard Swope, the flamboyant editor-reporter for the *New York World*.

Before he left for Paris, Krock had, at the owners' request, negotiated the sale of the Louisville newspapers to Judge Robert Worth Bingham, who was later to become United States ambassador to the Court of St. James's. Krock and his new publisher were unable to agree on editorial policy, however, and soon Krock resigned his editorship. He worked briefly in public relations; then, in 1923, he accepted Swope's invitation to join the *World*—at that time perhaps the country's most distinguished newspaper. The staff included Charles J. V. Murphy, one of the country's top reporters; Walter Lippmann; Alexander Woollcott; Heywood Broun; the historian Allan Nevins; the novelist James M. Cain; and the playwright Maxwell Anderson. It was heady company, but Krock, who had long since learned his craft, easily held his own.

Four years after joining the *World*, however, Krock resigned; he had been promoted to the position of assistant to the publisher and frequently found himself unhappily trapped between Ralph Pulitzer and his galaxy of reporting stars. Krock accepted an invitation from *New York Times* publisher Adolph S. Ochs to write editorials and to establish a national network of correspondents for the rapidly expanding Sunday paper. When the *Times*'s Washington correspondent, Richard V. Oulahan, died in 1931, Krock was named his successor.

Ochs, who had rescued the *Times* from near-bankruptcy and had steadily pointed it toward a position of national leadership, decided in 1932 that the newspaper should begin, as an experiment, a by-lined editorial-page column from the capital. The tone and content of the feature would have to be worked out, but Ochs instinctively felt that Krock was the writer he wanted to try it. The experiment was an unqualified success, as Krock's interpretative essays invariably commanded the attention of political leaders. A *Time* magazine writer, crediting Krock, Lippmann, and David Lawrence with institutionalizing the serious political column, put it this way: "Lippmann offered the perspective of history; Lawrence offered polemics; Krock encompassed both." Krock's column, "In the Nation," frequently began with a statement from a political figure, followed by the journalist's assessment of it. Krock's political conservatism often angered many readers, but the country's leaders carefully read the column. "He had a lot of clout where it counted," another columnist, William S. White, later recalled. "He sure as hell wasn't for the subway trade. He had enormous influence among the movers and shakers in Washington." "In the Nation," a mixture of reporting, analysis, interpretation, and commentary, became a fixture on the *Times*'s editorial pages, and hundreds of other newspapers moved to provide their readers with something similar.

For all his column writing, however, Krock remained at heart a reporter, dazzling the capital with one major scoop after another. His colleague Murphy provided a glimpse of the Krock style. Early in 1933, Krock broke the story that President Franklin D. Roosevelt had decided to take the country off the gold standard:

> Acting on a tip, Krock phoned Secretary of the Treasury William H. Woodin at his hotel. "Mr. Secretary, I hear we're going off the gold standard. When are you going to announce it?" he asked.
>
> Woodin, startled that the government's most closely guarded secret had reached the most influential and widely read journalist in Washington, asked innocently, "Don't you think we ought to let the President announce that himself?"
>
> "When is he planning to?"
>
> "Saturday."
>
> "I'll announce it myself on Friday." And Krock did.

Krock also got the beat on the establishment of the National Industrial Recovery Act, Roosevelt's ill-fated plan to pack the Supreme Court, and dozens of other exclusives. Frequently the editors of the *Times* would find Krock's column so newsworthy that they decided to put it on the front page. When that happened, Krock would rewrite the column as a news story, then swiftly research and write an entirely new column late that same evening to fill his usual spot on the editorial page. Krock also wrote the lead story for the *Times* on every biennial election from 1932 to 1952.

As bureau chief, Krock moved swiftly to shore up the *Times*'s presence in Washington and to cover the dramatic expansion of the government during the New Deal. Krock hired top people and encouraged them to develop their individual skills. At the same time, his own powerful personality shielded his correspondents from the demands of editors back in New York. His judgment—often tartly relayed to the home office—was that his Washington reporters knew what they were doing and were to be considered right until proven otherwise. His staff meetings were rare; he is believed to have called only three of them in the more than twenty years he headed the bureau. At one of these, he insisted that the correspondents develop their individual expertise: "We've got to specialize," he said. "You've got to know as much about the subject you're handling as the men who are making the news. And for God's sake, try to keep it simple." In his personal associations with colleagues, he maintained his distance, referring to most of them as "mister." When a newcomer asked him how long a person had to be on the staff in order to be called by his first name, Krock replied simply, "For as long as you care to remain here. I'm sorry, but that's the way I am."

Nor would he permit himself to become personally close to his news sources. He held that the newspaperman must "cheerfully accept the penalty of limitation upon friendships with those whose acts he must reveal and analyze." Krock was fond of quoting Frank R. Kent of the *Baltimore Sun* in this respect: when a senator once admonished Kent by referring to "your friends in the Senate," Kent replied: "Who said I wanted any friends in the Senate?"

Krock was of medium height, somewhat portly, and resembled an investment banker more than a hard-digging newspaperman. President John F. Kennedy, bruised by Krock's critical analysis of some New Frontier programs, invited the journalist to a private dinner and asked him: "Arthur, how can so benign-looking a fellow as you write such mean things?" Krock regarded himself as a gentleman of the old school, and his courtly manner brought him a reputation as something of a snob. "He yearned for social status, and put great store on the graces and symbols of life," colleague James Reston wrote of Krock. "And the paradox of this was that the reality of the man was so much better than the pretense." He shrewdly mined Washington's social scene for news, and could be counted on to convert lunches and dinner parties into significant news beats. "The mighty talked to him trustingly as a friend or warily as a critic," *Time* magazine noted, "but almost always they talked."

Krock's first Pulitzer Prize was awarded in

1935 for the "general excellence" of his reporting during the New Deal. Two years later President Roosevelt granted Krock an exclusive interview; the lengthy conversation earned Krock a number of news beats and his second Pulitzer.

His beloved Princeton—Krock maintained a lifelong interest in the university, and spoke there frequently—conferred upon him an honorary master of arts degree in 1937. He received honorary doctorates from a number of institutions, including the University of Kentucky, the University of Louisville, Northwestern University, Hamilton College, and Centre College of Kentucky.

Krock's wife died in 1938. They had been married twenty-seven years and had a son, Thomas Polleys Krock. His second wife was Martha Granger Blair, whom he married in 1939. A native of Chicago, she was a society columnist for the *Washington Times-Herald*. In one of her columns she mentioned Krock, describing him as one of Washington's "glamour boys." Six months later, they were wed.

An exclusive interview with President Harry S Truman in 1950 brought Krock a nomination for an unprecedented third Pulitzer; however, Krock was serving that year as a member of the Pulitzer advisory board, and he requested that the prize be withheld to avoid suggestions of favoritism. The Pulitzer board, determined to reward what it called "the outstanding instance of national reporting in 1950," presented him with a special commendation anyway. In 1955, Krock won his fourth Pulitzer award, a special citation for distinguished reporting from Washington. He also received the John Peter Zenger Award in support of freedom of the press, and a number of decorations from foreign nations.

Krock had critics both outside and inside the *New York Times*, and many of the objections to his work were related to his conservative political views. Although Krock never attempted to impose his opinions on the other *Times* correspondents in his Washington bureau, he was set upon frequently for letting his conservative bias creep into his news reports. Morris Ernst, a noted liberal of the period, bitterly criticized Krock for what he called a "hit and run" assault on a State Department official: "I have never met Krock as far as I can remember," Ernst wrote in the *Saturday Review*, "but I abhor his type of attack. I even prefer nasty, hard-hitting [Westbrook] Pegler, with whom, of course, I disagree on practically all his tactics as well as on matters of taste. I just don't like one-sided snipers. I like my opponents tough and direct." Others voiced similar views, but Reston took precisely the opposite

position. "Maybe the most remarkable thing about [Krock] was that, no matter how deeply he believed in his conservative philosophy, he did not allow his opinions to interfere with the reporting of the news," Reston wrote in the *Times*. "He was stiff and formal, and kept an air space between himself and his colleagues, and between himself and most officials, but he had standards as well as opinions."

In 1953, Krock agreed to step aside as chief of the Washington bureau. He was sixty-seven, but frankly admitted that he had "planned this move for a much later time." He yielded his title to Reston, whom he had hired during World War II; Reston had been approached by competitors with important job offers, and the bureau chief's position would keep him with the *Times*. Krock continued to write his column, although the *Times*'s leftward shift widened the gulf between him and the paper's top management. In 1966, when he was seventy-nine, he was asked to retire. His final column—it was estimated to be the 8,500th one he had written for the *Times*—concluded with a cliché line from television crime thrillers: "All right, Officer, I'll go quietly."

In his last years, he continued to keep regular hours at an office in the *Times*'s Washington bureau, where he worked on a succession of books. One of them, *Memoirs: Sixty Years on the Firing Line* (1968), enjoyed a run of six months on national best-seller lists. A devoted husband, he told friends he hoped to survive his wife—she was an invalid—so that he might take care of her throughout her lifetime. This was not to be: on 12 April 1974, following an illness of nearly six months, he died at his home in Washington. He was eighty-seven.

One of the country's leading reporters, Charles J. V. Murphy, spoke for many American journalists when he concluded an affectionate tribute to Krock with these words: "How to sum up Arthur Krock? As a man who, from the building of the Panama Canal to the walk on the moon, was always close to power, able himself to influence men of power, but never by power corrupted? A man whose every word, written or spoken, for more than 60 years, showed the bright glint of integrity? Perhaps the only way is simply to say that he was the finest journalist and one of the most decent men I have ever known."

References:

John Chamberlain, "*The Times*'s Loss, History's Gain," *National Review*, 23 (15 June 1971): 656;

Morris Ernst, "Strictly Personal: Hit and Run Journalism," *Saturday Review of Literature,* 28 (7 April 1945): 13;

"Grand Old Man," *Time,* 103 (22 April 1974): 61;

Charles J. V. Murphy, "Unforgettable Arthur Krock," *Reader's Digest,* 107 (March 1975): 101;

"Old School Ties," *Newsweek,* 83 (22 April 1974): 73.

Papers:
Arthur Krock's papers are at Princeton University.

David Lawrence
(25 December 1888-11 February 1973)

Ronald S. Marmarelli
Central Michigan University

MAJOR POSITIONS HELD: Washington correspondent, Associated Press (1910-1915), *New York Evening Post* (1915-1919); founder and owner, Consolidated Press Association (1919-1933); syndicated columnist (1919-1973); founder and editor, *United States Daily* (1926-1933), *United States News* (1933-1940);

BOOKS: *The Truth about Mexico* (New York: New York Evening Post, 1917);

The True Story of Woodrow Wilson (New York: Doran, 1924; London: Hurst & Blackett, 1924);

The Business Man and His Government (Washington, D.C.: United States Daily, 1929);

The Other Side of Government (New York: Scribners, 1929);

Industry's Public Relations (New York: American Management Association, 1930);

Beyond the New Deal (New York & London: Whittlesey House, McGraw-Hill, 1934);

Stumbling Into Socialism and the Future of Our Political Parties (New York & London: Appleton-Century, 1935);

Nine Honest Men (New York & London: Appleton-Century, 1936);

Supreme Court or Political Puppets? Shall the Supreme Court Be Free or Controlled by a Supreme Executive? (New York & London: Appleton-Century, 1937);

Who Were the Eleven Million? (New York & London: Appleton-Century, 1937);

Diary of a Washington Correspondent (New York: H. C. Kinsey, 1942);

The Editorials of David Lawrence, 6 volumes (Washington, D.C.: U.S. News & World Report, 1970).

David Lawrence

PERIODICAL PUBLICATIONS: "The President and His Day's Work," *Century,* 93 (March 1917): 641-652;

"International Freedom of the Press Essential to a Durable Peace," *Annals of the American Academy of Political and Social Sciences,* 72 (July 1917): 139-141;

"Government By Impression," *Century,* 96 (May 1918): 117-123;

"Crisis in the Leadership of President Wilson," *Outlook,* 120 (4 December 1918): 528-529;

"Peace By Publicity," *Scribner's,* 65 (June 1919): 702-709;

"The President and the Press," *Saturday Evening Post,* 200 (27 August 1927): 27, 117-119;

"Reporting the Political News at Washington," *American Political Science Review,* 22 (November 1928): 893-902;

"I Saw America," *Saturday Evening Post,* 209 (5 December 1936): 5-7, 96-98;

"The Cause That Failed But Lives On," *New York Times Magazine*, 93, 14 November 1943, pp. 3, 34-35;

"Shop Talk At Thirty," *Editor & Publisher,* 77 (27 May 1944): 64, 60.

As a reporter, columnist, publisher, and editor, David Lawrence stood at the top among his fellow journalists for more than sixty years. He was, the *New York Times* wrote in an editorial after his death in 1973, "one of the nation's most highly respected and warmly regarded newspapermen, and it is as such that he would want to be remembered." His work throughout his career was motivated in large part by a personal fascination with public affairs and a commitment to the ideal that citizens must be provided every means possible for keeping informed about the affairs of the nation and the world. His guiding belief was that there was a great need for "enlightened public opinion, steadily and persistently" and that it was the task of journalists to provide the means for enlightenment.

Lawrence was born on Christmas Day in 1888 in a room one floor below his father's tailor shop in Philadelphia, Pennsylvania. His parents, Harris and Dora Cohen Lawrence, had recently immigrated to the United States from England. The family soon moved to Buffalo, New York, where Lawrence attended the public schools. While preparing for an eighth-grade debate, he came upon the *Congressional Record* in the public library. "Long after my debate," he said years later, "I used to go to that library to read the *Record.* I just couldn't imagine anything finer than to be able to some day see those men in debate." When he was in high school, Lawrence began his newspaper career by selling photographs of local sports figures to the *Buffalo Express*; later he wrote general news for the paper during vacations from school.

In the fall of 1906, Lawrence set off for Princeton University with, he said later, "exactly $25 in my pocket and a pass on the railroad given me by my newspaper when I left Buffalo." He earned his way by working as an Associated Press correspondent, and also supplied seventeen newspapers with news of college sports and other activities during his years at Princeton. In 1924 he described the period as "four eventful years which embraced the reporting of the last two years of Grover Cleveland's residence there and his death, and the famous Graduate School controversy which led to Woodrow Wilson's withdrawal from the University [presidency] to accept the [Democratic] nomination for Governor of New Jersey." The association with Wilson that he developed as a reporter covering a major news figure (and as a student in Wilson's Constitutional Government course in the spring of 1909) prepared him well for later work that was to see him become, as one writer noted, "one of Wilson's chief journalistic interpreters." Wilson assisted Lawrence at one point in his work at Princeton by convincing the board of trustees to waive the rule prohibiting students from having telephones in their rooms; he agreed with Lawrence that a telephone was essential for his news work.

Lawrence's first major feat as a reporter came in June 1908 when he sent out the first word of the death of Grover Cleveland. Lawrence had stayed in Princeton that summer, and Mrs. Cleveland had agreed to keep the young correspondent informed about the condition of the former president, who was gravely ill. She sent him a telegram from Lakewood, New Jersey, on 24 June 1908: "Grover Cleveland died at 8:40 A.M." He said later, "I had a scoop. There wasn't any correspondent then in Princeton except myself. And as a result of the scoop and the work I did for the Associated Press during the funeral, I was given a job as vacation relief in the Philadelphia office." He returned to the Philadelphia AP bureau for summer work in 1909 and for full-time employment in 1910 after receiving his B.A. degree from Princeton.

After a few months in Philadelphia, Lawrence was assigned in October 1910 to the Washington bureau of AP. He worked the night shift at first. Years later, Cabell Phillips wrote that Lawrence had come to Washington "with the reputation of a prodigy, a handicap he promptly overcame by proving really to be one." His longtime friend and colleague Arthur Krock said of Lawrence: "The chief of the Associated Press bureau in Philadelphia must have had a good eye for promise when he recommended that Lawrence be transferred to Washington. It was not long before the slim, eager young man, with a most agreeable personality, was upsetting the complacent hierarchy of Washington correspondents—some of them wore silk hats then, and carried canes—with exclusive news stories written with . . . clarity and personal detachment. . . ." Krock wrote that Lawrence "combined the reportorial qualities of a ferret and a beaver. His hazel eyes seemed to reflect at once deep contemplation and a searching eagerness. When he smelled news, he was unrelenting until he found its origins; then he spared no labor in making its presentation clear and durable. His integrity, and the ability to listen, opened up many a reluctant source to him."

In 1911 Lawrence's enterprise, together with his knowledge of Spanish (gained by means of concentrated effort after he failed a college Spanish course the first time he took it; it was the only course he failed at Princeton), earned him the confidence of representatives in Washington of both the Mexican government of President Porfirio Diaz and Mexican rebel forces under Gen. Francisco Madera. He helped the two sides get together to begin negotiating an end to the fighting in Mexico and was assigned by the AP to go to that country to cover the armistice talks. While he was in Juarez, he found himself the only newspaperman on the scene of a three-day battle between government and rebel troops. He fired off a steady stream of bulletins to the AP, and when he returned to Washington, AP chief Melville Stone awarded the twenty-two-year-old reporter a gold watch for "exceptionally valuable service."

Lawrence was sent back to Mexico in 1912 to cover the continuing strife there, but in July he was ordered back to the United States to cover the presidential campaign of Democratic nominee Woodrow Wilson. "From that time forward," Lawrence wrote in 1924, "through the campaign and the preinaugural period at Bermuda, Trenton and Princeton, the author was writing daily dispatches for the Associated Press, and when Mr. Wilson was inaugurated, was assigned to the White House . . . to report almost hourly the incidents of that eventful administration." Lawrence recalled an early conversation with the nominee in 1912 at Wilson headquarters in Sea Grit, New Jersey:

> I had a frank talk with Mr. Wilson at the very outset stating that while we had known each other intimately at Princeton, my function as a reporter for the Associated Press would be disinterested, and that the organization I represented was, of course, not interested in advocating the candidacy of any man but simply in chronicling the news. . . .
>
> When I told Mr. Wilson that my purpose was to give him a "square deal," he said he wanted nothing else.

Wilson made himself readily available to the reporters covering his campaign, but he objected to their following him everywhere he went. In mid-August, Lawrence was selected to accompany Wilson on a private trip to New York City in lieu of having "a squad of newspapermen" follow him. "My sixteen keepers," Wilson wrote in a letter from the city that evening, "sent one of their number in with me. . . , the representative of the Associated Press, an old pupil of mine at Princeton, to keep an eye on me."

Lawrence soon acquired the reputation of being a confidant of the new president. "When Wilson moved into the White House, Lawrence, in a newspaper sense, moved in with him," wrote the author of a later profile of the journalist. "He became one of the recognized channels for semi-official expressions of Presidential opinion." On several occasions, however, Lawrence made a point of stressing that he had only as much direct, personal access to Wilson as any other journalist. In *The True Story of Woodrow Wilson* (1924), which Lawrence emphasized was a "dispassionate narrative," he wrote at length of the limited nature (in a journalistic sense) of his relationship with Wilson. He stated that "in all the years of [my] acquaintance with Woodrow Wilson, no favor was sought and none given. No obligation was incurred, no political allegiance established. Most of the time it fell to [my] lot as a newspaper reporter to see behind the curtain of events. It was a scrutiny necessitated by the never-ending demands of present-day journalism, a scrutiny resented at times by Mr. Wilson himself, tolerated upon occasions as a necessary evil, but never wholly accepted by him as a corollary of that 'pitiless publicity' which, in an unguarded moment of impromptu speech, he coined as a slogan for his first administration."

Wilson had no favorites among newspapermen when he was in the White House, Lawrence wrote. Wilson insisted that when he talked to individual newsmen, his statements be considered "off the record." But usually, according to Lawrence, "the same information was obtainable from other sources without strings." He said he found it to his advantage "not to ask for audiences with the President, but to get information about Mr. Wilson's activities from members of the Cabinet and other sources in Washington. . . . [which] often irritated

Mr. Wilson." Lawrence was on especially good terms with Joseph Tumulty, Wilson's secretary, who performed the role of press secretary. He said he realized that personal relations with Wilson would compromise his work as an impartial newsman covering the White House. "Although there were frequent charges that Mr. Wilson inspired my articles, especially after I left the Associated Press in 1915 to become a special correspondent, the truth is I saw him alone much less than did some other men in the newspaper business and I never received from him in private conversation any stories which could be used in the newspaper at the time." Nevertheless, Lawrence did obtain

> from other sources several items of news of a sensational character and published them and found no difficulty in reflecting the President's views without even seeing him. . . .
>
> Although Mr. Wilson occasionally sent me personal messages of regard and reposed in me sufficient confidence on two occasions to ask that I undertake delicate missions which related to our negotiations with foreign governments, I was never in any sense his "mouthpiece" or his "spokesman" in the press.

Lawrence asserted that the view of him as a channel for the White House negated his "journalistic enterprise" and his impartiality, two professional qualities of which he was always proud. "My own writings . . . were frequently distasteful to the President. Indeed, the Washington correspondent who allows friendships or antagonisms to influence his dispatches betrays the trust imposed in him by his newspaper and its readers. The general public expects fair-minded interpretation of the facts without regard to whether an individual or party is helped or hurt by the disclosure."

As part of his dealings with the press, Wilson formalized the practice of having regular presidential press conferences. Lawrence and other reporters assigned to the White House soon perceived a need for some means of accrediting correspondents. "It became necessary to make sure that men who regularly covered the White House were admitted [to the press conferences] because the space was limited," Lawrence recalled in 1953. As a result, the White House Correspondents Association was chartered on 25 February 1914 with William W. "Fatty" Price of the *Washington Evening Star* as chairman, Lawrence as vice-chairman, William B. Metcalf of the *Baltimore Sun* as secretary-treasurer,

and eight other charter members. (The association charter, framed by oval photographs of the eleven charter members, still hangs in the White House Press Room; Lawrence was the last surviving charter member.)

Meanwhile, strained relations between the United States and Mexico, which culminated in the United States Navy's occupation in April 1914 of Vera Cruz, resulted in additional tasks for Lawrence, including coverage of the conference at Niagara Falls, New York, at which diplomats from Argentina, Brazil, and Chile attempted to mediate between the two nations. With the outbreak of war in Europe in July, Lawrence was put in charge by the AP of news out of Washington related to the war, but developments in Mexico and continued tension in U.S.-Mexican relations continued to occupy part of his energy. He had cultivated sources among representatives of the new government in Mexico, and these were to be useful in Lawrence's subsequent activities for his employers and for the United States government.

In May 1915, Lawrence reported to Wilson by letter on his talks with the German ambassador and wrote him a memorandum on the situation in Mexico. Then on 9 June 1915 Lawrence scored one of his biggest scoops by reporting the resignation of Secretary of State William Jennings Bryan. He had heard a big story would be breaking but had no specifics. His news sense and his knowledge that Bryan was at odds with Wilson over the president's strong note to Germany on the sinking of the *Lusitania* in May led him to deduce that the big story was about Bryan. The manner in which he got the story has been recounted often; Lawrence himself told it this way: "I went to the office of my friend, the Secretary of War, Lindley Garrison. When I walked in and sat down with him, I said: 'Too bad about Bryan, isn't it?' He said: 'Yes, it is. I'm sorry to see him go.' And I said: 'When do you think it will be?' He said: 'Well, it's supposed to be tomorrow afternoon about 2 o'clock.'" Lawrence checked with another official and then went to the White House and got a confirmation from Tumulty. He called in the story from a phone booth in the press room at the State Department, then stayed inside the phone booth for twenty minutes. "I was afraid that I might reveal my excitement to colleagues sitting around the press room," he recalled.

In August 1915 the Associated Press sent him to Vera Cruz to interview Mexican president Venustiano Carranza about United States proposals for bringing peace to Mexico and improving relations between the two countries. Wilson and Secretary of

State Robert Lansing encouraged him to report to them on his talks with Carranza. Lawrence sent several confidential reports, using the code name "Laguirre," to Lansing, who passed them along to Wilson. When he returned to Washington in early September, Lawrence wrote further to Wilson about his journey, and he continued to report to the president of developments in Mexico throughout the month. Of particular interest to Lawrence and the White House was the extent of German influence in Mexico. Lawrence wrote later that he "recommended that the most effective way to counteract German influence and prevent Mexico being used as a base for hostilities, especially in the event the United States entered the war, was to recognize the Carranza administration and formalize the relations between the United States and Mexico."

Lawrence's career was boosted in December when he left the Associated Press to become special Washington correspondent for the *New York Evening Post*. His editor was his former bureau chief with the AP, John Palmer Gavit. One of his early dispatches for the *Post* on Col. Edward House's trip to Europe to carry an offer of mediation from Wilson to the warring powers aroused the ire of the president. "I am deeply annoyed by the *Evening Post*'s performance," Wilson wrote House on 24 December 1915. "David Lawrence is a nuisance."

Cabell Phillips described Lawrence's work: "His stint was to write the daily lead story out of Washington under his own by-line. This was not an uncommon assignment for Washington correspondents in those days. Lawrence, however, gave his stories a new twist by appending a shirttail of succinct interpretation. Not content to give simply the who, what, and where of Washington events, he gave the *why* also. He set the current happening in the larger canvas of what had gone before and what might reasonably be anticipated in the future." This "was an innovation in reporting. . . , and it caught on. Lawrence's stories came to be more and more interpretive and less and less spot news." The *Post* began syndicating Lawrence's dispatches in 1916.

Lawrence's involvement in Mexican-United States affairs, both as a reporter and as an unofficial adviser to Wilson, continued in 1916, when relations between the two nations were further strained by Pancho Villa's raids on American territory and by the army's subsequent punitive expedition into Mexico in March. Lawrence advised the president on the release to the press of information about American actions in Mexico and kept Wilson informed from May through July about his frequent talks with the Mexican ambassador.

At some point, Lawrence's activities apparently were perceived by administration officials as not useful. On 27 July 1916, in what Lawrence described as "my last communication on the subject to you," he wrote Wilson: "I am restrained by the circumstances from writing anything for my paper about Mexico. I cannot comment at all really on the situation and while that is not so essential really, for my paper understands that, I do not like to feel that my activity may be undesired by the Government." In November and December of that year, Lawrence got back to Mexico for the *Post* and wrote a series of articles that were republished in 1917 by the newspaper in a collection titled *The Truth about Mexico*.

Lawrence was not an active participant in the Washington social whirl, but he did attend White House receptions on occasion. In 1916 at one such affair, the only one "ever truly important to him," according to Arthur Krock, he met Ellanor Campbell Hayes, "the beautiful woman who two years later became my wife," Lawrence said. They were married on 17 July 1918 and had two sons, David and Mark, and two daughters, Nancy and Etienne.

Meanwhile, with 1916 an election year, Lawrence was busy covering Wilson's reelection campaign from the perspective of a Washington correspondent with friends among those around the president. In July he advised the president in a memorandum: "Recent happenings have demonstrated pretty clearly that we must take some definite steps in our foreign policy. We are at a turning point. In the sense that our course must be submitted to the voters at the polls next November, it is political. If we are fair and honest, we need have no fear of what their judgment will be. If we are not true to the trust they impose in us, we deserve to be disappointed." He called for a policy of even-handed neutrality in regard to both Great Britain and Germany, noting: " 'America First' must be our motto as you have well chosen it."

Although Wilson's reelection chances were not viewed as good by many journalists, Lawrence predicted a Wilson win, and his reputation as a seer was enhanced when Wilson's victory came close in scope to what Lawrence had forecast. But his relations with Wilson were strained again in mid-November when the president asked Tumulty, Lawrence's friend, to resign. Tumulty revealed that fact to Lawrence and to other journalists, and Lawrence went to Wilson to try to convince him not to fire Tumulty. Lawrence told Wilson that he would appear to be guilty of ingratitude and that he was wrong about his secretary's performance in his job. Wilson relented.

United States war policy and the development of Wilson's plans for the postwar world received most of Lawrence's journalistic attention in 1917 and 1918. After the Armistice in November 1918, a Lawrence story published in the 25 November *New York Evening Post* and run in several other newspapers and magazines angered Wilson. It stated that the president was facing a crisis and that many of his friends and supporters were concerned for a variety of reasons. Lawrence reported that Wilson faced a rebellion within the Democratic party, which would face defeat in 1920 if the problem were not solved. The article appeared shortly before Wilson sailed for Europe to attend the Paris peace conference. Lawrence wrote later: "Reports of the President's displeasure were carried to me but when I talked with him in Paris and later in Rome, he was cordial. On the Western trip in September 1919, I found him personally cordial."

Lawrence covered Wilson's trips to London and Rome and was on hand for much of the peace conference. He also made a trip across the United States in February 1919 to survey public sentiment on the League of Nations proposal. In September Lawrence was part of the press corps accompanying Wilson on his twenty-two-day, 8,000-mile, twenty-state trip to rally the public behind the Versailles Treaty. The trip ended with Wilson's collapse after his thirty-sixth speech.

In February 1920, Lawrence finally broke with Wilson:

> The dismissal of Secretary Lansing on the ground that he had called cabinet meetings without authority seemed to me unjust and I reported the facts as well as I knew them, suggesting that only a fit of temper could have prompted this action.
>
> From that time on Mr. Wilson was represented to me as again displeased with my writings and though I had no communication with him thereafter I was apparently so sympathetic with his ideals that editorial writers continued to accuse me of being inspired by him.

For Lawrence, the postwar years brought new successes. When new owners of the *New York Evening Post* told him that they no longer wished to continue syndicating his work, Lawrence went into business for himself. He organized the Consoli-

dated Press Association in 1919 and began sending out a Washington column of interpretation and analysis to subscribing newspapers. It is widely recognized as the first column to be syndicated by wire, and Lawrence, Mark Sullivan of the *New York Herald-Tribune,* and Frank R. Kent of the *Baltimore Sun* are credited with being pioneers of the political column in American newspapers.

To keep his leased wire busy and to earn income for his new business, Lawrence also provided news and feature services and financial news, including speedy market quotations. Years later, publisher John S. Knight recalled: "During the early 1920s when we were getting out a newspaper [the *Detroit Free Press*] with only an International News Service state wire, the old Consolidated Press Association was a lifesaver. It provided, as a supplementary news service, the stock-market reports, Dave Lawrence's column and the renowned foreign service of the *Chicago Daily News.*" Lawrence was credited in 1931 by Robert Allen and Drew Pearson with having "the business genius to see that a boom was rapidly crystallizing and that there would be enormous popular interest in stock market quotations and special business articles." An article in the October 1920 *Everybody's* commented: "The latest 'success' in Washington is young David Lawrence. He has just passed thirty, but he has developed a new idea in distributing Washington news. . . . Lawrence now serves some one hundred newspapers in the United States with a telegraphic story of analysis and interpretation. He has a large suite of offices in Washington with an office force larger than that of many newspapers, and assistants in many American cities. He has his own leased telegraph wires for distribution. Every weekday at 11 o'clock in the morning he puts on the wires in his office a simple-looking nine-hundred-word story which he has just written. For the next two hours that story scuttles throughout the wires of telegraphdom until he has reached every corner of the country. It is a story of the 'why' of the latest news incident in Washington. Lawrence has about three and a half million readers, and his present income tax is said to work out to about a cent a reader."

In 1926 Lawrence undertook another new project, a daily newspaper containing nothing but news of government and texts of official actions. Announcing that the *United States Daily* would begin publication on 4 March 1926, Lawrence stated, "The newspaper will concern itself with a complete presentation of facts covering the day-by-day activities of the legislative, judicial, and executive branches of the United States Government." The newspaper, whose motto was "All the Facts—No Opinion," carried no editorial page. In 1929, the *United States Daily* began publishing news about state governments. By the end of 1926, its circulation was 13,560; at its peak in 1930, circulation was 40,956.

Lawrence, meanwhile, in addition to writing his daily column and overseeing the operation of his press association and the newspaper, continued his frequent writing for magazines, especially the *Saturday Evening Post,* and in the late 1920s he moved into radio. He was among the first political commentators with a regular broadcast, presenting a Sunday program, "Our Government," on the National Broadcasting Company network from 1929 to 1933.

In June 1931 he made an unsuccessful attempt to purchase the *Washington Post* from the McLean family for $3 million. If his offer were accepted, the *New York Times* noted at the time, he would be "at 43 years of age, one of the leading newspaper publishers of the country."

Lawrence reorganized his enterprises in 1933. The Consolidated Press Association was ended, its financial news service turned over to the Associated Press and its features taken over by the North American Newspaper Alliance. His daily newspaper became a weekly, under the title the *United States News.* The newspaper's content continued to emphasize developments in Washington, but it was broadened to include general national affairs, more analysis, and an editorial page on which Lawrence presented his opinions. The weekly's circulation at the end of 1933 was 29,854; by 1940 it was up to 85,000. Lawrence also organized the Bureau of National Affairs to provide information services to businessmen and other professionals.

In the 1930s, the scope of his enterprises and his financial success, together with his support of Herbert Hoover and his unrelenting opposition to the New Deal, brought Lawrence criticism from several directions. It became common practice then and later to refer to his financial success as unique among reporters. This set him apart from most journalists. Allen and Pearson wrote in 1931 that he "is not popular among the correspondents. He is too commercial for the taste of the true reporter." Asserting that Lawrence, like some other commentators, had been in a gloom since Wilson's death, Charles Fisher wrote in 1945: "The Herbert Hoover Administration cheered him up for a while, it is true. At about that period he became the only working newspaperman in the country to own a yacht. The view from its deck was reassuring and,

until well along into the Depression, it was his habit to join the Great Administrator in announcing that prosperity was just around the corner." Allen and Pearson were also critical of his blind support for persons in high stations:

> David Lawrence [is a] shining example of what unremitting application, business acumen, and respectful regard for high authority and position will do for an ambitious man.
>
> Lawrence was a reporter once—and one of the very best in the game, too—but today as the result of the happy combination of the aforementioned talents, he is an editor, owner, and publisher.

They cited his yacht, his fashionable home off Massachusetts Avenue in Washington, his wife's limousine, and Lawrence's own expensive roadster.

Expressions of opinion appeared more and more openly in Lawrence's syndicated column in the 1930s. In a 1945 profile of Lawrence, John O'Brien wrote of his colleague: "He was so thoroughly indoctrinated with the Associated Press prejudice against editorializing in the news report that it had never occurred to him that publishers would buy opinion. When Walter Lippmann, shortly after moving from the Democratic *New York World* to the arch-Republican *New York Herald-Tribune* in 1932, came out for Roosevelt in flat contradiction of the paper's policy, Lawrence said that publishers would never stand for it. Discovering that they did, he decided to try airing his own views." Another journalist, Delbert Clark, wrote of him in 1941: "In some ways Lawrence is the most skillful of all the Washington columnists: he has the ability to appear sweetly reasonable while making the most highly prejudiced statements of opinion, unlike those others who never attack any person or policy without advertising the fact." Fisher commented that although Lawrence at times grew "moody and sorrowful," he was "seldom an ill-tempered critic."

His criticism of the New Deal dominated his columns and five books he wrote in the 1930s. Arthur Schlesinger, Jr., cited him as one of the newspaper commentators who "became faithful spokesmen of the [Anti-New Deal] cause." Lawrence called for the formation of a "Constitutional" Democratic party to oppose the "Socialist Democrats" of the New Deal. He asserted in *Stumbling Into Socialism* (1935) that the "maelstrom of centralized order-giving [of the New Deal] more strongly resembles the dictatorship of the Fascistic and Communistic states of Europe than it does the American system." His writing was not based only on pontificating from the nation's capital. From August through October 1936, he traveled more than 20,000 miles (nearly all of it by train) through forty-six states, talking with people in sixty-four communities to gather material for his columns and for magazine articles.

Lawrence's *Diary of a Washington Correspondent* (1942) consisted of his daily observations from May 1940 to May 1942 on developments related to World War II. He was critical of administration policy on the domestic front as it related to the war effort: "The responsibility of the critic is to point out the errors until correction is made. The aid and comfort that can be given the enemy by sheer incompetence or neglect in governmental office is far greater than can be given by scattered criticism in the press." He observed that his criticism was "nothing personal" against the president: "This writer has always had a feeling of personal friendship for Franklin Roosevelt."

In his own enterprises, meanwhile, Lawrence had made further changes. The *United States News* was changed to a magazine format in January 1940, and during World War II its coverage of national news greatly expanded. Circulation grew from 85,000 to 240,000 by 1943. In 1946 he founded the *World Report,* a weekly magazine devoted to international news and analysis, and in 1948, deciding that no distinction could logically be made between national and international news, he merged his two magazines into *U.S. News & World Report,* which he edited until his death. Its circulation in its first year was 378,776 and at his death in 1973 was 1.94 million. In 1962, Lawrence arranged for the magazine to be employee-owned (as he had done earlier with the Bureau of National Affairs). This was part of his effort, wrote the magazine's publisher, John H. Sweet, "to ease the transition and make sure that his successors would be able to carry on without him."

Lawrence continued to be a critic of liberal policies in government; he was staunchly anti-Communist and supported U.S. policy in Vietnam. The next-to-last editorial he wrote for *U.S. News & World Report* — in the familiar space at the end of the magazine, with the small photo of the U.S. Capitol in the upper right-hand corner — was "Peace with Honor," which praised presidents from Eisenhower through Nixon for keeping American commitments. The editorial appeared in the 12 February 1973 issue.

Lawrence received numerous awards and honorary degrees. In the later years of his life his long career and achievements were recognized on several occasions. At a National Press Club luncheon on 23 December 1963, two days from his seventy-fifth birthday. Lawrence was given a Certificate of Achievement. One member of the audience arose to say: "Do you know that every person here and many more who are absent have a real affection for you?" He was given the University of Missouri Honor Medal and inducted into the School of Journalism Hall of Fame in 1965. On 22 April 1970 President Nixon presented him with the Medal of Freedom, the nation's highest civilian award. The citation read in part: "He has won and held the respect of millions for his perception, his judgment, his fairness, and his devotion to the principles on which America was founded." In 1971 Lawrence was elected a charter member of the Hall of Fame of the Washington Chapter of Sigma Delta Chi, the professional journalists society.

In a tribute after Lawrence's death, John S. Knight recalled that Lawrence had told him not to stop writing. "Whether you know it or not, you and I would be nothing if we didn't write," Lawrence had said. Up to his death of a heart attack at the age of eighty-four in his winter home at Sarasota, Florida, on 11 February 1973, Lawrence had followed his own advice. The *Washington Star-News* noted that he had "kept busy to the end. No one at *The Star-News,* and probably none of his readers, was surprised that his usual Monday column was already in the office. But he did surprise us, for all that. The obituary in our early editions yesterday directed readers to Mr. Lawrence's 'last column' on that day's opposite-editorial page. And then, on the wire, right on time as usual, came what indeed is his last column, written a few hours before he died. It appears in its usual spot today — lucid, crisp, informative, the product of a wise and gentle mind which never stopped asking the right questions." Lawrence's last editorial for *U.S. News & World Report,* "Only the People Can Regulate Broadcasting" appeared in the 19 February issue.

Arthur Krock remembered that Lawrence did not like vacations because they took him away from the news; even a heart attack in 1968 and his wife's death on 13 June 1969 had not stopped him. "At an age when most men are content to relax, David Lawrence refused to bask in his accomplishments. He had news to report, complex events to explain and comment upon." Nothing for Lawrence "was more fascinating than the news. He devoured it as it clattered off the teleprinter machines that he kept operating around the clock at his summer and winter homes and at his farm near Washington. He capsuled it in concise and pithy table talk for his wife and four children. . . . As an old friend once noted, 'Dave never stopped being a reporter.' " As a reporter and editor, Lawrence held himself and his employees to strict professional standards: "A reporter should, he felt, set down the facts of a situation and leave judgment of its significance to the reader. When commentary is necessary, it should be plainly marked as such." His end-of-the-magazine editorials were headed by a note: "This page presents the opinion of the Editor. The news pages are written by other staff members independently of these editorial views." The reputation of *U.S. News & World Report,* Krock noted, was built "on the unadorned presentation of facts on national and international affairs. Any expression of opinion was confined to Lawrence's signed editorial. Indeed, lest his particular viewpoint influence the news section, he would not permit staff members to see his editorial until they read it in the magazine itself. Once, interviewing a new editor, he said, 'I would really rather you did not read my daily newspaper column. I don't want you to be influenced by my opinion.' "

Several eulogists emphasized Lawrence's integrity and his avoidance of pejorative criticism and hypocritical praise. At the memorial service for Lawrence on 14 February 1973 at the Washington Hebrew Congregation Temple, Rabbi Joshua O. Haberman stated that although Lawrence was a "tough-minded observer of the struggle for power . . . [he] never turned cynical." Krock commented that adherence to such standards as Lawrence observed "does not set the river of print on fire. But it helps greatly to keep that river clean, and sustain the flow of reliable information that serves our government process." Later, Krock wrote in *Reader's Digest*: "David Lawrence was a friend and colleague. I do not believe he ever did a petty thing. I know he never wrote a petty line."

As for his political views, *Time,* labeling him "The Durable Wilsonian," commented: "He was, above all, a keeper of vows and custodian of tradition." The *New York Times* obituary quoted Lawrence's comments at the National Press Club in 1963: "There are lessons to be learned from the past. But there is one doctrine that has emerged intermittently which I have never been able to accept. It is the doctrine that change is good for change's sake." The obituary writer then noted: "In prose that was neat and serviceable, although far from artistic—the prose of the old-time newspaper reporter, not the essayist—he proclaimed a conser-

vative credo with weekly certitude." Rather than being a conservative or a reactionary he was, as the *New York Times* observed, "a Woodrow Wilson-type liberal who simply declined to change his opinions to conform with most of the other national opinion-makers." Lawrence frequently called himself a "conservative liberal." Benjamin McKelway, a former editor of the *Washington Evening Star,* had stated on the occasion of Lawrence's receipt of the Medal of Freedom in 1970:

> No matter in which direction the tide may choose to flow, Dave is more inclined to buck it than float with it.
> This trait is—or at least it ought to be—a distinguished characteristic of sound and useful journalism, expressed by the readiness to say, "I doubt it," when everybody else is saying, "It's a sure thing."

The *Washington Star-News* summed him up this way: "He was the newsman in the classic mold. His opinions were firm, but they never overrode the reporter's instinct to get to the bottom of the story. He had the tenacity of the proverbial bulldog in his search for the facts, but with all he was the most forgiving and kindest of men. One of the best things that can be said about the profession of journalism is that, very occasionally, it produces a David Lawrence."

References:

Robert S. Allen and Drew Pearson, *Washington Merry-Go-Round* (New York: Liveright, 1931);

Delbert Clark, *Washington Dateline* (New York: Stokes, 1941);

"David Lawrence," *New York Times*, 14 February 1973, p. 40;

"The Durable Wilsonian," *Time,* 46 (26 February 1973): 46;

Charles Fisher, *The Columnists* (New York: Howell, Soskin, 1944);

John S. Knight, "A Farewell to an Old Pro," *Detroit Free Press,* 18 February 1973, 2 D;

Arthur Krock, "Unforgettable David Lawrence," *Reader's Digest,* 104 (January 1974): 75-79;

"Lawrence Announces Daily Paper," *New York Times,* 16 February 1926, p. 13;

"Lawrence May Buy Washington Post," *New York Times,* 9 June 1931, p. 29;

"The Lawrence Memorial Service," *U.S. News & World Report,* 74 (26 February 1973): 98, 97;

Arthur S. Link, ed., *The Papers of Woodrow Wilson,* volumes 25 and 33-37 (Princeton: Princeton

University Press, 1978, 1980, 1981);

F. B. Marbut, *News From the Capital* (Carbondale: Southern Illinois University Press, 1971);

John C. O'Brien, "Custodian of the New Freedom," in *Molders of Opinion,* edited by David Bulman (Milwaukee, Wis.: Bruce, 1945), pp. 121-131;

Cabell Phillips and others, eds., *Dateline: Washington* (Garden City: Doubleday, 1949);

Arthur M. Schlesinger, *The Coming of the New Deal* (Boston: Houghton Mifflin, 1958);

William G. Shepherd, "Our Ears in Washington," *Everybody's,* 43 (October 1920): 68-73;

John H. Sweet, "David Lawrence 1888-1973. A Message From the Publisher," *U.S. News & World Report,* 74 (26 February 1973): 3;

"Tributes to 'A Giant of Journalism,' " *U.S. News & World Report,* 74 (5 March 1973): 84, 82-83;

" 'Won Respect of Millions': Life Story of David Lawrence," *U.S. News & World Report,* 74 (26 February 1973): 93-96.

Max Lerner
(20 December 1902-   )

Clifford G. Christians
University of Illinois

MAJOR POSITIONS HELD: Editorial director, *PM* (1943-1948); columnist, *New York Post* (1949-present).

BOOKS: *It Is Later than You Think: The Need for a Militant Democracy* (New York: Viking, 1938; London & Edinburgh: Chambers, 1939; revised, New York: Viking, 1943);

Ideas Are Weapons: The History and Uses of Ideas (New York: Viking, 1939);

Ideas for the Ice Age: Studies in a Revolutionary Era (New York: Viking, 1941);

The Constitution and the Crisis State (Williamsburg, Va.: College of William and Mary Press, 1941);

International Organization after the War: Roads to World Security, by Lerner and Edna Albers Lerner (Washington, D.C.: National Council for Social Studies, 1943);

Public Journal: Marginal Notes on Wartime America (New York: Viking, 1945);

The Third Battle for France (New York: Union for Democratic Action Educational Fund, 1945);

World of the Great Powers and George Fielding Eliot on the Military Strength of the Big Five (New York: Foreign Policy Association, 1947);

Actions and Passions: Notes on the Multiple Revolution of Our Time (New York: Simon & Schuster, 1949; London: Kennikat, 1970);

America as a Civilization: Life and Thought in the United States Today (New York: Simon & Schuster, 1957; London: Jonathan, 1958);

The Child and Parent in American Civilization (New York: Child Welfare League of America, 1958);

The Unfinished Country: A Book of American Symbols (New York: Simon & Schuster, 1959);

The Age of Overkill: A Preface to World Politics (New York: Simon & Schuster, 1962);

Education and a Radical Humanism (Columbus: Ohio State University Press, 1962);

Tocqueville and American Civilization (New York: Harper, 1966);

Values in Education (Bloomington, Ind.: Phi Delta Kappa, 1976);

Ted and the Kennedy Legend (New York: St. Martin, 1980).

OTHER: Oliver Wendell Holmes, Jr., *The Mind and Faith of Justice Holmes: His Speeches, Essays, Letters, and Judicial Opinions,* edited with foreword and commentary by Lerner (Boston: Little, Brown, 1943; revised, New York: Modern Library, 1954);

Thorstein Veblen, *The Portable Veblen,* edited by Lerner (New York: Viking, 1948);

Essential Works of John Stuart Mill, edited by Lerner (New York: Bantam, 1961);

"The Triumph of Laissez-Faire," in *Patterns of American Thought,* edited by Morton White and Arthur Schlesinger, Jr. (Boston: Houghton Mifflin, 1963), pp. 147-166;

Alexis de Tocqueville, *Democracy in America,* translated by George Lawrence, edited by Lerner and J. P. Mayer (New York: Harper & Row, 1966);

Max Nicholson, *The System: The Misgovernment of Modern Britain,* introduction by Lerner (New York: McGraw, 1969);

Kiyoaki Murata, *Japan: The State of the Nation,* foreword by Lerner (Tokyo: Japan Times, 1979);

Marilyn Ferguson, *The Aquarian Conspiracy: Personal and Social Transformation in the 1980s,* foreword by Lerner (Boston: Houghton Mifflin, 1980).

SELECTED PERIODICAL PUBLICATIONS: "The Social Thought of Mr. Justice Brandeis," *Yale Law Journal* (November 1931): 1-32;

"The Supreme Court and American Capitalism," *Yale Law Journal* (March 1933): 668-701;

"The New Age of Despots," *Yale Review,* 24 (December 1934): 293-310;

"What is Usable in Veblen?," *New Republic,* 83 (15 May 1935): 7-10;

"Democracy With a Union Card," *Virginia Quarterly Review,* 14 (Spring 1938): 209-228;

"American Leadership in a Harsh Age," *Annals of the American Academy* (July 1941): 117-124;

"Russia and the Future," *Atlantic Monthly,* 170 (November 1942): 79-87;

"State Capitalism and Business Capitalism," *American Scholar,* 19 (Autumn 1950): 484-491;

"Ordeal of the American Woman," *Saturday Review of Literature,* 40 (12 October 1957): 13-15, 60-63;

"Climate of Violence," *Playboy,* 14 (June 1967): 99, 118, 162-166;

"Are the Experts Destroying Our Judgment?," *McCall's,* 95 (November 1967): 26, 132;

"The Negro American and His City," *Daedalus,* 97 (Fall 1968): 1390-1409;

"American Agonistes," *Foreign Affairs,* 52 (January 1974): 287-300;

"What is a Liberal-Who is a Conservative?," *Commentary,* 62 (September 1976): 77-79;

"Eros and Power," *Playboy* (December 1978);

"We Were All Reds in Those Days," *Vogue,* 172 (April 1982): 318- ;

"Jonathan Schell's *Fate of the Earth,*" *Vogue,* 172 (July 1982).

Max Lerner has combined journalism and teaching for nearly five decades. While he calls himself a newspaperman, Lerner has been recognized throughout his career as a member of America's intellectual elite. His column is still syndicated by the *Los Angeles Times,* and he continues to teach

Max Lerner

classes at the United States International University in San Diego. Lerner describes himself as a "working thinker," as a teacher in the public arena. "I'm trying to bridge gaps," Lerner says, "to relate the two worlds of journalism and academics. If you're going to write for the papers as a columnist, instead of just retell Washington gossip, . . . you ought to be pretty fundamentally based in the social and human sciences. For that reason I think my academic work is critical to my journalistic writing. On the other hand, I also feel as an academic that I don't want to write just for a small coterie of my fellow professors." Lerner sees his role as confronting the pressing cultural issues of the day in terms of democratic and constitutional values. Since the early years of the New Deal, Lerner has been an influential spokesman for the leftist segments of liberalism. More recently he has shifted to a centrist liberal position.

Mikhail Lerner was born on 20 December 1902 near Minsk, Russia, to Benjamin and Bessie Podel Lerner. Before his birth, his father had immigrated to New York City; as Jewish parents, Max Lerner wrote later, they "wanted their children to breathe a freer air and become someone." When Benjamin Lerner had scratched together enough money, Bessie took the four children across the Atlantic and the Lerner family established itself among the other one million immigrants of 1907. "America was the golden kingdom," Lerner recalls, "that's what the Jewish immigrants used to say, the golden kingdom."

The land of promise was not hospitable at first. Benjamin Lerner had saved $700 by working in a garment loft for $10 a week; but the run on the banks in 1907 made the family feel insecure. They foolishly purchased a farm in the Catskills from an uncle without seeing it. Lerner remembers the look on his father's face when they arrived "and saw that the land was covered with boulders, all stones. All of his savings were gone. He broke his back there, and broke his heart, too." Max's older brother, Hyman, developed a rheumatic heart and died on the farm.

The family settled in New Haven, Connecticut, in 1913 after the farm went bankrupt. His father opened a grocery store and delivered milk. At the age of seventeen Lerner entered Yale College on a scholarship. Although he was elected to Phi Beta Kappa in his junior year, he never felt that he achieved a fully satisfying educational experience. "There was a decided gap between the boys from New Haven and the boys from the outside," he recalled in an interview for *People* magazine. "You just didn't get into the clubs. You didn't become editor of the *Yale Daily News*. I was short and Jewish, and the beautiful girls didn't want anything to do with me." He graduated in 1923 as Maxwell Alan Lerner with his B.A. degree in literature. At one point he thought of becoming a professor of literature; but he was also interested in economics and social theory, and instead entered the Yale Law School.

Lerner dropped out before the end of the first year. He could not bear the thought of spending his life "fighting for somebody's house deed." During this year he read Thorstein Veblen's *The Theory of the Leisure Class* (1899). It was a revolutionary book for him. "I felt that I wanted to become an economic reformer," he said. "Then I saw a sign on a bulletin board which informed me of a fellowship out in St. Louis which would enable me to get a master's degree in economics at Washington University and then go on to the Robert Brookings Graduate School of Economics and Government in Washington, D.C." Lerner won the award; he received his M.A. from Washington in 1925 with a

thesis on "The Economic Theories of Thorstein Veblen" and his doctorate from Brookings (an adjunct to the Brookings Institution, discontinued since then) in 1927. He met Anita Marburg at Brookings and married her in 1928. They had three daughters: Constance, Pamela, and Joanna.

During his student days in the nation's capital, Lerner became acquainted with Justice Oliver Wendell Holmes; he lived next door to Holmes and often observed him and his close associates at close range. At Brookings his interests centered on constitutional law, so Holmes's work had a particular impact. Sixteen years after graduation he prepared an anthology of Holmes's writings with a commentary. *"The Mind and Faith of Justice Holmes,"* he wrote, "is sort of half Holmes and half myself." He took as his own creed that of the justice: "It is required of a man that he should share the passion and action of his time, at the peril of being judged not to have lived."

At twenty-five years of age Lerner settled in New York, where he joined the editorial staff of the *Encyclopedia of the Social Sciences*. Lerner had been profoundly influenced by Walton Hamilton, the economist who headed Brookings, and Hamilton located this first job for him. Lerner worked for five years on the *Encyclopedia*, first as assistant editor and then as managing editor. One of his colleagues on the project was Alvin Johnson, the former editor of the *New Republic* who had founded the New School of Social Research in 1923. Johnson also had a significant influence on Lerner.

In 1932 Lerner joined the social science faculty of Sarah Lawrence College in Bronxville, New York, where he fell in love with a "brilliant and beautiful student," Edna Albers. Nine years later he divorced his first wife to marry Edna. They had three sons: Michael, Stephen, and Adam. Edna Albers Lerner is at present a clinical professor of psychology at New York's Payne Whitney Psychiatric Hospital and Clinic.

While teaching at Sarah Lawrence, Lerner served as chairman of the Wellesley Summer Institute. He lectured on government at Harvard University in 1935 before becoming editor of the *Nation* in 1936. Only the intransigence of Harvard's president, James B. Conant, prevented Lerner from continuing to teach while editing the country's oldest liberal journal. He resigned from the *Nation* after two years to join the political science department at Williams College in Williamstown, Massachusetts, where he taught until 1943. In several of the summers during those five years, he was a professor of government at the Harvard Summer

School and served as contributing editor to the *New Republic*.

In establishing himself between 1932 and 1943 as an academic, Lerner maintained a heavy involvement in journalism and politics. In 1934 he directed the Consumers' Division of the National Emergency Council, and in 1942 he served as a consultant for the U.S. Office of Facts and Figures, working with Archibald MacLeish. Meanwhile he built a name for himself in the literary world as well. During these years he wrote dozens of articles on economic, political, and cultural issues for the *Nation* and the *New Republic,* but also for more technical journals such as the *Yale Law Journal* and the *Harvard Law Review.* Nearly all the tough battles of the 1930s and 1940s captured his attention—including the sitdown strikes in automobile plants, which he characterized as a "revolutionary development."

Lerner's thinking at that time was gathered into three books: *It Is Later than You Think* (1938), *Ideas Are Weapons* (1939), and *Ideas for the Ice Age* (1941). Together they persuaded *Current Biography* to label him in 1942 "one of the outstanding political thinkers and journalists of the Left Wing of American democracy." Thirty years before radicals of the 1960s announced liberalism's demise, Lerner, as a self-styled "neo-Marxian liberal," struggled with that very issue in *It Is Later than You Think.* Lerner recognized the tragedy of men with good intentions "who willed the ends they sought and could not will the means to achieve them." In order to defend democracy against fascism and communism, he called for a rapid transition to "democratic collectivism" in which basic industries would be carefully planned in the public interest. *It Is Later than You Think* reflects, in part, Lerner's involvement in the disputes over a basic social theory by which to guide the New Deal.

The sixty essays and reviews collected as *Ideas Are Weapons* explore the relationships between society and ideas. Composed over an eight-year span, they range from the Supreme Court to the novels of John Dos Passos. Most of the articles are journalistic portraits of people whose ideas shaped the modern West: Veblen, Holmes, Emerson, Thoreau, Lincoln, Roosevelt, Marx, Pareto, Hitler, and Swift. *Ideas for the Ice Age* struggles directly with the problems created by World War II and appeals for a confrontation with "those revolutionary events and forces of the past few years that have burst the bounds of our social forms, our international organization, our received ideas." These books are pivotal in understanding Lerner. As a writer and

teacher who traffics in ideas, he concludes in these books that ideas are instrumental: "I have increasingly sought to view them as weapons in the personal struggles that every individual has for the resolution of his tensions, and in the struggles for power and order that every age has and every culture."

The balance shifted from academia to journalism in 1943 when Lerner left Williams College to become the editorial director for the New York newspaper *PM.* Though he continued to teach part-time at the New School for Social Research, *PM* and some efforts at radio commentary dominated his time. *PM,* founded by Ralph Ingersoll in 1940 and funded by Chicago liberal Marshall Field III, stands as an important experiment in the history of American journalism—a serious, idealistic forerunner of the underground press of the 1960s and 1970s. *PM* operated off Field's fortune, carrying no advertising and determined to survive on subscriptions alone. Within eight years, it folded. However, *PM*'s reputation for good writing and photography, a crusading spirit, and well-developed feature departments had already been recognized. Journalism historian Frank Luther Mott observes that "though *PM* was financially a failure, it made an important contribution to the journalism of the decade. The editorials of Max

Lerner during the time he was editorial director for PM

Front page of PM, *the experimental New York tabloid for which Lerner worked in the 1940s. The paper lost money almost every year after it was founded in 1940. Three months after this issue appeared, its name was changed to the* Star; *it died in January 1949.*

Lerner were often high points in liberal writing. The coverage of medical, racial, and anti-monopoly matters was notable, though always angled, *PM*-style, by opinion. Income taxes and insurance scandals were specialties. A brilliant staff, of leftist tendency, worked for the paper, and gave it often an amateurish flavor—like the staff of a college paper having a wonderful time without too much feeling of responsibility." In the evaluation of Richard Louv, this was one of the few times that the stodginess of newspaper makeup and newswriting would be challenged in a lasting way. *PM* demonstrated the value of interpretation, departmentalized news, features, and prominently displayed columnists.

For one year after the demise of *PM,* Lerner wrote columns for its successor, the *New York Star.* Then, in 1949, he began his career as columnist for the *New York Post,* a role he continues to fulfill. His column appears in nearly 100 newspapers worldwide through *Los Angeles Times* syndication. Also in 1949, Lerner became professor of American Civilization at Brandeis University, a post he held until 1973; he served as dean of the graduate school from 1954 to 1956. The period 1949 to 1973 marks his richest and most productive years both as academic and journalist. As a tribute to his achievements, Wilberforce University in Ohio gave Lerner his first honorary LL.D. degree in 1962; six others have followed since then.

Two major books provide clues to his accomplishments during this era of maturity: *America as a Civilization* (1957) and *The Unfinished Country* (1959). The first represents his scholarly side—a dozen years of research and reflection written up into a massive work of more than 1,000 pages and nearly one-half million words. *The Unfinished Country* is a 733-page collection of Lerner's columns, mainly from the 1950s. After reading almost 2,000 of them, he chose the few hundred which comprise this book.

America as a Civilization— a veritable storehouse of facts and analysis on American life and thought—has sold nearly 100,000 copies since 1957. Now translated into five languages, it is an internationally recognized classic. In the foreword, Lerner writes: "Americans are beginning to turn a search light on themselves and their civilization, and interpret them both to the world. The present study is intended as a trial essay in that direction." He contends that America is more than a form of government, an economic system, or a racial mixture; its civilization is a composite of all three elements. For Lerner, the American is a new kind of person

on this planet—a special combination of gifts and powers about which we ought to remain optimistic. He has tried to see the nature and meaning of the American experience as a whole. "Whenever I have tried to chip off a fragment—on American government, on liberalism, on foreign policy, on morals—I found that it lost some of its meaning when torn from the rest."

Lerner's broad scope in *The Unfinished Country* differs little in comprehensiveness from his first collection, *Ideas Are Weapons*. One section deals with personal and family matters, while another traces current American phenomena such as novels, movies, cocktail parties, and patterns of marriage and divorce. Sandwiched among these social and cultural observations are Lerner's essays on politics and governmental crises—Truman and McCarthy, wiretaps, the Warren Court, Alger Hiss and John L. Lewis, Little Rock. Lerner considers himself a general columnist rather than exclusively a political commentator. He sees all phases of the human comedy or tragedy as available to him: "I am as likely to write about the death of a movie producer or the life and loves of a TV star as about the UN debates, about the arrest of a prostitute as about the visit of a head of state." *The Unfinished Country* is more informal than *America as a Civilization,* with a swinging cadence and occasional slang. Yet its erudition is as obvious as that of the latter book, which is intended to be more scholarly in tone.

These two volumes together have defined Lerner as a generalist. He self-consciously sees himself in this vein and insists on a holistic vision as an alternative to academia's rigid categories. "In Jefferson's day," he explains, "it was possible to have the sense of encompassing what was known and thought, but it is very hard now. For that reason I feel that if any writer, any thinker, has the urge to broaden out and try to do the over-arching, synthesizing work, it is all to the good. I have the taste for that."

Some academics have tried to damn his generalist position, and he is at pains to justify himself in the preface of *The Unfinished Country*. He observes that much of his own continuing interest in journalism stems from an aversion to the academic environment, which only encourages specialization. Lerner characteristically appeals to Justice Holmes, who taught him the value of seeing life whole by insisting that the business of thinkers is to show "the relation between your particular fact and the frame of the universe."

When he was seventy-one years old, Lerner

retired from the Brandeis faculty. However, he has continued uninterrupted his three-times-a-week column for the *Los Angeles Times* Syndicate. He has also been enticed into teaching at the Graduate School for Human Behavior, part of the United States International University at San Diego. Every other week during the school year he commutes to the West Coast from his East End Avenue apartment in Manhattan. Though small (3,000 students) and young, USIU has attracted several stars to its faculty in addition to Lerner—psychoanalyst Viktor Frankl, the late futurist Herman Kahn, and humanist Rollo May. Its individualized approach draws the creative students who greatly interest Lerner. As Distinguished Professor in the School of Human Behavior, he finds his classes a natural laboratory for trying out his latest ideas. Meanwhile, he is studying the California way of life: "This is the area of growth," he believes, "and I want to be where it is happening." A close friend of Hugh Hefner for two decades, he has an open invitation to stay at the Los Angeles Playboy Mansion whenever he is in southern California. This contact has earned him such unofficial titles as "the Hefner Mansion's in-house guru" and "the Henry Kissinger of the Playboy empire."

Lerner's interests remain broad. He is currently working on two books: "The Wounded Titans," a psychohistory of six presidents, and "Eros in America." Lerner wrote scores of columns on sexuality when the Kinsey reports were first released in the early 1950s. He is still a close observer of trends in sexual behavior and applauds the modern tendency to see sexual life-styles as part of an emerging cultural pattern rather than condemning all variation from middle-class conventions as perverted or criminal. Wanting to maintain an "element of the sacral in sexuality," he is preparing his book as part of his own search for meaning. Lerner seeks for all men and women not only greater freedom, but "whatever leads people to greater emotional depth." Most recently he has given priority to completing a memoir of his life.

On a visit to Poland, Lerner was asked to give in a single word the essence of America. "You know, one word, what is America?" Lerner recalls thinking "very hard, very fast, over all the various possibilities, equality, freedom, equity, justice, tolerance, all the rest, dynamism, and—I came up to my surprise with this word *access*." In Lerner's view, the United States gives everyone, on balance, an equal chance at life's opportunities. Working it out, he admits, is still an ongoing battle involving affirma-

tive action, reverse discrimination, and entrenched social disagreements.

Lerner prefers, however, not to call his attitude "optimism." "I'm a possibilist," he says, "I like to read history as possibility. When it comes to our collective living . . . our destiny as a people rests not in our stars but in ourselves. . . . I think it's going to be possible for us to cope, survive, in some way. I won't say we will resolve problems, you don't resolve them, but you change them so that they are more manageable. . . . More options are open for us than we dare admit. Everything depends on our collective intelligence in making choices, and our will to carry them out." George W. Bain summarizes Lerner's attitude: "Lerner seeks to work with what he believes to be the stream of history, to channel this fact of change in healthy directions and toward humanistic goals." Through his self-styled "possibilism" he pursues neither the "is" nor the "ought" but the "can be." Since his earliest immigrant days, Lerner has believed in America as the leading symbol of the modern age.

Thomas Jefferson saw education and the press as twin poles of the democratic order— trained minds plus reliable information as both essential to self-governance. Lerner embodies both domains in a manner that few besides Walter Lippmann have succeeded in achieving. He has always looked behind events to grapple with their social and historic meaning. The press today, in Lerner's judgment, has too much flabby tissue; it does not vigorously confront the basic issues of the time. Still, "between the two groups of people with whom I've spent my life, newspapermen and professors," he claims, "I much prefer the former. They're more compassionate, they share easier, they're earthier. Academics are so scared." "Perhaps," as Richard Louv observes, "Lerner's survival secret is that he has cut his own path between the two worlds, just out of reach of the stagnating and destructive qualities of each camp."

References:

George W. Bain, "Liberal Teacher: The Writings of Max Lerner," Ph.D. dissertation, University of Minnesota, 1975;

Dorothy Brockhoff, "A Conversation with Max Lerner," *Washington University Magazine* (Spring 1972): 26-30;

Sidney Hook, *Reason, Social Myths, and Democracy* (New York: Humanities Press, 1950), pp. 62-75;

Richard Louv, "Max Lerner: Lamenting and Loving America," *San Diego Magazine* (August 1978): 83;

Frank Luther Mott, *American Journalism: A History: 1690-1960,* 3rd edition (New York: Macmillan, 1962), p. 772;

Barbara Rowes, "Liberal Admirers. . . ," *People* (19 March 1979): 49-57;

I. F. Stone, "Max Lerner's Capitalist Collectivism," *Southern Review,* 4 (1938-1939): 649-664.

Walter Lippmann

Michael Kirkhorn
University of Kentucky

BIRTH: New York City, 23 September 1889, to Jacob and Daisy Baum Lippmann.

EDUCATION: B.A., Harvard University, 1910.

MARRIAGES: 24 May 1917 to Faye Albertson; divorced. 26 March 1938 to Helen Byrne Armstrong.

MAJOR POSITIONS HELD: Staff member, *New Republic* (1913-1922); editorial staff member, director of the editorial page, *New York World* (1922-1931); syndicated columnist (1931-1971).

AWARDS AND HONORS: Commander, French Legion of Honor, 1946; Legion of Honor, Officer of Order of Leopold (Belgium), 1947; Knight's Cross of the Order of St. Olav (Norway), 1950; Commander, Order of Orange Nassau (Netherlands), 1952; Overseas Press Club Award, 1953, 1955, 1959; Pulitzer Prize, 1958, 1962; George Foster Peabody Award, 1962; Gold Medal, National Academy of Arts and Letters, 1965; LL.D., Wake Forest College, 1926, University of Wisconsin, 1927, University of California and Union College, 1933, Wesleyan University and University of Michigan, 1934, George Washington University and Amherst College, 1935, University of Rochester, 1936, College of William and Mary and Drake University, 1937, University of Chicago, 1955, New School for Social Research, 1959; Litt.D., Dartmouth College and Columbia University, 1932, Oglethorpe College, 1934, Harvard University, 1944; Presidential Medal of Freedom, 1964; City of New York Bronze Medallion, 1974.

DEATH: New York City, 14 December 1974.

BOOKS: *A Preface to Politics* (New York: Mitchell

Walter Lippmann

Kennerley, 1913; London: Unwin, 1913);
Drift and Mastery: An Attempt to Diagnose the Current Unrest (New York: Mitchell Kennerley, 1914; London: Unwin, 1914; new edition with introduction and notes by William E. Leuchtenberg, New York: Prentice-Hall, 1961);
The Stakes of Diplomacy (New York: Holt, 1915);
The World Conflict in Its Relation to American Democ-

racy (Washington, D.C.: Government Printing Office, 1917);

The Political Scene: An Essay on the Victory of 1918 (New York: Holt, 1919; London: Allen & Unwin, 1919);

Liberty and the News (New York: Harcourt, Brace, 1920);

France and the European Setting (New York: Foreign Policy Association, 1922);

Public Opinion (New York: Harcourt, Brace, 1922; London: Allen & Unwin, 1922);

Mr. Kahn Would Like to Know (New York: Foreign Policy Association, 1923);

The Phantom Public (New York: Macmillan, 1925);

H. L. Mencken (New York: Knopf, 1926);

Men of Destiny (New York: Macmillan, 1927);

American Inquisitors: A Commentary on Dayton and Chicago (New York: Macmillan, 1928);

A Preface to Morals (New York: Macmillan, 1929; London: Allen & Unwin, 1929);

Notes on the Crisis (New York: Day, 1931);

The United States in World Affairs: An Account of American Foreign Relations, 1931, by Lippmann, W. O. Scroggs, and others, 2 volumes (New York: Harper, 1932-1933);

Interpretations, 1931-1932, edited by Allan Nevins (New York: Macmillan, 1932; London: Allen & Unwin, 1933);

A New Social Order (New York: Day, 1933);

The Method of Freedom (New York: Macmillan, 1934; London: Allen & Unwin, 1934);

Self-Sufficiency: Some Random Reflections, by Lippmann, and *Planning International Trade*, by G. D. H. Cole (Worcester, Mass. & New York: Carnegie Endowment for International Peace, 1934);

The New Imperative (New York: Macmillan, 1935);

Interpretations, 1933-1935, edited by Nevins (New York: Macmillan, 1936);

An Inquiry into the Principles of the Good Society (Boston: Little, Brown, 1937); republished as *The Good Society* (London: Allen & Unwin, 1938);

The Supreme Court: Independent or Controlled? (New York & London: Harper, 1937);

Some Notes on War and Peace (New York: Macmillan, 1940);

U.S. Foreign Policy: Shield of the Republic (Boston: Little, Brown, 1943; republished, with an introduction by D. W. Brogan, London: Hamish Hamilton, 1943);

U.S. War Aims (Boston: Little, Brown, 1944);

In the Service of Freedom (New York: Freedom House, 1945);

The Cold War: A Study in U.S. Foreign Policy (New York: Harper, 1947; London: Hamish Hamilton, 1947);

Commentaries on Far Eastern Policy (New York: American Institute of Pacific Relations, 1950);

Isolation and Alliances: An American Speaks to the British (Boston: Little, Brown, 1952);

Public Opinion and Foreign Policy in the United States (London: Allen & Unwin, 1952);

Essays in the Public Philosophy (Boston: Little, Brown, 1955); republished as *The Public Philosophy* (London: Hamish Hamilton, 1955);

America in the World Today (Minneapolis: University of Minnesota Press, 1957);

The Communist World and Ours (Boston: Little, Brown, 1959; edited by Edward Weeks, London: Hamish Hamilton, 1959);

The Confrontation (Stamford, Conn.: Overbrook, 1959);

The Coming Tests with Russia (Boston: Little, Brown, 1961);

The Nuclear Era: A Profound Struggle (Chicago: University of Chicago Press, 1962);

Western Unity and the Common Market (Boston: Little, Brown, 1962; London: Hamish Hamilton, 1962);

The Essential Lippmann: A Political Philosophy for Liberal Democracy, edited by Clinton Rossiter and James Lave (New York: Random House, 1963);

A Free Press (Copenhagen: Berlingske Bogtrykkeri, 1965[?]);

Conversations with Walter Lippmann, introduction by Edward Weeks (Boston: Little, Brown, 1965);

Early Writings, introduction by Arthur Schlesinger, Jr. (New York: Liveright, 1970).

OTHER: *A Modern Reader: Essays on Present-Day Life and Culture*, edited by Lippmann and Allan Nevins (Boston & New York: Heath, 1936);

Karl E. Meyer, ed., *Fulbright of Arkansas: The Public Positions of a Private Thinker*, introduction by Lippmann (Washington, D.C.: Luce, 1963);

Carl Sandburg, *The Chicago Race Riots, July, 1919*, introduction by Lippmann (New York: Harcourt, Brace & World, 1969).

Every career contains paradoxes and inconsistencies—great careers perhaps more than others. The contradictions of Walter Lippmann's career seem particularly revealing because they indicate how deeply he was involved in the complicated uncertainties of his time. He wrote continually of public opinion, yet he distrusted the expressions of popular will and always sought a counterbalance in the elevating, moderating, and uniting expression, through the designated authorities, of the "public interest." From his earliest writings to his last he argued that liberal democracy suffered from a debilitating and perhaps fatal sickness; men and women, he said, had been severed from the moorings of principle, tradition, and instruction; the lost arts of democracy had to be "revived and renewed" if democracy was to survive. He was the century's most influential political journalist and one of its finest critics of the press. He believed in the sacred character of serious journalism, once referring to the editing of a great newspaper as a "priestly" function. Yet his interpretation of the workings of the daily press restricted it severely. He held that the press could be no more than a "searchlight" which revealed for public scrutiny one corner of society, then another. The press, he said, could never provide a sure guide for public policy.

The fullest expression of his beliefs may be found in *Essays in the Public Philosophy*, which was begun in Paris during "the fateful summer of 1938," put away in 1941 with the realization that World War II would change everything, and finally published in 1955. Characteristically, the book opens with a skeptical examination of the ability of the people to arrive at sound judgments about public affairs. Forty years earlier, in *Drift and Mastery* (1914), he had suggested that the "clouds of accusation" produced by Lincoln Steffens and the other muckrakers had been thickened by a bewildered public, excited at the uncovering of misdoings, however conventional and harmless; and *The Phantom Public* (1925) declares that the public is "inexpert in its curiousity, intermittent" and able to discern "only gross distinctions." *Essays in the Public Philosophy* warns that the overvaluing of popular opinion is a sign of "a functional derangement of the relationship between the mass of the people and the government. The people have acquired power which they are incapable of exercising, and the governments they elect have lost powers which they must recover if they are to govern. . . . Where mass opinion dominates the government, there is a morbid derangement of the true functions of power. The derangement brings about the enfeeblement, verging on paralysis, of the capacity to govern. This breakdown in the constitutional order is the cause of the precipitate and catastrophic decline of Western society. It may, if it cannot be arrested and reversed, bring about the fall of the West."

Although it is decidedly uncharacteristic for Lippmann, whose values were embodied in words such as "civility" and "disinterest," to express militance, the conclusion of *Essays in the Public Philosophy* calls out militantly for the restoring of just and rational authority: "the signs and seals of legitimacy, of rightness and of truth, have been taken over by men who reject, even when they are not the avowed adversaries of, the doctrine of constitutional democracy. If the decline of the West under the misrule of the people is to be halted, it will be necessary" to present a "convincing demonstration" that the "principles of the good society" exist, and that they can be "discovered by rational inquiry, and developed and adapted and refined by rational discussion." The successful demonstration of this fact would "rearm all those who are concerned with the anomy of our society, with its progressive barbarization, and with its descent into violence and tyranny."

When Lippmann died at the age of eighty-five, he had been a prominent public figure for more than sixty years. *Time* magazine's obituary compared him with Voltaire and Gibbon and speculated that in political discourse, Lippmann and Edmund Burke "would have found themselves on the same aloof Olympian plane." This presumed aloofness, as well as the genuine pessimism of his political doctrine, belonged to a man noticeably eager and radiant in his earlier years, physically and emotionally robust throughout his life, and vitally concerned with every important public question.

Lippmann was born in his parents' home on Lexington Avenue in New York City. His father was a successful clothing manufacturer. Culturally active and socially confident, Lippmann's parents provided him with a childhood of concerts and plays, with summers spent at resorts or European spas. "Walter grew up in a gilded Jewish ghetto," according to his biographer, Ronald Steel. "Virtually everyone he knew was wealthy, Jewish and of German background. . . . Unlike the immigrant Jews on the Lower East Side, they did not feel cut off from the mainstream of American culture. Indeed, they were eager to be a part of it, and believed the path lay through assimilation. This meant submerging rather than affirming their Jewishness, relegating it to a small and unimportant part of their identity. For them Judaism was not a matter of pride or a question to be discussed, but an infirmity that could be rendered innocuous, perhaps unnoticeable, by being ignored. . . . But assimilation demanded a price. It meant being cut off from one's origins and trying to fit into a society where one was never fully secure."

Lippmann made an outstanding record at Sachs Collegiate Institute and moved on to Harvard, where he was inspired by professors such as Irving Babbitt and George Santayana. After William James dropped by Weld Hall to congratulate the nineteen-year-old Lippmann on an article he had written for an undergraduate magazine, the two met regularly for friendly discussions which left Lippmann impressed with the philosopher's zealous concern for social reform and experimentation. It was at Harvard also that Lippmann first encountered social discrimination. He soon saw that a Jew, however accomplished, wealthy, or personable, would not be admitted to the Harvard clubs. Neither was he invited to join the *Crimson* or the Signet Society. Responding energetically to this exclusiveness, Lippmann became a "brilliant outsider." He wrote articles; he formed a socialist club with eight other students, and delivered an impassioned speech at a rally challenging the clubmens' traditional practice of filling class offices with their own members. However, Lippmann's resentment was never strong enough to embitter him or to provoke a deep questioning of the values which had guided his upbringing. Discrimination, Steel says, led Lippmann to "put even greater emphasis on assimilation as an answer to anti-Semitism." He accepted "the values and style of the white Protestant majority. If being an outsider had led him to socialism, so later, when he ceased to be an outsider, he also ceased to be a socialist."

Never again would Lippmann be an outsider. His Harvard class of 1910 sometimes is described as the most illustrious the university ever produced. It included the poet T. S. Eliot and three other graduates who became famous journalists: Heywood Broun, columnist and founder of the American Newspaper Guild; John Reed, whose passion for revolution found shape in *Insurgent Mexico* (1914) and *Ten Days That Shook the World* (1919); and Hans von Kalterborn, the first great radio news reporter. From this promising start, Lippmann entered a career in which he was recognized as a prodigy in social and political thought and journalistic observation, and the road he trod almost immediately became one of ever-enlarged opportunity.

Lippmann's first job after leaving Harvard could be described as an interlude. His months as a cub reporter at the *Boston Common*, a high-minded but, Lippmann said, intellectually slack and "mechanical" progressive paper, were disappointing. When the famous muckraker Lincoln Steffens,

whom Lippmann had met in 1908, responded to a letter from Lippmann by offering him a job, the young reporter quit the *Common* and, in July 1910, became Steffens's assistant.

Steffens had agreed to do a new series of investigative articles for *Everybody's* magazine in which he would analyze the inner workings of great financial power. Steffens had asked around Harvard for an assistant who had "the ablest mind that could express itself in writing." Everyone agreed on Lippmann, who, Steffens recalled, "asked me intelligent, not practical, questions about my proposition. . . . He caught on right away. Keen, quiet, industrious, he understood the meaning of all that he learned; and he asked the men he met for more than I had asked for. He searched them; I know because he searched me, too, for my ideas and theories."

Lippmann was Steffens's legman, burrowing through New York's financial district for revealing information and traveling across the country to gather data. The first articles, expressing Steffens's conviction that great wealth resembled the concentrated political power he had found in Tammany Hall, were published by *Everybody's* in September 1910, as Lippmann turned twenty-one. Steffens left for England and Lippmann stayed for a while as a subeditor at *Everybody's*.

For four months in 1912 Lippmann served as secretary to the Reverend George T. Lunn, socialist mayor of Schenectady, but this was another interlude. In the years immediately following his Schenectady experience he truly launched his career. In 1913, Steffens introduced him to Mabel Dodge's Greenwich Village salon. Here Lippmann flirted with rebellious and unorthodox ideas. Whatever her other failings, the irrepressible Dodge was capable of astute judgment of the clever and contentious human beings who passed through her salon. After meeting Lippmann, well-mannered and in those days carefully tailored to conceal his stocky (fat, Dodge said) physique, she observed that he was "well-bred and in possession of himself. There was no incontinence there, no flowing sensuality. . . . Rather a fine poise, a cool understanding, and with all the high humor in the world shining in his intelligent eyes." Dodge took Reed as her lover; she relied upon Lippmann for intellectual coaching, and she admired his already mature strength of character.

The years 1913 and 1914 represented a crossroads for the precocious Lippmann. In his first two books, *A Preface to Politics* and *Drift and Mastery*, he began the explication of doubt and uncertainty—of "drift"—which would provide him with the central theme of his life's work; he strengthened the voice which would announce and argue these disturbing truths; and, at the *New Republic*, he found his first important job. It was *A Preface to Politics* which drew the attention of the magazine's founder, Herbert Croly. "The *Preface to Politics* is an astonishing book for a fellow three years out of college to write," Croly said, "but no matter how he turns out as a political philosopher he certainly has great possibilities as a political journalist." Croly offered Lippmann a chance to work on the staff of the new magazine, which was to be a journal devoted to the dispassionate and disinterested examination of public affairs, and Lippmann accepted immediately. One of the first staff members to be hired, Lippmann drafted the magazine's position on labor and spent some enjoyable months traveling in Europe for the purpose of employing European writers for the magazine. He returned to New York just in time to help with the details of getting the first *New Republic* into print. "I begin to see somewhat more clearly why administrators have not time to think, and why people who think often can't administer," he wrote in a letter to Graham Wallas as the magazine approached its first publication. After a year of experimenting and organizing subsidized by Willard and Dorothy Straight with their inherited Standard Oil royalties, the *New Republic*'s first issue appeared on 7 November 1914.

Lippmann's outlook was set early and his career was one of great continuity—of continued restatement and restudy of a few questions which he thought needed to be answered if Western institutions were to survive. The upheavals of his time required no seismographic intelligence to measure the shock; shock was evident everywhere. Lippmann's discerning intellect and moral sensitivity provided his readers with something more than another alarmed reciting of circumstances.

A Preface to Politics calls for the forthright recognition of the new conditions under which common life in an industrial democracy was unfolding. "We live in a revolutionary period and nothing is so important as to be aware of it," Lippmann told his readers. "The measure of our self consciousness will more or less determine whether we are to be the victims or the masters of change. Without philosophy we stumble along. The old routines and the old taboos are breaking up anyway, social forces are emerging which seek autonomy and struggle against slavery to non-human purposes."

A Preface to Politics also throws light on the development of Lippmann's later career, and particularly on the ways his career was interpreted. While he was directing the editorial page of the *New York World* he was accused by some of his critics of high-mindedly overlooking the corruption of Tammany Hall. In *A Preface to Politics* he revealed the analysis which underlay his acceptance of Tammany's methods. While working with Lincoln Steffens in their investigation of the "Money Power" which ruled Big Business, they learned, Lippmann said, that Big Business and Tammany Hall were "strikingly" similar: "the same pyramiding of influence, the same tendency of power to center on individuals who did not necessarily sit in the official seats, the same effort of human organization to grow independently of legal arrangements." Big Business may control politics, but, Lippmann wrote, "it certainly is not very illuminating to call the successful business men of the nation criminals. Yet I suppose that all of them violate the law. May not this constant dodging or hurdling of statutes be a sign that there is something the matter with the statutes? Is it not possible that graft is the cracking and bursting of the receptacles in which we have tried to constrain the business of this country? It seems possible that business has had to control politics because its laws were so stupidly obstructive." As for Tammany, Lippmann said, "You cannot beat the bosses with the reformer's taboo. . . . You can beat Tammany Hall permanently in one way—by making the government of a city as human, as kindly, as jolly as Tammany Hall. I am aware of the contract-grafts, the franchise-steals, the dirty streets, the bribing and the blackmail, the vice-and-crime partnerships, the Big Business alliances of Tammany Hall. And yet it seems to me that Tammany has a better perception of human need, and comes nearer to being what a government should be, than any scheme yet proposed by a group of 'uptown good government' enthusiasts."

A few years later *Time* would say that Lippmann learned to distrust the expression of popular will while editor of the *World*. It was overlooked that during his brief, early career as reforming public official and journalist, he also learned to distrust politicians. In some ways, he said, the public's indifference to politics is understandable. "If men find statecraft uninteresting, may it not be that statecraft is uninteresting? At first it was a hard confession to make, but the more I saw of politics at first-hand, the more I respected the indifference of the public. There was something monotonously trivial and irrelevant about our reformist enthusiasms, and an appalling justice in that half-conscious criticism which refuses to place politics among the genuine creative activities of men."

In *A Preface to Politics* Lippmann is backhandedly generous to business leaders; he saves his harshness for the reformers. Business leaders, together with politicians, govern the nation "in a rather absent minded fashion. Those revolutionists who see the misery of the country as a deliberate and fiendish plot overestimate the bad will, the intelligence and the singleness of purpose in the ruling classes. Business and political leaders don't mean badly; the trouble with them is that most of the time they don't mean anything. They picture themselves as very 'practical,' which in practice amounts to saying that nothing makes them feel so spiritually homeless as the discussion of values and an invitation to examine first principles."

Their adversaries, the reformers, leaven this intellectual ineptitude with their scoldings. Lippmann declares his dislike for the applying of empty self-righteousness to serious social problems. He describes Chicago's Hull House as "a little Athens in a vast barbarism—you wonder how much of Chicago Hull House can civilize. . . . As you walk those grim streets and look into the stifling houses, or picture the relentless stockyards, the conviction that vice and its misery cannot be transmuted by policemen and Morals Commissions, the feeling that spying and inspecting and prosecuting will not drain the marsh becomes a certainty. You want to shout at the forcible moralizer: 'So long as you acquiesce in the degradation of your city, so long as work remains nothing but ill-paid drudgery and every instinct of joy is mocked by dirt and cheapness and brutality—just so long will your efforts be fruitless, yes even though you raid and prosecute. . . .'"

A genuine, useful and humane politics "begins by accepting human nature," whereas "mechanical politics has usually begun by ignoring and ended by violating the nature of men." The statesman's business "is to provide fine opportunities for the expression of human impulses—to surround childhood, youth and age with homes and schools, cities and countryside that shall be stocked with interest and the chance for generous activity." A premium should be placed on inventiveness, "on the ingenuity to devise and plan. There will be much less use for lawyers and a great deal more for scientists." Lippmann believed that the ideal home for mankind already existed—but dormantly, obscured by habit, indifference, passion, and vileness. "The dynamics for a splendid human civilization are all about us. They need to be used. For that there must

be a culture practiced in seeking the inwardness of impulses, competent to ward off the idols of its own thought, hospitable to novelty and sufficiently inventive to harness power."

These hopeful meditations were interrupted by the unharnessing of a destructiveness unparalleled in human history. Lippmann was in London at the beginning of World War I, and as he prepared to join a war protest in Trafalgar Square he wrote to his friend Felix Frankfurter: "Ideas, books, seem too utterly trivial, and all the public opinion, democratic hope and what not, where is it today? Like a flower in the path of a plough." Yet this war, the portrayal of all he despised and the betrayal of all he believed, was to offer him an opportunity to confirm his identity as an insider with access to the sources of decision.

Painfully, Lippmann abandoned an early hero, Theodore Roosevelt, and established everstronger ties with the Wilson administration. He traveled back and forth to Washington to gather material for his *New Republic* column and was impressed by Wilson and by his close adviser, Col. Edward House. "They both have imagination and the courage of it, which is a good deal at this time," Lippmann reported. As the 1916 election approached, Wilson began to court Lippmann, hoping to persuade the *New Republic* and its progressive readers to support him. Lippmann was invited to Shadow Lawn, the president's New Jersey summer home. There Wilson expressed his intentions for social reform at home and neutrality abroad; but, he told Lippmann, neutrality was becoming more difficult in the face of unrestricted German submarine warfare and other provocations. Back in New York, Lippmann told Croly and Willard Straight that the nation was electing a "war president," and that he preferred Wilson to Charles Evans Hughes. Two months later, after finally convincing Croly and Straight that Hughes was trying to win German-American votes by taking a pro-German line, Lippmann told his readers that he would support "the Wilson who is evolving under experience and is remaking his philosophy in the light of it." Wilson, he said, was a "constructive nationalist" and the Democratic party he led was the only party "national in scope, liberal in purpose, and effective in action." Lippmann did not stop there: he wrote speeches for Wilson and campaigned for him in upstate New York from the back of a trailer truck. When Wilson declared war against Germany in 1917 he had no more fervent admirer nor loyal follower than Walter Lippmann. With the United States in the war, Lippmann wrote, the clash between empires "will dissolve into democratic revolution the world over."

Secretary of War Newton D. Baker was assembling a group of capable young assistants to serve during the war. Among them was Lippmann's friend, Felix Frankfurter. At Frankfurter's urging, Lippmann was invited to join the group, which included Eugene Meyer, later publisher of the *Washington Post*; Frederick Kappel, who would eventually head the Carnegie Corporation; and Stanley King, later president of Amherst College. "All were progressives," Lippmann's biographer observes, "infatuated with proximity to power, and eager to help in the war for democracy." Lippmann, on leave of absence from the *New Republic*, joined Baker in June 1917, and within six months his dedicated and articulate devotion to Wilson was rewarded when he was invited by House to join a group of experts who would work secretly in New York to draw up a peace plan to deliver the peoples of the world from militarism and irresponsible government.

In the same year he married Faye Alberton, the daughter of the Boston socialist parson who had given Lippmann his first job at the *Boston Common*. Faye was high-spirited and while, as some of Lippmann's friends noticed, she had little in common with Lippmann intellectually, their relationship proceeded quite rapidly to marriage on 24 May 1917, at his parents' home on East Eightieth Street in New York City.

Wilson's postwar planning group established offices at the New York Public Library—away from the capital, where its activities were more likely to be detected. It was called—its members hoped enigmatically—"The Inquiry." Within a few months of its establishment Lippmann was entrusted with a stupefyingly difficult challenge: from the ancient national and ethnic divisions, habitual antagonisms, and rivalries of a Europe now scorched by war and revolution he had to map the boundaries of the postwar continent in a way which would be acceptable to the warring parties. If realized, Lippmann's biographer notes, the redrawn frontiers would be "either the basis for a lasting peace or cause for another war." The weight of that responsibility was Lippmann's, and he was not yet thirty years old.

The Inquiry set to work. Maps showing concentrations of national groups were coordinated with national political movements to determine where self-determination could be recognized without provoking new antagonisms. These findings were correlated with provisions of the "secret

treaties," revealed to the world by the Bolsheviks. The secret treaties, negotiated by the Czar with the Allies, mostly during the first two years of the war, specified territorial gains for the victors: France would recover Alsace and Lorraine; Britain would get Germany's African colonies; Italy would gain Istria and Dalmatia; Japan would receive the Shantung Peninsula of China.

On 22 December 1917 Lippmann gave Colonel House his report, "The War Aims and Peace Terms It Suggests," illustrated with maps. Wilson requested clarification, and Lippmann's policy group complied. On 8 January Lippmann was rewarded: Wilson read to Congress his Fourteen Points address; many of the phrases he used were quoted from Lippmann's report.

On 13 December 1918 a delegation of 1,300 Americans, led by Wilson, stepped ashore at Brest. The Americans, greeted with uproarious happiness in Paris, included twenty-three members of The Inquiry, but one of its most brilliant members, wearing the uniform of an army captain, witnessed the welcome from the balcony of the Hotel Crillon. Lippmann had been persuaded to join an army propaganda mission in Europe, and as the German armies retreated he had been devising leaflets urging enemy soldiers to surrender. Both Lippmann and Straight, who was also serving with the army, had contracted influenza. Lippmann had recovered, but Straight, with Lippmann at his bedside, died a few weeks after Wilson's triumphant reception in Paris. Lippmann asked for an assignment with The Inquiry, but his forthrightness both as policymaker and propagandist had annoyed Isaiah Bowman, leader of The Inquiry, and Wilson. On 23 January, six months after setting sail for Europe, he left for New York. "What had begun as a crusade had ended in confusion and disillusion," Steel observes. "I am glad of the whole experience," Lippmann said, "and I am glad it is over."

In his second book, *Drift and Mastery*, Lippmann had argued that the old arrangements which had maintained social stability had vanished and that the common perceptions based on this stability had become useless. The problem was to rescue institutions from drift. When he looked at the press as it exercised its responsibilities in this tilting world he concluded that aggressive reporting might be considered just another expression of bewilderment. Muckraking "flared up at about the time when land was no longer freely available and largescale industry had begun to throw vast questions across the horizon. The muckrakers spoke to a public willing to recognize as corrupt an incredibly varied assortment of conventional acts. . . . These charges and counter-charges arose because the world has been altered radically, not because Americans fell in love with honesty." New necessities and changed expectations had produced "the clouds of accusation which hang over American life," but these suspicious accusations also revealed a deep confusion, an enshrouded response to mankind's new challenges. Lippmann wanted to untwist the confusion, to embolden mankind: "If we could know the inner history of weakness, of what disappoints us in leaders, the timidity of thought, the hesitancy and the drift, we should find in endless cases that the imagination had been blinded and the will scattered by the haunting horror of constructed evils."

Lippmann's exploration of the induced confusion of mankind was renewed in *Liberty and the News* (1920). Lippmann refers repeatedly to the subdued "anarchical" nature of mankind, and he believes that the world has become so complex that no individual can understand it fully. By themselves, these circumstances would make the job of informing the public a difficult one. The job is harder yet, Lippmann argues, when the press fails to meet its responsibilities. In this argument for clarity of understanding Lippmann aims directly at what he calls the "modern news problem."

The world's new intricacy defies the understanding of men and women prepared in the usual ways, through church and school, Lippmann wrote. Changing conditions cannot be grasped unless facts are quickly and steadily available, and the privately owned press is not providing those facts. Can democratic government survive, Lippmann asked, "when the manufacture of consent is an unregulated private enterprise?" The question is crucial because "in an exact sense the present crisis of western democracy is a crisis in journalism." Once again, as he did in his writing about Tammany Hall, Lippmann minimized the influence of corruption: journalists may be pressed or enticed by "moneyed control, caste pressure, financial and social bribery, ribbons, dinner parties, clubs, petty politics"—but none of this explains the condition of journalism.

More attractive to Lippmann was the idea that well-meaning arrogance had warped journalistic purpose. Since World War I, editors have come to believe "that their highest duty is not to report but to instruct, not to print news but to save civilization. . . . The work of reporters has thus become confused with the work of preachers, revivalists, prophets and agitators. The current theory of American newspaperdom is that an abstraction like

the truth and a grace like fairness must be sacrificed whenever anyone thinks the necessities of civilization require the sacrifice. . . . They [editors] believe that edification is more important than veracity." His experience as a propagandist had shown him how readily public opinion could be shaped by those determined to shape it; he applied his perceptions to the less purposeful activities of newspaper editors and reporters—and condemned them: "The news columns are common carriers. When those who control them arrogate to themselves the right to determine by their own consciences what shall be reported and for what purpose, democracy is unworkable. Public opinion is blockaded." He substantiated his assertions with an examination of the *New York Times*'s coverage of the Bolshevik revolution. The results of the study, done with Charles Merz, were published as a forty-two-page supplement to the *New Republic* in August 1920, and concluded that the paper's news stories, which reported ninety-one times that the Bolshevik regime was about to collapse, were "dominated by the hopes of the men who composed the news organization."

The next five years were eventful, even in a life as eventful as Lippmann's. In 1920 he began a regular column for *Vanity Fair*, an irreverent magazine of high literary quality whose contributors included Heywood Broun, Bill Bolitho, H. L. Mencken, and Dorothy Parker. He enjoyed writing the column so much that he continued it until 1934. Writing profiles and freewheeling commentary loosened the stylistic restraints imposed on Lippmann's natural lucidity by the ponderously serious *New Republic*. He decided to continue his study of public opinion and moved to an old house at Wading River, on Long Island, to write another book. Here he was handed another opportunity.

One afternoon Herbert Bayard Swope arrived at Lippmann's house in a chauffeured limousine. Swope, editor of the *World*, New York's most important liberal newspaper, needed an assistant for the eminent Frank Cobb, director of the editorial page. Swope offered Lippmann a large audience, a salary of $12,500 a year, and freedom to write what he pleased. Lippmann talked it over with publisher Ralph Pulitzer and agreed to start the job on 1 January 1922.

Lippmann always wrote swiftly, and the book he completed that summer would exert an influence as enduring as anything he wrote in his long career. *Public Opinion* (1922) and its sequel, *The Phantom Public* (1925), together constitute a contribution to understanding the practical workings of public opinion and the responsibilities of the press which remains unsurpassed.

The intentions of this influential work were foreshadowed in *Liberty and the News*, but Lippmann's focus was shifting from the press's violation of its canon of objectivity to the public's ability to understand even the most objective representations of reality. For Lippmann, a continual interplay existed between courage, imagination, and perception. Public perception was the key: a bold course of action could not be chosen or followed unless the facts which indicated it could be determined. So public opinion—the ability to decide—was crucial. But, he had said in 1920, the needed facts were not available, or they proceeded from situations so complex that no man or woman could understand them, or they were warped by the relentless partisanship of "special groups which act as extra-legal organs of government" and "conduct a continual electioneering campaign upon the unformed, exploitable mass of public opinion.... The government itself acts in reference to these groups far more than in reference to the district congressman." Liberty requires a process "by which men educate their response and learn to control their environment.... The task of liberty, therefore, falls roughly under three heads, protection of the sources of the news, organization of the news so as to make it comprehensible, and education of the human response." Journalism needed professional standards; the "untrained accidental witnesses" (reporters) would have to be replaced by trained observers, scoop merchants would have to give way to "patient and fearless men of science who have labored to see what the world really is."

In *Public Opinion* Lippmann's idealism yielded to a deeper and more skeptical analysis. He continued to insist that ordinary people are overwhelmed by complexity, but now he looked more closely at the process by which that complexity is simplified: "We are not equipped to deal with so much subtlety, so much variety, so many permutations and combinations. And although we have to act in that environment, we have to reconstruct it on a simpler model before we can manage with it.... The analyst of public opinion must begin then, by recognizing the triangular relationship between the scene of the action, the human picture of that scene, and the human response to that picture working itself out upon the scene of action."

We do not—can not—see things precisely as they are, Lippmann said. We require "stereotypes"—simplified pictures of events. Without these "pictures in our heads" the world is a swirling kaleidoscope of meaningless imagery. As they bear feeble witness to the bewildering play of events and personalities going on all around them, the best that ordinary human beings can hope for is that fairly reliable stereotypes will be provided, and that is one function of the press. But the press itself, Lippmann had observed in *Liberty and the News*, sees the world murkily and partially, and by the time he wrote *Public Opinion* Lippmann no longer believed that professionalization would clear the vision of editors and reporters. At best, he said, the press will be a searchlight traversing society, illuminating first one event and then another. This alert but essentially inattentive press can never provide the consistency of outlook needed to formulate policy; the governing elite, to whom Lippmann entrusts great power over the affairs of the bewildered mass, require other, special sources of information. Lippmann has been criticized for relying so completely on the wisdom of governing elites, but his argument left him no alternative conclusion.

"The world that we have to deal with politically is out of reach, out of sight, out of mind," Lippmann wrote. "It has to be explored, reported and imagined.... Those features of the world outside which have to do with the behavior of other human beings, in so far as that behavior crosses ours, is dependent upon us, or is interesting to us, we call roughly public affairs. The pictures inside the heads of these human beings, the pictures of themselves, of others, of their needs, purposes, and relationships, are their public opinions. Those pictures which are acted upon by groups of people, or by individuals acting in the name of groups, are Public Opinion with capital letters."

Lippmann's argument contained a repudiation of the traditional democratic idea that competent citizens who studied issues as they arose could make up their own minds about which courses of action they would support. In some of his earlier writings Lippmann had treated this ideal of the omnicompetent citizen as an innocent delusion; in *The Phantom Public* he seemed annoyed with the persistence of the ideal; by the time he summed up, in his *Essays in the Public Philosophy*, he regarded the reliance on the supposed understanding of the masses as an insidious deception—one which virtually crippled the decisiveness of democratic government. His distaste was outspokenly expressed in *The Phantom Public*: "We must assume that a public is inexpert in its curiosity, intermittent, that it discerns only gross distinctions, is slow to be aroused and quickly diverted; that since it acts by aligning itself, it personalizes whatever it considers, and is interested only when events have been melodramatized as conflict."

It may seem paradoxical that the bearer of these opinions should have become a mainstay of a great liberal newspaper, but in the decade preceding its demise Lippmann's was the voice of the *World*'s editorial page, and his definitely was not the voice of a swinger of searchlights. His biographer says that Lippmann wrote about 1,200 editorials, about one-third of these on foreign affairs. He brought to this writing a consistently large and intelligent viewpoint.

Cobb died at the end of 1923; Lippmann was named editor of the editorial page and given a raise to $20,000 a year, as well as three months off each year to write articles and books. He added to the editorial-page staff writers such as Allan Nevins and James M. Cain because he admired lucid writing and thinking. "The tough and graceful prose of the editorial team, together with the cartoons of Rollin Kirby, gave the *World* the best-written and most influential editorial page in the nation," Steel observed. In appearance, as well as intellect, Lippmann was an imposing figure to his colleagues at the *World*: "Lippmann did not correspond to the popular image of a frail intellectual or litterateur. He was big-boned, muscular and vigorous, with a heavy chest, a small waist, and strong hands. His 190 pounds lent a sense of power to his five-foot ten-inch frame. . . . Sensitive, even a bit vain, about his appearance, Lippmann had long since lost his chubbiness. . . . His squash and tennis partners were often surprised at the ferocity he brought to the game. His determination to win belied his normally placid manner. His bearing was sure, his hazel eyes expressive and sensitive. He was a handsome man, with the kind of presence that women were drawn to and men found impressive. Only the voice seemed out of key, a bit high-pitched for one built like a grand-opera baritone."

The decade of the 1920s was an emotional rollercoaster for most Americans. Lippmann did not miss the ride, but the turmoil never interfered with his productivity. He published nine books and many articles in addition to his *World* editorials. He nurtured the moral sensitivity which made *A Preface to Morals* (1929) one of the most, if not the most, profoundly knowing of any of his books. He tested his deepening distrust for the wisdom of the people in editorials written about the Scopes trial, "declaring that the efforts of popular majorities to rule over individual consciences was the 'chief tyranny of democracy.'" In a lecture at the University of Virginia in 1928 he observed that majority power

tended "to become arbitrary and absolute. . . . And therefore it may well be that to limit the power of majorities, to dispute their moral authority, to deflect their impact, to dissolve their force, is now the most important task of those who care for liberty."

Lippmann had just returned from Europe, where he had interviewed Mussolini and visited his old friend Bernard Berenson, when *A Preface to Morals* was published. The book struck a chord for a generation seeking recovery from the disillusionment of the late 1920s. It went through six editions before the end of the year, was translated into a dozen languages, and was Lippmann's first book to be chosen by the Book-of-the-Month Club. "The book was perfectly attuned to its times," Steel points out, "codifying the anxieties of a generation that had grown tired of its binge and was ready for a little renunciation."

In this book, Lippmann revives that feeling of estrangement—the awareness of *drift*—which he had evoked in *A Preface to Politics* and *Drift and Mastery*. Mankind's certainties, he declares, have been dissolved by "acids of modernity" which are "so powerful that they do not tolerate a crystallization of ideas which will serve as a new orthodoxy into which men can retreat. And so the modern world is haunted by a realization, which it becomes constantly less easy to ignore, that it is impossible to reconstruct an enduring orthodoxy, and impossible to live well without the satisfactions which an orthodoxy would provide." This uncertainty is accentuated by the encroachment on individual liberty of virtually all modern forms of government. With tempered cynicism Lippmann observes that, in power, communists, fascists, and democrats all claim the powers of coercion, confiscation, and control which characterize the modern state: "There is no theoretical limit upon the power of the ultimate majorities which create civil government. There are only practical limits. They are restrained by inertia, and by prudence, even by good will. But ultimately and theoretically they claim absolute authority. . . ." The moralist himself is confused: "He is no longer absolutely sure that he knows what is right." The populace does not know what is right or wrong, and "continues very frequently to prefer what was once regarded as wrong. . . . The result is that there no longer exists a moral code which the moralist can interpret, administer, and enforce. The effect of that is moral anarchy within and without."

The old virtues retain their validity, but the value of "courage, honor, faithfulness, veracity, justice, temperance, magnanimity, and love," must be recovered. The moralist has lost credibility because beliefs have lost substance. The attempt to impose empty dicta drives men, "especially the most sensitive and courageous, further away from insight into virtue and deeper and deeper into mere negation and rebellion. . . . For that reason the recovery of moral insight depends upon disentangling virtue from its traditional sanctions and the metaphysical framework which has hitherto supported it." Again and again, almost Nietzschean in his insistence, Lippmann hammers home his belief that the morality handed down by the sages has been warped through misuse: "Morality has become so stereotyped, so thin and verbal, so encrusted with pious fraud, it has been so much monopolized by the tender-minded and the sentimental, and made so odious by the outcries of foolish men and sour old women, that our generation has almost forgotten that virtue was not invented in Sunday schools but derives originally from a profound realization of the character of human life. . . . Only by deliberately thinking their way past these obstructions can modern men recover that innocence of the eye, that fresh, authentic sense of the good in human relations on which a living morality depends."

So, for Lippmann, his generation, corroded by modernity, was ancient in its need for virtue. The ideals have been stated again and again, but only mature and disinterested citizens are able to realize them. The moralist who "succeeds in disentangling that which men think they believe from that which it is appropriate for them to believe" also will reveal to men and women a moral theory consisting of "what the sages have prophesied as high religion, what psychologists delineate as matured personality, and the disinterestedness which the Great Society requires for its practical fulfillment." The mature and disinterested figure which emerges from this long exploration of modern man's moral dilemma moves through the world with philosophical detachment, afflicted neither by hope, doubt, ambition, frustration, nor fear. "And so whether he saw the thing as comedy, or high tragedy, or plain farce, he would affirm that it is what it is, and that the wise man can enjoy it."

The tone of this phrase suggests that Lippmann had arrived at a final stage of austerity, a maturity of outlook from which he could pass judgment on mankind. But, as it turned out, it was the expression of a transitional phase—and one which was not very happy. As he turned forty, things were dying in Lippmann's world: the inflated exuberance of the past decade was already dead; his newspaper, the *World,* was dying; his marriage

would last for several more years but it, too, was dying. (He had come, as his biographer puts it, to "an emotional dead end," and the best he could do for the married couples who read *A Preface to Morals* was to urge them to stoically accept wedlock as "a necessary affliction.") Ahead, however, lay personal rebirth and ever greater eminence.

By 1927 the *World*'s circulation had dropped from 400,000 to 285,000 and the paper was running a deficit. Its critics blamed the *World*'s failure on a divided identity: its crusading news coverage bothered readers who wanted objective coverage; Lippmann's subtlety and complexity confused readers accustomed to Cobb's unsubtle assaults. Cain observed that the *World* had "an editorial page addressed to intellectuals, a sporting section addressed to the fancy, a Sunday magazine addressed to morons, and twenty other things that don't seem to be addressed to anybody."

In the summer of 1929 Lippmann was made executive editor, replacing Swope, who had retired. On 27 February 1931, the *World* published its last issue. It had been sold to Scripps-Howard for $5 million and was to be combined with the chain's *Telegram*. Lippmann was invited by Roy Howard to be editorial director of the new combined newspaper; William Randolph Hearst offered Lippmann $50,000 a year to write a column for his newspapers; the *Times* was also interested. Lippmann finally chose to write a column for the conservative *Herald Tribune*, whose publisher, Ogden Reid, had convinced Lippmann that the *Herald Tribune* wanted the *World*'s Democratic readers. Lippmann's first column appeared on 8 September. He continued to write the column, under the title "Today and Tomorrow," for the *Herald Tribune* until 1962. By 1932 the column was being syndicated to 100 newspapers with a combined circulation of ten million readers; eventually more than 200 papers would run the column. It was an immediate and continuing success.

Reid's sincerity was tested when Lippmann decided that Franklin D. Roosevelt would be a better president than Herbert Hoover. Lippmann had been skeptical about Roosevelt's qualifications, but once he decided on Roosevelt his support was wholehearted—altogether too wholehearted for Ogden and Helen Reid, who demanded that he cut a column accusing Hoover of using emergency relief funds to improve his political position. Furious, Lippmann refused. The column went out as he had written it; then Lippmann relented and the offending paragraphs were cut before it was published widely.

So quickly were the vestiges of his doubts swept away by Roosevelt's decisive first days in office that Lippmann soon began speculating that the president might have to assume "dictatorial powers" to steady the nation and start recovery. Startled, and upset about the danger of agitating Congress with talk of a dictatorial executive, Roosevelt urged Felix Frankfurter to calm Lippmann. Unmoved, Lippmann replied with a paraphrase of the philosophy he had expressed in *Public Opinion* and *The Phantom Public*: "There are elements of corruption down deep in the electorate," and these are "part of the old Adam in every man." Wickedness and selfishness come not only from the top of society but also from the bottom. Emergency measures were needed and the "kindly and intelligent" Roosevelt was Lippmann's man. Having decided that Roosevelt approximated the enlightened and disinterested leader he had been seeking, Lippmann supported every early New Deal measure, including the abandonment of the gold standard.

By 1935, convinced that extraordinary executive powers no longer were urgently needed, Lippmann joined the opposition to further fundamental New Deal reforms, and even considered joining the Republican party. In the 1936 election, even though he regarded the Republican candidate as a dull person, he urged his readers to vote for Alf Landon against Roosevelt. Lippmann was aligned with most newspapers against FDR, but the people disagreed and Roosevelt swept all the states except Maine and Vermont. Lippmann's continued opposition to the New Deal as a program of reform and experimentation which was heading toward authoritarianism exposed him to criticism as a reactionary and a voice of Wall Street. Lippmann persisted, and within a few years, as it eclipsed all political controversy, the onset of World War II surged over Lippmann's differences with the liberal Democrats to whom he had been expected to appeal when he joined the Republican *Herald Tribune*.

Meanwhile, another sort of crisis was transforming Lippmann's personal life. The Lippmanns were discovering the depth of their incompatibility; their marriage was ending. Never a casual man, Lippmann sought relief from his frustration not in affairs but in friendship. He particularly valued the friendship of Hamilton Fish Armstrong; Lippmann and Armstrong were so close that they were known as Damon and Pythias. Helen Byrne Armstrong—his best friend's wife—was also Lippmann's affectionate companion. Quick-witted, interested in politics, she wore her brown hair cut short, was quick-tempered, and possessed, Steel says, "an inquisitive mind that ranged voraciously over politics, literature and the arts."

One evening when he was working late at the Council on Foreign Relations, Armstrong asked Lippmann to take his wife to dinner. Strangely nervous, Lippmann complied. They dined at the Rainbow Room in the new tower in Rockefeller Center. Helen Byrne Armstrong had recognized the emotional power—however disguised—which animated *A Preface to Morals* and as they talked she began to discern in this exemplar of the disinterested outlook a desire to unmask, to reveal feelings. He told her that he had been a lonely child, neglected emotionally, unloved by his mother; he said that his marriage had become cold and habitual. "He was," Lippmann's biographer observes, "bringing her into his life. A sense of complicity had grown between them. He allowed her into an inner sanctum where no one had ever before penetrated. He wanted something from her without quite knowing what it was. She did know. . . . By the time they left the Rainbow Room and hailed a cab on Fifth Avenue to take her home, they both knew that something irrevocable had happened." He called the next day. They arranged to have dinner again in a neighborhood restaurant. After dinner they went to a hotel.

They suffered through a period of dissembling (often the Lippmanns and the Armstrongs would attend the same social functions). Lippmann talked politics with Armstrong. Hitler's power was growing; the British and French, Armstrong told Lippmann, were "rotten with appeasement." Then, through a mixup in the mail, four love letters intended for Helen reached her husband instead. Lippmann and Helen decided to obtain divorces and marry. In the settlement, Faye Lippmann received almost everything Lippmann had: two country houses, the proceeds from the sale of a house in Manhattan, a $50,000 cash settlement, the family silver. She remarried and settled in Wading River; she and Lippmann never met again. Helen obtained a Reno divorce. In January 1938, Lippmann moved to Washington; on 26 March he and Helen were married. They honeymooned in the Blue Ridge Mountains. "Lippmann had what he wanted," Steel observes. "He had won the woman he loved. Faye, and all the depression that went with a bad marriage, was irrevocably behind him. He had lost Hamilton and had caused a good deal of scandal among his friends. But he was too happy to brood over that. Things had worked, he said in a letter to Berenson, 'perfectly.' "

Lippmann and his second wife, Helen, at their country home in Maine (Courtesy of Mrs. George Porter)

Lippmann was in Maine when Hitler invaded Poland on 1 September 1939. Lippmann urged aid to strengthen the French and British against the Germans. This, he concluded, was the best way to keep the United States out of a European war at a time when tension was increasing with Japan in the Pacific. With the shocking defeat of France at the hands of the invading Germans, Lippmann suggested that a standoff be negotiated with the Japanese, to allow the United States to concentrate its forces in the event of a war with Germany.

After the bombing of Pearl Harbor by the Japanese Lippmann traveled to the West Coast to survey the situation. He decided that the West Coast should be regarded as a combat zone, where normal civil liberties might be suspended. "This argument, coming from such a prestigious and normally calm observer, gave powerful impetus to the demand for relocation [of Japanese-American citizens], and may even have intensified the panic," Steel claims. Lippmann remained convinced that his judgment was correct, but he was never able to put the question entirely out of his mind.

Lippmann was no longer an agent of Wilsonian idealism, and in one of his two wartime books, *U.S. Foreign Policy* (1943), he rejected the idealists'

view of the importance of world law and international parliaments, arguing instead that security would be ensured by alliances against aggression. The book was a best-seller; the *Reader's Digest* printed a condensation, and paperback copies were distributed to American troops. "Lippmann's formula of great power cooperation seemed a realistic alternative both to bankrupt isolationism and to wishful universalism," Steel points out. When the Big Three foreign ministers, with China as an honorary member, met at Dumbarton Oaks in 1944 and decided on the structure of the United Nations, Lippmann was skeptical. International differences would not be settled by exertions of the imagination or by wishfulness, he said, but only by principles which applied to actual or likely points of conflict between nations.

On 7 April 1945, Lippmann wrote a column in which he said goodbye to Roosevelt, whose medical reports from Warm Springs, following the exhausting Yalta Conference, had alarmed his friends. Lippmann wrote a tribute which was, in effect, an obituary which the ailing president might read. FDR had, Lippmann said, "led this country out of the greatest peril in which it has ever been to the highest point of security, influence, and respect which it has ever attained." Five days later Roosevelt died. "If it took the war to make Roosevelt a truly great President, so the same war, and the cold war that followed, made Lippmann the nation's preeminent analyst of foreign affairs," Steel notes.

The postwar period saw both the forming of the alliances Lippmann desired and another try at international organization through the United Nations. At the conference in San Francisco at which the United Nations was launched, Lippmann, once again a mediating figure, persuaded the principal spokesman for isolationism, Sen. Arthur Vandenberg, to relent. He and James Reston of the *New York Times* wrote a speech in which Vandenberg endorsed the principles espoused at Dumbarton Oaks. He nevertheless retained his distrust, at times contempt, for the ability of international organizations to keep the peace, and he was never able to subscribe to disarmament or any device other than a favorable balance of power as a means of ensuring peace.

Lippmann's personal life remained perfectly happy. He and Helen traveled together and enjoyed a stimulating intellectual and social life. "Helen not only accompanied Lippmann on his trips abroad," according to Steel, "but she was his assistant, his interpreter, his private secretary, his guardian. She went along on his important interviews, translated where necessary, and took copious notes, which she transcribed as soon as they returned to their hotel. She arranged for the dinner parties. . . ."

In his professional life he enjoyed unbroken eminence, the access to heads of state and members of royalty, the close confidings of the "insiders" whom he had decided decades before were the truly important people in any society. Yet he was dissatisfied at times. In 1951 he took a six-month vacation from column writing to work on *Essays in the Public Philosophy*. When he returned to journalism he began to look around for an appealing successor for President Truman, who, as the 1952 elections approached, was embroiled in the Korean War, stalemated by the Europeans in his plan to rearm Germany, and dogged by the red-baiting of Sen. Joseph McCarthy, of whom Lippmann was an outspoken critic. Lippmann thought that Gen. Dwight Eisenhower was politically simpleminded; he preferred the Democratic nominee, Gov. Adlai Stevenson. But he was convinced that a military hero could negotiate peace in Korea and a Republican president could subdue the McCarthyite wing of the party. He was dismayed at Eisenhower's lack of clarity on the issues and his jumbled syntax during the campaign, but he remained a supporter of the general, who won by a landslide.

As the Cold War persisted Lippmann's commentary was marked at times by a curious detachment. He opposed McCarthy, but wrote relatively little about witch-hunting; he wrote nothing about the espionage trial of Julius and Ethel Rosenberg, which aroused political antagonisms of a kind not seen since the Sacco and Vanzetti trial. "Having only a guidepost of national interest, lacking a philosophical approach or ideological commitment, reluctant to accept the part that economic demands or imperial ambitions might play in explaining American foreign policy, Lippmann was unable to take a consistent approach to the issues he wrote about," in Steel's estimation. "He dealt with each situation on an *ad hoc* basis. . . . He believed that America's cold war policies were essentially defensive, that it had acquired its informal empire by 'accident,' and that the problem was primarily one of execution rather than conception. He criticized the policymakers, but rarely what lay behind their policies."

He had invested great energy over a prolonged period in the *Essays in the Public Philosophy*, and when the book failed to excite even his friends, Lippmann, overwhelmed with fatigue, suffered a nervous collapse which kept him in the hospital for three weeks in 1955, followed by five weeks of recuperation in California. His spirits were partly revived by praise from his old friend, Gen. Charles de Gaulle, who appreciated Lippmann's plea for a stronger executive. Lippmann later told Learned Hand that his breakdown had been the result of trying to counter the currents of public opinion. Wistfully, he said he sometimes wished he had a profession, such as law or medicine, with an established subject matter and methods.

Recovered, Lippmann returned to a robust life of activity (including physical activity; he was a good tennis player) and political involvement and commentary. He was resilient; he endured criticism and finally accepted even the indifference which greeted the publication of his essays. On his seventieth birthday he spoke at a luncheon meeting at the National Press Club. Journalists, he said, have the privilege in a democratic society of learning, inferring, deducing, imagining, guessing, and then informing the sovereign citizen who is supposed to inform himself but has neither the time nor the interest. "This is our job. It is no mean calling. We have a right to be proud of it and to be glad that it is our work."

Lippmann was infatuated with John F. Kennedy, and after the election of 1960 he became, Steel observes, "one of the shining ornaments of the Kennedy administration." He was consulted on speeches and on the incipient policies of the new government. As a New Frontier insider, Lippmann was invited to the Soviet Union, where he was strenuously feted and allowed to interview Chairman Khrushchev. Lippmann's three articles, including Khrushchev's forthright discussion about the need for a peace treaty recognizing the new boundaries of Eastern Europe, won for the columnist his second Pulitzer Prize. (Lippmann's first Pulitzer Prize, awarded in 1958, had been based on an earlier series of stories from Russia.) He retained his journalistic integrity, in spite of his closeness to the Kennedy administration, and criticized the United States-supported invasion of Cuba at the Bay of Pigs, as well as those who thought that a nation proved its virility by involving itself in wars such as the struggle which continued in Vietnam. He defended the administration's handling of the Cuban Missile Crisis and remained a Kennedy insider, seeing the president frequently at lunch or at parties.

When Lippmann's contract with the *Herald Tribune* expired in 1962 he was persuaded by Philip Graham, publisher of the *Washington Post*, to accept a lucrative contract which would require him to write only two columns a week for eight months a year and sixteen articles for *Newsweek*, which Graham had recently purchased. Lippmann's salary would be $70,000 a year, plus 90 percent of syndication revenues. The *Post* also offered a New York apartment and a staff of three. Lippmann began working for his new employer early in 1963.

As he entered his seventy-fourth year Lippmann was about to encounter his last formidable political adversary, the paradoxical Lyndon Johnson, who succeeded Kennedy as president after JFK was shot and killed in Dallas. Johnson courted Lippmann, who appreciated Johnson's true qualities—"a subtle and cunning mind" lurking beneath LBJ's loud, braggart manner. Lippmann supported Johnson's irresistibly persuasive advocacy for the civil rights bill of 1964; as the elections of that year approached, Lippmann—fearing Johnson's opponent, Sen. Barry Goldwater—"turned to LBJ almost as to a savior," according to Steel.

Johnson's decision to send a great army of Americans to Vietnam severed his relationship with Lippmann. Lippmann's objection to the United States' intervention was based on political and not moral considerations: he considered it foolish to fight a land war on the Asia mainland. He helped

Lippmann preparing to read a commentary on the radio
(Courtesy of the Boston Public Library)

persuade Katharine Graham, who succeeded her husband as publisher after his death, to change the *Post*'s prowar editorial position. His bitterness toward Johnson increased, Steel notes: "He had allowed himself to be drawn into Johnson's web, not by any bribes or rewards, but simply because he was flattered at being called in for advice, and because he thought the administration was seriously listening to him. When he discovered that the White House was merely trying to butter him up, he was hurt and angry." The national outrage which led to LBJ's demise confirmed Lippmann's judgment of the folly of involvement in Vietnam.

The withdrawal from Vietnam, evidence of crisis in the workings of the empire whose growth Lippmann had recorded, coincided with his own decline. He and Helen went through a restless period in which they sought a comfortable home in Europe, then returned to an apartment in New York. As he aged, Lippmann found for the first time in his life that he had to contend with idleness. As his career came to its end, the politicians who had courted him found that they had no time for him. He had no energy for long trips. He lost lucidity and deteriorated physically, and in 1973 Helen placed him in an elegant Park Avenue nursing home. She died, unexpectedly, on 16 February 1974. He followed on 14 December.

Lippmann was the century's great journalistic insider, a man who sought—testing and dismissing one president after another—the great disinterested leader who would rescue the people from themselves and the century from its turmoil. The leader never appeared, but Lippmann's search was an adventure worthy of that invisible figure.

When public relations counsel Ivy Lee was searching in 1932 for a respectable and respectful biographer for his client, John D. Rockefeller, Sr., one of the first names proposed was that of Walter Lippmann. Lippmann was not selected, but his early appearance on the list of possibilities attested to his reputation. That he was not a biographer mattered less than that he was a man of prominence, whose own stature assured a measured evaluation of Rockefeller's career, and whose conclusions would very likely be contrary to those of the reviling muckrakers whose opinions Lee hoped to undercut.

In any consideration of Lippmann the scope of his magnificently realized career must be considered. Even as they sought beneath the cultivated surface of his writing some deficiency in substance, Lippmann's critics acknowledged the power of his reputation. There is a backhanded compliment in

Benjamin Stolberg's observation that "there is something in his temper which tends to make him, as the years go by, more prominent than significant." Another writer who found in Lippmann the empty "illusion of intellectuality" admitted that he felt "awe" when he contemplated the great career, the weight of ambition and accomplishment, whatever the possible defects.

It would have been very nearly a perfect career if Lippmann had been able to conclude triumphantly his lifelong philosophical study of politics. But the *Essays in the Public Philosophy* fell short of being this culmination. As a very young man Lippmann had identified the problem he would study: the drifting indecision which revealed moral decay in the constitutional order. But the *Essays in the Public Philosophy* revealed no satisfactory solution. Lippmann, as *New York Times* columnist James Reston has observed, preferred to be judged as a philosopher, and he was deeply disturbed by the cool reception of the book, over which he had labored on and off for seventeen years. But he had available an enormous consolation, for flowing smoothly above the stony preoccupations of the political philosopher was a life in journalism which carried Lippmann's sparkling eminence through presidential elections, philosophers' studies, and the innermost chambers of palaces and capitals across the world. If this ceaseless attendance before the famous and powerful represented to another generation of critics a kind of subservience, provoking reporter Tom Wolfe to call Lippmann a "snoremonger," it provided newspapermen such as Reston with a "wider vision of our duty." Lippmann, Reston said, had "shown us how to put the event of the day in its proper relationship to the history of yesterday and the dreams of tomorrow."

Lippmann's philosophical speculations no longer are widely read, but the integrity of his outlook is evident in the determination with which he confronted the "barbarism" of his time, and even an age which some call "postmodern" could find guidance in Lippmann's examination of the corrosions and dislocations of his "modern age." His views on the press still reverberate in the universities and in the writings of press critics, though he is more likely to be quoted conveniently, without the context of doubt and social pessimism in which his judgments originally were clothed. Even stripped to axioms (his image of the press as a "searchlight" is most frequently cited), his thoughts stimulate reflection.

Those who wish to find acceptance for wider and deeper definitions of the duties of journalists sometimes feel burdened by the influence of Lippmann's austere rendering of the journalist as an agent of "disinterest" and objectivity. On the surface his view of the limitations of press and public may seem overly pessimistic and restricting. Here, once again, it is helpful to turn to the richly expressive career of this reporter, columnist, and philosopher, and see that Lippmann neither accepted these restrictions for himself nor imposed them on his readers, for whom he obviously felt respect.

An examination of Lippmann's career, from the years of radiant promise, to the decades of varied and prolific accomplishment, to his virtual enshrinement as the great statesman of twentieth-century American journalism, will carry one to the conclusion that his achievements eclipsed his shortcomings, and the shortcomings themselves resulted from his great reach. No journalist has been more confident; none has claimed a larger field of activity; none has had more to say.

Interviews:

William Attwood, "A Visit with Walter Lippmann," *Look,* 25 (25 April 1961): 100;

"Walter Lippmann: An Interview with Roland Steel," *New Republic,* 168 (14 April 1973): 16-21;

"Lippmann Speaks," *National Review,* 25 (22 June· 1973): 670-671.

Biography:

Ronald Steel, *Walter Lippmann and the American Century* (Boston: Little, Brown, 1980).

References:

Marquis Childs and James Reston, eds., *Walter Lippmann and his Times* (New York: Harcourt, Brace, 1959);

"The Columnists JFK Reads Every Morning," *Newsweek,* 58 (18 December 1961): 65-67, 69-70;

Doris Grumbach, "Fine Print," *New Republic,* 172 (25 January 1975): 33;

Amos Pinchot, "Walter Lippmann," *Nation,* 137 (5 July 1933): 7-10; (12 July 1933): 36-40; (19 July 1933): 67-70; (2 August 1933): 126-131;

Richard H. Rovere, "Walter Lippmann," *American Scholar,* 44 (Autumn 1975): 585-603;

David Elliott Weingast, *Walter Lippmann, a Study in Personal Journalism* (New Brunswick, N.J.: Rutgers University Press, 1949).

Marie Manning
(Beatrice Fairfax)
(22 January 1873?-28 November 1945)

Achal Mehra
University of Northern Colorado

MAJOR POSITIONS HELD: Columnist, *New York Evening Journal* (1898-1905); syndicated columnist (1930-1945).

BOOKS: *Lord Allingham, Bankrupt* (New York: Dodd, Mead, 1902; London: Stevens & Brown, 1902);
Judith of the Plains (New York & London: Harper, 1903);
Problems of Love and Marriage, as Beatrice Fairfax (Springfield, Mass.: McLoughlin, 1931);
Personal Reply, as Beatrice Fairfax (Philadelphia: McKay, 1943);
Ladies Now and Then, as Beatrice Fairfax (New York: Dutton, 1944; London: Gifford, 1949).

Beatrice Fairfax has been eulogized in songs and lyrics. Biographers have called her a national grandma, a one-person institution, a name "as familiar as the national anthem," and the "top-ranking purveyor of balm to the troubled." For decades, America confessed its transgressions and woes through her columns. Not since the public confessions in the early Christian church had there been anything like it. Her love forum, one of the first in the country, is the oldest surviving uninterrupted advice column in any American newspaper. Manning's column started nineteen years before Dorothy Dix's. At its peak, the column was syndicated to 200 newspapers by King Features, the syndicating agency of William Randolph Hearst's chain of newspapers. A Hearst biographer has written that in an age when the list of Hearst's employees read like a who's who of American journalism, Beatrice Fairfax was "one of Hearst's greatest acquisitions."

"Beatrice Fairfax," in fact, is a pseudonym for a string of women who have edited the column "Letters from the Lovelorn" that first appeared in the *New York Evening Journal*. The column was the creation of Marie Manning, then a staff reporter on the *Evening Journal*. The column has passed through a succession of hands, both during her

Marie Manning (Harris and Ewing)

lifetime and after her death, and continues to this day.

Marie Manning was born to English immigrants, Michael Charles Manning, an employee in the War Department, and Elizabeth Barrett Manning, in Washington, D.C., probably on 22 January 1873, according to information provided in her death record by her son Oliver Gasch. The date and year of her birth are disputed. Obituaries and biographies of her do not agree on her birthdate, and she is supposed to have kept her age secret even from her own family. In the only reference to her age in her autobiography, she wrote that she was twenty in 1898, suggesting that the year of her birth was 1878.

An older brother died in his youth, and her mother died when Manning was only six. She was educated in private schools in Washington, New York, and London, acquiring, as she was to later observe, "such oddments as were considered meet for a young gentlewoman to know." After her father's death, she studied at a ladies' seminary because, she recalled in her autobiography, "my guardian, Justice Martin F. Morris, didn't quite know what to do with a girl who was almost six feet tall, had no interest in clothes, and wouldn't go to 'pink teas,' as coming-out parties were apt to be called at the time."

According to some accounts, Manning joined the London bureau of the *New York Herald* in 1897 and then moved to the *New York World*. In her autobiography, however, Manning said she "stumbled" into journalism one evening when she was asked to fill in for an absent schoolmate at a dinner and found herself sitting beside Arthur Brisbane, editor of the *World*. He offered her a job on his newspaper. A few weeks later, after wringing consent from her guardian, she went to work on the *World*, earning between five and six dollars weekly under a space system in which payment depended upon the amount of her material used. At the time, the paper's lowest paid male reporter earned twenty dollars.

Manning got her first break when she was sent to interview ex-President Grover Cleveland, who had denied interviews to other *World* reporters. The Spanish-American controversy was heating up at the time, and publisher Joseph Pulitzer wanted Cleveland's reaction on the subject. Manning had a stroke of good luck: mistaken for a daughter of Cleveland's treasury secretary, Daniel Manning, she was brought before the former president. Cleveland took compassion upon the novice reporter and dictated a short statement to her, even lending her a pencil with which to jot it down. The scoop won her a fifty-dollar reward from Pulitzer and a thirty-dollar-a-week reporter's salary.

She did not stay with the *World* for long, however. Joining the exodus of Pulitzer employees, which included her mentor, Brisbane, she moved to Hearst's *Evening Journal* in 1898. There she was holed up in the "Hen Coop," otherwise known as the women's section. It was also infamous as a place where erring male reporters were sent to expiate their crimes. Being sent to the Hen Coop, Manning

wrote in her autobiography, was the equivalent of "standing a child in the corner." Together with two other women, she helped put out the women's page for what she called an "amiable little Victorian world." She also wrote book reviews, added the appropriate "women's angle" to sensational trials, and did some general reporting. She also interviewed celebrities, most notably the actress Mrs. Patrick Campbell, who was then at the height of her popularity.

One day in July 1898, the *Evening Journal*'s editor, Brisbane, brought three letters to the Hen Coop. The letters sought advice on personal problems, and Brisbane suggested that the letters be carried on the women's page. Manning, however, proposed opening a public confessional, a column inviting people to write to the newspaper about their love problems and personal and domestic difficulties. The idea impressed Brisbane. Manning signed the column "Beatrice Fairfax," a name she compounded from Dante's Beata Beatrix and Fairfax, a Virginia county where she owned property. Manning turned her back on cooking, beauty hints, and etiquette to produce the column, which made its first appearance on 20 July 1898, featuring a tiny pen-and-ink drawing of the gawky, six-foot amazon columnist in the upper left-hand corner.

The column was an instant success. Its popularity was understandable because it served a need for readers at a time when there were few social agencies to which people with desperate problems could turn. Victorian propriety permitted few commonsense solutions for such familiar personal problems as deserted wives, destitute families, or jilted lovers. Advice seekers could use the anonymity of the column to get impartial answers from an unknown and unprejudiced person. Reticent people who ordinarily would not have confided in anyone enjoyed seeing their own experiences mirrored in the column. As Manning wrote in her autobiography, "That old never-quenched curiosity about the secret springs of other people's lives got us hundreds of thousands of readers." She recalled that "circulation zoomed like an ascending airplane. Heartthrobs helped to outdistance the *New York Journal*'s old rival, the *Evening World*, leaving its figures far behind." In fact, so incredible was the column's popularity that several other newspapers founded "heart clinics" of their own.

Although she initially fabricated letters to simulate reader participation, Manning said she soon began to dread the sight of office boys straining under mail sacks brought over from the post office. With mail topping 1,400 pieces a day, the post office had disclaimed responsibility for delivery, and the *Journal* had to hire two workers just to perform the task.

Before long, Beatrice Fairfax—a role played by all three reporters in the Hen Coop, but mostly by Manning—was advising correspondents on a range of knotty problems from legal questions, for which she sought assistance from her former guardian, Justice Morris, to matters of love and marriage.

A punctilious young man was advised that he did not have to kneel while proposing and that it was better not to buy the ring until the girl accepted his hand. Young men tottering on the brink, but too timid to propose, were urged, "Do it now." A correspondent anxious to mend a lover's quarrel was advised to force the issue and thereby end the suspense: "If she deigns no reply, then he is answered, for she does not love him, and is none too well bred in her way of showing this."

Her advice was always strong and practical. Her simple formula was, "Dry your eyes, roll up your sleeves, and dig for a practical solution, battle for it; if the law will help, invoke the law . . . pick up the pieces and keep on going." At times, the practicality and seriousness of her advice came home to roost. She once advised a widower to court a widow in his building to help him raise his five children. When the widow declined, he came around to propose to Manning instead, bringing along his five children in an attempt to melt her heart.

Sometimes Manning took a personal interest in her correspondents' problems. When a woman who had come to New York to plead for a stay of her son's execution wrote to say that she could not find a place to stay, Manning intervened. She took the woman to the Salvation Army and visited her daily until the day of the execution.

While writing the column, Manning continued to report for the *Journal*. She interviewed celebrities such as William Jennings Bryan; covered sensational murder trials; and wrote occasional investigative reports, including one on the living conditions of poorly paid department store employees. She also wrote several short stories and one-act plays for *Harper's* magazine. The stories involved characters confronting problems similar to those of the correspondents to her column. The characters in her stories usually resolved their predicaments with the philosophy that underlay the advice Manning gave to her readers.

She also wrote two novels, *Lord Allingham, Bankrupt* (1902) and *Judith of the Plains* (1903), under her original name, Marie Manning. The first

novel, a romantic adventure, was a commercial failure even though *Harper's Weekly* called it "one of the strongest and most original novels that came from the pen of a new writer last year." *Judith of the Plains* won considerable critical acclaim and even went into a second printing. The novel revolves around a strong woman who fights to save her brother from an unjust death sentence. The book is a strong indictment of the repression of women in a male-dominated society. *Problems of Love and Marriage* (1931) is a collection of letters and her responses in her advice column. The book was published under her famous pseudonym, Beatrice Fairfax.

Manning left newspaper work and on 12 June 1905 married an old friend, Herman Gasch, a real estate agent. They had two sons, Oliver and Manning. For twenty-five years, except for a brief reunion during World War I, Manning was separated from her column and devoted herself to her family. Meanwhile, the column changed hands, remaining longest under Lilian Lauferty.

Manning continued to write prolifically for *Harper's, Harper's Weekly, Collier's,* and the *Ladies' Home Journal*. She wrote more than twenty short stories for these magazines, mostly for *Harper's*, between 1905 and 1930. Manning published all her short stories under her original name, and there is no evidence that readers connected that name to the legendary Beatrice Fairfax.

After the 1929 stock market crash, in which she saw all her inheritance from her father "melt like a cake of ice left unnoticed at the kitchen door in August," she returned to her column in 1930. The column was no longer confined to the pages of the *Journal*: it was syndicated by Hearst's King Features to nearly 200 newspapers all over the country. Manning simultaneously worked for the International News Service, another Hearst enterprise, covering Mrs. Eleanor Roosevelt's White House press conference and the woman's angle on Washington.

There was a marked change in the nature of the correspondence to her new column as compared with that received during the column's inception. "In the nineties," Manning recalled, "when a girl got married, practically all correspondence with Beatrice Fairfax ended. Now marriage is only the beginning." Correspondents wrote about illicit love affairs, restless wives, the impact of divorce on children. They worried about the war, separations, broken engagements, missing sweethearts, unmarried girls expecting babies. But the most nagging problem of all involved the dealings of women with the Office of Dependency Benefits. In 1943 she pulled together the "thousand and one questions most commonly asked by service men, their wives and their sweethearts" into a book, *Personal Reply*.

In May 1944, Manning's witty, chatty autobiography, *Ladies Now and Then*, was published. It deals mostly with the early years of her career as a reporter and says little about her personal life. The book is spiced with inane gossip but does provide insight into the struggles and sacrifices of all the women journalists who were trying to break out of the "latest society divorce scandal" and into the world of serious reporting.

The autobiography, which the *Library Journal* called "superficial but very readable," also provides insight into the movement for women's suffrage at a time when it was taken more or less as a joke. Although a confirmed suffragist herself, Manning was unable to take an editorial stand in her column because of the conservative beliefs of her publishers. She could not even approve the use of rainy

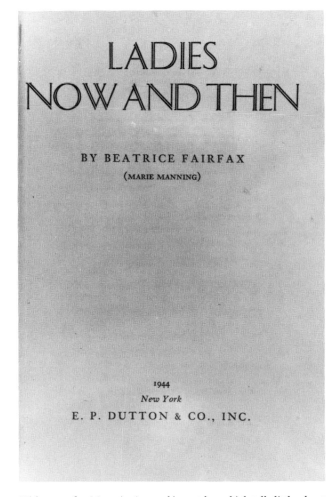

LADIES
NOW AND THEN

BY BEATRICE FAIRFAX
(MARIE MANNING)

1944
New York
E. P. DUTTON & CO., INC.

Title page for Manning's autobiography, which tells little about her personal life but provides insights into the problems faced by early women journalists and by suffragists

day skirts—skirts that ended four inches off the ground—in her column. Because the stories she wrote about parlor meetings on the suffrage movement were often discarded, she arranged altercations to make meetings newsworthy enough for coverage.

Although she was a founding member of the Women's National Press Club and the Newspaper Women's Club, she disapproved of the jostling that went on to get into these clubs. "Almost every woman in Washington who has progressed in her literary ambitions as far as having received a printed rejection slip, or burst into print with a cooking recipe," she wrote in her autobiography, "hungers and thirsts to belong to one or the other of the press clubs, as an honorary member, an out-of-towner, or a visiting fireman, if she is ineligible as an active member. The clubs are open sesame to so much that is socially intriguing, or just getting under an exclusive wire."

Until 1920, when women were finally given the right to vote, Manning was active in the suffrage movement. She led and joined delegations to plead for the vote, although looking back in 1944, she was amazed at her meekness in a just cause. Of several prominent women who were arrested for picketing the White House she said, "I've always felt a certain shame that I lacked the moral courage to go to jail with these women." But she felt she could take heart "as an inconspicuous private who has helped to fight the good fight for women even before I was legally of age."

Manning's even greater contribution was to those anonymous thousands of lovelorn people who turned to her for advice and comfort and solace year after year for decades. There is no record of the joy she gave to broken hearts, the hearts she mended, maybe even the lives she saved through her column, long before, as she herself boasted, Sigmund Freud and Carl Jung devised their schemes to relieve overburdened consciences.

The Beatrice Fairfax column is representative of those rare institutions in history that outlive the person who conceived them. Few readers of her column knew that after 28 November 1945, when Manning died, their problems were being answered by a person other than the one who originated the column. The column continued uninterrupted, lasting longest under Marion Clyde McCarroll, who took it over soon after Manning's death and produced it until her own death in August 1977.

Four decades after her death, the woman whose advice was closely read by millions all over the country has been reduced to a footnote in journalism history. The legendary Beatrice Fairfax, however, survives. Readers can still, as they have done since the turn of the century, write to the column. A popular rhyme from the early days of the column went:

> Just write to Beatrice Fairfax
> Whenever you are in doubt;
> Just write to Beatrice Fairfax
> And she will help you out.

References:

Oliver Carlson and Ernest Sutherland Bates, *Hearst: Lord of San Simeon* (New York: Viking, 1936), p. 88;

Ishbel Ross, *Ladies of the Press* (New York: Harper, 1936), pp. 79-83;

W. A. Swanberg, *Citizen Hearst* (New York: Scribners, 1961), pp. 197, 428.

Anne O'Hare McCormick
(16 May 1880-29 May 1954)

J. Douglas Tarpley
Evangel College

MAJOR POSITIONS HELD: Associate editor, *Catholic Universe Bulletin* (1898-1910); foreign correspondent, *New York Times* (1922-1954); editorial board, *New York Times* (1936-1954).

BOOKS: *St. Agnes Church, Cleveland, Ohio: An Interpretation* (N.p., 1920);
The Hammer and the Scythe: Communist Russia Enters the Second Decade (New York: Knopf, 1928); republished as *Communist Russia: The Hammer and the Scythe* (London: Williams & Norgate, 1929);
Ourselves and Europe (Poughkeepsie, N.Y., 1941);
The World At Home: Selections From The Writings Of Anne O'Hare McCormick, edited by Marion Turner Sheehan (New York: Knopf, 1956);
Vatican Journal 1921-1954, edited by Marion Turner Sheehan (New York: Farrar, Straus & Cudahy, 1957).

Anne O'Hare McCormick was the first woman to serve on the editorial board of the *New York Times* and the first woman to be awarded a Pulitzer Prize for journalism. She wrote a column for the *Times*, entitled "Abroad," that appeared three times a week. As an editorial board member, she wrote unsigned editorials twice a week in addition to her column. A foreign correspondent for the *Times* beginning in 1922, McCormick wrote almost exclusively for the newspaper after 1925, traveling around the world and "invading almost every head of state's office" to win an international reputation

as a knowledgeable and insightful foreign correspondent.

Anne Elizabeth O'Hare was born in Wakefield, Yorkshire, England, on 16 May 1880, the first of three daughters of Thomas J. and Teresa Beatrice Berry O'Hare. The family migrated to the United States shortly after her birth, ultimately settling in Columbus, Ohio. O'Hare was reared in a devout Catholic home and educated in private schools such as Saint Mary of the Springs Academy in Columbus, reflecting her family's strong Irish-Catholic heritage. Just before her 1898 graduation with a B.A. from the academy, her father encountered financial problems in his insurance business and permanently deserted his family. Teresa O'Hare struggled to support the family by operating a dry goods store and selling a book of her poetry door-to-door. That same year the family moved to Cleveland, where both Anne and her mother worked for the weekly *Catholic Universe Bulletin*. Teresa wrote a column and edited the women's section; Anne began her journalistic career as an associate editor.

Her marriage on 14 September 1910 to Francis J. McCormick, a Dayton importer and engineer, caused Anne to leave the *Bulletin*, because she traveled extensively with her husband on his frequent European purchasing trips. She continued to write, producing poetry that appeared in *Smart Set*, the *Bookman*, and other magazines; a short ecclesiastical history of her former parish church (1920); and free-lance articles published in *Catholic*

Anne O'Hare McCormick (Wide World Photos)

Throughout the 1920s, 1930s, and early 1940s McCormick displayed the broad knowledge and thoughtful insight about world affairs, the aggressive traveling, and the wide rapport with world leaders that would cause her to be recognized as an outstanding journalist at the top of her profession. In 1939 she visited thirteen countries in five months; during an aborted revolution in Huszt, Carpatho-Ukraine, she literally lived under the flags of three republics in twenty-seven hours. During that March day she watched the birth and demise of three nations, "perishing before they could draw breath." Hourly during the ordeal she cabled home what she observed, speaking to an international audience. In 1940 she traveled for six months along the front line of the war to get firsthand information. She traveled thousands of miles throughout the Continent, usually accompanied by her husband.

She became well known for her interviews with many of the world's most influential leaders, including Mussolini, Adolf Hitler, Sir Neville Chamberlain, Joseph Stalin, Sir Winston Churchill, Gustav Stresemann, Leon Blum, Franklin D. Roosevelt, Eamon De Valera, and Eduard Beneš. Her keen perception of personality, her rapport with world leaders, and her insights about issues and events of the day made her a favorite with many of her interview subjects.

An anecdote about her early encounter with Mussolini is typical. Before her initial interview with the dictator in the fall of 1926, she did her backgrounding by reading his new law of corporations in the Italian original. When Mussolini asked her what interested her most about Italy, she responded, "The new law for the corporate state." On discovering that she had actually read the statute, he rose from his chair, smiled, grasped her hand, and exclaimed, "My congratulations; you and I are the only ones who have." She later said of him: "Of all the public characters I have interviewed, Mussolini is the only one who seems interested not only in what he says himself but in what you have to say; he appears to weigh your suggestions, solicits your opinions." He told her on one occasion that he detested society because it was dominated by women, a statement that did not sit well with her.

Other leaders responded similarly. Franklin Roosevelt repeatedly broke his rule against private interviews because he "enjoyed chatting with her." Dwight Eisenhower said she was "a truly great reporter," one "held affectionately to be a warm person to whom we all responded." She enjoyed several private audiences with Pope Pius XI and Pope Pius

World, Reader magazine, the *Atlantic Monthly*, and others. The travels throughout Europe showed her the social and political changes occurring in the post-World War I era. In 1920, the same year she sold the *New York Times* a sonnet for $3.50, she wrote to Carr V. Van Anda, managing editor of the *Times*, proposing to send the newspaper some dispatches from abroad. Van Anda replied, "Try it," and in late 1920 her articles began appearing in the newspaper. The editors were so pleased with these vignettes of life abroad that they offered McCormick an assignment as a regular correspondent in 1922.

She accepted, writing stories which focused on the rise of fascism in Italy. In 1921, she had heard one of Benito Mussolini's first speeches in the Chamber of Deputies. Although his name was still relatively unknown throughout the world, she was struck by his oratory and the way he reduced the noisy audience to utter silence. Leaving the building, she said to a colleague, "Italy has heard its master's voice." This observation won admirers for her when it was quickly proved to be accurate, since most other journalists had dismissed the Fascist leader as just an upstart Milanese newspaper editor.

XII, ultimately reporting on the history, organization, and contemporary influence of the Catholic church. Her book *The Hammer and the Scythe: Communist Russia Enters the Second Decade* (1928) examines the Soviet Union during the decade after the Bolshevik Revolution.

McCormick was one of the few who understood the danger of a militant totalitarianism in Europe from the very beginning. Her early articles indicated her untiring efforts to awaken America to the threat presented by the Axis powers in Europe. Her awareness in 1921 of the danger of Mussolini moved her to warn Americans against a rearming Italy. Four years before the Nazi armies crashed into Poland and the dive-bombing Stukas roared over Danzig, she said, "Nothing better or more stable can be established by more war, but in the long view it is equally certain that there must be war— not all the sanctions in the world can stop it—until there is a league not only to enforce but to create peace."

In June 1936 she accepted an invitation to join the *Times*'s editorial board. Publisher Arthur Hays Sulzberger told her: "You are the freedom editor. It will be your job to stand up and shout whenever freedom is interfered with in any part of the world." American-European and American-Asian relationships became her beat. The assignment required that she write two unsigned pieces weekly for the newspaper's editorial pages. She moved into a roomy, sunlit office on the tenth floor at 229 West Forty-third Street as the only woman member of the daily's policymaking editorial board. A fellow newswoman said after visiting McCormick's office: "She saw me, as she saw everyone who knocked. . . . Seated alone in her big office and at a huge desk behind which she looked incredibly small," she talked "simply and with a twinkle." As the first woman on the *Times* editorial council her professional accomplishments challenged and encouraged other career-minded women of the day.

By February 1937, when she was assigned a regular *Times* column, McCormick was "must reading" both in Washington and in foreign capitals. Her thrice-weekly column "In Europe" alternated with Arthur Krock's column; it was later retitled "Abroad" and retained that title until her death. She traveled extensively throughout the United States covering national political conventions, describing life in the modern South, and relating the difficulties and hardships of the Depression in human, concrete anecdotes and images. A few months after she began her column, she became the first woman to be awarded a Pulitzer Prize in

journalism for her distinguished foreign correspondence.

A *Times* executive editor said that McCormick could sweat out her column, make a speech, sit up talking about international affairs until 3:00 or 4:00 in the morning—and then start out all over again at 9:00 A.M. She hated to write her column until the last minute. A *Times* executive said, "No matter whether she files from Claridge's in London, a press camp in Germany or the *Times*'s office in Rome, she has an uncanny way of getting her dispatches to the cable desk in Manhattan about 9:30 P.M., just before her deadline." Though *Times* copyreaders initially labeled her "Verbose Annie" and cut her dispatches down to size, she learned quickly to tighten and sharpen her copy so that it needed almost no editing.

When conducting interviews she preferred not to take notes so as not to distract her subjects. She said that she believed in treating interviewees as human beings, not expecting to get information from them: important statements would not be made to reporters, but would be held for public speeches. She believed that the interview is valuable only for the opportunity to study the personality of the subject.

Refusing to take unqualified credit for unearthing major news stories, she remarked on one occasion that since "crises were popping all over Europe at the time," it was not strange that she "bumped into a few." She did not believe that journalists should become celebrities and generally refused to authorize articles to be written about her during her lifetime. She feared that fame would interfere with her performance as a journalist, and she maintained that the public was not really interested in her anyway. A reporter's job, she declared, is to report objectively; to hold the mirror up to people and events of public concern. Once a reporter stands in the way and casts a reflection, he is lost.

McCormick's writing was sensitive but logical, often taking on a semiconversational tone. Describing Berlin in the early days of World War II, for example, she wrote: "Groping along the tunnel-like streets you almost never hear a voice. Other gropers are shadows and footsteps." A poet in her younger days, McCormick liked to use the tools of the poet, such as metaphor. She likened the war in Europe to the "Apocalypse of the long drawn-out fight of man to control the machine." Describing Respighi's "Pines of Rome" played in the Roman Forum on a moonlit night, she called the sound "moonlight put to music," and pictured the cypresses and pines each "listening in a separate radiance." She likened Italy's political atmosphere in March 1948 to "a warm day with an undercurrent of icy wind. . . . It is an odd combination of hopeful reconstruction and fearful suspense. Nowhere has the Communist victory in Czechoslovakia caused such reactions of glee among Communists and gloom among anti-Communists."

Her values of human life and peace, and her belief in an unchanging moral order based on universals and absolutes, strengthened her to refuse to embrace despair even in the darkest days of World War II.

Although not an activist on behalf of feminist causes, McCormick encouraged women to enter all professions and urged government and business leaders to employ them, capitalizing on their distinctive sensitivities and talents. Her correspondence with Dorothy Thompson and Clare Boothe Luce reveals her awareness of and interest in women's issues. Discussing her professional success and that of other prominent women journalists of the time, she said, "We had tried hard not to act like ladies or to talk as ladies are supposed to talk— meaning too much—but just to sneak toward the city desk . . . and even the publisher's office with masculine sang-froid."

She believed in the distinctive role of women in restoring and preserving spiritual and moral values to the benefit of society. She challenged women to this task a few months before her death, when she wrote in a foreword to *The Spiritual Woman –Trustees of the Future*, "Women, and particularly American women in a time when the United States is thrust into a position of unique power and influence, have the soul of the nation in their keeping. They have a special obligation to emphasize, preserve, and manifest in their own lives the spiritual values that are in danger of being lost in an age in which skepticism is a virtue and faith a vice."

In a piece for the *Times* in 1945, she sketched a concrete dramatization of the concept. She pictured a devastated town behind the fighting lines where a correspondent saw a woman emerging from a cellar and, though her house and land were in ruins, proceed to sweep away the rubble on her doorstep. Someone asked what she was doing with a broom among all the bombs. "Who's to take care of the [garden] cabbages and onions if I don't? They're all that's left of all the work of all my life," she said fiercely. "And, somebody has to begin clearing away this mess." McCormick observed that

It's pretty futile to start attacking the ruins of

great cities with a kitchen broom. Yet, . . . women instinctively seize their brooms in this age-old gesture of cleaning up the mess the men have made.

While there's no assurance that they can clear it up this time . . . we are the trustees of the future. We can't leave it to the next generation because they won't have seen what we have seen. . . . It isn't chance that women have been named for the first time to a conference called to set up the framework of international order.

McCormick believed in the goals of the United Nations, and her writing around 1945 offered a sincere appeal to the people of the world to make the organization work as a significant catalyst of peace.

During World War II she was named to the Advisory Committee on Post-War Foreign Policy, an elite governmental body. She served as a delegate to the UNESCO conferences in 1946 and 1948 and was considered for influential diplomatic positions.

McCormick's greatest influence occurred during the 1940s, based on her articles about America's position and role in the postwar world. As a recognized expert on current events, she was besieged by publishers eager to have her sign a contract with them to write books. "In love with newspapers" and convinced of the importance of getting accurate and perceptive information to the public during these years of crisis, she refused to take time away from her duties at the *Times*.

After the death of Stalin in 1953, when a thousand wild speculations were afloat as to what might occur next, she called on her knowledge of totalitarianism from the days of Mussolini and Hitler to suggest the way to meet the Communist threat to the free world. In a *Times* column, she declared:

It is tiresome to repeat it all the time, but the truth is that there is no way to meet provocation save to increase the strength and imperviousness of the stone wall it aims to pierce.

Unless they have lost Stalin's sense of caution, the new Soviet rulers cannot be "provoked" into total war, and the West cannot allow itself to be goaded into reckless action. Since the aim of our policy is to build up the force and cohesion that would discourage warlike adventure on the other side, we cannot afford to be diverted for a moment from our supreme task by pot shots and braggart dares. . . . The supreme task is to hold the free nations together.

A former correspondent for a newspaper syndicate, discussing how to judge the reliability of news stories, said, "If you see it in Anne O'Hare McCormick's column of analysis and comment on foreign news in the *New York Times*, you can be pretty sure it's so."

Over the years she received numerous honors, awards, and honorary degrees. In 1934 she received the *New York Evening Post*'s Medal of Service. In 1937 she was awarded the New York Newspaper Women's Club prize for the best feature story of the year, "Exploring The Hitler Legend." In 1939 the National Federation of Press Women, the American Women's Association, and the New York Career Women's Association named her Woman of the Year. With her characteristic modesty, she responded that she had only "stolen some of the thunder" from a year of "thunderous events." In 1940 she was recognized as the outstanding Catholic woman in the United States for that year and received the Theta Phi Alpha Siena Medal. In 1941 she received the Woman's Theodore Roosevelt Memorial Association Medal and in 1942 the Gold Medal of the National Institute of Social Sciences. In 1944 she was awarded the coveted Laetare Medal by the University of Notre Dame. In 1945 she was recognized by the National Press Club with that organization's Women's Award. That year she also received the Distinguished Service Award of International Altrusa. In 1946 she received the National Achievement Award of Chi Omega, and in 1947 the Overseas Press Club Award for Best Interpretive Foreign Correspondent. In 1947 she was also elected to the National Institute of Arts and Letters. In 1950 she received the Theodore Roosevelt Distinguished Service Medal and in 1952 the Silent Award for Journalism. She received some fourteen honorary degrees from American colleges and universities, including Columbia, Dayton, Fordham, Smith, New York, Wellesley, Villanova, Middlebury, Elmira, and Lafayette. She was even decorated by the French government.

Anne O'Hare McCormick died in Manhattan on 29 May 1954 of cancer. She was buried following a solemn requiem mass at the church of Saint Jean-Baptist.

At her death, McCormick was extolled in tributes from many people. Sulzberger summarized her achievements when he declared that those who read her writing relied upon her. The *Times* put black bars on her column and printed in it a tribute by Robert Duffus, who had worked with her for many years. It read in part:

> She was a reporter and gloried in the title. She could not understand how anyone could be satisfied with less than the personal observation on the spot. . . .
>
> In spite of all her genius for seeing, understanding and reporting, she was also a deeply feminine person and could not help being so and would not have wished not to be so. She had a great tenderness for people. She had a great compassion for those who suffered. War to her was not something abstract that destroyed nations. War was the thing that destroyed individuals. War was the thing that wrecked houses in which real people lived, that left children hungry and mothers hopeless. She saw beneath the surface of the events of the day and saw the effect of those events on families, on the old, on the young, on the sick.

Marion Turner Sheehan, in a preface to a 1957 collection of articles by McCormick about the Vatican and the Catholic church, declared that "she emerged as one of the world's greatest women journalists and her death . . . was a great loss to her profession."

Her friend and fellow journalist Helen Walker Homan said: "Anne McCormick really believed in the Fatherhood of God and the brotherhood of man—and worked at it. . . . Love your neighbor wasn't just a glib phrase. Love meant [to] find out what he needs, and do something about it! That's how she felt toward the far countries in whose behalf she raised her pen; that's how she felt about all people, from prime minister to peasant. . . . Wherever freedom was struck to earth, there lay her heart. And it was in freedom's defense that her words frequently rose." Homan told of attending mass in a small English village with McCormick and observing McCormick's normal practice of secluding herself from others for private and lengthy spiritual inspiration and worship. The retiring from others, Homan felt, "bespoke total dedication." Clare Boothe Luce, in an introduction to a collection of McCormick's work, says of the journalist: "In the secular, as well as in the religious sense, she had a catholic mind: she was interested in all areas of knowledge which could have an impact on the well-being of the West."

McCormick observed a time of social, economic, and moral change and worked to interpret it for her readers. Fiercely proud of American journalists and their successes in informing the world about Hitlers and Mussolinis, she observed a generation in a hurry and helped it think about where it was going. She always did so in an atmosphere of hope. In her last published essay she said, "In spite of this dark uncertainty, perhaps because of it, it is heartening to read that everywhere Easter was celebrated with unusual fervor." She saw hope in a speech Pope Pius XII had made appealing for an international ban on using atomic and hydrogen bombs except in self-defense, given on the eve of another attempt by the United Nations to "clear the decks" for a consideration of an international pool of atomic energy. She saw hope symbolized in the Easter Resurrection services held in the Church of the Holy Sepulcher in a tensely divided Jerusalem. Similarly, she found hope burning bright in the hearts and minds of people in Germany, Ireland, and "even Moscow."

She became the personification of her final published line, "And so it goes—a reminder that Easter flourishes as a sign that mankind will never relinquish hope."

References:

"Anne McCormick Crashes the Sacrosanct Portal," *Newsweek*, 7 (20 June 1936): 37;

"Deadlines & a Gold Watch," *Time*, 51 (22 March 1948): 75-78;

J. M. Gillis, "Enlightenment From Eleanor," *Catholic World*, 165 (July 1947): 293-298;

L. C. Gray, "McCormick of the *Times*," *Current History*, 50 (July 1939): 27-64;

Matthew Hoehn, ed., *Catholic Authors—Contemporary Biographical Sketches 1930-1947* (Newark, N.J.: St. Mary's Abbey, 1948), pp. 454-455;

John Hohenberg, *The Pulitzer Prizes: A History of the Awards* (New York: Columbia University Press, 1974), pp. 132-133;

Helen Walker Homan, "Anne O'Hare McCormick: An Appreciation," *Catholic World*, 180 (October 1954): 42-48;

Oliver Jensen, *The Revolt of American Women* (New York: Harcourt, Brace, 1952), p. 103;

"Kudos Champions," *Time*, 37 (30 June 1941): 47;

"Like Mother Used to Cook," *Better Homes & Gardens*, 16 (December 1937): 28, 70-75;

Marion Marzolf, *Up From The Footnote: A History of Women Journalists* (New York: Hastings House, 1977), pp. 54-58;

Robert McHenry, ed., *Liberty's Women* (Springfield, Mass.: Merriam, 1980), pp. 260-261;

"Mrs. McCormick's Thunder," *Newsweek*, 35 (20 March 1950): 47-48;

"Off To War," *Time*, 53 (10 January 1949): 45;

Ishbel Ross, *Ladies of the Press* (New York: Harper, 1936), pp. 150, 163, 360, 366-369;

"The Times' McCormick," *Newsweek*, 43 (7 June 1954): 80-81;

"U.S. At War," *Time*, 43 (20 March 1944): 17;

"Veteran to Rome," *Time*, 44 (28 August 1944): 71-72;

"Without Fear Or Favor," *Time*, 55 (8 May 1950): 68.

Papers:

Anne O'Hare McCormick's papers, including correspondence, lectures, editorials, columns, clippings, and pamphlets, are at the New York Public Library; a collection of McCormick's *New York Times* articles is on microfilm in the State Historical Society of Wisconsin.

Robert R. McCormick

Caryl H. Sewell

BIRTH: Chicago, 30 July 1880, to Robert Sanderson and Katherine Medill McCormick.

EDUCATION: B.A., Yale University, 1903; Northwestern University Law School, 1904-1906.

MARRIAGES: 10 March 1915 to Amie deHoule Irwin Adams. 22 December 1944 to Maryland Mathison Hooper.

MAJOR POSITION HELD: Publisher, *Chicago Tribune* (1910-1955), *Washington Times-Herald* (1948-1954).

AWARDS AND HONORS: Distinguished Service Medal for leadership, executive ability, and supervision of training and discipline, United States Army, 1923; LL.D., Northwestern University, 1947.

DEATH: Wheaton, Illinois, 1 April 1955.

SELECTED BOOKS: *With the Russian Army* (New York: Macmillan, 1915);
The Army of 1918 (New York: Harcourt, Brace, 1920);
Ulysses S. Grant, the Great Soldier of America (New York: Appleton-Century, 1934);
The Freedom of the Press (New York & London: Appleton-Century, 1936);
How We Acquired Our National Territory (Chicago: *Chicago Tribune*, 1942);
The American Revolution and Its Influence on World Civilization (Chicago: *Chicago Tribune*, 1945);
The War Without Grant (New York: Bond Wheelwright, 1950);
The Founding Fathers (Chicago: *Chicago Tribune*, 1951);
The American Empire (Chicago: *Chicago Tribune*, 1952).

It might be contended that Robert Rutherford McCormick was one of the few men in America—perhaps the only man—in whom the two divergent strains of American newspaperdom were combined. These two strains—personal journalism, as represented in the great editors of earlier days, and

Robert R. McCormick

hardheaded manufacturing and publishing with a sharp eye to profits—were both so strong in his character as to make him a unique and formidable force in his time. As one commentator put it, "He not only knows what will sell and how to manage his big business shrewdly; he also knows what he believes and is willing to go to hell for it."

McCormick, also known as "the Colonel," was editor and publisher of the *Chicago Tribune* for forty-five years. Although he earned the lasting hatred of many people for his isolationism and his staunch rejection of President Roosevelt and the New Deal, many of his policies and innovations had a lasting effect on the newspaper industry. Due to McCormick's endeavors, the Tribune Company invested in Canadian forests, built paper mills in Quebec and Ontario, and purchased a fleet of lake ships that enabled it to produce newspapers from the log to the finished product, a feat that was unequaled anywhere in the world. He was the first to invest in developing the northern side of the St. Lawrence River, and this business acumen enabled him and his paper to survive editorial faux pas (for example, his impassioned defense of one of his reporters—Jake Lingle—who had gangster connections and was gunned down on the street) that might have toppled a less well run enterprise.

McCormick made the *Tribune* one of the best papers to work for in America. He paid the highest salaries and offered irresistible benefits such as generous sick leave, pensions, speedy death benefits, cheap credit, group insurance and hospitalization, free dental care, free medical attention in office emergencies, and free lunch nightly for city room workers.

The outspoken, opinionated, stubborn McCormick, although best known as a journalist, was also a lawyer, public official, historian, soldier, radio performer, amateur polo player, and world traveler. He was born on 30 July 1880 at home on Ontario Street in Chicago, Illinois, the second son (an older sister died in infancy) of Robert Sanderson McCormick and Katherine Medill McCormick.

Bertie, as he was known in the family, was not the favorite son. Although he eventually followed in the footsteps of his mother's father, Joseph Medill,

who had made the *Tribune* a dominant force in American politics (he is credited with naming the Republican party and with helping to elect Abraham Lincoln to the presidency), Bertie was not expected to have a career with the newspaper. This position was reserved by his mother for his brother, Joseph Medill McCormick, on whom she lavished affection and whom she designated as heir to the *Tribune* throne.

Though related to the extremely wealthy McCormicks of the McCormick reaper (Cyrus Hall McCormick, its inventor, was his father's uncle), Bertie's family had no financial interest in the reaper or in the International Harvester Company. (Many people have mistakenly assumed that Robert McCormick's wealth came from this business.) So in 1889, when Bertie's father lost the small inheritance he had invested in the grain markets in Chicago, the family was momentarily without an income. Katherine's father used his influence to obtain an appropriately prestigious post for his son-in-law: Robert Todd Lincoln, the son of President Lincoln and a *Tribune* lawyer, had just been appointed minister to Great Britain; Lincoln was persuaded to take McCormick on as second secretary to the legation. The family moved immediately to London.

Once in England, Bertie and Medill were en-

McCormick's father, Robert Sanderson McCormick (left), as ambassador to France circa 1905, with his wife, Katherine Medill McCormick, and two aides at the U.S. embassy in Paris

rolled in several boarding schools. They stayed at the first one only a short time—it was typical of the harsh, cold environment for which British boarding schools have long been famous. Ludgrove, the second school they attended, was an oasis, and Bertie enjoyed it very much. This was also true of Elstree, the school to which he was transferred at the age of twelve. There, he explained later, he learned from the masters that despite the glories of England his duty was to his own country. Perhaps this was where he learned his intense patriotism. McCormick corresponded all his life with his British schoolmates who survived World War I and with the widow of the headmaster.

In 1893 the family returned to Chicago for the World's Fair; the next year, when McCormick was fourteen, his parents returned to England and he began his American schooling at Groton.

McCormick must have been very lonely during those years: his parents were abroad and his older brother was a student at Yale. He contracted pneumonia and missed a lot of school while being cared for by relatives. His great-aunt, Nettie Fowler McCormick (the widow of Cyrus), catered to his mechanical bent. She thought it would be useful to let him learn about electricity and gave him the opportunity to experiment. He learned, with a neighbor friend, to hang electric bells, and they ran a telegraph line between their homes.

During the summers, McCormick visited with his grandfather, Joseph Medill, either at Medill's Red Oaks Farm west of Chicago in Wheaton or in San Antonio, Texas. He was with Medill in Texas early in 1899 when, according to McCormick, his boyhood ended. His grandfather died after uttering his last words to McCormick one morning—last words that any great journalist would love to have credited to him: "What is the news this morning?"

In the fall of 1899, McCormick entered Yale University, following the academic footsteps from Groton to Yale of both his brother, Medill, and his cousin, Joe Patterson. McCormick earned a "gentleman's C average," joined many clubs, and spent his vacations hunting in Idaho; exploring Hudson's Bay, where he shot two polar bears; and visiting his parents in Europe, where his father had just become one of America's first ambassadors in a rather strange way. The elder McCormick's status as United States minister was suddenly upgraded by the emperor Francis Joseph of Austria-Hungary during his first visit to the court. The emperor, apparently impressed by the United States' easy victory in the Spanish-American War, had ordered the coach and four in which McCormick had ar-

Publishing dynasty founder Joseph Medill, with his grandsons Robert McCormick (seated, left), Joseph Patterson (seated, right), and Medill McCormick, and his granddaughter Eleanor (Cissy) Patterson (Private Collection)

rived at the palace to be replaced by the ambassadorial coach and six for the return trip to the legation, which had now been raised to an embassy.

In his later years, McCormick came to dislike the idle rich and avoided them and their clubs. He considered himself and his cousin Joe among the few genuine aristocrats in America, but it was an aristocracy based upon achievement and concern for the nation's future. He despised the wealthy who shirked their responsibilities, although he was not loath to accept any and all advantages that came his way. As one observer pointed out in 1944: "Though the McCormicks came to Chicago a hundred years ago, they originally were a Virginia family and the Colonel, despite frequent attacks upon Southern politicians, today retains a deep affection and kinship for many traditional Southern institutions—militarism, gallantry, paternalism, feudalism, and the landed aristocracy which champions states' rights."

After completing his four years at Yale, McCormick was at loose ends. He had been greatly influenced by the teaching of William Graham

Sumner, whose theory of Social Darwinism continued to influence McCormick's thinking for the rest of his life. Sumner believed that nobody had enough wisdom to be rational or just in developing and carrying out detailed social plans. Thus, the less meddling with the mysterious process of human affairs, the better. This idea and his famous "get capital, young man, get capital" are perhaps the sources of McCormick's stubborn resistance to the New Deal.

Although McCormick's talents appeared to lie in the areas of math and science, especially engineering, and he had been discouraged from writing by a professor who criticized his work, McCormick did not know what to do. His brother, Medill, and cousin Joe were both at the *Tribune*, but he had never thought about becoming an editor or publisher—these jobs had been reserved for the older boys. He considered entering the Naval Academy, but his eyesight fell short of the admission standard. Finally, partially influenced by the remark of a professor who told him that he was poor in physics but "would make a good lawyer," he decided to enter law school. This decision elevated him to a new class of supereducated Americans: in the early 1900s only four percent of the college-age population even attended college; few lawyers learned law at universities. The idea of topping a college education with a professional degree was very new.

McCormick enrolled in the Northwestern University Law School on the recommendation of his father, who felt that attending school in the community where he lived would give him the opportunity to introduce himself to important people. It was good advice: before he could even finish law school, McCormick was approached by political leaders and asked to run for city alderman from the twenty-first ward. He was elected in 1904. In 1906 he ran successfully for president of the sanitary district, and while directing the sanitary district he completed his law courses. In this position McCormick was able to use his considerable executive and organizational abilities. He oversaw the completion of the sanitary canal linking the Chicago sewage system with the Mississippi River. Construction had bogged down and the administration was ridden with graft and corruption when he was elected, but McCormick quickly fired unnecessary and unqualified workers and took the firm stance that would later become so familiar to those who worked for him at the *Tribune*. He is credited with changing the history of Chicago through his efficient and businesslike approach in completing this project.

Another McCormick innovation, a laboratory to study bacterial purification of sewage, put Chicago in the forefront with its sewage treatment system.

Despite the successful completion of this work, McCormick was defeated in the next election in 1910; the tide had turned against Republicans. His political ambitions—he had entertained thoughts of becoming mayor or governor someday—evaporated. He turned to the law practice he had opened with two partners, which was located in the Tribune Company building, and gradually found himself becoming more and more interested in the family business. On the other hand, Medill, a heavy drinker with emotional problems, was not all that interested in the paper. Upon graduation from Yale he worked halfheartedly at the *Tribune* in various positions, finally resigning in the spring of 1910 to the great relief of all who ran the *Tribune*. Medill's true interest was politics; he married the daughter of Mark Hanna, a power in the Republican party, and was elected to Congress in 1916 and to the Senate in 1918. He died prematurely, from the results of drinking, in 1925.

In the meantime, events were taking place which would have a profound influence on the rest of McCormick's life and thought. His father, after a

McCormick as a young attorney in 1910, shortly before he became publisher of the Chicago Tribune *(Photo by Dana Hull)*

brief stay as ambassador to the court of Francis Joseph, had been transferred to Russia. Also present in St. Petersburg was an agent of the British foreign office, Sir Cecil Spring-Rice. According to at least one biographer of McCormick, all those who spent so much time and energy in later years searching for the roots of McCormick's bitter hatred of the British could have found the answer if they had bothered to read the two-volume *Letters and Friendships of Sir Cecil Spring-Rice* (1929). Some have concluded that McCormick's dislike for the British must have come from his early childhood experiences at school in England. Others have pointed out the contradictions that make this explanation difficult to accept: he rode to work in a Rolls-Royce, spoke with a mild British accent, sported a British-style moustache, had a London tailor and shoemaker inherited from his father, and expressed undying affection for his English boarding schools. Even his three favorite authors—Rudyard Kipling, A. Conan Doyle, and P. G. Wodehouse—were English. Frank Waldrop, a former editor of the *Washington Times-Herald*, writes that McCormick's anglophobia grew out of loyalty to his father rather than personal experiences with the British. In *McCormick of Chicago* (1966), Waldrop suggests that it was Spring-Rice who destroyed McCormick's father's career: "Step by delicate step, Spring-Rice built an understanding through letters, first to the President, and then to the President's wife, to show that the McCormicks who saw themselves securely in favor because they were effusively pro-Russian, were thought at court some sort of a joke in poor taste on Roosevelt's part." In subtle, carefully chosen words, Spring-Rice warned Roosevelt that unless he was stopped, Kaiser Wilhelm of Germany, who was in league with the czar, would manipulate a peace between Russia and Japan in the Russo-Japanese War that would profit Germany at everyone else's expense. Spring-Rice was a close friend of Roosevelt's and had served as best man at his wedding, so when he ended the letter by saying, "How I wish you had a really good ambassador here. . . ," Roosevelt took the hint. Robert Sanderson McCormick was relieved of his duties. According to Waldrop, this was "simply and utterly the end." The McCormicks kept up appearances as well as they could at the next post in France. But two years later, all hope of a future career was destroyed.

Through the years, the rivalry between the two Medill sisters had grown. Beginning, undoubtedly, during their own childhoods, McCormick's mother, Katherine, and her sister Elinor had tried to outdo each other. Both, for example, had named their firstborn sons after their father—Joseph Medill McCormick, known as Medill, and Joseph Medill Patterson. Katherine planned from the beginning for Medill to take over the *Tribune*. But Elinor's marriage to Robert Patterson, who eventually became managing editor of the paper under his father-in-law, complicated matters. Joseph Medill had contemplated selling the *Tribune* as he grew older. He had been talked out of it by Robert Patterson and his daughter Katherine. Eventually, he had created a trust with 1,050 shares of *Tribune* stock. Both of his daughters' husbands and his attorney, William Beale, were made trustees. They held the power to vote the stock and receive its dividends, which were to be divided equally after expenses. The sisters were to succeed their husbands as trustees. In 1908, the sisters' pettiness and the lack of charity they felt for each other had new and malignant repercussions. Elinor also had a daughter named Elinor who, although she later changed the spelling to Eleanor, was known as "Cissy" throughout her life. Cissy had joined her Aunt Kate and Uncle Robert in St. Petersburg and had foolishly married a fortune-hunting Polish nobleman who wanted her money in return for his title. Later, she found herself unable to leave Russia with the child of this unhappy marriage. Katherine, desperate to leave the limbo in which she and her husband had found themselves in Paris, made a last attempt to achieve prominence in diplomatic circles. She tried to make a deal with Cissy's father, Robert Patterson. Katherine offered to use the influence they had with the czar to help Cissy leave Russia if Patterson would intervene with the new president, William Howard Taft, for a diplomatic post for her husband. Patterson responded with fury at this suggestion and in August 1908 he sent a letter to Taft. He told the president that he opposed the idea of a diplomatic post for McCormick, who had never done anything to warrant it in the first place, and that "President Roosevelt told me that he was compelled to remove McCormick from St. Petersburg during the peace negotiations because he was incompetent and a 'stronger man' was needed there." Also, Patterson added, Katherine had misled people into thinking that she owned the *Tribune* and that it gave the appearance of favoritism or bribery if such favors were traded.

Waldrop says that by 1910 Robert Sanderson McCormick was far gone into melancholia (depression) and that from time to time he "had to be dug out of retreat to a country hotel at Natural Bridge, in the Virginia county where he had been born."

Eventually, he was put into a nursing home in Hinsdale, Illinois, where he died of pneumonia in 1916. Other biographers have been less kind, pointing out that McCormick turned to the bottle.

The ruin of his father's life, according to Waldrop, was "without any doubt the most influential single experience of which Robert R. McCormick was ever conscious." Hardly anyone knew much of the story, Waldrop asserts, and even those who did never dared to risk McCormick's fury by mentioning it. McCormick was a private man and managed to keep much of his personal life hidden; even now, twenty-nine years after his death, archives at the Tribune Company offices containing his personal papers are not open to the public and an "official" biography has yet to be written.

The unexpected death of Robert Patterson on 1 April 1910 put the *Tribune* in crisis. McCormick heard about his uncle's death and rushed to the *Tribune* offices just in time to prevent the sale of the paper to Victor Lawson, publisher of the *Chicago Daily News* and *Record-Herald*. Patterson had arranged the meeting, and the sale undoubtedly would have occurred had he not died at that time. Instead, McCormick, who had been serving as treasurer of the business, talked the trustees into letting him and his cousin Joe Patterson take over the paper. Despite the difficulties between their parents, Bertie and Joe were good friends and remained so throughout their lives.

James Keeley, a hard-nosed editor who had been working under Robert Patterson, wanted the job of publisher. Keeley, who put "The World's Greatest Newspaper" onto the *Tribune* flag, even entertained the thought of signing on former president Roosevelt as a figurehead publisher. Instead, McCormick kept Keeley on as general manager, reserving the title of publisher for himself and his cousin. McCormick was made president of the *Tribune* in 1911; in 1912 he and Patterson were elected to the board of directors.

Keeley stayed on at the *Tribune* for a while, but he felt frustrated by the turn of events and quit in 1914 to buy the *Record-Herald* from Lawson. At that time, Keeley was recognized as Chicago's number one newsman and everyone wondered who could replace him. The answer was undoubtedly a surprise to all concerned. Who would have thought that a couple of amateurs like Robert McCormick and Joe Patterson could turn the *Chicago Tribune* into one of the nation's dominant papers?

At his full adult height, McCormick stood an imposing six feet, four inches. He became accustomed to dominating others, and perhaps it was partly his body build which led him to assume superiority over them. At any rate, neither McCormick nor Patterson seemed to have any doubts about their ability to run the *Tribune*. They divided the job of editor between them and then, to avoid arguing about day-to-day decisions, alternated on a monthly basis. Some writers have claimed that the arrangement was very confusing to readers because the two editors had opposite points of view on many issues, but others have pointed out that the variations in editorials are mostly too subtle to be detected.

Patterson, as it turned out, was a journalistic genius. He fathered most of the comic strips for which the *Tribune* became famous and also contributed the idea of continuity of comic strips—an idea that developed a loyalty to the strips that no one could have predicted. His many contributions to the *Tribune*'s fight for supremacy in the morning field in Chicago were not, however, nearly as decisive as the effort that McCormick put forth in developments in Canada.

A demographic study that had been done while McCormick was president of the sanitary district had convinced him that there was rapid population growth ahead for Chicago. The prediction was that over the next four decades the population of Cook County would grow to 4,500,000. He reasoned that if the paper was well managed and the price kept low, it could rise from a 1910 circulation of 241,000 to 500,000 by 1950. (Actually, by the beginning of World War II the circulation was well over a million.) In order to keep the price low, he proposed that the *Tribune* build its own paper mill at an investment cost of $1 million. His timing could not have been better: wood was growing scarce in the eastern United States, and a tariff on Canadian newsprint had just been removed. Ultimately, instead of just building a paper mill, he received permission from the trustees to build a pulp and paper mill. He settled on a spot in Ontario, ten miles from Niagara Falls, and, using Swedish electrical motors—no 12,000-volt motors were manufactured in the United States—began by early 1914 to turn out virtually the entire *Tribune* paper supply. He also leased vast timberlands in Canada and a fleet of lake freighters to carry the paper stock to Chicago. For the next forty years, McCormick led the construction of a great papermaking, power-generating, mining, and shipping industry which not only made the Tribune Company secure at its base but also initiated a complete change in the economy of the region.

Under the energetic, aggressive leadership of

Max Annenberg, whom the cousins lured from the Hearst circulation department, the newspaper began to boom. Many reporters carried guns, and bloody fights among circulation crews are believed by some historians to have given starts to many of the thugs who later became Chicago's Prohibition-era gangsters. Circulation continued to grow even without the use of circulation gangs: World War I produced exciting, violent headlines every day, and as demand for newspapers rose, newsprint became increasingly scarce. All of this made McCormick look like a genius.

Early in 1915, McCormick, who had been commissioned a colonel in the First Cavalry of the Illinois National Guard, went to England. On 10 March he married a Chicago woman, Amie Adams, who had divorced an alcoholic cousin of McCormick's (a son of Cyrus Hall McCormick) to marry him. They traveled together throughout Europe and then returned to the United States.

Later that year McCormick visited the Russian front with credentials identifying him both as an officer and as the son of the former ambassador and wrote *With the Russian Army* (1915), a diary of his visit. The book showed that he had a reporter's eye for detail: he noted things such as the storm windows with thermometers showing the temperature outside, between the panes, and inside the room where he met the czar. He went to the front with the czar's brother, the grand duke.

McCormick exchanged his temporary colonel's commission for a permanent commission as major when the First Illinois Cavalry was sent to Texas to pursue Pancho Villa in 1916. McCormick observed that the American army lacked automatic weapons, which even the Mexicans possessed, and persuaded banker Charles G. Dawes, a fellow officer, to raise money to buy six machine guns. He also bought some mobile field kitchens similar to ones he had seen in Russia.

In 1917 the United States entered World War I. McCormick was soon promoted to lieutenant colonel and then to colonel. It is not clear just what role he played in the battle of Cantigny, but after the war McCormick renamed Red Oaks, the farm in Wheaton, for this first major battle in which American troops participated. There has been some question as to whether or not he actually risked his life on the line, but he wrote afterwards in *The Army of 1918* (1920), "I have tasted the wine of death and its flavor will be forever in my throat." Although called a "tin soldier" by critics and caricatured in a rival newspaper's comic feature as "Colonel McCosmic," McCormick was a very serious student of military

McCormick in his colonel's uniform during World War I

affairs. He later wrote two books about the American Civil War: *Ulysses S. Grant, the Great Soldier of America* (1934) and *The War Without Grant* (1950).

In 1918, McCormick had a momentous meeting in France with his cousin Joe Patterson. Patterson—who, unlike McCormick, had scorned the opportunities that family connections could bring—had enlisted in the army as a private and had worked his way up to captain. It is a legend that they sat atop a manure pile in the backyard of a French farmhouse and decided that upon their return to America Patterson would begin a newspaper in New York City modeled on the successful tabloids he had seen in London. Thus Patterson masterminded the creation of the *New York Daily News*. It was an immediate hit and began earning money by its second year. Patterson remained in Chicago working on the *Tribune* and running the *Daily News* from afar until 1925, when he moved to New York.

McCormick continued the circulation war that finally eliminated Hearst from the Chicago morning field. At the critical point, McCormick bought up the last available newsprint in the United States while he developed his own sure source in Canada.

McCormick became famous for the battles in which he engaged. Some of these fights were childishly petty, while others revolved around the future of the nation and the nature of the government. No one could ever predict just what he would do or say in a particular situation. But he entered wholeheartedly into the fray, risking all to defend his point of view. During 1917 and 1918, Chicago Mayor William Hale ("Big Bill") Thompson sued the *Tribune* three times for a total of $1.35 million. He lost. In 1919, when the *Tribune* accused him of corruption and of bankrupting the city, Thompson filed a suit for $10 million in the name of the city, claiming the *Tribune* had damaged Chicago's credit. Ultimately the Illinois Supreme Court found for the *Tribune,* and the case became a landmark in press jurisprudence. *Tribune* lawyers had argued that the Thompson suit was alleging "libel upon government," a form which had never existed in the United States. The court ruled that this form was not legal. Newspapers, the court said, could not exist long without public confidence, while "the harm which would certainly result to the community from an officialdom unrestrained by fear of publicity is incalculable." Also in 1919, the *Tribune* was sued by Henry Ford for an editorial published at the time of the Mexican trouble in 1916. Ford had opposed calling out the national guard; the *Tribune* had charged that Ford workers who volunteered for service might lose their jobs, and had called Ford "an anarchistic enemy of the nation which protects him in his wealth." Although Ford won the suit, he was awarded only twelve cents—six cents in damages and six cents in costs.

The Tribune Tower was built in the early 1920s following a design competition with entries from all over the world. The final neo-Gothic design rose twenty-four stories, topped by another twelve stories of Gothic stonework with gargoyles and "grotesques." The pressroom in the new building was laid out in a pattern designed by McCormick. Instead of the traditional arrangement of five or six presses grouped together to produce a section of pages which had to be assembled later, McCormick had the twenty-five press units and six folders connected in a continuous line. He was granted three patents for this system, which later became standard for newspapers. Color printing

was also a *Tribune* innovation during these years. The *Tribune*'s "Coloroto" section came out for the first time on 9 April 1922. It consisted of four pages of color and eight of black and white. The *Tribune* maintained the lead in this area for many years.

During the years between the world wars, McCormick really began to develop his style. It was patterned upon that of Grandfather Medill, who was said to have run the paper like a frontier editor. He, too, had controlled the news as well as the editorial content and was probably more of an influence on his grandson than most biographers have realized. It was Joseph Medill who began the practice of simplified spelling for which the *Tribune* became famous. McCormick, beginning in 1934, introduced such innovations as "burocracy," "altho," "thru," "frate," "rime," and many others. These changes were finally eliminated in 1975, twenty years after McCormick's death.

According to *Time* magazine of 9 June 1947:

> It was a hectic era that found Colonel McCormick touting Fascism (a 1927 editorial: "Dictatorships frequently are constructive. This is the case with Mussolini." 1928: ". . . we can use that sort of government here.") He pooh-poohed the bomber (1926: ". . . the outlook for bombing plane versus battleship does not favor the plane"). In a careless moment, he even nominated Roosevelt II (1929: "In this role he might . . . from the White House, restore the rich heritage of constitutional order. . .").
>
> But it was on the flaming issue of war & peace that McCormick won his reputation as the most bitterly hated press lord of his time. Beginning in 1939, daily & Sunday, the *Trib's* eight-column banner lines screamed McCormick's ideas on the approaching conflict:
> WAR BLAMED ON U.S. ENVOY
> HALIFAX STEERS F.D.R. BILL
> HOUSE PASSES DICTATOR BILL
> FIGHT JAPS. BRITONS TO U.S.

After McCormick took over the *Tribune*, the paper was departmentalized more than it ever had been before. The idea of providing personal service, instituted at the *Tribune* under Keeley, was transformed under McCormick from an editorial conception into a promotional one. By 1926, the paper had twenty different departments, fourteen of which were *Tribune* inventions. The public responded positively to these innovations—the *Tribune* received about 700,000 letters to its departments that year. These features included a health column, a contributor's column, a law department, quiz questions, the "Voice of the People," cartoons, radio listings, women's page features, amusement coverage, day-by-day reports on the *Tribune*'s experimental farm, and a picture page. Many other newspapers had some of these features, but no other paper had all of them.

The paper also began to promote public events, such as the Golden Gloves boxing tournament, which it began in 1923. The *Tribune* got the publicity; the proceeds went to charity. It also held history essay contests, and fashion contests for American (not *French*) designs.

Another astute move involved McCormick's recognition of the importance that radio would have. He foresaw its value as early as 1921 and by 1924 was able to end the negotiations for the purchase of WDAP, then Chicago's most powerful radio station. Within a month its call letters were changed to WGN, for World's Greatest Newspaper. For a long time no one realized the potential that radio had for transmitting the news. The station broadcast dance music from the top of the Drake Hotel, and it was only by accident that the news potential was discovered. One day one of the broadcasters happened to glance outside at the lake. A boat was sinking within his view and, horrified, he scooped the papers as he quickly began to describe what he was witnessing to listeners.

Many Chicagoans still remember the Colonel's regular Saturday night broadcasts. During the intermissions of a popular show, "Theatre of the Air," McCormick loved to come on and talk. He broadcast travelogues, history lessons, and his memoirs; his talks were printed the following day on the editorial page of the *Tribune*.

McCormick, although often dull in his presentations, greatly enjoyed public speaking. He gave speeches in the space of ten days in Chicago, St. Louis, Oklahoma City, New York, and several Western states.

Always a firm defender of the freedom of the press, McCormick was considered an authority on the subject. In 1931 he became involved in a landmark U.S. Supreme Court case, *Near v. Minnesota*, when he came to the aid of a small Minneapolis publication which was shut down under a state libel law based on prior restraint. He brought in the American Newspaper Publishers Association (ANPA) and ultimately won national acclaim in the five-to-four decision. The *Tribune* spent $35,000 on the case. McCormick spoke frequently on the issue,

and many of his talks were compiled into a book, *The Freedom of the Press* (1936).

McCormick's loyalty to his employees led him into a scandal in the case of a *Tribune* police reporter. In 1930, Alfred "Jake" Lingle was murdered by a gunman as he entered the Illinois Central subway station on his way to the racetrack. Lingle had been on the staff of the *Tribune* since 1912. Although he did not actually write any articles, he did supply information on the activities of Chicago gangsters and was a personal friend of the police commissioner. At first, the *Tribune* and other newspapers in Chicago thought Lingle had been gunned down because of his journalistic activities. "What made him valuable to this newspaper made him dangerous to his killers," the *Tribune* declared. The paper demanded an investigation of his death and the capture and punishment of his killers and offered a reward.

Unpleasant truths were soon discovered. It appeared that Lingle, on a sixty-five-dollar-a-week salary, had been able to bank thousands of dollars. He had used his friendships with gangster Al Capone and Police Commissioner William Russell to serve as a middleman for those who desired privileges or wanted certain police officers transferred.

McCormick ordered the editorial staff to publish all of the facts. There was much concern that other dishonest people might be on newspaper payrolls at the *Tribune* and elsewhere in the city. Eventually, it was found that several newsmen at other newspapers had been receiving money for moonlighting in other jobs, some mob-controlled. But there was no evidence that news of gangster activity had been withheld—even at the *Tribune*.

According to historians, the *Tribune* had as long a honeymoon with the New Deal as any of the other papers of the time, but what finally estranged McCormick and most of his colleagues was the National Recovery Administration code of fair practices. The imposition of a code on the newspaper business bothered McCormick tremendously, and as chairman of the ANPA Freedom of the Press Committee, he urged a stand. The association finally accepted the code with the addition of a written stipulation reserving their First Amendment rights.

By 1936, McCormick was considered by many to be the leading reactionary publisher in the Midwest. Although many others in the press voiced the same sentiments about the New Deal—dislike of government interference with business, of the

bureaucracy, of the extravagances, of bungling, and of the possibility of a Roosevelt dictatorship—there was something about McCormick that drew attention to his opinions. He was arrogant, distant, and rubbed people the wrong way. The paper became famous for the virulence of its attacks, and as the New Deal continued, the attacks grew more strident. *Tribune* editorials accused Roosevelt and his aides of perverting the American way. The result, they predicted, would be similar to the results in Europe: anarchy, then dictatorship. In an editorial on 1 January 1936 McCormick began the battle to defeat Roosevelt in the next election with the headline "TURN THE RASCALS OUT":

> There is a new plank this morning in the *Tribune's* Platform. It is probably the most imperative of them all for the year 1936: "Turn the rascals out." The opportunity to get rid of the dangerous and unsavory conditions used by countless predatory politicians is offered this year in the campaign and the election. The people can vote the rascals out of office, out of Congress, out of alphabetical administrations, out of important missions, boards, and commissions, and out of the affairs of the nation.
>
> Get rid of the men who have broken faith, been false to their word, untrue to their promises, and dishonest with the American people. Turn out the wasters who have hoisted the national debt to the 30 billion dollar mark. Turn out the men who have abused their diplomatic immunity, traded secret information for profit, treated desperate situations vaingloriously and in high spirits dealt lightly with the miseries of their fellow countrymen. . . .
>
> Turn out the men who buy elections. Turn the rascals out. Clean house. Stop the spoliation and destruction. Call a halt while there is yet something to be saved and in time to save it. Restore the national honor. Return the national sanity. Give the people back their faith in government. Time still remains and the opportunity is at hand. It cannot be the destiny of the United States to run like the Gadarene swine violently down a steep place and perish in the sea.

A tragic riot on Memorial Day in 1937 at the Republic Steel plant in South Chicago and the distorted coverage given to the event by the *Tribune* ultimately made it notorious to liberals and to labor. To the end, even though the violence was clearly due to police aggression, the *Tribune* stubbornly stuck to the thesis that the strikers were responsible.

Although McCormick did not read every story in the paper before publication, the *Tribune* so closely reflected his personality that he was blamed or praised for everything in it. He had a talent for surrounding himself with excellent workers, and he labored "prodigiously" at newspapering. McCormick devoted the majority of his adult life to the Tribune Company and its various enterprises. It was almost his sole interest, and he went about his business with single-minded purpose. He ran the business like a military operation. His orders came down from his office on the twenty-fourth floor, where he sat in regal opulence in a paneled room behind a red and white marble desk. All editorials at the *Tribune* received his careful consideration. Each day at noon he held an editorial conference at which he told his ideas and views to the assembled staff. When the conference was concluded the staffers returned to their desks to write editorials and draw cartoons. At three o'clock McCormick would go over them and add ideas or make other changes. A frequently related story told of his delight in embarrassing visitors who would find when they turned to leave his abode that the door was hidden in the paneling. He would hit the kickplate (installed so that he could leave with his briefcase in one hand and the leash of his German shepherd in the other) only after maliciously watching the visitor fumble for the exit.

Each New Year's Day, McCormick invited the staff to a reception where he stood at the head of a receiving line in a cutaway, shaking hands and offering seasons' greetings. Cousin Joe Patterson, present at one of these receptions, was widely quoted as remarking smilingly to a companion, "Bertie certainly likes to crack the whip and march the serfs by." Apparently the "serfs" did not mind: "There was nothing rotten about the *Tribune* as a paper to work for," writes Joseph Gies in his biography, *The Colonel of Chicago* (1979). "It paid the highest salaries in Chicago or New York and gave the best fringes. Its Washington staff was the best paid in that city. Top people got contracts for top figures, and sometimes with exceptional throw-ins. Besides being paternalistic by nature, the Colonel was a believer in the philosophical cornerstone of free enterprise, that merit should be rewarded."

Many critics were sure that when McCormick entangled himself in ruinous self-contradictions he knew the truth but was so arrogant and self-centered that he thought the public would swallow anything he thrust at them. Although many have questioned McCormick's thinking, only one biographer, Frank Waldrop—an admittedly less than impartial observer—has suggested that McCormick had emotional problems: "When he came to Washington in his later years, he stayed with his cousin, Mrs. (Cissy) Patterson. He was a welcome guest . . . but she . . . learned to remove from his bedroom anything of importance to her that might break or be spoiled with stains or general abuse. In the dark hours, the terror could overtake him so that McCormick's shouts and battles with his demon would echo through the whole house. The next morning servants would find there was nothing to do but strip down and re-assemble the room. As for McCormick, his morning policy was to ignore the whole thing, never apologize and certainly never explain. His tips to the staff, on departure, were more than generous, so it was all taken as a matter of course by everybody. Mrs. Patterson, herself, was both discreet and sympathetic in saying it was 'Bertie's affliction,' something he could not help, and therefore, something for which he must never be embarrassed. Nor was he." Waldrop also suggests that McCormick preferred to avoid confrontations with people due to his fear of losing control of himself: "His need to hate and loathe, in conflict with his shame for such conduct . . . made a curious and understandably confusing spectacle to those who had little opportunity to observe his torments." The main force of his invective, Waldrop says, was depersonalized and abstracted so that he could really let himself go best against "super-natural malignancies" by denouncing "burocracy."

The Colonel emerged as a leading spokesman for conservative opposition to labor and the New Deal at the same moment that the issue of fascist aggression came to the fore. Perhaps much of the emotional reaction to McCormick's militant neutralism came because of America's loyalty to the British. There was little public support for American involvement in a war between the Nazis and the communists and little support for the French. But Britain was different, and part of McCormick's strategy, to minimize the differences between Britain and Germany, aroused a violent response. He was never able to convince his readers that Britain was nearly as bad as Germany (or soon to become as bad), and so McCormick fell back on blaming the greedy Allies for the fall of the Weimar Republic: "They killed liberalism, culture, intelligence, good will, and liberty. In the place of a friendly society they raised up dictatorship, brutality, ignorance, serfdom, and military power." Although no one wanted war, Britain's entry into the fighting caused the isolationists to become isolated. The psychology

had changed, and neutralism was "suddenly embarrassing, shading into suspicious."

McCormick was also becoming isolated in other ways during this time. His wife, Amie, died in August 1939 after a long illness; she was preceded in death by McCormick's parents and brother. He had no children and thus was left with only his German shepherd for close companionship.

McCormick fought vehemently against U.S. involvement in World War II until the bombing of Pearl Harbor. Just the week before, on 4 December 1941, the *Tribune* published secret government papers known as the Victory Program under the headline "FDR'S WAR PLANS." The publication of these secret plans for mobilization of American armed forces and an invasion to smash the Nazis caused a great uproar. Even though McCormick thought that this evidence proved that FDR had been deceiving the nation about his intentions, McCormick was accused of treason, and there was talk of indicting him for having printed the information. The bombing of Pearl Harbor on 7 December ended the commotion, and the *Tribune* entered into the war effort with an editorial titled "WE ALL HAVE ONLY ONE TASK": "All of us from this day forth, have only one task. That is to strike with all our might to protect and preserve the American freedom that we all hold dear."

In June 1942, a story on the great American naval victory in the Battle of Midway made McCormick vulnerable to the accusation of giving away military secrets. Information in the story identifying Japanese ships and their organization and classifications was parallel to information contained in a secret navy dispatch. This information had been gained by breaking the Japanese naval code, and the *Tribune*'s story seemed to give the secret away—even though it was others who actually referred to the code. It was asserted that this article had hurt the war effort because the Japanese had been alerted to the problem and had changed their code. In fact, the Japanese code was never changed, and part way through prosecuting McCormick the navy decided not to continue because they would have had to disclose the secret that they were accusing McCormick of revealing.

Critics, in analyzing the *Tribune*'s success, have never been able to reconcile their dislike of the paper (and of McCormick) with the fact of its enormous popularity in the area that McCormick liked to call "Chicagoland," encompassing the Chicago metropolitan area and parts of Michigan, Indiana, Iowa, and Wisconsin. Oswald Garrison Villard wrote of the *Tribune* in his 1944 book *The*

Disappearing Daily: "Since it is a newspaper obviously made above all else, to sell, and not to educate or to convey information, it constantly slights national, state, and municipal matters of great importance. In its local news it is as biased and inaccurate as many of our metropolitan dailies, and it has never hesitated to reveal malice in its reports of the doings and utterances of those whom it does not like; there are plenty to accuse it justly of falsification; its news reports are not beyond question."

Over and over observers have wondered what made the *Tribune* successful. McCormick wondered himself, and once had an informal grass-roots survey done by several staff members. They spent days talking to people in saloons, on the street, on commuter trains, in barbershops, and at home. They found that men liked the sports section, women liked the "How to Keep Well" section, and that both sexes liked the comics. Most people said that they read the *Tribune* because "it just seems like the thing to do." Some *Tribune* circulation men thought that it was because of its excellent comics ("Dick Tracy," "Harold Teen," "Winnie Winkle," "The Gumps," "Moon Mullins," "Smitty," "Gasoline Alley," "Smilin' Jack," and "Little Orphan Annie" all had their start on *Tribune* pages), and the faithful following they acquired in spite of the paper's politics. Others thought that perhaps it was read so widely because it antagonized so many people. "But," as *Harper's* magazine pointed out in 1944, "if nearly a million midwesterners believed it a sinister force, would they buy it? Hardly. The truth would seem to be different: the colonel's huge power in the midwest is largely based on the fact that millions of midwesterners are hospitable to his ideas. They may not go all the way with him, but his prejudices, his narrow nationalism, his distrust of foreigners and especially Europeans and more especially the English, and his detestation of many labor activities, of federal intervention in economic affairs, and of liberal ideas generally—coincide with and inflame their prejudices. This fact, added to the power which he wields by virtue of his inherited wealth, his great family prestige, and his sound business ability, makes him at the moment, one of the strongest forces in American public life." *Time* said the same thing three years later: "Its strident voice of command, always heard if not always heeded, is shrewdly pitched to pierce the eardrums and excite the ancient prejudices and suspicions of the Midwest heartland. . . ."

One suggestion for its success was simply that McCormick had made the *Tribune* indispensable. No other paper in Chicagoland could match its overwhelming coverage of the news. "When a big story breaks," *Time* explained, "the *Trib.* can throw a score of men on it to outreport and outwrite the opposition. In sports, in comics, women's pages, signed columns and display ads it offers all things to all people. It is the housewife's guide, the politician's breakfast food, a bible to hundreds of small-town editorial writers. A classless paper, it is read on the commuter trains from swank Lake Forest, and on the dirty 'El' cars taking workers to the stockyards."

In 1945, Louisville publisher Mark Ethridge made an appraisal: "I have always felt that those who said [the *Tribune*'s] great hold came from comic strips and other features were wrong: it possesses an animal vigor." Responded the *Tribune*, "Comes the dawn. It ain't Orphan Annie. It's the hair on our chest."

Late in 1944 McCormick surprised everyone by marrying the beautiful Maryland Mathison Hooper, a vivacious friend who, like his first wife, had divorced another man to marry him. The wedding took place in Chicago at the home of a cousin, and McCormick's life changed. With Maryland as his hostess and companion there were, once again, parties at Cantigny and trips throughout the world. Journeys over the next ten years took the McCormicks from Canada to Latin America, from Europe to Africa and easternmost Asia. After each trip, in his ten-minute spot on the radio, McCormick would recount his experiences, mixing travelogue with history and comments on the current political scene. Those who missed the broadcast could read the script the following day on the *Tribune*'s editorial page.

Time characterized the Colonel in 1947 in the following way: "A realistic portrait would show a tall (6 ft. 4 in.), ruddy, 200-lb. man of 66 who can still get into his World War I uniform. The haughty eyes, ice-water blue, would window an inordinately shy, insufferably proud, incredibly prejudiced mind, acutely aware of its heritage." The Colonel, *Time* asserted, had a brilliant mind with "some appalling blind spots." Although well-read in history, he had "learned from it only his single-track, narrow-gauge approach to world affairs."

When Joe Patterson died suddenly in 1946, the Colonel persuaded his cousin Cissy Patterson to become chairman of the board of the *New York Daily News*. She had done a fine job running the *Washington Times-Herald* for many years, but disagreements with McCormick led to the point where she was about to sue him when she suddenly died in 1948. Now McCormick was, as he told his wife (quoting from a poem by Oliver Wendell Holmes),

Joseph Medill's Red Oak Farm near Wheaton, Illinois. His grandson, Robert McCormick, renamed the estate Cantigny Farm after a French town where he saw action in World War I.

"the last leaf on the tree." Cissy left the paper to its top seven executives. But the *Times-Herald* was losing money and they did not want to keep it. McCormick bought it at a low price, changed a few things, and made his niece, Medill's daughter Basie McCormick, editor. Nothing seemed to help, however, and it remained a loser.

When Harry Truman defeated Thomas E. Dewey for the presidency in 1948, the *Tribune* became the source of malicious pleasure for critics. The famous photo of the *Tribune* headline "Dewey Defeats Truman," triumphantly held aloft by a victorious Truman, added another embellishment to the legend of Colonel McCormick.

Since the days of the New Deal, the *Chicago Tribune* had repeatedly warned that communism was gradually penetrating American life at all levels, including government. Thus it was no surprise to observers when the *Tribune* staunchly supported Wisconsin senator Joseph McCarthy in his communist witch-hunts. The *Tribune* continued to defend Senator McCarthy until his death in 1957.

By 1954, McCormick was becoming less active.

His WGN broadcasts had ceased and his by-lines disappeared from the Sunday editorial page. A long illness that year forced him to sell the *Washington Times-Herald* to Eugene Meyer of the *Washington Post*. This was the only business failure of McCormick's long career. His formula for success at the *Tribune* had simply not worked in Washington.

McCormick spent his last months at Cantigny, where he died on 1 April 1955 at seventy-four—nearly the same age as his greatly admired grandfather, Joseph Medill. Medill had been a staunch Midwesterner who had never had any use for Easterners, Englishmen, or kowtowing to anyone. McCormick was cut from the same cloth.

Throughout his career, McCormick waged campaigns for military preparedness even while he promoted isolationism: he was against the United States entering World Wars I and II, and against the formation of the League of Nations and the United Nations. The Colonel was never afraid to ask a question or to promote an original idea: he wore automobile seat belts years before the idea became acceptable—in fact, *Time* wrote with amusement of this practice. He once wondered aloud if the sap rose in trees due to the pumping motion of their branches in the wind.

An incident recounted in 1941 in the *Saturday Evening Post* gives a revealing illustration of McCormick's character: the general assembly of Rhode Island loaded its supreme court with Democrats while shelving the five Republican justices who had constituted a majority on the court. McCormick was so angry about this action that he decided to punish Rhode Island by expelling it from the Union. He cut a star out of the flag in the lobby of the Tribune Tower and was preparing to run an editorial on the subject when a guard suggested that it was probably illegal to deface the flag. McCormick consulted with his lawyers and then quickly retreated; Rhode Island's star was returned to the *Tribune* flag.

As Joseph Gies points out in *The Colonel of Chicago*, "If one quotes some of the things McCormick said over his lifetime, he can be, and has been, made to sound like a fool, but so can anybody who expressed himself freely during the era of two world wars and the depression.... Being wrong out loud or in print is an inevitable privilege of the leaders of opinion."

The *Tribune*, under McCormick, fought corruption in government wherever it appeared. He tried, through the newspaper, to make Chicago a better place in which to live.

Although the *Tribune* sponsored many events, such as the Chicagoland Music Festival, the Golden Gloves Tournament, and the civic opera, as well as drives for civic beautification, McCormick's own personal philanthropies were largely unknown during his lifetime. "If the Colonel makes large contributions to charities or other public causes from his large private fortune, he does so anonymously...," John B. Martin wrote in *Harper's* magazine in 1944. But McCormick did give his own money. He gave to Passavant Hospital, to Northwestern University's Medical College in Chicago, and to the Medill School of Journalism at the Evanston campus.

Although McCormick felt that he used the *Tribune* justly, many people disagreed. But in the end, there was peace. In November 1960, an exhibition hall on the Chicago lakefront was opened with great ceremony. It was named McCormick Place after the strong-willed Colonel who had made Chicago a better city because he had lived in it his way. The name had been suggested by a reporter on the staff of a competing newspaper.

McCormick never lost the loyalty of his staff members. Walter Trohan, an employee for forty years, wrote this epitaph in 1959 for the Illinois State Historical Society: "Certainly he had his idiosyncrasies, but they became our idiosyncrasies and we loved him for them, even when we smarted under them. He was the greater editor for being human and having faults common to all. With all his faults he was a better editor and a better man than those who mocked and derided him."

In the years since McCormick's death, the *Tribune* has undergone many changes. The growth of the suburbs made it clear that the patterns of advertising and distribution would have to change. New conditions and the changing interests of readers were also reflected as additional specialists were hired to write on religion, science, medicine, and culture. Although it has continued to maintain a conservative stance, the policy of slanting the news for partisan purposes—the hallmark of McCormick's personal style—has come to an end.

Biographies:
Frank Waldrop, *McCormick of Chicago* (Englewood Cliffs, N.J.: Prentice-Hall, 1966);
Joseph Gies, *The Colonel of Chicago* (New York: Dutton, 1979).

References:
"The Colonel's Century," *Time*, 50 (9 June 1947): 60-66;
Alexander Jack, "The Duke of Chicago," *Saturday Evening Post*, 214 (19 July 1941): 10-11, 70-71;
Jack, "The World's Greatest Newspaper," *Saturday Evening Post*, 214 (26 July 1941): 27, 80-89;
John Bartlow Martin, "Colonel McCormick of the Tribune," *Harper's*, 189 (October 1944): 403-413;
John Tebbel, *An American Dynasty* (Garden City: Doubleday, 1947);
John H. Vivian, "Through with Thru at the Chicago Tribune: The McCormick Spelling Experiment," *Journalism History*, 6 (Autumn 1979): 84-87, 96;
Lloyd Wendt, *Chicago Tribune: The Rise of A Great Newspaper* (Chicago: Rand McNally, 1979).

Papers:
Robert R. McCormick's papers are in the *Tribune* archives. They are held by the McCormick Charitable Trust, which has not set a date for them to be opened.

Ralph McGill

(5 February 1898-3 February 1969)

Beverly M. Bethune
University of Georgia

MAJOR POSITIONS HELD: Reporter, sports editor, *Nashville* (Tennessee) *Banner* (1922-1929); assistant sports editor, sports editor, executive editor, editor, publisher, *Atlanta Constitution* (1929-1969).

BOOKS: *Two Georgians Explore Scandinavia: A Comparison of Education for Democracy in Northern Europe and Georgia,* by McGill and Thomas C. David (Atlanta: State Department of Education, 1938);
Israel Revisited (Atlanta: Tupper & Love, 1950);
The Fleas Come with the Dog (Nashville: Abingdon Press, 1954);
A Church, A School (Nashville: Abingdon Press, 1959);
The South and the Southerner (Boston: Little, Brown, 1963);
The Best of Ralph McGill Selected Columns, compiled by Michael Strickland and others (Atlanta: Cherokee, 1980).

SELECTED PERIODICAL PUBLICATIONS: "My First Boss," *Atlantic,* 203 (February 1959): 68-70;
"Agony of the Southern Minister," *New York Times Magazine,* 27 September 1959, p. 6+;
"Where We Stand: Emancipation," *Look,* 27 (15 January 1963): 72-73;
"Speaking Out," *Saturday Evening Post,* 234 (14 December 1963): 8+;
"The Case For the Southern Progressive," *Saturday Review,* 47 (13 June 1964): 17-20.

Time called him "the conscience of the South." His profession gave him journalism's highest award, the Pulitzer Prize. The nation's universities showered him with honorary degrees. The Ku Klux Klan named him "Southern enemy number one." Many readers peppered him with hate mail. One writer noted that he was often treated in the South "much like some social disease—not to be discussed in public." No matter how one may have felt about Ralph McGill, however, one would have to agree with his biographer, who said that in the almost forty years McGill wrote for the *Atlanta Constitution,* "the paper, the town, and the South he loved and lectured and chastised and tried to lead out of its old ways, all were moved and shaken and changed because of him."

Ralph Waldo Emerson McGill was born to Benjamin Franklin and Lou Skillern McGill on 5 February 1898 in an eastern Tennessee farming community about equidistant from the towns of Soddy and Daisy. Soddy had a post office, so it was claimed as his birthplace, but when people asked where Soddy was, McGill would say, "Just three miles from Daisy—and everybody knows where Daisy is." McGill's maternal grandfather, Anderson Skillern, had been an itinerant newspaperman who soon deserted his family, but the McGills had farmed in the area almost seventy-five years.

When McGill was a year old, his father decided the farm could no longer support all the McGill brothers and sisters who then owned it. So he moved his family into Soddy and worked in the coal mines there. In five years they moved again, this time to Chattanooga, where his father became a clerk in a roofing company. Although McGill grew up in the city, he spent most of his summers on the family farm. His deep love of the land and his sympathy for the small Southern farmer grew out of these early days.

A frail child, he was tutored at home for the first few years of his schooling. Encouraged by his father, he became an omnivorous reader—later, as a journalist, he would read several books a week and fourteen or fifteen newspapers each day. His mother kept him amused by teaching him to cook, a hobby he would enjoy the rest of his life. The McCallie brothers of Chattanooga had recently founded a preparatory school in the city, and when McGill was of high school age, his father borrowed the tuition money and sent the boy to the private school. He graduated from McCallie in 1917 with many honors. He had been captain of the football team, editor of the school newspaper and the literary magazine, and a leading actor in most of the school plays. The stage was his intended career until a prominent director told him that his voice, described by a friend as "somewhat reminiscent of an asthmatic bullfrog," would prevent his ever getting lead roles.

McGill went on to Vanderbilt University that year but dropped out after Christmas to enlist in the Marine Corps. His eagerness as a boot at Parris Island, as well as his previous education, sent him to noncom school in the United States when his fellow recruits went to France. The war was over before he finished school.

Back at Vanderbilt he switched his course of study from medicine to law and finally to general arts and sciences. He associated with a group of writers and poets who called themselves "The Fugitives" and who were interested in contemporary poetry and literature. Among them were John Crowe Ransom, Robert Penn Warren, Allen Tate,

and Merrill Moore. Their enthusiasm fired McGill, but his poetry was never good enough to make him a full-fledged member of the group, and he soon turned to journalism. He wrote for the school newspaper, founded the campus humor magazine, and worked part-time for the *Nashville Banner* as a copyboy and occasional sportswriter. Shortly before he was to graduate in 1922, he was suspended for a fraternity prank and a column he wrote for the school newspaper accusing the administration of embezzling a bequest. He never returned to the university.

Instead, McGill became a full-time reporter for the *Banner,* a job he held for the next seven years. Prohibition had made Nashville a little Chicago, according to McGill, and it was a tremendously exciting place for an eager cub. He was groomed as a political reporter and covered the campaigns of various candidates in whom the paper's owner, Edward Bushrod Stahlman, was interested. But with great versatility he also covered the police beat, interviewed visiting celebrities, reviewed plays and concerts, covered general news, and wrote sports pieces. For his last five years with the *Banner*, he was officially the sports editor. However, he continued to cover politics, and the Will Rogers-type column "I'm the Gink," which he originated, ranged over many topics.

In 1929 Ed Danforth, who was moving as sports editor from the *Atlanta Georgian* to the *Atlanta Constitution*, called McGill in Nashville to ask him to become his assistant. McGill accepted and began work in Atlanta in the spring of that year.

He returned to Nashville in September to marry Mary Elizabeth Leonard, a warm, generous, courageous woman who had just been released from a two-year stay in a tuberculosis sanatorium when McGill met her. The couple shared many years of happiness in spite of her frequent illnesses and the deaths of two daughters. Their first daughter, born prematurely in January 1936, lived only thirty-six hours. Their second daughter was adopted, chosen because she had been born at the approximate time the first daughter would have been born at full term; she died of leukemia in December 1939. Years later they would have a son, Ralph, Jr., who would live to manhood.

McGill covered many sports events for the *Constitution* and wrote about them in his column "Break O' Day." As at the *Banner*, however, the column treated other subjects under the thin guise of sports, and McGill soon found that owner-publisher Clark Howell, Sr., like Major Stahlman, wanted to make use of his talent for political re-

McGill discussing the New Deal with a Georgia farmer. The series of articles he wrote on agriculture in the state for the Atlanta
Constitution *won McGill a Rosenwald Fund grant in 1937 which enabled him to spend six months in Europe.*

porting. Howell assigned him to the 1936 reelection campaign of young Senator Richard Russell, who was being challenged by Governor Eugene Talmadge and seemed to be in some difficulty. Howell implied that Russell could use a little help from McGill, which McGill provided in fiery prose. Russell won the election and remained a friend of McGill's until the civil rights battle put the two on opposing sides.

At about the same time as the Russell campaign, other events turned McGill to broader topics than sports. He began to travel around the state with economists and agricultural experts from the state universities, financed largely by federal funds. The travelers' purpose was to discuss and interpret New Deal farm policies to the Georgia farmer and other interested persons. A strong Democrat and an avid admirer of Franklin Roosevelt, McGill was happy to be a part of the implementation of the New Deal.

Out of these trips came a series of articles on farm problems in the South, particularly Georgia,

and the need for cooperative marketing for small farmers. McGill asked his readers to recognize that the old days of farming were over forever, that King Cotton was indeed dead, and that it was time to acknowledge this fact and to move on to other crops and other ways. The farm articles led to the great turning point in McGill's life, for they won for him a grant from the Julius Rosenwald Fund in late 1937 which enabled him to travel with his wife for six months in Great Britain and Europe. The purpose of the fund was to encourage improvement in rural education in the South by providing promising young teachers and journalists with fellowships.

The McGills spent much of their time in Scandinavia, where he visited and wrote about farms and farm cooperatives. But they also went to Berlin, where they watched an armed, closely guarded motorcade bearing Hitler to a three-hour speech at the opera house. And they went to England, where McGill heard Churchill speak at the House of Commons. McGill later wrote, "I . . . heard him, like a prophet of old crying in the wilderness, warn against the course of appeasement pursued by the Chamberlain government."

Leaving an ill Mary Elizabeth in England, McGill went to France and then to Austria. He arrived in Vienna only a few days before the plebiscite on Hitler's Anschluss was held, and swastikas and the tramp of boots were everywhere. Back in England he found his wife feeling well again, and they journeyed to Ireland, home of some of McGill's ancestors, on the last leg of their travels.

On their return to the United States in late spring 1938, McGill was made executive editor of the *Constitution*, a position created for him by Howell. He was in charge of the news, sports, and society departments and was to write a daily column for the editorial page. "Break O' Day" disappeared, and "One Word More" began. His mind broadened immensely by his international travels, McGill wrote about anything that caught his attention: most often politics, but also the weather, economics, poker, bees, religion, the military, bookkeeping, ballet, hunting dogs, ancient Greece, education, the 4-H Club, and sometimes, even yet, sports. He took on the KKK, declaring, "The Klan breeds crime and intolerance and bigotry and never a single good thing." In the 1938 elections he supported Senator Walter George against former governor Talmadge and Roosevelt's handpicked candidate, Lawrence Camp; George went back to the Senate.

In 1942 McGill was named editor in chief of the *Constitution*, completely in charge of the editorial policies of the paper. In 1943 he went to England with a small group of editors invited to see how England was holding up after four years of warfare. In 1945 he was back again, this time on a world tour sponsored by the American Society of Newspaper Editors. He and two companions traveled 50,000 miles to twenty-two countries urging foreign editors and government information officers to support a freedom of information treaty after the war.

His 1937 farm tour and his wartime travels were only the beginnings of a lifetime of journeys for McGill. The birth of Ralph, Jr., kept him home briefly in 1945, but it was not long before he was off again. The Overseas News Agency sent him to Palestine to "do the real story" in early 1946. He began that trip with a stopover in Nuremberg,where he observed the trials of Nazi war criminals, then visited the camps for displaced persons. In Cairo, he discussed the new Arab nationalism with leaders of the movement and found their ideas "reactionary." In Palestine he was sold on the country as a Jewish national home, and he visited the area again in 1950 at the invitation of the new Israeli government. He

went to India in 1951, to Germany and England in 1954. In 1959 he went with Vice-President Nixon to Russia.

But he had a standard to bear, a battle to fight, a crusade to lead, however reluctantly, and they kept calling him home from his travels. In 1954 the United States Supreme Court handed down its historic decision making illegal the South's "separate but equal" school systems. The nation, especially the South, was forever changed. McGill's public stance on civil rights to that date appeared to be a conservative one: in 1946 he had written that "separation of the races" was still "the best and only workable system" and vowed that "there will be no mixing of the races in the schools." In 1948 he had said, "This newspaper and this writer have not, and do not, favor or advocate ending education segregation." Yet in these same years he had also written, "I have always regarded a Negro as a person . . . entitled to complete justice and economic opportunity. . . . Our failure even today to give the Negro equal justice in our courts; to make him safe from police brutality; to give him his due in education, in playgrounds and the usual civic facilities such as paved streets, public health, sewers and so on, is another example. . . . I am on the side of human rights and believe it is the obligation of the South to so be and to positively assert itself."

To have spoken with a stronger voice at that time, however he may have felt, would probably have resulted in his having no voice at all. McGill acknowledged this when he wrote in 1957 that moderates "must learn to run on the fence—not merely sit on it . . . the moderate develops a sort of technique of survival. He knows just how far he can go in telling his people the truth. . . ." Instead, there were small beginnings. On his first day as executive editor at the *Constitution* he had sent a memo to the staff that in the future the paper would print the word "Negro" with a capital *N*. Two printers had quit and a few subscribers had canceled, but McGill and the capital *N* had prevailed. In 1944 he and thirteen others had founded the Southern Regional Council, a fact-finding group which brought together blacks and whites from all occupations. Their purpose was to identify problems and to start a dialogue about how to solve them. A year before the Supreme Court school decision was announced, McGill was trying to prepare his readers for it. In a column entitled "One Day It Will Be Monday" (Mondays are the days on which Supreme Court decisions are announced), he pointed out that one Monday the Court would hand down a ruling which would probably outlaw the South's dual school system. "So, somebody," he said, "especially those who have a duty so to do, ought to be talking about it calmly and informatively." But most important, "there is no reason for violence, whatever the decision. Leadership everywhere in the South must talk about this and make it clear. Anger and violence solve nothing." Later that year he wrote, "Segregation is on its way out, and he who tries to tell the people otherwise does them great disservice. The problem of the future is how to live with the change."

Finally it was Monday. For McGill the issue now became peaceful compliance with the law. "There is only one alternative," he warned, "and that is secession by armed force."

Peaceful compliance was not to be. As scattered violence broke out across the South, the KKK was revitalized and White Citizens Councils were organized to resist the Court's decision. McGill battled them all. Appalled by the bombing of the Atlanta Jewish Temple in 1958, he wrote an editorial titled "A Church, A School":

Dynamite in great quantity ripped a beautiful temple of worship in Atlanta. It followed hard on the heels of a like destruction of a handsome high school at Clinton, Tennessee. The same rabid, mad-dog minds were, without question, behind both. They are also the source of previous bombings in Florida, Alabama, and South Carolina. The schoolhouse and the church were the targets of diseased, hate-filled minds.

Let us face the facts. This is a harvest. It is the crop of things sown.

It is the harvest of defiance of courts and the encouragement of citizens to defy law on the part of many Southern politicians. It will be the acme of irony, for example, if any one of four or five Southern governors deplore this bombing. It will be grimly humorous if certain attorneys general issue statements of regret. And it will be quite a job for some editors, columnists, and commentators, who have been saying that our courts have no jurisdiction and that the people should refuse to accept their authority, now to deplore.

It is not possible to preach lawlessness and restrict it.

Gates Opened To be sure, none said go bomb a Jewish temple or a school. But let it be understood that when leadership in high places in any degree fails to support constituted authority, it opens the gates to all those who wish to take law into their hands.

There will be, to be sure, the customary act of the careful drawing aside of skirts on the part of those in high places. "How awful!" they will exclaim. "How terrible. Something must be done."

But the record stands. The extremists of the citizens' councils, the political leaders who in terms violent and inflammatory have repudiated their oaths and stood against due process of law have helped unloose this flood of hate and bombing.

This too is a harvest of those so-called Christian ministers who have chosen to preach hate instead of compassion. Let them now find pious words and raise their hands in deploring the bombing of a synagogue.

You do not preach and encourage hatred for the Negro and hope to restrict it to that field. It is an old, old story. It is one repeated over and over again in history. When the wolves of hate are loosed on one people, then no one is safe.

Hate and lawlessness by those who lead release the yellow rats and encourage the crazed and neurotic who print and distribute the hate pamphlets—who shrieked that Franklin Roosevelt was a Jew—who denounce the Supreme Court as being Communist and controlled by Jewish influences.

The Harvest This series of bombings is the harvest, too, of something else.

One of those connected with the bombing telephoned a news service early Sunday morning to say the job would be done. It was to be committed, he said, by the Confederate Underground.

The Confederacy and the men who led it are revered by millions. Its leaders returned to the Union and urged that the future be committed to building a stronger America. This was particularly true of General Robert E. Lee. Time after time he urged his students at Washington University to forget the War Between the States and to help build a greater and stronger union.

For too many years now we have seen the Confederate flag and the emotions of that great war become the property of men not fit to tie the shoes of those who fought it. Some of these have been merely childish and immature. Others have perverted and commercialized the flag by making the Stars and Bars, and the Confederacy itself, a symbol of hate and bombings.

For a long time now it has been needful for all Americans to stand up and be counted on the side of law and the due process of law—even when to do so goes against personal beliefs and emotions. It is late. But there is yet time.

McGill's column had been syndicated by the North American Newspaper Alliance not long before "A Church, A School" was written, and at last he had a national audience. Even more national recognition came when he won the Pulitzer Prize the next year; the temple column was specifically cited as an example of his prizewinning editorial writing. Many other awards would come to him, among them *Atlantic*'s Non-Fiction Award, the Lauterbach Award for Distinguished Service in the Field of Civil Liberties, the Presidential Medal of Freedom, the Medallion of Valor from the government of Israel, and the National Newspaper Publishers Association's Distinguished Editors Award. He was also awarded honorary degrees from Harvard, Columbia, Notre Dame, Morehouse College, and fourteen other universities and colleges. The year after he won his Pulitzer Prize, he was asked to serve on the Pulitzer Advisory Board, which makes the final decisions on Pulitzer jury selections of prizewinners.

Not everyone wanted to honor McGill. He received an almost daily outpouring of hate mail, his mailbox at home was riddled with bullets, someone shot into his home when everyone was out (the

bullet hole in the window pane and the bullet in the sofa back were found later), garbage was dumped on his lawn and driveway, and his telephone rang incessantly with abusive and obscene messages. So many of the callers asked for "Rastus McGill" that he named his dog "Rastus"; when a caller asked for Rastus, McGill would put the receiver in front of the dog and command, "Speak, Rastus!" The dog would then bark loudly into the caller's ear.

Sensitive to criticism when he was a young reporter, McGill's hide toughened with age. Later in life he worried when the hate mail slowed down because he was afraid he was losing his effectiveness. Frequently he would choose a topic because he knew it would bring a reaction from some of his more hotheaded readers. It was his job as a writer, he felt, to spark such discussion.

For one at the pinnacle of his profession, however, he remained oddly sensitive to the security of his job. He was terrified of retirement, which was mandatory for editors at age sixty-five, and he began to worry about it before he even reached sixty. Then in 1960 the younger Clark Howell (Clark Howell, Sr., had died in 1936) moved from publisher to vice-chairman of the board of Atlanta Newspapers, Inc., and McGill was made publisher, no longer subject to editors' retirement rules. Life continued much the same for him, since his old friend and staunch supporter Jack Tarver, president of the *Constitution,* continued to handle most of the publisher's duties as he had for Howell.

Still, whenever McGill made an error or his memory slipped, he was certain senility was setting in and he would be forced to retire. Eugene Patterson, then editor of the *Constitution*, came to his office one day in 1967 to find McGill literally sobbing at his desk. An unpleasant incident at which McGill was present had taken place between Jack Tarver and some black leaders, including Martin Luther King, Jr., the previous day. The blacks accused Tarver of dragging his feet in hiring blacks. Tarver's dander rose, and in his retort he said the word "Nigra" instead of "Negro." King pounced on him (figuratively) and forced him to say "Nee-grow," then walked out with an ultimatum that there would be more black faces at the paper or there would be a black picket line outside. At a dinner with the McGills that night, Tarver had remarked, "McGill, you'd better start filling out your retirement papers. We wouldn't want you to be embarrassed having to cross the picket line your Negro friends are going to put around us." Tarver meant the remark to be the usual sort of jesting that he and McGill indulged in, but McGill's sensitivity turned the words into an

VOL. LXXXVI, No. 145

RALPH

McGILL

ATLANTA, GA. — One summer Sunday afternoon I sat in a rocking chair under an oak tree in front of Uncle Cade Worley's home. It rested on a shelf of the Blue Ridge Mountains, which thrust into North Georgia as the southern buttresses of the Appalachians.
Uncle C

long since at rest in a tain grave, was the
As a young boy he the sound of ca throug his hills

McGill's column, which was written for the Atlanta Constitution *and syndicated nationwide*

McGill, his first wife, Mary Elizabeth, and Ralph, Jr., at a Constitution *Labor Day picnic in 1959*

ominous threat. Nothing Patterson said could console the grieving McGill.

McGill was much loved by his friends, and they were legion—from Carl Sandburg and Adlai Stevenson to the black waitress in his favorite downtown restaurant. But his greatest pleasure came from his bantering relationships with such colleagues and friends as Harry Ashmore, editor of the *Arkansas Gazette*, later at the Center for the Study of Democratic Institutions in California; John Popham of the *Chattanooga Times*; Bill Baggs of the *Miami Daily News*; John Griffin of the Southern Educational Foundation; and Tarver. They treated him with great irreverence, sometimes calling his secretary to request to speak to "the Conscience of the South" or to ask, "Is he who is without sin among us today?" These relationships helped to sustain him in his sorrow and loneliness following the death of his wife in 1962.

McGill had spent the last months of Mary Elizabeth's long illness sitting beside her bed day and night, much of the time working on his book *The South and the Southerner*. Published in 1963, the book is a mixture of personal reminiscence, South-

ern history, and commentary. It was well received and brought McGill further national recognition and the Atlantic Non-Fiction Award.

Following Mary Elizabeth's death, he assuaged much of his loneliness in travel. He and Ralph, Jr., went to Japan; McGill then went to Africa and later traveled the United States promoting his book. In 1966 he went to Vietnam and again to Japan; in early 1967 he returned to Africa. Later that year his loneliness ended when he married Dr. Mary Lynn Morgan, an Atlanta children's dentist whom he had known for many years.

His travels continued, however—to Mexico City, to Russia, and to the political conventions of 1968. He had just returned from Mexico City when he learned of the murder of Martin Luther King, Jr., and he wrote a series of columns in the next days discussing the civil rights movement led by King. Once again, as he had so many times before, he called on Southerners to meet their moral obligations: "The white South—the white population in all the country—must now give answer. If injustice and inequity, if racist prejudices and discriminations now become the targets of all decent men and

McGill and his second wife, Dr. Mary Lynn Morgan, after their wedding in 1967 (Photo by Reeves)

women, Dr. King's death may bring about what he sought for himself, his people and country. If this does not happen, then slaves who serve masters of hatred, fear, and evil will have to be put down mercilessly and immediately. Out of martyrdom must come the right answer."

For several years McGill had suffered from atrial fibrillation, a condition in which the heart suddenly pauses, then flutters rapidly for a number of beats. Diet and medication had improved the condition, but in the late summer of 1967 the fibrillation began again. He went to Emory University for shock treatments to restore the regular rhythm of the heart, but the treatments did not work. So he added exercise to his regimen and went on with his life as before.

On 3 February 1969 he and Mary Lynn were dinner guests at the home of friends when McGill's heart simply stopped. Attempts to revive him were not successful.

Great masses of people attended McGill's funeral. Vice-President Hubert Humphrey was there, as was Senator Talmadge. There were winos and waitresses, the wealthy and the influential, blacks and whites, young and old. Some were among the many young people he had helped get started on their careers. There were many at the funeral he had never met. In the midst of it all, there was a bomb threat. Secret Service men searched the pews quietly without finding anything. The procession to Westview Cemetery was through a predominantly black section of town. At every intersection along the way were groups of blacks standing bareheaded and sorrowful, saying a last goodbye to their friend.

McGill had not concerned himself only with civil rights. His restless, inquiring mind explored almost every topic imaginable, and politics was always an overriding interest. He had very actively supported the war in Vietnam, for example, and his dogmatic position had brought a coolness between him and some of his dovish friends. But he will be remembered most for his writings on civil rights, for his prodding of the Southern conscience, for his great moral outrage, and for his kind and understanding heart which led him to say in 1966, "But it is true, now, that we see, I think, clearly and painfully, how ugly and what a great weight and burden this policy of segregation put upon the Southern people. . . ."

He was the South's leading social critic of his time, a mover and shaker of men and ideas. The last words that he wrote are most appropriate for such a man. He had written a column urging the secretary of Health, Education, and Welfare to reject the freedom-of-choice school plan that Southern school boards were presenting to him. McGill felt that such a plan would simply cloak segregation and encourage tokenism. The column was not quite long enough to fill the front page space allotted to it, so McGill's secretary, Grace Lundy, gave it back to him to add the final lines, the last he would ever write: "You may be assured, sir, that the freedom-of-choice plan is in fact neither real freedom nor a choice. It is discrimination."

Biographies:

Calvin McLeod Logue, *Ralph McGill, Editor and Publisher*, 2 volumes (Durham, N.C.: Moore, 1969);

Harold H. Martin, *Ralph McGill, Reporter* (Boston: Little, Brown, 1973).

References:

"Death of a Conscience," *Time*, 93 (14 February 1969): 68;

Eugene C. Patterson, *Ralph McGill: Rock in a Weary*

Land (Athens: Henry W. Grady School of Journalism and Mass Communications, University of Georgia, 1979);

Celestine Sibley, "They Don't Scare McGill," *Saturday Evening Post*, 231 (27 December 1958): 25, 51-52;

"Voice of Moderation," *Newsweek*, 61 (25 March 1963): 110.

Papers:
Ralph McGill's papers are in the Woodruff Memorial Library at Emory University, Atlanta, Georgia.

H. L. Mencken

J. James McElveen

See also the Mencken entry in *DLB 11, American Humorists, 1800-1950*.

BIRTH: Baltimore, Maryland, 12 September 1880, to August and Anna Abhau Mencken.

MARRIAGE: 27 August 1930 to Sara Powell Haardt.

MAJOR POSITIONS HELD: Reporter, *Baltimore Herald* (1899-1901); editor, *Baltimore Sunday Herald* (1901-1903); city editor, *Baltimore Morning Herald* (1903-1904); city editor, *Baltimore Evening Herald* (1904-1905); editor in chief, *Baltimore Herald* (1906); news editor, *Baltimore Evening News* (1906); editor, *Baltimore Sunday Sun* (1906-1910); editor, *Baltimore Evening Sun* (1910-1916); coeditor (with George Jean Nathan), *Smart Set* (1914-1923); editor, *American Mercury* (1924-1933); columnist, political correspondent, *Baltimore Sunpapers* (1919-1941).

DEATH: Baltimore, 29 January 1956.

BOOKS: *Ventures into Verse* (Baltimore: Marshall, Beck & Gordon, 1903);

George Bernard Shaw: His Plays (Boston & London: Luce, 1905);

The Philosophy of Friedrich Nietzsche (Boston: Luce, 1908; London: Unwin, 1908);

Men versus the Man: A Correspondence between Robert Rives La Monte, Socialist, and H. L. Mencken, Individualist (New York: Holt, 1910);

A Book of Burlesques (New York: John Lane, 1916; revised edition, New York: Knopf, 1920; London: Cape, 1923);

A Little Book in C Major (New York: John Lane, 1916);

A Book of Prefaces (New York: Knopf, 1917; London: Cape, 1922);

Damn! A Book of Calumny (New York: Philip Goodwin, 1918); republished as *A Book of Calumny* (New York: Knopf, 1918);

In Defense of Women (New York: Philip Goodwin, 1918; revised, New York: Knopf, 1922; London: Cape, 1923);

The American Language: A Preliminary Inquiry into the Development of English in the United States (New York: Knopf, 1919; revised and enlarged, 1921; London: Cape, 1922; revised and enlarged again, 1923; corrected, enlarged and rewritten, New York: Knopf, 1936; London: Paul, 1936); *Supplement I* (New York: Knopf, 1945); *Supplement II* (New York: Knopf, 1948);

Prejudices: First Series (New York: Knopf, 1919; London: Cape, 1920);

Heliogabalus: A Buffoonery in Three Acts, by Mencken and George Jean Nathan (New York: Knopf, 1920);

Prejudices: Second Series (New York: Knopf, 1920; London: Cape, 1921);

Prejudices: Third Series (New York: Knopf, 1922; London: Cape, 1923);

Prejudices: Fourth Series (New York: Knopf, 1924; London: Cape, 1925);

Selected Prejudices (London: Cape, 1926; New York: Knopf, 1927);

Notes on Democracy (New York: Knopf, 1926; London: Cape, 1927);

Prejudices: Fifth Series (New York: Knopf, 1926; London: Cape, 1927);

Prejudices: Sixth Series (New York: Knopf, 1927; London: Cape, 1928);

James Branch Cabell (New York: McBride, 1927);

Selected Prejudices: Second Series (London: Cape, 1927);

Treatise on the Gods (New York & London: Knopf, 1930);

Making a President: A Footnote to the Saga of Democracy (New York: Knopf, 1932);

Treatise on Right and Wrong (New York: Knopf, 1934; London: Paul, 1934);

The Sunpapers of Baltimore, 1837-1937, by Mencken, Gerald W. Johnson, Frank R. Kent, and Hamilton Owens (New York: Knopf, 1937);

Happy Days, 1880-1892 (New York: Knopf, 1940; London: Paul, Trench & Trubner, 1940);

Newspaper Days, 1899-1906 (New York: Knopf, 1941; London: Paul, 1942);

Heathen Days, 1890-1936 (New York: Knopf, 1943);

Christmas Story (New York: Knopf, 1946);

A Mencken Chrestomathy (New York: Knopf, 1949);

The Vintage Mencken, edited by Alistair Cooke (New York: Vintage, 1955);

A Carnival of Buncombe, edited by Malcolm Moos (Baltimore: Johns Hopkins Press/London: Oxford University Press, 1956);

Minority Report: H. L. Mencken's Notebooks (New York: Knopf, 1956);

The Bathtub Hoax, and Other Blasts & Bravos from the Chicago Tribune, edited by Robert McHugh (New York: Knopf, 1958);

H. L. Mencken on Music, edited by Louis Cheslock (New York: Knopf, 1961);

The American Scene: A Reader, edited by Huntington Cairns (New York: Knopf, 1965);

H. L. Mencken's Smart Set Criticism, edited by William H. Nolte (Ithaca, N.Y.: Cornell University Press, 1968);

The Young Mencken: The Best of His Work, edited by Carl Bode (New York: Dial, 1973);

A Gang of Pecksniffs, and Other Comments on Newspaper Publishers, Editors and Reporters, edited by Theo Lippman, Jr. (New Rochelle, N.Y.: Arlington House, 1975);

Mencken's Last Campaign: H. L. Mencken on the 1948 Election, edited by Joseph C. Goulden (Washington, D.C.: New Republic Book Co., 1976);

A Choice of Days: Essays from Happy Days, Newspaper Days, *and* Heathen Days, edited by Edward L. Galligan (New York: Knopf, 1980).

OTHER: Henrik Ibsen, *A Doll's House,* edited with introduction by Mencken (Boston & London: Luce, 1909);

Ibsen, *Little Eyolf,* edited with introduction by

H. L. Mencken (National Archives)

Mencken (Boston & London: Luce, 1909);

Ibsen, *The Master Builder, Pillars of Society, Hedda Gabler,* introduction by Mencken (New York: Boni & Liveright, 1917);

Friedrich Wilhelm Nietzsche, *The Antichrist,* translated with introduction by Mencken (New York: Knopf, 1920);

Americana, edited by Mencken (New York: Knopf, 1925);

Menckeniana: A Schimpflexicon, edited by Mencken (New York: Knopf, 1928);

Sara Powell Haardt, *Southern Album,* introduction by Mencken (New York: Doubleday, Doran, 1936);

A New Dictionary of Quotations on Historical Principles from Ancient and Modern Sources, edited by Mencken (New York: Knopf, 1942);

Theodore Dreiser, *An American Tragedy,* introduction by Mencken (Cleveland & New York: World, 1946);

"The American Language," in *Literary History of the United States,* volume 1, edited by Robert E. Spiller, Willard Thorp, Thomas H. Johnson, and Henry Seidel Canby (New York: Macmillan, 1948), pp. 663-675.

SELECTED PERIODICAL PUBLICATIONS:
"Newspaper Morals," *Atlantic Monthly,* 113 (March 1914): 289-297;

"The Motive of the Critic," *New Republic,* 27 (26 October 1921): 249-251;

"Footnotes on Journalism," *Nation,* 114 (26 April 1922): 493-494;

"Three Years of Prohibition in America," *Outlook,* 131 (24 June 1922): 502-503;

"What I Believe," *Forum,* 84 (September 1930): 133-139;

"Future of English," *Harper's,* 170 (April 1935): 541-548;

"Some Opprobrious Nicknames," *American Speech,* 24 (February 1949): 25-30.

During his lifetime H. L. Mencken was called the Great Iconoclast and the Sage of Baltimore, appellations he gained because of his journalistic writing in newspapers and magazines. However, his contributions to American letters were more extensive than those ordinarily found in one who gained fame—or, as some would describe it, notoriety—as a reporter, editor, and columnist. For Mencken was the author of at least thirty books and collections of essays and criticism, including his highly acclaimed philological study, *The American Language* (1919, 1945, 1948); the popular autobiographical trilogy, *Happy Days, 1880-1892* (1940), *Newspaper Days, 1899-1906* (1941), and *Heathen Days, 1890-1936* (1943); and the fascinating volumes on politics, religion, and ethics: *Notes on Democracy* (1926), *Treatise on the Gods* (1930), and *Treatise on Right and Wrong* (1934).

Henry Louis Mencken was born in Baltimore, Maryland, on 12 September 1880. When he was three years old, his parents, August and Anna Abhau Mencken, moved to 1524 Hollins Street. There Mencken lived for all of his life except the five years of his marriage. Mencken recalled his "Introduction to the Universe" in *Happy Days, 1880-1892*, as he described Baltimore's Summer Nights' Carnival of the Order of Orioles on the evening after his third birthday: "At the instant I first became aware of the cosmos we all infest I was sitting in my mother's lap and blinking at a great burst of lights, some of them red and others green, but most of them only the bright yellow of flaring gas."

The Menckens were by any standards a closely knit family, and "Harry" and his three younger siblings, Charles, Gertrude, and August, knew a childhood fraught with the usual pleasures and perplexities of living in late nineteenth-century Baltimore. Mencken recalled the days of his nonage in the backyard of the Hollins Street row house: "Along with my brother Charlie, who followed me into this vale when I was but twenty months old, I spent most of my pre-school leisure in it, and found it a strange, wild land of endless discoveries and enchantments. . . . In Spring we dug worms and watched for robins, in Summer we chased butterflies and stoned sparrows, and in Autumn we made bonfires of the falling leaves. At all times from March to October we made a Dust Bowl of my mother's garden."

When he was six years old, Mencken was en-

The house at 1524 Hollins Street, Baltimore, where Mencken lived almost all his life

rolled at Professor Friedrich Knapp's Institute, "a seminary that catered to boys and girls of the Baltimore bourgeoisie for more than sixty years." There his recitations were sufficiently impressive for him to receive his first fifty merits, entitling him to a keenly sought prize at the close of the school year in 1888: a copy of *Grimms' Fairy Tales* "for industry and good deportment." Mencken's "academic orgies," as he termed them in his memoirs, were punctuated with pleasant experiences, especially the institute's annual picnic and the yearly parade signaling the arrival of the circus. But to Mencken the "crown and consummation" of the year at Knapp's was the annual exhibition that came soon after the picnic in June. His part on the program was usually to stand at the blackboard and display his mathematical skill by multiplying or dividing several complex numbers, to the delight of his father.

Three experiences were very likely important in Mencken's choice of a career in newspaper work. On 26 November 1888, August Mencken had dispatched his bookkeeper to the Baltimore firm of J. F. W. Dorman to purchase a Baltimore No. 10 Self-Inker Printing Press and a font of No. 214 type. These basic tools of the trade were a gift for Harry. Receipts discovered years later by Mencken indicated that the press cost $7.70 and the type $1.10. Mencken said that the details of this purchase were "of a degree of concern bordering upon the super-colossal, for that press determined the whole course of my future life. If it had been a stethoscope or a copy of Dr. Ayers' Almanac, I might have gone in for medicine; if it had been a Greek New Testament or a set of baptismal grappling-irons, I might have pursued divinity. As it was, I got the smell of printer's ink up my nose at the tender age of eight, and it has been swirling through my sinuses ever since." On Christmas Day Harry and his father tried out the new equipment, and the results of their efforts were far from successful. Because both possessed a minimum of mechanical dexterity, they managed to smash most of the type. A few days thereafter, however, the eight-year-old printed his first calling card, shortening his name to H. L. Mencken because he had insufficient usable type to spell out his full name.

Mencken claimed in later years that "aside from the direct and all-powerful influence of that Baltimore No. 10 Self-Inker. . . , I was probably edged toward newspapers and their glorious miseries by two circumstances, both of them trivial." One was his discovery of the printing office of the *Ellicott City Times,* the weekly newspaper of the Maryland village where the Menckens spent the summers of 1889 and 1890. He recalled watching a young man and a boy operate an ancient Washington handpress in getting out the *Times.* Their press day was Thursday, and Mencken was there to gaze at the process at every opportunity. Mencken also remembered overhearing a conversation between his father and uncle and his father's Washington agent, Mr. Cross. After discussing the transitory eminence of the congressmen, senators, justices, and military men he met in the nation's capital, Mr. Cross said that the "real princes of Washington" were the newspaper correspondents. Mencken attributed his lifelong reverence for "the gentlemen of the Washington corps" to that conversation.

The evolution of Mencken as writer, editor, and critic can also be traced to his early discovery of his father's small library, which was shelved in "an old-fashioned secretary in the sitting room" of the Hollins Street residence. Mencken devoured the collection and was drawn especially to a set of volumes by Mark Twain. Throughout his career he asserted that *Huckleberry Finn* had a "genuinely terrific" impact on him and referred to his discovery of the work as "probably the most stupendous event of my whole life." After completing what he called the "Biblioteca Menckeniana," Mencken began raiding the shelves of Baltimore's Enoch Pratt Free Library, to which he had a card beginning when he was nine years old. He continued his voracious reading until he reached adolescence, inhabiting "a world that was two-thirds letterpress and only one-third trees, fields, streets and people."

Mencken credited Professor Knapp and his staff at Knapp's Institute with preparing him so well that he was advanced a full year when he entered Baltimore Polytechnic Institute in 1892. His interests at the polytechnic, chemistry and journalism, were apparent in his first attempt to get a manuscript published in 1894. He submitted an article describing a platinum toning bath for silver photographic prints to several photography magazines, but the editors rejected it. Mencken said that had he "encountered a competent teacher of chemistry at the Polytechnic, I'd have gone in that science, and today I'd be up to my ears in the vitamins, for it was synthetic chemistry that always interested me most. But the gogue told off to nurture me succeeded only in disheartening me, so I gradually edged over to letters. . . ." He recalled that although his record at the polytechnic was "pretty good," he had little interest in most of the subjects taught. Despite that attitude Mencken excelled in the school's general examination at the end of his four years. He did so well, in fact, that he finished at the head of his class and therefore spoke at the commencement exercises in June 1896. He reminisced in *Heathen Days, 1890-1936*, "That speech must have been a dreadful thing, indeed, for I was still very young in those days, and had not yet acquired my present facility for rabble-rousing." Mencken was the youngest member of his graduating class, being three months short of his sixteenth birthday.

Mencken took the first, albeit unsuccessful, step in beginning a career in journalism the Monday after his father died on Friday, 13 January 1899. August Mencken had not viewed favorably his son's oft-expressed interest in journalism, assuming that his offspring would continue the cigar-manufacturing business he and his younger brother had begun as Aug. Mencken & Bro. in 1875. But on that 16 January Mencken appeared in the newsroom of the *Baltimore Herald* to beg a reporting job from Max Ways, the city editor he later described as "a very competent man." Even though Ways was in no hurry to satisfy Mencken's wish to join the staff, he perceived the young man's eagerness and persistence. After more than a month, during which he trekked daily to the *Herald* office after his labors at the cigar factory, Mencken's chance came. On 23 February, Ways sent him to Govanstown on the outer reaches of Baltimore to seek out the news, since the *Herald*'s regular correspondent had not reported in for six days. A tremendous blizzard had just left much of the city and its environs covered with ice and snowdrifts.

Mencken's first published news story was a product of that assignment. He wrote: "A horse, buggy and several sets of harnesses, valued in all at about $250, were stolen last night from the stable of Howard Quinlan, near Kingsville. The county police are at work on the case, but so far no trace of either thieves or booty has been found." Ways also had him prepare a notice from information that had been submitted to the *Herald* about a "kinetoscope or cineograph" exhibition of war scenes. Thus, Mencken began his career in journalism much as young reporters always have, by composing an innocuous news account and rewriting a publicity release. His forays into Baltimore's remoteness did not last long, however. Shortly Ways was assigning him to the usual variety of meetings, interviews, rallies, and concerts that young reporters also glean as part of their introduction to journalism. By summer Mencken had earned a staff position on the *Herald* at seven dollars a week. Only then did he resign his job at the cigar factory. Thus began a forty-three-year experience in the news-

paper field for the man who would become a premier writer, editor, and critic, known as well for his singular writing style as for his prodigious outpouring of information and ideas. Mencken admitted in his preface to *Newspaper Days, 1899-1906* that young reporters led "a gaudy life": "I believed then, and still believe today, that it was the maddest, gladdest, damndest existence ever enjoyed by mortal youth. At a time when the respectable bourgeois youngsters of my generation were college freshmen, oppressed by simian sophomores and affronted with balderdash daily and hourly by chalky pedagogues, I was at large in a wicked seaport of half a million people, with a front seat at every public show, as free of the night as of the day, and getting earfuls and eyefuls of instruction in a hundred giddy arcana, none of them taught in schools."

Mencken's career at the *Herald* spanned seven years, and his rapid rise through the ranks is a clear indication of his growth as a skilled and competent newspaperman. He covered the police and city hall beats and wrote drama criticism as well. During his first year at the *Herald* Mencken witnessed his first hanging when four felons were executed in the Baltimore jailyard. Later, when he was the waterfront reporter for the *Herald*, Mencken and two other reporters adopted a practice he called "synthesizing news" that assured that all three wrote identical stories. A *Baltimore American* reporter with the curious name of Leander J. de Bekker offered to supply from his vivid imagination any details missing from their daily report, saving them needless legwork. "The labor-saving device was used the whole time I covered South Baltimore for the *Herald*, and I never heard any complaint against it," Mencken said. Their city editors occasionally commended the creative reporters for their accuracy.

Mencken said he developed his "theory that Service is mainly only blah" when he journeyed to Jacksonville, Florida, in May 1901 to cover his first out-of-town story. Most of the city had been destroyed by fire, and Mencken was sent to file stories about the efforts by various cities throughout the United States to help the residents. The paper was especially interested in Baltimore's relief offering, since it was produced at the instigation of the *Herald*. However, he found that the train carloads of horse blankets and Maryland rye whiskey, however well-intentioned as aid for victims of the conflagration, created more mirth than satisfaction. During those years Mencken also received assignments that introduced him to legislative reporting in Washington and in the state capital at Annapolis.

When he was elevated to Sunday editor in 1901, he scrapped several undesirable features, changed writers of the long-favored travel article, and, in general, enlivened the pages. His writing for Sunday editions consisted primarily of pieces about the theater.

When Mencken was twenty-three, he was made city editor of the *Herald*, the position he held during the great fire that engulfed downtown Baltimore on 7 February 1904. He devoted an entire chapter of his *Newspaper Days, 1899-1906* memoir to that harrowing experience, explaining the change it wrought in him: "It was brain-fagging and back-breaking, but it was grand beyond compare—an adventure of the first chop, a razzle-dazzle superb and elegant, a circus in forty rings. When I came out of it at last I was a settled and indeed almost a middle-aged man, spavined by responsibility and aching in every sinew, but I went into it a boy, and it was the hot gas of youth that kept me going." The *Herald*'s building was destroyed by the flames that consumed a square mile of the city, necessitating a search for a new home for the paper. During the first three days after the fire began, the staff used the facilities of the *Washington Post*, the *Baltimore World*, and the *Catholic Mirror*. Then for five weeks the *Herald* contingent worked in the plant of the *Philadelphia Evening Telegraph*, traveling as often as necessary the 100 miles between the cities. Mencken said his "opening burst of work without a stop ran to sixty-four and a half hours, and then I got only six hours of nightmare sleep, and resumed on a working schedule of from twelve to fourteen hours a day, with no days off and no time for meals until work was over."

After the fire the *Herald* experienced several upheavals in its organization and operation. Because it was difficult to get enough advertising, due to competition with the morning *Sun* and *American* and with the *Evening News*, the *Herald*'s publisher decided during the summer of 1904 to add an evening edition. After a week, the morning edition was discontinued except on Sundays. Mencken became managing editor in 1905 and, in addition to directing the newspaper's operation, often helped with the editorial page.

While he labored at the *Herald*, Mencken's writing was not devoted solely to journalistic efforts. Though he had written verse during his teenage years, he did not make his first free-lance poetry sale until the fall of 1899. He had submitted the selection anonymously, claiming it was his only after it had appeared; he was paid ten dollars. Mencken said his first poem "to make high literary society . . .

Mencken as editor of the Baltimore Morning Herald *in 1904 (Mencken Room, Enoch Pratt Free Library, Baltimore)*

was a rhymed address to my hero Kipling, urging him to forget politics and go back to Mandalay." His other extracurricular writing consisted of features and news stories which he submitted to other newspapers, including the *New York Telegram*, the *New York Sun*, and the *Philadelphia Inquirer*. Mencken also tried his hand at more mundane forms of creative writing, such as advertising copy for a cemetery and jokes for a syndicate. He sold about two dozen short stories in the early 1900s to such magazines as *Munsey's*, *Youth's Companion*, and *Frank Leslie's Popular Monthly*. During this same period he completed seven chapters of a novel set in Shakespearean England, complete with a fistfight between his protagonist and the Bard himself. The manuscript was never published.

Mencken's first column writing also took place while he worked at the *Herald*. The column, "Rhymes and Reason," appeared on the editorial page of the Sunday edition beginning in 1900, and contained some of his poetry. He said later: "I had a drawer full of verse, but I was making fewer and fewer additions to it. A large part of it consisted of dreadful imitations of Kipling, who was then my god. . . . In the Autumn of 1900, when I was given a weekly column on the editorial page, and invited to do my damnedest, I unearthed a lot of these *Jugendwerke,* and so saved the labor of writing new stuff. They were all pretty bad, but they seemed to be well received in the office, and in December I received the singular honor of being invited by the new managing editor, [Robert I.] Carter, to do a poem for the first page. . . . It was blowsy stuff, God knows, but Carter professed to like it, and, good or bad, there it glowed and glittered in long primer italic on page one—glory that no other American poet, however gifted, has ever achieved, at least to my knowledge." Subsequently his columns appeared under other titles—"Terse and Terrible Texts," "Knocks and Jollies," and "Untold Tales"—and contained humor and verse and later a series of what Mencken called "buffooneries," in which he featured Baltimore politicians in the guise of ancient Romans. But probably the best of his column writing at that time was in "Baltimore and the Rest of the World," which reflected not only Mencken's humor but his personal view of his hometown.

Mencken's first book, *Ventures into Verse* (1903), was published in an edition of 100 copies by two young printers and an artist who had sought out his work for one of their first efforts at advanced typography. He recalled receiving fifty of the small volumes containing mostly the verse he had used on the *Herald*'s editorial page. Mencken said the copies he sent to the chief critical publications drew good reviews but only three orders. "My presentation copies seem to have been preserved in odd corners," he wrote in *Newspaper Days,* "for when American firsts began to bring fantastic prices, in 1925, a good many appeared in the market, and at one time a clean specimen brought as much as $225."

Another of Mencken's editorial interests at the *Herald* was drama criticism; he was a second-string theater critic during Carter's tenure as managing editor, beginning in late 1900. Carter reviewed the serious plays staged in Baltimore, leaving the comedies and musicals to Mencken. Thus it was that Mencken's thought was focused on plays by George Bernard Shaw, an interest that he said led him to begin his first real book in 1904. *George Bernard Shaw: His Plays* (1905) was the first critical study of the dramatist's works. Mencken remembered the day the book's proofs arrived for his perusal. He showed them to Carter's successor as managing editor, Lynn R. Meekins, on the pretense of asking about a questionable passage, whereupon Meekins

insisted that the young author take the day off to read the galleys. Mencken recalled: "So I locked myself in as he commanded, and had a shining day indeed, and I can still remember its unparalleled glow after all these years." Biographer Carl Bode maintains that Mencken's true style emerged during the writing of the Shaw book: "Many different ingredients went into it but the combination was unique. There was the love of words . . . seen at its earliest in the school exercise at the Polytechnic and at its fanciest in the aborted novel on Shakespeare. There was the readiness at writing which was cultivated by his reams of copy at the *Herald* and the *Sun,* copy nearly always pushed by a deadline. And there was the urge to write clearly, in part because he needed to make the mass of newspaper readers understand him but also because he early acquired an admiration for clarity for its own sake." In January 1906 Mencken was elevated to editor, but the *Herald* closed in June. Mencken moved to the *Evening News* as news editor, but his work for his former competition was short-lived. The *Baltimore Sunpapers* hired him in July as Sunday editor, beginning an association that would continue until 1941, with a brief interruption during World War I and the addition of a short period in 1948 for political convention reporting.

Mencken brought his vibrant style and exuberant spirits to the *Sun* on 30 July 1906. Within a month he had evoked a response from the subject of one of his editorial page pieces, Col. Henry Watterson, editor of the *Louisville Courier-Journal*: "Think of it! The staid, old Baltimore *Sun* has got itself a Whangdoodle. Nor is it one of the bogus Whangdoodles which we sometimes encounter in the side-show business—merely a double-cross betwixt a Gin-Rickey and a Gyascutis—but genuine, guaranteed, imported direct from the Mountains of Hepsidam." During his first four years on the *Sun,* as he found editing the Sunday edition less demanding, Mencken began writing editorials and reviewing plays. He asked to be relieved of the theatrical critiques, however, after he had written twenty-three consecutive unfavorable reviews during the first year. He also found the editorial writing a frustrating chore because of the anonymity and uninspired subject matter inherent in such essays.

The experience of writing his Shaw book gave Mencken the impetus to start a large volume in 1907, *The Philosophy of Friedrich Nietzsche* (1908). Two years later he brought together his correspondence with Robert Rives La Monte, a Marxist and organizer for the Socialist party, in *Men versus the*

Man (1910), a debate on socialism. Mencken said that after these two nonfiction efforts, he was strictly a critic of ideas.

When the *Sun* was taken over by another owner in April 1910, Mencken was elevated to associate editorship of the new *Baltimore Evening Sun*. His duties included writing two editorials every day. He also grabbed the opportunity to begin a daily column, which he signed "H.L.M." His inimitable style—direct, humorous, and iconoclastic—found a milieu and an appreciative audience. In May 1911 Mencken was asked by the *Sunpapers'* management to write a by-lined column—unusual in that day—in the manner of the British columnist Horatio Bottemly, whose irreverent essays had caught the eye of a son of one of the newspaper's major stockholders. Mencken was given the mandate to be blunt, witty, and controversial. He could direct his barbs at anyone, except perhaps the church—though that institution, too, became fair game after Mencken was attacked frequently from the pulpit.

The "Free Lance" columns began appearing in the *Evening Sun* on 8 May 1911—the first day's title, "The World in Review," was dropped after that one use—and continued until 23 October 1915. Mencken's tack was to ridicule and heap abuse on every conceivable social scheme, idiotic practice, and public or private individual, whether politician, "Uplifter," or civic leader (Honorary Pallbearer, in Mencken's lexicon). He roared, hooted, and bawled; his sarcasm and derision were rarely subtle, usually bombastic in tone. William Manchester, another Mencken biographer, notes that "it was his outrageous attitude which distinguished Mencken. He opposed everything respectable, mocked everything sacred, inveighed against everything popular opinion supported." He included these two paragraphs in the "Free Lance" for 9 May 1911, the first day on which the column's title was officially used:

> After all is said and done, how many victuals are as genuinely and constantly appetizing as pigs' feet in jelly?

> Blackamoors smear the tree trunks with whitewash and elegant Neapolitans, laying aside the razor and the pushcart, practice fearful cadenzas upon the E flat clarinet. In brief, the summer parks prepare for trade. Three weeks will see them all open. A heavy miasma from singeing popcorn and hot frankfurters. Barkers barking. The sextet from *Lucia.* Young devils ogling the girls.

> Babies bawling. The crowded trolley. Comedians.

A Mencken device for calling attention to absurdities or to underline his opinion was the use of exclamations, interrupting other brief, usually audacious, observations on morals, habits, books, or whatever drew his sharp eye. One such paragraph appeared in the "Free Lance" of 15 March 1913: "Boil your drinking water! Cover your garbage can! Down with rum! Down with cocaine! Down with caffeine!" After a discussion of the relative merits of caffeine and alcohol Mencken concluded: "The cigarette! The cigarette! Beware, or it will get you yet! Oh, many and many a mother's pet hath perished in its awful net! On every hand its snares are set! The cigarette! The cigarette!" Because his new column was signed—not with just initials, as had been his earlier editorial-page efforts—Mencken gained a reputation for his impudent, devil-may-care pageant of mockery and satire. Bode characterizes the "Free Lance": "But allowing for comic exaggeration, Mencken meant what he said. The rebellion was real, the criticism purposeful. The point is that it was never heavy. In its largest dimension the Free Lance represented his basic attitude towards newspaper work and toward life. He treated both like his gaudy girls in the red-light district—whom he enjoyed thoroughly but disrespectfully." With the "Free Lance" Mencken had begun "stirring up the animals," his intention from the start, and as a result he gained a notoriety that led to his pronouncements being quoted throughout the United States.

During his years with the *Sunpapers* Mencken took on other writing and editing tasks, enough to tax the endurance and skill of even the most talented journalist. But his work on books and magazines was suitable and altogether appropriate for a man with such an immense fascination with ideas and the continuing carnival of humanity. In 1914 he became coeditor with George Jean Nathan of the *Smart Set,* a magazine known for its risqué content appealing primarily to the so-called society crowd. The *Smart Set* had been founded as "A Magazine of Cleverness" in 1900 by Col. William D'Alton Mann, whose lack of success with the publication forced him to sell it in 1908 to John Adams Thayer. The publication experienced a series of editors and declining circulation during the next fourteen years. Willard Huntington Wright, predecessor of Mencken and Nathan, had become editor in 1913. He had changed the magazine's slogan to "Its Prime Purpose Is to Provide Lively

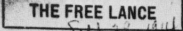

THE FREE LANCE

RISING to a question of personal privilege, I beg to assure those gentlemen of the Letter Column who mistake my defense of the slandered and hard-pressed Germans for a laudable (or heinous) manifestation of patriotism that I am not a German and am not bound to Germany by sentimental ties. I was born in Baltimore of Baltimore-born parents; I have no relatives, near or remote, in Germany, nor even any friends (save one Englishman!); very few of my personal associates in this town are native Germans; I read the German language very imperfectly, and do not speak it or write it at all; I never saw Germany until I was 23 years old; I have been there since but twice; I am of English and Irish blood as well as German.

WHAT is more, the most massive influences of my life have all been unmistakably English. I know Kinglake's "Crimea" and Steevens' "With Kitchener to Khartoum" a great deal better than I know any history of the American Revolution or Civil War; I make a living writing the language of Thackeray and Huxley, and devote a good deal of time to studying it; I believe thoroughly in that imperialism for which England has always stood; I read English newspapers and magazines constantly, and have done so for 15 years; I regard the net English contribution to civilization as enormously greater than the German contribution; I am on good terms with many Englishmen, always get along well with them, and don't know a single one that I dislike.

ALL this by way of necessary explanation. But the Englishman upon whom the glory and greatness of England rests is not the Englishman who slanders and blubbers over Germany in this war. The England of Drake and Nelson, of Shakespeare and Marlow, of Darwin and Huxley, of Clive and Rhodes is not the England of Churchill and Lloyd-George, of Asquith and McKenna, of mongrel allies and bawling suffragettes, of "limehousing" and "mafficking," of press-censors and platitudinarians, of puerile moralizing and silly pettifogging. The England that the world yet admires and respects was a country ruled by proud and forthright men. The England that today poses as the uplifter of Europe is a country ruled by cheap demagogues and professional pharisees. The slimy "morality" of the unleashed rabble has conquered the clean and masculine ideals of the old ruling caste. A great nation has succumbed to mobocracy, and to the intellectual dishonesty that goes with it.

WHAT is the war really about? Why are the nations fighting one another? In so far as Germany and England are concerned, the cause is as plain as a pike-staff. Germany, of late years, has suddenly become England's rival as the boss of Europe, and with Europe, of the world. German trade has begun to prevail over English trade; German influence has begun to undermine English influence; even upon the sea, the new might and consequence of Germany have begun to challenge England's old lordship. The natural result is that the English have grown angry and alarmed, and the second result is that they yearn to crush and dispose of Germany before it is too late—i.e., before the Germans actually become their superiors in power, and so beyond their reach.

SUCH a yearning needs no defense. It is natural, it is virtuous, it is laudable. National jealousies make for the security, the prosperity and the greatness of the more virile nations, and hence for the progress of civilization. But did England, filled with this yearning, openly admit it, and then proceed in a frank and courageous manner to obtain its satisfaction in a fair fight? England did not. On the contrary, she artfully dissembled, her mouth full of pieties, until Germany was beset by enemies in front and behind, and then she suddenly threw her gigantic strength into the unequal contest. And did she, even then, announce her cause, state her motive, tell the truth? She did not. She went into battle with a false cry upon her lips, seeking to make her rage against a rival appear as a frenzy for righteousness, shedding crocodile tears over Germany's sins, wearing the tin halo and flapping chemise of a militant moralist.

I DO not like militant moralists, whether they be nations or individuals. I distrust the man who is concerned about his neighbor's sins, and who calls in the police (or the Turcos, or the Sikhs, or the Russians) to put them down. I have never known such a man who was honest with himself, nor is there any record of such a one in all history. They were a nuisance in the days of Christ, and His most bitter denunciations were leveled against them. They are still a nuisance today, though they impudently call themselves Christians, and even seek to excommunicate all persons who object to their excesses. That their shallow sophistries appeal to the mob, that they are especially numerous and powerful under a mobocracy, is but one more proof that mobocracy is the foe of civilization, and not only of civilization, but also of the truth.

FOR the manly, stand-up, ruthless, truth-telling, clean-minded England of another day I have the highest respect and reverence. It was an England of sound ideals and great men. But for the smug, moralizing, disingenuous England of Churchill and Lloyd-George, of hollow pieties and saccharine protestations, of Japanese alliances and the nonconformist conscience—for this new and oleaginous England, by Gladstone out of Pecksniff, I have no respect whatever. Its victory over Germany in this war would be a victory for all the ideas and ideals that I most ardently detest, and upon which, in my remote mud-puddle, I wage a battle with all the strength that I can muster, and to which I pledge my unceasing enmity until that day when the ultimate embalmer casts his sinister eye upon my fallen beauty.

WHEN I think of this new, this saponaceous, this superbrummagem England, so smug and slick without and so full of corruption and excess within, I am beset by emotions of the utmost unpleasantness. I snort; I swear; I leak large globulous tears. It is my hope and belief that this sick and bogus England will be given a good licking by the Deutsch, to the end that truth and health may prevail upon the earth. If the Mailed Fist cracks it, I shall rejoice unashamed. The Mailed Fist is dedicated to the eternal facts of life, to the thing behind the mere word, to the truth that is above all petty quibbling over theoretical rights and wrongs. I am for the Mailed Fist, gents, until the last galoot's ashore.

MEANWHILE, the Hon. William Jennings Bryan continues to make sheep's eyes at the Nobel prize. Like all uplifters, a thrifty fellow!

READ the Towsontown *New Era*, and escape the Sunday drought.—
Adv.   H. L. MENCKEN.—

Mencken's column in the Baltimore Sun *for 29 September 1914 (The* Sun, *Baltimore, Md.)*

Entertainment for Minds That Are Not Primitive," beginning some of the changes that Mencken and Nathan would embrace. William Manchester, in his Mencken biography, says that Wright should receive full credit for having published for one year "that magazine now considered a literary milestone." Before selling the *Smart Set* to Eugene Crowe, the owner of *Field and Stream,* Thayer fired Wright, who became a columnist for the *New York Evening Mail*. Crowe appointed Eltinge F. Warner, formerly with *Field and Stream,* to be publisher of the *Smart Set*. Warner, meeting Nathan during a voyage from Europe, asked Nathan to become editor of the magazine. Nathan agreed but insisted that Mencken be coeditor. Mencken had been book editor for the magazine since November 1908, a task he approached with his usual bluster and erudition. Nathan, a former reporter who had studied languages and the theater in Europe, had become drama editor at about the same time. Under their coeditorship the *Smart Set* became a ready market for the creative efforts of young and talented writers and an important force in the literary taste of the time.

In the fifteen years he wrote for the *Smart Set,* Mencken reviewed about 2,000 books. In his final essay in December 1923 he said he had composed 182 articles during those years, or more than 900,000 words of criticism. William H. Nolte says that Mencken "was the most powerful literary critic, in his own lifetime, that this country has produced; and his judgment of individual writers and his analysis of our literary heritage were nigh unerring." The vitality, originality, and iconoclasm of the Mencken style showed through in every essay. In December 1909, for example, he wrote under the headline "A Novel Thus Begins": *"Apologies for Love*—by F. A. Myers. ' "Do you remain long in Paris, Miss Wadsworth?" Earl Nero Pensive (!!!) inquired, as he seated himself beside her. His eyes, like beaming lights out of shadowless abysm, were transfixed upon her as by magic force. . . .' Thus the story begins. God knows how it ends!" Mencken's sure touch with ridicule is apparent in these opening sentences of a review titled "Lachrymose Love" in February 1915: "Have you tears? Do you leak easily? Are you a weeper? Then wrap yourself in a shower-bath curtain before you sit down to *Innocent,* by Marie Corelli, for the tale wrings the lachrymal ducts with exquisite and diabolical art. Sadness, indeed, stalks through the countryside; it is a sure cure for joy in every form. I myself, a mocker at all sweet and lovely things, a professional snickerer, a saucy fellow by trade, have moaned and blubbered

over it like a fat woman in *La Dame aux Camelias*. My waistcoat is a sponge. My beard is white with salt. My eyes are a brilliant scarlet. . . ."

Mencken was considered something of a patriarch in the German-American community, but biographer Edgar Kemler says that "His allegiance was, after all, to a Germany that existed in its pure state only in his mind, and it was highly distressing for him to be reminded how much the German-Americans resembled other Americans." As Mencken's columns were thought to be more and more pro-German in the early years of World War I, the *Sunpapers'* management grew apprehensive that the "Free Lance" would have a volatile influence on its audience. Bode notes that Mencken, in the "Free Lance," defended the commander of the German submarine that torpedoed the *Lusitania* and predicted that Paris would be captured and London destroyed by German armies. Announcing that the war was nearing its end, Mencken proclaimed "Deutschland Über Alles!" In October 1915 the *Sun* dropped the column, and for the next year Mencken wrote on music, literature, and the arts. He was sent to Germany as a correspondent in January 1917, and for two months dispatched accounts covering aspects of life among the troops in the trenches and the generals in Berlin. He returned to Baltimore by way of Cuba, from where he smuggled out accounts of an impending revolution through his contacts in Havana. Mencken broke with the *Sun* in March 1917 and did not resume writing for it until 1919.

Meanwhile, Mencken's sardonic and entertaining views, on subjects as varied and controversial as those in the "Free Lance," appeared in the *New York Evening Mail,* with which he had a contract for three columns a week. One of the Iconoclast's *Evening Mail* columns which gained notoriety—and provoked an especially fierce uproar from one region of the country—was "The Sahara of the Bozart," which appeared on 13 November 1917. The title of the essay, a permutation of the French *beaux arts,* was evidence of Mencken's penchant for wordplay. He phrased his scorn audaciously, true to his style of overstatement: "Nearly the whole of Europe could be lost in that stupendous region of worn-out farms, shoddy cities and paralyzed cerebrums: one could throw in France, Germany and Italy, and still have room for the British Isles. And yet, for all its size and all its wealth and all the 'progress' it babbles of, it is almost as sterile, artistically, intellectually, culturally, as the Sahara Desert. There are single acres in Europe that house more first-rate men than all the states south of the

Potomac; there are probably single square miles in America. If the whole of the late Confederacy were to be engulfed by a tidal wave tomorrow, the effect upon the civilized minority of men in the world would be but little greater than that of a flood on the Yang-tse-kiang. It would be impossible in all history to match so complete a drying up of a civilization." After he included "Sahara of the Bozart" in his 1920 collection, *Prejudices: Second Series,* Mencken became the object of hostile editorials. From Atlanta to Richmond, from Charleston to Little Rock, the outpourings of furious Southerners likened him to Satan incarnate and labeled him "an insufferable excrescence on the body of American literature," "an infernal and ignorant mountebank," and "a miserable, uninformed wretch." Mencken recalled: "It produced a ferocious reaction in the South, and I was belabored for months, and even years afterward in a very extravagant manner.... On the heels of the violent denunciations of the elderly Southerners there soon came a favorable response from the more civilized youngsters, and there is reason to believe that my attack had something to do with that revival of Southern letters which followed in the middle 1920s." Such was the influence Mencken was beginning to wield on public opinion.

On 18 December 1917 one of Mencken's most memorable creations—for a creation is precisely what it was—appeared in the *Mail.* The famous "bathtub hoax" was a cleverly contrived column entitled "A Neglected Anniversary." Mencken later said he composed the column with its seemingly well-documented canard because in wartime "more serious writing was impossible." The bathtub history found its way into medical reference books, other news and magazine accounts and, in later years, onto television. Mencken lamented that no matter how much he tried to explain away his foolishness, the story contined to thrive. His essay detailed the tub's construction by Adam Thompson, a cotton and grain merchant, in Cincinnati in December 1842. The huge tub was designed to hold the body of an adult and was constructed of highly polished mahogany lined with sheet lead. The magnificent container weighed 1,750 pounds. Mencken wrote gravely that the public and the medical fraternity denounced the invention as "an epicurean and obnoxious toy from England" and as "dangerous to health." He went so far as to claim that acceptance of the tub by President Millard Fillmore was responsible for bringing the device "recognition and respectability in the United States." Fillmore was said to have visited Cincinnati when he was vice-president, and after

inspecting the bathtub proceeded to bathe in the Thompson original. When he became president, he ordered a similar tub for the White House. Mencken's account had all the marks of an authentic chronicle. It sounded momentous with all its dates and names, and to the gullible reader it had credibility.

Mencken's association with the *Mail* ended when the newspaper's pro-German sympathies led to its suppression in July 1918. He then directed his literary efforts to completing *Damn! A Book of Calumny* (1918) and *In Defense of Women* (1918). At the same time he began what many consider his most notable achievement, *The American Language,* a philological study that has been highly praised since the first edition was published in 1919. Mencken himself believed the work would "outlast anything else that I have ever written." He had first written about the subject in his *Sun* column and in a subsequent series for the *Smart Set,* and he carried this intense interest in language over to the massive project that consumed thirty-eight years—from 1910 to 1948—while he was engaged in other editorial and writing projects. Mencken produced a thorough, penetrating, and, as always, readable analysis of enormous significance to the understanding of American English idiom. His observations about and examples of American English vocabulary, spelling, pronunciation, grammar, and syntax earned praise from scholars as well as ordinary readers. Four editions of *The American Language,* along with two Supplements, reveal the orderly, systematic method of a writer enthralled by the complexities of language. In each succeeding edition, Mencken incorporated suggestions from thousands of letters and information from linguistic publications and other sources devoted to language study. The fourth edition of *The American Language* appeared in 1936, and the two Supplements were published in 1945 and 1948.

Mencken became general editorial adviser for the *Baltimore Sun* after rejoining the organization in 1919. His extraordinary energy and genius for editing and writing gave value to his guidance of the *Evening Sun,* particularly after Hamilton Owens became managing editor in 1922. Mencken helped improve both the content and the appearance of the newspaper and offered counsel and instruction in both major and inconsequential matters. In editorial conferences and in conversations with reporters and other staff personnel Mencken revealed his skill in management.

Mencken agreed also to write occasional articles when he went back to the *Sun,* and the famous

George Jean Nathan and Mencken in 1923, shortly before they launched the American Mercury
(Photo by Alfred Knopf)

"Monday Articles" were born. His weekly columns on the editorial page helped identify Mencken as a premier journalist, a newspaperman of the first order. From 1920 until 1938 he wrote of politics, literature, personalities, places—any subjects that events or encounters suggested to his fertile journalist's mind. By the end of the series of "Monday Articles" in 1938 Mencken had moved through the Depression and into Franklin D. Roosevelt's presidency. As the "Free Lance" had brought his ideas to the attention of his hometown, the "Monday Articles" imprinted his particular brand of commentary on the psyche of America. Mencken entertained and angered, engendering responses in extreme degrees among his readers. They delighted, despised, hooted, and whooped, but they always noticed.

In 1923 both Mencken and Nathan left the *Smart Set* to become coeditors of the *American Mercury,* the periodical that, more than any other, became a bible to collegians of the 1920s. Mencken reached the pinnacle of his popularity and influence during the ten years he edited the *American*

Mercury. With its Paris-green cover, the magazine was simply designed by standards of later decades but was a superb typographical specimen in its day. It was not only a status symbol but a voice of critical significance during the wild, unabashed decade of prosperity and Prohibition. When Alfred A. Knopf, Mencken's publisher since 1916, was eager to begin a new magazine, he sought Mencken to be editor. Mencken insisted that Nathan also be part of the enterprise, and so his coeditor from the *Smart Set* made the transition to the *American Mercury* to provide drama criticism and comments on the foibles of humanity. The first issue, dated January 1924, indicated editorially the course Baltimore's "bad boy" intended to follow: "The editors are committed to nothing save this: to keep the common sense as fast as they can, to belabor sham as agreeably as possible, to give a civilized entertainment." The flavor of that sentence typified the *American Mercury*'s profound and audacious tone. Mencken was an imaginative editor, and his special writing style, along with his keen insight and trenchant wit, gave the *American Mercury* a lively and intellectually stimulating quality that appealed to sophisticated and perceptive readers. He used submissions from a variety of writers, the recognized talents of the day as well as virtual unknowns.

The *American Mercury's* mélange of criticism, fiction, poetry, and essays on all manner of topics—always satiric and provocative with a note of humor, occasionally sarcastic and ironical—affected the thinking and taste of a mass of readers in the 1920s. Largely as a result of the magazine's impact, Walter Lippmann remarked in 1926 that Mencken was "the most powerful personal influence on the whole generation of educated people." Each issue of the *American Mercury* contained the "Americana" column, which consisted of brief notes taken from news clippings, wire reports, church bulletins, publicity releases—an assortment of sources from throughout the United States. The passages reflected the idiocies, imbecilities, and prejudices of the populace and appeared under state name headings with sardonic introductory sentences. The first issue's "Americana" included:

ALABAMA

Final triumph of Calvinism in Alabama, October 6, 1923:
> Birmingham's exclusive clubs—and all other kinds—will be as blue hereafter as city and State laws can make them. Commissioner of Safety W. C. Bloe issued an order today that Sunday golf, billiards, and *dominoes* be stopped, beginning tomorrow.

VIRGINIA

Examples of neo-Confederate English from examination papers submitted by Virginia schoolmarms attending the Summer School at the University of Virginia:
> He run down the street, but it was too late to cought him . . .
> I like James Witcomb Riley, becuse he is not dead, and writes poems in the paper that one can see all right . . .
> The flames shot into the sky a few foot above the house . . .

WASHINGTON

Hurrying on the Kingdom in the Chinook State, as reported by the *Editor and Publisher*:
> Newspaper advertising was the best invest- (sic) made in 1923 by the Garden Street Methodist Episcopal Church, Bellingham, Wash., according to the pastor, the Rev. Dr. J. C. Harrison, who added that $100 worth of advertising had brought in more than $1,700 in silver plate collections.

Readers were amused by "Americana," and they found other regular features—Nathan's column on "The Theatre," Mencken's "The Library," and their collaboration on "Clinical Notes"—similarly entertaining and informative. The *American Mercury's* contents had appeal that few other periodicals of that time could claim. The first issue was indicative of what was to come in the next 120 issues, all of which contained 128 pages. In addition to Mencken's and Nathan's efforts, the twenty-two selections ranged from essays on "The Lincoln Legend" by Isaac R. Pennypacker and "Stephen Crane" by Carl Van Doren to four poems by Theodore Dreiser and "Four Generations," a story by Ruth Suckow.

Mencken's own writing was direct, and his turns of phrase and superb use of language rendered his subjects memorable. On 8 December 1924, he described chiropractors in his *Baltimore Sun* column: "That pathology is grounded upon the doctrine that all human ills are caused by the pressure of misplaced vertebrae upon the nerves which come out of the spinal cord—in other words, that every disease is the result of a pinch. This, plainly enough, is buncombe. The chiropractic therapeutics rest upon the doctrine that the way to get rid of such pinches is to climb upon a table and submit to a heroic pummeling by a retired piano-mover. This, obviously, is buncombe doubly damned." Mencken summed up his feelings about religionists, particularly the more zealous, in his definition of Puritanism as "The haunting fear that someone, somewhere, may be happy." The succinct observation embodied his reaction to many of the pious causes célèbres of his time, but the furor raised by the Scopes trial in Dayton, Tennessee, in 1925 was one of Mencken's great moments, both as reporter and as social critic. The so-called monkey trial grew out of the indictment of John Thomas Scopes, a high school biology teacher who disobeyed the Tennessee law against teaching evolution. In *Heathen Days, 1890-1936,* Mencken recalled going to Dayton to cover the trial. He wrote that after the event stories about his being run out of town were pervasive, but "nothing of the sort ever happened. It is a fact that my dispatches from the courtroom were somewhat displeasing to the local susceptibilities, and that my attempts to describe the town and its people were even more so, and it is also a fact that there was talk among certain bolder spirits of asking me to retire from the scene, but beyond that it did not go." Indeed, Mencken's dispatches to the *Evening Sun* caught the flavor of the place and the event. One of them began: "It was hot weather when they tried the infidel Scopes at Dayton, Tenn., but I went down there very willingly, for I was eager to see something of evangelical Christianity as a going concern. In the big cities of the Republic, despite the endless efforts of consecrated men, it is laid up with a wasting disease. The very Sunday-school superintendents, taking jazz from the stealthy radio, shake their fire-proof legs; their pupils, moving into adolescence, no longer respond to the proliferating hormones by enlisting for missionary service in Africa, but resort to necking instead. Even in Dayton, I found, though the mob was up to do execution upon Scopes, there was a strong smell of antinomianism. The nine churches of the village were all half empty on Sunday, and weeds choked their yards. Only two or three of the resident pastors managed to sustain themselves by their ghostly science; the rest had to take orders for mail order pantaloons or work in the adjacent strawberry fields; one, I heard, was a barber."

A prime target of Mencken's acerb pen was William Jennings Bryan, the prosecutor in the Scopes trial. Mencken attacked Bryan, hero of the fundamentalists, in a notable piece for the *Evening Sun* of 27 July 1925 that began: "Has it been duly marked by historians that William Jennings Bryan's last secular act on this globe of sin was to catch flies? A curious detail, and not without its sardonic overtones. He was the most sedulous fly-catcher in American history, and in many ways the most successful." Bryan had died the day before.

Among the hundreds of targets of his observations, caustic criticism, and ironic comments, Mencken also counted members of the press as particularly appropriate objects of scorn. Although he was a member of their breed, he had no difficulty in focusing on their shortcomings. In 1927 he wrote: "It is this vast and militant ignorance, this widespread and fathomless prejudice against intelligence that makes American journalism so pathetically feeble and vulgar, and so generally disreputable. A man with so little intellectual enterprise that, dealing with news daily, he can go through life without taking in any news that is worth knowing—such a man, you may be sure, is lacking in professional dignity quite as much as he is lacking in curiosity."

The controversy surrounding publication of

"Hatrack" in the April 1926 *American Mercury* brought Mencken increased notoriety. Herbert Asbury's relatively innocuous story of a small-town prostitute stirred the Boston censors. Mencken subsequently confronted the Reverend J. Franklin Chase, secretary of the Watch and Ward Society of Boston, selling him a copy of the offending issue of the *American Mercury* on Boston Common. Mencken openly sought arrest so that he could test the obscenity charge in court. He won an injunction against Chase and a similar action against the New York postmaster, who, at Chase's urging, had sought a Post Office ban on the *American Mercury*.

Mencken commented on comedians in his *Sun* column for 18 November 1929: "Relatively few reflective persons seem to get any pleasure out of acting. They often, to be sure, delight in comedians—but a comedian is not an actor: he is a sort of *reductio ad absurdum* of an actor. His work bears the same relation to acting properly so called as that of a hangman, a midwife or a divorce lawyer bears to poetry, or that of a bishop to religion."

The surprise announcement that H. L. Mencken would marry Sara Powell Haardt of

Mencken and his wife, Sara Powell Haardt, just after their wedding in August 1930. She died in May 1935 (Baltimore News American).

Montgomery, Alabama, in September 1930 produced much hilarity among the acquaintances of Baltimore's premier curmudgeon. The press treated the impending nuptials with high good humor and, in some cases, scorn, as headlines trumpeted the Great Iconoclast's fall from professional bachelorhood. Editorials quoted Mencken's *In Defense of Women,* which had been considered proof of his aversion to the matrimonial state. The wedding took place in Baltimore on 27 August, a week earlier than the announced date of 3 September, to avoid the confusion the event could possibly have created.

Mencken had met Sara Haardt in 1923 when she was teaching English at Goucher College. A writer of fiction and articles in her own right, she had won over the great debunker with her wit, charm, and Victorian manner. Her frail health, although not a totally debilitating influence, always hovered over their courtship and marriage.

Before the end of its fifth year in 1928 the *American Mercury* had numerous imitators, espe-

cially among college publications, but the magazine's popularity was beginning to wane. Its circulation, more than 77,000 in 1927, was down to almost 74,000. By the close of the 1920s and the onset of the Depression, Mencken's and consequently the *American Mercury*'s influence had declined severely: circulation dropped to 67,000 in 1929. Criticism of Mencken from many quarters pointed to his failure to adjust to the times. His columns did not have their usual vitality, and much of the writing by contributors reflected a Menckenian formula. Nathan had departed the *American Mercury* in 1925, though he continued to write his theater column and to contribute to "Clinical Notes" until early 1930.

Mencken's bite was not totally gone, however. His suggestion for choosing legislators was published in the *Sun* on 13 April 1931: "So I propose that our Legislatures be chosen as our juries are now chosen—that the names of all the men eligible in each assembly district be put into a hat (or if no hat can be found that is large enough, into a bathtub),

Mencken covering the 1936 Republican National Convention in Cleveland

and that a blind moron, preferably of tender years, be delegated to draw out one. Let the constituted catchpolls then proceed swiftly to this man's house, and take him before he can get away. Let him be brought into court forthwith, and put under bond to serve as elected, and if he cannot furnish the bond, let him be kept until the appointed day in the nearest jail."

Mencken left the *American Mercury* in December 1933. After five years of marriage—the only period of Mencken's life that he lived away from Hollins Street—Sara died of tubercular meningitis on 31 May 1935. Mencken wrote that he was "dashed and dismayed" by her death. Their life together, he said, had been "a beautiful adventure."

In addition to his work on the *Evening Sun* and the *American Mercury,* Mencken also wrote essays for the *Chicago Tribune* from November 1924 to January 1928 and for the *New York American* from July 1934 to May 1935.

Mencken's favorite continuing news story was the political campaign. From the first two conventions he covered in 1904 for the *Herald* until his final campaign in 1948, he gloried in the hoopla and circuslike atmosphere of the quadrennial orgies. Beginning in 1920 he covered every political campaign until 1940. Although he left the *Sun* in 1941—an echo of the experience of a quarter of a century before, as he realized his feelings about the war in Europe were at odds with those of the newspaper—Mencken agreed to revel just once more in the orators, crowds, and steaming auditoriums in 1948. He ground out his usual perceptive and colorful copy on the Democratic, Republican, and Progressive conventions that year. A dispatch in June 1948 from the Republican gathering in Philadelphia revealed the old Mencken touch, as he viewed the arrival of a new technology:

> Television will take its first real bite at the statesmen of America tomorrow, and this afternoon there was a sort of experimental gumming or rehearsal in Convention Hall.
>
> It passed off well enough, all things considered, and no one was actually fried to death.
>
> But I doubt if any politician, however leathery his hide, survives that unprecedented glare of light without a considerable singeing. I was sitting quietly in the almost empty press-stand when the first 10,000-watt lamp was turned on.

Mencken's campaign coverage continued into

Mencken returning from the hospital with his nurse, Lois Gentry, in 1951

November and the election of Democrat Harry S Truman to the presidency.

On 23 November 1948, Baltimore's Sage had a severe stroke, which left him unable to read or comprehend well what he saw or heard. His speech was also impaired. For the next eight years Mencken suffered the ultimate disability for one whose life had been built on a rare ability to communicate, a skill for choosing the right word and formulating the most colorful, the most potent statement. He died in his sleep on 29 January 1956, leaving among his millions of words a brief epitaph: "If, after I depart this vale, you ever remember me and have thought to please my ghost, forgive some sinner and wink your eye at some homely girl."

It would be possible to assign H. L. Mencken to some esoteric category that would encompass what he contributed to American letters: journalist-editor-critic-author-satirist-philologist. It would be simple enough, as many authors have found, to expound his "meaning" by quoting at length from his voluminous correspondence or his extraordinary outpouring of columns, articles, and books.

Both approaches merely prove that Mencken cannot be compartmentalized; his works cannot be described in simple terms or limited to preconceived notions. The constant stream of commentary about Mencken, dissecting his ideas on everything from religion to ethics to politics and reviewing his life in detail, never really captures the man himself.

A great part of Mencken was his inimitable style. His words and, as a result, the works that those words produced, pulsate with pungent and potent good humor and common sense. Mencken remarked on his style in his notebooks, which have been collected in *Minority Report* (1956): "The imbeciles who have printed acres of comment on my books have seldom noticed the chief character of my style. It is that I write with almost scientific precision—that my meaning is never obscure. The ignorant have often complained that my vocabulary is beyond them, but that is simply because my ideas cover a wider range than theirs do. Once they have consulted the dictionary they always know exactly what I intend to say. . . ."

Mencken's ideas may not always have been original; his conservative-libertarian philosophy sometimes seemed contradictory. But he could grab the public's attention by stating an issue in terms that pointed up the inanity and the foolishness of man. His iconoclasm knew no limits; everything he encountered—person, object, or idea—was fair game for his particular brand of debunking. All elements of the persona of H. L. Mencken—his boisterous humor, his incisive wit, his healthy skepticism, his seemingly limitless gusto, and his innate rebelliousness—were inseparable from his thinking, his way of seeing the universe.

Mencken's dissent—his way of demolishing society's hypocrisy, of smashing the idols of human folly—set him apart from other writers of his day. His thought embraced the whole range of issues and problems that beset the first half of the twentieth century; and his writings have not aged, because mankind is subject to the same shortcomings and foibles that prevailed in his day.

Mencken's life as a journalist doubtless made him conscious of the peculiar position of those in the writing profession. In his notebooks he commented about the "unhappy man of the pen": "His feelings torture him far more than any other man is tortured, but soon or late he is able to work them off. They escape by way of his writings. Into those writings, if he lives long enough, he gradually empties all his fears and hatreds and prejudices—all his vain regrets and broken hopes—all his suf-

ferings as a man, and all the special sufferings that go with his trade. The world, to such a man, never grows downright unbearable. There is always a sheet of paper. There is always a pen. There is always a way out." As long as there are those who long for a well-turned phrase that probes subjects that really matter, that breaks the mold of the commonplace, then there will be an audience for H. L. Mencken.

Recording:
H. L. Mencken Speaking (New York: Caedmon Records TC 1082, 1960).

Letters:
Letters of H. L. Mencken, edited by Guy J. Forgue (New York: Knopf, 1961);

The New Mencken Letters, edited by Carl Bode (New York: Dial, 1977).

Bibliography:
Betty Adler and Jane Wilhelm, *H. L. M.: The Mencken Bibliography* (Baltimore: Johns Hopkins University Press, 1961); *Ten-Year Supplement, 1962-1971* (Baltimore: Enoch Pratt Free Library, 1971).

Biographies:
Isaac Goldberg, *The Man Mencken: A Biographical and Critical Survey* (New York: Simon & Schuster, 1925);

Edgar Kemler, *The Irreverent Mr. Mencken* (Boston: Little, Brown, 1950);

William Manchester, *Disturber of the Peace: The Life of H. L. Mencken* (New York: Harper, 1950);

Charles Angoff, *H. L. Mencken: A Portrait from Memory* (New York: Thomas Yoseloff, 1956);

Sara Mayfield, *The Constant Circle: H. L. Mencken and His Friends* (New York: Delacorte, 1968);

Carl Bode, *Mencken* (Carbondale: Southern Illinois University Press, 1969);

Douglas C. Stenerson, *H. L. Mencken: Iconoclast from Baltimore* (Chicago: University of Chicago Press, 1971);

H. Allen Smith, "A Friend in Baltimore," in *The Best of H. Allen Smith* (New York: Trident, 1972);

Charles A. Fecher, *Mencken: A Study of His Thought* (New York: Knopf, 1978).

References:
Charles Angoff, "H. L. Mencken: A Postscript," *South Atlantic Quarterly*, 63 (Spring 1964): 227-239;

Robert Bendiner, "Mencken Blunderbuss," *Reporter,* 16 (24 January 1957): 42-43;

Van Wyck Brooks, "Mencken in Baltimore," *American Scholar,* 20 (Autumn 1951): 409-421;

William Henry Chamberlin, "Mencken, Scourge of Boobs," *New Leader,* 39 (19 March 1956): 29;

Louis Cheslock, "At Home With Henry Mencken," *Gardens, Houses and People,* 32 (August 1957): 12-13;

Alistair Cooke, "The Baltimore Fox," *Saturday Review,* 38 (10 September 1955): 13, 63-64;

Jonathan Daniels, "Nonage of an Iconoclast," *Saturday Review of Literature,* 31 (27 January 1940): 6;

John Dorsey, ed., *On Mencken* (New York: Knopf, 1980);

Joseph Epstein, "Rediscovering Mencken," *Commentary,* 63 (April 1977): 47-52;

Willliam Evitts, "The Savage South: H. L. Mencken and the Roots of a Persistent Lineage," *Virginia Quarterly Review* (Autumn 1973): 596-611;

Guy Jean Forgue, "Myths about Mencken," *Nation,* 193 (16 September 1961): 163-165;

Fred C. Hobson, Jr., *Serpent in Eden: H. L. Mencken and the South* (Chapel Hill: University of North Carolina Press, 1974);

Gerald W. Johnson, "Reconsideration: H. L. Mencken," *New Republic,* 173 (27 December 1975): 32-33;

Walter Lippmann, "H. L. Mencken," *Saturday Review of Literature,* 3 (11 December 1926): 413-414;

William H. Nolte, *H. L. Mencken, Literary Critic* (Middletown, Conn.: Wesleyan University Press, 1966);

Louis D. Rubin, Jr., "H. L. Mencken and the National Letters," *Sewanee Review,* 74 (Summer 1966): 723-738;

Edward S. Shapiro, "The Southern Agrarians, H. L. Mencken and the Quest for Southern Identity," *American Studies,* 13 (November 1975): 75-92;

M. K. Singleton, *H. L. Mencken and the American Mercury Adventure* (Durham, N.C.: Duke University Press, 1962);

Douglas C. Stenerson, "Mencken's Early Newspaper Experience: The Genesis of a Style," *American Literature,* 37 (May 1965): 153-166;

Carl Van Doren, "Smartness and Light, H. L. Mencken, a Gadfly for Democracy," *Century,* 105 (March 1923): 791-796;

Edmund Wilson, "The Aftermath of Mencken," *New Yorker,* 45 (31 May 1969): 107-115.

Papers:
The Enoch Pratt Free Library, Baltimore, has H. L. Mencken's personal library, including manuscripts, typescripts, and scrapbooks; and his correspondence, except that with twentieth-century authors and non-Marylanders, which he gave to the New York Public Library. Thirty-four other institutions and libraries are listed in Betty Adler, *A Descriptive List of H. L. Mencken Collections in the U.S.* (Baltimore: Enoch Pratt Free Library, 1967) as holding first editions of Mencken's books, original issues of magazines, or manuscripts.

Eugene Meyer
(31 October 1875-17 July 1959)

Elizabeth Brown Dickey
University of South Carolina

MAJOR POSITIONS HELD: Publisher, *Washington Post* (1933-1946); chairman of the board, *Washington Post* (1946-1959), *Washington Times-Herald* (1954-1959).

BOOKS: *The New Anaconda* (New York: E. Meyer, Jr., 1916);
Some After-War Economic Problems (New York, 1916);
War Profiteering: Some Practical Aspects of Its Control (Washington, D.C., 1917);
Address to the Sixth National Foreign Trade Convention at Chicago, April 24, 1919 (Washington, D.C., 1919);
Address on International Finance and Trade to the Association of Foreign Press Correspondents in the United States (New York, 1920);
Signs of Hope (Philadelphia: Railway Business Association, 1922);
Agricultural and Live Stock Conditions and Finance: Report to the President (Washington, D.C.: Government Printing Office, 1922);
Report to the President on the Wheat Situation (Washington, D.C.: Government Printing Office, 1923).

Eugene Meyer in 1937

Eugene Meyer, who distinguished himself in three careers, worked out a plan of life at a very young age: twenty years for schooling; the next twenty to earn a living, marry, and start a family; another twenty for public service; and at sixty he would retire and enjoy growing old. He kept to his schedule for much of the first sixty years, but as retirement age approached, he bought the bankrupt *Washington Post* and for the next two decades worked hard to create a reputable and profitable newspaper in the nation's capital.

Eugene Meyer was born on Halloween 1875 in Los Angeles to Eugene and Harriet Newmark Meyer. His father had immigrated to the United States from Alsace-Lorraine, France, in 1859. After many years as a merchant in Los Angeles and a banker in San Francisco, the senior Meyer became a partner in the international banking firm of Lazard Frères in New York City.

Young Meyer spent a year at the University of California, then compressed three years of study into two after transferring to Yale. He was graduated at age nineteen and worked for his father's bank for a year before going to Europe for two years to study banking and languages. On his return, he went back to work for Lazard Frères.

In 1901, at twenty-six, Meyer started his own brokerage and investment banking house, Eugene Meyer, Jr. and Company. He bought a seat on the New York Stock Exchange and invested in the oil, copper, and automobile industries. Meyer was extremely successful; financier and industrial magnate J. P. Morgan once advised a partner, "Watch out for this fellow Meyer, because if you don't, he'll end up having all the money on Wall Street." In 1910 he married Agnes Elizabeth Ernst, a twenty-three-year-old New Yorker, in a Lutheran ceremony; by this time he had dropped his Jewish faith.

Meyer's wife, Agnes Elizabeth Meyer, who occasionally wrote articles for the Washington Post

The couple had five children: Eugene III, Florence, Elizabeth, Katharine, and Ruth. Meyer later organized the Allied Chemical and Dye Corporation. He gave up a chance to become one of the two largest stockholders in General Motors, but he made money with the Fisher Auto Body Company. By the time he was forty, he had a fortune of $50 to $60 million.

Meyer believed that a person who is successful should help others: "I always had a theory that men who achieved a competence and reasonable success in business owed a period of public service." Because of color blindness, he was unable to join the armed services, so in 1917, during the Wilson administration, he moved his family to Washington in order to serve with the Council of National Defense and the War Industries Board. He began his public service career as a dollar-a-year adviser to the army in the purchase of shoes and cotton duck. A Republican, he also served under Presidents Harding, Coolidge, Hoover, Roosevelt, Truman, and Eisenhower.

"If you want to get ahead in politics, keep out until you have made your pile," he told associates. "That's what I did. Once you have money, everything opens to you." His responsibilities increased: he joined Bernard Baruch's War Industries Board

and directed the War Finance Corporation and the Federal Farm Loan Board. He was appointed the first chairman of the Reconstruction Finance Corporation and governor of the Federal Reserve Board.

While the Meyers lived in Washington, they entertained and were entertained by the highest echelons of society. However, near the end of the Hoover administration he was accused by the radical radio commentator Father Charles E. Coughlin of being one of the financial Four Horsemen of the Apocalypse, along with J. P. Morgan, Andrew Mellon, and Ogden Mills. Following Roosevelt's election, Sen. Huey Long called Meyer "an ordinary tinpot bucketshop operator up on Wall Street—not even a legitimate banker." Meyer worked with the Roosevelt administration for only two months because he "didn't believe in monetary manipulation as a method of recovery."

After retiring from sixteen years of government service at age fifty-seven, Meyer spent two weeks recovering from exhaustion and mental fatigue at Mt. Kisco, his farm in Westchester County, New York. There he began to annoy his wife, and one morning after finding dust on a bannister he reprimanded her, "This house is not run properly." Agnes Meyer responded, "You'd better

The auctioning of the Washington Post *on 1 June 1933. Meyer, acting through his attorney, bought the paper for $825,000 (Arthur Ellis,* Washington Post*).*

go buy the *Washington Post.*" In 1929 he had secretly offered *Post* publisher Ned McLean $5 million in cash for the paper, but McLean had refused to sell. In the early 1930s the *Post* foundered and McLean was forced out. By 1933 the *Post,* with a circulation of only 52,000, could print only fourteen pages a day. It went into receivership when it could not pay its newsprint bills to the International Paper Company.

On 1 June 1933, the *Post* went on the auction block. The bidding began at $250,000. Such notables as Alice Roosevelt Longworth, Victor Kaffman of the *Washington Star,* Eleanor (Cissy) Patterson of the *Herald,* and David Lawrence of *U.S. News* watched the proceedings. The publisher's estranged wife, Evalyn Walsh McLean, who wore the Hope diamond, bid $600,000 for the paper through her attorney. Ned McLean was in a Montreal hospital suffering from an "unsound mind because of excessive use of alcohol." The bidding closed at $825,000. George E. Hamilton, Jr., an attorney, had purchased the *Post* for an "undisclosed principal." Meyer had authorized him to go up to $2 million. Other Washington newspapers speculated as to who the new owner might be, and several days later the *Star* printed a statement from Meyer to the Associated Press in New York denying

that he was the purchaser. At the end of a ten-day period the court declared the sale legal and final, and on 13 June, the *Post* ran a two-column headline: "Eugene Meyer Announced As Washington Post Buyer."

Meyer knew little about newspapers, but he established four rules early on:

A newspaper must serve as the conscience of its community.

The opinions of the *Washington Post* must appear on its editorial page, not in its news columns.

The primary interest of a newspaper must be the welfare of the immediate community which supports it.

The *Washington Post* is a public institution. Its duty is to its readers, and not to the private interests of its owners.

Meyer, a lifelong Republican, wanted readers to know that "I acted entirely on my own behalf, without suggestion or discussion with any person, group, or organization." Previously the *Post* had been a Republican newspaper, but Meyer wanted it to be independent politically. Executives of the new Washington Post Company included Meyer as president, his wife as vice-president, and Floyd R. Harrison, a longtime friend and associate, as secretary-treasurer.

For his investment, Meyer had purchased little more than membership in the Associated Press. The *Post*'s main claim to fame was a march in its honor written by John Philip Sousa.

Although Meyer made many mistakes the first two years, he worked hard to create a vigorous, independent newspaper with a national reputation. He intended to do this by building a dynamic editorial page and a bureau that would cover all branches of government. Meyer gave his staff the freedom to do their jobs well. Although he offered suggestions, he avoided interfering in day-to-day activities. He set the standards, and his staff produced a stimulating newspaper. Felix Morley, a Rhodes scholar and former editorial writer and foreign correspondent for the *Baltimore Sun,* became Meyer's first editorial page editor, and in 1936 he won the *Post*'s first Pulitzer Prize for editorial writing. The paper's editorial writers had to be gatherers of news as well as writers of opinion pieces; Morley insisted that they spend more time on Capitol Hill than in their offices. The paper filled its editorial pages with the most prominent columnists of the day: Walter Lippmann, Sumner Welles, Marquis Childs, and Paul Winker. Critics claimed the newspaper printed too many syndicated columns. At the time of his entry into the newspaper world, Meyer faced competition in Washington from three major papers: the *Herald,* the *Star,* and the *Daily News.* But other papers across the country began reprinting *Post* editorials, and this helped the *Post* to become a national newspaper. *Post* stories were frequently reprinted in the *Congressional Record,* and the newspaper had the highest readership in Congress among Washington daily newspapers.

Alexander F. (Casey) Jones from Minneapolis was hired to direct the news staff in 1935 and maintained a balance between items of general interest and stories for intellectual readers. *Fortune* magazine described Jones as "cyclonic, convivial, incurably romantic about his profession." He liked sensational, flashy news stories and told reporters to "write what the man said" and leave interpretative writing to another part of the paper.

During the early years Meyer checked nightly at 9:30, either in person or by phone, to see what would be in the next day's paper. He also began publishing the results of polls conducted by George Gallup's American Institute of Public Opinion. The

Post displayed the weekly polls in the "Outlook" section of the paper along with the editorials and columns.

In 1935 the *Post* helped make the name of Alfred M. Langdon of Kansas known in his bid for president against Franklin D. Roosevelt. Yet the paper did not endorse him because citizens in Washington could not vote. As Meyer said, "The major part of our constituency does not vote." When FDR did win the election, the *Post*'s public relations man, Charles F. Moore, Jr., promoted a homecoming with headlines screaming, "Let's Give the President a Real Welcome." Roosevelt received "the biggest, noisiest and most enthusiastic welcome the capital ever gave a President" with more than 200,000 people lining the streets to cheer him.

In the late 1930s Morley and Meyer had opposite beliefs about the war in Europe. A pacifist and a Quaker, Morley opposed American participation and said, "We should maintain neutrality in order to use our impartial influence in favor of a constructive peace." Meyer believed that the United States would be involved in the war, and Morley resigned to become president of Haverford College in Pennsylvania. Meyer then hired Herbert Ellison, an editor and columnist with the *Christian Science Monitor,* to head the editorial page and named himself editor.

Ellison wrote about fiscal matters, exposing waste and extravagance in the government. While the *Post* supported the idea of Social Security, it found other projects undesirable. The paper continually criticized the Works Progress Administration and its director, Harry Hopkins. Editorial writer Raymond Clapper wrote: "The dominating fact in Washington is the complete supremacy for President Roosevelt. . . . It comes close to being a dictatorship, though one which does not in any sense rest upon force or terrorism or suppression as is the case with European dictators. If what we have is a near dictatorship it rests upon the common consent of the American people." When Clapper resigned to become a columnist for Scripps-Howard papers, he wrote a tribute to Meyer which included the comment: "He has never sought to influence the writer's interpretation, or to see the copy before it appeared in print the next morning. If he had seen this before it got into the paper, he might have broken his rule and killed it."

In 1937 the *Post* fought against Roosevelt's attempt to "stack" the Supreme Court by expanding it, without waiting for retirements or deaths of the justices. FDR claimed the court members were behind in their cases because of their age. A *Post*

Meyer wearing pressman's hat, starting the presses for the merged Washington Post *and* Times-Herald *on 17 March 1954*
(Charles Del Vecchio, the Washington Post*)*

reporter—after saying it was against precedent to interview a justice and being told by Meyer that he himself would do it—began an investigation, and his articles revealed the problem was not the age or health of the justices, but with district and circuit court personnel.

By 1938 *Post* circulation had doubled from 50,000 to 100,000. For ten years Meyer put more than $1 million a year into the *Post*, and in 1943 it finally made a profit—$13,732 from "open presentation" ads. Meyer had suggested that the newspaper run these ads as a way of telling both the government and the public of a company's wartime accomplishments and difficulties. These ads, now called public service ads, were tax deductible for the advertisers. The *Post* received revenue for the ads, many of which were full page, and the profits grew.

In the 1920s Oswald Garrison Villard, the editor and journalism critic, had examined newspapers in Washington and found "a capital without a Thunderer." Newspapers at that time were "timid" and "provincial" and inadequate in presenting the news. Those who wanted to keep up with current events bought papers from New York, Baltimore, or Philadelphia. Twenty years later Vil-

lard returned to Washington and found the situation vastly improved. The *Washington Post* had "earned the respect of the newspapermen . . . and made notable contributions to the national welfare." By this time the *Post*'s influence had grown so that it was required reading in the White House.

Although Mrs. Meyer had little to do with the daily activities of the *Post*, she occasionally wrote an article or a series of articles for the paper. *Journey through Chaos* (1944), a collection of her articles published in the *Post* in 1943 and 1944, depicts the effect of World War II on men, women, and children in American war centers.

In 1946, Meyer retired as publisher of the *Post*, turning the job over to his son-in-law, Philip Graham, the husband of his daughter Katharine; Meyer remained as board chairman. He also gave half a million dollars of *Post* stock to 711 veteran employees. In addition, Meyer had given the paper three ingredients of success: integrity, decency, and idealism. In 1950, on his seventy-fifth birthday, staff members gave "Butch" Meyer, as they affectionately called him, a plaque inscribed "Newspaperman of Conscience."

By 1954 circulation was 200,000, and Meyer purchased the rival *Times-Herald* from Col. Robert R. McCormick for $8.5 million. Meyer combined the *Times-Herald* with the *Post* to create a morning newspaper monopoly.

Except for six months in 1946 when Meyer headed the World Bank, he served the *Post* as editor, publisher, or chairman of the board from 1933 until his death in 1959. He spent a great deal of time outside the corporate offices, once even questioning taxi drivers about their reading habits. Occasionally he reported on events in the capital. He liked to tell staffers he was a publisher who became a reporter. He received honorary doctorate degrees from Yale University in 1932, Syracuse University in 1934, the University of California in 1942, and Georgetown University in 1958. He died in George Washington Hospital, Washington, D.C., at the age of eighty-three.

Meyer started the *Post* on its way to greatness and power. Philip Graham committed suicide in 1963; today Katharine Meyer Graham and her son Donald carry on Meyer's legacy.

References:

Agnes Elizabeth Meyer, *Out of these Roots: The Autobiography of an American Woman* (Boston: Little, Brown, 1953);

"The Rise of the Washington Post," *Fortune*, 30 (December 1944): 132-138, 258, 261-262;

Chalmers M. Roberts, *The Washington Post* (Boston: Houghton Mifflin, 1977);

Kenneth Stewart and John Tebbel, *Makers of Modern Journalism* (New York: Prentice-Hall, 1952), pp. 450-455;

"They Called Him 'Butch,' " *Newsweek*, 54 (27 July 1959): 53;

Oswald Garrison Villard, *The Disappearing Daily* (New York: Knopf, 1944), pp. 186-192;

Villard, *Some Newspapers and Newspaper-Men* (New York: Knopf, 1923), pp. 184-188;

Carol Williams and Orwin Touster, *The Washington Post* (Englewood Cliffs, N.J.: Prentice-Hall, 1976).

Webb Miller
(10 February 1892-7 May 1940)

Harry H. Griggs
University of Florida

MAJOR POSITIONS HELD: Reporter, war correspondent, foreign correspondent, United Press (1916-1940); general European manager, United Press (1938-1940).

BOOK: *I Found No Peace: The Journal of a Foreign Correspondent* (New York: Simon & Schuster, 1936; London: Gollancz, 1937).

OTHER: "The Little World War in Spain," in *We Cover the World*, edited by Eugene Lyons (New York: Harcourt, 1937), pp. 413-441.

PERIODICAL PUBLICATION: "Bluebeard of Paris," *Reader's Digest*, 30 (February 1937): 91-94.

Webb Miller worked for the United Press news service for nearly a quarter of a century—most notably as a foreign correspondent. He covered wars and great world social changes from the punitive expedition against Pancho Villa to the early months of World War II. He was the first correspondent to report the actual beginning of the 1935 Italian campaign in Ethiopia. He believed in firsthand reporting wherever there was action, and he was nominated three times for the Pulitzer Prize in journalism.

Webster Miller was born 10 February 1892 on a run-down tenant farm outside Pokagon, five miles from Dowagiac, in the southwest corner of Michigan. He was the oldest of the five surviving children of Jacob H. and Charlotte Alexander Miller. His family lived on different farms in that general area as he was growing up, and he yearned for a way of life that would provide more excitement than farming did. He was a voracious reader, recalling later that for many years he averaged more than one book a day. Since his home was five miles from the library and his school, he often read and studied his lessons while making these walks back and forth.

As a boy he sometimes wandered alone in the woods, watching birds and animals. He did not hunt because the sight of blood made him physically ill. He was greatly influenced by Henry David Thoreau's *Walden*, usually keeping a copy by his bedside throughout his life. He used it as an antidote against what he saw and felt during his years of reporting. He had no religious training because both his father and grandfather were agnostics.

Hard farm work toughened the growing Miller and in a way conditioned him for the rigorous physical demands he often met in his later life as a foreign correspondent. In high school he ran the quarter-mile on the track team and was a back on the football team.

Miller's dream from boyhood was to become a writer, and his first writing attempts dealt with nature. Then, despite abnormal shyness and hypersensitivity, he made it his ambition to become a newspaper reporter. The pull of the activity and excitement of the outside world was strong enough to overcome his diffidence. After he finished high school he taught one year in a rural school to accumulate a stake to support himself while he looked for newspaper work in Chicago. He later admitted that except for being an above-average writer he could hardly have been worse equipped for the hurly-burly of big-city reporting.

He was hired as a cub reporter on the *Chicago American* in 1912 at twelve dollars a week. In his autobiography, *I Found No Peace* (1936), Miller relates that he began to expand his intellectual horizons after he had been in Chicago a while. He bought a set of forty volumes—*Dr. Eliot's Five-Foot Shelf of Books*—and from them he became interested in religion. For the first time he came into contact with good music and on Sundays often went to the Art Institute. He grew a mustache to make him look older, and he changed his given name from Webster to Webb because it made a better by-line. He deliberately altered his signature to a bold self-confident one and selected suits and accessories he thought were distinctive and noticeable.

He proved enterprising in covering the criminal courts, and his editor wanted to assign him to this beat permanently. Despite the security offered, and a salary increase to twenty-five dollars, he decided early in 1916 to seek new challenges as a free-lance reporter covering the Pancho Villa disturbance on the border of Mexico and the United States. In his autobiography Miller says, "The regular staff correspondents who flocked in from all over the country were busily occupied with the main

story; they had no time to develop feature angles. I picked out human interest stories susceptible of development, covered them, and sold the resulting stories outright to the staff correspondents, who were glad to get them and paid liberally." His longtime association with United Press began when E. T. Conkle, in charge of the United Press staff on the border, offered Miller a regular job covering the base of the Punitive Expedition. He accepted eagerly.

Miller formed the ambition to become a foreign correspondent when he took the train to Mexico City and followed up on his border coverage. During the remainder of his life he was to cover assignments in more than thirty countries and report on practically every war and squabble on the globe.

Miller covered World War I both before and after the United States got into the conflict. He was in the front-line trenches at the hour of the armistice and noted that there was little excitement or joy; the front just became silent. As he raced back from the front by automobile to file his story he would lean out and yell to the troops marching forward that the war was over. He later said that

Webb Miller (right) with Raymond Clapper in New York City in 1932

bringing the soldiers the most important news they would ever hear was his biggest thrill of the war.

After the war, Miller became a foreign correspondent. He lived much of the time in London, where he met and became engaged to Mary Alston, an English girl; they were married in England in 1920 just before he was transferred to France. They became the parents of a son, Kenneth.

From 1925 to 1935 Miller was assistant European manager of United Press. During this period he continued to live in London but took frequent trips to other parts of the world. He interviewed Adolf Hitler and Benito Mussolini, visited Spain and Portugal, and spent four months in South America. In 1930 he traveled nearly 16,000 miles by air to cover M. K. Gandhi's nonviolent political rebellion, a story that caused a sensation when it appeared in newspapers throughout the world. During the trip he was in the air for fifteen days and visited sixteen different countries in Europe, Africa, and Asia.

Miller's best-known reportorial coup probably was his early coverage of the 1935 Italian campaign in Ethiopia. He observed the Italian army massed for invasion, and he saw the elaborate war preparations being made. Using a mixture of cablese, journalistic jargon, and other obfuscatory devices, he managed to slip a dispatch of some 2,000 words past the censor. His United Press editors fully grasped the situation and were able to get his story out to client newspapers eighteen hours before the war actually started.

He watched the war begin at five o'clock in the morning as Italian troops waded across the Belesa River. He had been an eyewitness to the start of a war, an experience he believed at that time to be unique in the history of journalism. He then wrote a story that reached the outside world forty-four minutes before any other dispatch about the beginning of the war. He later explained that his "scoop" resulted from his technical knowledge of the operation of the lines of communication to Europe, which he had studied closely for many years.

Motorized travel was impossible through the mountains and Miller was unable to obtain a mule, so he set out on foot to follow the action. On painful, blistered feet he marched with the Italian troops, often near the point of exhaustion. To get his story out to the world he rode mules and trucks to Asmara. There he wrote the first complete account of the beginning of the Italian campaign against Ethiopia. He followed the action until physical privation and the high altitude completely exhausted him.

During the summer of 1936 Miller took a leave of absence, living alone on a farm in northern Connecticut, where he had an idyllic interlude of peace. The serene valleys and wooded foothills seemed a special contrast to the extremely active, sometimes dangerous, and always pressured life he had led as a wire service reporter and executive. During that summer he wrote his autobiography, *I Found No Peace*, in which he said that the most important thing he had learned professionally was that the truth about anything is difficult to obtain; that the more he studied the various aspects of any particular subject the more qualified and less clear-cut his opinions became:

> Even when I witnessed an event myself I saw it differently from others. When I questioned eyewitnesses, persons who had no reason to distort the truth, each told a somewhat different story. I had to strike an average of their stories and temper this with my judgment of the circumstances and interests involved to come somewhere near the truth. I found that even when people with the best will in the world tried to tell the truth and nothing but the truth they could not do it. Each one saw something different. Every man's imagination unwittingly distorted what his eyes saw.
>
> When the persons involved had a direct interest in distorting, magnifying, or concealing facts, as happens in a large proportion of the daily news, the task of arriving somewhere near the truth was greatly increased.

Miller said that he had come to understand the "overwhelming obscenity and futility" of war only when he returned to the World War I battlefields eight years after the armistice. He concluded that the eight and one-half million men who lost their lives had died in vain. When Italy invaded Ethiopia, he did not condone the deliberate aggression, but at the same time he considered this particular land grab no worse than earlier ones by which European nations gobbled up almost the entire continent of Africa: "Although the invasion was doubtless morally indefensible, I felt after I came to know more about actual conditions that perhaps domination of the country by the white man was less reprehensible than it at first seemed. . . . I concluded that the mass of people would undoubtedly be no worse off and probably much better off under white rulers and that the world in general would be likely to benefit, politically and economically, from the modern development of the country." Miller added that although he detested authoritarian or regimented forms of government, he had concluded that economic activity would have to come more and more under governmental control.

Reviewers noted the vividness of Miller's writing—"all his scenes stand out clear and cameo-like"—as well as his "rare economy in the use of language," saying that the book was "written as though it all had to be sent by cable at a dollar a word."

As soon as he completed his manuscript Miller sailed to Spain to report the agony and terror of the Spanish Civil War. Once again he went into danger to get firsthand information about what was happening. He wrote a description of the survivors of the Alcazar in Toledo who had lived through a weeks-long siege only by killing and eating several horses and mules. He reported the evidence of foreign intervention and interviewed survivors of bombardment from the air. His description of what he saw in Spain was a graphic warning of what was to come on a much larger scale in Europe and the world. He described how the 70,000 persons in the beleaguered city of Oviedo slowly starved. He wrote of how rifles cracked continually while people going about their affairs hugged the sides of buildings to avoid bullets. Especially poignant was his description of what war had done to the children. Some, still wearing bandages covering wounds, played in the safer streets. He described two little girls near his hotel who played a game of shooting one another with fingers imitating revolvers, merrily shouting, "Ping, ping." Another game was called "bombing." A boy lay on the ground while his companion held a half-brick above, then dropped it; the excitement lay in rolling over before the brickbat hit him.

Most of the events Miller covered tended to be serious, and his writing reflected this seriousness. Yet he could find humor in relatively grim situations. For instance, when he was reporting the war in Spain he had to dive into a ditch along with soldiers and other newsmen when a group of warplanes came flying in their direction. The officer in charge yelled at him to keep still lest his movements give the position away. He yelled back, "Damn it, I'm lying in thistles and can't keep still." On another occasion he was sleeping when the warning of bombers came. By the time he reached the stone arch of a ruined bridge where others were taking shelter, this spot of relative safety was quite crowded and he could get only his head and shoulders under the masonry. He admitted later that his protruding parts felt remarkably large and exposed.

"I came out of Spain badly shaken by the atmosphere of blood, tears and terror and profoundly discouraged about the future of Europe," Miller wrote in 1937. "What I saw and heard of the wide development of the use of terrorism as a definite weapon in warfare was sickening. In merciless ferocity on both sides it resembled in some ways ancient religious wars in which it was an act of piety for a Christian to kill an infidel or vice-versa. Never in modern times has there been such a holocaust of cold-blooded slaughter of prisoners, of wounded and of helpless hostages in thousands. Terrorism of civilian populations by indiscriminate bombing has largely wiped out the distinctions between combatants and non-combatants. Among the dead and wounded on both sides were many thousands of women and children." In a speech before the American Society of Newspaper Editors in April 1937, Miller predicted that the Spanish war would end eventually through exhaustion and collapse of morale of one side or the other rather than by victory of arms. He expressed doubt that compromise or negotiation could end the conflict. Of six wars he had seen up to that time he declared that none, not even the First World War, was so ghastly.

After he returned to London from Spain, Miller had a brief respite from war. He witnessed and reported on three major events that swayed the throne of England—the abdication of King Edward VIII, the coronation of George VI, and the wedding of the Duke of Windsor to a divorced American woman. In 1938 he was appointed general European manager of United Press.

The following year Miller watched the Nazi takeover of Czechoslovakia and was a correspondent with the British army in France. He also reported from the bitterly cold front of the Russo-Finnish War. As general European manager he was partly responsible for developing the channels which made it possible for United Press to scoop other news services by some three hours in reporting the German blitzkrieg into the Low Countries.

Miller has been described as "well-muscled." This would not be unusual for a farm boy who played football. Undoubtedly his physical stamina was important in many instances when he had to undergo extreme rigors to cover a story. The "crow's feet" around his eyes revealed the hours he spent squinting in the sun all around the globe. In his mature years he wore a thin mustache, and his hairline was beginning to recede. He was a smart dresser and looked jaunty even when dressed in the uniform of a war correspondent.

On 7 May 1940, Miller covered Prime Minister Neville Chamberlain's struggle before a heckling House of Commons—the Parliamentary showdown that was to take Chamberlain out of power and put Winston Churchill in—and left by train after dark for his suburban home. He planned to get a night's rest before returning to cover the next day's House of Commons session. Miller's body was found the next morning some ten yards from Clapham Junction station, at which the train had stopped. The coroner ruled Miller's death an accident, saying the newsman probably held the door of his coach open for some reason and was pitched out onto the track by the train's gathering speed as it drew out of the station. London was under blackout, and no one saw the accident. He died instantly of a fractured skull. His ashes were buried at the family plot in Dewey Cemetery south of Dowagiac, Michigan.

Shortly before his death Miller had sent his wife and eighteen-year-old son to the United States to select a university for the young man to attend. In his will Miller made his wife the beneficiary of his estate.

During World War II a series of Liberty ships bore the names of war correspondents who lost their lives. First in the series was the *Webb Miller*, launched on 5 December 1943 in South Portland, Maine. The ship was cosponsored by Miller's wife and son, who at that time was a private first class in the army. When she received an engraved silver plate during the ceremony, Mrs. Miller said, "If that ship brings home the bacon as well as Webb did, it will have to break all records."

In the end it was not the discomfort and privations such as going without food and rest or the pressure of delivering the news first that corroded Miller's spirit; it was the pain of observing the horrors people inflicted on other people. He could see clearly the price many individuals were paying, but he could not perceive any benefit to humanity for the price paid. His experiences in Spain and elsewhere in Europe on the eve of World War II were behind his cry of despair: "Poor Spain, poor Europe—yes, poor Human Race!"

References:

"Death of a Correspondent," *Time*, 35 (20 May 1940): 61-62;

"Faces of the Month," *Fortune*, 18 (July 1938): 18;

"Webb Miller, 1892-1940," *Newsweek*, 15 (20 May 1940): 54-55.

Edgar Ansel Mowrer

(8 March 1892-2 March 1977)

Maurice R. Cullen, Jr.
Michigan State University

MAJOR POSITIONS HELD: War correspondent, Rome correspondent, chief of Berlin bureau, chief of Paris bureau, Washington correspondent, *Chicago Daily News* (1914-1941); syndicated columnist, *New York Post* (1943-1969).

BOOKS: *Immortal Italy* (New York & London: Appleton, 1922);

This American World (New York: Morrow, 1928; London: Faber & Gwyer, 1928);

Sinon: Or the Future of Politics (London: Kegan Paul, Trench, Trubner, 1930);

Germany Puts the Clock Back (New York: Morrow, 1933; revised, Harmondsworth, U.K.: Penguin, 1937; revised, 1938; revised, 1939; revised, New York: Morrow, 1939);

The Dragon Wakes: A Report from China (New York: Morrow, 1939); republished as *Mowrer in China* (Harmondsworth, U.K.: Penguin, 1939);

Global War: An Atlas of World Strategy, by Mowrer and Marthe Rajchman (New York: Morrow, 1942; London: Faber & Faber, 1943);

Our State Department and North Africa (Chicago: Union for Democratic Action, 1943);

The Nightmare of American Foreign Policy (New York: Knopf, 1948; London: Gollancz, 1949);

Challenge and Decision: A Program for the Times of Crisis Ahead, for World Peace Under American Leadership (New York: McGraw-Hill, 1950);

A Good Time to Be Alive (New York: Duell, Sloan & Pearce, 1959);

An End to Make-Believe (New York: Duell, Sloan & Pearce, 1961);

Triumph and Turmoil: A Personal History of Our Time (New York: Weybright & Talley, 1968; London: Allen & Unwin, 1970);

Umano and the Price of Lasting Peace, by Mowrer and Lilian T. Mowrer (New York: Philosophical Library, 1973).

PERIODICAL PUBLICATIONS: "Fascisti and Italy's Economic Recovery," *Forum,* 69 (February 1923): 1198-1206);

"Rule of the Fascisti," *Forum,* 69 (March 1923): 1299-1307;

"Treason in the German Republic," *Nation,* 120 (11 March 1925): 259-260;

"Our Imaginary Isolation," *Forum,* 75 (February 1926): 186-195;

"How the Dawes Plan Works," *Harper's,* 153 (October 1926): 592-599;

"Germany Comes Back," *Harper's,* 155 (July 1927): 203-209;

"Germany after Ten Years," *Harper's,* 158 (December 1928): 61-69;

"Unseating Kultur," *Survey,* 61 (1 February 1929): 589-590, 629-631;

"Swiss Rearmament," *Foreign Affairs,* 14 (July 1936): 618-626;

"France of Leon Blum," *Survey Graphic,* 25 (November 1936): 612-615, 635;

"Minorities of Opinion," *Survey Graphic,* 28 (February 1939): 83-84);

"Education of a Democrat," *Nation,* 152 (8 March 1941): 272-273;

"Informing the Citizen in a World at War," *Publishers' Weekly,* 142 (4 July 1942): 21-26;

"Dumbarton Hopes," *Survey Graphic,* 34 (January 1945): 5;

"Genial Blackmail," *Time,* 45 (22 January 1945): 32-33;

"Finer World by Partnership Capital," *Saturday Review of Literature,* 31 (18 December 1948): 14;

"The Only Way to Handle Russia," *Coronet,* 25 (February 1949): 72-76;

"Human Destiny Is Paging Truman," *Coronet,* 25 (April 1949): 37-41;

"Reports," *Fortune,* 39 (June 1949): 63-64;

"Why Advertise God's Country?," *Saturday Review of Literature,* 33 (21 October 1950): 8-10, 36-39;

"Who Is with Uncle Sam?," *Reader's Digest,* 58 (February 1951): 120-125;

"Our Lives, Our Fortunes and Our Sacred Honor,"

Reader's Digest, 58 (March 1951): 120-124;

"What Asia Wants," *Harper's,* 203 (October 1951): 67-72;

"Good Time to Be Alive," *Saturday Review of Literature,* 34 (22 December 1951): 6-8;

"Saviors of a Decaying Profession," *Saturday Review,* 35 (14 June 1952): 13;

"Third Man," *Saturday Review,* 35 (5 July 1952);

"Italy in the Red: A Lesson in Foreign Aid," *Reader's Digest,* 62 (March 1953): 98-108;

"If Not Containment, What?," *Saturday Review,* 36 (18 April 1953): 16;

"Our Three-Story Heritage," *Saturday Review,* 36 (1 August 1953): 9-10, 40-41;

"City Hall Politics in Italy," *Atlantic,* 192 (December 1953): 59-61;

"France Needs a New Revolution," *Collier's,* 133 (22 January 1954): 19-23;

"New Frontier for Freedom," *Collier's,* 133 (25 June 1954): 34-40;

"The Reds Hold Five Big Cards, but We Can Trump Them," *Collier's,* 134 (29 October 1954): 50-51;

"Braver and Newer," *Saturday Review,* 38 (8 January 1955): 22;

"Return to Integrity," *Saturday Review,* 38 (5 February 1955): 7-8, 38-41;

"Recreation for What?," *Recreation,* 48 (December 1955): 466-468;

"Berliner Biographies," *Saturday Review,* 39 (13 October 1956): 11-12;

"Sawdust, Seaweed and Synthetics," *Saturday Review,* 39 (8 December 1956): 11-13, 54-56;

"How Many People Are Too Many?," *Science Digest,* 41 (March 1957): 57-62;

"Four Men's Stories," *Saturday Review,* 40 (13 April 1957): 19;

"Open Universe," *Saturday Review,* 41 (19 April 1958): 11-13;

"New Concepts of an Old Enemy," *Saturday Review,* 42 (30 May 1959): 16-17;

"Brinkmanship Is Necessary," *National Review,* 14 (26 March 1963): 229-231;

"The Fifth Europe," *Horizon,* 5 (March 1963): 4-9;

"Will to Survive?," *National Review,* 16 (21 April 1964): 321-323;

"Analysis of Appeasement," *National Review,* 19 (10 January 1967): 40-41;

"The Power of Arrogance," *National Review,* 19 (4 April 1967): 367-368.

Edgar Ansel Mowrer was born on 8 March 1892 in Bloomington, Illinois, to Rufus and Nell Scott Mowrer. He was the younger brother of Paul

Scott Mowrer, the first Pulitzer Prize winner for foreign correspondence. As Edgar recalled the relationship, "Until I was about ten, the most influential person in my life was unquestionably my brother Paul. He embodied all that seemed most desirable." The younger Mowrer had such regard for his brother that he, too, became a prizewinning foreign correspondent. Despite the four years and eight months that separated them, Paul Mowrer occasionally permitted Edgar to join in with the older boys for rough-and-tumble games of cowboys and Indians, with Edgar, long blond curls draped over his shoulders, playing a Texas steer. That role required allowing himself to be "lassoed and thrown to the ground while running at full gallop." "Yet," Edgar later recalled, "I so relished the society of the bigger boys that I willingly accepted the bumps and bruises."

In the fall of 1898, the family moved to Chicago's South Side. Rufus Mowrer saw to it that his sons learned to cope with the hazards of life, both in the city and the wooded backcountry of Michigan, where they spent their summers. When their mother once protested that a particular venture might be too risky, the father responded firmly: "Nell, if a boy has not learned to look out for himself by the time he is ten, he never will."

At Hyde Park High School Edgar excelled in literature, languages, and mathematics. When he was sixteen girls "exploded" into Mowrer's life. He fancied one in particular, a girl named Ruth who appeared "interested" in him, although she also looked kindly upon a certain member of the football team. Mowrer took up athletics on the spot. Before graduation, he had lettered in football, tennis, and golf. "Thereafter, I regularly appeared in classes wearing the blue and white blazer of the successful athlete," he said. He also became an accomplished boxer. Mowrer was, however, first and foremost a consummate reader, beginning before he attended a formal school. His earliest conquests included *Peterkin Paul, The Prince and the Pin Elves, The Wizard of Oz, Treasure Island,* and *Gulliver's Travels.* Under the guidance of the superior Hyde Park faculty, he excelled in literature and writing. In his senior year, he served as editor of the yearbook.

The University of Michigan turned out to be a disappointment, so he transferred to the University of Chicago in the fall of 1910. That winter Paul, then Paris correspondent for the *Chicago Daily News,* invited Edgar to visit him. In Paris he could experience true culture, sharpen his French, and take courses at the Sorbonne. Edgar arrived in France in mid-January 1911. In Paris he pursued the schol-

Edgar Ansel Mowrer (Wide World Photos)

arly life and became acquainted with the city and her people. Captivated by it all, he worked feverishly. Paul noted that in "the intervals of attending lectures at the Sorbonne, he read, and his mind was as ravenous as his stomach. He read everything within reach, swiftly and with enthusiasm."

When his Paris study had ended, Edgar headed for Liverpool and the train that would carry him on the first leg of his trip home. He took a seat in the crowded car. The train lurched forward, and a suitcase slipped from the baggage rack above the head of a pretty young woman. With uncanny timing, Mowrer leaped from the opposite end of the carriage and caught the valise, saving the woman from injury. The two chatted about themselves and other topics, each delighted with the charm and intelligence of the other. Upon parting, Mowrer held her hands in his. "Well good-bye," he said sadly. "You are the first Englishwoman I've met who didn't act like a clam." "And you," she smiled, "are the first American I've met who didn't tell me his golf score. . . ." The young woman was Lilian

Thomson. Five years later she and Mowrer would marry.

Mowrer decided to go back to the University of Michigan, from which he received the B.A. degree in 1913. He then returned to Paris to continue his pursuit of the arts. With the onslaught of World War I in September 1914, Paul Scott Mowrer had to go to the front to cover the action firsthand, and someone was needed to run the *Daily News* bureau. After considering various options, Paul searched Edgar out and demanded that he take charge of the Paris office as head correspondent; nobody else on the staff could write effectively in English. "I'll teach you the rudiments of newspaper work before I leave," Paul said. He added that the salary was twenty-five dollars a week, a veritable fortune to Edgar, who liked the challenge even more than the money.

Edgar threw himself into the vital tasks that required attention while Paul raced to Belgium to cover developments there. The younger Mowrer outdid himself. Though a rank beginner, even his earliest dispatches to America caught the reality of the war. Paul said that the "dispatches my brother Edgar had composed . . . astonished our editors." His artistic younger brother, Paul said, "took to journalism like a squirrel to a tree."

Upon Paul's return from the front, Edgar went to see the war for himself. Carrying a bogus Belgian passport and dressed in a tattered raincoat and Belgian army hat, he entered Ypres. He had no official pass to enter combat areas and, if discovered, could be sent back or arrested as a spy. To offset such possibilities, he tried "the old pipe trick" he had picked up along the way: as he neared a checkpoint he would stop short of the sentry and casually fumble with a pipe and matches, smiling and waving to the sentry as he puffed smoke. Presumably, one so casual in a combat zone had to be a soldier! It worked for a time, but Mowrer eventually ran out of luck at Ypres and landed in a Belgian jail as a spy. Hours later German gunners zeroed in and began shelling the jail. British soldiers hauled Mowrer free, carried him to the rear, relieved him of the phony passport, and shipped him to England. There he talked his way out of further difficulty and eventually returned to Paris, battered but better for his experiences. His courageous efforts had not gone unnoticed: Paul offered him his choice of Rome or Vienna as chief correspondent for the *Daily News*. The paper would double his salary, which would make him a man of means. Mowrer chose Rome. He and Lilian were married in London on 8 February 1916 and left immediately for Rome.

While many public figures in Italy were demanding that the nation stay neutral, others called for intervention on the side of the Allies. In his dispatches to the *Daily News,* Mowrer decried the practice of a nation going to war to justify its claim to be a "great power." Italy finally entered the war on the Allied side. As he had in Belgium, Mowrer witnessed combat up close at the disastrous battle at Caporetto and the attendant rout of Italian forces by disciplined Austrian troops. He wrote of dispirited civilians and soldiers shuffling through a small town, some of them carrying loot from stores and private homes, others drunk on the supplies of pillaged wineshops. The sight of officers was "rare, and their men were taking orders from no one. A few sang antiwar songs and others popular tunes. Others talked in small groups of twos and threes, chiefly about peace. . . ." Mowrer added with disgust, "There were enough Italian soldiers on that road to have repulsed a division had they kept their arms. But they thought only of flight."

Mowrer got to know Benito Mussolini in 1915. He recognized Mussolini's personal courage and superb oratorical skills. At the same time, Mowrer noted that Mussolini admired the "Superman" ideal popular among some European leaders of the time. Mowrer came to regard the future dictator with distaste mixed with alarm. In time Mowrer's views were borne out as young Italian Fascists rioted in the streets under the protection of the authorities. Ultimately Italian public opinion swung to support them and, in Mowrer's words, "they moved to conquer the country."

Mowrer soon fell victim to the Spanish influenza epidemic that had been ravaging the war's survivors. Hospitals filled beyond intended capacities with the patients consigned to mattresses on corridor floors. Understaffed personnel with too few medical supplies attempted to stave off the suffering. Mowrer's illness turned into pneumonia, at which point he became "delirious in three languages." He recovered, then came down with empyema. Mowrer lingered on the brink of death, then rallied after major surgery. He regained his health after a lengthy recuperation.

In early January 1924, shortly after the birth of their daughter, Diana Jane, the Mowrers took up residence in Berlin, where Mowrer had been appointed chief of the Berlin bureau for the *Daily News*. Mowrer had long sympathized with the German people and their struggle to renew their country, given the restrictions of Versailles. But once he was able to assess firsthand the political and social currents active there, his notions began to change.

He learned that popular opinion was equally divided for and against the Weimar Republic. The major difference was that supporters tended to be workers and other ordinary citizens while opponents consisted of powerful individuals such as professionals, business leaders, diplomats, and influential civil servants. For nine years Mowrer wrote about the major changes within Germany, noting the growth of powerful groups which vied for dominance of the German people. His book *Germany Puts the Clock Back,* published in December 1932 but dated 1933, traced the disintegration of the Weimar Republic by conservative forces. Lilian read the manuscript and commented that "it was like peeping behind the curtain where a monstrous drama was being acted." A month after the book was published, Adolf Hitler became chancellor; he ordered it banned in Germany.

In early 1933, Mowrer was elected president of the prestigious Foreign Press Association. At that point the German government began to apply pressures on the foreign news corps within the Third Reich. Offensive foreign correspondents were banned from the country. Veiled threats of personal violence against individual correspondents became commonplace, particularly against Mowrer. A natural scrapper, Mowrer stood up to the Nazi leadership, who suggested that he leave the country while he was still able to do so. Mowrer's 1933 Pulitzer Prize for the best correspondence from abroad brought a sudden change in Nazi dealings with him, a cooling-off effort with platitudes and new fellowship. That posture lasted only until the Germans realized that he would not toady to their blandishments. The Nazis then resumed their threats and their suggestions that he leave the country. He refused until the authorities arrested Dr. Paul Goldman, a journalist of Jewish-Austrian birth and a close friend of Mowrer's, as a ploy to run him out. In order to secure Goldman's release, Mowrer resigned and left Germany in the summer of 1933. At a going-away party, American and British correspondents presented him with a silver bowl inscribed to "a gallant fighter for the liberty of the press."

As the first American journalist to be banished from Germany, Mowrer returned to Chicago in great demand as a public speaker. He went on tour to reveal to concerned audiences the madness then gripping Germany. He was then informed that he would replace his brother Paul as chief correspondent in Paris while the latter returned to Chicago to become editor of the *Daily News.*

The Edgar Mowrers returned to Paris to witness French fascists parading through the streets. Demonstrations and protests against the existing order had become commonplace. As Lilian Mowrer described it, "The crowds surged, defying the police who were getting more and more jittery every day. It almost seemed as though someone were organizing trouble." The City of Light had become a battleground. In England, Mowrer watched with outrage as moviegoers cheered a newsreel which depicted Nazi troops being welcomed into the Rhineland by "liberated" Germans. He felt that the world had gone mad.

Mowrer resumed his journalistic duties in Europe in time to hear Hitler demand annexation of the Sudeten Germans of Czechoslovakia. The Nazi Führer had already seized Austria on a diplomatic bluff and was ready to try again. Timid negotiators from Britain traveled not to Berlin for a showdown with the Germans but to Prague to discuss with the Czechs what more they would be willing to concede to keep the peace. Hitler switched his "bluff" diplomacy into high gear. A year previously, the U.S. ambassador to Russia, William Christian Bullitt, had approached Mowrer about becoming ambassador to Czechoslovakia, and had offered to personally present Mowrer's credentials to President Roosevelt. Mowrer had declined; now that Germany would obviously move against the Czechs, he mused about his decision with a heavy heart.

Mowrer then decided to take a personal look at Spain, then writhing in civil war between fascist elements and the monarchy. He was repelled by what he saw. Barcelona he found peaceful enough, even orderly, despite the ruins of shell-blasted churches and convents standing stark against the sky. Most private automobiles had been commandeered by "workers in overalls" who bore the insignia of revolutionary organizations. He interviewed representatives of the various factions that were hoping to seize control of the country. He also met several "rifle wenches," women soldiers brandishing military hardware. In Toledo, he and a fellow correspondent drew gunfire which pierced the backseat of their car. During the return flight to Paris, Mowrer composed a dispatch for the *Daily News* which read in part: "The rebels butcher women and intellectuals, the Republicans kill priests, fascists and monarchists. . . . The war will be fought to a bloody and bitter end, with no quarter given by either side."

After a brief sojourn in the United States, Edgar and Lilian went to the Soviet Union via Austria and Poland. He found Moscow "disappointing." Even the new buildings about the city appeared "rickety"; old Russian acquaintances seemed fear stricken. "Russia," he later wrote, "was in the grip of the most gruesome terror the world had ever seen."

In 1938 Mowrer accepted an invitation to visit China, where he sized up the Japanese-Chinese conflict. He also learned that international posturing for peace notwithstanding, "no Great Power did anything serious to save China" from the slaughter and destruction inflicted by the invading Japanese. Based on his observations and conversations there, he wrote another book, titled *The Dragon Wakes* (1939) for the American market and *Mowrer in China* for the British. The book offered a hopeful view of China ultimately becoming a united people and a world power in its own right. He noted that the danger to democracy was immediate, not in some distant future when barbarism would have either triumphed or disappeared. The answer would be more democracy. As Mowrer saw it, China was defending civilization itself.

The times grew more ominous. The Allies appeased Germany with further concessions in Czechoslovakia. Appeasement muffled the anti-Hitler element within Germany; even so, the majority of the French and British sighed with relief that they had maintained "peace with honor." So pleased were the English that they signed a "nonaggression" pact with the Nazi master as well. A Conservative member of Parliament told Mowrer: "I find the Munich settlement quite right. Ever since Versailles, we have treated Germany badly. I think we owed something to the Germans and I am glad we have paid it." Mowrer responded that if it had been up to him, he would have given Germany something "that belonged to me rather than the territory of another." "And what would you give them?," the M.P. asked. "Give them the county of Kent," Mowrer retorted. In March 1939, Hitler wolfed down the remainder of Czechoslovakia. To that Mowrer commented sardonically: "I smiled bitterly at the consternation of those Englishmen who had believed that they had really purchased peace in their time at the modest price of Czechoslovakia's independence."

In 1939, Italy joined Germany in a "Pact of Steel" to split the spoils of conquest. Mowrer wrote that the League of Nations' new home, the "Palace of Nations," had already "become haunted by the ghosts of braver men" who had struggled for permanent peace in the world.

The Second World War erupted along the German-Polish border on 1 September 1939,

blitzkrieg versus horse cavalry. While their ally bled, Britain and France fidgeted. In Paris, Mowrer chafed at Allied inaction, which seemed to border on cowardice. Journalists were barred from all combat zones, but Mowrer and three others ignored the order and set out in an automobile "to find the war." They got through most checkpoints by displaying their American passports; when turned back at others, they selected seldom-used side roads and pressed on. Upon reaching the Saar River, they left the car and walked over a bridge into Germany—unchallenged. Mowrer wrote of this: "It was uncanny. Were there no French troops between us and the German lines? . . . How could one win a war by doing nothing?" In such fashion Mowrer and his fellow reporters filed dispatches "from the fighting front."

Ultimately Hitler turned the so-called "phony war" into flame and destruction, and France fell in six weeks. Mowrer, certainly no friend of the Führer since his time in Berlin, made ready to leave the country, first sending Lilian to Lisbon and safety.

As the French armies retreated in confusion, they blew up bridges to stall the enemy. In the process, they stalled thousands of refugees and foreign nationals. Though constantly on the move, Mowrer kept up a steady stream of dispatches to the *Daily News*. Some he wrote on tables in cafés and private homes under chaotic conditions. Once he typed a story on the hood of a car with columns of refugees staggering by. Mowrer wanted to remain in the country long enough to cover the German takeover of Bordeaux, but friends warned him against doing so, given his old rifts with the Nazi leadership. Mowrer finally agreed. He rejoined Lilian in Lisbon, and they returned to Chicago. After a rest, he took up a new assignment as Washington correspondent for the *Daily News*. With America's entry into the war, he became deputy director of the U.S. Office of Facts and Figures (OFF) under Archibald MacLeish. He enthusiastically opposed the internment of Japanese-Americans from the West Coast as "loyalty risks"; that decision particularly galled him as German-Americans and Italian-Americans remained untouched even though their mother countries were also enemies of the United States. In time, various government agencies came together to form the Office of War Information (OWI), headed by former newsman Elmer Davis. Mowrer served the OWI as interim director of operations for the Pacific area. But the inner turmoils of government bureaucracy ultimately took their toll, and in 1943

Mowrer resigned to become "commentator on world affairs" for the *New York Post*. His position on international affairs became increasingly conservative.

In March 1944, Mowrer returned to Europe aboard the *Queen Mary,* now a troopship ferrying American GIs to Normandy. He served in the European Theater until war's end. Then he toured much of the postwar world before settling into retirement.

In 1951, Edgar and Lilian purchased a country house in Tamworth, New Hampshire, in the Sandwich Mountains near his brother, Paul. Then, at sixty-five years of age, he became North American editor of a new opinion magazine, *Western World,* the title reflecting the scope of the publication's coverage. The magazine would be printed in Utrecht and was conceived as "something between *Realités* and *Newsweek*." Mowrer's personal goal for the publication "was not to entertain but to convince: to fortify Atlantic unity, liberate captive peoples, and hasten the coming of a world under enforceable law." The first issue of *Western World* appeared in April 1957 and was a rousing success. Still, funds remained in critically short supply, and with the March 1960 issue, *Western World* ceased

publication. As Mowrer sadly noted, it "was conceivably the most successful failure in the history of magazines."

Mowrer and Lilian traveled and maintained active writing careers. In later years Mowrer came to appreciate profoundly "the good fortune that made me a free citizen of a literate society, and for the chance that, in an age of triumph and turmoil, made me a foreign newspaper correspondent."

Mowrer died in his sleep on 2 March 1977 on the Island of Madeira, Portugal, several days before his eighty-fifth birthday. He left his wife, their daughter, Diana Jane Beliard, and two grandchildren. He had worked as a journalist for fifty-five years and had, as he said, "occupied a ringside seat at most of the major scenes of history." Vincent Sheean, a fellow reporter, characterized Mowrer as "the most persistently engaging conversationalist I know . . . passionate, gloomy, explosive with biases . . . the best-educated American I ever met."

References:

Stuart W. Little, "Mowrer's Great Events," *Saturday Review,* 51 (14 September 1968): 145;

Lilian Thomson Mowrer, *Journalist's Wife* (New York: Morrow, 1937).

Paul Scott Mowrer
(14 July 1887-7 April 1971)

Maurice R. Cullen, Jr.
Michigan State University

MAJOR POSITIONS HELD: Paris correspondent, war correspondent, head of European service, associate editor, editor in chief, *Chicago Daily News* (1910-1944); European editor, *New York Post* (1945-1949).

BOOKS: *Hours of France in Peace and War* (New York: Dutton, 1918);

Balkanized Europe, A Study in Political Analysis and Reconstruction (New York: Dutton, 1921);

The Good Comrade and Fairies (New York: Dutton, 1923);

Our Foreign Affairs: A Study in National Interest and the New Diplomacy (New York: Dutton, 1924);

Red Russia's Menace (Chicago: *Chicago Daily News,* 1925);

The Foreign Relations of the United States (Chicago: American Library Association, 1927);

Poems between Wars: Hail Illinois! France Farewell (Chicago: Mariano, 1941);

The House of Europe (Boston: Houghton Mifflin, 1945);

On Going to Live in New Hampshire (Sanbornville, N.H.: Wake-Brook, 1953);

And Let the Glory Go (Sanbornville, N.H.: Wake-Brook, 1955);

Fifi; or, Something Entirely New: A Comedy in One Act (Sanbornville, N.H.: Wake-Brook, 1956);

Twenty-One and Sixty-Five: Poems (Mill Valley, Cal.: Wings Press, 1958);

The Mothering Land: Selected Poems (Francestown, N.H.: Golden Quill, 1960);

High Mountain Pond (Francestown, N.H.: Golden
    Quill, 1962);
School for Diplomats (Francestown, N.H.: Golden
    Quill, 1964);
This Teeming Earth (Francestown, N.H.: Golden
    Quill, 1965);
The Island Ireland (Francestown, N.H.: Golden
    Quill, 1966);
Six Plays (Boston: Branden, 1968);
The Poems of Paul Scott Mowrer, 1918-1966 (Fran-
    cestown, N.H.: Golden Quill, 1968).

OTHER: "Press and the Public," in *Interpretations of
    Journalism*, edited by Frank Luther Mott and
    Ralph D. Casey (New York: Crofts, 1937), pp.
    315-323;
"Life of Dwight Morrow," in *Essays of Three Decades*,
    edited by Arno L. Bader and Carlton F. Wells
    (New York & London: Harper, 1939), pp.
    462-463;
"War in Journalism," in *Books and Libraries in War-
    time*, edited by Pierce Butler (Chicago: Univer-
    sity of Chicago Press, 1945), pp. 67-87;
A Choice of French Poems, edited by Mowrer (Fran-
    cestown, N.H.: Golden Quill, 1969).

SELECTED PERIODICAL PUBLICATIONS:
    "New Tactics," *Harper's*, 186 (February 1943):
    297-307;
"Call of the Quai d'Orsay," *Newsweek*, 24 (18 De-
    cember 1944): 86-87;
"Cub Reporter," *Scholastic*, 48 (4 February 1946):
    17-18;
"France After de Gaulle," *New Republic*, 114 (18
    February 1946): 243-244;
"Same Old Story," *Forum*, 105 (June 1946): 909-
    910.

Paul Scott Mowrer (Wide World Photos)

Early in his memoirs Paul Scott Mowrer commented: "There is German in me, and Dutch, and
Scotch, and Welsh, and for aught I know, much
else. I put this down, not because I think it important, but because I believe it typical." Mowrer reflected the strength of a growing turn-of-the-
century middle class in America. Comprised of
hardy farmers and mercantile folk, they were
churchgoers who sometimes took to counting the
numbers of Revolutionary War stalwarts in their
family trees. The Mowrers also had hired help, albeit part-time, a mark of their solvency.

Paul Scott Mowrer was born in Bloomington,
Illinois, on 14 July 1887 to Rufus Mowrer, a merchant, and Nell Scott Mowrer. On 8 March 1892
his younger brother, Edgar, came along, and, de-

spite the difference in age, the two became lifelong
friends. Paul remembered the feeling between
them: "When I would remonstrate with him, his
tear-filled eyes would take on such a look of re-
proach as would cut my heart." The two would be
mutual admirers throughout their lengthy and ad-
venturesome lives.

Visiting his uncle in Chicago one summer,
young Paul envied the newspaperboys hawking the
latest editions to the city crowds. In time he persuaded his aunt to permit him to indulge in this
madness, and for an hour every afternoon he sold
the *Chicago Daily News* to commuters on the cable
cars along Garfield Boulevard. As he later wrote,
"Fortunately for the career that was to be mine with
this same paper, it sold well."

Returning to Bloomington at summer's end,
Mowrer became caught up in news of the Spanish-
American War. Each day he read eagerly the
chalked-up bulletins in front of the local newspaper
office. But the victory over Spanish forces in Cuba
took a backseat to his father's sudden business mis-
fortunes that forced the family to move to Chicago

when Paul was in the sixth grade.

Mowrer entered Hyde Park High School, where he began to write poetry at the instigation of a dedicated teacher who recognized this talent in the youngster. Much of his early writing reflected his love for the glories of summer in Michigan, where the family vacationed. In these formative years, Mowrer also labored as coeditor of the *Hyde Parker*, the school's literary magazine. The art editor was Bud Fisher, who would one day launch the comic strip "Mutt and Jeff" into national syndication.

Due to excessive enrollments Mowrer's class was graduated in February rather than the traditional June; thus he would have to wait nine months to enter college. Astonishing his family, he decided to seek employment in some challenging field to prepare himself for college. The favorite newspaper in the Mowrer household had long been the *Chicago Daily News,* and Paul had been its most dedicated reader. He had already met Charles Faye, the paper's managing editor, through a school chum, and decided to use that tenuous association as a means of getting a foot in the door. But Faye waved him away; certainly the *Daily News* would never add someone with no experience to its illustrious staff. In fact Faye advised him to avoid journalism, with its long hours and skimpy pay, altogether. But Mowrer insisted that he was ready. Finally Faye suggested that the young man try the City Press Association and ask for a man named Saylor.

At the City Press Association, the would-be journalist met a wall of resistance. Saylor told him flatly that he already had a thousand or more applicants, most of whom would never make the grade. Even if he were hired, the pay would match a pauper's income. But again Mowrer persisted, and finally Saylor agreed to take his name. The following week, Mowrer received a one-day assignment from City Press to cover the local election results. Throughout the day, which featured a howling snowstorm and freezing winds, Mowrer raced from precinct to precinct, jotting down the returns at one before stumbling and sliding to the next. Finally he staggered back to City Press with the vital figures. Saylor handed him a one-dollar bill and went back to his desk. But Charles Faye, impressed by Mowrer's zeal, sent for him and hired him as a full-time reporter for the *Daily News*. Thus Mowrer became a bona fide "picture chaser" for a major newspaper at a salary of five dollars a week. In time the young zealot gained assignments of greater challenge, from the eerie gloom of a medium's sanctum in a back-alley slum to the violence of a teamsters' strike.

During that time Mowrer began to acquire an appreciation of the arts, beginning with a performance of the opera *Parsifal*. As he recalled the experience, the "music seemed to take hold of my bowels, and pull with delectable intensity." He also found time to write poetry, some of which found its way into the *Daily News*. More important, however, he was gaining stature as a reporter. His mentors assigned him to a wide range of assignments, to which he responded with hard facts strung together with highly readable prose. His salary soared to thirty dollars a week. He also courted three young women at the same time before settling on one of them.

With all his successes, he recognized the need to expand his intellectual horizons in order to make a significant contribution to journalism. Though it pained him to do so, he left the *Daily News* in 1906 and entered the University of Michigan, where he remained until 1908 as a special student. That classification permitted him to select courses which appeared particularly challenging to him without concern about earning a degree.

At Michigan he applied the same diligence to his studies as he had to his reporting and excelled academically, particularly in the liberal arts. Observing the drinking bouts of his roommates, he became convinced that to consume alcohol in large quantities was sheer madness. He joined the staff of the *Michigan Daily,* the university student paper, as writer and editor. At the end of his time there and because of his journalistic contributions he was awarded a special gift from the board of $300. With little hesitation he decided to use the money for a bicycle trip through Europe with a college friend. The Continent entranced him; as he wrote years later, "The impressions of that summer in Europe bit into my memory like drypoint."

Upon his return to Chicago, he applied to the *Daily News* for his old job. But Faye was one of the "anticollege" editors who were legion at the time: to them, a college education was an abomination in the newsroom. After a lengthy discussion, Faye agreed to reinstate Mowrer, but at fifteen dollars a week rather than the thirty he had previously earned. The pay cut failed to deter Mowrer; he possessed sufficient poise and self-confidence to believe he could return to his former level—and move beyond it.

Mowrer worked on the story of Ella Gingles, a young Irish lacemaker who charged that she had been chloroformed and sexually abused "for the White Slave Market." He zealously reserved time for his poetry, which began to gain acceptance by some of the better periodicals. On 8 May 1909 he married Winifred Adams, a former college classmate. Mowrer developed a special talent for interviewing, to him the very heart of newsgathering; he coined a motto: "Good questions bring good answers." Andrew Carnegie had a reputation among reporters for being an uncooperative subject, but Mowrer interviewed him with ease. The steel magnate balked, however, at having his picture taken. Mowrer assured him that his photographer was no run-of-the-mill shutterbug: "This man is an *artist*," he confided. "Well," Carnegie said, "if he's an artist, all right. Go ahead." Mowrer got his picture.

In 1910 Lamar Middleton, the *Daily News*'s Paris correspondent, died. Against a tide of warnings from those who felt that the young reporter was not ready for such responsibility, publisher Victor Lawson asked Mowrer to replace Middleton. At twenty-two Mowrer was a noticeable cut above most journalists, and Lawson knew it. The Mowrers set sail for France.

In the *Daily News* quarters at the corner of the Place de l'Opéra, Mowrer was confronted by a steady flow of Americans and others, most of them asking for favors, money, or jobs. A few were swindlers. The English clerk who supervised the office, Mowrer quickly discovered, had embezzled over £1,000 from petty cash to play the horses. Mowrer dealt with each problem in turn and gradually reorganized the office. He welcomed the high and the mighty, foreign and American, to the *Daily News* office. A stream of meaningful stories began flowing back to Chicago, all written with an uncommon flair that pleased readers back home. The *Daily News* management was pleased as well. Mowrer adhered to the paper's dictum of concentrating on "feature stories, quaint episodes illustrative of French life, human interest stories, stories of Americans abroad." He kept to his schedule and he came to know Paris and her leading citizens well. As busy as he was transmitting news of French events and opinions to *Daily News* readers, Mowrer reserved time for his poetry and fiction, both of which received praise from editors of prestigious American and foreign literary publications.

Shortly after their arrival in Paris, Winifred and Paul Mowrer became the parents of a son, Richard ("Scotty"), who would one day also become a foreign correspondent. The new father summed up his feelings: "How, I asked myself, can any man have the effrontery to expect others to listen to his opinions until, by working at a job, marrying a wife, and begetting a child, he has earned the right to an opinion?" Later a second son, David, was born; he grew up to become a newspaperman in Seattle.

Talk of war was rife throughout Europe. Mowrer found a New Year's trip to Berlin unsettling, observing that "about every fifth man wore some kind of uniform. Army officers in their long gray coats never got out of the way on the sidewalk. If you saw an army officer coming, it was best to step aside, otherwise he would push you, and in addition he might have you arrested." International tensions continued to mount as war broke out in the Balkans and North Africa. But, Mowrer discovered, Americans evinced little interest in the embroilments of backwater peoples in no-account wars. American newspapers and magazines sent not a single correspondent to cover the carnage in this dress rehearsal for the larger drama about to engulf all of Europe. The big news at home, Mowrer learned from his editors, was the coming World Series. Mowrer noted that "a single murder in Galveston, Texas, was worth as much space in Chicago as a shambles in Africa." Nonetheless, as the violence spread, Mowrer received word from Chicago: Cover the Balkan war! He turned over the bureau to his brother, Edgar, who was not yet a journalist but who happened to be visiting Paris at the time, and left for the war zone. Paul Mowrer's initial battle experiences impressed him profoundly, particularly the terrible toll among civilians. By freight car and horseback and on foot, he followed the armies of Serbs, Croatians, and Bulgarians that hoped to drive the German-supported Turks from the Balkans. He roamed through once-quaint villages that had been reduced to charred rubble and fertile farmlands pitted by the shallow graves of young men. He gained knowledge of the fundamentals of tactics and strategies that would serve him well in the future. The bloodletting and devastation he witnessed also created permanent changes in him. He read voraciously the works of leading thinkers past and current—Rousseau, Rimbaud, Rabelais, Goethe, Schiller, and Nietzsche. He learned "about the superman, a man who is above common morality and answerable only to his all-powerful will." Mowrer's experiences in the Balkans—the burned-out villages, the wooden crosses, the awesome human suffering—"I could only reject with loathing." Human nature, he determined, is not dedicated to peace but to violence; therefore, "must an outbreak of war always come upon us . . . as an utter surprise?" He trained himself in military strategy by studying accounts of historical and recent actions, the better to serve his readers, and became a military expert.

When World War I broke out, Mowrer

headed for the front. Via assorted cloak-and-dagger strategies, he managed to enter Brussels, then occupied by German troops who were hostile to all correspondents. He collected valuable information even as other foreign correspondents were being arrested and jailed. With cunning and daring, he moved freely about the city, committing his observations to memory. When he felt his luck was beginning to run out, he escaped to England, and ultimately returned to Paris unruffled and unscathed.

Back at his desk, Mowrer organized a network of *Daily News* correspondents to cover the elongated battle lines of the Western Front. He humanized his dispatches by recreating war scenes as he had seen them. His interviews with civilian and military participants of high and low station became regular front-page fare in the paper. Soon other American newspapers were pleading for permission to run the dispatches in their pages.

He made repeated forays to the French front, though it frequently meant violating the military regulations of the various belligerents. Fascinated, he stood on hilltops observing artillery fire directed at the slits in the mud where French troops tried to stay alive. He visited the trenches while they were under bombardment, as well as airfields and hospitals, and wrote in detail of his observations, always including vivid portrayals of individuals. Because of his youthful appearance he grew a Vandyke beard to impress his foreign hosts during press conferences. It worked, for the generals began addressing him instead of some of the older correspondents.

Mowrer continued to be appalled at the slaughter of young French soldiers with little or nothing to show for their sacrifice: "Verdun was a holocaust. Half the women in France were wearing black. . . . I hardly knew anyone anymore who hadn't been wounded once."

On 6 April 1917 the United States entered the war, even as Germany boasted that no Yankee troops would ever reach France. On 1 July Mowrer was officially accredited to the French armies as official correspondent until the end of the war. He prepared a series of articles for the *Daily News* on American infantry tactics and also provided explanations of how German forces operated. But his major contributions proved to be his detailed accounts of battles. Even rival newspapers singled them out with lavish praise: the *Chicago Evening Post* said Mowrer's dispatches were "as good as the best that had been written about the war, not even excepting those of Kipling and Richard Harding Davis!" For his penetrating coverage of the French

army during the war, Mowrer became one of eight correspondents decorated with the Legion of Honor by French General Headquarters in April 1918. (In 1933 he was promoted to "officer" in the Lègion of Honor.)

After the war's end, Mowrer covered the international complications of forging and maintaining the peace. He paraded before his readers all the petty quarrels at the conference table and predicted that the likely impact of the negotiations on future generations would be a new world war. His book *Balkanized Europe, A Study in Political Analysis and Reconstruction* (1921) traced the postwar carving up of Europe into small, weak states "economically dependent and a prey to intrigue." The work was enthusiastically received. His by-line began to appear regularly in the *Atlantic, Harper's,* the *New Republic,* and *Forum,* among others. He also did articles for *Time* and *Newsweek* and prestigious foreign journals.

He spent most of 1922 traveling through the new countries created by the Versailles Treaty, the Balkans in particular, and found eastern Europe plagued by revolution and starvation. The international threats to peace posed by Japan's seizure of foreign territories caused him grave concern; Japan, in Mowrer's view, had become "the Prussia of Asia, fanatical, ruthless, determined." In 1924 his book *Our Foreign Affairs* was published, and his superiors at the *Daily News* were sufficiently impressed to make him head correspondent in Europe, in charge of all *Daily News* personnel.

With world problems foremost in his thinking and writing, he managed to reserve time for his poetry, including a collection, *The Good Comrade and Fairies* (1923).

Although the political intrigues in Europe were sufficient to keep any dedicated correspondent occupied, Mowrer longed for new places and adventures. In 1925, he found what he was looking for in Africa. The Riffs, a group of Moroccan Arabs, were fighting a two-front war against the Spanish at one end of their domain and the French at the other. This was a "little" war, snubbed by the outside world, but it caught Mowrer's imagination. He decided to work his way through the battle lines, interview the Riffian leadership, and tell their story to the world. The Riffs detested outsiders, and Mowrer would have to wind his way through other hostile tribal realms to get to the Riffs; any of those might take his life as a matter of course. Despite the odds Mowrer sallied forth. "I had lived more, I told myself, at thirty-seven, than most at seventy. And a bold resolution, if executed with prudence, would usually succeed." Mowrer would attempt to visit Abd-el-Krim, the Riff chieftain, and size matters up for the outside world. He donned Arab dress and let his skin bake brown under the desert sun. He injured his ankle at the outset, which caused intense pain; traveling by camel added to his discomfort, as he and a guide stared death down on numerous occasions. Eventually he managed to reach Abd-el-Krim and conduct a series of interviews before sullen-faced Riff warriors. In short order, the world was reading about the Riffs' resistance against the invaders. Mowrer's articles described the unique methods of warfare employed by the Riffs, the character of the people, and the country itself.

Following his return to Paris from Morocco, Mowrer explored firsthand the impact of the Russian Revolution on adjacent countries, particularly on Sweden, Finland, and Germany. Ultimately he put his observations and concerns into a *Daily News* pamphlet, *Red Russia's Menace* (1925). Mowrer's reporting left few questions about Soviet intentions for the future.

In October 1925 Mowrer was one of 200 correspondents in Locarno, Switzerland, covering the formal acceptance of Germany into the League of Nations, "not as beaten culprits guilty of having caused untold misery, but as equals," which to Mowrer meant trouble for the future. There he also saw the Fascist dictator of Italy, Benito Mussolini. Mowrer came away with unsettled feelings about the increasing likelihood of another world war, which Germany, Italy, and Japan appeared to favor. In the months that followed Mowrer observed firsthand the ominous growth of fascism in Europe—particularly in Italy, where it was then most visible. The barbarity its adherents unleashed against those who disagreed with them violated his sensibilities. Evidence indicated that similar events were happening inside Germany.

In 1928 Mowrer received the Pulitzer Prize as best foreign correspondent, the first prize to be awarded in that category. The Pulitzer citation commended "his high distinction as a specialist in foreign affairs."

In 1931, as Mowrer had predicted, Japan invaded Manchuria, drawing the first blood in what would become World War II. With Hitler's rise to total power in Germany in 1933, Mowrer attacked the "New Order of National Socialism" and the obvious designs of the new Führer for conquest. "To complete the rearming of Germany," Mowrer wrote, "he would defy, if need be, the universe. . . . Gangs of exultant Nazis roamed the streets, chasing Jews, terrorizing citizens."

His first marriage having ended in divorce in 1933, Mowrer married Hadley Richardson Hemingway, former wife of Ernest Hemingway, on 3 July of the same year. The following year the couple returned to Chicago, where Mowrer was made chief editorial writer for the *Daily News*. A year later he became the paper's editor. He retired from the paper in 1944 and became European editor for the *New York Post*.

In addition to his numerous books on international political issues, Mowrer also produced ten volumes of poetry and several plays, some of them produced in New York. In 1949 Mowrer retired to the mountain country of New Hampshire, subsequently being named poet laureate of that state. He died on 7 April 1971 at eighty-three years of age, while vacationing in Beaufort, South Carolina.

Reference:

"Mr. Mowrer Remembers," *Time*, 46 (24 September 1945): 62.

Theodore W. Noyes

(26 January 1858-4 July 1946)

Charles A. Fair
Sam Houston State University

MAJOR POSITION HELD: Editor in chief, *Washington Evening Star* (1908-1946).

BOOKS: *The National Capital* (Washington, D.C.: B. S. Adams, 1893);

Newspaper Libels and Reprinted Notes of Travel (Washington, D.C.: B. S. Adams, 1894);

War of the Metals; Washingtonia; Mexico, Hawaii and Japan (Washington, D.C.: T. W. Cadick, 1899);

Conditions in the Philippines (Washington, D.C., 1900);

Oriental America and Its Problems (Washington, D.C.: Judd & Detweiler, 1903);

Fiscal Relations between the United States and the District of Columbia (Washington, D.C.: Government Printing Office, 1916);

The Presidents and the National Capital (Lancaster, Pa.: New Era, 1917);

The World's Great Waterfalls (Washington, D.C.: Judd & Detweiler, 1926);

Our National Capital –And Its Unamericanized Americans (Washington, D.C., 1951).

Theodore W. Noyes followed in his father's footsteps. As the successor to Crosby Noyes in the editor's chair at the *Washington Evening Star,* Theodore Noyes exhibited the same driving dedication to objective reporting and to the improvement and development of the nation's capital that had brought his father fame and the *Star* its position of dominance among Washington newspapers. Noyes was editor in chief of the *Star* for thirty-eight years, only two years less than his father, and had been long involved in the editorial leadership of the paper before his father died in 1908.

Theodore Noyes enthusiastically joined his father in various editorial campaigns for improving the nation's capital, and for getting the federal government to pay its fair share of operating the District of Columbia. Many of the physical assets that are today enjoyed by Washington residents and tourists were first championed by Noyes on the pages of the *Star.* Noyes felt equally at home with his pen—he never used a typewriter in his fifty years with newspapers—and as a persuasive speaker in the halls of Congress and in numerous radio addresses.

Theodore Williams Noyes was born in 1858 to Crosby Stuart Noyes, then an assistant editor on the *Star,* and Elizabeth Selina Williams Noyes. His brother, Frank Brett Noyes, who was to become the first president of the modern Associated Press in 1900, was born in 1863.

Unlike his father, Theodore Noyes had the advantage of a formal education. After attending the public schools in Washington, he entered the preparatory program at Columbian College (which later became George Washington University) at age twelve. When he was nineteen he began his career as a reporter for the *Star,* of which Crosby Noyes had become part owner and editor in chief in 1867. After four years, he returned to Columbian to attend law school, receiving his LL.B. in 1882 and his LL.M. in 1883.

Upon graduation, he was in poor health, and so he did not return to the *Star* but accepted a job with a law firm in the drier climate of Sioux Falls, Dakota Territory. He wrote a weekly column for the *Sioux Falls Press,* helped draft the plan for state government for the territory, and was elected county judge; but before taking office, he returned to Washington in 1886 to accept the associate editor's post at the *Star* and to work closely with his father, who was then sixty-one years old. In that same year, he married Mary E. Prentice. They had three children, Ruth, Elizabeth, and Theodore Prentice.

Theodore Noyes wrote many editorials calling for the elimination of railroad grade crossings which created massive traffic problems and resulted in a number of deaths. He assailed the railroads for "squatting" on the Mall for free with their tracks, and called for the establishment of a Union Station to consolidate train traffic in the capital. The *Star* was one of the most financially independent newspapers in America, with advertising linage often leading the nation. Noyes was not worried, therefore, when one railroad threatened to withhold its advertising from the *Star:* "The Pennsylvania Rail-

Theodore W. Noyes

road is a very rich and powerful corporation. But it has not enough money to buy a line of editorial opinion in the *Star,* and this it very well knows."

Noyes has been described as gentle, courteous, generous, caring—and stubborn. His stubbornness was exhibited best in his *Star* editorials that sought to get Congress to pay debts incurred by the district on behalf of the federal government. Writing in March 1888, at a time when Congress was paying half the annual operating costs of the capital city, Noyes said: "The nation's 'bantling' no longer fears sudden death. Congress fulfills its obligations in respect to the improvement of the District with fidelity. . . . The ward of the nation is properly clothed and fed." He reminded Congress that while its current efforts were appreciated, there were

debts incurred over many years that had been left unpaid. He noted that the federal government had received more than $700,000 from the sale of land that had been pledged to the district for the benefit of improvements there, but that for thirty years Congress had spent less than $700 per year to improve the streets, which was a federal responsibility. He berated Congress for continuing its direct control of the capital city without giving it due consideration. While it favored representation for the district in Congress and the Electoral College, he did not favor popular election of officials to govern Washington. He pointed to examples of other cities with home rule, and noted that elected officials ineptly obligated those communities to debts that could not be paid. He also feared that election of local government officials in Washington might lead to an end to the shared costs of operation with Congress. He wanted Washington to be governed by a commission appointed by the president.

Just as his father had done, Noyes assumed the role of ombudsman for the residents of Washington. Through his use of the editorial pages, his prominence on many important civic committees, and his personal visits to Congress, he fought to get the streets cleaned regularly, to have utility lines placed underground, and for an end to the practice of dumping Washington's garbage in the Potomac River. The latter campaign went on for two years before a contract was let for a disposal plant in 1900. Some of his campaigns were carried on even longer. His battle for a tax-supported public library began in 1891; it was five years before Congress passed the proper legislation, and another two years before the library was included in the federal budget. The library building, donated by Andrew Carnegie, was finally opened twelve years after Noyes began his campaign. He served as president of the library board for fifty years. Another of his campaigns that was slowly realized was the construction of an office building for the district government. He began that effort in the 1880s; Congress approved the project in 1902, and the building opened in 1908, the year Crosby Noyes died and Theodore took over as editor in chief of the *Star*.

Some of his other major efforts included campaigns for the establishment of a national arboretum, a district war memorial, a ban on billboards on major approaches to the city, the elimination of diploma mills from the capital, the establishment of the Community Chest, and the building of a monument to President Lincoln.

Although many of his editorials were unsigned, collections of them were later published in book form and distributed to new Congressmen and other opinion leaders.

A major victory of his father—the arrangement whereby the federal government shared half the cost of operating the district—appeared to be in trouble in the early 1920s, when Congress cut its contribution from 50 to 40 percent, and then, in 1924, to a lump sum payment. In 1925, Noyes hired accountants who proved that $5 million in the fed-

eral treasury belonged to the city. The money was returned, with half of it going toward schools, and $600,000 to buy land to connect the Rock Creek and Potomac parks, which had been established as a result of earlier editorial campaigns by the *Star*.

Noyes traveled extensively, including trips to Europe, the Arctic, the Orient, the Philippines, and Australia. He wrote for the *Star* from these locations, and had a hand in the campaign to gain the Hawaiian Islands for the United States in 1898.

Noyes and his partners—his brother Frank, who became president of the Star Company in 1910, and the descendants of Samuel H. Kauffmann and George W. Adams, who had been Crosby Noyes's partners—have been credited with some innovative employee-relations achievements. *Star* employees could take advantage of a variety of benefits, ranging from dental care to home mortgages provided by the company.

Noyes's employees learned to expect his orders to come scrawled on the backs of envelopes or on galley proofs. When ill health beset him in later years, he kept in constant touch with the office by an old-fashioned two-hand telephone. Even though his nephew, Newbold Noyes, the associate editor, had assumed some of the daily tasks of the editor in chief in the last few years, Theodore outlived his nephew by four years, and continued at the helm of Washington's dominant newspaper. During his lifetime, the *Star* did not place heavy emphasis upon national and international news, but depended upon the Associated Press, whose office was in the *Star* building, to provide that coverage. The *Star* staff concentrated upon providing local coverage. By the time of Noyes's death in 1946, nearly 96 percent of the paper's circulation was in the District of Columbia and the immediate trading area, 79 percent of it by home delivery.

References:

Samuel H. Kauffman, *The Evening Star (1852-1952): A Century at the Nation's Capital* (Washington: Newcomen Society, 1952);

Kenneth Stewart and John Tebbell, *Makers of Modern Journalism* (New York: Prentice-Hall, 1952), pp. 455-457.

Eleanor Medill Patterson
(7 November 1881-24 July 1948)

Jean C. Chance
University of Florida

MAJOR POSITIONS HELD: Editor/publisher, *Washington* (D.C.) *Herald* and *Times-Herald* (1930-1948).

BOOKS: *Glass Houses*, as Eleanor M. Gizycka (New York: Minton, Balch, 1926);
Fall Flight, as Eleanor M. Gizycka (New York: Minton, Balch, 1928).

If a movie or television show were to be made about a successful woman executive in the traditionally male world of American publishing, Eleanor Medill Patterson would be an ideal model for the heroine; her life contained most of the basic dramatic elements needed to capture and keep a contemporary audience. She was a wealthy socialite, playing a leading role on the social stages of Chicago and Washington, D.C.; she was once married to a Polish count and cavalry officer. Her grandfather developed the *Chicago Tribune*. As a widow, she asked an old friend, William Randolph Hearst, for a job, and he handed her the editorship of a failing Washington, D.C., newspaper, despite her lack of journalistic experience.

Surprisingly, in light of her seeming disinterest in life outside the social scene, Patterson quickly assumed the role of activist editor: she interviewed Al Capone, boosted reader interest by running a gossip box on the front page, and stimulated running feuds with President Franklin Roosevelt and Washington socialite Alice Longworth Roosevelt. In 1940 Patterson was the only woman editor/publisher of a large metropolitan daily newspaper in the United States.

Patterson was born Elinor Josephine Patterson in Chicago on 7 November 1881; she later changed the spelling of her first name to "Eleanor," adopted "Medill" as her middle name, and lied about her age so many times that her obituary listed her birth date as 1884. She was born to Chicago wealth and society: her mother, Elinor, was the daughter of Joseph Medill, owner of the *Chicago Tribune*; her father, Robert Wilson Patterson, was managing editor of the paper and Medill's designated successor. Her older brother, Joseph Medill

(United Press International)

Patterson—who was later to found the *New York Daily News*—nicknamed her "Cissy."

By her own admission, red-haired Cissy was a willful, spoiled child whose socialite mother groomed her solely for an elitist life that included schooling at Miss Hersey's School in Boston and Miss Porter's in Farmington, Connecticut. Cissy's social debuts were in Chicago and Washington. As she grew up, Patterson's home life revolved around an indulgent father and a mother who aimed at becoming Washington's official hostess from the

Patterson with Arthur Brisbane, who persuaded William Randolph Hearst to let her take over the Washington Herald
(Chicago Tribune *photo*)

family mansion on Dupont Circle in the capital city.

When Patterson was nineteen, her uncle, Robert Sanderson McCormick, was ambassador to Austria-Hungary, and he introduced her to Viennese society. She met Polish count Joseph Gizycki in Vienna at a ball; they were married in Washington on 14 April 1904. He was thirty-five; she was twenty-two. The marriage was stormy, and the couple separated in 1907. The custody battle over their daughter, Felicia, kidnapped by Count Gizycki, reflected the media sensationalism of the period. President Taft intervened personally, and Patterson recovered the child in 1908. The marriage was officially dissolved in 1917.

During the years before and after her divorce from Gizycki, Patterson led the life of the rich, idle socialite. She spent time in Chicago, New York, Europe, and at her parents' home on DuPont Circle in Washington. She dated a number of prominent men, including the German ambassador, Count von Bernstorff, before he was expelled from the United States during World War I. She appeared in amateur plays, and traveled throughout the country in her custom-built private railroad car. She bought a vacation ranch near Jackson Hole, Wyoming, where she had an affair with a cowboy

and former rustler and took up big-game hunting.

In April 1925 she married a Jewish New York lawyer, Elmer Schlesinger, and commenced a career as a novelist. Her first novel, *Glass Houses* (1926), satirized life in Washington; her second and last book, *Fall Flight* (1928), is a thinly disguised account of her marriage to Gizycki. Both novels were published under the name Eleanor M. Gizycka (the feminine form of Gizycki). Her second marriage was crumbling, and she had already asked Schlesinger for a divorce, when he died of a heart attack on a golf course in Aiken, South Carolina, in February 1929.

True to her unpredictable nature, a year after her second husband's death, Patterson made a mid-life career change that left its mark on American journalism history. Arthur Brisbane talked Patterson's friend William Randolph Hearst into hiring her to take over his failing *Washington Herald*. She took the job of editor-publisher seriously and even covered many stories herself, including interviews with Albert Einstein and mobster Al Capone. Patterson crusaded for humane treatment of animals (she had given up hunting), hot lunches for schoolchildren, the cleaning up of the Potomac River, and home rule for the District of Columbia. In ten years

Front page of the Washington Herald, *23 July 1930, announcing Patterson's appointment as editor in chief*

she hired and fired seven editors, and in six years—by 1936—Patterson doubled the circulation of the *Herald*. The newspaper featured gossipy items, including a front-page box, "Interesting But Not True." She engaged in a highly publicized feud with *Washington Post* publisher Eugene Meyer. Journalism historian James Boylan describes the *Herald* as "exciting, gossipy, unpredictable," and "operating on the standards of yellow journalism and regressive politics."

In 1937 Patterson leased the morning *Herald* and the afternoon *Times* from Hearst with an option to buy, and despite warnings of failure from her brother Joseph at the *New York Daily News*, she combined both papers into the first all-day daily newspaper in the country: the new *Washington Times-Herald* featured six editions daily. Patterson exercised her option to buy the paper in January 1939. The *Times-Herald* was showing a profit by 1943; two years later, the paper made a $1,000,000 profit.

The turbulent political climate of the late 1930s to the mid-1940s was reflected in Patterson's dramatic disenchantment with Franklin Roosevelt. She had supported his presidential race in 1940, but his lend-lease policy enraged her. Along with her brother Joseph in New York and her cousin Col. Robert McCormick, publisher of the *Chicago Tribune*, Patterson was acidly labeled by FDR as part of a "McCormick-Patterson axis." Three days before Pearl Harbor was attacked, on a tip from sources in the armed services, the *Times-Herald* and the *Chicago Tribune* published American secret war plans. Government charges of betraying U.S. secrets were later dropped.

Columnists Drew Pearson and Walter Winchell also drew Patterson's wrath over World War II issues. Pearson repeatedly argued with Patterson about his support of Roosevelt's foreign policy; in return, Patterson's nickname for Pearson was "The Headache Boy." (One factor in this animosity may have been the fact that Pearson was married to Felicia Patterson from 1925 to 1928.) Patterson accused Winchell of excessive Nazi-hunting, and often would cancel Winchell and Pearson columns; both columns were finally dropped from the paper.

In 1943 Patterson was described as lonely, fat, and suffering from alcoholism and heart disease. She had six homes with a total of ninety rooms. Her personal and business payroll totaled 1,300 employees. Life in her final years was lonely and friction-filled. In 1945 she formally split from her daughter, Felicia.

On 24 July 1948, Patterson died in her sleep at her estate in Maryland, apparently from a heart attack. She willed $25,000 a year to her estranged daughter and divided the *Times-Herald* among eight company executives. The will was disputed, with Felicia Patterson's lawyers urging her to claim that her mother was mentally unsound when she died. To avoid tarnishing her mother's reputation, Felicia agreed to settle for $400,000.

During the year following Patterson's death, the *Times-Herald* was sold to Colonel McCormick. In 1954 he sold it to Eugene Meyer, who merged the paper with the *Washington Post*.

James Boylan evaluates the mark that Eleanor Medill Patterson left on American journalism: "If the public good of her life had been weighed at age fifty, it might not have been substantial. If she had lived out her days as she had lived her first five decades, she would probably not be remembered much more vividly than, say, her cousin Medill McCormick (who was, after all, a United States senator). But she is remembered, and it is largely because she ran the *Herald* (later the *Times-Herald*), the first woman, it is said, to head a major American daily newspaper."

Biographies:

Paul F. Healy, *Cissy: The Biography of Eleanor M. "Cissy" Patterson* (Garden City: Doubleday, 1966);

Alice Albright Hoge, *Cissy Patterson* (New York: Random House, 1966);

John W. Tebbel, *American Dynasty: The Story of the McCormicks, Medills and Pattersons* (Westport, Conn.: Greenwood, 1968);

Ralph G. Martin, *Cissy* (New York: Simon & Schuster, 1979).

References:

James Boylan, "No Sissy She," *Columbia Journalism Review*, 19 (May-June 1980): 81-82;

Stanley Walker, "Cissy Is a Newspaper Lady," *Saturday Evening Post*, 211 (6 May 1939): 22-23.

Papers:

The *Washington Post* has an extensive collection of material about Eleanor Medill Patterson from the files of the old *Washington Times-Herald*. The *Chicago Tribune* library and the Medill Library in Chicago also have papers of the Patterson, Medill, and McCormick families.

Joseph Medill Patterson

Ronald S. Marmarelli
Central Michigan University

BIRTH: Chicago, Illinois, 6 January 1879, to Robert W. and Elinor Medill Patterson.

EDUCATION: B.A., Yale University, 1901.

MARRIAGES: 19 November 1902 to Alice Higinbotham; children: Elinor, Alicia, Josephine, James; divorced. 5 July 1938 to Mary King.

MAJOR POSITIONS HELD: Reporter, editorial writer, assistant editor, Sunday editor, coeditor and copublisher, *Chicago Tribune* (1901-1905; 1910-1925); founder, editor, publisher, *New York Daily News* (1919-1946); publisher, *Liberty* magazine (1924-1931); publisher, *Detroit Mirror* (1931-1932).

DEATH: New York, 26 May 1946.

BOOKS: *A Little Brother of the Rich* (Chicago: Reilly & Britton, 1908);
Rebellion (Chicago: Reilly & Britton, 1911; London: Holden & Hardingham, 1914);
The Notebook of a Neutral (New York: Duffield, 1916).

PLAYS: *The Fourth Estate*, by Patterson and Harriet Ford, New York, Wallack's Theater, 6 October 1909;
A Little Brother of the Rich, by Patterson and Ford, New York, Wallack's Theater, 27 December 1909;
Rebellion, New York, Maxine Elliott Theater, 3 October 1911;
By-Products, New York, Lyceum Theater, 9 November 1913;
Dope, New York, Forty-eighth Street Theater, 4 January 1924.

PERIODICAL PUBLICATIONS: "Confessions of a Drone," *Independent*, 61 (30 August 1906): 493-495;
"The Socialist Machine," *Saturday Evening Post*, 179 (29 September 1906): 5, 19;
"The Nickelodeons," *Saturday Evening Post*, 180 (23 November 1907): 10-11, 38;
"Mission of College Snobbishness," *Collier's*, 49 (1 June 1912): 29.

Joseph Medill Patterson (Jackie Martin)

Joseph Medill Patterson created the *New York Daily News* in 1919 and led it within a short time to the top in daily and Sunday circulation among newspapers in the United States. With a tabloid format filled with features, pictures, and news that was highest in popular interest, the *Daily News* appealed to the broadest base of the population in the nation's largest city. The key to its phenomenal and unprecedented success was Patterson's ability, which some said was uncanny—even mystical—to identify with the interests of the people to whom his newspaper spoke. He knew what people wanted in their newspaper and how they wanted it to be presented to them. Patterson, said his daughter Alicia, was "born to understand why people behave as they do; why they laugh and cry and hate and love; and why they buy some newspapers but ignore others." If he was a genius, he was also a hard worker who learned well from experience and association with people and applied what he learned in creating and shaping his newspaper. A *Time* writer noted this in a 1939 article observing the twentieth anniversary of the first appearance of the *Daily News*, commenting that the newspaper's "formula for success is to give the people what they want, but the reason it works so well on the *News* is that he knows the people's tastes infinitely better than any other newspaper publisher. Since he got out of college he has studied in only one textbook: the People."

Family background also had something to do with Patterson's success in journalism. Born on 6 January 1879 in Chicago, he was the first child and only son of Robert W. Patterson, Jr., who was at that time a subeditor at the *Chicago Tribune,* and Elinor Medill Patterson, a daughter of *Tribune* editor Joseph Medill. His father was the son of a prominent Presbyterian minister. On his mother's side there was a long tradition of newspaper work dating from 1819, when his great-grandfather, Judge James Patrick, established the weekly *Tuscarawas Chronicle* in eastern Ohio. Patrick's daughter Catherine married Joseph Medill, who organized the *Cleveland Leader,* then moved to Chicago. In 1855 Medill bought into the *Chicago Tribune,* which had been established eight years earlier. He became editor in chief in 1863 and was one of the giants of nineteenth-century American journalism. His two daughters gave him three other grandchildren be-

sides Joseph M. Patterson: Eleanor "Cissy" Patterson, Joseph's younger sister; and Robert Rutherford McCormick and Joseph Medill McCormick, sons of Katherine Medill McCormick. All four achieved high status in journalism, although Medill McCormick became more prominent in politics. "I would wager money in matching the four grandchildren against the production of any family," wrote "Doting Grandpa" to Cissy in the mid-1890s. Joseph Medill died in 1899, leaving his daughters an estate of $2 million and *Tribune* stock in a trust for them and their heirs.

Robert Patterson had joined the *Tribune* in 1873 and moved up to become general manager in 1890. After Joseph Medill's death, Patterson became president of the Tribune Company and editor in chief of the newspaper. He is credited with making the *Tribune* less of a personal organ and more of a general newspaper. His interest was in presenting news rather than in influencing public opinion by means of editorial content.

For Joseph Medill Patterson childhood meant living in comfort in fashionable Chicago neighborhoods. In 1892 the family moved into a ninety-one-room Stanford White mansion Joseph Medill had built them. Educated in private schools in Chicago and, briefly, in France, Patterson went off to Groton School in 1890. After graduating from Groton he spent a year on a ranch in New Mexico before en-

Patterson's parents, Robert W. and Elinor Medill Patterson

tering Yale University in the fall of 1897. He later wrote of having made his "leisurely, gentlemanly way through boarding-school and university." He explained: "I don't think it was entirely natural aptitude that marked me out for a university education, since I remember that frequently I had to pay money to tutors to drill into my head information of a remarkably simple character. I was fond of a good time—and that I had." In 1900 Patterson took time off from Yale to go to China, where he assisted correspondents covering the Boxer Rebellion. (Sources differ as to whether he was working for the *Tribune* or for Hearst's *New York Journal* at this time.) He received his B.A. from Yale in 1901, then went to work at the *Tribune* as a reporter for fifteen dollars a week. He was, he wrote later, "the greenest cub on the staff," who had an allowance of some $10,000 a year in addition to his salary. Patterson also worked as an editorial writer and an assistant editor of the Sunday edition in those early years. In 1902 he married Alice Higinbotham, daughter of Harlow Niles Higinbotham, a partner in the Marshall Field department store. They had three daughters, Elinor, Alicia, and Josephine, and an adopted son, James.

The young journalist was elected to the Illinois House of Representatives as a Republican in 1903. He became a vocal advocate of municipal reform and was involved in at least one near-brawl that arose in the House chamber during heated argument about public ownership of Chicago's transit system. Patterson learned later that his election had been rigged by his father in a deal with a Republican district boss, and in 1905 he resigned from the *Tribune*.

He soon joined the campaign of Judge Edward F. Dunne, Democratic candidate for mayor in 1905, whose Republican opponent was supported by the *Tribune*. Patterson was an active campaigner for Dunne and was appointed commissioner of public works in the Dunne administration. Dunne wrote later, "I doubt if in its history the Department was more honestly, efficiently, or ably conducted." Patterson was an activist as commissioner, "a spitfire," according to one observer, "who could go so far as to call great corporations anarchists, and accuse them of stealing water. He even proposed to cure the stockyards smell." He fought the department stores over the extension of basements under city streets and fought newspapers over circulation wars. At one point he had a number of newsstands hauled away to the city dump to pressure the *Daily News* and the *American* to halt their violent tactics. But Patterson was impatient, and became dis-

illusioned with regular politics and municipal government. In a letter to Dunne dated 28 February 1906 and widely circulated by Patterson to the newspapers, Patterson resigned as public works commissioner and declared that "as I understand it, I am a socialist." Patterson caused another stir six months after he resigned with an article titled "Confessions of a Drone" in the 30 August 1906 issue of the *Independent*. An editor's note identified Patterson as "a young man who has lately surprised his wealthy friends in Chicago by coming out publicly as a Socialist," and described the article as an explanation of his position. Patterson stated that he was writing of "the *type* of the idle, rich young man," who produces no wealth but consumes a great deal of it. He wrote that he spent between $10,000 and $20,000 annually but "I produce nothing—am doing no work. I (the type) can keep on doing this all my life unless the present social system is changed."

Shortly after this appeared, an article by Alfred Henry Lewis in the 15 September 1906 *Saturday Evening Post* described a speech Patterson delivered in Milwaukee in support of socialism. Lewis noted in the speech a rhetorical style that, decades later, many would say was characteristic of Patterson editorials in the *Daily News*: "There was no straining for metaphor, no effort at effect. His phrases, like his manner, were straightforward, sincere, earnest, wanting embellishment. He told them they were serfs. He told them they might free themselves. . . ." Lewis also described Patterson's physical appearance: "Of middle height, straight as a lance, sinewy, wide of shoulder, knit like a boxer, lean of flank and panther-wise, the natural athlete, one understands at a glance his reputation as a breakneck polo player of the dreadnaught sort. . . . The eyes were deep luminous, replete of a staring, unblinking honesty. They were the home of energy, courage, and a kind of fiery radicalism that finds virtue in the new. . . . [His was] the face of a thinker and a fighter—a face wanting utterly in the passive—the face of a rebel rather than a revolutionist."

In 1906 Patterson withdrew from a full-time role in public life and took up farming in Libertyville, Illinois, after completing a short course in agriculture at the University of Wisconsin. He wrote occasional articles for magazines and turned out pamphlets and other literature for the Socialist cause. In 1907 he supported the Socialist candidate against Dunne and in 1908 he served as national campaign manager for Eugene V. Debs's presidential campaign. He also produced several modestly successful novels and plays during this period: *A*

Little Brother of the Rich (novel, 1908; play, with Harriet Ford, 1909); *The Fourth Estate* (play, with Harriet Ford, 1909); *Rebellion* (novel and play, 1911).

In April 1910, Patterson was drawn back into active participation in the daily affairs of the *Tribune* following the death of his father. Robert Patterson had been negotiating to sell the newspaper to Victor Lawson, publisher of the *Daily News* and the *Record-Herald,* for $10 million. Patterson and Robert McCormick persuaded their mothers and the other stockholders to drop the idea of a sale by offering to become involved in running the newspaper on a full-time basis. Patterson wrote his mother: "Bertie [McCormick] and I are perfectly capable of safeguarding your interests in the paper. . . . I know not a little about newspaper work from inheritance, environment, and active work. . . ." In a 1 March 1911 resolution, the board of directors of the *Tribune* elected Patterson chairman and McCormick president and chief executive officer. James Keeley, the veteran managing editor, who had largely run the news operation at the paper for many years, was elected a vice-president and given power over daily management of the *Tribune.* By May 1914, Keeley was out. Patterson and McCormick made formal their roles and authority in directing the *Tribune* in a handwritten agreement drafted by McCormick which concluded: "The ironbound agreement lasts until we both are dead." They agreed to share responsibility in management and policymaking, and for several years they actually alternated monthly in exercising authority over editorial policy.

Patterson and McCormick revitalized the *Tribune.* Any lingering notions about selling off the newspaper were soon laid to rest. Total daily and Sunday circulation nearly doubled between 1914 and 1920 as the *Tribune* outdid its competitors in heated circulation wars. The newspaper was modernized, its content was made livelier, and its appeal was broadened with the adding of new special features and the undertaking of vigorous crusades against social and political ills.

Overall management of the company was largely in McCormick's hands; Patterson concentrated his attention on the newspaper's content. The Sunday *Tribune* was of special interest to him. According to Burton Rascoe, who worked at the *Tribune* during this period, Patterson had in mind to develop the Sunday paper into "a comprehensive magazine embodying nearly every type of reading matter and picture appeal that individual magazines carried as their own speciality. He hoped to make the purchase of magazines redundant."

Rascoe attributed to Patterson "a fecundity in journalistic ideas" about how to achieve his notion of what the newspaper should be. Responsibility for carrying out many of these ideas fell to Mary King, the Sunday editor.

The products of Patterson's talent for developing circulation-building features included Sidney Smith's "The Gumps," which made its debut in February 1917 as the first continuing-story comic strip, and a motion picture section, which capitalized on readers' growing interest in news and gossip about Hollywood. Another addition to the Sunday *Tribune* was the *Pictorial Weekly,* printed on one of the first rotogravure presses imported from Germany.

Patterson, meanwhile, found his time increasingly taken up by military affairs and international conflict. In April 1914 he went to Vera Cruz, Mexico, to cover the United States military occupation there. The following year he went to Europe to observe the war, spending three months in England, France, Belgium, and Germany. Returning to the United States on a slow steamer he penned a series of articles that ran in the *Tribune* under the title "The Note Book of a Neutral." The series was published in book form in 1916.

In June 1915 Patterson enlisted in the Illinois National Guard field artillery, and one year later, as a corporal, he was shipped with his unit to Texas during the border crisis with Mexico. He was promoted to sergeant in Texas and was commissioned a second lieutenant in February 1917. Five months later his battery was mobilized as part of the Forty-second (Rainbow) Division and shipped to France, arriving in November. After several weeks of training, Patterson, by then a first lieutenant, moved to the front with his unit. In thirteen months overseas, the battery was involved in five major campaigns and was on the front lines for about 200 days. Patterson was hospitalized briefly after being caught in a gas attack. He was a favorite among his men because of his close attention to their welfare and his willingness to share in front-line action with them.

It was while he was in Europe that Patterson developed his ideas about starting a tabloid newspaper in New York City. He was impressed by the success of Lord Northcliffe's *Daily Mirror* in London, and he visited with that publisher. Patterson and McCormick had had ideas about buying a newspaper in New York, but moves in this direction had been put off because of the war. In July 1918, McCormick, a colonel on General Pershing's staff, was heading back to the United States, and visited with his cousin at a farmhouse near the front where Patterson's unit was stationed. Patterson told McCormick that he would like to start a tabloid in New York after the war, and the two agreed that such an undertaking would be worthwhile. In September 1918 William Field, retired business manager of the *Tribune,* began preparations for the project. In October, Patterson was promoted to captain, thus acquiring the title by which he was widely known in later years. (He preferred being addressed as "Mr. Patterson" rather than as "Captain Patterson," however.) He returned from Europe in December and was discharged from active duty in January 1919.

In New York City, Field rented office space on the fifth floor of the Evening Mail Building at 25 City Hall Place; he also arranged for use of the *Evening Mail*'s composing room and pressroom. Arthur Clarke, city editor of the *World* and a former *Tribune* man who was enthusiastic about tabloids, was hired by Field to be managing editor. On 10 May 1919 the board of directors of the Tribune Company unanimously adopted a resolution: "That the officers of the company be empowered to take the steps necessary in their discretion to institute a subsidiary pictorial newspaper enterprise in New York City." Patterson was elected president of a new corporation, News Syndicate Company, Inc., with the agreement that he would continue to share in the direction of the *Tribune.* He would supervise operation of the New York paper from Chicago by means of letters, telegrams, phone calls, and periodic visits.

Financial support for the new venture was not as readily forthcoming as verbal endorsement of the idea. Mrs. Patterson and Mrs. McCormick were not as enthusiastic about the plan as their sons were and were unwilling to be generous in funding it. It was agreed that the new venture would be financed with money loaned to it by the parent company through demand notes.

The first edition of the *Illustrated Daily News,* as the newspaper was to be called, was scheduled to be published in August 1919. However, the debut date was moved up to June when word got around that William Randolph Hearst might be coming out with a tabloid. There were already seventeen other dailies in New York, including seven morning papers. Patterson decided to make the *News* a morning newspaper, telling Field that this would mean all-day sales, a better newsstand position, and cheaper delivery costs. He added: "Also, all morning New York papers are alike and none of them prints pictures." There would be no Sunday edition at the start. Daily price was set at two cents, Patterson reasoning that if other papers lowered their price to one cent to undercut the new paper, the *News* could then cut its price to one cent.

"The *Illustrated Daily News* is going to be your newspaper. Its interests will be your interest," an editorial headed "Who We Are" told readers of the first edition on 26 June 1919. It contained sixteen pages, its front page taken up almost wholly by a photograph of the Prince of Wales, who was soon to visit the United States, riding a horse; the photo was outlined by a filigreed border. Aben Kandel recalled a few years later that at the appearance of the first issue, "the wiseacres of Park Row picked it up gingerly, felt the heft of it, observed its pallor, listened for faint heart beats, and sadly wagged their nicotine-stained beards. 'It cannot live a month,' the bulletin ran." But the *News* editorial emphasized that the newspaper was

> not an experiment, for the appeal of news pictures and brief well-told stories will be as apparent to you as it has been to millions of readers in European cities.
>
> We shall give you every day the best and newest pictures of the interesting things that are happening in the world. Nothing that is not interesting is news. The story that is told by a picture can be grasped instantly. . . .
>
> With the pictures we shall give you short concise news stories, covering every happening recorded by news gatherers. Pictures and stories together will supply a complete understanding of the events of the day, and that is liberal education.

The editorial noted also that the tabloid size of the *News,* its larger text type, and its policy of not running stories from one page to another would make for easier reading on the subway. It promised an aggressive editorial policy "for America and for the people of New York," with "no entangling alliance with any class whatever." It also promised a society column, "the best and newest" fiction, and "the best features that are to be found." The masthead listed Patterson and McCormick as editors and publishers. Managing editor Clarke and his assistant Merton E. Burke headed an editorial staff of twenty-seven. In all, the first day payroll numbered sixty-eight, including thirty-three circulation personnel.

Features and news stories borrowed from the *Chicago Tribune* were especially prominent in the *Illustrated Daily News* at the start. These included editorial cartoons by John T. McCutcheon;

Front page of first issue of Patterson's New York Daily News, *under its original title*

Washington correspondence from Arthur Henning; "A Line O' Type or Two" by Bert Leston Taylor; and "The Gumps," the first of many Patterson-inspired comic strips to appear in the *News*. But those early issues also carried several items that were representative of the special character of the new paper and of Patterson's ideas for providing content that would be of interest to many readers. Page three of the first issue, for example, carried sketches of the judge, defendant, and courtroom visitors at a trial of a physician accused of murdering his wife. Page four carried a small boxed notice offering cash for usable snapshots. Page five, the editorial page, offered readers one dollar for submitting items on the theme "Most Embarrassing Moment of My Life." On page eleven, there were two additional reader contribution features, "Real Love Stories" and "Bright Sayings of Children"; the latter had been started by Patterson at the *Tribune*. The big feature for the first issue and for the next sixty-five days was a beauty contest offering a first prize of $10,000. The back page of the first issue carried photos of five contest entrants with a caption promising a full page of candidates every day. Full-page advertisements in other newspapers promoted the contest and the *News*. One in the *New York Times* declared in bold capital letters: "SEE NEW YORK'S MOST BEAUTIFUL GIRLS EVERY MORNING IN THE ILLUSTRATED DAILY NEWS." The promotions, coupled with the novelty of the *Illustrated Daily News*, helped it average 115,888 circulation daily through the end of June, after a 150,000 first-day circulation, which was a virtual sell-out of the first pressrun. In July, however, average daily circulation dropped to about 27,000; in August, it was 26,000. One day in August, paid circulation reached its lowest point: 11,000. Patterson watched closely what was going on in New York, and kept his editors busy with a daily stream of memos. In the newspaper's second week, Patterson was stressing the need for more pictures. To Clarke he wrote: "In reference to news pictures, please, PLEASE get a larger percentage." He advised:

> You can frame pictures when necessary. For instance, on July 1 you could have had a picture or several pictures of people taking their last drink. [Manufacture of liquor after 30 June 1919 was forbidden under a wartime prohibition measure.] Try and get in a couple of crime pictures every day; that is, you can direct action pictures showing how the crime was committed, or at least get in pictures of

people connected with crime either as victim or criminal.

> It is essential to get more news pictures. That is our life blood and if we do not excel in that we are done for.

To get more pictures, Patterson suggested hiring "picture chasers. Green reporters who do leg work and can get a lot of good news pictures every day by hunting around and asking for them."

On another matter, Patterson directed, "For goodness sakes remember to publish knocks, and vicious ones, every day." These were letters of complaint or criticism of the *News* for publication in the "People's Voice" column on the editorial page. Over the years, it became one of the most popular features in the newspaper.

In his directives to Clarke and others in New York, Patterson expressed a consistent determination to work hard to make the *News* a success, even though circulation in the first few months was on a steady decline. "This thing has got to go and the paper has to get better every day," he wrote during the second week of business. At another time he stated: "Remember one thing and don't ever forget it. I want results in this paper and I don't care what it costs to get those results. Any time you think you MIGHT get results don't worry about the cost. And where speculation is concerned always remember that even the best of us makes mistakes."

The downturn in circulation, which continued until late August, prompted Patterson, McCormick, and others to suggest a number of ideas for dealing with the crisis, including closing down the newspaper. A new start with a new name, the *Mirror*, was suggested, as was changing to afternoon publication. In late August, however, the newspaper expanded from sixteen to twenty pages, and by September Patterson was sure the *News* would make it. Circulation went over 32,500 in September and over 41,000 in October. It was then that the directors of the Tribune Company agreed to continue financial support of the *News*, which was running a deficit of about $40,000 a month. For the staff in New York, the decision removed a troubling cloud of uncertainty.

Further evidence that the *News* was on the way up for good was provided by the response to the newspaper's limerick contest in November. Four lines of a limerick were published, and a daily prize of $100 was offered for the best fifth line. In the 100 days the contest ran, the *News* received more than 1.2 million entries, and circulation in November averaged 60,000. In December, average circulation was 98,900, and on some days more than 100,000 copies of the paper were sold. The contest was clearly the sort of thing Patterson had in mind for building circulation. Leo McGivena, who for many years was the *News*'s advertising and marketing expert, wrote later that the limerick contest established for the *News* "the structure of a circulation stimulant; an artificial attraction, plus money prizes, induced non-readers to try the paper." He reported that experience showed it took three weeks on the average to induce a person to become a regular reader of the *News*.

In a report to Patterson on 10 December 1919, William Field wrote that success seemed certain: "In my judgment, by the end of 1920, our circulation will be better than 200,000. I think also that, within three years, we shall reach or top the maximum daily circulation in this town." By the first anniversary of the debut of the *Illustrated Daily News* ("*Illustrated*" was dropped from the title on 20 November 1919), circulation was 233,000, sixth among dailies in New York. Patterson told *News* employees in an anniversary message, "The *News* will be a success. I don't think one can say that it is already a success because it is not yet self-sustaining." He said he expected the newspaper would "pass from red figures to black on our balance sheets" in less than a year. The black figures were recorded in September 1920, and by the end of the year the newspaper was making a steady profit. Advertising totaled 1,723,000 lines for the year. Soon, the debt to the Tribune Company, which amounted to slightly more than a million dollars, was retired. Patterson's newspaper was clearly a success.

Some observers then and later found a ready explanation for the success of the *News*, linking it to the character of the 1920s in America. "It had the good fortune to come into existence when the astonishing capers of the post-war morals revolt were starting," commented the writer of a 1938 *New Yorker* profile of Patterson. "The *News* and the tabloids which came after it emphasized this type of news with a magnificent sense of disproportion. . . . Patterson conceived his tabloid's primary function to be that of purveying to the masses the forbidden thrills enjoyed by the few." McGivena agreed but went further to explain the popularity of the *News:* "The *News* reflected the spirit of the times. It was frivolous, irreverent, often outrageous, but it won intense reader interest and loyalty, [and] did more to serve readers personally than other papers."

More than good fortune and good timing were involved. Patterson worked hard at making

sure his newspaper would be interesting to large numbers of readers. He insisted on measuring public taste directly. On his trips to New York from Chicago in the early years and also after he moved permanently to New York, Patterson went out among the people in the city, alone or with a group of *News* executives, to do a form of marketing research. They would watch at newsstands and subway stations and peer through subway train windows to see who was reading the *News* and what they were reading. "The idea of these tours," he told the *News* executives, "is to make you fellows realize that every line you put in the paper ought to be aimed directly at these people." Patterson spent a lot of time over the years in the places where the people could be found: drugstore lunch counters and soda fountains, movie theaters, and subways. He talked with people and advised his employees to do the same. "You know, you fellows could learn a lot if you talked more with truck drivers," Patterson told one writer. His practice of going out among the people was not indicative of eccentricity, A. J. Liebling wrote after Patterson's death; rather, Patterson "studied people as closely as the Plains Indians studied the buffalo herds—and for much the same reason."

He was also skillful in choosing his employees, especially the executives who were given the task of seeing that his ideas and wishes were carried out. He was generally successful in gaining their loyalty and cooperation, partly by conveying his enthusiasm for ideas and partly by the manner in which he treated them. John Chapman, a longtime *News* writer and columnist, described Patterson as "austere but not distant or forbidding;" he "rarely summoned anybody to his presence; he went to see the one he wanted to see." Chapman stated that "once his mind was made up, and it made itself up very quickly, he got what he wanted; but, military man though he was, he never barked an order. His approach was 'Let's try this' or 'Don't you think it would be a good idea if we' or even 'What do you think about. . . .' Almost everybody knew this was an order." He "rarely showed anger, rarely chewed out anybody either in private or in public." One of the rare occasions was described in Patterson's obituary. His plan for handling a story was disputed by an executive, who was informed by Patterson: "The fact that I decided against you is no proof that I'm right and you're wrong. It may be true that I'm wrong and you're right. The fact that I decide against you is no proof that there's anything wrong with your judgment. It's purely because of an accident of birth that

I happen to be in a position where I get my way. But I do get my way, and don't ever forget that." He ended with a bang of his fist on a desk.

In 1921, the *News* moved to new quarters in a renovated building at 23-25 Park Place. Operations were underway there on 16 April, and two weeks later, on 1 May, the first issue of the Sunday *News* rolled off the presses. Its first-day circulation was about 200,000. Soon, it achieved new highs in circulation, as its daily counterpart had.

Part of the continued efforts to boost circulation involved contests with ever-increasing amounts of cash to be awarded. In December 1921, after a fierce competition with Hearst papers in Chicago and New York, the *Tribune* and *Daily News* joined their competitors in acceding to Postmaster General Will H. Hays's request that they consider discontinuing the contests. Total prize money had reached $700,000 in New York in less than a month.

Despite the popular success of the *News,* however, advertisers displayed a reluctance to buy large amounts of space in the tabloid. They remained to be convinced that the readership of the *News* offered them a good market for their products and services. In 1922, McGivena undertook a promotional campaign aimed at convincing them. In advertisements in newspapers and trade journals, the *News* used readership studies and demographics in making its case that "Sweeney," the statistically average New Yorker and typical *News* reader, had purchasing power. "In New York, Tell It To Sweeney! (The Stuyvesants Will Understand.),", the first of the advertisements read. A series of "Tell It To Sweeney!" ads followed. Patterson took an active interest in this promotional effort. He tied it in with his own newsstand and subway investigations by having a movie cameraman shoot film of people buying the *News;* he used the film to convince reluctant advertisers. In another campaign the *News* promoted its distinction as the newspaper least likely to be discarded on subways, a fact it uncovered by counting discarded papers maintenance men had saved.

Circulation continued to climb through 1922 and 1923, reaching an average of more than 630,000 daily and almost 600,000 on Sunday. "By 1923," McGivena wrote in his history of the *News,* "there were indications that the *News* was getting better as a newspaper." News coverage was better. The writing was more colorful and sharper in its terseness, as were headlines and picture captions. "The pictures were better, with more life and contrast." In short, the *News* was becoming more in accord with Patterson's vision of the ideal popular newspaper. By 1924 daily circulation hit 750,000, making the *News* the top daily in circulation in the United States.

In April 1926, by which time Patterson had moved permanently to New York, daily circulation passed the million mark for good; it had already averaged more than one million on Sunday since 1925. Patterson moved into what McGivena described as a "small cubbyhole of an office" on the fourth floor of the *News* building. "Most of the time he spent at the *News* plant was in the newsroom. His presence prevented many of the frictions and delays that occurred while he was based in Chicago."

The success of the *News* and the continued soundness of the *Chicago Tribune* enabled Patterson and McCormick to plan and undertake other ventures in the 1920s. They founded Pacific and Atlantic Photos, Inc., a picture gathering and distributing service, and organized the Coloroto Company in 1924 to publish *Liberty* magazine, which they planned as a weekly competitor of the *Saturday Evening Post* and *Collier's;* the magazine eventually reached a circulation of about 2.5 million. Patterson and McCormick talked about starting another tabloid newspaper in Los Angeles or moving into Washington, D.C., if *Liberty* showed a reasonable margin of profit. They gave up in April 1931, selling the magazine to Bernarr Macfadden and taking over Macfadden's *Detroit Daily* and changing its name to the *Detroit Mirror.* Edward Doherty, a *Liberty* writer, recalled that Patterson gathered the magazine's writers and editors in his office and, "grave and unsmiling," told them of the transaction. "We can't make a go of the magazine," Patterson said. "We've lost thirteen million dollars on it." Patterson and McCormick published the *Detroit Mirror* until 6 August 1932, when they closed it down.

Patterson continued developing ideas for comic strips for the Tribune-News Syndicate, following up on the success of "The Gumps." One observer commented in 1938 that "Patterson sets up comic-strip artists as a sort of aristocracy, pays them enormous salaries, and coaches them in developing their strips. Possibly this is because he rates pictures far above the written word as conveyors of ideas." Patterson had a hand in the creation of "Gasoline Alley," "Winnie Winkle, the Breadwinner," "Smitty," "Harold Teen," "Moon Mullins," and later "Smilin' Jack" and "Terry and the Pirates." Two other strips were the biggest successes of all. In mid-1924 Harold Gray, who had assisted on "The Gumps," approached Patterson with an idea for a new strip about an orphan boy named Otto. Patterson felt the character should be a girl because there were already enough strips about boys, and suggested naming her "Little Orphan Annie." That strip made its debut in the *News* on 5 August 1924. In 1931, Patterson told Chester Gould to change the name of the strip he was trying to sell from "Plainclothes Tracy" to "Dick Tracy," and outlined the way the story should begin. It first appeared in the *Daily News* on 12 October 1931. Lloyd Wendt says in his official history of the *Chicago Tribune* that "Patterson became an acknowledged genius in the world of syndicated strips. He insisted that the characters depict the lives and dreams, hardships and accomplishments of the kind of people who could be found in mass newspaper readership. He suggested ideas, coached the artists, and provided promotional stunts and campaigns to sell the comic wares. His formula was simple: 'Youngsters for kid appeal, a handsome guy for muscle work and love interest, a succession of pretty girls, a mysterious locale or a totally familiar one.' "

Another distinctive characteristic often noted about the *News* under Patterson's leadership was the plain style and forthrightness of its editorial page, which, an *Editor & Publisher* writer noted, reflected Patterson's personality. On that page, "the Captain daily holds council with New York's masses as no editor has done before or since his time." Stanley Walker, city editor of the *New York Herald Tribune,* wrote that it seemed as if the paper were saying, "Well, pal, I'll tell you how we feel about things." Patterson insisted on simple, even colloquial language and on editorials devoid of dogmatism and cant. When his chief editorial writer was on vacation, Patterson rejected the substitute's first effort because it read "as though an editorial writer had written it." Reading a typical *News* editorial has been described as being "something like listening to a hardheaded discussion by an intelligent and well-read barber." Reuben Maury became Patterson's chief editorial writer in 1926, and it was he who put on paper the views Patterson directed that the editorials should express. Patterson's wishes were passed on to Maury and to C. D. Batchelor, editorial cartoonist starting in 1931, in daily sessions at 11 A.M. on weekdays. (Both Maury and Batchelor won Pulitzer Prizes for their work.) The editorial conferences, according to John Chapman, "consisted mainly in Patterson saying what tomorrow's editorial should declare—and although Maury did the writing, the editorial would be almost entirely in Patterson's words." Maury had to hold the words in his memory because Patterson disliked anyone taking notes while he talked. Except on very rare occasions, the editorial *we* was used, a convention Patterson commented upon in one editorial: "The trouble is that the editorial 'we' is a clumsy convention. As a matter of fact almost every editorial is written by one man plus a policy."

The dominance enjoyed by Patterson's tabloid in the New York market was challenged for a time in the mid- and late 1920s by two new tabloids which appeared in 1924: Hearst's *Daily Mirror* in June and Macfadden's *Evening Graphic* in September. In the sensational competition of the period of "Jazz Journalism," the *News* kept pace with and often outdid its counterparts in the ballyhoo manner in which it covered the antics and follies of celebrities and the titillating and grisly revelations of sex crimes and murder trials. It all seemed perfectly in tune with Patterson's formula, which was to provide a thoroughly interesting newspaper for a mass audience. The *News* "played up whoopee and the crowd loved it," Patterson's obituary noted.

At times, Patterson expressed reservations about excesses in coverage, and occasionally *News* editorials questioned the conduct of the tabloids. During a controversy in January 1927 about censorship of stage plays, a suggestion that this could lead to control of the press prompted an editorial that asked, "Well, why not?" It went on: "In this Peaches-Daddy Browning trial some of the publications reporting it have gone so far beyond the line of decency as to seem insane. . . . Far be it from us to pin a lily on our coat. The *News*, also, has gone too far." But, it noted, "We see no end to competition in the New York newspaper field. Hence, we see no end to the smut parade unless the authorities intervene." The editorial commented that the "censorship, of course, should extend only to matters of common decency. Free speech as to public affairs must be free as now."

Still, in 1927 the *News* gave thorough and detailed coverage to the murder trial of Ruth Snyder and Judd Gray, and in January 1928, "New York's Picture Newspaper," as the *News* labeled itself, carried on its front page one of the most famous news photos in history: the execution in the electric chair of Ruth Snyder. The photograph, which was shot by a hidden camera attached to a photographer's leg, was carried first on 13 January 1928, under the headline, "DEAD." It was then reprinted on the front page of the Saturday and Sunday editions of 14 and 15 January, and again a week later as a Sunday centerfold. Several years later it was revealed that it was Patterson who had suggested getting a photograph of Snyder in the electric chair. "If

WHEN RUTH PAID HER DEBT TO THE STATE!—The only unofficial photo ever taken within the death chamber, this most remarkable, exclusive picture shows closeup of Ruth Snyder in death chair at Sing Sing as lethal current surged through her body at 11:06 Thursday night. Its first publication in yesterday's EXTRA edition of THE NEWS was the most talked-of feat in history of journalism. Ruth's body is seen straightened within its confining gyves, her helmeted head, face masked, hands clutching, and electrode strapped to her right leg with stocking down. Autopsy table on which body was removed is beside chair.

Story and another electrocution picture on p...

Front page of the New York Daily News *for 14 January 1928, with the famous photograph of the electrocution of Ruth Snyder, who had been convicted of murdering her husband. The picture was taken by* Daily News *photographer Tom Howard with a camera strapped to his ankle.*

this woman dies, I want a picture of her," he said. After it ran the first time, Patterson, who was in Chicago, rebuffed protests of the business office that it would cause the *News* to lose advertising. It appears, however, that even though Patterson had asked for the photo, he had second thoughts after actually seeing it in print; for soon after, he reportedly told his managing editor that he would not have known whether to run the photo or not. He added: "But since you used the picture, okay." The photo was a good circulation builder.

The *Daily News* made history again in November 1928 when it published photos from the S. S. *Vestris* sinking off the coast of Virginia. Its front page of 15 November, under the headline "CALL VESTRIS DISASTER 'MURDER!,'" carried what has been described as one of the greatest action pictures of all time. It showed the sharply angled deck of the *Vestris* as crewmen, some of whose faces reflected the fear they felt, attempted to make ready a lifeboat. The British steamer had sunk on 12 November with the loss of 110 lives. A *News* picture chaser had obtained an undeveloped roll of film from a crew member on one of the rescue ships that had brought survivors into New York.

In 1929, as the *News* moved into its second decade, Patterson sensed that the stock market crash and the onset of economic hard times would mean a change in people's interests. "We're missing the bus," he told members of his editorial staff. "People don't care so much about playboys, Broadway, and divorces. They want to know how they're going to eat. From now on we'll pay attention to the average man and his family." The *News* maintained its overall light touch and tone, but it offered "more bread while maintaining the supply of a pleasing dessert."

For the *News*, the most conspicuous sign of its solidity was its new $10 million, thirty-six-story building on East Forty-second Street. Designed by Raymond Hood, who had designed the Tribune Tower in Chicago, the building was completed in November 1929; operations commenced there in February 1930. The clean lines of its white brick exterior (a look Patterson insisted on) made it one of the most striking buildings in Manhattan at the time. Its four-story circular lobby was walled with panels of black glass; at its center was a globe seventeen feet in diameter. Patterson directed that all manner of weather, time, and geographic information be made available to users of the lobby. The facade over the main entrance on Forty-second Street had eight panels with "THE NEWS" at the top and "HE MADE SO MANY OF THEM" at the

bottom, with representations of men and women in between. The words were taken from a statement attributed to Abraham Lincoln: "God must have loved the common people, he made so many of them." *Time* magazine reported that "curious crowds stood in front of the new *News* building last week, eyeing a procession of laborers, beggars, children, flappers, photographers, marching in light relief across the building's grey-green granite facade over the tabloidally cryptic excerpt: 'He made so many of them.' " The building's cost forced Patterson to incur a $4 million mortgage, but that was paid off within four years, despite the general business decline of the Depression.

In 1934 Patterson paid $750,000 to help get Associated Press Wirephotos started and was granted exclusive use of the photos in New York for five years. (Seven years earlier he had obtained an Associated Press franchise by purchasing the *Commercial Bulletin* from Ridder Brothers for $500,000.)

By the time of its fifteenth anniversary in 1934, the *News* could editorialize without reservation that doubt about whether it would succeed "has been largely laid to rest, if we may say so." The tabloid's continuing growth in respectability in the eyes of the journalistic community was widely noted. "The *Daily News* was built on legs," Patterson said in 1938, "but when we got enough circulation we draped them." On the newspaper's twentieth anniversary, Walter E. Schneider wrote in *Editor & Publisher:* "That infant prodigy of American Newspapers, the *New York Daily News*, into whose veins a journalistic genius named Joseph Medill Patterson is still injecting his own magic that gave it early manhood and gigantic stature, bids *adieu* to its fabulous teen-age this week-end." At that point, daily circulation averaged 1.8 million (the largest in the United States) and Sunday circulation was 3.3 million (the second largest in the world).

Patterson married Mary King, women's editor of the *News*, in July 1938, after his divorce from his first wife became final. He and his first wife had been separated since 1925, when Patterson moved to New York from Chicago. Patterson and King had worked together for more than twenty years, starting at the *Chicago Tribune*. He said at one point: "I never had a good idea in my life that she wasn't at least the first half of it."

Almost as widely acknowledged as Patterson's genius was his quirkiness. Especially in the 1930s, as Patterson and the *News* became more actively and vociferously involved in advocating positions on important domestic and foreign policy issues, the examination of numerous oddities and unpleasant features of his personality was a frequent exercise among writers and critics. The 1938 *New Yorker* profile of Patterson, for example, began: "The theory that the man of genius is necessarily an odd fish fits the case of Joseph Medill Patterson. . . . He abounds in whims, caprices, phobias, and other psychological quirks, the most pronounced of which is a recurrent fondness for wearing disreputable-looking clothes." It added: "To intimates he exhibits a shy, charming side. Most others who encounter him find him dictatorial, muleheaded, contrary, unstable, and ruthless." Burton Rascoe described his former boss as "impulsive, erratic and impatient, unpredictable, a man who acts and works on hunches. He is devoid of all except the most elementary reasoning powers; and his mistakes have been made through the initial errors of assuming that he was thinking when he was merely feeling, and of attempting to apply a logical process to matters of pure instinct and emotion." Observers also noted his tendency toward excessive heroworship; his severe claustrophobia; his restlessness, which was evident, it was suggested, in his taking up flying; and his suspicion of anything foreign.

Patterson was a maverick among newspaper publishers in the 1930s, especially in his support for Franklin D. Roosevelt in three elections and his approval of much of the New Deal. Shortly after the 1932 election the *News* organized a campaign to collect donations for the building of a swimming pool in the White House, where Roosevelt could exercise his crippled legs. A 6 March 1933 editorial carried "A Pledge to Support Roosevelt," and one year later an editorial read: "We are glad to report today that we have never regretted that pledge; that we have been in sympathy with almost everything the President has done or tried to do or proposed to do." Patterson was a frequent guest at the White House and on the president's yacht, and Roosevelt often sought his advice and opinions. After the 1936 election, Roosevelt wrote Patterson that "I do not have to tell you how very splendid you have been throughout. I have a strong feeling that the *News* was worth more to us in the city in the way of votes than all the political meetings and speeches put together."

Differences over what the United States should do in response to the onset of war in Asia and Europe eventually caused a break between Patterson and Roosevelt. "Father hated war so much that it made him a different man," Patterson's daughter Alicia said. "I think it was because of what he went through in the first war." Even as general war loomed, Patterson, in a message in June 1939 on the twentieth anniversary of the founding of the *News*, stated, "My most earnest hope is that the next five or ten years will not include for American newspapers the coverage of a great war." But his abhorrence of war did not cause Patterson to argue against American preparedness for it. As early as 1934 he had called for building two ships to every ship the Japanese built. He also advocated a bigger air corps. Roosevelt recognized Patterson's influence and support in July 1940 when the president signed the "Big Navy" bill. He sent Patterson one of the pens he had used in signing the bill, noting Patterson's "great and helpful interest in this legislation" and expressing his "sincere appreciation."

Patterson became concerned that the Roosevelt administration was considering economic reprisals against Germany and Japan, seeing these as actions that usually lead to war. Although he thought that war with Japan was probably inevitable, he did not want the United States to cause it to happen any sooner than necessary. Just as he had in 1916, Patterson felt that the United States should stay out of the European war. However, after Roosevelt told him about it in advance, Patterson supported the arrangement in August 1940 whereby the United States traded Great Britain obsolete destroyers for bases. The break started after the election, when Roosevelt asked Congress for broad lend-lease authority. By 22 January 1941, Patterson, who felt betrayed by Roosevelt, had joined his cousin Robert McCormick and his sister Cissy Patterson, who had taken over the *Washington Times-Herald* in 1939, in opposing Roosevelt's policy and attacking lend-lease. In an editorial of that date, the *News* declared that the bill would "make the President a dictator of the United States, and hence its right name is the 'dictatorship bill' instead of the lend-lease bill." *News* editorials thereafter frequently criticized the president and questioned his respect for the truth. Critics saw the cousins as forming a "McCormick-Patterson Axis," a charge Patterson attempted to refute in a two-part editorial on 7 and 8 October 1941 titled "Family Portrait." Patterson traced the family's long history of isolationist sentiment and stressed the differences of opinion among the cousins, especially between McCormick and himself; he stated that the disagreements had influenced his move to New York. He also emphasized the independence in operation of the three newspapers.

After Pearl Harbor, Patterson laid aside his reservations about involvement in war. On 8 December 1941, the *News* editorial stated: "Well, we're in it. God knows Americans didn't want it. But let's gct behind our President and fight for America first." Three days after the attack on Pearl Harbor Patterson formally requested readmission to the army in a letter to the War Department. At sixty-two he expressed a willingness to serve in any capacity. The following day, he went to the White House to meet with Roosevelt. Patterson stood briefly in the president's study while Roosevelt signed documents, then stood for another fifteen minutes "while he gave me a pretty severe criticism for the way the *News* had conducted itself during the year 1941," Patterson recalled in a memorandum. "He said he would give me a task, which was to read over the *News* editorials for 1941." Later that day, at Cissy's home in Washington, Patterson said angrily, "That man did things to me that no man should ever do to *any* man. . . . All I want to do now is outlive that bastard." Patterson received no wartime assignment from Roosevelt and remained bitter at the president.

The Pattersons and McCormick and their newspapers were frequently criticized during the war for their opposition to the Roosevelt administration. One of the most widely noted incidents began in August 1942 when Representative Elmer Holland, a freshman Democrat from Pennsylvania, attacked the Pattersons as "America's No. 1 and No. 2 exponents of the Nazi propaganda line . . . doing their best to bring about a fascist victory, hoping that in the victory they were to be rewarded." Patterson replied bluntly the following day with an editorial headed "You're a Liar, Congressman Holland." It was signed "Joseph M. Patterson" and was the only editorial he ever signed. Holland responded with another attack, moving Patterson's daughter Alicia Patterson Guggenheim to speak out for her father in an editorial in her two-year-old Long Island newspaper *Newsday*. Although she and her father had strong disagreements about Roosevelt at the time, she defended Patterson, stating that she had "seen him under all sorts of circumstances," including "when he came back from France in 1918 looking older and grimmer; when he fought for the Roosevelt Administration because he believed that the underprivileged of the country should get a better break. . . . As long as I can remember, he was carrying the torch for the U.S.A." Patterson defended Father Charles E. Coughlin and other right-wing critics of the war in *News* editorials. In 1942 he was named to Gerald L. K. Smith's Hall of Fame, along with Coughlin, Martin Dies, William Randolph Hearst, Robert McCormick, and Eleanor Medill Patterson. By 1944, Patterson had been estranged from Roosevelt

for almost four years, and the *News* editorialized in that year "No Fourth Term for Caesar."

The closest Patterson got to the war was after its end when he went to Japan at the invitation of Gen. Douglas MacArthur. After his return his health steadily declined. He had little to do with active management of the *News* in the months before he died in Doctor's Hospital in New York on 26 May 1946. At the time of his death, which was attributed to a liver ailment, Patterson had been preparing for the fiftieth reunion of his class at Groton School. Services were conducted in his big house on his 108-acre estate in Ossining, New York, and his body was taken to Washington for a military burial in Arlington National Cemetery. The *News* editorial column for 27 May 1946 bore one brief notice:

> Joseph Medill Patterson, publisher of this newspaper and the man who directed this page from the day the *News* began June 26, 1919, is no longer with us. The story of his death will be found in the news columns.
>
> Those who are left behind will do their best to keep this page and the paper what we believe he would want them to be.

At the time of Patterson's death, circulation was more than 2.25 million daily and more than 4.5 million on Sundays. Those figures suggested that the *Daily News* was without question on solid footing, but for many observers the death of Patterson raised questions about the future. This concern had been expressed earlier, in the 1938 *New Yorker* profile by Jack Alexander: "So thoroughly is the *News*, from first page to last, the expression of one man's personal bias that it is difficult to imagine how its essential flavor will survive when Patterson dies or retires." Patterson himself had once stated that the *News* "won't last five years after I die." Observed the *New York Times* after his death: "The *Daily News* was so peculiarly Captain Patterson's individual creation from day to day that it will be interesting to watch what changes, if any, his death will bring."

Beyond speculation about the future of his newspaper, Patterson's death also brought forth numerous attempts to evaluate him and his journalism. To *Time* he was "the maverick journalistic genius who sired the slick, expert, irritating, irreverent, gamy newspaper with the largest circulation in the United States," whose "journalism owed more to P. T. Barnum than to Adolph Ochs." Others were more reserved, acknowledging his creativity and independence but withholding judgment on his place in journalism history. Another view was expressed by the *New York Herald Tribune*: "Whatever may be the historian's verdict on Joseph Medill Patterson, he certainly forced the newspapers of his day to test their old concepts anew, and, whether in competition or opposition to his ideas, to exert themselves to the utmost."

In 1947 the *Daily News* reached its peaks of circulation: 2.3 million daily and 4.7 million on Sundays. But by 1981, when daily circulation was down to 1.5 million and Sunday circulation down to 2.1 million, Tribune Company executives announced that they were considering closing the paper unless a buyer could be found. By November 1982 they had reconsidered and determined to keep the newspaper going for at least five more years.

References:

Jack Alexander, "Vox Populi," *New Yorker*, 14 (6 August 1938): 16-21; (13 August 1938): 19-24; (20 August 1938): 19-23;

"All in the Family," *Time*, 37 (24 February 1941): 46, 48;

"America Firster," *Time*, 43 (29 May 1944): 56-58;

Simon M. Bessie, *Jazz Journalism: The Story of the Tabloid Newspapers* (New York: Dutton, 1938);

John Chapman, *Tell it to Sweeney: The Informal History of the New York Daily News* (Garden City: Doubleday, 1961);

Irvin S. Cobb, *Exit Laughing* (Indianapolis: Bobbs-Merrill, 1941);

Richard G. DeRochemont, "The Tabloids," *American Mercury*, 9 (October 1926): 187-192;

Edward Doherty, *Gall and Honey: The Story of a Newspaperman* (New York: Sheed & Ward, 1941);

Edward F. Dunne, *Illinois: The Heart of the Nation, Volume 2* (Chicago: Lewis, 1933);

"Father and Daughter," *Time*, 15 (26 May 1930): 66;

"Five-Man Board Will Continue to Function on *New York News*," *Editor & Publisher*, 79 (1 June 1946): 9;

Herb Galewitz, ed., *Great Comics Syndicated by the New York Daily News and Chicago Tribune* (New York: Crown, 1972);

Oliver H. P. Garrett, "The Gods Confused," *American Mercury*, 12 (November 1927): 327-334;

Joseph Gies, *The Colonel of Chicago* (New York: Dutton, 1979);

Ben Gross, *I Looked and Listened* (New Rochelle, N.Y.: Arlington House, 1970);

John Gunther, *Inside U. S. A.* (New York: Harper, 1947);

Paul F. Healy, *Cissy: The Biography of Eleanor M.*

"Cissy" *Patterson* (Garden City: Doubleday, 1966);

Alice Albright Hoge, *Cissy Patterson* (New York: Random House, 1966);

Helen MacGill Hughes, *News and the Human Interest Story* (Chicago: University of Chicago Press, 1940);

"Joe Patterson of the 'News.' The Master of American Tabloid Journalism Dies at 67, Arch-Isolationist to a Bitter End," *Life*, 20 (10 June 1946): 47-50;

"Joseph Medill Patterson," *Chicago Tribune* (27 May 1946): 18;

"Joseph Medill Patterson," *New York Times* (27 May 1946): 22;

"Joseph M. Patterson Dies," *Editor & Publisher*, 79 (1 June 1946): 9, 60;

Aben Kandel, "A Tabloid a Day," *Forum*, 77 (March 1927): 378-384;

Alfred Henry Lewis, "Joseph Medill Patterson: An Apostle of Hope," *Saturday Evening Post*, 179 (15 September 1906): 3-4;

Lloyd Lewis and Henry Justin Smith, *Chicago: The History of Its Reputation* (New York: Blue Ribbon, 1933);

A. J. Liebling, "The Wayward Press: Mamie and Mr. O'Donnell Carry On," *New Yorker*, 22 (8 June 1946): 90, 92, 98;

James Linn, *James Keeley, Newspaperman* (Indianapolis: Bobbs-Merrill, 1937);

Ferdinand Lundberg, *America's 60 Families* (New York: Vanguard, 1937);

Ralph G. Martin, *Cissy* (New York: Simon & Schuster, 1979);

Leo E. McGivena, *The News: The First 50 Years of New York's Picture Newspaper* (New York: News Syndicate Company, 1969);

"N. Y. Papers Praise Patterson as 'Unique Force,'" *Chicago Tribune* (28 May 1946): 4;

"1,848,320 of Them," *Time*, 34 (3 July 1939): 30-31;

"Passing of a Giant," *Time*, 47 (3 June 1946): 87-88, 90-91;

Alicia Patterson as told to Hal Burton, "This is the Life I Love," *Saturday Evening Post*, 231 (21 February 1959): 19, 21, 44-45, 50-51;

Eleanor M. Patterson, "Sister Says Patterson Was 'Born With Genius,'" *Editor & Publisher*, 72 (24 June 1939): 7;

Burton Rascoe, *Before I Forget* (New York: Literary Guild, 1937);

Arthur Robb, "Shop Talk at Thirty," *Editor & Publisher*, 72 (24 June 1939): 52;

Walter E. Schneider, "Fabulous Rise of N.Y. Daily News Due to Capt. Patterson's Genius," *Editor*

& Publisher, 72 (24 June 1939): 5-7, 45-48;

George Seldes, *Lords of the Press* (New York: Blue Ribbon, 1941);

"So Many of Them," *Time*, 15 (21 April 1930): 26;

"Staff Tells Patterson's Concern for Masses," *Editor & Publisher*, 79 (1 June 1939): 60;

Kenneth Stewart and John Tebbel, *Makers of Modern Journalism* (New York: Prentice-Hall, 1952), pp. 217-238;

John Tebbel, *An American Dynasty* (Garden City: Doubleday, 1947);

Dana L. Thomas, *The Media Moguls* (New York: Putnam's, 1981);

Oswald Garrison Villard, "Are Tabloid Newspapers A Menace? I. Tabloid Offense," *Forum*, 77 (April 1927): 485-491;

Villard, *The Disappearing Daily* (New York: Knopf, 1944);

Frank C. Waldrop, *McCormick of Chicago: An Unconventional Portrait of a Controversial Figure* (Englewood Cliffs, N.J.: Prentice-Hall, 1966);

Stanley Walker, *City Editor* (New York: Stokes, 1934);

Coulton Waugh, *The Comics* (New York: Macmillan, 1947);

George Y. Wells, "Patterson and the *Daily News*," *American Mercury*, 50 (December 1944): 671-679;

Lloyd Wendt, *Chicago Tribune: The Rise of a Great American Newspaper* (Chicago: Rand McNally, 1979).

Papers:

Joseph Medill Patterson's papers are collected at the *New York Daily News* Library and in the *Chicago Tribune* archives.

Joseph Pulitzer, Jr.

(21 March 1885-30 March 1955)

Ronald T. Farrar
University of Kentucky

MAJOR POSITION HELD: Editor and publisher, *St. Louis Post-Dispatch* (1912-1955).

BOOK: *A Report to the American People* (St. Louis, 1945).

Joseph Pulitzer, Jr., who emerged from the shadow of his illustrious father to become a towering journalistic figure in his own right, headed the *St. Louis Post-Dispatch* for forty-three years. Far more than a caretaker of a family tradition, he was a forceful presence in the field of crusading journalism. Pulitzer's style and temperament differed sharply from those of his flamboyant father, but the two men shared the same publishing philosophy: a newspaper should do more than merely print the news; it should aspire to be a force for the public good. "Sooner or later, public opinion will crystalize," the younger Pulitzer once said during a *Post-Dispatch* crusade. "When it speaks, there can be heard the roar of a great tidal wave. The tidal wave is the inexorable, majestic force that in this country we know as the power of public opinion. Another name for it is American democracy." Joseph

Pulitzer, Jr., knew many such climactic moments in his career; under his leadership the *Post-Dispatch* won more journalistic battles, perhaps, than any other American daily of the era.

Pulitzer was born in New York City, the second of three sons of Joseph and Kate Davis Pulitzer. The elder Pulitzer, born in Hungary, had immigrated to the United States as a young man; settling in St. Louis, he stumbled into journalism and eventually launched his spectacular publishing career in 1878 by gaining control of two failing newspapers, the *Post* and the *Dispatch*. He merged them, and under his aggressive command the *Post-Dispatch* quickly established editorial supremacy and a solid financial footing. Pulitzer drove himself hard, and the incessant work took its toll on the high-strung journalist. By 1883 the thirty-six-year-old publisher's health had begun to crack; his eyesight was failing and his nerves were impaired. He was further discouraged in St. Louis by a tragedy in the *Post-Dispatch* editorial rooms: Pulitzer's editor, John A. Cockerill, shot and killed a prominent local attorney whom the paper had attacked in its columns. Cockerill acted in self-defense, but the public

Joseph Pulitzer, Jr.

backlash against the newspaper stung the sensitive Pulitzer and soured him on the city. Pulitzer moved to New York and, pledging the *Post-Dispatch* as collateral, took over the ailing *World*. In that much larger arena, Pulitzer became an immediate success. His "New Journalism"—crusading reporting, hard-hitting editorials, bright features, expanded coverage, intense promotion—filled a newspaper vacuum in New York and attracted new readers by the tens of thousands. By the time Joseph Pulitzer, Jr., was born in 1885, the *World* was the most powerful and most prosperous newspaper in America.

As a boy, Joseph Jr. displayed neither his father's feverish intensity nor his consuming intellectual curiosity; his easygoing manner frequently put him at odds with the harsh discipline imposed by his father, and the two often quarreled. He was sent to St. Mark's School in Southboro, Massachusetts, and then to Harvard; but in the wake of another family argument, he was yanked out of college in 1906 and exiled by his father to St. Louis to learn the newspaper business. Upon his arrival, the young man was ignominiously introduced to editor in chief George S. Johns with this letter: "Mr. Johns: This is my son Joseph. Will you try to knock some newspaper sense into his head?"

Authorized a salary of only fifty dollars a

week, young Pulitzer dutifully undertook to learn the business end of the operation, although his true interests lay in the news and editorial offices. Virtually an apprentice, he maintained a low profile. One incident later that year, however, evoked an outburst in the true Pulitzer tradition. That occurred when William Randolph Hearst, his father's archenemy since the "yellow journalism" days of the 1890s, paid a hurried visit to the *Post-Dispatch* newsroom. Hearst, passing through St. Louis on a train trip to Mexico, had granted an interview to the Associated Press; the wire service offices were situated in the *Post-Dispatch* building. Bristling at the sight of the controversial press magnate, young Pulitzer confronted Hearst. "I guess you don't know me," he said, "but I'm Joseph Pulitzer, Jr. I'd like to inquire whether you meant what you said about my father." Hearst's reply was curt: "I usually mean what I say." Pulitzer, an athletic youth who had taken boxing lessons, responded by delivering a powerful punch to Hearst's midsection, sending the large man reeling. Hearst dropped his overcoat and rushed his attacker, but the *Post-Dispatch* staff members separated the two men and escorted Hearst safely away. In New York, the senior Pulitzer was swiftly notified of the incident; he said nothing, but it was clear that he approved of his son's rousing defense of the family honor.

On 1 June 1910, Pulitzer married Elinor Wickham; they had three children, Joseph Pulitzer, III; Kate; and Elinor.

Pulitzer, Jr., still had not earned his father's full confidence by the time of the latter's death in 1911, a fact reflected in the elder Pulitzer's will. Pulitzer, Sr.'s complex division of his wealth may be regarded as his assessment of his sons' relative executive abilities. Herbert, the youngest son—he was only fifteen at the time—was awarded a six-tenths share of the family trust. The oldest son, Ralph, thirty-two, received two tenths. One tenth was divided among the chief editors and department heads of the two Pulitzer newspapers. Joe, Jr., the least favored, received the remaining tenth.

In 1912, the family named Joseph editor and publisher of the *Post-Dispatch,* presumably signaling an end to his apprenticeship. The titles remained largely honorary for years, however, for he was reluctant to snatch away the management of the paper from older and more experienced men, particularly where editorial judgments were concerned. He did spend a great deal of time on the business side, and as his financial, business, and general managers were lost through death, retirement, and resignation, Pulitzer assumed their responsibilities. His brothers—their hands full attempting to sustain the *World* against heavy competition in New York—virtually gave over to him control of the *Post-Dispatch*, and he gradually moved to take charge of his legacy. His steady progress was interrupted briefly by World War I: he had attempted to enlist in the navy as early as 1916, but had been rejected for poor eyesight; eventually he did receive a commission as an ensign in the aviation corps, but his weak vision precluded him from the flight duty he had hoped for. The war ended two months later.

Following the war Pulitzer began to assert himself more prominently in the operations of the the *Post-Dispatch*. He imposed a strict acceptability code for advertising—one of the first and most stringent measures of its kind. False or misleading ads were rejected outright—often over the anguished protests of the paper's own advertising executives—and questionable product claims were carefully verified by the paper's own censor and review board before the *Post-Dispatch* would run them. This strict bit of self-regulation, coming at a time when advertising abuses were rampant throughout the industry, caused the *Post-Dispatch* to refuse more than $200,000 a year in advertising, but it enhanced the credibility of the paper and won its publisher some deserved prestige.

Pulitzer also developed a keen interest in newspaper machinery and production techniques. Largely through his urging, the *Post-Dispatch* became a pioneer in the development of rotogravure photography sections. He was quick to grasp the journalistic possibilities of radio: the *Post-Dispatch*-owned station, KSD, went on the air in the spring of 1922; it was the first commercial radio station in Missouri and the first in the United States to be operated by a newspaper. His subsequent interest in television, evident as early as 1936, led to the establishment in 1947 of KSD-TV, the first television station operated by a newspaper. Pulitzer fought hard against broadcast advertising messages that interrupted the news—"plug-uglies," he called them—and insisted that commercials be placed only at the beginning and the end of his stations' newscasts.

His consuming interest, though, was in the news and editorial operations of the *Post-Dispatch*. He felt keenly the responsibility of upholding the mandate for the paper cabled by his father from Europe in 1907: "I know my retirement will make no difference in its cardinal principles; that it will always fight for justice and reform, never tolerate injustice or corruption, always fight demagogues of all parties, never belong to any party, always oppose privileged classes and public plunderers, never lack sympathy with the poor, always remain devoted to the public welfare; never be satisfied with merely printing news; always be drastically independent; never be afraid to attack wrong, whether by predatory plutocracy or predatory poverty." That platform has been repeated every day atop the editorial page since November 1911; Pulitzer insisted that it was the only guide that the paper had or needed. Although he actively managed the business affairs of the corporation, Pulitzer liked to be thought of as the editor rather than the publisher. "If somehow you could establish my identity a little more clearly as an active newspaper man," he once told an interviewer, "contributing with suggestions, criticism, editing, and occasional rewriting, to the news, features, and editorial contents of the paper from day to day, I should be glad to see that done." His memoranda, always on distinctive yellow sheets, flooded the desks of his chief editors. Usually the messages were worded in the form of polite questions—to which, as one *Post-Dispatch* man put it, "intelligent activity was the wisest reply."

Elinor Pulitzer was killed in an automobile accident on 13 March 1925. On 7 April of the following year, Pulitzer married Elizabeth Edgar. They had one child, Michael.

Pulitzer's managing editor was Oliver Kirby Bovard, a legendary newspaperman who developed on the *Post-Dispatch* one of the most admired reporting and editing staffs of the day. *Post-Dispatch* investigations uncovered graft and corruption at every level—including the Teapot Dome scandal—and the staff's handling of the day-to-day news set standards for completeness and accuracy. The editorial page, under the immediate supervision of George S. Johns and later Clark McAdams, was an unwavering voice for liberalism throughout the 1920s and earlier 1930s. A passionate champion of civil liberties and civic ownership, McAdams wrote stirring editorials that were widely quoted throughout the country. One memorable example came in his biting endorsement of Franklin Roosevelt over Herbert Hoover in 1932: "The issue," he declared, "is between the Country and the Country Club."

Yet, as Irving Dilliard, another brilliant editorial page editor of the *Post-Dispatch*, would later observe, Pulitzer did exert a restraining influence on those editors who sought to push beyond positions he was willing to take. Midway through Roosevelt's first term, Pulitzer decided to moderate the paper's liberal stance; he replaced McAdams as

ST. LOUIS POST-DISPATCH

FINAL   SEVENTH WAR EXTRA

The Only Evening Newspaper in St. Louis With the Associated Press News Service

ST. LOUIS, MONDAY, DECEMBER 8, 1941—32 PAGES   PRICE 3 CENTS

CONGRESS DECLARES WAR ON JAPAN
1500 KILLED IN ATTACK ON HAWAII

BATTLESHIP CAPSIZED, DESTROYER BLOWN UP, WHITE HOUSE REVEALS

Other American Ships Damaged, Many Planes Destroyed — U. S. Fighting Back — Manila Fort and Airfield Are Heavily Bombed.

"Unprovoked and Dastardly Attack"---Roosevelt

PRESIDENT ROOSEVELT delivering his war message to Congress today. Behind him sit VICE-PRESIDENT HENRY WALLACE (left) and HOUSE-SPEAKER SAM RAYBURN (center.)

JOINT SESSION ACTS QUICKLY ON REQUEST FROM THE PRESIDENT

Representative Jeannette Rankin Casts Only Opposing Vote in Either House—'We Will Gain the Inevitable Triumph,' Says Roosevelt.

JAPANESE CLAIM THEY SANK TWO U.S. BATTLESHIPS

TEXT OF ROOSEVELT'S MESSAGE TO CONGRESS

BRITAIN DECLARES WAR ON JAPAN IN ALLIANCE WITH U.S.

TODAY'S WAR NEWS

FAIR AND COOLER TONIGHT, ABOUT 31; HIGH TOMORROW 48

TREND OF TODAY'S MARKETS

Front page of the St. Louis Post-Dispatch *as it appeared during Pulitzer's years as publisher*

editorial page editor with the more conservative Charles G. Ross. To the astonishment of many, the *Post-Dispatch* endorsed Alf Landon for president in 1936—just as it would endorse another Republican candidate, Thomas E. Dewey, in 1948.

Pulitzer ultimately lost a measure of confidence in Bovard, the managing editor to whose judgment he had deferred for many years. Following the stock market crash of 1929, Bovard's political views had taken a sharp left turn, and the ambitious managing editor longed for more power on the paper as well as a more activist editorial policy for it. In time Pulitzer's own moderate instincts prevailed; he overruled Bovard on a number of occasions, and in 1938 the managing editor resigned, citing "irreconcilable differences" between himself and Pulitzer as the cause. Bovard was succeeded by Benjamin H. Reese.

Physically, Pulitzer resembled his father. He stood just over six feet tall and weighed 200 pounds. When not involved with *Post-Dispatch* business, he spent much of his time outdoors. He inherited his father's weak eyesight; he became entirely blind in one eye and retained only about twenty percent vision in the other. He carried on, like his father before him, by having secretaries read the newspapers to him, then dictating by the hour letters and his famous interoffice memoranda. He could read ordinary newspaper print only with the aid of a magnifying glass. Doctors told him he could postpone the onset of complete darkness by taking good care of himself. As a result, Pulitzer restlessly pursued the outdoor life, either on his yacht or at hunting lodges from Canada to the Gulf Coast. Wherever he went, his secretaries and his files were with him, and he kept in close and continuous contact with the affairs of the paper. "My professional life is what I live for," Pulitzer said, "and I have a perfectly swell time living it and would not swap it for any other kind of life."

The *Post-Dispatch* and its broadcast properties flourished, and Pulitzer became one of the highest-paid executives in the Midwest, frequently drawing salary and bonuses in excess of a quarter-million dollars a year. His business acumen proved just how wrong his father had been in sizing up his sons; by 1931 Herbert and Ralph Pulitzer had sold the floundering *New York World* to the Scripps-Howard chain, but back in St. Louis Joseph Jr., the ugly duckling, had not only survived but had been able to nurture his newspaper to a prestigious national reputation and enormous profits. Throughout the years, the *Post-Dispatch* had attracted talented people to its staff, including reporters Bart

WITNESSES FOR THE PROSECUTION
APRIL 30, 1945

A commentary on the horrors of the Nazi concentration camps in a 30 April 1945 political cartoon by the Post-Dispatch's *Pulitzer Prize-winning cartoonist Daniel R. Fitzpatrick*

Howard and Paul Y. Anderson, columnist Marquis W. Childs, and political cartoonist Daniel Fitzpatrick. In 1945, on the occasion of his sixtieth birthday, Pulitzer convened a massive reunion of present and former employees. The party attracted national attention, and the guest list included many of the glittering names in American journalism.

Though he rarely sought publicity for himself, Pulitzer in 1945 undertook a determined personal crusade to focus American public opinion on the atrocities committed by the Nazis against Jewish, Polish, and Russian political prisoners. One of a team of American journalists invited by Gen. Dwight Eisenhower to visit European concentration camps, Pulitzer arrived at Buchenwald just twelve days after it had been liberated by American troops. "I came here in a suspicious frame of mind," Pulitzer cabled from Paris, "feeling that many of the terrible reports were exaggerations and largely propaganda. It is my grim duty to report that the descriptions of the horrors of this camp, one of the many which have been and will be uncovered by the Allied armies, have given less than the whole truth. They have been understatements. The brutal fiendishness of these operations defies description." Upon returning to the United States, Pulitzer was instrumental in obtaining the release of classified pictures taken by Signal Corps photographers documenting the tragedies; he arranged for public showing of these films, and accepted speaking engagements in which he advocated ridding the world of "the cancer of Nazism and German militarism." The articles he had written from Europe were collected as *A Report to the American People* (1945).

Like his father, Pulitzer never wrote his memoirs; he seemed more concerned with the present and future than the past. He was convivial but not garrulous, as courteous with his employees as his father had been overbearing. In 1951 he bought out an old competitor, the *Star-Times,* to give the *Post-Dispatch* clear sailing in the afternoon field in St. Louis. He had received an award from the University of Missouri School of Journalism in 1947; in 1952 he was given an honorary doctorate of laws degree by Columbia University.

Pulitzer died on the evening of 30 March 1955, following a full day of work at the *Post-Dispatch.* The cause of death was a ruptured blood vessel in the abdomen. His ashes were scattered over Frenchman's Bay, near his summer home in Bar Harbor, Maine. Tributes to his long and distinguished career came in from leading political figures and journalists throughout the world, but perhaps the one he might have cherished the most had already come from within the *Post-Dispatch* family: a statement from his employees that had been read to him on his seventieth birthday, less than two weeks before his death. The hand-lettered testament, the frontispiece of a leather-bound gift book containing reproductions of the newspaper's front pages, said in part: "If you are exacting in your requirements, as you must be, you have never breached the rule of courtesy in being so. Your respect for a man because he is human and needs a certain pride in himself includes a certain respect for his ideas. We have learned that anyone who is true to his work can be true to himself with no risk to his sensibilities or his aspirations. . . ."

Pulitzer's older son, Joseph Pulitzer III, succeeded him as editor and publisher of the *Post-Dispatch.*

References:

Jack Alexander, "The Last Shall Be First," in *Saturday Evening Post. Post Biographies of Famous Journalists,* edited by John E. Drewry (Athens: University of Georgia Press, 1942), pp. 85-106;

Silas Bent, *Newspaper Crusaders: A Neglected Story* (New York & London: McGraw-Hill, 1939);

Roger Butterfield, "An Editor Must Have No Friends," *Collier's,* 126 (23 December 1950): 30-31, 47-49;

Butterfield, "The *St. Louis Post-Dispatch*—Pulitzer's Prize," *Collier's,* 126 (16 December 1950): 26-27, 76-83;

Ronald T. Farrar, *Reluctant Servant: The Story of Charles G. Ross* (Columbia: University of Missouri Press, 1968);

James W. Markham, *Bovard of the* Post-Dispatch (Baton Rouge: Louisiana State University Press, 1954);

Charles G. Ross, *The Story of the* Post-Dispatch (St. Louis: *St. Louis Post-Dispatch*, 1954);

Papers:
Joseph Pulitzer, Jr.'s papers are at the Library of Congress.

Ernie Pyle

Mary Alice Sentman
University of North Carolina

BIRTH: Near Dana, Indiana, 3 August 1900, to William Clyde and Maria Taylor Pyle.

EDUCATION: Indiana University, 1919-1923.

MARRIAGE: 7 July 1925 to Geraldine Elizabeth Siebolds, divorced 14 April 1942. Remarried 12 March 1943.

MAJOR POSITIONS HELD: Reporter, *La Porte* (Indiana) *Herald* (1923); reporter, desk man, *Washington* (D.C.) *Daily News* (1923-1926); desk man, *New York Evening World* and *New York Evening Post* (1926-1927); telegraph editor, *Washington Daily News* (1928); aviation editor and columnist, *Washington Daily News* and Scripps-Howard Newspapers (1928-1932); managing editor, *Washington Daily News* (1932-1935); roving columnist, Scripps-Howard Newspapers (1935-1940); war correspondent, Scripps-Howard Newspapers (1940-1945).

AWARDS AND HONORS: Pulitzer Prize, 1944; LL.D., University of New Mexico, 1944; L.H.D., Indiana University, 1944; Medal of Merit, 1945.

DEATH: Ie Shima Island, in the Ryukyus, 18 April 1945.

BOOKS: *Ernie Pyle in England* (New York: McBride, 1941);
Here Is Your War (New York: Holt, 1943);
Brave Men (New York: Holt, 1944);
Last Chapter (New York: Holt, 1946);
Home Country (New York: Sloane, 1947).

Ernie Pyle became a well-known and widely read columnist during the Second World War. Following the path of the fighting from England to Africa, then to Italy and France, and finally to the Pacific, Pyle wrote the story of the ordinary soldier. His daily columns told of the details of war life, of danger, sadness, fear, heroism, and humor. Pyle was awarded the Pulitzer Prize in 1944 for "Distinguished Correspondence" in 1943. He was killed in

Ernie Pyle

action on Ie Shima in the Pacific on 18 April 1945. At the time of his death, the column was carried by more than 300 daily and 400 weekly newspapers.

Born on a small farm near Dana, Indiana, Ernest Taylor Pyle grew up in an early twentieth-century midwestern rural setting. He was an only child and spent a great deal of time alone. Regularly assigned his share of chores, he fed chickens, plowed the fields from the age of nine, chopped wood, and attended to the routine daily tasks of farm life. He accompanied the family to town on Saturday nights and to church on Sunday mornings. Observing the patterns of small-community life may have fostered the keen sense of finding, observing, and writing detail which later made his journalistic columns so appealing and realistic. These early days also provided material for later writing, and he told his readers of his mother, his father, his boyhood fear of snakes, the incessant midwestern wind, and the heat and laziness of summer country days.

Years later he would write home commenting on his parents' attendance at the state fair or suggesting that the foreign stamp on his letter be given to a neighborhood child. About his mother he wrote in one of his columns: "My Mother would rather drive a team of horses than cook a dinner. But in her lifetime she has done very little of the first and too much of the latter. She has had only three real interests—my Father, myself, and her farm work. . . . My Mother probably knows as little about world affairs as any woman in the neighborhood. Yet she is the broadest-minded and most liberal of the lot."

His understanding and compassion for ordinary people and those left out of the mainstream of life may have had its beginnings in his youth as well. He was small as a child and did not participate in the sports and games of his schoolmates; he remained short and slight as an adult. About his hometown experiences, he wrote, "I never felt completely at ease in Dana. I suppose it was an inferiority hangover from childhood. I was a farm boy, and town kids can make you feel awfully backward when you're young and a farm boy. I never got over it. I should have, of course. . . ."

Pyle attended a country school, which he reached by horse and buggy. He graduated from Helt Township High School in 1918 and joined the navy, in which he served only a few months before the First World War ended. He never left the United States during that war and later, when asked to fill in his military duty on a form, wrote that it was "too slight to mention."

In September 1919, he registered as a student at Indiana University in Bloomington. He started college with no idea of a future job or an academic major, and drifted into journalism on the advice of a new acquaintance, Paige Cavanaugh. The two were to become lifelong friends and confidants. Cavanaugh told the freshman that he had heard journalism was easy and so the two signed up. Since there was no formal major in the subject, Pyle officially majored in economics, taking a concentration of journalism courses. (Cavanaugh did not continue in journalism; he later moved to California, where he was involved in the filming of a movie about Pyle toward the end of the Second World War. The two remained friends and exchanged letters and visits until Pyle's death.)

Pyle's newspaper writing career began as a staff reporter for the university paper, *The Student*. He covered routine assignments—one of the first was an article on the university bookstore—and wrote in such a simplistic and ordinary manner that the editors sometimes complained.

In his junior year, he was appointed city editor of *The Student* one semester and news editor the next. But he became known for his travels rather than for his university beat. In the fall semester of his junior year, he briefly exchanged jobs with the sports editor and drove to Boston in an old car with a friend to attend an Indiana-Harvard football game. The car, a Lozier, burned up, and the two would-be sports reporters hitchhiked back to Indiana. Pyle wrote nothing about the game he had planned to cover, although his own experiences were reported in the paper by another student who stated that the two had ridden in more than fifty cars on the return trip.

Later that same year, Pyle and three other students traveled to the Far East to follow the Indiana University baseball team and report the games with various Japanese universities. But no stories were filed from those games, for the travelers had worked their way over on a ship and their contract did not permit them to leave that ship until the journey was completed at Manila. The 28,000-mile trip, however, did provide Pyle with a story which earned his first by-line. In its careful chronicling of the details of ship life, it foreshadowed the detailed reports he was later to send from his travels throughout the United States and then from the battlefronts of the Second World War. His concern for people showed itself when he helped a Filipino boy stow away on the return trip and, later, helped him gain an education. Pyle's easy style and conversational writing may be seen in his story of the trip: "Within a few hours the ship started rolling slightly and it was not long until the first terrible feelings of sea sickness began to creep over the majority of the voyagers. Everyone was in bed early that night, since that seemed the only way to avoid the inevitable. The sea was no better the next morning, and the few of those who were bold enough to venture on deck were not able to remain long." About his own role and those of his companions, he said: "A word about the four adventurers. Kaiser and I are serving as bell boys on the ship; we take turns working, so that neither of us is overburdened with our labors. We carry ice water, shine shoes, deliver packages, fix bath tubs, and tend to the innumerable queer wants of the passengers."

Pyle became editor in chief of *The Student*

during the following summer session and was well known on the campus. The next fall, he was elected to a number of campus organizations and assumed the duties of football team manager. He also became editor of the *Smokeup*, a monthly humor sheet that used campus activities and figures for its material.

Pyle did not finish his senior year. Rejected by the girl he loved, he left the campus to take a job as a reporter at the *La Porte* (Indiana) *Herald*. While there he covered a Ku Klux Klan rally and refused to be intimidated by threats into not writing about it. His story was published. He stayed in this job only three months, leaving for Washington, D.C., and a better job as a reporter at the *Washington Daily News*.

After a stint as a reporter, he moved to the copydesk of the *News*. In 1925 he married Geraldine ("Jerry") Siebolds, a young woman from Minnesota who was working in Washington. They led an almost bohemian life of late hours, many friends, and little furniture.

In 1926 Pyle quit his job and the two embarked on a car tour of the United States, a forerunner of the "Roving Reporter" tours they were to make. Returning to the East ten weeks later with no money and no job, Pyle found work on the copydesk of the

Pyle's wife, Jerry (Fred Payne, Memphis Press-Scimitar*)*

New York Evening World, moving later to the *New York Evening Post,* again on the copydesk.

At the invitation of a friend from Washington days, Lee G. Miller (later Pyle's biographer), Pyle returned to the *Washington Daily News* as telegraph editor in December 1927. According to all reports, he was superb in the job. Miller remembered that "he was as fast and clean a copy-handler as I ever knew, and worked a tense shift of eight hours." But Pyle was restless at a desk job and asked to write an aviation column as well. For several months he worked at both jobs, leaving the paper in the midafternoon when his telegraph work was finished and going to the airfields. Finally, in June 1929, the paper made him a full-time aviation writer.

Although he was to become best known for his writings about the common man, Pyle was somewhat of a hero worshipper at this time, admiring the pioneer aviators in much the same way as he had the Indianapolis Speedway drivers in his youth. The fliers and he were great friends and he spent many hours with them, both on duty at the flying fields and socially. His home was a gathering place for those in the aviation world. His column appealed to people interested in flying and to others who were fascinated by the human interest aspects.

Pyle wrote of a young flier who crashed and nearly died just one day after his marriage, and of his subsequent struggle to build a new life. He wrote of daring and successful mail flights. He wrote of the women who waited for men who never returned: "Missing—that is aviation at its worst. Sudden news of death is like a knockout blow; it hurts and bewilders and then it gradually diminishes. But missing—that is the torture screw, with each hour that passes giving the screw another turn. You can't resign yourself to grief; you must hang alone by the tips of your hope—dangling, imagining, lying to yourself, waiting."

The aviation column was Pyle's first step to becoming nationally known. When he wrote of the crash of pioneer pilot Floyd Cox, he received emotional mail from all over the country. One unsigned letter praised Pyle for his columns about "pioneers breaking the earthbound instincts of many years and now taking us up to the clouds." The subjects were wide ranging—from heroes to on-the-ground workers to air fares to the air mail debates in Congress. In 1932 he wrote a series on the use of planes in war in which he addressed the rumors and fears of the public concerning air warfare: "If this country were to go to war tomorrow, it is extremely

Pyle in Washington State during the tour of the United States he took with his wife in 1926. Similar automobile trips later supplied material for his early columns.

doubtful whether any cities would be 'blown off the map.' The worst horror would be within the first few days or weeks."

When Pyle left the aviation job in 1932 to be *Daily News* managing editor, he received letters from senators, from government officials, from pilots, and from ordinary people who read his columns day by day. His final column summarized his feelings about the purpose of the column: "This column has tried to feel with those who fly. It has recorded the surprised elation of those who have risen rocketlike into renown, has felt despair with those who have been beaten down by the game, has shared the awful desolation of those who have seen their close ones fly away and come back only in the stark blackness of the newspaper headlines."

As managing editor, Pyle had few opportunities to write, but he held his staff to the standards he had developed for himself. In one of his early memos, written in lieu of a staff meeting (he called such meetings "odious"), he outlined his philosophy of what the paper should be:

> A friend of mine, a very great editor, once said that inevitably in any organization inertia and lethargy develop, and that in a newspaper they are fatal.
>
> I feel that has happened here. As individuals, we are not especially conscious of it. But it is here. The paper shows it. Today the columns lack youth, the sparkle and the fire that they once had.
>
> This lethargy is explainable. You know your jobs too well. . . . you write, as the drama critics would say, adequately.
>
> On an old, established paper, that might be good enough. But on this paper it isn't. . . . We have to *make* people read this paper by making it so alert and saucy and important they will be afraid of missing some things if they don't read it.

Along with his standards, Pyle maintained a keen interest in the welfare of those under him and worked for raises for the staff. His memos show lists of salary figures and suggested increases along with reasoning to support the changes. There is record of him firing only one person during his years as managing editor—a "new and spectacularly inept" copyboy.

Despite his affection for aviators, Pyle was more loyal to his reporters. He became angered by Lindbergh who, himself angry with the press for hounding him, stopped his plane after a landing at Washington in such a way that the still-revolving propeller covered the waiting reporters with mud. Later, when the Lindbergh baby was kidnapped, Pyle put the story on page five of the first edition of the *News*. By the second edition, cooler heads had prevailed and the story appeared on page one.

The inside desk work wearied Pyle, who preferred to be out among the people chasing stories. In late 1935, he became ill with the flu and, as part of his convalescence, traveled to the Southwest with his wife. They searched in vain for sunshine during a particularly cold and wet winter. It was on this trip that Pyle met a man who was to become a good friend: Ed Shaffer, then editor of the Scripps-Howard *Tribune* in Albuquerque. The Pyles were to build a house in that city just before Ernie went to London to write the first of his war columns.

They sailed on a freighter, the *Harpoon,* from Los Angeles to Philadelphia; the cruise took three weeks. Pyle went back to work as managing editor, but also wrote eleven pieces about his recent travels. These first columns were written to fill space for the regular Heywood Broun column while Broun was on vacation. The columns were a success and, within four months, he had convinced the paper that he should initiate a full-time six-day-a-week column, traveling where the mood took him and writing whatever stories he found along the way. He and Jerry, who was to become known through the columns as "that girl who rides beside me," started out across the United States, driving to Maine, New Jersey, New Orleans, Los Angeles, Portland, the Dakotas, and Ohio. The first year they spent almost entirely in the car. Pyle talked to anyone and everyone, finding stories in the lives of the common and the great, and telling the stories with humor, compassion, insight, and detail. He could poke fun at life and at himself. In one of his funniest columns he wrote about a new pair of pants with a zipper that "ran like a cog wheel off the track." One evening he found that he could not get the zipper to move at all; he reported: "We had a dinner guest that night, a big fellow who thought he could zip the zipper all right. He was just a fool; he couldn't even get it started." He went on to describe a grueling process of putting the zipper tab on the kitchen table and pounding it open a half inch at a time. He concluded:

We got the zipper open in a little less than half an hour.

I didn't put on the other pair of pants, the one with the buttons. I didn't eat any dinner, either. Didn't feel like dinner, somehow. I just went to bed and turned out the lights and lay there with my jaws clenched, glaring at the darkness.

Pyle worked painstakingly on the columns, often feeling that they were no good and despairing over his ability to write. When she was with him, his wife offered criticism, and performed editing and typing tasks as well. He was sensitive about having the columns cut or changed and once wrote his editor that "the whole thing flows together like music in my head. I'll write less, if you want, but I don't want it cut."

The job was demanding. His friends thought it sounded easy—write one column a day, write whatever you want, go wherever you want. Once when he became chagrined at these sentiments, he wrote Lee Miller: "Takes me about half a day to write a column. Other half to dig it up. Other half seeing old friends in various cities. Other half traveling. Other half sleeping." In actual practice, he searched for stories for several days and then wrote a number of columns at one time. As in his later writing days in the war, he attempted to keep a cushion of stories ahead and became depressed when it would become depleted.

His letters to his old friend Cavanaugh recounted problems with his writing and worries about the column. He had other worries, too: his personal life was unhappy due to his wife's more and more frequent depressions. Pyle himself was melancholy much of the time, although he kept his low moods out of the columns.

He crossed the country many times, visiting all forty-eight states, Alaska, Hawaii, Canada, and Mexico. In Alaska he interviewed a man who had made himself a set of false teeth using bear teeth for the back molars. He also wrote several Alaska columns about a woman and her three daughters who lived alone in the wilderness and trapped for a living. He visited the leper colony at Molokai and wrote about his conversations with a young man who had contracted leprosy just a few days after graduating from the university. In September 1938 Pyle flew to South America, where he found his inability to communicate well in Spanish limited story possibilities.

Pyle was becoming well known and was increasingly followed by people who wanted to talk or wanted autographs. It was difficult to reserve any private time, for his friends visited often.

Scripps-Howard decided to syndicate the column. When G. B. (Deac) Parker, editor in chief for Scripps-Howard, sent Pyle his first syndication check in June 1939, it was for $136.57. Parker commented in his letter, "While the sum is not of such size as to cause you to think of buying a yacht, nevertheless, it would be a lot of money if you had won it on a horse."

In August 1940, Pyle visited Brown County, Indiana, not far from Bloomington, where he had gone to school. He wrote a series of columns about the area and in one of them commented: "I want to come back sometime to Brown County when the slope turns into the bitter beauty of dying summer. Come back and hunt squirrels with the boys, and listen to the quartet at night, and go far out into the dirt roads where the cabins still lean. There is an accumulation of generations of dignity about these rolling hills and their peoples that gives me a nostalgia and a feeling of deep respect." Instead he left late that fall for London to cover the war and write the first of the columns that would make him famous.

The decision to go to Europe had not been an easy one. Pyle's wife had been against it, but slowly they both realized that it was what he should do. The danger in the job was great and he knew it. In letters to friends, he confessed to being "already so damned scared I wish I'd never thought of it in the first place." He sailed 16 November 1940 on the American Export Line ship *Exeter*.

Pyle began his series of columns on the ship but was unhappy with the writing. The copy was sent back airmail, except for urgent material, which was sent by cable. The ship docked in Lisbon, where he had to wait twelve days before leaving for London. He arrived in London on 9 December carrying "a yellow bag, a typewriter, and a sugar sack" filled with belongings.

He thought his first columns were dull and felt unemotional and drifting. But the column written after the 29 December firebombing of London was charged with emotion: "For on that night this old, old city—even though I must bite my tongue in shame for saying it—was the most beautiful sight I have ever seen. It was a night when London was ringed and stabbed with fire. They came just after dark, and somehow I could sense from the quick,

bitter firing of the guns that there was to be no monkey business this night . . . there was something inspiring in the savagery of it." He described the hundreds of fires, the grinding of plane engines, the pinpoints of white-hot incendiary bombs, and summarized the experience: "These things all went together to make the most hateful, most beautiful single scene I have ever known."

There were less exciting days and nights as well. Pyle explored the everyday scenes of a city and country at war. His descriptions of these were detailed and far more serious than the writings of his peacetime sojourns, but at the same time they were conversational, making the war meaningful for the readers. In one column, soon after the firebombing, he asked his readers to "just shut your eyes, try to transfer the details to your own city and see how odd it looks to you." The column went on to describe the underground shelter signs, the surface-level concrete street shelters, the tanks of water and buckets of sand for fighting fires, and the daily cleanup operations following the nights of bombings.

Although he was in the war daily in London, Pyle had no desire to be any more involved in physical danger or heroics than was necessary. In early January 1941, he wrote: "Although I've had my big 'night of fire' and plenty of bombs, too, I have not yet achieved any intimate acquaintance with a bomb. And I am quite willing to have the introduction filed under 'things pending.' "

As he always had, he filled his columns with the life around him and told the everyday stories of the people who lived it. He wrote of existence in the bomb shelters, of the nighttime bombing and antiaircraft artillery, of the blackouts, and of the British struggle to carry on despite the war. He attempted to bring the scope and reality of the war to his readers. Roy Howard sent him a cable: "Ernie Pyle. Your stuff not only greatest your career but most illuminating human and appealing descriptive matter printed America since outbreak battle Britain. . . ."

The columns were not without humor. One related the bomb damage to Westminster Abbey and to Parliament. Commenting on the damage to the House of Commons, Pyle wrote: "and the same bomb damaged the behind of Richard the Lionheart's bronze horse and bent Richard's upheld sword, but he still rides on."

The columns were a success in America, but Pyle remained unsure of himself and his work. He wrote his wife of his "timidity and inferiority complex." Later, in a column, he wrote that he never seemed to be at the center of the danger, adding, "It's probably just as well. I'm too old and weak to be a hero anyhow."

He met other newspapermen, both British and American. He visited David Low, the British cartoonist, and wrote in letters of Low's family, home, and humor. Pyle had taken with him a cartoon by Low, given to him after it had had a hole blown in it by a bomb blast; Low, delighted, had inscribed the cartoon, "Dear Hitler, Thanks for the criticism. Low."

Pyle returned to the United States in early summer 1941. For close to a year, he traveled and again wrote domestic pieces for Scripps-Howard. He deprecated his own importance and shunned celebrity life. The Scripps-Howard Alliance published a book of his columns, *Ernie Pyle in England* (1941). A planned trip to the Far East was canceled when the Japanese attacked Pearl Harbor.

The time in the United States was marred by his wife's illness, and Pyle was forced to take a three-month leave of absence during the most difficult time. Jerry had suffered increasingly severe bouts of depression for several years. She was both alcoholic and suicidal and would recover for a time, but then slip back into depression. Their life together was chaotic, and they finally decided on divorce as "an experiment" to see if that would shock Jerry into working to cure herself. If she could, Pyle felt they could later be remarried. During this time, Pyle considered resigning from his job and just doing free-lance work. They were divorced on 14 April 1942.

Finally, on 19 June, Pyle again flew to Europe. His column was resumed on 16 July. From July to November, he forwarded material from Ireland and England. In November he left by convoy for North Africa, where the American invasion had begun two weeks earlier. He was beginning his life as a battlefront correspondent.

He attempted to generalize some of his observations, so that those reading them at home could envision the lives of their loved ones. About the convoy trip he wrote: "This will be a series on our convoy trip from England to Africa. As you read it, you can apply it to any other convoy, for they are essentially the same, and they are sailing all the oceans this very moment." He continued to report on the everyday life of the soldier, although he did write two columns criticizing the Americans for allowing pro-Nazi Frenchmen to stay in their former political offices in North Africa: Pyle was very much opposed to the American policy of not recognizing the French Committee of National Liberation. These volatile columns were passed by the censors and sent on to America, possibly because the censors were accustomed to rubber-stamping the nonpolitical content of Pyle's columns. He wrote of the men and of the equipment they used, saying that the Jeep "does everything. It goes everywhere. It's as faithful as a dog, as strong as a mule, and as agile as a goat."

But he remained discouraged about himself and his column, writing his wife, whom he had remarried by proxy in March 1943: "I feel confused and inadequate among all the younger men with much more enthusiasm and purpose. I'm sad at not being able to do a wonderful job with the column, but I just can't seem to," and, later: "I guess the last struggling vestige of my will to write has finally gone, for the recent columns have been utterly lifeless, although I'm really in a section where everything is exciting and interesting." He continually misspelled *Tunisia* in the copy he forwarded to Scripps-Howard.

He wrote of planes that barely made it back to airfields and of planes that did not, of the heat and the cold, of guns, helmets, and jeeps, of eating food from tin plates, of not bathing for weeks, and of the dogs that followed the soldiers in their camps. But most often he wrote about the men themselves. As the war continued, Pyle found he was most comfortable when he was around the ordinary soldiers. His writing was filled with names and events that made it read like a letter home. The African columns were published by Holt as *Here Is Your War* in 1943; the book was later the basis for a movie, *The Story of G.I. Joe* (1945).

In April 1943 he returned to the front after being with other troops for a time, and he noted a change in the men: "They have made the great psychological transition from the normal belief that taking human life is sinful, over to a new professional outlook where killing is a craft." He recognized that his own situation made him view the war and himself differently from those he was with every day. He became hardened to the life and could usually face the casualties with a reporter's equanimity. Sometimes, however, the continuing volume of injured and dead overwhelmed him. He wrote to his friend Cavanaugh that "the enormity of all those newly dead strikes me as a living nightmare . . . there are times when I feel I can't stand it and will have to leave."

He wrote his wife of his daydreams about what they could do after the war: "a little travel still and some sittin' and some dog-playing and some daily chores and through it all something definite to tack on to that has some purpose to it." But he went on to Sicily with the troops, writing home that "the only justification I can find for myself is that at least I'm making it the hard way and not sitting in New York or Washington, pontificating over a typewriter."

Pyle went on to Italy, writing what was to become his most famous column on the death of Capt. Henry T. Waskow of Belton, Texas, a company commander of the Thirty-sixth Division who was killed in mountain fighting near San Pietro. The story was given front-page display across the United States; the *Washington Daily News* made it the entire front page.

The war went on to the hard-fought Anzio beachhead, and Pyle followed. There the house where he and other war correspondents were staying was blasted by 500-pound German bombs, which fell thirty feet away. Pyle made that shelling the subject of a column in which he reported not feeling nervous, but then realized he had taken his handkerchief out of his pocket and was attempting to comb his hair with it. "Me nervous?," he wrote, "I should say not." He later wrote a friend, "I was tremendously lucky to come out of that alive." Always frail, Pyle was suffering from anemia in Italy and continued to take liver shots on the beachhead.

From Italy he flew to England, from where he embarked two months later as one of the twenty-eight correspondents to cover the D-Day invasion. Walking along the beach on the day following, he wrote of the "vast and startling wreckage" of war. "I walked slowly," he reported, "for the detail on that beach was infinite." He was with the army at Saint-Lo when the air corps mistook its target and bombed American troops. He huddled with an officer under a heavy wagon in a shed and reported in his column later, "We said nothing. We just lay sprawled, gaping at each other in futile appeal."

The army reached Paris, and Pyle was with them. In a last column from France, he wrote of the coming end of the war in Europe and the rebuilding to follow. But he reminded his readers that the war in the Pacific could be long. He had already decided to go there. "The others," he wrote in a letter, "write the stark drama of events. Many of them write it better than I do. But no one else does what I do."

Pyle was awarded the Pulitzer Prize in 1944 for distinguished correspondence in 1943. He learned of it while he was in London waiting to cover the D-Day invasion of Normandy.

On a trip to the United States, Pyle received two honorary degrees: the University of New Mexico awarded him a doctorate of laws on 25 October 1944; Indiana University, the site of his own academic career, awarded him a doctorate of humane letters on 13 November, the first such degree ever given by that university. Pyle did not speak in public and so did not make a speech on either occasion. At one point in the Indiana ceremony, he leaned over to President Herman B. Wells, a former fellow student. The audience thought he might have changed his mind and be planning to speak after all. But what he said to Wells was, "Hermie, do I take my hat off or keep it on when I get the degree?"

The trip home was once again marred by his wife's relapse. She attempted suicide and had to be hospitalized, but was recovering when he left for the Pacific. Pyle felt he could not back out of the trip.

Pyle left for the Pacific in January 1945, spending several weeks at sea. His columns were filled with details of life on a carrier, of preparations in the Philippines, and stories of the marines and navy men. One of his columns described the landing formations and procedures for planes returning to the carrier deck after a mission. After talking about the precision required and the precariousness inherent in the landing signal officers' jobs, he commented on his own experience standing with them while an entire flight of planes landed. "You would swear every plane was going to land right on top of you. Before it was over, I decided that if I were running the Navy, I'd let them all land in the water."

The Okinawa invasion was ahead. Pyle dreaded it, but felt that the only way to cover the marines was to be with them on their maneuvers. The landing was far easier than expected, for the beach was undefended. On 15 April, Pyle wrote what turned out to be the last column he ever filed. Ironically, it concerned the death of a fellow correspondent, Fred Painton, who had died of natural causes on Guam. He wrote: "The war and weariness of war is cumulative. To many a man in the line today, fear is not so much of death itself, but fear of the terror and anguish and utter horror that precede death in battle . . . somehow I'm glad he didn't have to go through the unnatural terror of dying on the battlefield."

Two days later, Pyle went ashore at Ie Shima in the Ryukyus. It was the day following the invasion of that island. He slept there that night in a former Japanese dugout and the next day set out in a jeep on a narrow island road for the forward positions attained by the troops. The group dived for the ditches when a sniper opened fire with a machine-

Pyle aboard an aircraft carrier on his way to the fighting in the South Pacific (Official U.S. Navy Photograph from Press Association Inc.)

gun. After a moment, Pyle and Colonel Coolidge raised their heads to check on the others in their party. The sniper opened fire again. Coolidge was unharmed, but Pyle was killed by three shots that went under his helmet and struck him in the left temple.

In his pocket was found a draft of the column he had planned to file when V-E day was finally announced. In part, it said: "Last summer I wrote that I hoped the end of the war could be a gigantic relief, but not an elation. In the joyousness of high spirits, it is easy for us to forget the dead. Those who are gone would not wish themselves to be a millstone of gloom around our necks. But there are many of the living who have had burned into their brains forever the unnatural sight of cold dead men scattered over the hillsides and in the ditches along the high rows of hedge throughout the world."

Pyle was buried on Ie Shima with the soldiers killed on the island. On the spot where he was killed, a marker was erected:

At this spot
The 77th Infantry Division

Lost a Buddy
Ernie Pyle
18 April 1945

After the war, his body was moved to the National Memorial Cemetery in Punchbowl Crater, near Honolulu. He was awarded the Medal of Merit posthumously by President Truman; it was presented to his wife in a 3 July ceremony following the Washington preview of the movie *The Story of G.I. Joe,* based on his columns.

Geraldine Pyle died in November. Their home in Albuquerque was left to the city as a branch library and bears Pyle's name. The journalism building at Indiana University has also been named after him, as has an elementary school in Indianapolis. His birthplace near Dana, Indiana, is kept as a memorial.

Ernie Pyle's writing was appreciated by the readers of his time and still stands as finely crafted journalistic writing today. His prewar work was often humorous, although it could be poetic as well. His columns were filled with names and places, and he attempted to capture the personalities of those he wrote about. Much of his early work reads as though he had just leaned over the back fence to tell an interesting story; his conversational style involves the reader in his tale. After his second trip to Portland, Oregon, he wrote: "Do you know what Portland is? It's Paradise on earth. At least, that's what people in Portland said. Personally, I had never thought so and I'll tell you why." The column went on to recount how, on his first trip, he had been eating watermelon at a roadside stand when an old codger came along and badgered him for eating watermelon and smoking cigarettes on Sunday. He continued, "Of course the incident was on my mind as we drew near Portland this time. But I said, 'No, let's be fair. We'll start all over again with Portland and see what happens.' About that instant we came around a bend, and there staring us in the face was an expensive signboard, as big as the side of a house, saying in huge letters: 'All Hath Sinned.' That's all it said. Now, I don't know whether all hath sinned or not. But supposing all hath, why put up a signboard about it? After that, it took my friends five days to convince me that I was wrong about Portland."

The columns from his "Roving Reporter" days

Memorial erected to Pyle on Ie Shima Island (U.S. Army Photograph from Acme)

were poignant as well. A summer trip into Iowa reminded him of his own rural days:

> I don't know whether you know that long, sad wind that blows so steadily across the thousands of miles of Midwest flat lands in the summertime. If you don't, it will be hard for you to understand the feeling I have about it. Even if you do know it, you may not understand. Because maybe the wind is only a symbol.
>
> But to me the summer wind in the Midwest is one of the most melancholy things in all life. . . .
>
> You could, and you do wear out your lifetime on the dusty plains with that wind of futility blowing in your face.

In 1939, J. W. Raper of the *Cleveland Press* called Pyle "just about the best reporter in the United States."

But it was his writing on the war that made Pyle famous and that is remembered today. His most famous piece—on the death of Captain Waskow—told of bringing dead men down from the mountains on mules. Pyle wrote: "I don't know who that first one was. You feel small in the presence of dead men, and you don't ask silly questions."

He continued the story of the dead men arriving by mule and of Captain Waskow being brought down:

> The men in the road seemed reluctant to leave. They stood around, and, gradually I could sense them moving, one by one, close to Captain Waskow's body. Not so much to look, I think, as to say something in finality to him, and to themselves. I stood by and I could hear.
>
> One soldier came and looked down, and he said out loud, "God damn it!"
>
> That's all he said, and then he walked away.
>
> Another one came, and he said, "God damn it to hell anyway!" He looked down for a few last moments and then turned and left.
>
> Another man came. I think he was an officer. It was hard to tell officers from men in the dim light, for everybody was bearded and grimy. The man looked down into the dead captain's face and then spoke directly to him, as though he were alive, "I'm sorry, old man."
>
> . . . he reached down and took the captain's hand, and he sat there for a full five minutes holding the dead hand in his own and looking intently into the dead face. And

he never uttered a sound all the time he sat there.

In writing of the D-Day invasion, he told of the beach and of what was left lying there. By describing in great detail the belongings of those who had died in the invasion, Pyle presented a vivid picture of what had happened only hours before: "There were socks and shoe polish, sewing kits, diaries, Bibles, hand grenades. There were the latest letters from home, with the address on each one neatly razored out—one of the security precautions enforced before the boys embarked. . . . snapshots of families back home staring up at you from the sand. . . . I picked up a pocket Bible with a soldier's name in it and put it in my jacket. I carried it half a mile or so and then put it back down on the beach."

In the column he intended for V-E day, he wrote that his heart was still in Europe and that the column was written for those who had fought there. He said that those who had stayed at home could never understand the impact of the war upon its soldiers. He told of seeing "dead men by mass production—in one country after another—month after month and year after year. Dead men in winter and dead men in summer. . . . We saw him, saw him by the multiple thousands. That's the difference."

In reviewing *Brave Men* (1944), the collection of his columns from Europe, the *Los Angeles Times* said that "reading this book is something like covering all the invasion fronts at once, talking with men from every city and hamlet in the United States. . . . You see at once that Pyle is writing for the common man and his mother—and that about includes all of us."

Biographies:

Lee G. Miller, *An Ernie Pyle Album: Indiana to Ie Shima* (New York: Sloane, 1946);

Miller, *The Story of Ernie Pyle* (New York: Viking, 1950).

References:

"Anniversary of Famed War Correspondent's Death," *Newsweek*, 66 (2 August 1965): 47;

D. Armstrong, "Boswell of the G.I.s," *Saturday Review of Literature*, 27 (25 November 1944): 7;

L. Barnett, "Ernie Pyle," *Life*, 18 (2 April 1945): 95-108;

"Correspondent Prepares to Resume Indefatigable Travels," *Life*, 15 (15 November 1943): 57;

"Dana Boy Makes Good," *Time*, 43 (12 June 1944): 64;

M. Duffield, "Ernie Pyle in Africa," *Nation*, 57 (20 November 1943): 589-590;

"Ernie," *Time*, 45 (30 April 1945): 61;

"Ernie Pyle's War," *Time*, 44 (17 July 1944): 65-72;

"Ernie Shared the Doughfoot's Lot," *Newsweek*, 25 (30 April 1945): 78-81;

"Ernie was tired," *Newsweek*, 24 (18 September 1944): 88;

G. B. Hovey, "This Is Ernie Pyle's War," *New Republic*, 111 (11 December 1944): 804-806;

R. Jarrell, "Ernie Pyle," *Nation*, 160 (19 May 1945): 573-576;

Philip Knightley, *The First Casualty: From the Crimea to Vietnam: The War Correspondent as Hero, Propagandist, and Myth Maker* (New York: Harcourt Brace Jovanovich, 1976);

A. J. Liebling, "Pyle set the style," *New Yorker*, 26 (2 September 1950): 69-73;

"Man about the World," *Time*, 41 (31 May 1943): 44-48;

F. C. Painton, "The Hoosier Letter Writer," *Saturday Evening Post*, 216 (2 October 1943): 17, 109-110;

D. L. Pillsbury, "Little White House on a Hill Top Where People Stop a While," *Christian Science Monitor Magazine*, 26 November 1949, p. 16;

"Remembering Ernie Pyle," *Newsweek*, 26 (3 September 1945): 67;

"Rover Boy with Typewriter," *Newsweek*, 21 (15 February 1943): 76-79;

"Tourist in the War Zone," *Time*, 37 (13 January 1941): 50.

Papers:

A collection of Ernie Pyle's papers is at Ernie Pyle Hall, School of Journalism, Indiana University, Bloomington, Indiana.

Helen Rogers Reid

(23 November 1882-27 July 1970)

Steven D. Lyons
Louisiana State University

MAJOR POSITIONS HELD: Advertising manager, *New York Tribune* (1918-1922); advertising manager and vice-president, *New York Tribune* (1922-1924), *New York Herald Tribune* (1924-1947); president, *New York Herald Tribune* (1947-1953); chairman of board of directors, *New York Herald Tribune* (1953-1955).

Helen Rogers Reid was a small woman who made a large impact on the world of newspapers as advertising solicitor, manager, and president of the *New York Tribune* and the *Herald Tribune*. Her innovativeness and energy were a major influence in the development of current journalism, especially in the field of advertising.

Helen Rogers was born in Appleton, Wisconsin, on 23 November 1882, the youngest of eleven children of Benjamin Talbot Rogers, a merchant who died when she was three, and Sarah Johnson Rogers. The family maintained a modest standard of living after her father's death. From the age of eleven through sixteen Rogers studied at Grafton Hall, a boarding school in Fond du Lac, of which her brother, the Reverend Benjamin Talbot Rogers, was headmaster. After graduating from Grafton, she entered Barnard College in New York City in 1899. She intended to become a teacher of Greek, but changed her major to zoology. Although her money ran out at the end of her sophomore year due to family complications, she had no intention of retreating to Appleton, and instead started working.

By assisting in the bursar's office, helping to manage her dormitory, and tutoring, she was able to earn enough to cover part of her expenses. She was chosen as business manager of the Barnard yearbook, the *Mortarboard*, in her senior year; that was the first time the yearbook did not show a deficit. The class poet summed up her no-nonsense personality: "We love little Helen, her heart/is so warm/And if you don't cross her she'll do you/no harm./So don't contradict her, or else if you do/Get under the table and wait/till she's through."

After receiving her bachelor of arts degree in 1903, Rogers became the social secretary to Mrs.

Helen Rogers Reid (Culver Pictures)

Whitelaw Reid, wife of the publisher of the *New York Tribune*. In 1905 Reid was appointed ambassador to Great Britain, so Rogers traveled frequently between London and the United States. During this time she met the Reids' only son, Ogden Mills Reid, named after his maternal grandfather who had been a prominent financier. Reid had joined the *Tribune* after graduating from the Yale University Law School in 1907. He and Rogers were married in Wisconsin on 14 March 1911.

The new Mrs. Reid worked as hard on her marriage as on any job she had undertaken. Since her husband enjoyed swimming, tennis, shooting, and sailing, she put her mind to excelling in all those sports. She took only a passing interest in the *Tribune*, which her husband inherited on his father's death in 1912. The Reids had three children: Whitelaw; Elizabeth, who died in childhood; and Ogden. Helen Reid was a leader in the suffrage campaigns in New York, helping to raise $500,000

301

Helen Reid, Ogden Reid (far right) and New York Mayor Fiorello La Guardia applaud Eleanor Roosevelt after a speech at a Herald Tribune *Forum on Current Problems (Whitelaw Reid)*

for the movement. "When I was at Barnard, working my way through," she explained later, "the necessity for complete independence of women was borne in on me." During World War I she had the 800-acre Reid estate, Ophir Hall, planted with alfalfa, corn, and oats, turning it into a producing farm.

In 1918 Ogden Reid asked his wife to "come down to the office and work out the paper's success with me," and she became an advertising solicitor for the *Tribune,* into which $15 million of the Reid family fortune h? `seen poured since 1898. Mrs. Reid attacked the job with as much fervor as she had the position of business manager of her college yearbook. Within two months she was made advertising director. Calling on clients or having them to lunch, she would bombard them with facts, figures, and flattery; according to one of her colleagues, "She had the persistence of gravity." She hired more salesmen, and drove them as hard as she did herself, motivating them with weekly sales meetings, pep talks, and contests. Between 1918 and 1923, despite competition from four other morning

newspapers, the *Tribune* more than doubled its advertising linage.

Mrs. Reid added the title of vice-president to that of advertising director in 1922, and although her influence continued to be felt mainly in the advertising department, she had an impact on the editorial side of the paper as well. She played a major role in the *Tribune*'s decision to purchase the letters of Woodrow Wilson and the memoirs of Col. Edward House, and in the hiring of several columnists. She also pressed for improvements in the paper's typography. One battle she lost was her attempt to make the *Tribune* support the "dry" side during Prohibition; Ogden Reid adamantly refused to go along with this. Mrs. Reid always denied the story that her husband had once told her to "get the hell back to your department and run it while I run mine" and that she had left his office meekly: "In the first place, my husband wouldn't speak to me that way. In the second, I wouldn't leave meekly."

The newspaper enjoyed a large gain in circulation in 1924 when Frank A. Munsey, failing to persuade the Reids to sell the *Tribune* to him, sold them his *New York Herald*, with its European edition, for $5 million. The *Herald Tribune* retained most of the *Herald*'s subscribers, and finally began to show a profit. The newspaper's annual Forum on Current Problems was started in 1930 by Mrs. Reid and Mrs. William Brown Meloney, the editor of *This Week*, the *Herald Tribune*'s Sunday magazine. The forum was originally designed to promote the interest of women's clubs in current events, but was expanded to include the general public. The forums were held in the Waldorf-Astoria ballroom, where prominent speakers would discuss national and world affairs. They were discontinued after 1955.

Mrs. Reid added women's columns and society pages to the paper. She cherished the idea of equal rights for women and set herself as an example of what women could achieve. She advocated the drafting of women during World War II, and was appointed to the Advisory Committee on Women in the Services.

The European edition of the paper suspended publication in 1940, when Paris fell to the Germans. It was resumed on 22 December 1944, after the liberation of the city.

When Ogden Reid died in January 1947, his widow succeeded him as president of the *Herald*

Helen and Ogden Reid leaving a motion picture premiere in 1943 (Culver Pictures)

Tribune. She became chairman of the board of directors in 1953; her elder son, Whitelaw, who had joined the staff in 1940 and had been named vice-president in 1947, succeeded to the presidency. During her years as chairman her editorial judgment was influential in making the paper attractive to women and suburban readers and helped transform the *Herald Tribune* into a modern newspaper; Mrs. Reid is given credit for supporting the testing kitchens which supplied readers with recipes. She frequently suggested story ideas and advised on coverage of others. By 1952 the *Herald Tribune* had a circulation of 343,000 on weekdays, 262,000 on Saturdays, and 596,000 on Sundays. In 1955, at the age of seventy-two, Mrs. Reid resigned as chairman but continued as a member of the board. Whitelaw succeeded her as chairman, and her other son, Ogden, who had joined the staff in 1950, became president, publisher, and editor. During the 1950s the *Herald Tribune* was regarded highly for its Washington and foreign correspondence, with syndicated columnists such as Walter Lippmann, Joseph Alsop, Roscoe Drummond, and Marquis Childs; two of its Korean War correspondents, Marguerite Higgins and Homer Bigart, won Pulitzer Prizes in 1951. A *Saturday Review of Literature* poll in 1951 judged the *Herald Tribune,* along with the *New York Times* and the *Christian Science Monitor,* as providing the fairest coverage of the controversial firing of Gen. Douglas MacArthur by President Truman.

Despite its prestige, the *Herald Tribune* suffered losses during the 1950s. In 1958, the Reids were forced to sell the paper to millionaire John Hay Whitney. (Ironically, at the time he bought the paper, Whitney was ambassador to Great Britain—as the first Whitelaw Reid had been.) The *Herald Tribune* was changed to a magazine format after Whitney assumed direct control in 1960, but it continued to lose money and was badly hurt by a 114-day strike in 1963. In 1966 the paper was merged with the Scripps-Howard *World-Telegram and Sun* and the Hearst *Journal-American* to form the *World Journal Tribune*. The *Herald Tribune* was intended to retain its identity as the morning edition of the new paper, but labor problems prevented the plan from being carried out. The final edition of the *Herald Tribune* appeared on 24 April. The evening *World Journal Tribune* appeared from September 1966 until May 1967. The European edition of the *Herald Tribune* was jointly owned by Whitney, the *New York Times,* and the *Washington Post* beginning in 1967.

Helen Rogers Reid was honored by numerous organizations during her lifetime, including the American Women's Association, the Cuban Red Cross, the Hundred Year Association of New York, the Council Against Intolerance, and the American Academy of Arts and Sciences. She also received honorary degrees from a number of colleges and universities.

At the time of her death in 1970 a *New York Times* editorial summarized her life and accomplishments by stating that "she had the curiosity and wide-ranging interests which are the hallmarks of a born journalist. She had, too, the energy, persistence and acumen of a good business executive. She brought all of these attributes to the service of the *New York Herald Tribune*, for nearly four decades. A

dedicated internationalist and a convinced Republican, she was a civilized and enlightened influence in the politics of her time as a publisher, a hostess, and an organizer of public forums."

References:

Harry W. Baehr, Jr., *The New York Tribune Since the Civil War* (New York: Dodd, Mead, 1936);

Mona Gardner, "Queen Helen," *Saturday Evening Post* (6 May 1944): 9;

"Helen Reid's Forum," *Newsweek*, 28 (11 November 1946): 74;

"Portrait," *Newsweek*, 7 (13 June 1936): 19;

"Successful Woman and Successful Businessman," *Newsweek*, 6 (23 November 1935): 19.

Grantland Rice

(1 November 1880-13 July 1954)

George Everett
University of Tennessee

MAJOR POSITIONS HELD: Sports editor, *Atlanta Journal* (1902-1905), *Cleveland News* (1905-1907), *Nashville Tennessean* (1907-1910); sportswriter, *New York Evening Mail* (1910-1913); syndicated columnist (1913-1954).

BOOKS: *Base-Ball Ballads* (Nashville: Tennessean, 1910);

Songs of the Stalwart (New York & London: Appleton, 1917);

Sportlights of 1923 (New York & London: Putnam's, 1924);

Songs of the Open (New York & London: Century, 1924);

The Duffer's Handbook of Golf, by Rice and Clare Briggs (New York: Macmillan, 1926);

Understand Football, by Rice and John W. Heisman (Bronxville, N.Y.: Mac-Hill, 1929);

Only the Brave, and Other Poems (New York: Barnes, 1941);

Steel and Flame: A Collection of War Poems (New York: Barnes, 1942);

The Bobby Jones Story, by Rice and Oscar Bane Keeler (Atlanta, Ga.: Tupper & Love, 1953);

The Tumult and the Shouting: My Life in Sport (New York: Barnes, 1954);

The Final Answer, and Other Poems (New York: Barnes, 1955);

Curtain Call [*The Lost Path*], edited by Charles C. Fleming and Martha Fleming (Richmond, Va.: Press of the Hicuppy Herring, 1956).

OTHER: *The Boy's Book of Sports*, edited by Rice (New York: Century, 1917);

The Omnibus of Sport, edited by Rice and Harford Powel (New York & London: Harper, 1932);

Reveille: War Poems by Members of Our Armed Forces, edited by Rice, Daniel Henderson, and John Kieran (New York: Barnes, 1943).

Grantland Rice covered sports throughout the first half of the twentieth century, a period that can aptly be designated sportswriting's Golden Age. He got his first newspaper job at the age of twenty, in a day when a sports editor was expected to write a newspaper's entire sports content in addition to covering more important beats. By the time of his death in 1954, he was widely dubbed the "dean" of sportswriters, with an established reputation in newspapers, magazines, radio, and film. As one who wanted to devote his lifetime to writing about

Grantland Rice

sports, he arrived on the American scene at just the right time.

Rice was born in Murfreesboro, Tennessee, in 1880 to Bolling and Beulah Grantland Rice. His family was dominated by Civil War veteran Major Henry Grantland, his mother's father. When Rice was four the family moved to Nashville. He was about eight when the family moved to a farm outside Nashville and an event occurred which Rice recalled almost seventy years later:

> It was my first Christmas on Vaughan Pike when a football, a baseball and a bat landed under the tree—for me. No glove. My hands have been calloused ever since.
>
> Those three presents were the sounding instruments that directed my life. I can still hear the echoes from far away and long ago. They were the Pied Piper in my march through life.

He pursued the two sports enthusiastically at the

two military academies he attended during his adolescence, the Nashville Military Institute and the Tennessee Military Institute. (The latter school was still supplying husky backs and linemen to the University of Tennessee varsity in the 1980s.) But Rice did not have the build for football: as he neared six feet in height, he weighed 120 pounds.

The family moved back into the city when Rice was fifteen, and after a final year of prep school at Wallace University School, he entered Vanderbilt University at the age of sixteen. The zealous youth persisted on both diamond and gridiron. In four years he missed no baseball practices, and by his junior year he had earned a letter in football. But he never weighed more than 134 pounds in college, and his participation was costly: he suffered a broken foot, a broken arm, a broken collarbone, and a broken shoulder blade, and had four ribs torn loose from his spine. The shoulder injury forced him to throw the baseball underhand during his senior year as a shortstop.

Upon graduation in 1901 he began barnstorming Tennessee with a semiprofessional baseball club, but his father summoned him home to try for a job at the *Nashville News,* which had been founded that year. The youth had made Phi Beta Kappa at Vanderbilt, and his father recognized that his stringbean son had a more promising future as a writer than as an athlete. The twenty-year-old applied for the sports editor position on the fledgling newspaper, and got it—along with the responsibilities of covering the state government, the produce market, and the customs house.

After a few months Rice went to Washington, D.C., to accept a job offer from *Forester* magazine, but appendicitis sent him back to the South. In 1902 he got a job writing the *Atlanta Journal* sports page at $12.50 a week, more than twice his *Nashville News* salary. He covered his first big running story, the rise of the Georgia Peach, Ty Cobb, and went north to cover his first World Series. When the *Cleveland News* offered him fifty dollars a week in 1905, he accepted, deciding that he could now afford to marry Katherine Hollis. The wedding took place on 11 April 1906 in her hometown of Americus, Georgia. It was a freewheeling day for sports journalists, and Rice thought nothing of accepting as a wedding present a barrel of china from Cleveland Indians manager Nap Lajoie, whose team he covered daily through the 1906 season. The Rices had a daughter, Florence, who became a movie actress.

The new *Nashville Tennessean* lured Rice back to Tennessee for seventy dollars a week in 1907, but the assignment was not an easy one. Besides putting

Rice (center) in 1896 with (left to right) his brother Bolling, Jr.; his father; his mother, Beulah; and his brother John

together two pages of sports daily and four on Sunday with no assistant, Rice had also to write a daily column of verse and paragraphs for the editorial page and cover the theater beat. The editorial page assignment was not an unpleasant one, for Rice doted on the turn-of-the-century custom of sprinkling a daily newspaper's pages with poetry. As a student he had liked Keats and Shelley, but his verse especially reflected his recent discovery of Kipling. He later recalled, "The meter and jungle drums inherent in Kipling's verse captured my ear and my imagination and never let go. My dear and departed pal O. B. Keeler of the *Atlanta Journal* could recite my stuff by the yard—but whatever verse I've written, more than 6,000 pieces, I've forgotten almost as quickly as I wrote it. Believe me, it just flowed." Poems punctuated his columns for many years, in newspaper syndication and then in his magazine writings, and many appear in book-length compilations. His best-known lines appeared in a poem titled "Alumnus Football," which typifies the idealistic outlook of a generation of sportswriters brought up on Frank Merriwell and the Victorian Era: "For when the One Great Scorer comes to mark against your name,/He writes—not that you won or lost—but how you played the game."

In 1910 Rice was beckoned to the center of the American newspaperman's universe when he was offered fifty dollars a week to write sports for the *New York Evening Mail*. The afternoon daily, an also-ran in New York journalism with not many years left, was nevertheless an important stepping-stone for an ambitious twenty-nine-year-old. There he worked with Franklin P. Adams, O. O. McIntyre, Heywood Broun, Homer Davenport, and Rube Goldberg. He moved into an apartment at 450 Riverside Drive and lived there for twenty years. In the same building lived Walter Trumbull, Irvin S. Cobb, and Deems Taylor, and nearby were Damon Runyon, Herbert Bayard Swope, and Harry Hershfield. The salary was less than in Nashville, but the hours were better and the contacts were priceless. Affable and intriguing with his gravelly voiced style, he moved easily in a cocktail circuit that was to be near the mainstream of the Roaring Twenties.

Adams suggested the name "Sportlight" for Rice's column, and in 1913 Ogden Reid offered $280 a week to syndicate it if Rice would come over to the *New York Tribune*. The column was offered through the *Tribune* (and later the *Herald Tribune*) Syndicate for more than fifteen years.

Rice joined the army in 1917, was made a drill

instructor because he "was older than most and knew my left foot from my right," and applied for officer training; he was commissioned a first lieutenant in the artillery. When he arrived in France he made more literary contacts by working for the *Stars and Stripes*, edited by Harold Ross, who later founded the *New Yorker*. The nature of these contacts in the wartime context is reflected in lines penned by Capt. Franklin P. Adams: "One night I slept on a terribly full cot/My partner being Alexander Woollcott."

Rice's literary contacts, maintained by frequent elbow-bending during Prohibition, identified him clearly with the smart set. When Harold Ross came up with an advertising campaign for the new *New Yorker* in the mid-1920s, Rice was one of the "in" New Yorkers whose testimonials he displayed. When a group of artists and writers formed for purposes of meeting socially in Palm Beach each year, Rice was nominated as president. The gathering included Rube Goldberg as treasurer, George Ade, Clarence Budington Kelland, Arthur Somers Roche, Frank Crowninshield, and Fontaine Fox.

Knute Rockne, the Notre Dame football coach whose exhortation to his team to "win one for the Gipper" was made famous by Rice

Using these contacts to dig up material for his column, Rice had many of them over to his Riverside Drive apartment to drink what he called "Tennessee milk." But the procession of sports figures which paraded within his reportorial reach was even more remarkable. He spent many hours with Babe Ruth, Knute Rockne, Bobby Jones, Jack Dempsey, and other heroes of the 1920s sports boom. It was in one of these quiet meetings that he heard Rockne tell how his team was going out to "win one for the Gipper" the next day at the Notre Dame-Army game, in response to a request made by halfback George Gipp as he lay dying in the arms of his coach. As Rice recalled in his memoirs,

> Rockne's "Let's win this one for the Gipper," is ancient history. It's the kind of history, however, that American sports thrived on during an age when school spirit, college try, or what-you-will, added up to a great deal more than cynicism—which has no place in collegiate football.
>
> That evening, sitting by the fire, Rock said he expected to be up against it—but good, next day.
>
> "You recall Gipp," said Rock. "He died—practically in my arms—eight years ago next month. He's been gone a long time but I may have to use him again tomorrow."

Rockne told Rice how Gipp died of pneumonia after playing in the rain during the last part of his great 1920 season:

> "Gipp looked up at me and after a moment, he said, 'Rock, I know I'm going . . . but I'd like one last request. . . . Some day, Rock, some time—when the going isn't so easy, when the odds are against us, ask a Notre Dame team to win a game for me—for the Gipper. I don't know where I'll be then, Rock, but I'll know about it and I'll be happy.'
>
> "A moment later Gipp was gone.
>
> "Grant, I've never asked the boys to pull one out for Gipp. Tomorrow I might have to."
>
> The following day that '28 Army-Notre Dame game played, as always, to an overflow sellout. At the half it was 0-0. The rest is history.
>
> A sobbing band of fighting Irish raced out for the 3rd quarter. When Notre Dame lined up for the kickoff, I knew they were playing with a 12th man—George Gipp. . . .
>
> Notre Dame carried that day, 12-6. Somewhere, George Gipp must have been very happy.

Such stories were a specialty of Rice's, and they were in high demand by an audience that wanted the inside dope on as unusual a set of heroes as sport has ever known. Babe Ruth's drunken sprees, Bobby Jones's temper, Tex Rickard's gargantuan boxing promotions provided ample copy suited to Rice's anecdotal style. Flamboyant golfer Walter Hagen was an excellent source, and the realistic Rice recognized his value: "Color no matter how it's spelled out, means gold for the newspapers. Hagen had more color than a lawn full of peacocks."

But Rice was not at a loss when the time came to write a straight follow-up story about a sporting event. During the 1924 football season, he wrote a lead the morning after the Notre Dame-Army game that gave four players a celebrated label they would carry with them the rest of their lives: "Outlined against a blue-gray October sky, the Four Horsemen rode again. In dramatic lore they are known as Famine, Pestilence, Destruction and Death. These are only aliases. Their real names are Stuhldreher, Miller, Crowley and Layden. They formed the crest of the South Bend cyclone before which another fighting Army football team was swept over the precipice at the Polo Grounds yesterday as 55,000 spectators peered down on the bewildering panorama spread on the green plain below." As the *New York Times*'s Arthur Daley wrote in Rice's obituary, "There was an era in the Twenties when every young writer tried to emulate Grantland Rice. None could."

Stanley Walker, the great city editor of the *New York Herald Tribune*, had a somewhat different view of Rice's style:

> Grantland Rice, perhaps the most popular and respected gentleman ever to write sports, came out of the South long before the war bearing an unusual equipment—he had a good education, he was a poet at heart, and he had a genuine, almost fanatical love for sport. His career probably has been the most successful of all sports writers, although he, like (Charley) Dryden, set an example for many a young man, who, seeking to be a word-painter, loaded his pop-gun with red paint and fired at the rainbow.
>
> Rice wrote much poetry, some of it good; much of his prose was poetry, too. His leads sang of sunsets which displayed the colors of the victorious college football team, which was an advantage, because except on rainy days the crimson of Harvard or the blue of Yale may be found in the late afternoon sky.

A football team in a desperate stand near the goal-line reminded Rice of the French at the Marne, the Spartans at Thermopylae or Davy Crockett and his boys at the Alamo. A fighter like Jack Dempsey, a former hobo, might carry the hammer of Thor or the thunderbolts of Zeus in his right fist ("maulie" or "duke"). A half-back, entering the game belatedly to turn defeat into victory, would remind Rice of Phil Sheridan at Winchester. Walter Johnson, Washington pitcher, was the Big Train roaring through. There were ghosts there too, strange but lovable visitors from that Valhalla where all good sportsmen go, hovering about in the dun light, advising the gladiators and making themselves useful around the place. Sometimes the reader had to wade through half a column of this fetching literature and mythology before getting any very clear idea of who won, and how they won. It was magnificent and, may God bless us all, pretty terrible.

This is an uncharitable assessment, but it probably is true that Rice not only inspired thousands of novice sportswriters but also frustrated a number of city editors who wanted only the score and a few other facts wrapped in a tight, unpretentious package.

As his career developed, Rice became involved increasingly in other media. When Walter Camp, originator of the *Collier's Weekly* magazine's All-America team, died in 1925, the editors immediately looked to Rice to continue the selections. Rice did so, with some advice from friends, for twenty-seven years, until the task was turned over to the country's coaches. Rice also wrote sports for *Vanity Fair* and *Liberty*, and with some fellow investors he started the *American Golfer*, which soon became a victim of the Great Depression. Rice was an active and accomplished golfer and wrote books on how to play the newly popular sport. He also became involved in films in the 1920s, producing and narrating a series of one-reelers called the *Sportlights*; one of them won an Academy Award in 1943. Rice was also featured regularly on "Cities Service Concert," an early network radio program, and helped with play-by-play broadcasts of the World Series.

But his newspaper column continued to be his anchor. He switched to the Bell Syndicate in 1930, and later to the North American Newspaper Alliance, but always kept the "Sportlight" heading. He wrote more than 18,000 daily columns and once estimated that he had written one million words a

Rice at his typewriter in 1954, the year of his death

year for fifty years, in addition to several books of verse and hundreds of magazine articles and book introductions.

In his seventy-fourth year he suffered a stroke while typing his column and died within hours. His column was carried by about 100 daily newspapers at the time. His honorary pallbearers read like a Who's Who in letters and sports; included were Bobby Jones, Bill Corum, Rube Goldberg, Herbert Bayard Swope, Toots Shor, Red Smith, Tim Cohane, Gene Tunney, Ford Frick, Col. Earl "Red" Blaik, and Jack Dempsey. Daley observed, "It's to be doubted that any man had a more profound effect on the sportswriting profession than our beloved dean." Red Smith said, "He put us all in white collars."

Grantland Rice knew more of the top sports figures (and many of them rather intimately) than any other sportswriter in American history. He was a prolific writer, and yet kept contacts in the literary community which gave his work an extra touch of class and respectability. He did all this with a gentlemanly cordiality that was rare and refreshing in the aggressive world of competitive sports and sportswriting.

References:

Frank Buxton and Bill Owen, "Sports and Sportscasters," in their *The Big Broadcast* (New York: Viking, 1966), pp. 287-289;

Arthur Daley, "Grantland Rice," *New York Times*, 15 July 1954, p. 30;

"The Dean, 1880-1954," *Newsweek*, 44 (29 July 1954): 50-51;

"An Evangelist of Fun," *Time*, 64 (26 July 1954): 38-39;

John Lardner, "Laureate of Sunshine," *Newsweek*, 49 (1 April 1957): 74;

Stanley Walker, *City Editor* (New York: Stokes, 1934), pp. 123-124.

Adela Rogers St. Johns

(20 May 1894-   )

Jean C. Chance
University of Florida

MAJOR POSITIONS HELD: Reporter, *San Francisco Examiner* (1913), *Los Angeles Herald* (1914-1918), International News Service (1925-1949), *Chicago American* (1928), *New York American* (1929).

BOOKS: *The Skyrocket* (New York: Cosmopolitan, 1925; London: Methuen, 1925);
A Free Soul (New York: Cosmopolitan, 1927);
The Single Standard (New York: Cosmopolitan, 1928; London: London Book Co., 1930);
Field of Honor (New York: Dutton, 1938);
The Root of All Evil (New York: Dutton, 1940);
Never Again, and Other Stories (Garden City: Doubleday, 1949);
How to Write a Story and Sell It (Garden City: Doubleday, 1956);
Affirmative Prayer in Action (New York: Dodd, Mead, 1957);
First Step Up Toward Heaven: Hubert Eaton and Forest Lawn (Englewood Cliffs, N.J.: Prentice-Hall, 1959);
Final Verdict (Garden City: Doubleday, 1962);
Tell No Man (Garden City: Doubleday, 1966);
The Honeycomb (Garden City: Doubleday, 1969);
Some Are Born Great (Garden City: Doubleday, 1974);
Love, Laughter and Tears: My Hollywood Story (Garden City: Doubleday, 1978);
No Good-byes: My Search into Life beyond Death (New York: McGraw-Hill, 1981).

SCREENPLAYS: *Broken Laws*, story by St. Johns, Ince, 1924;
Inez from Hollywood, story by St. Johns, First National, 1924;
Lady of the Night, story by St. Johns, M-G-M, 1925;
The Wise Guy, adaptation by St. Johns, First National, 1926;
The Broncho Twister, story by St. Johns, Fox, 1927;
The Arizona Wildcat, story by St. Johns, Fox, 1927;
Singed, story by St. Johns, Fox, 1927;
The Patent Leather Kid, adaptation by St. Johns, First National, 1927;
The Heart of a Follies Girl, story by St. Johns, First National, 1928;

Adela Rogers St. Johns (© Engstead)

Miss Fane's Baby Is Stolen, Paramount, 1934;
Back in Circulation, story by St. Johns, Warner Bros., 1937;
The Great Man's Lady, story by St. Johns, Paramount, 1942;
That Brennan Girl, story by St. Johns, Republic, 1946.

Adela Rogers St. Johns has the unofficial title of veteran "sob sister" of American journalism due to the years she spent covering the Hollywood scene between 1913 and 1928. Her days at Hollywood High School prepared her for her work as a profile writer for the Hearst movie magazine *Photoplay*, where she cultivated an image of "mother confessor of Hollywood" and wrote about such stars as Garbo and Valentino. Following a recess to raise her family, she returned to her newspaper career and was assigned to some of the major news and sports stories of the day; she is considered the first woman sportswriter in the United States. Her sensational and personal writing style suited the tastes of the 1920s and 1930s. She wrote for Hearst publications for forty years.

Adela Rogers was born in Los Angeles on 20 May 1894. Her father, Earl Rogers, was a prominent trial lawyer who once defended Clarence Darrow on a jury tampering charge. St. Johns was devoted to her father; the tempestuous marriage of Earl and Harriet Greene Rogers caused her virtually to grow up in her father's law office. In *Final Verdict* (1962), her biography of her father, St. Johns says that she was content to be raised by him and her paternal grandparents. "I can't connect her with anything," she says of her mother. "My memory has rejected her, eliminated her, cannot apparently bear to remember her." Earl Rogers's father, Lowell Lynch Rogers, tutored her from an early age. He was a Methodist minister and college president. At the age of nine, she sold her first fiction story to the *Los Angeles Times*. She attended Hollywood High School, but dropped out after failing a math course; in 1951 the school conferred an honorary diploma on her.

In 1913 Rogers introduced his eighteen-year-old daughter to William Randolph Hearst, who hired her for seven dollars a week to write for the *San Francisco Examiner*. In 1914 she joined the staff of Hearst's *Los Angeles Herald* and covered city hall, police, sports, society, and features.

On Christmas Eve of 1914, Adela Rogers married the chief copy editor of the *Herald,* William Ivan ("Ike") St. Johns. Four years later, she left the *Herald* to raise their children: William Ivan II, who was to die in World War II; Elaine; McCullah; and Richard Rogers. She balanced raising babies with occasional writing, mostly features and magazine articles. She contributed numerous free-lance short serials to the *Saturday Evening Post, Good Housekeeping, McCall's, Ladies' Home Journal, Cosmopolitan, American Weekly, This Week, Redbook, Reader's Digest, Harper's Bazaar*, and the London *Daily Express* and *Evening Standard*. She also wrote profiles of movie stars for *Photoplay,* plus stories or screenplays for two westerns for cowboy star Tom Mix, three serials, and several feature films. She returned to daily newspaper work in 1925 to cover sports and news. Her assignments for the Hearst newspapers included the World Series, Kentucky Derby, Rose Bowl, Olympic Games, and the Forest Hills Tennis Tournament. She and Ike St. Johns were divorced

in 1929. Adela St. Johns was remarried twice, to Richard Hyland and to airline executive Francis Patrick O'Toole. Both later marriages ended in divorce, and her official biographies omit references to Hyland and O'Toole.

When St. Johns covered the 1935 trial of Bruno Richard Hauptmann for the kidnapping and murder of the Lindbergh baby, she filed stories for thirty-one consecutive days and was called "the world's greatest girl reporter" in Hearst promotions. At this time she was forty years old, and women journalists were scarce beyond the boundaries of the society department. She was moving quickly away from her old Hollywood "mother confessor" beat with assignments that included the abdication of Edward VIII, the disputed Dempsey-Tunney long-count boxing match, and the assassination of Sen. Huey Long. In the mid-1930s St. Johns moved from California to Washington, D.C., to cover politics. A key assignment for her as a developing political writer in 1940 was to cover the Democratic national convention. In 1949, a six-part series about India's Mahatma Gandhi just before his assassination was her final story for the Hearst International News Service.

In an *Editor & Publisher* magazine interview St. Johns talked about her reporting style. "I was a feature writer and would spend very little time on each one. Mr. Hearst would put in new staffs like ball clubs put in new players. I don't remember what all the names of the papers were, they kept merging and consolidating so much and their names kept changing all the time."

Her writing had a personal tone, as in her observations of fighter Jack Dempsey: "He knew his own strength and the murderous temper that had given him the name of the 'Manassas Mauler.' The reason he had the most beautiful manners I ever saw was because he felt an inner necessity to be a GENTLE man."

"Retirement" for St. Johns just meant moving into a new journalistic field. From 1950 to 1952, she was the first woman faculty member of the graduate school of journalism at the University of California at Los Angeles. She also taught journalism at the University of Missouri, the California Polytechnic Institute, Pepperdine University, Stephens College, Stanford University, and Loyola University. In the 1950s and 1960s, she devoted her writing interest to books, including *How to Write a Story and Sell It* (1956); *Affirmative Prayer in Action* (1957); *Final Verdict*, a 1962 biography of her father; and *Tell No Man* (1966), a novel.

Fellow Californian Richard Nixon awarded

her the Medal of Freedom in 1970. Probably her most revealing account of her own life, in addition to her autobiography, *The Honeycomb* (1969), which took four years to complete, is her 1974 book *Some Are Born Great*. Here she notes that she is not a feminist, but believes in "the superiority of American women." The book is based on the idea that if she could choose some great American women of the past to join Damon Runyon's "Tavern at the End of the Road," she would include Amelia Earhart, Carry Nation, Judy Garland, Margaret Mitchell, Elsie Parrish, Margaret Sanger, Rachel Carson, Dr. Miriam Van Waters, and Bess Truman. St. Johns said the two women then living whom she most admired were Anne Morrow Lindbergh and Rose Kennedy. St. Johns claims that she never felt discriminated against during her career in the traditionally male newspaper field. Despite critical mail accusing her of being antiwoman, she considers herself "too pro-woman . . . I am the only one who is sure woman's gallantry in covered wagons, transatlantic flights and having babies has never faltered." St. Johns states as her ultimate position on women: "As the controlling factor of the world's destiny, all women are born great. Greater. Greatest." In *Some Are Born Great,* she applies a humorous, critical look back at her early writing style, crediting the judgment of her editor, Ferris Mack, with preventing "any slipping too far back into the sob sister."

Hollywood entertainment writer Joyce Haber wrote in the *Cleveland Plain Dealer* for 25 October 1974 about her impressions of St. Johns after appearing with her on Merv Griffin's television show when St. Johns was touring the country to promote *Some Are Born Great*. "For more than 60 years in journalism, writing, teaching, delivering sermons and lecturing, this remarkable intelligent woman who recently turned 80 has had the last word," Haber noted. St. Johns told Haber after the television appearance that her marriage to Ike St. Johns failed "because I had no interest in it." Repeating her claim to have forgotten her second husband's name—"and so has everyone else"—St. Johns declared, "I think every woman's entitled to a middle husband she can forget."

In 1976, at age eighty-two, she came out of retirement to cover the bank robbery and conspiracy trial of William Randolph Hearst's granddaughter Patty for the *San Francisco Examiner*. Only recently, as she approached her ninetieth year, has St. Johns lived in true retirement in Malibu, California.

References:

Paul F. Healy, *Cissy: The Biography of Eleanor M. "Cissy" Patterson* (Garden City: Doubleday, 1966), pp. 177-181, 188, 238-239, 315-316;

John Jakes, *Great Women Reporters* (New York: Putnam's, 1969);

Don Maley, "Adela Rogers St. Johns Talks of Journalism and W. R. Hearst," *Editor & Publisher,* 102 (29 November 1969): 15;

Ralph G. Martin, *Cissy* (New York: Simon & Schuster, 1979), pp. 178, 180, 283, 285, 293-294, 301-302, 303, 360;

J. Edward Murray, "From Sensation to Meditation," *Editor & Publisher,* 90 (17 August 1957): 57;

Ishbel Ross, *Ladies of the Press* (New York & London: Harper, 1936), pp. 251-253.

George S. Schuyler

(25 February 1895-31 August 1977)

Nickieann Fleener
University of Utah

MAJOR POSITIONS HELD: Reporter, columnist, chief editorial writer, New York edition editor, associate editor, *Pittsburgh Courier* (1924-1966); special correspondent, *New York Evening Post* (1931); syndicated columnist, Spadeau Columns (1953-1962), North American Newspaper Alliance (1965-1977).

SELECTED BOOKS: *Racial Intermarriage in the United States* (Girard, Kans.: Haldeman-Julius, 1929);

A Negro Looks Ahead (N.p., 1930);

Black No More: Being An Account of the Strange and Wonderful Workings of Science in the Land of the Free AD 1933-1940 (New York: Macauley, 1931);

Slaves Today: A Story of Liberia (New York: Brewer, Warren & Putnam, 1931);

The Communist Conspiracy Against the Negroes (New York: Catholic Information Society, 1947);

The Red Drive in the Colonies (New York: Catholic Information Society, 1947);

Fifty Years of Progress in Negro Journalism (Pittsburgh: Pittsburgh Courier, 1950);

The Van Vechten Revolution (Atlanta, 1951);

Black and Conservative: The Autobiography of George S. Schuyler (New Rochelle, N.Y.: Arlington House, 1966).

SELECTED PERIODICAL PUBLICATIONS: "Hobohemia I: The World of the Migratory Worker," *Messenger,* 5 (June 1923): 741-744;

"The Negro-Art Hokum," *Nation,* 122 (16 June 1926): 662-663;

"Blessed Are The Sons of Ham," *Nation,* 124 (23 March 1927): 313-315;

"Racial Intermarriage in the United States," *American Parade,* 1 (Fall 1928);

"Woof," *Harlem,* 1 (November 1928): 17-20;

"Keeping The Negro In His Place," *American Mercury,* 17 (August 1929): 469-476;

"Emancipated Woman and the Negro," *Modern Quarterly,* 5 (Fall 1929);

"Traveling Jim Crow," *American Mercury,* 20 (August 1930): 423-432;

George S. Schuyler

"Black America Begins to Doubt," *American Mercury,* 25 (April 1932): 423-430;

"Freedom of the Press in Mississippi," *Crisis,* 43 (October 1936): 302-303, 306;

"Not Gone With The Wind," *Crisis,* 44 (July 1937): 205-206;

"What The Negro Thinks of the South," *Negro Digest,* 2 (May 1945);

"Jim Crow in the North," *American Mercury,* 68 (June 1949): 663-670;

"What's Wrong With Negro Authors," *Negro Digest,* 7 (May 1950): 3-7;

"Why I Want to Stay in America," *Negro Digest,* 9 (June 1951): 52-56;

"The Phantom American Negro," *Reader's Digest,* 59 (July 1951): 61-63;

"Do Negroes Want to be White?," *American Mercury,* 82 (June 1956): 55-60;

"Freedom Through Finance," *Sepia,* 11 (May 1962): 55-58.

George S. Schuyler, *Pittsburgh Courier* associate editor, columnist, and reporter, was one of the first black journalists to gain national prominence in the twentieth century. Considering himself an American and a citizen of the world as well as a black man, Schuyler traveled extensively during his career of over fifty years. He was one of the first black reporters to serve as a foreign correspondent for a major metropolitan newspaper and was particularly familiar with social, economic, and political conditions in Africa and Latin America. Because of his unique position in the black press, the strength of his satirical style, and the diversity of his subject matter, numerous newspapers and magazines sought his work until the late 1960s. However, Schuyler's dogmatic conservatism ran in absolute contrast to the philosophies expressed by virtually every major spokesperson of the civil rights movement. As the movement grew, the outlets for Schuyler's work shrank until he was in virtual obscurity at the time of his death in 1977.

Schuyler did not plan to be a writer. His childhood and early years were spent in a variety of pursuits. To each experience, Schuyler brought a strong sense of humor, keen powers of observation, and an active curiosity. He put these characteristics to good use, and drew frequently in his later writings from the memories of his youth. Always a rebel, Schuyler began his career as a socialist and ended it as an ultraconservative. His life and his career are studies in contrast.

George Samuel Schuyler was born 25 February 1895 in Providence, Rhode Island, and was reared in Syracuse, New York. His family took pride in having been free as far back as any could remember. His father, George F. Schuyler, head chef at a local hotel, died when Schuyler was three years old. His mother, Eliza Jane Fischer Schuyler, remarried three years later. Schuyler's stepfather, Joseph E. Brown, worked as a cook and porter for the New York Central Railroad. The family lived in a fourteen-room home on the outskirts of the Brighton community. Schuyler's family stressed the values of hard work, self-reliance, and determination. His mother maintained a small library in the home and taught Schuyler to read and write before he entered grade school. As a child, Schuyler par-

ticularly enjoyed reading Joseph T. Wilson's *The Black Phalanx* (1888), a history of black soldiers and sailors.

Schuyler was brought up and educated entirely in neighborhoods and schools where whites greatly outnumbered blacks. He indicated in his autobiography that he did not find this racial isolation detrimental, but that he believed it would be detrimental for most young blacks never to see blacks in positions of leadership or authority. To help remedy this problem, Schuyler made black accomplishments throughout history a frequent theme in his later columns and magazine articles.

Throughout his youth, Schuyler added to the family income by taking odd jobs. His introduction to the newspaper business came with a paper route. Schuyler found selling newspapers to be not only an excellent source of extra money but also an exciting introduction to current events. Schuyler always saved one paper for himself and became an avid newspaper reader.

Although he was an excellent student and enjoyed school, Schuyler left formal education behind in 1912, when he dropped out of high school to join the army. He was only seventeen, but his mother signed the necessary papers. Schuyler later explained that he thought opportunites for young black men in Syracuse were severely limited and he wanted to advance himself. After basic training, Schuyler was assigned to Company B of the segregated Twenty-fifth U.S. Infantry Regiment, stationed at Fort Lawton near Seattle. Three months later Schuyler's mother died. Her death left Schuyler feeling isolated and he made Company B his family. In November 1912, the Twenty-fifth Infantry was transferred to Schofield Barracks, Hawaii. Schuyler was discharged in mid-July 1915, but remained in Hawaii and started a taxi service.

In November, Schuyler reenlisted in the army. His first attempts at newspaper writing came during this second-duty tour. In addition to occasional pieces for the *Honolulu Commercial Advertiser* and the *Service* magazine, Schuyler produced a typed newspaper which was tacked on camp bulletin boards. The primary purpose of the paper was entertainment, and Schuyler used this newspaper as a training ground for the development of his satirical style. He continued producing the paper until he was discharged from the service immediately after the end of World War I. During his time in the service, Schuyler collected experiences and personalities about which he later wrote. For example, his first sergeant, William Glass, was the subject of "Woof," a profile which appeared in the November 1928 issue of *Harlem* magazine. At the time of his discharge in 1919, Schuyler was a first lieutenant.

For the next several years, Schuyler worked in New York City as a civil service clerk processing military prisoners. The job gave him much free time, which he spent primarily in reading. Politically, Schuyler was leaning more and more toward socialism. After the civil service appointment ended, Schuyler held a series of odd jobs including factory work and dishwashing. Although not satisfied with any of the jobs, Schuyler also drew from these experiences when he wrote later articles. One restaurant in which he worked was the subject of an *American Mercury* article, "Memoirs of a Pearl Diver," written and published ten years later.

Increasingly dissatisfied with twelve-hour workdays filled with steam, kitchen odors, and dirty dishes, Schuyler quit his dishwashing job, left New York City, and returned to Syracuse. He moved in with his cousins Lila and Mary Louise Watson, and began working as a handyman. Schuyler noted in his autobiography that he did not particularly enjoy the work, but his flexible schedule allowed him to do a lot of reading. Many of the books he read were about socialism, and in November 1921, he joined the Socialist Party of America. Within a short time he was elected education director of the Syracuse chapter, and he launched an ambitious campaign designed to bring socialism to his hometown. As part of his educational program, Schuyler wrote several short pamphlets praising socialist principles. Several of these were written primarily for black audiences.

Schuyler tired rather quickly of being a handyman. He also began to question some of the basic teachings of socialism. For a short time, he worked in Syracuse as a hod carrier and building laborer. When the construction job ended, Schuyler returned to New York in December 1922 with little money and a determination to meet a different type of black than he had previously. To this end, he rented a room in the Phillis Wheatley Hotel, which was operated by Marcus Garvey's Universal Negro Improvement Association. He attended several UNIA meetings and found that he did not share Garvey's belief that the solution to the race problem was for blacks to go back to Africa. Schuyler also attended meetings of other black organizations and became familiar with the philosophies of many of the movements of the early 1920s. Eventually he became heavily involved with the black socialist group Friends of Negro Freedom, headed by A. Philip Randolph and Chandler Owen.

Through Schuyler's association with Randolph and Owen came the actual start of his journalistic career. In 1923, Randolph offered Schuyler the job of general assistant on the *Messenger,* the official magazine of the Friends of Negro Freedom. Although the salary was only ten dollars a week, Schuyler accepted the job because the idea of being associated with what he considered an important publication fascinated him. He wrote a monthly page called "Shafts and Darts: A Page of Calumny and Satire," which lampooned the fads and foibles of the day. Schuyler thought that most black publications were too somber; his goal was to bring humor to black journalism.

Shortly after beginning work on the *Messenger,* Schuyler began free-lancing. His initial effort, "From Job to Job," a first-person account of his work experiences in New York, was published in the April issue of *The World Tomorrow,* the official magazine of the Christian socialist group Fellowship of Reconciliation. Schuyler was elated over the acceptance because he felt that writings by blacks were too infrequently found in magazines.

While working at the *Messenger,* Schuyler met a variety of black writers and intellectuals, including Ira F. Lewis, general manager of the *Pittsburgh Courier.* In 1924, Lewis asked Schuyler to write a regular column for the *Courier,* which had the second largest circulation of the black weeklies. Although the salary was only three dollars a week, Schuyler was delighted to accept; and thus began an association with the *Courier* which lasted over forty years.

During this period, Schuyler became increasingly disenchanted with socialism and began his political march to the right. He also developed a passionate hatred for communism and turned this hatred into a lifelong campaign against what he believed to be a Communist conspiracy to take over the United States. As is reflected in his 1939 *American Mercury* article "Negroes Reject Communism," Schuyler came to believe that Communist claims of brotherhood were hypocritical and that Communists were trying to enlist the support of blacks only to polarize further black and white Americans and thereby weaken the country. In his autobiography, Schuyler wrote that he felt compelled to use all of his energies to fight "this conspiracy to destroy the Negro population to ensure a Communist victory." More than any other factor, this anti-Communist obsession dominated Schuyler's writings and shaped the direction of his career.

In November 1925, Schuyler began his first major *Courier* assignment. He was sent below the Mason-Dixon line to report on the condition of blacks in the South and to bolster *Courier* circulation in the area. The *Courier* heavily publicized the tour prior to his departure, explaining that Schuyler's basic task was to present an accurate picture of the conditions and progress of the black population in the form of a word photograph. Schuyler remained on the assignment until July 1926. He later described the tour as hectic, without incident, and vastly educational.

Although he remained with the *Messenger* until the publication died in 1928, Schuyler's involvement with the *Courier* and his free-lancing both increased after he returned from his trip. Perhaps the most significant free-lancing breakthrough occurred when his work captured the attention of H. L. Mencken, who solicited Schuyler's work for the *American Mercury*. The two men became lifelong correspondents. Another significant step in Schuyler's career came in August 1926 when Lewis asked him to write *Courier* editorials. Schuyler continued as *Courier* chief editorial writer for thirty-eight years.

On 6 January 1928, he married an artist, Josephine E. Lewis, the daughter of a prominent white Texas family. Shortly after their marriage, the Schuylers moved to Chicago, where he edited a weekly magazine insert for some of the larger black newspapers. However, he quickly became dissatisfied with the position and returned to New York, where he continued his *Courier* work and his free-lancing; in addition, he went on the lecture circuit, speaking on the topics he wrote about. In August 1930, he taught a two-week newswriting and reporting course to about 150 farm and home demonstration agents at South Carolina State College at Orangeburg. Also in 1930 he wrote the satirical novel *Black No More* (1931), which presented a mythical solution to the race problem: blacks were turned permanently white by the use of a cream. The book focused on the reaction of black leaders who saw their powers eroded as fewer and fewer followers existed. Although the characters had fictional names, the similarities to major black leaders of the times were obvious. Former National Association for the Advancement of Colored People (NAACP) director Henry Lee Moon said, "I remember W. E. B. Du Bois laughing about recognizing himself in George's book."

Toward the end of 1930 came one of the major breaks of Schuyler's early career: publisher George Palmer Putnam asked him to go to Liberia and write a book about the contemporary slave trade there. The project was also sponsored by the *New York Evening Post*. *Post* editor Julian Mason arranged the sale of a newspaper series based on Schuyler's findings. Schuyler arrived in Liberia's capital, Monrovia, in late February 1931. He was appalled by the conditions he found and described the squalor thoroughly in his newspaper series. For the next two months, Schuyler and his guides traveled over 600 miles throughout Liberia. In each village, Schuyler interviewed the leaders. He found all to be cooperative and heard story after story about leaders being forced to turn young men over to the government. Schuyler traveled with a portable typewriter and spent the days interviewing and the nights typing his notes. At the end of his stay, he contracted malaria and did little actual writing until he had recovered back in the United States. He wrote six newspaper articles which were published during June and July 1931 in several newspapers, including the *New York Evening Post,* the *Washington Post,* and the *Philadelphia Ledger.* The *New York Evening Post* also ran several of Schuyler's photographs of Liberian life. The project represented one of the first times a black journalist had served as a foreign correspondent for a major metropolitan daily; Schuyler noted the accomplishment as one of the highlights of his career. After he completed the newspaper series, Schuyler wrote the book, *Slaves Today: A Story of Liberia* (1931), promised to Putnam.

Schuyler became increasingly obsessed with what he regarded as a Communist conspiracy to win over blacks during the early 1930s. He was particularly concerned with what he believed to be Communist involvement in the "Scottsboro boys" case, in which nine black teenagers had been indicted on rape charges. The case was receiving widespread publicity when Schuyler returned from Liberia in spring 1931. Although the NAACP initially handled the defense, the International Labor Defense organization quickly took over the case. Schuyler believed the ILD to be a Communist front organization plotting to incite the American black population into civil war against the whites. In his columns and editorials, Schuyler repeatedly attacked the ILD, the handling of the Scottsboro case, and individuals who supported either.

One of his first individual targets was William N. Jones, managing editor of the *Baltimore Afro-American*. Beginning in August 1931, Jones and Schuyler exchanged editorial barbs. Schuyler also spoke against black boycotts of white merchants because he believed the tactic to be Communist-inspired. Schuyler's voice was a lonely one. Very few writers joined in his attacks; on the contrary, a number of black newspapers accused him of being an Uncle Tom and joining with the lynchers who wanted to see the Scottsboro boys executed. Schuyler responded by attacking the entire black press for what he termed its "gullibility in swallowing the propaganda and boresome lies and calumnies of the Communists . . . with very few exceptions, Negro newspapers have thrown discrimination to the winds and carried practically all of the lying Communist 'news' releases that have been sent them." Later, Schuyler criticized the handling of the Angelo Herndon case. Herndon had been sentenced to a Georgia chain gang for organizing and leading marches of hungry and unemployed workers in Georgia, but had been released on bail. Schuyler wrote that Herndon would probably jump bail as other Communists arrested on similar charges had done. The Communist journal *Negro Liberator* called Schuyler the "most vicious of the pen prostitutes plying his trade in the Negro press." The *Negro Liberator* sent a letter calling for Schuyler's immediate dismissal from the *Courier* because of his "disruptive and slanderous attacks which have appeared in his column upon the militant struggles of the Negro workers." *Courier* officials did not publicly respond to this demand, and Schuyler continued his attacks.

The early 1930s were full years for Schuyler both personally and professionally. On 2 August 1932, his only child, Philippa Duke, was born. A child prodigy, Philippa wrote her first composition for piano at age four and the following year won first prize in the New York Philharmonic children's concert series. In his autobiography, Schuyler wrote that his home life with Josephine and Philippa gave him the confidence he needed to contend with society and those who criticized him.

During this period, Schuyler completed several special assignments for the *Courier* and the NAACP. In December 1932, the NAACP sent him to investigate labor conditions on the Mississippi Flood Control Project. Schuyler and Roy Wilkins, the NAACP assistant secretary, traveled incognito to Mississippi and attempted to obtain work on the project. Schuyler visited a series of labor camps and observed working conditions. He returned to New York after Mississippi police mistakenly arrested him in connection with a robbery. Schuyler wrote extensively about his adventures in his *Courier* columns.

When he returned to New York, Schuyler went to work part-time in the NAACP's publicity office. One of his projects was an eighteen-article history of the organization which was published by a number of black newspapers. He remained with the publicity office until 1935, when budget cuts eliminated his job.

In autumn 1934, Schuyler researched and wrote what he believed to be a highly significant series of articles for the *Courier*: a study of Harlem schools, illustrated with his own photographs. Schuyler believed that Harlem was one of the most misunderstood neighborhoods in America, and hoped to show the strength of the schools and the quality of the black students. He believed the series to be the first dealing exclusively and objectively with black schools.

During the summer of 1935, the *Courier* sent Schuyler to Mississippi to improve the newspaper's circulation in the state. He was allotted two pages in each issue for news, features, and photos of Mississippi life. *Courier* circulation in the area rose from 2,000 to 10,000 during the six-month assignment.

In July 1937, the *Courier* assigned Schuyler a series of articles on the impact of the industrial labor union drive on black workers and vice versa. He spent three months traveling through eighteen states and visiting over forty industrial centers. In each city, he visited union headquarters and strike centers and interviewed labor leaders, organizers, and black workers. Each week one page of the *Courier* was devoted to his findings. Horace Clayton and George Mitchell quote liberally from this important series of articles in their study, *Black Workers and the New Unions* (1939). In addition to writing the series, Schuyler continued to write editorials, his "Views and Reviews" column, and a one-column front-page summary of general news. He also continued free-lancing and lecturing around the country. Later in 1937, he became business manager of the NAACP magazine, *Crisis*. He continued in that position until the spring of 1944, when his other work with the *Courier* became so demanding that he resigned from the *Crisis* staff.

In spite of the fact that Schuyler researched and wrote at least three highly significant investigative series during the 1930s, he later wrote that he felt his most significant pieces during the period were those which predicted World War II and its potential impact on the international color conflict. In both the *Courier* and *Crisis*, Schuyler repeatedly predicted that the probable impact of World War II on the black colonies would be eventual liberation.

Throughout the decade from 1940 to 1950, Schuyler remained a highly productive writer, and his involvement with the *Courier* deepened. The

Courier was reaching a nationwide audience of 250,000 each week, which consistently placed it among the top three in readership and geographical distribution among black newspapers. In 1942, the *Courier* gave Schuyler the title of associate editor; thus, during the decade Schuyler fulfilled at least four major roles for the *Courier*: editor, reporter, columnist, and editorial writer. He saw these functions as discrete and interpreted the role of each to be different. As an editor, Schuyler felt the most important objective of the black newspaper was education. He thought that most black Americans were isolated and undereducated and that the black press should help educate the black masses. As a reporter he considered his role to be that of objective observer; he said that he "tried to present an accurate picture, not a caricature, to remain an observer, not become a partisan." As an editorial writer, Schuyler tried not to forget that he was speaking for the newspaper and not for himself; therefore, his editorials were much more restrained than his columns. As a columnist, he felt free to let go completely and express his personal views.

Although Schuyler wrote on a variety of topics during the 1940s, his most frequent theme remained communism. Out of this constant harangue came what he called the only direct interference he ever experienced from the *Courier* management. In the New York edition, Schuyler was running a series of articles by Communist defector George Hewitt which revealed dates and places of Communist meetings in the United States and the names of participants. Three or four articles into the series, William Nunn, *Courier* managing editor, ordered that the series be terminated, without explaining to Schuyler why he wanted the series canceled. Schuyler complied without an argument.

In May 1943, Schuyler became associate editor of a monthly magazine, the *African,* contributing a page on events in Africa to each issue. This assignment kept Schuyler in more direct contact with black African life, and this closer perspective was reflected in his *Courier* writings.

During World War II, Schuyler became increasingly concerned about the growth of racial intolerance in America. Alerted to the problem by many of the union contacts he had made during his 1937 investigation, he found that the influx of black and white workers from the South to the Northern industrial centers for war jobs was causing much racial tension. He decided that the solution was the reeducation of the white masses with scientific propaganda; to conduct the campaign, he founded the Association for Tolerance in America. Schuyler devoted much time and energy throughout 1943 developing an ambitious publicity campaign using pamphlets, press releases, transit cards, matrices, advertising, and postcards; the association generated over 30,000 individual pieces. However, after only one year of existence, the organization folded because it had not been able to attract sufficient membership or financial backing.

After the failure of the association, Schuyler directed his energy to the *Courier* and his fight against communism. In his columns, he repeatedly criticized blacks for their stupidity in permitting themselves to be attracted into the Soviet orbit. He also attacked black leaders who exhibited what he believed to be Communist leanings. In particular, he attacked W. E. B. Du Bois for his close association with Communists. For example, when Du Bois became a contributing editor to *New Masses* in 1946, Schuyler wrote: "Agitation is the food and fuel of Communism and all of its organs of propaganda. So when Dr. Du Bois joins *The New Masses* he is more definitely than ever committed to that policy. . . . After all perhaps it is appropriate that Du Bois should join Stalin's literary gendarme where inconsistency, backbiting, and charlatanism are crowning virtues and political irregularity is the only vice." Schuyler also used his column to expose the United Negro and Allied Veterans of America organizations as Communist fronts. He was virtually the only member of the black press to attack so doggedly and consistently communism, and he was not without his critics. Nevertheless, in February 1944 he was made editor of the *Courier*'s New York edition.

During the late 1940s Schuyler undertook several major reporting assignments for the *Courier*. The first assignment came from managing editor Nunn during the winter of 1947-1948. Nunn asked Schuyler to generate a series of articles comparing the civil rights picture in each state capital with the situation in the federal capital. Schuyler traveled to each state capital and assessed the civil rights situation. He found the assignment in many ways comparable to his survey of the South twenty-two years earlier. Once again, his major problem was securing suitable lodging. He observed in his stories that the vast area from the Missouri River to the Pacific Coast was virtually a no-man's-land for the black traveler and that finding overnight accommodations was almost impossible. While on the road he continued to write *Courier* editorials and columns.

Almost immediately after completing this assignment, Schuyler began another in New York: a survey of living conditions in Harlem. He hired an assistant to help him conduct an in-depth study of the area. Schuyler had lived in and near Harlem for many years, and thought the area had been much maligned by the white press. His research consisted of interviewing Harlem residents and consulting a variety of published sources, including the U.S. Census and data from the New York departments of education, housing, police, fire, sanitation, and hospitals. The data revealed that in 1948, Harlem was far less congested than it had been in 1916, when it was predominantly populated by whites. Also, 1948 Harlem contained more owner-occupied dwellings than any other district in Manhattan. Schuyler concluded that the prevailing myth that Harlem was overcrowded came from an antiblack bias among newspaper and magazine editors, who ran pictures of only the worst blocks and alleys. The resulting series, "The Truth About Harlem," ran in the *Courier* for several months and remains a significant historical study.

Schuyler's next major assignment of the decade came on the heels of his Harlem series. In mid-June 1948, *Courier* editor Lewis sent him on a tour of Latin America. In addition to writing about the countries he visited, Schuyler was to try to broaden the paper's circulation base and attract foreign advertisers. During this six-week tour of Cuba, Venezuela, Colombia, Panama, Ecuador, Peru, Chile, Argentina, Uruguay, and Brazil, Schuyler found color prejudice and discrimination to be widespread throughout Latin America. For example, he reported that rigid regulations against black immigrants existed throughout the area and that in Venezuela visiting blacks were allowed to stay only twenty-four or forty-eight hours. Hotel accommodations were difficult to obtain in most countries. The series was titled "Racial Democracy in Latin America" and focused on the role of blacks in government and the military.

After he returned to New York, Schuyler was asked to write a series of articles titled "What's Good about the South?" To write this series, Schuyler had to visit fourteen states, and in each one he interviewed one urban and one rural black family about living conditions. Because the series praised parts of the South, it aroused the ire of several black leaders who were appalled that anyone would praise the region. Tremendous debate in the black press accompanied the publication of the series.

While "What's Good about the South?" was running, Schuyler renewed his attacks on communism. Some of his columns focused on the fate of Jews in the USSR, the services of W. E. B. Du Bois and Paul Robeson to the Communist cause, the Red conspiracy against NAACP, and the ouster of

eleven unions from the CIO because the unions were allegedly Communist led.

In the spring of 1949, Schuyler convinced the *Courier's* management to send him on another major overseas assignment. In May, he covered a conference on the problems of blacks in Brazil held in Rio de Janeiro. Schuyler covered the conference and wrote in greater depth about life for blacks in the Brazilian capital. Schuyler's findings concurred with the viewpoints presented by the speakers: discrimination was rampant. In his articles, Schuyler likened the situation to the worst conditions in America. After leaving Brazil, Schuyler toured the West Indies and wrote a series of articles titled "The New West Indies." Schuyler later commented that one of the major dividends of his tour was the large number of stringers he accumulated. The stringers airmailed weekly stories to Schuyler, and he put the stories together to form at least one page of timely news from the region each week. Because many black immigrants came from the area and few black newspapers covered the area in such depth, the page attracted many new readers to the *Courier*.

Schuyler began a weekly radio program over New York station WLIB in December 1949. "The Negro World" emphasized news from Africa and the Caribbean and featured interviews with non-white United Nations delegates and visiting dignitaries from the region. The program prospered, and Schuyler remained associated with the station in various capacities until the late 1960s.

Schuyler was a delegate from the United States to the Congress of Cultural Freedom in Berlin in June 1950. He viewed the congress as the largest and most important gathering in the history of anticommunism. During the congress he presented an address on "The Negro Question Without Propaganda," an analysis of the black experience in capitalist America and a spirited defense of the free enterprise system. In part, Schuyler said, "Actually, the progressive improvement of interracial relations in the United States is the most flattering of the many examples of the superiority of the free American civilization over the soul-shackling reactionism of totalitarian regimes. It is this capacity for change and adjustment inherent in the system of individual initiative and decentralized authority to which we must attribute the unprecedented economic, social and educational progress of the Negroes of the United States." The speech was published as Congress Paper twenty-three and was distributed by every United States embassy and consulate and inserted into the *Congressional Record* by Congresswoman Frances Bolton. Also in 1950,

Schuyler's seven-page pamphlet *Fifty Years of Progress in Negro Journalism* was published by the *Pittsburgh Courier*'s publishing company.

In 1951, Schuyler condensed his Cultural Freedom address and rewrote it under the title "The Phantom American Negro." The thesis of the piece was that the dire picture of the position of the American black painted in many quarters was false and only aided and comforted the Communist propagandists. The article was published in the June 1951 issue of the *Freeman* magazine. The article attracted immediate attention. Seventeen American and foreign publications, including the *Christian Science Monitor,* requested permission to reprint it. *Reader's Digest* reprinted the article in its July 1951 American edition and also ran the piece in nine later foreign editions. The *Courier* realized its publicity value and reprinted the article with a prominent note identifying Schuyler as a member of the *Courier* staff.

In early 1952, Schuyler received a citation of merit from Lincoln University School of Journalism. The following November, he attended another organizational meeting of the Congress for Cultural Freedom in Brussels, Belgium. In addition to being a delegate, Schuyler covered the conference as a reporter and wired stories to New York following each session. While in Belgium, he also investigated the lives led by African immigrants. After the congress, he remained in Europe to cover the Nobel Peace Prize ceremonies for Dr. Ralph J. Bunche. While traveling to the ceremonies, he investigated living conditions of blacks in Holland, Denmark, and Norway. Based upon his findings, he wrote *Courier* articles and recorded programs for WLIB.

Schuyler became a columnist for Spadeau Columns when the syndicate was formed in 1953. He was the only black journalist originally invited to join the syndicate, and he accepted because of the large audience he anticipated reaching. For the next several years, his "For the Record" column reached a potential audience of more than six million. Schuyler identified two major purposes for his column: exposing the Communist conspiracy (as in columns titled "Castro's Butcheries Follow Leftist Patterns" and "Bolivia's Red Bosses Love US Generosity") and presenting blacks in a light rarely seen by mass white audiences (as in columns titled "Negro Education Pays Dividends" and "Growing Southern Negro Votes").

Schuyler remained a student of African affairs, and in the late 1950s he toured French West Africa, Angola, Nigeria, and Mozambique and wrote articles about African life for the *Courier* and for a variety of magazines. His position on African independence irritated many black leaders in both America and Africa: he vehemently contended that the African nations were not ready for independence. In his *Courier* columns, he commented that Africans were in the main ravaged by disease, ignorant, and torn by tribal rivalries, and insisted that these problems could only be solved by foreign capital and Christian missionaries. He argued that only after an extended transitional period would the African nations be ready for independence and that anyone who thought otherwise had never been there.

Schuyler's position on Africa, his unwavering attacks on the Communist conspiracy, and his racial attitudes, which were viewed as paternalistic at best by many black leaders, strained his relationship with the *Courier* during the 1950s. He continued to write *Courier* editorials, columns, and articles, but an ever-deepening trench was being dug between Schuyler and his employers. The *Courier* began running a statement of content disavowal with each of his columns; at the time, his was the only column to carry such a statement. From 1957 to 1961, Schuyler experienced three pay cuts, but he chose to stay with the paper.

The *Courier*'s first overt attempt to curtail Schuyler's power came in September 1960 when he was replaced as editor of the New York edition. In his autobiography, Schuyler said he never received any formal notification that he had been replaced; he learned from a rumor that George F. Brown had been given the job. Schuyler continued as columnist and editorial writer. During 1960 Schuyler was interviewed for Columbia University's Oral History Collection.

In November 1961, Schuyler was one of the founders of the New York State Conservative Political Association; he was active in the party throughout the remainder of his life. Also in 1961, Schuyler began to write for the John Birch Society's *American Opinions.* In 1964, he was chosen by the party to run against incumbent Adam Clayton Powell for the eighteenth Congressional District seat. During the campaign, Schuyler publicly blamed the Harlem race riots on the incessant incitement of civil rights leaders. His views were widely published in an interview given to the North American Newspaper Alliance and in a letter to the *New York Times.* The *Times* printed the letter and identified Schuyler as an associate editor of the *Pittsburgh Courier. Courier* editor P. L. Prattis then wrote a letter to the *Times* denying that Schuyler held such a position with the paper; Prattis said that Schuyler was only a columnist. He admitted that at one time Schuyler had held the title of associate editor, but the title was no longer his. Schuyler was shocked by the letter because he had not received notification from the *Courier* that the title he had been given in 1942 had been removed.

Later in the campaign, Schuyler supported Sen. Barry Goldwater's presidential aspirations. This stance resulted in another storm of protest, since the vast majority of civil rights groups were openly fighting Goldwater because of his opposition to the Civil Rights Act. Frequently thereafter, the *Courier* editorially stated that Schuyler was connected to the paper only as a columnist and that his opinons did not reflect the policies of the paper. However, the *Courier* failed to mention that Schuyler was still writing editorials for the paper.

After Schuyler lost the election to Powell, his *Courier* columns were increasingly critical of virtually every aspect of the growing civil rights movement. He thought that most leaders of the movement were professional agitators and Communist inspired. He spoke against all of the marches on Washington and other forms of public demonstration. He warned blacks that any form of mob action, nuisance provocation, or civil disobedience would worsen rather than better conditions. The strength of his position and the prose is reflected in such statements as "Under the influence of their white or (Red) mentors, a contaminated Negro leadership snapped at the Communist bait, received the support of white 'liberals' charting a course of disaster, and like pied pipers led the lunatic fringe astray." Not only did Schuyler oppose virtually every aspect of the movement, but he also spoke strongly against media coverage of the movement; he said that all of the communications media "not only surrendered to the hysteria religiously and monotonously repeating all of the self-serving fictions of the civil rights agitators, but virtually excluded contrary comment." In doing so, he felt, the media did not fulfill their proper journalistic responsibility. He was particularly irritated that he was not interviewed as a spokesperson for an alternative point of view. Schuyler also contended that because American blacks were in a better position than were blacks elsewhere in the world, agitation could only hurt. He did not deny that discrimination still existed, but argued that statesmanship, not protest, was the solution. Until his death, Schuyler continued to hold this belief and never felt that any lasting good came from the 1960s civil rights movement.

Shortly after Martin Luther King, Jr., won the Nobel Peace Prize in 1964, Schuyler devoted an entire column to King's unworthiness for the award. He held that King was quite undeserving of any prize as an apostle of peace because his activities were quite to the contrary. The *Courier* refused to run the column. However, the *Manchester Union Leader* did run the piece on 10 November 1964, and it was reprinted in other newspapers. Schuyler became a regular contributor to the *Manchester Union Leader* after its publication of his King article. Schuyler was the second member of his family to write regularly for the *Union Leader*. His daughter, Philippa, had begun working for the paper in the early 1960s as a roving correspondent. Shortly after the King column was published, Schuyler wrote his last editorial for the *Courier,* and he also ceased doing his weekly world news summary for the paper. He continued to write book reviews, occasional columns, and what he termed inspirational pieces for two more years.

In spring 1965, Schuyler became associated with the North American Newspaper Alliance. Through the syndicate he distributed a lengthy feature in which he attacked the Watts rioters and attributed the riot to the leadership of the civil rights movement. The article appeared in more than 200 publications and was the subject of heated debate; the *Philadelphia Bulletin* carried pro and con letters to the editor in response to the piece for more than a month after it was run. The *Crisis* ran an editorial denouncing Schuyler as an iconoclast who had gone too far and said that because of the wide coverage given the article it had harmful effects.

Schuyler's autobiography, *Black and Conservative,* was published in 1966 by Arlington House. That same year, Schuyler's association with the *Courier* ended.

In early 1967, Schuyler became analysis editor and film reviewer for the John Birch weekly *Review of the News,* and literary editor of the *Manchester Union Leader.* On 9 May 1967, Schuyler's only child, Philippa, was killed in a helicopter crash in Viet Nam. Philippa had been working in Viet Nam as a war correspondent for the *Union Leader* and giving piano concerts. At the time of her death, she was helping ferry Vietnamese children from Hue to Da Nang, where she planned to enroll them in school. One of the children was also killed in the crash, which was attributed to mechanical failure. *Union Leader* publisher William Loeb described Schuyler at Philippa's funeral as "a composed man. Whatever he felt inside he knew that a gentleman doesn't bare [his feelings] to the rest of the world." Two years later on 2 May 1969, Schuyler's wife died.

During Schuyler's last years, his outlets were more restricted, but he did continue to write and to lecture. He wrote book reviews and literary pieces for the *Union Leader* and remained a contributing editor of *American Opinion*. As a speaker, he was particularly popular with white conservative organizations. In 1966, he told the Denver chapter of the John Birch Society that American blacks should be grateful because they were better educated and healthier than African blacks.

Throughout the late 1960s and early 1970s, Schuyler received a variety of honors. In 1968, he received the American Legion Award, and the following year he was awarded a citation by the Catholic War Veterans. In the early 1970s, Schuyler was chosen for inclusion in *Ebony* magazine's biographical work *1,000 Successful Blacks*. In February 1972, he was guest of honor at the New York Conservative Party's annual George Washington's Birthday Dinner and received the Freedom's Foundation Award at Valley Forge.

Schuyler died on 31 August 1977 in New York Hospital. A journalist who once had an audience in the hundreds of thousands, he died in virtual professional obscurity. Black historian John Henrik Clarke perhaps best explained Schuyler's life: "I used to tell people that George got up in the morning, waited to see which way the world was turning, then struck out in the opposite direction. He was a rebel who enjoyed playing that role."

Interviews:

"The Reminiscences of George S. Schuyler," New York: Oral History Collection of Columbia University, 1960;

Steve Cannon and Michael Peplow, "George S. Schuyler, Writer" (October 1972), in Ishmael Reed, *Shrovetide in Old New Orleans* (Garden City: Doubleday, 1978).

References:

"Author George S. Schuyler Dies at 82 in New York," *Jet* (29 September 1977): 56;

Guy J. Forgue, compiler, *Letters of H. L. Mencken* (New York: Knopf, 1961);

George Goodman, Jr., "George S. Schuyler, Black Author," *New York Times*, 8 September 1977, p. 40;

Martin Mayer, "Meet the George Schuylers: America's Strangest Family," *Our World* (April 1951): 22-26;

1,000 Successful Blacks, The Ebony Success Library, Volume 1 (Chicago: Johnson, 1973), p. 275;

Michael W. Peplow, *George S. Schuyler* (Boston: Twayne, 1980);

Hollie West, "A Black Biting John Bircher," *Washington Post*, 6 September 1973.

H. Allen Smith
(19 December 1906-24 February 1976)

James E. Murphy
Southern Illinois University

See also the Smith entry in *DLB 11, American Humorists, 1800-1950.*

MAJOR POSITIONS HELD: Rewrite man and feature writer, United Press (1929-1934), *New York World-Telegram* (1936-1941).

BOOKS: *Robert Gair: A Study* (New York: Dial, 1939);

Mr. Klein's Kampf; or, His Life as Hitler's Double (New York: Stackpole, 1939);

Low Man on a Totem Pole (Garden City: Doubleday, Doran, 1941; London: Barker, 1947);

Life in a Putty Knife Factory (Garden City: Doubleday, Doran, 1943; London: Barker, 1948);

Lost in the Horse Latitudes (Garden City: Doubleday, Doran, 1944; London: Barker, 1949);

Rhubarb (Garden City: Doubleday, 1946; London: Barker, 1950);

Three Smiths in the Wind (Garden City: Doubleday, 1946);

Lo, the Former Egyptian! (Garden City: Doubleday, 1947; London: Barker, 1955);

Larks in the Popcorn (Garden City: Doubleday, 1948; London: Barker, 1948);

We Went Thataway (Garden City: Doubleday, 1949;

H. Allen Smith

London: Barker, 1951);

Low and Inside: A Book of Baseball Anecdotes, Oddities and Curiosities, by Smith and Ira Lepouce Smith (Garden City: Doubleday, 1949);

People Named Smith (Garden City: Doubleday, 1950);

Three Men on Third: A Second Book of Baseball Anecdotes, Oddities and Curiosities, by Smith and Ira Lepouce Smith (Garden City: Doubleday, 1951);

Mister Zip (Garden City: Doubleday, 1952; London: Barker, 1952);

Smith's London Journal; Now First Published From the Original Manuscript (Garden City: Doubleday, 1952; London: Barker, 1953);

The Compleat Practical Joker (Garden City: Doubleday, 1953; London: Barker, 1954; revised, New York: Morrow, 1980);

The Rebel Yell (Garden City: Doubleday, 1954; London: Barker, 1956);

The World, the Flesh, and H. Allen Smith, edited by Bergen Evans (Garden City: Hanover House, 1954);

The Age of the Tail (Boston: Little, Brown, 1955; London: Barker, 1956);

Write Me a Poem, Baby (Boston: Little, Brown, 1956);

The Pig in the Barber Shop (Boston: Little, Brown, 1958);

Don't Get Perconel with a Chicken (Boston: Little, Brown, 1959);

Let the Crabgrass Grow: H. Allen Smith's Suburban Almanac (New York: Geis, 1960);

Waikiki Beachnik (Boston: Little, Brown, 1960);

How to Write without Knowing Nothing: A Book Largely Concerned with the Use and Misuse of Language at Home and Abroad (Boston: Little, Brown, 1961);

To Hell in a Handbasket (Garden City: Doubleday, 1962);

A Short History of Fingers and Other State Papers (Boston: Little, Brown, 1963);

Two-thirds of a Coconut Tree (Boston: Little, Brown, 1963);

Poor H. Allen Smith's Almanac: A Comic Compendium Loaded with Wisdom and Laughter, Together with a Generous Lagniappe of Questionable Natural History, All Done up in Style (New York: Fawcett, 1965);

Son of Rhubarb (New York: Trident, 1967);

Buskin' with H. Allen Smith (New York: Trident, 1968);

The Great Chili Confrontation (New York: Trident, 1969);

The View from Chivo (New York: Trident, 1971);

The Best of H. Allen Smith, edited by Elton Miles (New York: Trident, 1972);

Low Man Rides Again (Garden City: Doubleday, 1973);

Return of the Virginian (Garden City: Doubleday, 1974);

The Life and Legend of Gene Fowler (New York: Morrow, 1977).

OTHER: *Desert Island Decameron,* edited by Smith (Garden City: Doubleday, Doran, 1945);

Gene Fowler, *Lady Scatterly's Lovers,* edited by Smith (Secaucus, N.J.: Lyle Stuart, 1973).

H. Allen Smith, humorist and reporter par excellence of the foibles of human behavior, was in his heyday one of the most popular and productive writers in America. During a newspaper and freelance career of more than fifty years, he wrote thirty-seven books—several of them best-sellers— hundreds of articles in leading national magazines, and untold numbers of feature stories for a dozen American newspapers and the United Press wire service. Most of his writings consist of true-to-life stories and musings about celebrities, eccentrics, "ordinary mortals," and himself. He looked for the

Smith (second from left) in the newsroom of the Huntington *(Indiana)* Press

humorous in everything and everyone, and could deftly turn the observation into a funny, often barbed, story. He laughed at pomposity and delighted in deflating pretension wherever he found it. A master storyteller, Smith has often been called a modern-day Mark Twain. He was rarely off the best-seller lists in the 1940s, his books reportedly selling nearly 1.5 million copies between 1941 and 1946. The *New York Times* called him one of the best-known Americans of the 1940s. Although less well known in his later years, Smith continued to write prodigious amounts during the 1950s and 1960s, having a book published nearly every year while turning out major feature articles for national magazines, often at the rate of one a month.

Smith was generally labeled a humorist, but he said that he did not particularly care for the designation: "I prefer to think of myself as a reporter, a reporter with a humorous slant. I am funny only in the sense that the world is funny."

He was born Harry Allen Smith in McLeansboro, Illinois, on 19 December 1906, though for the first half of his life his parents led him to believe that he was actually born in 1907. A cousin turned up the correct date in 1941 in a search of Hamilton County records. Even today, Library of

Congress listings and most biographical sketches give 1907 as his birth date. With nine children in the family, the confusion of Henry Arthur and Adeline Allen Smith over the birth date of their son is perhaps understandable.

Smith spent only his earliest childhood in the small southern Illinois town before the family moved north to Decatur in 1913, from there to Defiance, Ohio, in 1919, and, in 1922, to Huntington, Indiana. Despite his tenuous southern Illinois roots, the area figured prominently in his later writing in a number of stories about "Egypt" or "Little Egypt," the unofficial designation of that part of Illinois between the Mississippi and Ohio Rivers.

After eight years of Catholic parochial education and a few weeks of public high school, Smith retired from the academic life. He then became, by his own account, "a chicken picker in a poultry house (hens 2½ cents, roosters, 3 cents), then became a shoeshine boy and sweeper-up of used hair in a barber shop." The barbershop soon gave way to the print shop of the *Huntington Press,* where he hired on as a proofreader. At the age of fifteen he moved from the backshop to become a reporter on the *Press.* His mother suggested "H. Allen Smith" for his by-line to add some distinction among the overabundance of American Smiths.

His stint at the *Press* hooked Smith on a writing career. Within six months he was writing a column under the by-line of "Miss Ella Vator." The paper's editor wanted Smith to write sports, but Smith rejected what he considered the senseless symbolism of sportswriting. His job at the *Press* came to a hasty end after Smith was found to be the author of a ribald, though unpublished, piece entitled "Stranded on a Davenport." As he was later to tell the story of his departure from Huntington, Smith wrote the story as a lark. A coworker managed to get girls at the local high school to type copies of the manuscript: from that point, "Stranded" made a quick trip through the typing instructor to the school principal and thence to the local judge. Fined $22.50, ordered to read the Scriptures, and feeling not a little infamous, Smith soon departed Huntington for a brief stint on the *Jeffersonville* (Indiana) *Bulletin*. From there he moved to Louisville, Kentucky, where he worked on the *Post* and the *Times*.

From the mid-1920s until 1941, Smith worked for a succession of newspapers throughout the country. As he described his peripatetic life in his autobiographical *To Hell in a Handbasket* (1962), he "came into the business at the tail end of a great tradition—the tradition of the itinerant newspaperman." From Louisville he moved to the *Tampa* (Florida) *Telegraph*. At the age of nineteen he became the editor of the *American*, a small daily in Sebring, Florida. There he met Nelle Simpson, the society editor of the paper. The *American* folded in 1926, and Smith caulked boats in Florida and sold town directories in Texas before taking a job with the *Tulsa* (Oklahoma) *Tribune*. A few days after his arrival in Tulsa he was joined by Nelle, and they were married on 14 February 1927. Smith worked for only a short time with the *Tribune* before moving to Denver in the summer of 1927 to work for the *Morning Post*. When that paper folded, he moved to the *Denver Post,* an evening paper. While outspoken in his later criticism of Denver newspaper publisher Frederick G. Bonfils, Smith was to write very highly of the other newspapermen he worked with in Denver. The Smiths' two children were born in Denver: Allen Wyatt in 1928 and Nancy Jean in 1929. The Denver years also marked the period when Smith discovered literature. Conscious of what he felt was a deficient formal education and lack of exposure to books, Smith asked his colleagues' advice on what to read. They steered him to H. G. Wells, Dickens, and Plutarch. He had his introduction to H. L. Mencken in *The American Language* and some of the *Prejudices;*

in time, Mencken became his idol.

Although he would later look back on his Denver experiences as the highlight of his journalistic career, after two years there Smith was ready to move again. He was convinced he had the talent to make it in the Big Town of American journalism, so in mid-1929 Smith headed for New York, leaving his wife and children with Nelle's family in Missouri. In September, down to his last ten dollars, Smith landed a job with the United Press. He began as a rewrite man, but was soon writing by-line features and perfecting his style as a humorist. He made his mark especially with his unconventional, witty accounts of interviews with celebrities and assorted oddball characters. Smith stayed with the United Press until 1934.

After a brief and none-too-happy hiatus doing public relations and other work with radio and film companies in 1935, Smith hired on with the *New York World-Telegram* in 1936. Here, too, he was a rewrite man, gaining a reputation among newspaper people as one of the best in the business. But while the rewrite desk helped him to hone his writing, his humor articles continued to enhance his public reputation. As at the UP, his focus at the

Smith taking reports as a rewrite man on the New York World-Telegram *(World Telegram & Sun)*

World-Telegram was on "major and minor celebrities, human oddities, and ordinary mortals." One of his later reminiscences about the period, noteworthy for what it says about his growing fame and about his own values, involves a dinner with five contemporary sports "greats": "What a stupendous thing for a callow young man from the Midwest to stumble upon! Ruth, Gehrig, Rockne, Johnson, and Grange! If I had been a normal American boy I'd have wet my pants. But my worship of authors was so dominant that these sports characters had little appeal for me."

In his celebrity interviews, Smith typically portrayed the human, fallible side of famous people such as Gypsy Rose Lee, Marlene Dietrich, Gary Cooper, and Vivien Leigh. He was the master of the inside story, telling his readers about his own reactions and conveying a tongue-in-cheek, you-should-have-been-there feeling. In several books he tells various versions of his interview with stripper (and former newspaperwoman) Kay Fears. Much of the story involves Smith's feigned nonchalance in the presence of his totally unclad interviewee.

While becoming well known with his celebrity interviews, Smith was grinding out miles of copy as a rewrite man—traditionally the job that papers assign to their best wordsmiths. While at the *World-Telegram,* Smith was writing or rewriting thirty to fifty stories a day, on everything from christenings to stockholders' meetings, murders, and lawsuits.

Smith wrote three books while working at the *World-Telegram.* The first was a commissioned biography (1939) of industrialist Robert Gair; it was well reviewed but did not sell well. The second was a novel, *Mr. Klein's Kampf* (1939), an ill-timed spoof of Hitler that fell flat when, soon after its publication, Hitler invaded Poland and rendered the subject unfunny. Smith's third book—his first literary success—was *Low Man on a Totem Pole* (1941), a series of vignettes, musings, and character portrayals with the Smith stamp firmly upon them. The book received generally good reviews (although the *New Republic* found it insubstantial), and it fast became a best-seller. Comedian Fred Allen, who by this time had become a friend of Smith's, wrote the introduction, in which he referred to the author as the "screwball's Boswell." The label was used often in subsequent biographical and critical material about Smith. "Smith never knows," wrote Allen, "where his next screwball is coming from. The world is his laboratory, the human race his clinic, the nearest disciple of monomania's story his immediate concern. He will walk twenty miles to hear a cliché—and frequently does." Allen also referred

to Smith as the "biographer of the dispensable man." The book's title made the expression "low man on a totem pole" an American idiom. (However, Smith did not suggest the title, according to Elton Miles, a personal friend of Smith's and the author of an unpublished biography of the humorist. An editor at Doubleday found the expression in Allen's introduction—"If Smith were an Indian he would be low man on any totem pole"—and proposed that as the title.)

As the book established Smith as a successful humorist, it also induced him to become a full-time free-lance writer, and he left the *World-Telegram* in 1941. He later described the book's success and the change it had wrought in his life: "In 1939 I wrote a book and in 1940 I wrote another. Their publication led me to seek employment as a crossing guard for a railroad. Before I could make such a connection, a man asked me to put together some flippant newspaper reminiscences and these were published under the title *Low Man on a Totem Pole.* People lost their heads. They bought it. I quit newspapering and wrote another one, *Life in a Putty Knife Factory.* Madness seized the populace. They bought it."

Before writing *Life in a Putty Knife Factory* (1943), however, he signed with United Features Syndicate to do a daily column, "The Totem Pole," but found it too taxing and pulled out of the contract after six months. He also dabbled in radio, serving as master of ceremonies on a network program called "Swop Nite." He left that job after only ten weeks and turned his full attention to writing books and articles.

Life in a Putty Knife Factory was, indeed, another best-selling success, and led to a call from Paramount Studios in Hollywood, where he went to write scripts. He was unhappy in the job and stayed for only eight months, but he gleaned enough material about Hollywood to write *Lost in the Horse Latitudes* (1944), his third best-seller in three years.

Between 1945 and his death in 1976, Smith turned out thirty-two more books, most of them in the same nonfiction, humorous, anecdotal genre as his first three successful books. There were also three novels: *Rhubarb* (1946), which became a Paramount Pictures film in 1951; *Son of Rhubarb* (1967); and *The View from Chivo* (1971). In 1952 came *Smith's London Journal,* based on material he gathered during a trip to England. Included in the book was the text of an essay written by Mark Twain for a 1907 British book. Smith was the first American writer to discover the essay and report it in the United States. An anthology of Smith's writing, *The World, the Flesh, and H. Allen Smith,* compiled by

Bergen Evans, appeared in 1954. In his introduction, Evans sees Smith as one who "sympathizes with the defeated, the frustrated and the hopeless. Nobility and absurdity are often intertwined and the pathetic and the ludicrous are frequently inseparable." According to Evans, this "deeper perceptiveness" of Smith's made him a great reporter: "As an observer of the passing scene he has few equals." He also finds in Smith a sense of detachment, and sees that as the basis of his honesty as a writer. Evans puts Smith squarely in the Midwestern humorist tradition of Mark Twain—along with Booth Tarkington, Damon Runyon, Ring Lardner, and James Thurber.

In 1962 Smith wrote his autobiography, *To Hell in a Handbasket,* which deals with his early life and his years as a newspaperman. It is filled with tales about the inner world of the daily newspaper and the often eccentric men and women who work at the craft of journalism. Smith paints a picture of a hardworking, hard-drinking, glamorous, and adventurous way of life, much like that depicted by Ben Hecht and Charles MacArthur in their play *The Front Page* (1928). *To Hell in a Handbasket* ends with Smith leaving newspapering for full-time free-lance writing. In its concluding chapter he facetiously promises a second volume that will trace "the details of all these events and my subsequent doings at home and abroad." The sequel never appeared.

As his first book had been a biography, so was his last: *The Life and Legend of Gene Fowler,* published posthumously in 1977, traces the life of the famous newspaperman, with whom Smith had worked in Denver and New York. The book reveals a passionate and poignant side of Smith rarely glimpsed elsewhere in his work.

The Smiths made their home in Mt. Kisco, New York, for more than twenty years after he left the newspaper business. In 1967 they moved to Alpine, Texas. The outspokenly caustic side of Smith's character was played in high relief when *Time* magazine came looking for him three years after he arrived in Alpine. He reported to *Time* that he was suffering mightily from "people pollution," and that he had never before seen "such a goddamned bunch of bigoted, pious, lying, cheating bastards in my life." Local furor ensued.

In Alpine Smith became acquainted with Elton Miles, a professor at Sul Ross State University. Eventually, Miles wrote "H. Allen Smith: Reporter of the Human Farce," a book-length biography that has not been published. "In the final analysis," Miles said in an interview, "Smith thought of himself more as a humorist than a journalist. He was a

humorist who used journalistic techniques." Like Evans, Miles puts Smith into the tradition of realism that flourished under Mark Twain and W. D. Howells. In his personal life, Miles found, Smith was a "homebody" who led an extremely uneventful life. "Like numbers of other writers, Allen was uneasy in social situations." He would do no lecturing, dreading both the public exposure and the inevitable receptions that followed. The Evans collection of Smith's writings includes the "letter of regret" that Smith sent to his publisher with instructions to mail it to whomever sought the humorist's services as a speaker: "Mr. Smith informs us that he recently has acquired a skin disease called impetigo which requires periodic and vigorous scratching. . . . Mr. Smith has had his affliction for six months. I'm sure you would be interested to know that during those six months he has found it impossible to take a bath."

Miles and others describe Smith as an extremely nervous person. He also suffered periodic and sustained bouts of drinking that, according to Miles, occasionally required medical help. In his introduction to *Low Man on a Totem Pole,* Allen reported that Smith did not drink: "He has nothing against alcohol, save that it arouses in his breast an urge to fly kites in two-room apartments." In *Current Biography 1942,* Smith denied Allen's "libel" that he did not drink. The *New York Times* obituary of Smith said he was "a ready carouser who amazed his friends by his ability to overcome sobriety with a single glass of beer."

Whatever the nature of his private life may have been, Smith's public medium was the printed page, and he attacked it with talent, gusto, and speed. "Unlike most scribblers," he said in 1942, "I enjoy writing." Aside from the "pure, lilting beauty of my prose, the essential quality of my writing is speed." Editors would call on Smith when they needed a piece in a short time, not only because they knew he would do a good job but because they knew that he would meet the deadline.

During the thirty-five years in which he was turning out nearly a book a year, Smith also wrote and published hundreds of shorter pieces that bore the same stamp of anecdotal humor and perceptivity. His magazine credits ran the gamut from *Cosmopolitan* to *Playboy, Family Weekly* to *True,* and included *Reader's Digest, Saturday Review,* and *Variety.* Appended to the Miles biography is an extensive, "almost complete" bibliography of Smith's magazine articles through 1972. The number of published articles listed is 196, including two excerpts from his books that were carried in *Cosmopolitan.*

The list does not include newspaper articles, though some stories for Sunday newspaper supplements, such as *Empire* magazine of the *Denver Post,* are included.

To gather material for his articles and books, Smith traveled fairly extensively, visiting England, Mexico, Hawaii, Tahiti, and much of the United States. "Travel for journalistic research," says Miles, "was about the only thing that could stir Allen from his home." While in San Francisco on one of his research trips, Smith suffered a fatal heart attack. He died on 24 February 1976 at the age of sixty-nine.

Smith's writing career spanned half a century, including twenty years on the proving ground of newspaper journalism and more than thirty years as an author on his own. In terms of popularity, the high point of his career came in the first few years after he left newspapering in 1941. Though his writing remained popular at least through the 1960s, he never again experienced the adulation and public following that marked his early books. The irony is that his writing, in its humor and its crispness of expression, improved as he got older. The masses, however, were turning their attention to other writers and other media in the 1950s and 1960s. He acknowledged the slippage himself in an interview in *Call* magazine in 1967: he said of his writing that "the overall quality has gotten better, but I've lost ground with the reading public."

Miles thinks that Smith is not widely appreciated today largely because his writing deals with the commonplace aspects of human behavior. His material is not sensational, sordid, or violent; it highlights what is ludicrous about all of us. Perhaps we no longer have a tolerance for seeing our foibles in print.

Whatever his ultimate reputation may turn out to be, Smith has left an extensive record of his attempts at depicting human behavior. He saved virtually everything he ever received, collected, jotted, or read. "I've got squirrel blood; I keep everything," he once told an interviewer. The bulk of this material—27.5 cubic feet of it—is housed in the Special Collections Division of the library of Southern Illinois University at Carbondale.

Perhaps the most fitting epitaph for Smith was written by Bergen Evans in the introduction to *The World, the Flesh and H. Allen Smith*: "Along with Chaucer, Swift, Mark Twain, Mister Dooley, Ring Lardner and H. L. Mencken, he is a cynic. He believes that dishonesty is firmly embedded in the human character and that men have petty larceny forever in their hearts and lies forever in their mouths. He believes that deceit and mistrust are the essence of human relationships. His years of interviewing the great, those who set the styles for the rest of us in apparel, manners and, to some extent, in thoughts, left him with no faith in idols or idolizers. To him one of the greatest philosophers who ever lived was an unknown Thinker who on a steel pillar in the Fourteenth Street I. R. T. subway scribbled 'Nuts to people' and then faded into the crowd."

Interview:

Robert van Gelder, "An Interview with Mr. H. Allen Smith," *New York Times Book Review,* 24 August 1941, pp. 2, 22.

References:

Red Gibson, "H. Allen Smith Lives Here in Alpine, Texas. What? Alpine, Texas? Why, of All Places, Alpine, Texas? Here's Why," *Texas Magazine* (supplement to *Houston Chronicle*), 27 October 1968, pp. 8-11, 24, 26;

Richard Maney, "Rhubarb in the Dugout," *New York Times Book Review,* 4 August 1946, p. 7;

Merle Miller, "Mr. Smith, and Not So Funny," *Saturday Review of Literature,* 29 (3 August 1946): 19;

Robert van Gelder, "Mr. Smith, the Screwballs' Boswell," *New York Times Book Review,* 8 June 1941, p. 5.

Papers:

The major collection of Smith's papers is housed in the Special Collections Division of Morris Library at Southern Illinois University at Carbondale. Included are photographs, along with three chapters of the Elton Miles biography. Other papers and all of Smith's personal library (more than 2,000 volumes) are at Sul Ross State University in Alpine, Texas.

Red Smith

(25 September 1905-15 January 1982)

S. M. W. Bass
University of Kansas

MAJOR POSITIONS HELD: Sports reporter and columnist, *Philadelphia Record* (1936-1945); sports columnist, *New York Herald Tribune*, merged to form *World Journal Tribune* (1945-1967), Publishers-Hall Syndicate (1967-1971), *New York Times* (1971-1982).

BOOKS: *Terry and Bunky Play Football*, by Smith and Dick Fishel (New York: Putnam's, 1945);
Out of the Red (New York: Knopf, 1950);
Views of Sport (New York: Knopf, 1954);
Red Smith's Sports Annual (New York: Crown, 1961);
The Best of Red Smith, edited by Verna Reamer (New York: Watts, 1963);
Red Smith on Fishing around the World (Garden City: Doubleday, 1963);
Strawberries in the Wintertime: The Sporting World of Red Smith (New York: Quadrangle, 1974);
To Absent Friends from Red Smith (New York: Atheneum, 1982);
The Red Smith Reader, edited by Dave Anderson (New York: Random House, 1982).

OTHER: *Sports Stories*, edited with introductions by Smith (New York: Barnes, 1949);
This Was Racing, edited by Smith and Joseph Hill Palmer (New York: Barnes, 1953);
Red Smith's Favorite Sports Stories, edited by Smith (New York: Norton, 1976).

PERIODICAL PUBLICATIONS: "Doghouse to Let: Apply Newhouser and Trout," *Saturday Evening Post*, 217 (31 March 1945): 22-23;
"Corn Pays Off at Yale," *Saturday Evening Post*, 218 (17 November 1945): 18-19;
"Little Man With Big Horses," *Saturday Evening Post*, 218 (25 May 1946): 20;
"What Broke Up the Yankees?," *Saturday Evening Post*, 219 (29 March 1947): 23;
"Has Baseball Forgotten the Fan?," *Saturday Evening Post*, 220 (4 October 1947): 25;
"No Crying Towels at Dartmouth," *Saturday Evening Post*, 222 (12 November 1949): 36;
"Reluctant Yankee," *Collier's*, 126 (8 July 1950): 30-31;
"New Yorkers Are Really Hayseeds," *Saturday*

Red Smith (New York Herald Tribune)

Evening Post, 223 (23 September 1950): 36-37;
"Anyone for Basketball?," *Collier's*, 127 (3 March 1951): 24-25;
"Pop Secol's Ice Cream League," *Reader's Digest*, 59 (July 1951): 89-90;
"Mountain Boys at Yale," *Collier's*, 128 (29 September 1951): 22-23;
"Moscow Olympics," *Collier's*, 128 (27 October 1951): 41;
"Mucha Trucha," *Outdoor Life*, 111 (April 1953): 33-35;
"Paradise for Horseplayers," *Saturday Evening Post*, 229 (29 June 1957): 26-27;

"Good Clean Fun in Finland," *Reader's Digest*, 92 (June 1968): 133-135;

"Tequila," *Holiday*, 44 (July 1968): 77-78;

"Red Smith on Politics," *Harper's Bazaar*, 105 (January 1972): 94;

"Super Sunday," *New York Times Magazine*, 12 January 1975, p. 79;

"The House that Ruth Built-Rebuilt," *New York Times Magazine*, 11 April 1976, pp. 60-61;

"Fan as Designated Sitter," *Saturday Review*, 3 (26 June 1976): 26-27;

"Olympic Games," *Horizon*, 18 (Summer 1976): 109-112;

"Perfect Beauty of a Ninety-Foot Field," *Horizon*, 19 (March 1977): 92-93;

"Four!," *American Heritage*, 31 (August/September 1980): 76-80.

Red Smith came to write about sports somewhat by accident. Even so, few have done it better or exerted greater influence on sports journalism in the twentieth century. His career spanned fifty-four years, beginning in 1927. During this time, Smith reported on sports from almost every continent in the world, from Africa to Australia.

Although he wrote for New York newspapers for thirty years, his column was syndicated around the world. In 1951, six years after he joined his first New York newspaper, the *New York Herald Tribune*, Smith's column went to twenty-four newspapers in the United States and foreign countries; by 1962, his readership reached 15 million in more than 100 newspapers. At the time of his death in January 1982, Smith's syndicated column went to 275 United States newspapers and to 225 papers in thirty other countries.

To Red Smith readers, a good many of whom were not, even by loose definition, sports fans, he was first a clever and careful writer, a craftsman of the English language. Smith, however, saw himself primarily as a spectator and commentator. He had a good ear for conversation, a full appreciation for the vagaries of human nature, and a relish for the absurd in everything. He rarely failed to see, and to share, the humor in any given situation. Sports was Smith's beat, but to him the world of sport was not a world apart, not a play world: "I think it's the real world. The people we're writing about in professional sports, they're suffering and living and dying and loving and trying to make their way through life just as the bricklayers and politicians are. . . . Games are a part of every culture we know anything about. And often taken seriously. It's no accident that of all the monuments left of the Greco-Roman culture the biggest is the ballpark, the Colosseum, the Yankee Stadium of ancient times."

Walter Wellesley Smith was born on 25 September 1905. His parents, Walter Philip and Ida Elizabeth Richardson Smith, lived in Green Bay, Wisconsin, a small paper-mill town with a population of 25,000. Red—he hated the name Walter Wellesley—had an older brother, Art, and a younger sister, Katherine. His father ran a third-generation wholesale produce and retail grocery business, Smith Bros. Company. It was here that Smith had his first job, at the age of nine: he weeded onions for three cents an hour. After one week he collected his pay and quit. Later on, he held other jobs to earn pocket money and to pay for college.

Smith's childhood days were not filled with sports activities or sports heroes, although he took advantage of the nearby outdoor resources, hiking in the woods, swimming, skiing, skating, and fishing. In neighborhood baseball games, he served as umpire because neither team wanted him; he was the smallest kid in the crowd, as well as being slow, uncoordinated, and nearsighted. In college, Smith did not finish his only one-mile race. Fishing, by himself, was his sport, or actually, his relaxation. "I never played golf, and when I was young enough to play tennis, any girl could beat me."

While in high school, Smith met a student from Notre Dame who happened to be a journalism major. Vincent Engels impressed Smith. He taught Smith a few fine points of flycasting, and left him with a mind-set to go to Notre Dame and to become a writer. Smith graduated high school in 1922 and went to work for Morley Murphy Hardware as an order filler. A year later, in September 1923, he had saved enough money for one year at Notre Dame. For the other three years, he scrounged. He majored in journalism, edited the *Dome*, the college yearbook, and received his B.A. in 1927.

Eager to get started as a journalist, Smith wrote to 100 newspapers; the only response seems to have been a letter of rejection from the *New York Times*. Despairing of finding work as a reporter, he applied for a job with a local company that made aluminum pots and pans. In a last-ditch effort, he wrote to Ed Hart, former managing editor of the *Green Bay Press-Gazette*, who was then with the *Milwaukee Sentinel*. Smith later described the letter as containing errant flattery, but Hart responded. Although the pots and pans outfit also offered Smith a job, he went to work at the *Sentinel* as a cub reporter at a starting salary of twenty-five dollars a week. Smith later said that he covered everything from murder to society-page news in that first year, and that was where he learned about journalism. He credited his night city editor, Alvin Steinkopf, and rewrite man, Edgar Brown, with teaching him how to do a story.

Nearly a year later, in 1928, Smith heard about an opening on the copydesk of the *St. Louis Star*. He wired an application, saying that he was an all-around newspaperman. A return wire offered him the job at forty dollars a week. He took it, even though it meant moving west; he wanted to go east, in particular to New York. He joined the *Star* in June 1928. He had had no experience writing headlines or reading or editing copy, so he had to work harder, as he said later, to keep his ignorance from showing.

In November, the managing editor, having fired nearly the entire sports department, detailed Smith to sports as he seemed the most expendable copyreader. Smith's only previous sportswriting had been to write up two big-league baseball games. His first sports assignment for the *Star* was a night football practice at Washington University. He covered that assignment just as he would cover many others over the years, with an eye out for the different viewpoint: this time he saw the story from the point of view of a low-down glowworm. His report brought favorable reader response, as did his coverage of the St. Louis Browns baseball team. In fact, Smith reported so well that he was assigned to cover the better-ranked St. Louis Cardinals.

By January 1933, however, Smith had become bored with the *Star*'s sports department. He especially disliked the winter months when there was nothing to cover but hockey and basketball, two of his least favorite sports. Smith asked to go back to the city room and to work as a general assignment reporter. On 11 February he married Catherine Cody. At about the same time, Smith, like many others, lost all his savings when his bank failed. His financial situation worsened when he received a ten percent salary reduction. He had been querying the Eastern newspapers, looking for better openings; finally, in 1936, one query resulted in an offer from the *Philadelphia Record*. The Smiths left immediately for Philadelphia, even though Smith had no idea whether he would be working as a general assignment reporter or as a sportswriter.

During his nine years at the *Record*, Smith covered every kind of sport and wrote a daily column as well. By 1945, Smith, with eighteen years' experience as a journalist, had begun to let the notion of New York fade, but Stanly Woodward, sports editor for the *New York Herald Tribune*, had other plans. He offered Smith a job as sports columnist. Woodward,

an inveterate reader of the nation's sports pages, knew both of Smith's workload and the quality of his work at the *Record*. Woodward planned to cut Smith's workload, figuring that an already good product would become even better. Smith went to work for the *Herald Tribune* in 1945 and remained there until, as the *World Journal Tribune*, it folded in 1967.

Smith's "Views of Sport" became the most widely syndicated and most widely read column in the country. *Cosmopolitan*, in a 1959 article about writers who made big money, indicated that Smith earned more than $45,000 a year—a good deal more than the three cents an hour he had earned as a boy, considerably more than his first reporting job, and an appreciable amount more than many career journalists ever earn. Dollars, to be sure, provide a quantitative rather than a qualitative measure of worth; still, earnings do indicate a writer's value to his publisher. Smith's value could be gauged better by his readers, who followed his reports and columns not only because of what he had to say but also because he could say it so well. Most of Smith's books were published between 1946 and 1967—five collections of his columns, and three others that he either edited or on which he collaborated.

This productive period came to a sad close for Smith, both personally and professionally. On 19 February 1967, Smith's wife, Catherine, died after a long illness. Red and Catherine Smith had had two children. Their daughter, Catherine, had married J. David Halloran and lived in Wisconsin. Their son, Terence Fitzgerald, became a journalist; currently, he edits the Washington page of the *New York Times*. Smith's professional loss came with the closing of the *World Journal Tribune* in the same year that Catherine died. The daily association with a New York paper was one he missed very much. It would be four years before he was again associated with a New York newspaper, but his columns continued to appear around the country through the Publishers-Hall Syndicate. In New York, the *Long Island Press* and *Women's Wear Daily* carried his column. On 8 November 1968 Smith married Phyllis Warner Weiss, an artist. They lived in Martha's Vineyard, Massachusetts, and New Canaan, Connecticut, where Smith continued to produce his syndicated columns.

Smith celebrated his sixty-sixth birthday in 1971, the year that he went to work for the *New York Times*. For the next ten years he wrote four columns each week under the title "Sports of the Times." He announced in his column of 11 January 1982 that he would cut back to three columns a week—Sunday, Monday, and Thursday. He did not live to put the new schedule into effect. Smith had once said that he envied his friend Grantland Rice, who died at his typewriter; Smith hoped that he, too, would leave this world mid-phrase. He almost had his wish. Just four days after writing his 11 January column, Smith died in a Stamford, Connecticut, hospital following a brief illness.

Red Smith enjoyed a lifetime of sports that included forty-five World Series games. Part of what made Smith good was his vast personal history and his staggering memory of all that history's events and characters. He absorbed, rarely to forget, the people, the games, the bust plays, and the spectacular finishes, and all of this added depth and breadth to his reporting. Beyond that, Smith cared about how he wrote. During one World Series game he said to another writer, "You don't want to be lousy during the World Series. If you've got to be lousy, let it be June. And believe me, I was very lousy yesterday. I had nothing to say, and, by God, I said it."

Smith comes across in his writing, and in the recollections of others, as a modest man, uncomfortable to have much made of him or his work. When he won the Pulitzer Prize in 1976, he said he was "only a newspaper stiff trying to write better than I can." Smith never considered himself an expert, only a spectator. He saw himself first as a reporter who relied on facts, and this judicious adherence to facts accounts for his spare, uncluttered style. Not the least of his contributions to sports journalism was his ability to avoid the superlative, a fault that garbles much sportswriting. Smith always advised young would-be sportswriters to do a stint in the city room to learn something about newspapers before moving into sports. For those who refused to learn reporting first, Smith had only this to say: "There's no hope for them. They just want a free pass to the ball park."

Smith was an observant reporter. He got the details and seemed to delight in sharing them with his readers, with clarity and imagination. Usually, he found some unique way of putting the picture across, as in his description of a scene from a Yankee-Dodger World Series game: "In the eighth, Hermanski smashed a drive to the scoreboard. Heinrich backed against the board and leaped either four or fourteen feet into the air. He stayed aloft so long he looked like an empty uniform hanging in its locker. When he came down he had the ball."

Coronet magazine published a portrait of Smith in February 1953. The article described Red Smith as "the rarest of creatures, a literate, rational sports writer" who was never tempted to call a base hit by any other name, such as a "bloop, a bingle, or a one-base bash." It is his simplicity, his directness, and his use of fact that makes Smith's 800-word columns read as though they had written themselves. Not that Smith could not turn a phrase: he particularly enjoyed inventing collective nouns, embellishing upon fifteenth-century terms of venery. Some of his inventions possibly indicate his own opinion of the group to which he referred, such as "a bibulation of sports writers, a gangle of basketball players, a yammer of radio announcers, a guilt of umpires, or, an indigence of writers."

Over the years, Smith spoke to many journalism students and at professional seminars. In the American Newspaper Institute's spring 1982 newsletter, J. Montgomery Curtis recapitulated some of the things Smith said about sportswriting: "Create in the reader the impression that you were there. You saw. You heard. Don't be pompous, not even authoritative. Don't strut. Be tolerant and compassionate, even to those who may not deserve it. Write about people always. Make the reader see the people, hear them." The reader always had a friend in Red Smith. Smith was a writer the reader could rely on, a writer who would speak plainly, and with whom, on occasion, the reader could have great fun. Smith kept working at being a writer. "I have tried to become simpler, straighter and purer in my language. I look at some of the stuff I wrote in past years, and I say, 'Gee, I should have cooled it a little more.'"

There are, in sportswriting, as in tennis, various levels of the game. There is the naive freshman sportswriter and the rooter just out of college; there are the cheerleaders and the shills, the bored and the cynical. Harry Stein, in his article on Smith in *Sport* magazine, describes those who play at the highest level: they are "reporters, journalists with the responsibility to cover the business of game playing every bit as seriously as other journalists cover politics or finance." Smith played at this level of the game, or, as he would probably say, he tried to play at that level.

Smith preferred some sports to others; he liked most to cover boxing, horse racing, baseball, and football. Dave Anderson of the *New York Times* says Smith's favorite spectator sport was racing, and that Smith could write about horses as if they were people—as he did in his obituary for Seabiscuit: "If this bureau had a prayer for use around horse parks, it would go something like this: Lead us not among bleeding-hearts to whom horses are cute or sweet or adorable, and deliver us from horse-lovers. Amen. . . . With that established, let's talk about the death of Seabiscuit the other night. It isn't mawkish to say, there was a racehorse, a horse that gave race fans as much pleasure as any that ever lived and one that will be remembered as long and as warmly. If someone asked you to list horses that had, apart from speed or endurance, some quality that fired the imagination and captured the regard of more people than ever saw them run, you'd have to mention Man o'War and Equipoise and Exterminator and Whirlaway and Seabiscuit. And the honest son of Hard Tack wouldn't be last."

In his last years, Smith wrote more sharply about some sports issues and sports figures. He said that as he got older he got more liberal; the world seemed a less pretty place to him, and he felt that that was a condition about which something ought to be done. In particular, Smith found the owners of professional teams to be lacking in quality and character. One of his columns on the subject was bitterly entitled: "Lively Times in the Slave Trade." Smith particularly objected to George M. Steinbrenner, owner of the New York Yankees, for his heavy-handed and overbearing manner. Smith often referred to Steinbrenner as a "potentate" and called him "George III."

Smith began to criticize television in his later years, seeing it as having an undermining influence on sports. In his New Year's Day 1982 column, Smith said he was appalled by the anticipated $17.5 million that would be earned in the five major college bowl games. He believed that such large sums of money, in large part, accounted for the increasing violations of recruiting rules, for academic abuses, and for other unethical practices. Smith wanted college football to be more sport and less salaried. He held the notion that college was a place where students learned that "reading maketh a full man, conference a ready man and writing an exact man." Football's place was to "add a patina of character, a deference to the rules and a respect for authority." Smith objected to the way the recruiters ran the show, promising fame and fortune and easy courses. "They tell the kid he's a chump if he doesn't take the best offer, and they demonstrate that rules, promises and ethics are false values."

Smith was not a puritan or dogmatic moralist, but it mattered to him how any game was played. While he made allowances for the foibles of hu-

man nature—he never, for example, expected prizefighters to act like choirboys—he could not forgive a collapse of character. He expected the best of sport, of athletes, and of their countries. He was the first to call for a boycott of the 1980 Moscow Olympics because of the U.S.S.R.'s invasion of Afghanistan.

His writing was not limited to sports. He once wrote a minor treatise on tequila for *Holiday*. On several occasions he covered the Democratic and Republican national conventions, spectacles which he thought had a good deal in common with sports events. He once compared the conventions of the two parties: "In entertainment value, the Democratic clambake usually lays it over the Republican conclave like the ice cream over parsnips. . . ." It was the 1968 Democratic convention, however, that affected Smith most and seems to have taken away his former zest for political reporting. "In the past, it seemed to make sense for a sportswriter on sabbatical from the playpen to attend the quadrennial hawgkilling when Presidential candidates are chosen, to observe and report upon politicians at play. After all, national conventions are games of a sort, and sports offers few spectacles richer in low comedy. . . . It is sadly different this week in the police state which Richard (The Lion-hearted) Daley has made of the city he rules. There is no room for laughter in this city of fear."

Smith usually got along well with the people he reported upon. He could separate the personal and the professional, maintaining a civil, if not always a warm, association with his subjects. Smith liked people and most people liked him. He was often asked who his favorite athletes were, and he seemed always hard put to answer. He liked many athletes, he said, most of whom were not necessarily among the great. He gave high marks to the jockey Bill Shoemaker; and he seemed to hope, even anticipate, that one day there would be another Joe DiMaggio. One of Smith's favorite people was Grantland Rice, "the nicest man I ever knew." Rice, for his part, wrote that Smith and Frank Graham of the *New York Journal American* were "marvelous companions in every detail," adding that they were also "experts whose opinions have been useful on many occasions. I hope they will be around at the last march." Rice died shortly thereafter in 1954.

Two years later Smith won the Grantland Rice Memorial Award from the Sportsmanship Brotherhood of New York. Smith won many awards for his work, but the Rice award was one of perhaps two that he most treasured. The other was the Pulitzer Prize for commentary, which he won in 1976. In granting this award, the Pulitzer committee cited Smith's work for its erudition, its literary quality, and its freshness of viewpoint. Other awards included the journalism award from the National Headliner's Club and the George Polk Award. He was the first recipient of the Red Smith Award, established in his honor by the Associated Press sports editors. Smith's alma mater, Notre Dame, honored him in 1968 with an honorary LL.D. degree. He was selected five times as the nation's best sportswriter. Smith did not see himself as special in any way and did not make much of awards; one report had it that he pried the metal off most plaques, chunked it into a box, and used the wood in his fireplace.

When he died in 1982, newspapers across the country carried Red Smith's obituary. Many of his friends and colleagues wrote about their friend and mentor; they wrote on the sport page, on the front page, and on the editorial page. Smith was a sportswriter whose grace, wit, and craftsmanship made him a welcome addition to any publication, on any page, on any day.

References:

Pete Axthelm, "Masters Touch," *Newsweek*, 87 (17 May 1976): 75;

"Behind Those Columns," *Coronet*, 33 (February 1953): 120-121;

C. Einstein, "Case for the Red Smith Irregulars," *Harper's*, 210 (March 1955): 82-86;

R. Kahn, "Red Smith of the Press Box," *Newsweek*, 51 (21 April 1958): 77-80;

L. Lerman, "Bouquet for Red Smith," *Mademoiselle*, 45 (May 1957): 149;

"One of a Kind," *New York Times Magazine*, 16 September 1973, pp. 42-44;

"One Was the Brightest," *Newsweek*, 48 (27 August 1956): 70;

R. Poe, "Writing of Sports," *Esquire*, 82 (October 1974): 176;

"Portrait," *Newsweek*, 2 (30 September 1933): 8;

"Red From Green Bay," *Time*, 55 (15 May 1950): 82-83;

J. D. Scott, "Big Money Writing," *Cosmopolitan*, 147 (August 1959): 38;

"Sight Unseen," *Outdoor Life*, 111 (May 1953): 40-41;

"Smith the Bleeder," *Newsweek*, 34 (10 October 1949): 62.

Papers:

The papers of Red Smith, should there be any, will be given to the University of Notre Dame; Mr. Smith, according to his wife, did not save such things. His books, some photographs, old columns, a few letters from treasured friends, and his old, battered typewriter are still in the old barn-workshop at his home in New Canaan, Connecticut.

Thomas L. Stokes
(1 November 1898-14 April 1958)

Charles C. Self
University of Alabama

MAJOR POSITIONS HELD: Washington correspondent, United Press (1921-1933), *New York World-Telegram* (1933-1936), Scripps-Howard Alliance (1936-1944); political columnist, United Features Syndicate (1944-1958).

BOOKS: *Chip off My Shoulder* (Princeton, N.J.: Princeton University Press, 1940);
The Savannah (New York: Rinehart, 1951).

Thomas L. Stokes covered Washington, D.C., for Scripps-Howard organizations for more than thirty-five years. His work included reporting, editing, and column writing, and his contributions won him a variety of honors ranging from election as president of the Washington Gridiron Club to a Pulitzer Prize in 1939 for his 1938 coverage of corruption in the Kentucky Works Progress Administration program. Stokes was briefly a war reporter in the 1940s but is chiefly known for his coverage of virtually every phase of national government during the 1920s and 1930s and for his political columns beginning in 1944.

Thomas Lunsford Stokes, Jr., was born 1

November 1898 in Atlanta, Georgia, near the home of Evan P. Howell, who had retired the previous year as editor of the *Atlanta Constitution* and later became mayor of Atlanta. His youth, as recounted in his autobiography, *Chip off My Shoulder* (1940), was filled with poignant scenes of a quiet Southern childhood among fragrant magnolias and oaks in middle-class Atlanta. His father was part owner of an Atlanta department store; his mother was Emma Layton Stokes. He was descended from colonial families on both sides. He vividly recalled Civil War stories recounted by his grandmother, scenes of interactions with Southern blacks, and memories of "missionary work" his family participated in for poor mill workers and their children in Atlanta. He said in his autobiography that these early experiences created in him a sense of a society of classes. He was repulsed by that sense. This discomfort later manifested itself in the crusades he mounted as a reporter exposing corruption or covering injustice in national labor activities. Stokes became a writer "who tilts hopefully on the side of the little guy," Fletcher Knebel wrote. Cabell Phillips called him an "evangelist."

Stokes worked his way through the University of Georgia with a job in the college library and as a correspondent to the *Atlanta Constitution* and the *Atlanta Georgian* for sports and college news. He was editor of the college literary magazine his senior year and graduated after three years, Phi Beta Kappa, in 1920.

Upon graduation, Stokes went to work for the *Savannah Press*. There he developed a love of the Savannah River and later wrote a book about the river and its historical importance to the South. In October 1920 he went to work for the *Macon News*, and he moved to the *Athens Herald* in May 1921. In September Stokes covered a rape-murder for which a black man was arrested. He then covered the story of a mob that took the man from his jail cell and lynched him. The lynching so affected Stokes that he left the South that month with $200 borrowed from his father and letters of introduction from newsmen at the *Constitution*, including Frank L. Stanton and Clark Howell, the editor. Stokes left with a sense of sadness about the South that would always be with him. He left, too, with a sense of injustice that would characterize his political writing for the next thirty-seven years.

His letters of introduction were to editors of New York newspapers; however, on his way north, he stopped in Washington, D.C. Through the intercession of Lowell Mellett, head of the Scripps-Howard Newspaper Alliance and editor of the

Thomas L. Stokes

Washington Daily News, Stokes landed a job with Scripps-Howard's United Press as a rewrite man. However, he soon was assigned to cover Congress, then the White House, and then to UP's night service for morning newspapers, United News. His bureau manager was Raymond Clapper, to whom Stokes later attributed his knowledge of the workings of politics.

Stokes had arrived in Washington something of an idealist, but his illusions began to be shattered as he watched the Harding cabinet fill government posts with political appointees. He was covering the White House when Attorney General Harry M. Daugherty brutally stopped the 1922 rail strike. In 1923 Stokes covered the funeral of Warren Harding; during the next two years, he covered the hearings that slowly revealed the scandals of the Harding administration. He watched as the Senate paraded a series of witnesses who recounted vast extravagance, waste, and graft involving Harding's cabinet officers. He was present when Teddy Roosevelt's son Archie recounted a payoff from the Union Petroleum Company to Secretary of the Interior Albert B. Fall's New Mexico ranch. This revelation was widely believed to have led to the uncovering of the Teapot Dome scandal, although Stokes said Sen. Thomas J. Walsh resented this notion since he had built evidence of the scandal even without Roosevelt's testimony.

The numerous scandals of the Harding administration and the influence of business in the Coolidge administration began to take their toll on Stokes's idealism. He wrote in his autobiography:

> Gradually, during my early years in Washington my eyes had been opened to certain rude and somewhat surprising actualities; among them, the influence exerted by powerful outside forces upon the political figures who conducted government there . . . Anyone who raised his voice against this invasion was classed as a radical.
>
> So I was no longer naive.
>
> . . . It was low-down, blatant thievery of the strictly American variety, not heretofore in my time associated with the national government—by blunt straightforward crooks who figuratively were ready to deliver the Goddess of Liberty off the Capitol Dome for a price.
>
> . . . It washed away, too, my idealism about the national government, coming as a climactic chapter in the process of education which had included courses in the gentler and less discernable purchase of favors.

Stokes was married to Hannah Hunt on 10 January 1924. The couple had a son, Thomas Lunsford III, and a daughter, Layton, who died young.

Stokes's first convention coverage experience was the 1924 Democratic National Convention in New York City. The long, drawn-out affair split hopelessly between Al Smith and William Gibbs McAdoo and over a minority plank pledging the party "to oppose any effort on the part of the Ku Klux Klan, or any organization, to interfere with the religious liberty or political freedom of any citizen, or to limit the civic rights of any citizen or body of citizens because of religion, birthplace or racial origin." Stokes was repelled by what he saw. He likewise found the Republican endorsement of Coolidge farcical. The only convention that impressed him favorably that year was the Conference for Progressive Political Action, which nominated Wisconsin senator "Fighting Bob" La Follette as its candidate in a simple ceremony that, for Stokes, provided a telling contrast to the uproarious Democratic convention.

In 1928 Stokes again covered the conventions and saw Herbert Hoover and Al Smith nominated. Stokes was assigned to cover the Hoover campaign; after the election he was one of eleven correspondents who accompanied the president-elect on his 1928 goodwill mission to South America. Stokes also covered the White House, Congress, and government agencies during the difficult years that followed the October 1929 stock market crash which swept all of Hoover's plans aside.

By the end of the Hoover administration, the sensitivities produced by Stokes's Georgia upbringing, his disillusionment with the successive Republican administrations, and his perception of a conflict in government between the interests of big business and the public interest had created in Stokes a receptiveness to the change that the American public embraced in Franklin D. Roosevelt. As Stokes put it in his autobiography: "Ignorant and faithless stewardship lay back of this catastrophe. As a reporter and an observer I saw the curtain torn away."

Stokes's coverage of the Roosevelt era is considered superb. "A liberal disillusioned with Republican conservatives, Mr. Stokes greeted the Roosevelt era with enthusiasm. His dispatches caught and communicated the early spirit of the first 'Hundred Days' of national unity in 1933," the *New York Times* observed in its obituary of Stokes in 1958. His reporting won him the position of Washington correspondent for the *New York World-Telegram*, a key newspaper in the Scripps-Howard chain, in August 1933. In June 1936 he advanced to Washington correspondent for the Scripps-Howard Alliance, covering general politics, national conventions, and presidential campaigns. He traveled the nation with FDR in 1936 and caught the spirit of optimism the nation drew from the president. "I think Franklin D. Roosevelt's chief service has been to show America to itself, to open its eyes," he wrote.

But in 1938 Stokes wrote a series of exposé articles in response to tips that abuses were to be found even among the beloved programs of FDR. Stokes traveled through Kentucky collecting evidence to show that the WPA was being used by politicians to collect votes in what Stokes called "a grand political racket in which the taxpayer is the victim." The articles won a Pulitzer Prize for him in 1939.

The WPA exposé had provided an opportunity for Stokes to return to the South. What he saw depressed him, although he continued to hold out hope for a better future for the region. "The trip was a revelation," he wrote. "It made me bitter. I had come up from the South. Now I saw it again first-hand. It was alien, and yet it was very familiar.... Democracy still does not exist in the South.... But a change is working in the South. Roosevelt started it.... There are signs of a renaissance."

In 1944 Stokes moved to United Features Syndicate and began writing a political column. Soon more than 100 newspapers were running the column to represent the liberal viewpoint. This column was the center of Stokes's work for the rest of his life. He was a chief defender of the Roosevelt programs when the reaction against many of those programs began. He became known for his political perception and knowledge of Washington. He was regarded as the watchdog of the liberal point of view.

Stokes was interested in environmental issues before such concerns became fashionable. He traveled extensively, and would occasionally comment in his column on the beauty of the land and the importance of preserving it. This interest also manifested itself in his 1951 book, *The Savannah,* in which he recounted the history of the Savannah River and its role in the development of the state of Georgia.

Stokes died on 14 April 1958 of brain cancer. His funeral was held at the National Cathedral in Washington and was covered by the national press. He was buried in Arlington National Cemetery.

Stokes's work in Washington is perhaps best measured by the kinds of awards he received. Aside from the Pulitzer Prize, he received the Raymond Clapper Award in 1947 for excellence in Washington reporting and crusading based on a "consistently good record for hard, intelligent and conscientious work." In 1950 he was elected president of the Gridiron Club in Washington. He also held offices in the National Press Club and the Standing Committee of Congressional Correspon-

dents and was cited for "unvarying high standards in newspaper work" in 1958. Most of his awards were granted by colleagues who understood and appreciated the strength of his coverage of Washington. A poll of Washington correspondents conducted in 1944 by the *Saturday Review of Literature* placed Stokes first as "the correspondent with the greatest influence both in Washington and in the nation, and the best all-around man in terms of reliability, fairness, and ability to analyze news." Both as a columnist and as a reporter, he set standards for covering Washington that have served as the measure for those who have followed.

His column was carried by more than 100 newspapers nationwide. He was so popular that United Features Syndicate used his name and column in advertisements designed to attract buyers for the service. He was considered tough and thorough, and whether readers agreed with him or not, his was a column that they found they needed to read.

His influence was as powerful in his time as that of any Washington correspondent. As a reformer who believed in the "New Deal" promised by Franklin D. Roosevelt, despite the corruption that Stokes himself uncovered in those programs, Stokes was one of the most important newspaper writers extolling the merits of FDR's approach to government.

References:

Delbert Clark, *Washington Dateline* (New York: Stokes, 1941);

Frank Luther Mott, *The News in America* (Cambridge, Mass.: Harvard University Press, 1952);

Cabell Phillips, ed., *Dateline: Washington* (New York: Greenwood, 1968);

A. Gayle Waldrop, *Editor and Editorial Writer* (New York: Rinehart, 1948).

Leland Stowe
(10 November 1899-   )

Jack Schnedler
Northwestern University

MAJOR POSITIONS HELD: Foreign correspondent, *New York Herald Tribune* (1926-1939); war correspondent, *Chicago Daily News* (1939-1943).

BOOKS: *Nazi Germany Means War* (London: Faber & Faber, 1933); republished as *Nazi Means War* (New York: Whittlesey House/McGraw-Hill, 1933);
No Other Road to Freedom (New York: Knopf, 1941; London: Faber & Faber, 1942);
They Shall Not Sleep (New York: Knopf, 1944);
While Time Remains (New York: Knopf, 1946);
Target: You (New York: Knopf, 1949);
Conquest by Terror: The Story of Satellite Europe (New York: Random House, 1952);
Crusoe of Lonesome Lake (New York: Random House, 1957);
The Last Great Frontiersman (Toronto: Stoddart, 1984).

Leland Stowe, one of the most renowned foreign correspondents of the 1930s and the 1940s, worked for the distinguished foreign services of the *New York Herald Tribune* and the *Chicago Daily News*. He won the Pulitzer Prize for correspondence in 1930 for his reporting for the *Herald Tribune* on the Paris Reparations Commission and the formation of the Young Plan and the Bank for International Settlements. His stalwart reputation as a war correspondent for the *Daily News* from 1939 to 1943 was established with a remarkable series of exclusive reports on the German conquest of Norway in April 1940.

Stowe was born on 10 November 1899 in Southbury, Connecticut, to Frank Philip and Eva Sara Noe Stowe. His father was a forester and lumberman. His first journalistic work came as a campus correspondent for the *Springfield* (Massachusetts) *Republican* while he was attending Wesleyan University, from which he graduated with a B.A. in 1921. With the goal of eventually becoming a novelist, he took a twenty-dollar-per-week reporting job with the *Worcester* (Massachusetts) *Telegram* in July 1921 to learn more about life and people.

"To my good fortune, The Telegram of

Leland Stowe

1921-23 was an exceptional training ground for cub reporters," Stowe wrote many years later. In November 1922, he set out for New York City and soon was hired as a reporter on Frank Munsey's *New York Herald*. When Munsey sold the *Herald* to Ogden Reid in 1924 and it was merged to become the *Herald Tribune*, Stowe was one of a half-dozen *Herald* staff members retained by the new paper.

A few months later, he left—for a salary increase from fifty dollars to eighty dollars a week—to become foreign editor of the Pathé News newsreel company. In later years, he liked to describe the position as "alleged foreign editor," maintaining that he was nothing more than a glorified caption writer. In working with the newsreels, Stowe recalled years later, "For the first time I was exposed, daily and visually, to major events in Europe and on other continents.... Surely a foreign correspondent's life must be as exciting and adventurous as those of newsreel cameramen—and how else to get abroad and be paid for working there?" Stowe was married on 27 September 1924 to Ruth F. Bernot. The marriage, which ended in divorce, produced two sons: Bruce B. and Alan A. Stowe.

Stowe returned to a reporter's job on the *Herald Tribune* in February 1926, eager to wangle an overseas assignment. In a few months there was an opening in the newspaper's Paris bureau, and he was named to the position. He sailed on the S.S. *Pennland* for Cherbourg, France, in July. He started out as an assistant to Wilbur Forrest, a noted World War I correspondent, and became chief of the bureau in 1927. He covered the League of Nations between 1927 and 1931, and the end of the Spanish dictatorship and founding of the Spanish Republic between 1929 and 1931. His coverage of the Paris Reparations Commission and the formation of the Young Plan and the Bank for International Settlements, for which he was awarded the Pulitzer Prize, was a complicated and exhausting four-month enterprise from February into June 1929. With the assistance of a junior *Herald Tribune* colleague, Ralph Barnes, he scored almost two dozen exclusives on the intentions and strategies of the diplomats assembled in Paris. The Pulitzer award, announced on 12 May 1930, cited him for "the best example of correspondence during the year, the test being cleanness and terseness of style; judicious, well-balanced and well-informed interpretative writing, which shall make clear the significance of the subject covered in the correspondence or which shall promote international understanding and appreciation." Ogden Reid happened to be in Paris when the Pulitzer was announced. He took Stowe to dinner, but the correspondent remembered years later that he offered no salary increase over the $100 a week Stowe was making. Stowe covered the return to the Rumanian throne of King Carol II in June 1930, the World Disarmament Conference in Geneva in 1932, the World Economic Conference in London in 1933, and the Reichstag fire trial in Berlin in 1933. His first book, a prophetic volume called *Nazi Germany Means War*, which had very few sales, was published in 1933.

Stowe returned from Europe in 1935 and was a roving Western Hemisphere correspondent for the *Herald Tribune* from 1936 to 1939, also going back to Spain in 1937-1938 to investigate the plight of the nine million homeless and war-orphaned

children in the Republican areas. His Latin American assignments included Franklin D. Roosevelt's visit to Brazil and Argentina and the Inter-American Peace Conference in Buenos Aires in 1936, and the Pan-American Conference in Lima, Peru, in 1938.

When Hitler sent the German armies into Poland on 1 September 1939, Stowe, prematurely white-haired at age thirty-nine, was working from the *Herald Tribune*'s home office in New York. He immediately determined to go overseas again. Wilbur Forrest, Stowe's predecessor as chief correspondent in Paris, was by then executive assistant to Reid. As Stowe later told an interviewer, he approached Forrest in a corridor outside the paper's bustling newsroom on 3 September, the day England and France declared war on Germany. "I've reported how Hitler was certain to start this war," Stowe told Forrest. "So I feel I'm equipped to report it for the Herald Tribune, not to stay home on the sidelines. After my years in Paris, I think I'm best prepared to cover the front in France. But I'd go anywhere you might prefer to send me." "I'm sorry, Lee," answered Forrest. "You and I have reported our wars, but we're too old to cover this one."

Later that day, Stowe received a telegram from Col. Frank Knox, owner of the *Chicago Daily News*, inquiring whether he would like to cover the war in Europe for the *Daily News* and its more than fifty foreign-service subscribers across the country. Stowe caught an evening train to Chicago, reached quick agreement with Knox and editor Paul Scott Mowrer on terms of employment, and departed for England by flying boat on 11 September 1939 with another *Daily News* war correspondent, the redoubtable Robert J. Casey.

The *Chicago Daily News* foreign service, under foreign editor Carroll Binder, was at the peak of its prowess when Stowe came aboard. Its roster when the war began included Edgar Ansel Mowrer, Wallace R. Deuel, William H. Stoneman, John Whitaker, M. W. Fodor, Frank Smothers, A. T. Steele, and Helen Kirkpatrick. These were not the colorful and romantic Richard Harding Davis types of previous wars, as John Hohenberg observed in his book, *Foreign Correspondence* (1964), but rather "calm, determined, professionally trained" reporters. By tradition, the *Daily News* correspondents meshed as a team, and "all of the men on this team were convinced that ours was the best all-round foreign service operated by any American newspaper," Stowe wrote in his 1941 book, *No Other Road to Freedom*.

Stowe did two seventeen-month overseas

tours for the *Daily News* as part of the last generation of newspaper war correspondents before the advent of television. By the end of the war, he had traveled with the armies of seven different nations, reporting in forty-four countries and colonies on four continents, and being bombed by five different air forces.

A breezy feature from London on the rigors of the blackout, dated 14 September 1939, was Stowe's first dispatch for the *Daily News*. By December he was on his way to Finland, where the invasion by the Soviet Union was being repulsed in the winter snows by the courageous soldiers of a much smaller nation. Finnish reluctance to admit reporters to combat areas provoked Stowe to declare after several weeks, "On the Western front, they have war without combat. On the Finnish front, we have war without correspondents." But the *Daily News*'s front page on 3 January 1940 displayed a Stowe dispatch, later reprinted in *Reader's Digest*, that gained a reputation as a paragon of fine war writing. The story was headlined "Finland's Snows Shroud Slaughtered Russ Legion," and datelined "With the Finnish Army in the East; the Battlefield of Tolvajarvi." It began: "In this vast solitude lie the dead: Uncounted thousands of Russian dead. They lie as they fell—twisted, gesticulating and tortured. But they lie beneath a kindly mask of fallen snow. Now they are one with the cold, white shapes of the illimitable pine and spruce trees. An unknown legion of the fallen, they have been sacrificed by winter's hands and covered over with winter's spotless sheet. They will not go back to the earth now for many months."

Stowe stayed in Finland until the weight of Russian manpower forced the Finns to sue for peace in March. At the start of April, he was in Stockholm with reservations to fly to Riga, capital of still-independent Latvia. But on instinct, he and Edmund Stevens of the *Christian Science Monitor* went instead to Oslo, where the Norwegian government was arguing with the British about the naval blockade. That decision led to the most remarkable of Stowe's World War II reporting exploits, a series of exclusives that dominated the attention of the world press in April 1940. As John Hohenberg described it in *Foreign Correspondence*, "Leland Stowe of the Chicago Daily News scored over all others as the Nazi blitz spread to Norway." In *The First Casualty* (1975), a probing study of war reporting, Phillip Knightley wrote, "It was left to a neutral correspondent, Leland Stowe of the Chicago Daily News, fresh from the fiasco in Finland, to report the war in Norway as it really was."

And Joseph J. Mathews, in his *Reporting the Wars* (1957), rated Stowe's Norway work "among the outstanding achievements of the period."

Stowe, Stevens, and Warren Irvin of NBC were the only foreign correspondents in Oslo on the morning of 9 April when German bombers appeared over the city. Stowe managed to transmit a dispatch that appeared on the front page of the 10 April *Daily News*, headlined "Oslo Natives Fraternizing With Nazis." It reported that a force of no more than 1,500 German troops, landed by plane, seemed to be in control of the confused Norwegian capital. Despite German censorship, Stowe managed to send one paragraph the next day: "The Germans have clinched their hold on Oslo with the arrival of five transports carrying more than 20,000 troops. Three of the largest, jammed to their rails, began disembarking at 4:45 p.m. today."

By 12 April, as Stowe reported in *No Other Road to Freedom*, "it was no longer necessary for us to linger in Oslo. . . . Since we now had the big and all-important story, Irv [Warren Irvin] and I decided to gamble everything on getting to Sweden." A gallant American woman of their acquaintance chauffeured them to the border past Nazi columns and roadblocks, and Stowe was in a position to file his exclusives. The 13 April *Daily News* carried a warm-up story, datelined "Gothenburg, Sweden," and beginning, "We have just emerged from German-occupied Oslo and we have just seen German troops pushing their field-grey columns northward, eastward and southward out of the Norwegian capital in the audacious, high-speed thrusts that are intended to dominate all of southeastern Norway within 48 hours."

On Monday, 15 April, came the first blockbuster, spread across all eight columns of the *Daily News*'s front page with a banner headline: "BETRAYAL OF NORWAY!" The subheadlines said: "Amazing Acts That Gave Oslo to Hitler; Norse Traitors Helped Nazi Spies Silence Forts." Datelined "Stockholm," the story began: "For the first time the story behind Germany's paralyzing 12-hour conquest of Norway on Tuesday, April 9, can be told. Between midnight and noon of that bewildering day, Norway's capital, all her principal seaports and her most strategic coastal defenses fell into German hands like an overripe plum. By bribery and extraordinary infiltration on the part of Nazi agents, and by treason on the part of a few highly placed Norwegian civilians and defense officials . . . the German dictatorship built a Trojan horse inside of Norway." Introducing American readers to Maj. Vidkun Quisling, whose role as a

Nazi collaborator added an epithet to the English language, Stowe called the German actions "among the most audacious, most perfectly oiled political plots of the last century."

Stowe ended this account by calling it "the most important newspaper dispatch I have ever had the occasion to write." A few days later, he went back into Norway to find the British expeditionary troops who were supposedly fighting their way south from Namsos to Trondheim in central Norway. After a grueling excursion that ended with a ten-mile hike through mud and snow over a mountain range, he and a photographer got back to Sweden. "I had had two meals in four days and I had slept less than seven hours in the past ninety-six," he recounted in *No Other Road to Freedom*. "But we had some pictures and a story which might be of considerable interest to the outside world, and we now knew beyond any likelihood of contradiction that the Allies had bungled their campaign in Norway irretrievably."

That story was bannered in the *Daily News* of 25 April with another "Exclusive" tag and a headline, "BRITISH DEFEAT TOLD." The subheadlines said: "Stowe Sees 1,500 in Nazi Death Trap; Soldiers Mired in Snow at Mercy of Foes' Planes." Stowe's story started: "Here is the first and only eyewitness report on the opening chapter of the British expeditionary troops' advance in Norway, north of Trondheim. It is a bitterly disillusioning, and almost unbelievable story." The troops, he wrote, "were dumped into Norway's deep snows and quagmires of April slush without a single anti-aircraft gun—without one squadron of supporting airplanes—without a single piece of field artillery." A follow-up story on 27 April on the British failures was headlined "Germans Bomb Steinkjer Into Black Skeleton," and another story on 30 April wrapped up the situation under the headline "Stowe Pictures Perilous Trip to Bring News of British Rout; Notes Defeatist Norse Attitude."

As Mathews summed it up in *Reporting the Wars*, "Stowe's personal courage and physical endurance, aided by an element of luck and the proximity of neutral Sweden from which he dispatched his stories, enabled him to achieve a series of scoops and brought from Editor and Publisher the prematurely optimistic statement that his work had 'blasted the fallacy that modern warfare and its censorship spell doom for the war correspondent.' "

The caliber of Stowe's achievements in Norway easily merited consideration for a second Pulitzer Prize, but the correspondence category the next year was a general award to American correspondents on war fronts. In a 1982 letter, Stowe commented, "Frankly, I knew I had earned it. . . . Then, I rashly dreamed, I'd be the only foreign correspondent to win two Pulitzers (chiefly blocked, I was later informed, reportedly by very top NY Timesman, or men)."

In May 1940, Stowe finally did get to see Riga briefly, on his way to Bucharest by way of Moscow and Odessa. He spent the summer and early fall of 1940 in the Balkans, where governments were under intense pressure from the Germans, and then arrived in Athens in November to cover Mussolini's invasion of Greece from the Italian protectorate of Albania. Among the other correspondents in Greece was Ralph Barnes of the *Herald Tribune*, who had assisted Stowe in the coverage that garnered his Pulitzer in 1930. "The most harrowing story I ever had to write," Stowe later recalled, "was from Athens, recording Ralph Barnes' death in an RAF bomber crash into a southernmost Yugoslavian mountain peak."

In February 1941, Stowe returned to the United States after a roundabout flight across Africa. He wrote a heavily promoted eight-part series that ran in the *Daily News* from 24 February to 4 March, aiming to "summarize his impressions." The series was a virtual encyclopedia of World War II up to then, as can be judged from the headlines: "Stowe Tells of Greek War"; "How Duce Lost Egypt War"; "Scandinavia's Tragedy Told"; "Stalin Biding Time—Stowe; Feels War With Nazis Inevitable"; "Hitler in Zero Year—Stowe; Nazis Must Beat Britain Quickly or Lose—Is View"; "Common Man Will Defeat Hitler: Stowe"; "Europe Views America as a Guide: Stowe"; "Tide Will Turn Against Hitler in 1942: Stowe." These stories, all on the front page, were followed by three days of front-page stories in which Stowe answered an outpouring of reader questions.

In the summer of 1941, after completing the manuscript of *No Other Road to Freedom,* his second book, Stowe was sent by the *Daily News* to replace A. T. Steele in the Far East. He did considerable reporting from China on the Burma Road, including a controversial series—only partly published—that spotlighted inefficiency and corruption in the operation of the lifeline between Chiang Kai-shek's regime and the West.

Reporting from the Nationalist capital of Chungking on 6 December 1941, he wrote with prescience, "the feeling grows here that the Far Eastern showdown may be a matter of hours or days." The Japanese attack on Pearl Harbor came the next day. Orders from his editors kept him from going after 7 December to Singapore, where he likely would have become a Japanese prisoner.

By way of Burma, India, and Iran, Stowe reached his next assignment in Moscow in mid-May 1942, at a time when the Germans were pressing their second summer of offensives. The highlight of his six months in the wartime Soviet Union was an opportunity—then unique for a Western correspondent—to visit the front lines alone rather than as part of a group of reporters. Traveling with the noted Soviet writer Ilya Ehrenburg, Stowe spent nine days on the Rzhev front in late September and early October. The visit produced a series of twenty-two reports that began in the *Daily News* on 13 October 1942 with this lead: "At last I have seen and lived with the Red Army. I have seen the front in several sectors and have the feel of those Russian soldiers and officers who have amazed the world. I really know in personal terms how the Russian people at the front, along the front and in recaptured villages inside the combat zone, are fighting the war." He called what he had seen "the only Allied front that never ceases to burn and bleed."

Back in the United States, Stowe completed for Alfred Knopf publishers another war book, *They Shall Not Sleep* (1944). In 1944 he became a correspondent for the ABC radio network and wrote for the *New York Post* Syndicate. He also did commentary for the Mutual Broadcasting System.

After the war, Stowe left daily journalism for a variety of other reporting and writing experiences. He worked as a free-lance magazine writer and lecturer from 1946 to 1948; foreign editor of *The Reporter* magazine in 1949 and 1950; director of Radio Free Europe's News and Information Service in Munich, Germany, from 1952 to 1954; roving editor of *Reader's Digest* from 1955 to 1976; and professor of journalism at the University of Michigan from 1956 to 1969. During his affiliation with the university, he taught autumn semesters on the Ann Arbor campus and traveled for *Reader's Digest* the rest of the year. He continued to write books: *While Time Remains* (1946), *Target: You* (1949), *Conquest by Terror: The Story of Satellite Europe* (1952), and *Crusoe of Lonesome Lake* (1957). In 1984, his eighth book, *The Last Great Frontiersman,* was published in Canada.

Stowe had met Theodora Calauz in the Balkans in 1940; they were married on 17 June 1952. Stowe presently lives in Ann Arbor.

Along with the Pulitzer Prize, his roster of honors includes the University of Missouri School of Journalism medal for outstanding war correspondence in 1941 and the Sigma Delta Chi medal

Stowe in his study in 1969, on the occasion of his retirement as professor of journalism at the University of Michigan (State Historical Society of Wisconsin)

and award for his Norwegian reporting in 1940. He was made a member of the French Legion of Honor in 1931 and received the Military Cross of Greece in 1945. In 1963, he was given Wesleyan University's James L. McConaughty Memorial Award. His honorary degrees include an M.A. in 1936 and an LL.D. in 1944 from Wesleyan University, an M.A. from Harvard University in 1945, and an LL.D. from Hobart College in 1946. In 1982, he endowed the annual Leland Stowe Journalism Award at the University of Michigan with a cash prize of $1,000 for the best analytical or critical essay based on the collection of 280 books by American foreign correspondents that he had previously donated to the university's communication-department library.

Stowe's World War II achievements, particularly in the Norwegian campaign, earned him a lasting place of honor on the list of what Hohenberg in *Foreign Correspondence* called "calm, determined, professionally trained men."

References:

John Hohenberg, *Foreign Correspondence* (New York: Columbia University Press, 1964);

Phillip Knightley, *The First Casualty* (New York:

Harcourt Brace Jovanovich, 1975);
Joseph J. Mathews, *Reporting the Wars* (Minneapolis: University of Minnesota Press, 1957).

Papers:
Leland Stowe's papers are at the Mass Communications History Center in Madison, Wisconsin.

Dorothy Thompson
(9 July 1893-30 January 1961)

Jo R. Mengedoht
University of South Carolina

MAJOR POSITIONS HELD: Chief of Central European service, *Philadelphia Public Ledger* (1920-1928); political columnist, *New York Herald Tribune* (1936-1941), Bell Syndicate (1941-1958).

BOOKS: *The New Russia* (New York: Holt, 1928; London: Cape, 1929);
I Saw Hitler! (New York: Farrar & Rinehart, 1932);
Concerning Vermont (Brattleboro, Vt.: Hildreth, 1937);
Once on Christmas (London & New York: Oxford University Press, 1938);
Dorothy Thompson's Political Guide: A Study of American Liberalism and Its Relationship to Modern Totalitarian States (New York: Stackpole, 1938);
Refugees: Anarchy or Organization? (New York: Random House, 1938);
Let the Record Speak (Boston: Houghton Mifflin, 1939; London: Hamish Hamilton, 1939);
Christian Ethics and Western Civilization (New York: Town Hall, 1940);
A Call to Action (New York: Ring of Freedom, 1941);
Our Lives, Fortunes, and Sacred Honor (San Francisco: Windsor, 1941);
Listen, Hans (Boston: Houghton Mifflin, 1942);
To Whom Does the Earth Belong? (London: Jewish Agency for Palestine, 1944);
I Speak Again as a Christian (New York: Christian Council on Palestine and American Palestine Committee, 1945);
Let the Promise Be Fulfilled: A Christian View of Palestine (New York: American Christian Palestine Committee, 1946);
The Developments of Our Times (De Land, Fla.: John B. Stetson University Press, 1948);
The Truth about Communism (Washington: Public Affairs Press, 1948);
The Crisis of the West (Toronto: University of Toronto Press, 1955);

The Courage to Be Happy (Boston: Houghton Mifflin, 1957).

OTHER: Joseph Roth, *Job: The Story of a Simple Man*, translated from the German by Thompson (New York: Viking, 1931);
Karl Zuckmayer, *Second Wind*, introduction by Thompson (New York: Doubleday, Doran, 1940; London: Harrap, 1941).

SELECTED PERIODICAL PUBLICATIONS: "Refugees: A World Problem," *Foreign Affairs*, 16 (April 1938): 375-387;
"How I Was Duped by a Communist," *Saturday Evening Post*, 221 (16 April 1949): 19, 75-76, 180;
"America Demands a Single Loyalty," *Commentary*, 9 (March 1950): 210-219;
"My First Job," *Ladies' Home Journal*, 74 (April 1957): 201;
"I'm the Child of a King," *Ladies' Home Journal*, 76 (November 1959): 11, 16, 23.

Dorothy Thompson, newspaper columnist and political commentator, was a respected virtuoso of her craft. Vitality was the outstanding quality of her writing, her broadcasts, and her life. For those who read her column in the *New York Herald Tribune* and listened to her broadcasts, she was a voice of courage and exceptional fluency.

Thompson was born in Lancaster, New York, the eldest of three children of Peter and Margaret Grierson Thompson. Her mother died when Thompson was eight; two years later her genial father, an English-born Methodist preacher, married the church organist, Elizabeth Abbott, a plain and unpleasantly solemn spinster of forty. In 1905 the family moved to Gowanda, New York, where Thompson entered high school. However, hostility

Dorothy Thompson (Syracuse University Library)

between Thompson and her stepmother resulted in the girl's being sent to live with relatives in Chicago. While there she was enrolled in Lewis Institute, a school noted for high educational standards. Her academic record was excellent and she demonstrated exceptional ability in English, history, Latin, and German.

In 1912 Thompson transferred to Syracuse University on a scholarship for children of Methodist ministers. Her classmates were impressed with her versatility: "She could compose a poem to order, deliver an eloquent sermon at vespers, and also run up a handsome party dress out of a bargain remnant. But she was not always lovable," according to her biographer, Marion K. Sanders. Some of her peers considered her an intellectual

snob, and she often demonstrated a propensity for monopolizing conversations—a lifelong trait that would annoy many of her future colleagues. While at Syracuse Thompson became active in the women's suffrage movement, a cause that was gaining fresh momentum at that time. Following her graduation in 1914 she became a publicist and lecturer in the suffrage movement for three years. Of her first employment Thompson recalled, "My first job would have been teaching, but I flunked my teacher's exam in English. So I went to work for the Women's Suffrage Movement in Buffalo, N.Y. We were radicals, liberals and reactionaries; raving beauties and plain as pikestaffs; demanding the vote or sweetly pleading for it. Leaders, speakers and organizers, paid and unpaid, came from every social group and embraced as many political and social ideas as there are in the nation. It was an education in politics, publicity, public speaking, organization and an insight into every variety of the human condition . . . a natural stepping stone to the field where by then I knew my chief interest lay: journalism." Thompson did not, however, move directly into journalism, but spent several years as publicity director for a reform organization financed by members of the liberal-philanthropic establishment in Cincinnati.

In 1920 Thompson and a friend, Barbara De Porte, sailed on the S.S. *Finland* for Europe. While free-lancing for the *International News Service,* the *New York Post,* and the *Christian Science Monitor,* Thompson earned her regular bread and butter as a publicist for the Red Cross. She also acted as an unsalaried Vienna correspondent for the *Philadelphia Public Ledger* under Paris chief Wythe Williams. Her biographer quotes John Gunther's essay "A Blue-Eyed Tornado": "Two things happened to central Europe during the decade of the 20s, people in Vienna still say—the world economic crisis and Dorothy Thompson. She was brimful of excitement and freshness and saw stories that were not stories to more experienced correspondents. . . ." Her writing was crisp and free-flowing, establishing her lifelong literary style. With Marcel Fodor of the *Manchester Guardian* Thompson wrote a firsthand account of the unsuccessful attempt of Charles, Franz Josef's grandnephew, to reestablish the Hapsburg monarchy. This scoop helped earn Thompson a salaried position with the *Ledger.* She was paid fifty dollars a week, plus a small expense account; her journalistic responsibilities extended to nine middle European countries. According to her biographer, "this was the beginning of the Thompson legend in which the intrepid girl re-

*Thompson at age twenty-eight during her tour of Europe
(Syracuse University Library)*

porter, braving unimaginable perils to get the news, becomes as much a part of the story as the events she is covering." Although many Thompson anecdotes became distorted in the retelling, it was clear from the start that she had a gift for walking in where news was breaking and for pursuing the story without regard to the effort or danger involved. She seemed to enjoy nothing more than an unscheduled jaunt to an unlikely or perilous place.

In 1922 Thompson married the first of her three husbands, a dark-eyed Hungarian Jew named Josef Bard. He was slender, suave, and strikingly handsome. His good looks and promise as a writer and philosopher brought together all that the impressionable Thompson sought in a husband. That summer Thompson was offered a job as acting chief of the *Ledger*'s Berlin bureau. This era of astronomical currency inflation and social and political ferment provided Thompson with the most challenging assignment of her early career. When the Berlin post was made permanent in 1924,

Thompson was the first woman to head a major American news bureau overseas. Although her career flourished during this period her relationship with her husband did not. Frequent separations contributed to the instability of the floundering marriage. The unabashed infidelity of the bohemian Bard caused Thompson severe emotional problems. They were divorced in 1927, leaving Thompson disconsolate. In May of the same year her work took her to Geneva to cover a fifty-nation economic conference; after this assignment her old joie de vivre returned.

At her thirty-fourth birthday party, Thompson was introduced to the novelist Sinclair Lewis. During their courtship Thompson traveled to Russia to report on the tenth anniversary of the Bolshevik Revolution on 7 November 1927. She produced a series of articles for the *New York Evening Post* that, according to biographer Sanders, gave her readers "the sense of sharing an exciting trip as seen through the very American eyes of a keen observer who made no claim to infallibility." Her articles were published as *The New Russia* (1928). Following the Russian assignment, Thompson resigned from her job; she and Lewis were married on 14 May 1928. They returned to the United States and purchased a Vermont estate that they christened Twin Farms. Their turbulent marriage years are

Thompson and her first husband, Josef Bard

Thompson with her second husband, Sinclair Lewis, and their son Michael (Syracuse University Library)

amply reported in Vincent Sheean's *Dorothy and Red* (1963). A son, Michael, was born on 30 June 1930; Wells Lewis, Lewis's son by his first marriage, was a frequent visitor in their home. Wells was killed by a sniper's bullet during World War II.

Retirement from her position with the *Ledger* was not, for Thompson, a retirement from writing. In 1929 she wrote a series of articles on Canada and another series on Prohibition. In 1930 the Lewises returned to Europe, Thompson bent on demonstrating that she was still an important figure in contemporary journalism. In articles for the *Saturday Evening Post* and other magazines she documented and interpreted the alarming events in central Europe. In 1931, on an assignment from *Cosmopolitan*, Thompson interviewed Adolf Hitler, the leader of the National Socialist Workers Party of Germany. The interview was expanded into *I Saw Hitler!* (1932). Thompson's usually astute judgment failed her in the case of Hitler, whom she assessed as a man of "startling insignificance" who would never rise to power.

During the 1932 Christmas holidays in Austria, Thompson conceived a second child, which was later miscarried. On the same holiday she renewed her friendship with the Austrian Baroness Hatvany, a talented sculptress and witty raconteur, whom she had met during the 1920s. Thompson and the baroness, who under her real name Christa Winsloe had written a lesbian novel, *Mädchen in Uniform*, developed an erotic relationship. "So it has happened to me again after all these years," Thompson wrote in her diary, alluding to two brief earlier episodes. "To love a woman is somehow ridiculous. *Mir auch passt as nicht. Ich bin doch heterosexuel.* [It doesn't suit me. I am heterosexual]. . . . Well then, how account for this which has happened again. The soft, quite natural kiss on my throat. . . . What in God's name does one call this sensibility if it be not love?" Although the relationship developed into just a warm friendship, the baroness remained in Thompson's life as a traveling companion and frequent houseguest until the baroness returned to Europe in 1935.

Christa Winsloe, with whom Thompson had an affair during the early 1930s (Syracuse University Library)

The Thompson-Lewis marriage suffered long and frequent separations as Thompson started writing regularly on foreign affairs for the *Saturday Evening Post.* "Between Hitler's rise to power in 1933 and the United States' entry into war in 1941, Dorothy Thompson emerged as one of the nation's most powerful voices denouncing Hitlerism and demanding American interventionism against the fascist threat," according to Paul Boyer. In 1934 she again traveled to Germany, but she was summarily expelled. The expulsion attracted international attention and triggered a deluge of lecture invitations from throughout the United States. She wrote articles on fascism for *Foreign Affairs* which enhanced her reputation as an astute political writer. In 1936 she began writing the column "On the Record"

three times a week for the *New York Herald Tribune.* In 1937 she began a monthly column in the *Ladies' Home Journal* and became a regular radio commentator on NBC. Thompson's fame in the late 1930s was matched among women only by that of the president's wife. "She and Eleanor Roosevelt are undoubtedly the most influential women in the U.S.," *Time* magazine confirmed in a cover story about Thompson.

As Thompson's professional star continued to rise, her husband's began to wane. Lewis's drinking produced intolerable conflicts between them; after 1933 they rarely lived together and by 1937 they had officially separated. They were divorced in 1942.

Thompson became a one-woman crusade against fascism. In the foreword to *Let the Record Speak* (1939), a collection of her newspaper columns, Thompson outlined her convictions concerning Nazi Germany: "National Socialism is not modification [of the social order]; it is total revolution. It is the repudiation of the whole past of western man, it is far more 'radical' than Communism, which at least, pays lipservice in however distorted form to certain humane ideas inherited from Christianity and from the French Revolution." She urged her readers to assume the responsibility for doing everything that "a great nation can do to maintain a world order in which the interests of its people, and the values that they cherish, can survive and improve. To be conscious of the serious danger, and to be ready to look it in the eye, is not pessimism. It is the way one gathers one's strength. For when one looks it in the eye, it becomes interestingly less ominous." But most Americans in the 1930s were opposed to involvement in the troubles of Europe, and Thompson's fiery, interventionist prose was denounced or ignored by those who preferred isolationism.

Thompson assisted numerous European colleagues and friends who were fleeing Hitler in securing visas to the United States, and often opened Twin Farms to them upon their arrival. In April 1938, she wrote an article for *Foreign Affairs,* "Refugees: A World Problem," in which she said: "As anti-Semitic policies spread through Europe it becomes clearer and clearer that charity is not enough. The problem, it should be repeated, must be regarded and treated as one of international politics. The only approach to a solution must be a political approach. And, as things are at present, it can be made only by an organization headed by outstanding personalities of the democratic world, with the full collaboration of Jewish organizations ev-

"And remember — no more Dorothy Thompson!"

A cartoon from the Scarsdale *(New York)* Inquirer *during the late 1930s indicating the effect Thompson's columns had on those who disagreed with her views (Whitelaw Reid)*

erywhere, and enjoying the sympathetic collaboration and support of the democratic governments. Such an organization would be listened to both by the anti-Semitic governments and by governments that need well-equipped and politically reliable settlers to develop their empty lands." It has been suggested that Thompson's work on behalf of refugees had significant influence upon President Franklin D. Roosevelt's decision to call an international conference that led to the creation of the Intergovernmental Committee on Refugees.

Thompson was often unsympathetic and critical toward FDR's domestic policies. She opposed Social Security taxes and the New Deal's floundering social and economic programs. Characterized by the liberal press as a self-appointed antifascist Joan of Arc, she was often called upon to defend her creed of social justice. As the 1940 election neared, she and other moderates found themselves in a political dilemma, because the isolationist Sen. Robert Taft was not acceptable as a presidential candidate. Thompson proposed a bipartisan ticket of Roosevelt for president and moderate Republican Wendell Willkie for vice-president, but such a ticket was acceptable to neither politicians nor vot-

ers. Subsequently, Thompson enthusiastically campaigned for and applauded Willkie's nomination for president on the Republican ticket. However, feeling that Roosevelt's world leadership role was more important than the domestic policies to which she was opposed, she had a change of heart and at the eleventh hour supported FDR's reelection. This political flip-flop cost her the renewal of her contract with the *Herald Tribune;* however, she signed on as a columnist with the Bell Syndicate. In New York City, her column appeared in the liberal *Post.*

As Hitler's troops rolled across Europe, Thompson's crusading intensified: she wrote, lectured, and initiated freedom organizations. She was honored at a dinner in New York on 6 May 1941 by a group calling itself the Committee of 1,000; representatives of countries under Nazi domination paid tribute to her, and FDR sent greetings. Following Pearl Harbor, Thompson's prestige and influence were at their zenith. In an effort to provide timely news to Europeans Thompson delivered a weekly shortwave broadcast in German, addressed to an imaginary friend named Hans. A compilation of these messages is found in her book *Listen, Hans* (1942).

On 16 June 1943 Thompson married Maxim Kopf, an Austrian emigré painter and sculptor, after they persuaded Kopf's third wife to agree to a divorce. The charming and easygoing Kopf was not interested in competing with his wife for fame or attention. He good-naturedly performed the role of prince consort to his Dorothy, and they maintained an intimate relationship until his death in 1958.

After World War II, Thompson focused her attention on the Middle East and the struggle between Israel and the Arab countries. In May 1945, the Kopfs visited the Holy Land, where Thompson was honored by Jewish leaders for her staunch championing of the Zionist movement. However, when she returned to the United States her zeal for the Zionist cause diminished. Her new position was put forth for the *Post* on 9 July 1946 in a column titled "The Palestine Tragedy." Her emphasis was on Zionist zealotry and Jewish acts of terrorism against Arabs. Her new position was highly unpopular with her editor, publisher, and readers. In November 1946, the *Post*'s Readers' Forum carried a letter from Rex Stout under the heading "FEELS THOMPSON COLUMN DOESN'T BELONG IN POST." It has been suggested that Thompson's opinions in 1946 were viewed by her readers and employers through the eyes of a nation recently jolted by the horrors revealed at Nuremberg: it was not an auspicious time to criticize Jewish actions. Thompson's position on Palestine caused her column to be dropped from the *Post* in 1947.

In the early 1940s Thompson had employed as a research assistant a homeless European refugee, only to discover several years later that he was a Russian Communist. Her forthright honesty compelled her to write of this embarrassing association in "How I Was Duped by a Communist" in the *Saturday Evening Post* in 1949.

As Thompson's pro-Arab position became more fixed, she was eagerly embraced by a small circle of Americans concerned about the plight of displaced Palestinian Arabs and about America's pro-Zionist policy. In 1950 she visited the Middle East on a trip financed by the State Department. Upon her return she sought a forum for her observations, but even the *Saturday Evening Post* refused to print her material. There were few outlets for her reports on this subject, although she finally placed a lengthy article in *Commentary*—published by the American Jewish Committee! In 1951 she became president of the American Friends of the Middle East (AFME). This organization was purportedly dedicated to publicizing the accomplishments of

Middle Eastern states, but in practice it served as a conduit for anti-Zionist pronouncements. It was reportedly funded by the Arabian-American Oil Company (Aramco) and—unknown to Thompson—by the United States Central Intelligence Agency. Thompson's editors and readers began to feel that she had become a propagandist for the Arabs. She was urged to resign as president of AFME if she wanted to continue to be a newspaperwoman.

Thompson's politics in the 1950s were veering steadily to the right, and in October 1952 she endorsed Eisenhower for president. Her columns, carried by only a small number of newspapers, became contradictory and lacked the fire and spark of earlier days. Following the sudden death of Maxim Kopf in 1958 at the age of sixty-five, Thompson suspended her column for two weeks; she struggled to resume it, but her enthusiasm for such taxing work was gone. Her farewell column appeared on 22 August 1958. She planned in her retirement to undertake an autobiography. This task was never completed, however, as her health rapidly deteriorated and she died of a heart attack in Lisbon, Portugal, in 1961.

For twenty-four years Thompson had written a monthly article for the *Ladies' Home Journal*. Her columns covered materials of domestic and personal interest to her readers. *The Courage to Be Happy* (1957) is a collection of thirty-one such essays published between 1937 and 1957. In the introduction, Thompson describes her attempt to write, for a magazine, about more enduring subjects than those appropriate for newspapers. In reviewing the monthly essays, she says, "I have been startled at the revelations of myself. I realize how deeply rooted I am in my own country, the home out of which I came, how all the experiences of my more adult years are checked and appraised against that background, how deeply skeptical I am of technical progress as the promise of human salvation and of many of the Shibboleths that accompany it and promise by one means or another to bring about the millennium." The subjects of her magazine pieces were far removed from politics: gardening, child rearing, the importance of loving animals, and the advantages of growing old. Her engaging and witty prose is the antithesis of the writing of the strident evangelist who in political arenas could overpower and exhaust her colleagues and friends.

Thompson was a prodigious worker, a reporter with insatiable curiosity. To her sound reportorial instincts she added an astonishing capacity to absorb vast quantities of printed matter. Possessed with a divine restlessness, Thompson earned a place in journalistic and twentieth-century history.

Biographies:
Vincent Sheean, *Dorothy and Red* (Boston: Houghton Mifflin, 1963);

Marion K. Sanders, *Dorothy Thompson: A Legend in Her Time* (Boston: Houghton Mifflin, 1973).

References:
"All Thompson Columns to Be Saved," *Editor & Publisher,* 84 (24 November 1951);

Paul Boyer, "Dorothy Thompson, Journalist," in *Notable American Women: The Modern Period,* edited by Barbara Sickerman and Carol Hurd Green (Cambridge, Mass.: Harvard Univer-

sity Press, 1980), pp. 683-686;

"Cartwheel Girl," *Time,* 33 (12 June 1939): 47-51;

"Columnist Bows Out," *Newsweek,* 52 (1 September 1958): 39-40;

Robert Neville, "A Talk with Vincent Sheean," *New York Times Book Review,* 17 November 1963, p. 63;

Ishbel Ross, *Ladies of the Press* (New York & London: Harper, 1936), pp. 360-366;

William L. Shirer, "Marriage Was Quite Another Story," *New York Times Book Review,* 17 November 1963, p. 1.

Papers:
Dorothy Thompson's papers are at the Syracuse University Library.

Robert L. Vann
(27 August 1879-24 October 1940)

Philip B. Dematteis

MAJOR POSITION HELD: Editor/publisher, *Pittsburgh Courier* (1910-1940).

The career of Robert L. Vann combined journalism, law, politics, and civil rights activism with varying degrees of success. Vann rose from rural Southern poverty to become a struggling black lawyer in Pittsburgh, and fell into journalism when friends asked him to draw up incorporation papers for a black weekly they were trying to establish. Vann was soon forced to take over the paper himself, and after years of struggle, he built the *Pittsburgh Courier* into the leading black weekly in the United States. Shrewdly using the newspaper to advance his law career, he tried to parlay his success in both fields into prominence in politics and civil rights leadership. In these endeavors he achieved some success, but also met with frustration and disappointment. His personality a complex mixture of conservatism, optimism, idealism, and opportunism, Vann switched political allegiances when it seemed to him expedient to do so, and engaged in well-publicized feuds with other black spokesmen. At the end of his life he had lost much of his influence and was generally regarded as something of an anachronism; but the *Courier* had the highest circu-

lation of any black newspaper in the country.

Robert Lee Vann was born in 1879 near Ahoskie, North Carolina, on a farm where his mother was employed as a cook. He was probably illegitimate; his mother, Lucy Peoples, named him Vann after her first employer, and Robert Lee after her grandfather. Lucy Peoples was light-skinned, which enabled her to procure the relatively high-status job of cook; Vann was also light in color, and in addition had straight hair and a long, straight nose that made him look more American Indian or Middle Eastern than Negro. In later life he refused to "pass" on several occasions when the possibility was suggested to him, but his appearance undoubtedly made him more acceptable in the white world of business and politics.

Vann remembered the first ten years of his life as rather idyllic. He was not conscious of suffering from discrimination; the various wealthy families for whom his mother worked were kind to him, and he played with their children as an equal. His mother, a proud woman, was determined to show that she could raise her son alone, and disciplined him strictly; she instilled in him a set of moral values and ideals which he tried to live up to for the rest of his life. At the age of six, he started at the

Robert L. Vann

Springfield Colored School; like most black schools in the South at the time, it was only open four months a year, and the education offered there was extremely rudimentary. Vann was an eager and a bright pupil, however, and soon was teaching his mother to read and write.

Vann's happy childhood came to an end when he was ten: his mother married a poor dirt farmer named John Simon who lived in an area of Hertford County called Red Hill. For the next six years, when he was not in school, Vann had to work on the farm or be hired out to cook for lumber crews, pick tobacco, or perform other physical labor. He looked back on this period as the most miserable of his life, and regarded his stepfather as "the world's most worthless man."

Vann graduated from the Springfield Colored School in 1892. In the summer of 1895, he was able to get a part-time job as a clerk at the Harrellsville post office from one of the few black postmasters in the South. At the end of the summer, having saved sixteen dollars, he persuaded Simon to allow him to enroll at the Waters Training School in Winton, the county seat of Hertford County. The tuition was four dollars for students who did not board at the school on weekends, five dollars for

those who did; so Vann signed up for four months and walked the twenty-two-mile round trip to Simon's farm each weekend. When his money ran out in January, he went back to tobacco picking and seine fishing for the spring, and worked at the post office again in the summer, until he had saved up another sixteen dollars; in October 1897 he returned to Waters, planning to stay another four months. One weekend, however, he collapsed after trudging back to the school through the snow; impressed by his spirit, the headmaster arranged for him to do odd jobs around the school so that he could afford to stay for the entire academic year, including weekends.

In the summer of 1898, Vann borrowed enough money for a train ticket to Boston, where he stayed with an aunt while working as a waiter at the Copley Square Hotel and doing odd jobs in his off-hours. In Boston he acquired some sophistication, and adopted the immaculate mode of dress that characterized him for the rest of his life. He graduated valedictorian from Waters in 1901 and enrolled at Wayland Academy, the preparatory school for Virginia Union University in Richmond. He entered the university itself the following year.

Vann got his first taste of journalism while at Virginia Union. He contributed poetry and prose to the *University Journal,* and took announcements for the debate team to the office of the *Richmond Planet.* He also acquired more social polish by hobnobbing with the black elite of Richmond.

Vann did not remain at Virginia Union long; in 1903 he won a scholarship to the Western University of Pennsylvania in Pittsburgh (the name was changed to the University of Pittsburgh in 1908). He arrived in the booming industrial city in the fall; registering for a liberal arts course of study, he rejected the registrar's suggestion that he enroll at the mostly white school as an Indian rather than as a Negro.

His studies were interrupted that winter when he received word from his stepfather that his mother was seriously ill. He returned to the farm to visit her and stayed as long as he could, then returned to school; but on the trip back to Pittsburgh, Vann himself became ill with either pneumonia or malaria, and was confined to a sickbed until spring. When he recovered, he learned that his mother had died. He spent the rest of the spring mourning and convalescing, then went to Maine to work for the summer as a waiter in a resort, where he heard a speech by Booker T. Washington. Returning to Pittsburgh, Vann began making contributions to the university magazine, the *Courant*; he was named editor in chief of the publication his senior year.

It was also in his senior year at the Western University of Pennsylvania that Vann first became involved in politics. Like most blacks in the post-Civil War period, Vann favored the Republican party—the party of Lincoln; also, at that time Pennsylvania was dominated by the Republicans. In the Pittsburgh mayoral election of February 1906, Vann worked for the candidate of the Republican machine run by William Magee and William Flinn. In the first of what was to be a long series of political disappointments, Vann saw the machine candidate lose to a reform Democrat who had the support of a rebellious faction of Republicans.

On graduation in 1906, Vann briefly considered trying to go to the Pulitzer School of Journalism in New York City, but decided that it would be more practical to stay in Pittsburgh and attend the Western University School of Law. To support himself, Vann got a job as a waiter on the Pittsburgh and Lake Erie Railroad. After he got out of class at six o'clock each evening, Vann would serve dinner in the dining car on the train to Connellsville; he would stay overnight in Connellsville and study, then serve breakfast on the train back to Pittsburgh in the morning. He completed his courses in June 1909 and passed the bar exam in December.

Vann immediately went into practice, specializing in criminal law both because he enjoyed the field and because this was the most likely area for a black attorney to make a living. On 17 February 1910 he married Jesse Ellen Matthews, a girl he had met at a dance two years previously; they had set their wedding for 16 February, but postponed it for a day so that the struggling young lawyer could handle a case that came up at the last minute.

In 1907 Edwin Harleston, a black guard at the Heinz food plant, had started putting out a weekly newspaper as an outlet for the poetry he wrote in his spare time. He had ten copies a week printed at his own expense and tried to sell them for five cents a copy. In late 1909 he decided to put his enterprise on a more businesslike footing and found some partners; they named the paper the *Courier* after the *News and Courier* in Harleston's hometown of Charleston, South Carolina. The first issue appeared on 15 January 1910; two of its four pages consisted of syndicated material, the other two containing locally produced matter. After three months, Harleston's savings were running out; his original partners, who had never had any money to put into the paper, pulled out, and Harleston found four backers. The five hired Vann, who had written some pieces for the *Courier*, to draw up papers of

incorporation. Instead of a fee, Vann was given ten shares of stock valued at five dollars apiece. The *Courier* was expanded to eight pages, and had a pressrun of about 3,000 copies a week. Harleston left the paper in the fall after some bickering among the partners, and Vann was asked to take over the editorship. His salary was $100 a year in *Courier* stock.

Vann continued his legal practice, and his successful cases appeared as front-page news stories in the *Courier;* this built up his clientele, and judges started appointing him to defend murder suspects. The paper also began giving notice of Vann's speaking engagements, and then reporting on them afterward, thereby increasing his prominence in the black community.

The *Courier* struggled for the first few years. Its offices were located above a funeral parlor; it had a staff of five, including Vann. White newsstands would not carry the paper, which was sold on the streets by high school boys and elderly men, and stocked by some black businesses. Advertising was primarily for low-cost products that blacks could afford, and brought in little revenue; occasionally the white department stores would advertise special sales and clearances. The *Courier* ran subscription contests, and then sometimes was unable to afford the promised prize to the winner, who was paid off in stock instead. Most other black weeklies in the country had similar problems, and many of them built up their circulation through sensationalism; but the somewhat prudish Vann would not permit this in the *Courier*.

In 1914 Ira F. Lewis, a part-time stenographer in Vann's law office, was hired as a sportswriter for three dollars a week; he was also offered a 25 percent commission for any advertising he brought in. Lewis immediately pulled out a sheet of paper, saying, "Well, I've already started to work. There's my first ad and I've got the payment for it in my pocket." In his first year with the *Courier* Lewis brought in more advertising and almost doubled circulation; he soon became business manager both for the paper and for Vann personally. The *Courier* moved into larger quarters that year.

During the next few years, Vann used the *Courier* to advance the cause of black improvement. In editorials, he chided blacks for not actively supporting civil rights groups such as the National Association for the Advancement of Colored People, the National Equal Rights League, and the Pittsburgh Council of Social Services among Negroes. (Vann was a charter member of the latter organization when it was formed in 1915; three years later it became the Pittsburgh branch of the Urban League.) He called for better housing conditions for blacks in Pittsburgh, particularly in the dilapidated and unsanitary Hill District, where most of the city's 25,000 blacks lived; in keeping with his free-enterprise, self-help philosophy, Vann advocated the formation of a black-owned building and loan association and real estate development business. Vann also attacked the problem of inadequate health care for blacks: only one of the twenty-eight hospitals in Pittsburgh would admit black patients except in rare cases; none of the white hospitals would accept black doctors or interns; and the University of Pittsburgh admitted very few black medical students. Vann tried to get a black hospital established, as had been done in Philadelphia, Chicago, and Washington, but the project never materialized. Vann's editorials also concerned themselves with the inferiority of educational facilities for blacks in Pittsburgh, where in 1915 there were 4,000 black students but not one black teacher. He admonished students not to drop out of school and exhorted parents to take an active interest in their children's education; he criticized a white teacher who told her students that *nigger* was a proper abbreviation of *Negro;* he advocated in two long editorials the hiring of a young black woman who had recently received her teaching certificate (she was not hired). He crusaded for more job opportunities for black workers in the steel mills and other industries, and called for boycotts of businesses with unfair hiring and firing practices. Basically distrustful of labor unions, which generally excluded blacks, Vann sometimes urged black workers to take jobs that had been vacated by strikers; at other times, rather inconsistently, he wrote that blacks should not undervalue themselves by becoming scabs. He exhorted those blacks who were employed to save their earnings.

Crime was rampant in the depressed, overcrowded black sections of Pittsburgh, especially in the Hill District. Vann pointed out editorially that the all-white police force was generally tolerant of crimes committed against blacks and of vice in the black areas; but when whites were victimized—or when elections were coming up—the police would swoop into the black areas in force and arrest masses of people indiscriminately. In one case, after a Jewish merchant was murdered in a holdup attempt, allegedly by two blacks, the police arrested 200 blacks on vagrancy charges. Vann railed against the injustice in the *Courier* and joined with two other black lawyers in getting the men released on writs of habeas corpus. Vann also criticized the white press

of Pittsburgh for its biased coverage of blacks. The white papers, he pointed out, ignored events of interest to blacks; when blacks did appear in the papers, it was usually in the role of criminals, and even then the coverage tended to be exaggerated. The *Pittsburgh Press,* for example, carried an item which claimed that two white women, after each being brutally raped by fifteen blacks, immediately ran to call the police and gave competent, rational accounts of the assault. Vann commented: "Any person of any intelligence will recognize this condition as a PHYSICAL IMPOSSIBILITY." Finally, Vann called for the passage of an equal-rights bill to outlaw discrimination against blacks in restaurants, theaters, department stores, and other places of public accommodation. One such bill, the Bass bill, had been defeated in 1911; another, the Stein bill, was introduced in 1915. Vann supported the Stein bill editorially and even went to Harrisburg to lobby for it; it passed the legislature but was vetoed by the governor. After that, Vann tended to be skeptical of the chances of passing such bills.

The Magee-Flinn Republican machine, which had been defeated in the mayoral elections of 1906, had come back to power in 1909, with William Magee himself being elected mayor. Despite the corruption of the machine, Vann and most other Pittsburgh blacks supported it because blacks received some patronage jobs from it, and also because the reformers tended to be contemptuous of blacks. In the 1917 mayoral election, however, Vann defected from the Magee-Flinn group to another Republican faction for two reasons: public outcry against the machine's corruption had reached such a level that Vann did not think Magee could win; and Magee's opponent in the primary, Edward V. Babcock, had promised Vann a political appointment in return for his support. Babcock was elected, and Vann, who had supported him heavily in the *Courier* and in public appearances in black districts, was named fourth assistant city solicitor, the highest position ever achieved by a black in Pittsburgh's government.

Vann took office in March 1918—confirmation of his appointment had been held up for over two months by the machine-dominated city council—and he quickly rose from handling routine cases involving blacks to trying appeals from the police department and all jury cases involving property. In his four years in the job he never lost a case, including one he argued before the state supreme court.

The *Courier* supported American entry into World War I; like most other black editors, Vann thought that blacks would improve their position in society by showing themselves to be good soldiers. Vann participated in Liberty Loan drives and other campaigns and gave them publicity in the *Courier,* and received good response from Pittsburgh blacks. Vann was appointed to a Committee of One Hundred to report on treatment of blacks in the armed forces, and succeeded in getting a black war correspondent sent to the front to report on black military achievements. On 23 August 1917, 100 black soldiers from Camp Logan near Houston, Texas, rioted in reaction to provocations from white civilians and police; seventeen whites and one black were killed. Thirteen of the black soldiers were hanged and the rest were sent to a federal prison. In the *Courier,* Vann acknowledged that black soldiers were subjected to insult and abuse near Southern military installations; still, he defended the severe sentences: "The honor of the Army must be upheld. Mutiny and murder are crimes that merit death upon conviction. Soldiers who participate in lawlessness must take the consequences." When the war was over, Vann said it had been too short to allow blacks to prove their merit as soldiers, and expressed the wish that the fighting had continued for another two to five years: "Had there been a larger percentage of the 'flower of America' cut down on the field, and corresponding larger opportunity thereby offered the black soldiers of the world to fill the vacancies, a higher and nobler sense of appreciation for our sacrifices would have been obtained after the Armistice."

In July 1919 a black youth was stoned when he accidentally swam into an area of the Chicago lakefront that was reserved for whites; in the riots that followed, twenty-three blacks and fifteen whites died. Race riots soon broke out in over twenty other cities. Vann's editorial response was surprisingly moderate: he blamed the whites for starting the Chicago riot, but mainly bemoaned the economic damage the riot had done to the city. After the riots had ended, the Justice Department launched an investigation which concluded that the black press had inflamed the situation and that many black newspapers were Communist dominated. The *Courier* was not named in the report, both because of its limited circulation and because of the moderate, patriotic sentiments Vann had expressed in his editorials; Vann had proved his anticommunism by supporting the deportations of Emma Goldman and other anarchists and socialists.

In the five-month strike by the American Federation of Labor against the steel industry that began in September 1919, Vann's editorials were both antiunion and xenophobic. He accused Eastern European immigrants—whom he called "hyphenated" Americans—of leading the strike, and praised blacks for staying at work and for taking the jobs vacated by the strikers. He also implied that AFL leader Samuel Gompers was a Communist. Vann shared the conservative, free-enterprise philosophy common to many self-made men; he believed that America could be a land of opportunity for blacks just as it had been for other oppressed minorities, such as the Jews, Irish, and Italians. The motto he placed on the *Courier*'s masthead reflected this outlook: "Work, Integrity, Tact, Temperance, Prudence, Courage, Faith"—personal qualities which would guarantee success. He gave extensive coverage to Booker T. Washington's self-help group, the National Negro Business League, and put the success stories of black entrepreneurs on the front page. He advised blacks to "hire yourselves, produce for yourselves, and sell something for yourselves. Let's stop going to the white man with nothing and ask them to loan us something." He pointed out that American blacks spent $2 billion a year, and said that black businesses should get a share of that wealth.

In January 1920 Vann launched a slick, heavily illustrated monthly magazine, the *Competitor,* featuring articles by eminent blacks on all facets of black life. However, at twenty cents a copy, the magazine was too expensive for most blacks; in addition, it appealed only to the small minority of highly literate blacks. Unable to secure sufficient advertising, the publication folded after eighteen months.

In July 1920 Vann made another risky move: at Ira Lewis's urging, he doubled the *Courier*'s price to ten cents in order to increase its size and add photographs. Circulation immediately dropped from 12,000 to 8,000, with some of the *Courier*'s readers going over to the *Pittsburgh American,* another black weekly which had been started in 1919. Within a year, however, the improved quality of the *Courier* brought circulation back to almost its previous level.

In 1921, Vann lost his city solicitor's job when funds for the position were cut from the budget by the city council, most of whose members still belonged to the Magee-Flinn machine. He ran unsuccessfully for a county judgeship in September; in the same election, William Magee became mayor of Pittsburgh again, eliminating Vann's chance for an appointment to another city office for the time being. Just after the election Vann became involved in a sensational murder case. A black bootlegger named Joe Thomas had been convicted of killing a white woman and had been sentenced to death; several black organizations raised the funds to hire Vann to try to have the sentence commuted to life imprisonment. Vann argued before the state pardon board that a change of venue should have been granted because of prejudicial pretrial publicity; that the mayor had made inflammatory statements before the trial; that Thomas's black lawyer had unaccountably put up no defense; that Thomas had an alibi for the night of the murder; that property of the victim found on Thomas had been planted; and that the evidence pointed to the victim's husband, who had quarreled with her the night before the murder and had hurriedly left the state, as the real killer. Vann's petition was turned down and Thomas was executed; but Vann's fame was enhanced by his able presentation, and circulation of the *Courier*—which had covered the case in detail—was increased substantially.

Vann was involved in some nonjournalistic business fiascoes in the mid-1920s. He lost several thousand dollars on a scheme to import manganese, animal hides, rubber, and cocoa from West Africa; an attempt to set up a black-owned bank also failed.

After these disasters, Vann concentrated his efforts on the *Courier* for the next few years. The paper joined the Associated Negro Press wire service in 1925, enabling it to carry more national news. Vann began to allow more sensationalism to creep into the *Courier,* although it still carried less sex and crime news than most black weeklies. Advertising from national companies such as Gulf, Lever Brothers, and Pillsbury began appearing in the paper due to the efforts of the William B. Ziff Company, a white-owned agency which handled national ads for most major black weeklies. Ziff charged exorbitant commissions of 35 to 50 percent, but guaranteed payment and eliminated collection problems for the papers. Vann hired a number of talented staffers, including the acerbic conservative columnist George S. Schuyler, who was referred to as the black H. L. Mencken. Vann estimated that Schuyler's nine-month tour of the South in 1925-1926 to report on conditions among Southern blacks and conduct circulation drives increased the *Courier*'s circulation by 10,000. Other additions to the staff included cartoonist Wilburt Holloway, features editor Floyd J. Calvin, entertainment writer Sylvester Russell, society reporter Julia Bumbrey Jones, and sportswriters Chester "Ches" Washington, Cum Posey, and Rollo Wilson. The paper also carried serialized novels and feature articles by noted black writers such as Blanche Taylor

Dickinson and Walter White. Circulation was further increased by controversies in which Vann became embroiled with other black leaders. In 1926 he accused NAACP leaders James Weldon Johnson and W. E. B. Du Bois of maintaining a slush fund; the dispute drew most of the nation's black press in on one side or the other before the principals buried the hatchet in 1929. An even more controversial issue was A. Philip Randolph's efforts to organize the Brotherhood of Sleeping Car Porters and Maids to secure better treatment of workers from the Pullman Company. Vann reversed his antiunion stand and supported the Brotherhood from 1925 until April 1928, when he suddenly turned on Randolph and demanded that he resign as head of the union. The reason, Vann claimed, was that the Pullman Company would not deal with Randolph because of his history as a socialist. Randolph replied publicly that Vann had known that he was a socialist for the past three years, and that his sudden turnabout made no sense. After that, Vann became a critic of the porters' union. Various explanations for Vann's reversal have been suggested, ranging from the theory that he wanted to control the union himself to the allegation that he was paid off by the Pullman Company.

At the end of 1929, the *Courier* completed construction of its own printing plant at a cost of $104,000. The money was raised by selling stock and by running contests, but a large part of it was either loaned or donated—it is still not clear which—by philanthropist Michael L. Benedum, head of the Benedum-Trees Oil Company. The new plant could handle any projected circulation increase and could bring in extra income from job printing, as well as saving the $25,000 a year the *Courier* had been paying a local printing company. Although furnished with secondhand equipment, the plant was one of the most modern possessed by any black newspaper in the nation.

During the 1920s, Vann had remained involved in politics as a Republican, but he had become progressively alienated from the party. Not only did the Republicans do nothing to improve the lot of blacks, feeling that they could count on the black vote anyway, but they consistently refused to reward Vann's efforts with any sort of political appointment. After campaigning for Coolidge in 1924 as vice-chairman of the Eastern Division of Colored Voters with headquarters in New York City, Vann felt sure he would be appointed to a treasury position; but he was not. In 1928 he sent out feelers to the Democrats, offering to support Al Smith instead of Herbert Hoover; but the Democrats, feeling that

Offices of the Pittsburgh Courier *around 1930. The new printing plant is at right.*

the black vote was lost anyway, failed to respond, so Vann gave lukewarm support to the Republicans once again. Hoover carried the black wards of Pittsburgh by a large margin, and Vann looked expectantly for a federal job; again he was disappointed. Hoover did offer Vann a place on a commission to plan a memorial in Washington to the black contribution to America, but Vann declined, pointing out in the *Courier* that the federal government's appropriation of $50,000 toward the memorial was contingent on the public's first raising half a million dollars. Vann backed a Republican one more time when he campaigned for Gifford Pinchot for governor of Pennsylvania in 1930; even though Pinchot carried every ward in Pittsburgh, and even though the black vote might have provided the balance of power, the victorious Pinchot offered Vann no political appointment. That was the end of Vann's allegiance to the GOP.

By the early 1930s the *Courier* had become a national paper with a local, northern, eastern, and southern edition; it was distributed in every state, as well as in Canada, Europe, the Philippines, Cuba, the Virgin Islands, and the West Indies. Each issue consisted of twenty pages. Nevertheless, the *Courier* had severe financial problems during the first few years of the Depression, and Vann was forced to cut staff salaries, ask friends for personal loans, and beg creditors for more time to pay bills. Two other black weeklies had gone out of business in Pittsburgh—

the *American* in 1928 and the *Vanguard* in 1929; another, the *Crier,* was founded in 1933, but folded in 1938. Black papers were suffering all over the country; even Robert S. Abbott's *Chicago Defender,* the leading black weekly, saw its circulation more than cut in half between 1925 and 1935.

Vann tried various schemes to increase circulation. One was the hiring of Marcus Garvey to write, without pay, a column explaining his black separatist philosophy. Garvey, the former head of the Universal Negro Improvement Association, had been convicted of mail fraud in 1923 in connection with a shipping business he had established; he had spent two years in a federal prison and then been deported to Jamaica. Even though Vann had opposed many of Garvey's positions in the past, he felt that there would be reader interest in the exiled leader's ideas. Garvey's "Negro World" column began on 15 February 1930 and ran until 31 May.

Early in 1931, the *Courier* began a campaign to have the most popular radio show in the country, "Amos 'n Andy," taken off the air on the ground that it perpetuated black stereotypes and portrayed blacks in a demeaning light. The crusade continued until the fall, and about 600,000 signatures were collected on petitions to have the program driven from the air; but the goal had been a million signatures, and the campaign died out by the end of the year.

While the "Amos 'n Andy" controversy was

going on, the *Courier* became involved in the more serious "Scottsboro boys" case. Nine young blacks had been convicted in Alabama, on shaky evidence, of raping two white women on a train, and all but the youngest had been sentenced to death. During the appeal process, the Communist-led International Labor Defense stepped in and tried to take control of the case away from the lawyers appointed by the NAACP. The anti-Communist *Courier* was one of the few black papers to come out strongly against the ILD, maintaining that the Communists were trying to advance their own interests rather than those of the Scottsboro boys, and that their inflammatory tactics would only make matters worse.

In 1932, at the urging of oilman Benedum and Pennsylvania Democratic leader Joseph Guffey, Vann came out for Franklin D. Roosevelt in a speech that rocked black America and made Vann nationally famous. In Cleveland on 11 September he said in part:

> So long as the Republican party could use the photograph of Abraham Lincoln to entice Negroes to vote a Republican ticket they condescended to accord Negroes some degree of political recognition. But when the Republican party had built itself to the point of security, it no longer invited Negro support. . . . Instead of encouraging Negro support, the Republican party, for the past twelve years, has discouraged Negro support. . . . The Republican party under Harding absolutely deserted us. The Republican party under Mr. Coolidge was a lifeless, voiceless thing. The Republican party under Mr. Hoover has been the saddest failure known to political history. . . .
>
> It is a mistaken idea that the Negro must wait until the party selects him. *The only true political philosophy dictates that the Negro must select his party and not wait to be selected. . . . I see millions of Negroes turning the picture of Lincoln to the wall.* This year I see Negroes voting a Democratic ticket. . . . I, for one, shall join the ranks of this new army of fearless, courageous, patriotic Negroes who know the difference between blind partisanism and patriotism.

The speech was, of course, printed in the *Courier;* it was also reprinted by other black papers, and Vann gave variations of it throughout the Northeast all during the campaign. In *Courier* editorials, Vann repeatedly attacked Hoover for being insensitive to black feelings and interests.

Nationwide, most blacks remained faithful to the Republicans, but in the part of Pennsylvania where Vann's influence was greatest, they came out solidly for Roosevelt. As a result, Vann finally received the federal job he had so long desired. After Joseph Guffey assured the president-elect that the appointment would not have to be confirmed by the Senate—where it might run into opposition from Southern Democrats—Roosevelt named Vann special assistant to the attorney general.

Before Vann went to Washington to take up his new post, he was chosen to act as the representative of the NAACP in the Beaver County deportation case. In January 1933, forty blacks had been arrested for disorderly conduct at a dance in Industry, Pennsylvania. After spending the night on the floor of the Beaver County jail, they were driven 117 miles in two trucks to the West Virginia border, put out into the rain, and told not to come back to Pennsylvania for two years. The incident created an uproar in the Northern white press, and a delegation from the NAACP, including Vann, presented a petition to Governor Pinchot. After an investigation, Pinchot demanded that the Beaver County district attorney prosecute the county officials on kidnapping charges, but the district attorney said he found insufficient evidence to do so. Since it was a county matter, there was nothing more Pinchot could do. Vann later tried to file charges against the Beaver County officials in federal court on the grounds that some of those arrested were residents of West Virginia. This move annoyed the NAACP leaders, who thought Vann was using the case to advance his own interests. Vann's efforts accomplished nothing, but his prestige was increased by the case.

Vann went to Washington full of enthusiasm, but quickly became disillusioned. He was not greeted by his boss, Attorney General Homer Cummings, and may never even have met him. His office was small and inadequate, and he had a hard time getting secretarial help. His duties were menial and routine, mostly having to do with checking land titles. Most of the younger attorneys in the Justice Department considered him an old-time political hack. He was able to secure a few patronage jobs for his friends back in Pittsburgh, but not as many as he had expected. Having little to do in Washington, Vann spent part of each week in Pittsburgh working on the *Courier*.

Outside the Justice Department, Vann was named chairman of the Negro Advisory Committee of the Advisory and Planning Council for the Department of Commerce in September 1933. The committee, consisting of ten prominent blacks, met for two days, hearing reports on the situation of blacks in American society. After the meetings, Vann left for Pittsburgh; in Maryland, Vann—who was a somewhat reckless driver with a long history of accidents—tried to pass a truck on a hill, collided with an oncoming car, and spent six weeks in the hospital with a skull fracture. When he had recovered, he was appointed chairman of another committee, the Inter-Departmental Group Concerned with the Special Problems of Negroes. The committee met for four months, hearing reports on how blacks were faring under the New Deal. Many examples of inequities and injustices were uncovered, but the group had no real power to do anything to change the situation. Vann finally concluded that Roosevelt was not particularly interested in the problems of blacks or committed to solving them.

In March 1934 the *Courier* launched a drive for a "Self-Respect Fund," asking readers to clip a coupon and send it in with a dollar. Initial response was good, and in April the *Courier* fund was allied with the NAACP Legal Defense Fund, which had been depleted by the Scottsboro case. A successful benefit show was held in May at the Apollo Theater in New York City with stars such as Stepin Fetchit, Bill "Bojangles" Robinson, Ethel Waters, and Cab Calloway, but similar shows in other cities, where the *Courier* did not have direct control, were financial failures. The drive soon ended, far short of its million-dollar goal.

In 1934, after long urging by business manager Ira Lewis, Vann finally broke the *Courier*'s advertising contract with the William B. Ziff Company—a move which resulted in a three-year lawsuit—and signed with the H. B. Crohn Company of New York City. Crohn's terms were much more favorable to the paper than Ziff's 35 to 50 percent commissions.

Vann and the *Courier* took an active part in the 1934 election in Pennsylvania, which resulted in the Democrats finally breaking the power of the Republicans in the state. George Earle was elected governor and Joseph Guffey, Vann's political mentor, was elected to the United States Senate. Vann was named to five state committees and was able to secure more patronage appointments. Governor Earle also pushed for and got a state equal-rights bill in 1935, something Vann had advocated since the Stein bill was defeated in 1915; however, the law carried only minor penalties, was openly defied by hotels and amusement parks, and was never enforced.

In July 1935 Vann was named to the Virgin Islands Advisory Council in the Department of the Interior, but did not take much interest in the committee's efforts to prepare the islands for independence. In September he and his wife took a cruise from New York through the Panama Canal to California. While they were in Los Angeles, the *Courier*'s pressrun reached 100,000 for the first time; the staff sent Vann an initialed copy of the final issue off the press in commemoration of the event. Vann promptly resigned from his position as assistant attorney general, using as his excuse the need to devote more attention to his newspaper.

It was the *Courier*'s continuing coverage of two stories which finally made it the country's leading black weekly. One of these was the Italian invasion of Ethiopia, which began on 26 October 1935. Ethiopia was a symbol of a proud racial heritage to many American blacks, and the *Courier* played up the invasion as a case of white imperialism against blacks. The only correspondent covering the fighting for any black American weekly was the *Courier*'s J. A. Rogers. Rogers sent back melodramatic reports depicting the Ethiopians as heroic fighters and the Italians as subhuman brutes; covered the exploits of Col. William T. Robinson, an American black who commanded Ethiopia's five-plane air force; and interviewed Emperor Haile Selassie. *Courier* coverage continued at a reduced level after the Italians took Addis Ababa and Selassie escaped to England on 5 May 1936.

The other major story which built the *Courier*'s circulation in the 1930s was the rise of Joe Louis. The paper had discovered the Brown Bomber in 1934, and began covering his every move, even calling itself the "Joe Louis paper." Virtually an entire issue was devoted to Louis's knockout of ex-heavyweight champion Primo Carnera in June 1935. Black America was plunged into mourning the following year when its hero was knocked out in the eleventh round by the German Max Schmeling; but the *Courier* covered Louis's comeback, culminating in his knockout of Jimmy Braddock for the heavyweight championship in June 1937. The following year, in a rematch against Schmeling, Louis knocked out the German in the first round.

The coverage of Ethiopia and Joe Louis, together with other features such as Vann's own reports from the Berlin Olympics in 1936 and a column by W. E. B. Du Bois the same year, made the *Courier* the leading black weekly in the nation by 1937 with an average weekly circulation of 149,000; it had briefly been as high as 250,000. The paper paid its first common stock dividend in seven years in 1936. Vann celebrated his prosperity by buying from his banker an eleven-room Tudor house, known as "Oakmont," on a large lot in the Pittsburgh suburbs.

Although his newspaper had reached a pinnacle of success, Vann's personal influence declined during the last three years of his life. In the 1938 Democratic primary election, Vann backed the losing candidates for governor and senator. The results meant that Vann's mentor and patron, Joseph Guffey, was no longer the head of the party in Pennsylvania. While vacationing in Europe that summer, Vann plotted an odd maneuver to try to put Guffey back in power. In keeping with his theory of the "liquid vote"—that idea that blacks should not let either party take their votes for granted, but should use their support as leverage to win concessions—Vann decided to come out for the Republican ticket in the general election. He reasoned that if the Republicans won, the anti-Guffey faction in the Democratic party would be discredited, and Guffey would assume the leader-

A poster advertising one of Vann's political appearances

ship again. Vann made his move two weeks before the election, and it backfired: he was roundly denounced for his defection; Guffey, the man he had been trying to help, was especially severe in his criticism, and the friendship between the two was ended. The Republicans did win, but Vann's support was not the reason: most blacks remained loyal to the Democrats. As Vann had foreseen, the Republican victory did return Guffey to dominance within the state party; but since he had now broken with Guffey, Vann received no benefit from the fact. The new Republican administration offered Vann nothing but a word of thanks for his support, and its policies were less favorable to blacks in general than those of the previous Democratic administration had been.

Vann spent most of 1939 crusading for equal treatment of blacks in the military. Realizing that complete integration of the armed forces was politically impossible, he pushed for the creation of a separate black division. Though Roosevelt made some token gestures, nothing significant was done about the matter during Vann's lifetime.

In May 1939, Vann realized a longtime dream by buying the assets of the Howard B. Crohn Company and forming the Interstate United Newspaper Company, the first black-owned newspaper advertising agency. The new company was not very successful at first, since most black weeklies preferred to stay with the Ziff Company. Had he been able to sign up the number two black paper, the *Chicago Defender,* others would have fallen into line; but the management of the *Defender,* resentful at having been toppled from first place by Vann's *Courier,* declined to purchase his company's services.

Vann's last political campaign came in 1940, when he made his break with the Democrats complete by supporting Wendell Willkie for president. He had several motives for doing so: the Democrats already regarded him as a turncoat, so that he had nothing to gain from a Roosevelt victory; he resented Roosevelt for not supporting equal treatment of blacks in the military in any meaningful way; he was opposed to a third term for any president; he objected to Roosevelt's "soak-the-rich" tax measures, which had affected him personally (he had been involved in disputes with the Internal Revenue Service since 1937); and he admired Willkie, who was, like Vann himself, a self-made man.

But before the election, Vann died of a recurrence of the stomach cancer for which he had been operated on in January. He went into the hospital on 14 October and died ten days later at the age of sixty-one. He was buried in a mausoleum he had designed with stained glass windows illustrating the important aspects of his life: the Book of Knowledge, representing his education; the scales of justice, symbolizing his legal career; and the Gutenberg press, representing his work in journalism. The *Courier* published a memorial edition on 2 November filled with tributes to Vann, including one from Wendell Willkie. Schools were named after him in Ahoskie and Pittsburgh, scholarships were established in his name at Virginia Union University and the University of Pittsburgh, a tower was erected in his memory at Virginia Union, and the Liberty ship *Robert L. Vann* was christened in 1943.

The *Pittsburgh Courier* was taken over by Vann's wife, Jesse, after his death, and remained the leading black American weekly into the 1950s. It sent ten war correspondents to cover World War II, and achieved its all-time peak in circulation, 357,212, in May 1947. Business manager Ira Lewis died the following year, and the paper's circulation began to decline, falling to 100,000 by 1960. That year the paper was taken over by a board of directors, including Mrs. Vann; but in 1965 it was sold to John H. H. Sengstacke, the nephew of Robert Abbott and owner of the *Courier*'s rival, the *Chicago Defender*. Jesse Vann died in 1967.

Biography:

Andrew Buni, *Robert L. Vann of the* Pittsburgh Courier: *Politics and Black Journalism* (Pittsburgh: University of Pittsburgh Press, 1974).

References:

"Black Purge," *Time*, 32 (31 October 1938): 13-14;

James H. Brewer, "Robert Lee Vann and the *Pittsburgh Courier*," M.A. thesis, University of Pittsburgh, 1941;

Frederick G. Detweiler, "The Negro Press Today," *American Journal of Sociology*, 44 (November 1938): 391-393;

Henry G. LaBrie III, "Robert Lee Vann and the Editorial Page of the *Pittsburgh Courier*," M.A. thesis, University of West Virginia, 1970;

Vishnu V. Oak, *The Negro Newspaper* (Yellow Springs, Ohio: Antioch Press, 1948);

George S. Schuyler, *Black and Conservative: The Autobiography of George S. Schuyler* (New Rochelle, N.Y.: Arlington House, 1966).

Papers:

Robert L. Vann's papers are at the Carnegie Library in Pittsburgh. The collection includes an unpublished biography: Harry Webber, "Vann of Pittsburgh, or the Third Emancipation," commissioned by Mrs. Vann.

Walter Winchell
(7 April 1897-20 February 1972)

Richard M. Brown

MAJOR POSITIONS HELD: Columnist, *New York Evening Graphic* (1925-1929), *New York Daily Mirror* (1929-1963), *New York Journal-American* (1963-1966).

BOOK: *Winchell Exclusive—Things That Happened to Me—And Me to Them* (Englewood Cliffs, N.J.: Prentice-Hall, 1975).

Walter Winchell developed the modern gossip column, employing a brash, sensational style to deal more intimately with the personal affairs of celebrities than other journalists had ever dared. His breezy, racy style came from his vaudeville background, and his clever neologisms became popular slang. One of the most highly paid columnists of his time, he was also able to combine an urgent delivery and show-business presentation to become a leading radio newscaster in the 1930s and 1940s.

Changing public taste, the decline of Broadway, and Winchell's espousal of a far-right political position all contributed to the demise of his career in the 1950s and early 1960s. Vendettas carried on with screeching attacks in both columns and broadcasts and touting of stock and horse tips made communications executives increasingly wary of him. He found himself isolated from his associates

Walter Winchell (United Press International)

and increasingly ignored by the media. In 1968, Winchell left New York for a lonely and reclusive life in Los Angeles and Arizona until his death from cancer in 1972.

Winchell was born near the corner of New York's Madison Avenue and 166th Street, a Harlem slum neighborhood. His parents, Jacob and Janette Bakst Winchel, were poor Russian Jewish immigrants. (Winchell later added the second *l* to the family name following a theatrical misspelling.) Jacob Winchel opened and closed several hole-in-the-wall shops on upper Broadway in an attempt to earn a living; defeated, he turned to playing pinochle and left the burden of supporting the family to Janette. After a series of separations and reconciliations, Jacob finally deserted his wife and two sons. Winchell's home life was erratic and unhappy. Often he and his younger brother, Albert, were boarded out with strangers or sent to stay with their grandmother, who ran a candy store, while their mother undertook a variety of jobs. Whenever

they could, other relatives pitched in to help Janette keep the family together. Winchell became a street-smart gang leader, and by the age of ten he was channeling his energy into gang fights and moneymaking chores.

Winchell was bored and rebellious in school. He played hookey to hawk newspapers and to indulge in his favorite pastime, vaudeville shows. When his mother, on complaint from the neighbors, forbade him to practice the songs and dances he imitated for hours, he transferred his activity to school. A failure as a pupil, he was a success as the class entertainer. After being hired as an usher at the Imperial Theater, along with George Jessel, he formed a trio which led the audience in sing-alongs during intermissions. Dreaming of a stage career, Winchell continued to fail in school and finally quit after he was held back in the sixth grade for the third time. He was twelve when he left home to join a vaudeville act, "Gus Edward's School Days." Besides Winchell and his pal Jessel, the act included Eddie Cantor, George Price, Jack Weiner, and Lila Lee.

Winchell's school became the theater, where he developed a taste for the backstage gossip with its tangy jargon, malice, and sexual innuendo. He was entranced with the headliners and acquired a lifelong adoration of stars. He was also learning showmanship—what excited people and how to manipulate them. Recognizing that he was reaching an age at which he must leave the "School Days" act, Winchell was developing a solo song-and-dance routine spiced with patter so he could go on his own. After four years, he left the act in December 1914 in Detroit and returned to New York. He got a few good bookings, then in 1916 he teamed with Rita Greene as a song-and-dance duo. He enlisted in the navy that year and spent his time in the service as an admiral's receptionist at the New York custom house.

After his discharge from the navy, he married Greene in 1920 and the two went back on the road. The act, however, never rose above second billing. It was in Chicago that Winchell pinned a typewritten gossip sheet, "Newsense," to a backstage bulletin board. It was an immediate hit and turning out these vaudeville gossip bulletins became almost an obsession with him. By the end of 1919, he was submitting items to *Variety* and the *New York Vaudeville News*. When the Winchells' act finally foundered in Birmingham, Alabama, he gave up his ideas of reaching vaudeville stardom and sought work with the *Vaudeville News*. His marriage fell apart in 1922.

Bursting with energy, the talkative young man lost no time in attracting attention. He became both columnist and advertising manager on the *Vaudeville News,* coupling the two jobs by giving advertisers favorable mention in his columns "Merciless Truth" and "Broadway Hearsay." He was resourceful in gathering material and was beginning to develop an unusual style. To compensate for the weaknesses in his formal education, he developed unique phonetic spellings and began to coin words. While still rough and rather bland, the Winchell column was beginning to emerge.

In 1923 Winchell met Elizabeth June Magee and, after a short courtship, they married. They had a son, Walter, Jr., and a daughter, Walda.

With the rapid growth of the racy, sensational tabloids in New York, it was almost inevitable that the ambitious Winchell would seek to enter the field. In 1925 he was hired by Bernarr Macfadden's *New York Evening Graphic,* primarily as a good source of stories rather than for his column. Hired at $100 per week plus a percentage of any advertising he solicited, he eventually held down five jobs at the *Graphic*: Broadway columnist, amusement editor, amusement-advertising manager, drama critic, and drama editor.

When Winchell first spiced his column with intimate gossip, he met resistance from the city editor; when he defied the editor and spiced the column again, Emil Gauvreau, the managing editor, urged Winchell to write more of the same. Within two months, the column was the paper's biggest mail puller and Winchell was given a sixty-five-dollar-a-week raise. It was not long, however, before conflict erupted between Gauvreau and Winchell as the younger man's popularity rose. The managing editor's blue-penciling led to almost daily clashes. Each man considered the other egotistical and insufferable and relations between them were glacial. Winchell was almost invulnerable to criticism, however, and was as aware as the paper's management that he was the mainstay of the *Graphic*'s circulation. Late in 1928, with the *Graphic* beginning to weaken, Winchell began to entertain ideas of switching to the William Randolph Hearst newspapers. They were offering him $500 a week, plus a $500 bonus when he signed their contract; however, Winchell's contract with the *Graphic* still had several years to run and Macfadden refused to release him. Winchell attacked the problem with his characteristic aggressiveness, harassing his publisher with phone calls at three and four o'clock in the morning. When this failed, he threatened to reveal that he, and presumably others, had seen

Winchell as a gossip columnist on Bernarr Macfadden's tabloid, the New York Evening Graphic, *during the 1920s*
(United Press International)

Macfadden, the leader of a widespread vegetarian health fad, eating meat. Macfadden capitulated and Winchell was fired on 3 May 1929. His first column appeared in the *Mirror* on 10 June.

As a top-salaried journalist, he no longer had to hustle up and down Broadway wheedling bits of gossip. Rather, he took to sitting in New York nightclubs, particularly the Stork Club, assured that the news would gravitate to his table. He wrote his items in a brash style filled with neologisms. Divorce became "cancellation" or "Reno-vation"; bandleaders were "batoneers"; people in love were "cupiding." Café proprietors invariably refused to present checks, hopeful of favorable mention. Since gangsters were deeply involved in the clubs of the era and often had girl friends in show business, Winchell's association with the underworld increased. He was on a first-name basis with the criminal world and they vied for his favor. This led to such exclusives as an interview with Al Capone and news of the gangs' plans to gun down Vincent ("Mad Dog") Coll. The latter revelation put Winchell in danger from the gunmen, and he left town, dropping his column for six weeks. Intercession by Owney Madden, a gang overlord, and a Madden-provided bodyguard eased the situation. With growing success, Winchell built an image as a supremely self-assured, tough reporter, a combative smart aleck who would take on anyone. Stung by his remarks about their shows, the Shubert brothers sought to ban him from their theaters; they soon found that his column was a more potent weapon than they could handle. They capitulated, as did Flo Ziegfeld in a similar incident. Mention in Winchell's column could make or break stars, shows, and nightclubs. He was becoming a legend.

In 1932, Winchell began to move in new directions. In spite of his belief that he talked too fast, Winchell allowed William Paley, president of CBS, to persuade him to do a radio show. Fusing his breezy writing style with his dynamic speech, he made the show an immediate success and was on his way to becoming number one in the broadcast ratings. His greeting, "Good evening, Mr. and Mrs. America and all the ships at sea, let's go to press!," together with his telegraph-key sound effects and staccato delivery at 237 words per minute, became the national model for radio news. The public loved his compressed, ungrammatical style and his ingenious word coinage. In 1951, he was able to gain a lifetime contract with ABC which guaranteed him $10,000 a week, or $1,000 a week if he became unable to perform.

In 1934, Winchell's intrusion into the Lindbergh kidnapping gave him tremendous publicity and increased his image of omniscience, convincing his readers and listeners that he had an inside track with the Federal Bureau of Investigation. When Bruno Hauptmann was arrested, however, Winchell withheld the news at FBI director J. Edgar Hoover's request, sacrificing his scoop to give the G-men a chance to get certain evidence. On two other occasions Winchell used his unique position with both the criminal world and law enforcement. In 1939 he brought Louis (Lepke) Buchalter in for the FBI when the head of Murder, Inc. feared he would be gunned down if he attempted to surrender, and in 1950 he arranged the surrender of Benedicto Macri for the murder of a labor organizer.

A far more significant change was taking place in Winchell's career during the early 1930s than his expansion into radio or his forays into the under-world. Winchell was awakening to the world of national and international politics and, although his political knowledge was shallow, his knowledge of human nature provided him an intuitive grasp of what was happening outside his own world. His columns of personals began to change to a column of principles, although the new material was sandwiched between items of gossip. He was among the first to attack the "ratzis," as he called the Nazis, and he evaluated Hitler as no different than the racketeers he had known on Broadway. In spite of the efforts of Hearst and CBS to shut him up, he was defiant of censorship and broadened his attacks to damn the "Hitlerrooters," as he referred to Fritz Kuhn and the German-American Bund, and the "Assolationists," as he branded the "America First" movement. Winchell's hatred for the Nazis and their supporters was vitriolic, strident, and unceasing. Even Hearst, whose 1934 visit to Germany had given him a more sanguine view of Hitler, could do nothing but fume and advise his editors to edit Winchell's material more carefully.

At the same time as the Nazis were the target for his hatred, President Roosevelt became the object of Winchell's adoration. In the columnist's view, his idol could do no wrong. A lasting personal friendship between the two began in 1937, when Roosevelt invited Winchell to visit him at the White House.

As the decade waned, Winchell was a force to be reckoned with because of his wide audience and considerable credibility. He had set out to warn America and to block Hitler's designs. He was succeeding and his blows, although seemingly small, were telling. He attacked not only Hitler but British Prime Minister Neville Chamberlain and those who sought accommodation with Germany. He scored beats in revealing the roles of Charles Lindbergh and Joseph M. Kennedy in the events leading to the Munich accord. He took on the isolationist senators who were out to destroy him and contributed heavily to their political ruin. Particularly noteworthy was Montana Sen. Burton K. Wheeler's attempt to knock him off the air with a bill to prohibit commentators on advertiser-supported broadcasts. Winchell attacked the bill as a First Amendment threat, and it died quickly and quietly.

Winchell spent the World War II years in a combination of naval service as a lieutenant commander, support of the administration and the war effort, and continuing vendettas with the conservatives and the isolationists. He had made many enemies, and his besting of them in many skirmishes had increased their determination to de-

Winchell and his daughter Walda at Winchell's table at the Stork Club (United Press)

stroy him. More and more of his time was spent in contention and, as time passed, he began to lose friends and supporters. When Harry S Truman became president, he sought to win Winchell's support but failed; Winchell judged Truman against his image of Roosevelt and considered him a pigmy. Winchell suffered a personal tragedy in 1946 when Damon Runyon, one of his few close friends and the only one from whom Winchell could take personal criticism and kidding, died of cancer; Winchell founded the Damon Runyon Fund for Cancer Research to memorialize his friend. Feuds developed between Winchell and columnists Leonard Lyon and Ed Sullivan and *New York Post* publisher Dorothy Schiff. Behind them all was Winchell's tremendous ego and his combativeness whenever he was challenged even slightly.

As the Cold War progressed, the Communists replaced the Nazis as the target for Winchell's hatred. Again the extremism that characterized the columnist's viewpoints was present. While Winchell had consistently reduced issues, groups, and personalities to dichotomies—all good or all bad—in the past, those he had supported were generally popular and his extremism had won considerable support. He had long been a champion of the

underdog and a staunch defender of individual rights, particularly those encompassed by the First Amendment. Now, he found his image under attack in the very areas he considered himself most invulnerable. Present at the Stork Club when the club was accused of a snub to Josephine Baker because of her race, Winchell found himself accused of tacit complicity in racism and, although he was defended by both Sugar Ray Robinson and Walter White, president of the NAACP, he had been damaged.

Winchell's strident anti-Communism led him to support Sen. Joseph R. McCarthy's Red witchhunts. An intense patriot, Winchell saw the senator as a likable individual performing a critically important task in seeking out Communist infiltrators in high places; besides, McCarthy was anti-Truman. At the same time, ironically, Winchell was denouncing Sen. Estes Kefauver and his organized crime committee for badgering Frank Costello and infringing on his civil rights. He proceeded to do an exclusive interview with the gangster, allowing Costello to present himself in the best possible light.

In January 1952, the *New York Post* opened a twenty-four-part series on Winchell, hitting heavily at his faults. Winchell collapsed into a deep depression that immobilized him for three months; then he came out swinging, attempting to categorize the *Post* as a Communist smear sheet. In December 1952, the *Post* filed a libel suit against Winchell, the Hearst Corporation, ABC, and Winchell's radio and television sponsors. The case dragged on for two years. More and more Winchell made common cause with McCarthy, and his columns were filled with forecasts of McCarthy's charges. When McCarthy fell into disgrace in 1954, Winchell was also discredited. At about the same time, the *Post* won its libel suit, and Winchell was forced to retract his statements about its Communist sympathies. He asked ABC to increase his libel insurance and when the network refused, he impulsively resigned from his lifetime contract. To his surprise, ABC accepted his resignation.

While Winchell's right-wing political swing explains his fall in part, it is far from the complete explanation. By 1960, his syndication had fallen from 1,000 to fewer than 150 papers and was continuing to collapse. The public's preoccupation with New York nightlife had faded under the impact of television, and once-brilliant Broadway had become tawdry and garish. The gossip which once titillated the public had become dull in a society where sexual matters were being openly discussed and frankly admitted.

Winchell with his former rival, Ed Sullivan

Winchell was finished, but with his extreme egotism, he saw his friends and sycophants abandoning him; he did not realize how he had changed and lost contact with reality. He found little sympathy at King Features: in his heyday he had gotten 100 percent of the syndication profits, the firm gaining only the advantage of packaging its other offerings with his popular column; now that his advantage was gone, he was a losing proposition. He tried several short-lived television news and variety shows, and even attempted to turn the clock back to his vaudeville days with a two-week stint as a dancer in Las Vegas. His only success during this period also capitalized on his fame in earlier days: he was the narrator of the popular television show, "The Untouchables," during the early 1960s. Winchell's voice lent an air of authenticity to the program, which concerned the fictionalized adventures of a group of Treasury agents battling gangsters in the Prohibition era. In his column, he continued his feuds, attacking talk-show host Jack Paar and famed party hostess Elsa Maxwell. He also took on the Kennedy administration for trying to manage the news.

The final chapter in Winchell's career began on 15 October 1963 when his flagship paper, the *New York Mirror,* ceased publication after a long printers' strike. His column was switched to the afternoon Hearst paper, the *Journal-American,* where it suffered from bad editing. In October 1965, the ailing Sherman Billingsley closed the Stork Club, which had been the seat of Winchell's power during his days of glory; Billingsley died a year later. Shortly after the closing of the Stork Club, the *Journal-American,* in a cost-cutting move, reduced the length and frequency of Winchell's column and slashed his salary. In September 1966, the *Journal-American* was merged with the *Herald Tribune* and the *World-Telegram and Sun* into the *World Journal Tribune,* and Winchell's column was cut from three times a week to one. Less than a year later, the *World Journal Tribune* folded, and Winchell's column disappeared from New York. Winchell heard that Hearst executives were planning to drop the column from syndication, but he begged for and won a reprieve. In early 1968 King Features did drop him; after being turned down by the Bell Syndicate, Winchell signed with the McNaught Syndicate.

At Christmas 1967, Winchell's son, Walter,

who had had a history of emotional illness, committed suicide at his home in California; he was thirty-five years old. Staggered, Winchell moved to his home in Scottsdale, Arizona, for a rest. He announced his retirement on 5 February 1968. Exactly a year later, his wife, June, suffered a fatal heart attack.

Winchell underwent surgery in Los Angeles for a prostate tumor in November 1969; the tumor was malignant, but he may not have been told this, because after his convalescence he was bursting with plans for a comeback. In early 1971 the *New York Mirror* was briefly revived, and Winchell was scheduled to write three columns a week; but he soon fell ill again, and returned to Los Angeles for treatment. His daughter, Walda, was his only frequent visitor at the hospital, where he died of cancer on 20 February 1972.

Brash, loudmouthed, and combative, Winchell brought a vaudeville approach to journalism and represents a high point in both tawdry sensationalism and personal journalism. Yet his career was not without positive contributions. His freewheeling approach to news gathering forced his competitors into intensified efforts, and his detestation of censorship and fearless publication of what he gathered led to important defenses of the First Amendment. While simplistic in his political views,

he was a major force in mobilizing opposition to Hitler and in winning support for the Roosevelt administration.

Winchell was a complex individual whose successes and failures both reflect the unhappy, impoverished childhood he endured. Abrasive and cynical, he was quick to criticize but could not endure criticism. Personally insecure, he hid his lack of self-confidence under a mask of toughness. Rising from poverty and impotence, he was driven by a love for wealth and power. Having grown up as a street urchin with little normality at home, he was unable to maintain normal human relationships with either his family or his friends. Needing the spotlight in his journalism as in his stage career, he had an ego that flourished when he was at center stage but failed when the spotlight dimmed.

Biographies:

St. Clair McKelway, *Gossip* (New York: Viking, 1940);

Lyle Stuart, *The Secret Life of Walter Winchell* (New York: Boar's Head, 1953);

Edward H. Weiner, *Let's Go To Press* (New York: Putnam's, 1955);

Herman Klurfeld, *Winchell: His Life and Times* (New York: Praeger, 1976).

Alexander Woollcott
(19 January 1887-23 January 1943)

Elizabeth Brown Dickey
University of South Carolina

MAJOR POSITIONS HELD: Drama critic, *New York Times* (1914, 1919-1922); reporter, *Stars and Stripes* (1918); drama critic, *New York Herald* (1922-1925), *New York World* (1925-1928).

SELECTED BOOKS: *Mrs. Fiske—Her Views of Actors, Acting, and the Problems of Production* (New York: Century, 1917);

The Command is Forward (New York: Century, 1919);

Shouts and Murmurs (New York: Century, 1922);

Mr. Dickens Goes to the Play (New York & London: Putnam's, The Knickerbocker Press, 1922);

Enchanted Aisles (New York & London: Putnam's, The Knickerbocker Press, 1924);

The Story of Irving Berlin (New York & London: Putnam's, The Knickerbocker Press, 1925);

Going to Pieces (New York & London: Putnam's, The Knickerbocker Press, 1928);

Two Gentlemen and a Lady (New York: Coward McCann, 1928);

While Rome Burns (New York: Viking, 1934);

The Dark Tower: A Melodrama, by Woollcott and George S. Kaufman (New York: Random House, 1934);

Long, Long Ago (New York: Viking, 1943);

Alexander Woollcott (photograph by James Abbe, courtesy of the Viking Press)

As You Were (New York: Viking, 1945).

PLAYS: *The Channel Road,* by Woollcott and George S. Kaufman, New York, Plymouth Theatre, 17 October 1929;

The Dark Tower, by Woollcott and George S. Kaufman, New York, Morosco Theatre, 25 November 1933.

Alexander Woollcott believed there was merit in a journalist using every available medium to further his career, and he proved his point by excelling as a reporter, drama critic, founder of the Algonquin Round Table, actor, playwright, world traveler, author, witty speaker, brilliant conversationalist, and radio's "Town Crier." But although Woollcott wrote more than fifteen books, compiled anthologies, wrote hundreds of magazine articles, appeared on radio programs, and covered opening nights of plays for fourteen years, he is most remembered not for his achievements but for his personality.

Woollcott began his journalism career as a fifteen-dollar-a-week reporter for the *New York Times.* In time, he was credited with "discovering" Katharine Cornell, Ruth Gordon, Lynn Fontanne, Alfred Lunt, Paul Robeson, and Fred and Adele Astaire. Comic W. C. Fields juggled for a living when Woollcott first wrote about him. Will Rogers was a comedian but Woollcott encouraged him to become a writer. "Nobody before, during, or since ever affected book sales as did Alexander Woollcott," according to John J. Delaney, senior editor at Doubleday. "Every bookseller in the country gathered before the radio on Sunday night to hear what books Woollcott would talk about or even mention. Even a mention by Woollcott was enough to sell thousands of copies." Writer E. B. White commented that "Nothing Woollcott did or thought escaped notice." Critic Percy Hammond called him "a mountainous jelly of hips, jowls, and torso, but with brains sinewy and athletic." He was an idol to high school and college students and has been credited with raising the role of the drama critic from that of harlot to respected professional.

Alexander Humphreys Woollcott was born on 19 January 1887 at The Phalanx, New Jersey, to Walter and Frances Bucklin Woollcott. His parents were members of a cooperative Fourierist group that lived in an eighty-five-room house. The Phalanx had been founded by Woollcott's grandfather, John Bucklin. Other newspaper people involved in this experiment in communal living included Horace Greeley and Charles A. Dana; Albert Brisbane, the father of Arthur Brisbane, also participated.

Woollcott's father, a lawyer, accountant, government clerk, and stock exchange operator, and never much of a success, uprooted the family and moved to Kansas City, Missouri, when Woollcott was two. "The son of a bitch left us dangling from the brink of insecurity over the pit of poverty," Woollcott told historian Margaret Leech Pulitzer. "What on God's good earth was there for me to love about my father? Or even admire?"

An early influence was the brother of poet Eugene Field. Roswell Field was a drama critic in Kansas City and took six-year-old Woollcott to see *Sinbad the Sailor.* Woollcott also grew close to his first-grade teacher, who predicted that he would go far.

The family moved back to The Phalanx in 1895, and the senior Woollcott went to Philadelphia seeking work. Young Alexander boarded with a family in Philadelphia so he could attend Central High School. While there he wrote book reviews and essays for the *Philadelphia Evening Telegraph* and *Record*. Never very popular in school, Woollcott turned his energy to reading. At seventeen he decided he would become a drama critic, but his dream was some ten years away. Meanwhile, he attended Hamilton College near Clinton, New York. Because of his pear-shaped body and high-pitched voice—he had been born with a hormonal imbalance and an inadequate testicular system—he avoided social gatherings and turned his attention to literary pursuits. His fraternity brothers are said to have used him to frighten away undesirable coeds. He edited the college literary magazine, joined Phi Beta Kappa, and eventually became popular with his fellow students. He founded, directed, and acted in the drama club.

He looked for work on a Philadelphia newspaper before graduation. Instead of formally interviewing with the managing editor, he visited the wife of the editor in chief. She agreed to telephone the managing editor, and as Woollcott eavesdropped, he overheard her say, "Mr. Dwyer, I don't know whether the boy will be able to write, but he should make a good reporter because he is the damnedest, nosiest person I have ever met."

Woollcott's physical problems were made worse when he suffered an attack of the mumps shortly after graduating from college in 1909. He was left permanently impotent.

After recovering from the mumps, Woollcott took a job as a messenger-clerk in the Chemical National Bank in New York. He disliked his menial duties and began hounding Carr Van Anda of the *New York Times* for a job. Eventually Van Anda hired him as an obituary writer and court reporter. He went to Halifax, Nova Scotia, to cover the sinking of the *Titanic* in 1912, and made his name as a reporter as he wrote vividly about "corpses stacked like deadwood on the wharf." However, he sometimes became too involved in his stories, and after spending weeks covering a murder case he had a nervous breakdown. Wolcott Gibbs, an editor with the *New Yorker*, found fault with Woollcott's early reporting: "He was not exactly hostile to facts, but was apathetic about them."

When the *Times* drama critic married an actress, his resignation made room for Woollcott, who began writing reviews in the winter of 1914. At that time, one unpleasant job of the drama critic was to sell advertising space to the management of the plays he reviewed. Woollcott requested that he be relieved of this responsibility, and publisher Adolph Ochs changed the policy.

Woollcott believed in writing about both strong and weak points of plays, but in 1915 he ran into some trouble with the owners of the Shubert theaters. The Shubert brothers were concerned about reviews the play *Taking Chances* might receive and ran the following advertisement:

TO THE PUBLIC

Do not believe everything you see in the notices today. And though some of the critics, lacking in humor, may try to make you believe that somewhere there is something a little bit off the line in "Taking Chances," the management is not taking any chances in extending its assurances to you that the impression is decidedly wrong. You will like "Taking Chances" just as the rest of the audience did last night, when the play scored one of the most sensational comedy hits ever known in the American theatre.

THE MANAGEMENT

Critics from fifteen weekly and daily newspapers attended the opening of the play, which received one good review from a Shubert-owned newspaper. Six writers merely explained the plot and named the actors and actresses; eight, including Woollcott, panned it. Shortly thereafter, the Shuberts gave the *Times* managing editor tickets to another play and requested that someone other than Woollcott review it. Woollcott went to the play anyway but was not allowed to enter the theater. The next morning Ochs filed for an injunction to stop the Shuberts from barring his theater critic. The *Times* also notified the Shuberts the paper would no longer accept their advertising. The battle for freedom of the press was on.

The Shubert brothers had attacked the *Times*, a relatively weak newspaper, because they wanted to teach critics and the newspaper industry a lesson. But the *Times* won the first round in the lower court. The court of appeals ruled in favor of the Shuberts, but by this time the story had been printed throughout the country. As the fight continued, Woollcott was barred twenty-two times from Shubert Theaters, but the *Times* accepted no advertising. At the end of a year, attendance was down and the Shuberts decided to allow Woollcott to review their productions. As a friendly gesture, the brothers sent him a box of Havana cigars. Woollcott remarked, "The whole thing went up in a puff of smoke." Woollcott biographer Edwin P. Hoyt credits the critic and his paper with bringing "the American theater to maturity. Before Woollcott's battle theater criticism was pap and promotion for the most part and small beer for the rest. After-

VERDUN BELLE, MARINE'S PAL, FINDS HER OWN

Trench Broken Mother-Dog Waits for Master on Battle's Rim

RETRIEVES OFFSPRING, TOO

Happy Family Reunion, Human and Canine, Is Held in Field Hospital

SEPARATED AFTER LONG HIKE

Young Soldier Started for Front With Seven Unweaned Puppies Added to His Pack

"THE COMMAND IS 'FORWARD'"

It was late in the afternoon, and a tireless Yankee regiment that had already pursued the retreating Germans across more than ten miles of France was resting for a few moments in a roadside ditch, a battered old road that wound its shady way through the ancient forest of Fère. You would have seen them all luxuriating in their breathing spell, the young lieutenants lounging comfortably, the battalion commander sitting with his back propped against a tree.

His name was Leahy—Capt. Francis M. Leahy of Lawrence, Mass., one who had done his turn in the ranks and who used to tell of the days when he was orderly to Capt. Pershing out in the Philippines. He had just caught the signal from down the road that the regiment was to fall in and move on when, whining out of space, came a German shell.

It plowed up the earth and stretched on the ground several men who were just getting to their feet, wounding some of them. It hit the tree against which the captain was leaning and snapped it off like an asparagus stalk. A piece of the shell struck the captain in the back and tore its way through his chest.

"Goodbye, boys," he said, and his head sagged forward.

Then it was as if, somewhere in the universe, a Commander Invisible had called "Attention!" Captain Leahy raised his head. With clearing voice, he spoke the name of the officer to whom it would be his duty to turn over the battalion in the event of his being called away.

"Lieutenant Hansen," he said, "the command is 'Forward.' See the boys through."

Then he died.

Two of Woollcott's anonymous contributions to the American military newspaper Stars and Stripes *during World War I* wards theater criticism rose to its stature as legitimate journalism."

In 1917, the year Woollcott's first book, *Mrs. Fiske –Her Views of Acting, Actors, and the Problems of the Stage,* was published, he joined the army medical corps as a private. After a brief stop at Base Hospital Number Nine in Paris, he was transferred to the military newspaper *Stars and Stripes.* Woollcott wrote poignant pieces about the First World War from the front lines. At that time, Pvt. Harold Ross, who later founded the *New Yorker,* was among other young soldiers on *Stars and Stripes* who would become famous journalists.

Woollcott wrote one of the most famous articles ever printed in *Stars and Stripes,* the story of Verdun Belle, a stray dog that adopted a marine. The soldier had been wounded at the battle of Château-Thierry:

> Then one evening they lifted out a young marine, listless in the half stupor of shell shock. To the busy workers he was just Case Number Such-and-Such, but there was no need to tell anyone who saw the wild jubilance of the dog that Belle had found her own again at last.
>
> The first consciousness he had of his new surroundings was the feel of her rough pink tongue licking the dust from his face. And those who passed that way on Sunday last found two cots shoved together in the kindly shade of a spreading tree. On one the mother dog lay contented with her puppies. Fast asleep on the other, his arm thrown out so that one grimy hand could clutch one silken ear, lay the young marine. . . .

By the end of the war, Woollcott had been promoted to sergeant. Returning to New York, he quickly made the transition from war reporter back to drama critic. His second book, *The Command is Forward,* a collection of his articles from *Stars and Stripes,* was published in 1919.

In 1922 he received an offer from the *New York Herald* to become drama critic at a salary of $2,000 a month; he was making about $100 a week at the *Times.* He wept as he cleared out his desk. He soon became known as one of the "Three Fat Fates of Broadway"; the others were his *Herald* colleagues Percy Hammond and Heywood Broun. In his autobiography, playwright Noel Coward wrote, "Alexander Woollcott, in a rage, has all the tenderness and restraining of a caged cobra, and when striking, much the same admirable precision." Woollcott's words became powerful. In 1921 Katharine Cornell

was playing a leading role in *A Bill of Divorcement,* which was scheduled to close after less than a week. Woollcott said to her, "This cannot close, this play. I will see that it does not close." He then told Broun, "Pull everything out for Sunday. Make your whole page 'A Bill of Divorcement.' " The play ran for two years, and Miss Cornell gave all the credit to Woollcott.

When Alfred Lunt and Lynn Fontanne first appeared together, Woollcott wrote, "They have youth and great gifts and the unmistakable attitude of assent, and those who saw them last night bowing hand in hand for the first time may well have been witnessing a moment in theatrical history. It is among the possibilities that we were seeing the first chapter in a partnership destined to be as distinguished as that of Henry Irving and Ellen Terry." Woollcott also liked the Astaires, and when Fred's musical *Apple Blossoms* opened on Broadway, he told his friends, "There is a kid hoofer at the Globe that you ought to look over." When they heard actor Paul Robeson singing at a party, Woollcott and Broun insisted he sing professionally. The former All-American football player and Phi Beta Kappa from Rutgers became a famous basso. Woollcott told friends that Ruth Gordon was the woman with whom he would most like to be stranded on a desert island, and he encouraged her to write. In 1925 Woollcott moved to the *New York World,* where his assistant was Jeffrey Holmesdale, an unassuming Englishman who took a leave of absence from the paper in order to return to England to see his sick father. The father died, Holmesdale became the fifth earl of Amherst, and a few days later he returned to his desk to resume his duties.

While Woollcott's reviews could make or break plays, his writing sometimes lacked professionalism. Most of his reviews were short and written under deadline pressure in less than an hour. He once told a critic who complained about the writing in his reviews: "If I had twice as much time, my blossom, my pieces would probably be half as long." In 1927 the actors' union, Equity, voted Woollcott "the most discriminating of all drama critics," but when his contract at the *World* expired a year later he left the daily drama reviewing forever. Years later he told Lynn Fontanne why: "My profession made me hard on watches. In my nights as a dramatic critic I used to prop mine beside the typewriter as I wrote and about once a month would knock it off onto the concrete floor. My bills for repairs at Tiffany's took about all my income. I decided I must get something cheaper and less fragile and picked out a nice plain one, in a Fifth Avenue shop, that seemed to be

THE REVIEWING STAND

By Alexander Woollcott

For the Minority, Indeed.

PUNCH AND JUDY THEATER—First bill of the Forty-niners, with sketches by Montague Glass, Heywood Broun, Franklin P. Adams, Ring Lardner, Robert C. Benchley, Dorothy Parker, George S. Kaufman, Marc Connelly, Morris Ryskind, Walt Kuhn, Howard Dietz, Bertram Blochy, Deems Taylor, Lewis Gensler and Arthur H. Samuels. In the company are May Irwin, Roland Young, Beryl Mercer, Sidney Toler, Denman Maley, Howard Lindsay and Ruth Gillmore.

An expectant audience packed the little Punch and Judy Theater last evening for the pre-release showing of "The Forty-niners," due to hold their first public revels there to-night. Here, we said, would be fine fooling. Here were some of the most gifted and most fantastic humorists of their time, summoned, for once in a way, to write their prankful whimsies under the thrall of no dull commercial manager and without a thought for that huge threatening, hydra headed halfwit—the public. Here were Ring Lardner, Franklin P. Adams, George Kaufman, Marc Connelly, Heywood Broun, Robert C. Benchley, Dorothy Parker and Montague Glass, turned loose in a little theater and bidden to cut loose. My, what fun! And then it wasn't. It wasn't fun. Not at all.

It is not any too easy to say just why. It is true that there was hit or miss showmanship about it. It is true that, like that precious "Zuleika Dobson," of which any twenty pages was always enough for us, it ran too much in the single vein—rather like a dinner consisting of five courses of perfectly splendid lemon meringue pie. It is true that it seemed depressed rather than buoyed up by the person chosen to be its Balieff—none other than May Irwin, returning to town and floundering around between the scenes, quite hopelessly out of her element. There must have been more than one old timer out front last night who yearned to call out: "Dear old friend, push this foolish little show into the wings.

get a piano hoisted up and clear the old throat for "I'm Looking for That Bully Must Be Found," or "When Mr. Shakespeare Comes to Town."

After this melancholy admission that "The Forty-niners" plunged us into a very abyss of boredom it should immediately be admitted that there were gleams of engulfed and enshrouded gayety on which we stumbled from time to time. There was one patch of delightful nonsense by Benchley—tolerably well delivered by one Denman Maley. Also a moment or two of mad humor in a languid adventure in nonsense by Ring Lardner. Also a passable vaudeville sketch by Mr. Glass which was at least second rate. And a bright morsel of a sketch by Kaufman. Also a fair to middling travesty on all the musical comedies of the last twenty-five years—this last by Franklin P. Adams. But it came at a time when its facetiousness groaned under the extra burden of waking an already hopelessly bemused audience. Indeed it must be recorded that the one thoroughly entertaining episode in all the dozen numbers of the evening was a foolish little nursery imitation of an equestrienne act, done very much a la Chauve-Souris and credited by the program to one Walt Kuhn, of whom we never heard before.

Involved in the proceedings were several excellent actors, of whom Sidney Toler seemed the best equipped for goings on of the sort invoked. His cheerfully idiotic smile could be glimpsed from time to time through the fog that settled over an evening of which we carried away this as our most definite impression—a lot of extremely clever people being given too much rope, a lot of celebrated comedians of the printed page under orders to romp around in an elfin manner and not presenting a too edifying spectacle.

As we sneaked away disconsolate into the drizzling November rain there seemed to come to us across the wet housetops a strange and embarrassing sound. It was the sound of George V. Hobart—laughing himself sick.

Woollcott's review of a production written and performed by his friends. He panned it.

encased in gun metal. Obviously it was better than a mere dollar Ingersoll watch but what if it cost $5 or $10? They told me the price was $1,500. So I went out onto the sidewalk, did some figuring on the back of an envelope and decided it would be cheaper to give up being a dramatic critic."

He began writing a column, "Shouts and Murmurs," for the *New Yorker* and wrote free-lance articles for other magazines. He demanded about $400 per printed page and usually got it. His by-line ran in the *American Mercury, McCall's, Vanity Fair, Cosmopolitan, Collier's,* and *Pictorial Review.*

Since 1925 he had been presiding over meetings of the Thanatopsis Literary and Inside Straight Club at the Algonquin Hotel. Other members of the famous "Round Table" included Broun, George S. Kaufman, Franklin P. Adams, Dorothy Parker, Robert Sherwood, Harpo Marx, Robert Benchley, Harold Ross, Ring Lardner, and Marc Connelly. When the group started to disband, Woollcott kept it together by whisking the members off to Neshobe Island, his hideaway in the middle of a lake near Bomoseen, Vermont. He invited many of his "900 best friends" and spent the summers playing croquet and exchanging gossip. He avoided inviting husbands and wives together, preferring to have the undivided attention of his friends.

Woollcott at his leisure on Neshobe Island, his hideaway in Vermont (Richard Carver Wood)

The Algonquin Hotel, site of the famous Round Table, as it looked when Woollcott and his friends met there in the 1920s (Brown Brothers)

Woollcott had become wealthy, but the 1929 stock market crash caused heavy losses. To make money he wrote advertising copy, lectured, wrote books and magazine articles, and began his love affair with radio. William S. Paley of the fledgling CBS network hired Woollcott in October 1929 as "The Town Crier" at a salary of $2,000 a week. Woollcott quickly became a national celebrity. He began the show, "This is Woollcott speaking." His comments seemed directed to an audience made up entirely of his dearest friends. He also reviewed books over the airwaves as "The Early Bookworm." A 1939 article in the *Nation* called him "the most influential salesman of books in the United States." If he said he was "quietly mad" about a book, bookstore managers ordered extra copies. He also recommended his own book, *While Rome Burns,* which received rave reviews and sold 290,000 copies in 1934.

For the next several years he edited collections of his favorite writers including Thornton Wilder, William Allen White, and Clarence Day. While some critics found fault with his selections, Archibald MacLeish, the librarian of Congress, asked

Woollcott to recommend books to go on shelves outside the study of the president. At the same time Woollcott was turning his interest toward writing plays and acting. Critics panned his first play, *The Channel Road* (1929), written with George S. Kaufman; one called it "fine writing, the sort of fine writing that turns into lead in the theater." Woollcott was the model for Sheridan Whiteside, the main character in Kaufman and Moss Hart's play *The Man Who Came to Dinner* (1939). He played the role in the West Coast company for four months in 1940 before having a heart attack. After an eight-month recovery, he traveled to England in 1941 and charmed everyone from Lady Astor to the Winston Churchills. He demanded $3,500 for a speech in America but gladly met the British for $100 a performance. Later that year, he stayed in the White House as a guest of his good friend Eleanor Roosevelt.

Woollcott enjoyed practical jokes. A friend once asked him to recommend his daughter to a prestigious private school. Woollcott wrote, "I implore you to accept this unfortunate child and remove her from her shocking environment." One evening during Woollcott's broadcast, Sigmund

Woollcott and Moss Hart at the Boston tryout of The Man Who Came to Dinner. *Hart and George S. Kaufman based the central character in the play—an insufferable drama critic—on Woollcott (Courtesy of the Algonquin Hotel).*

Romberg and the NBC Symphony Orchestra serenaded Woollcott outside his CBS studio door. A week later Woollcott took the CBS orchestra to "The Romberg Hour." Announcer Deems Taylor and Woollcott exchanged compliments until, with only five seconds of air time remaining, Woollcott said, "Deems, dear. I may throw up." This was an extremely shocking expression for radio in the 1930s.

Woollcott never completely regained his health. But he continued to invite friends to Wit's End, as he called his New York apartment, or to Neshobe Island. He sometimes greeted friends with "Hello, repulsive," and dismissed them with "I find you are beginning to disgust me, puss. How about getting the hell out of here?"

On 23 January 1943, Woollcott appeared on a CBS panel with mystery writer Rex Stout, chairman of the Writers' War Board; two college presidents; and a novelist. They were discussing the book *Is Germany Incurable?* Woollcott remarked, "I do think it's a fallacy to think that Hitler was the cause of the world's present woes. Germany was the cause of Hitler." He then wrote "I am sick" on a piece of paper and died of a heart attack.

Woollcott's obituary made the front page of nearly every newspaper in America. Even though a snowstorm stopped all traffic in New York City, more than 500 people came to his memorial service at McMillin Theatre at Columbia University. The Algonquin group gathered afterwards. George Kaufman read aloud a tribute from critic Harry Hansen: "The writing world is always beset by owlish men who demand uniformity. Woollcott's whole career contradicted them. When he told a good story mathematicians chuckled, watchmakers forgot the time and engineers put aside their blueprints. Now the landscape seems a bit grayer and more cheerless. It can't all be the fault of bituminous coal."

At the time of his death, Woollcott was a powerful literary figure—loved, hated, but above all respected for his power over the reading and listening public. He was an idol to students, a counselor to senior citizens, a public personality, a household word. But less than twenty-five years after his death, he was virtually unknown because his work was in the transitory media—radio, magazines, and newspapers—and his books were out of print, their contents dated.

Although he wrote or compiled more than fifteen books and anthologies, wrote thousands of theater reviews, hosted countless radio programs, and wrote hundreds of magazine articles, he is best remembered as the model for "the greatest critic in America" in *The Man Who Came to Dinner*.

Letters:

The Letters of Alexander Woollcott, edited by Beatrice Kaugman and Joseph Hennessey (New York: Viking, 1944).

Biographies:

Edwin P. Hoyt, *Alexander Woollcott: The Man Who Came to Dinner* (New York: Abelard-Schuman, 1944);

Samuel Hopkins Adams, *A. Woollcott* (New York: Reynal & Hitchcock, 1945);

Howard Teichmann, *Smart Aleck: The Wit, World and Life of Alexander Woollcott* (New York: Morrow, 1976).

References:

"Beginning of a Legend," *New Yorker* (30 January 1944): 11;

Wayne Chatterton, *Alexander Woollcott* (Boston: Twayne, 1978);

Noel Coward, *Present Indicative* (Garden City: Doubleday, Doran, 1937);

Calder M. Pickett, "A Paper for the Doughboys: *Stars and Stripes* in World War I," *Journalism Quarterly* (Winter 1965): 60-68;

"Wit's End," *Time* (1 February 1943): 36.

Papers:

Some of Alexander Woollcott's papers are in the New York Public Library; others are in the Houghton Library, Harvard University.

Checklist for Further Reading

Abrams, Alan E., ed. *Journalist Biographies Master Index.* Detroit: Gale Research, 1978.

Arndt, Karl J. R. and May Olson. *German-American Press Research from the American Revolution to the Bicentennial,* volume 3 of *German Language Press of the Americas.* Detroit: Gale Research, 1980.

Bartow, Edith Merwin. *News and These United States.* New York: Funk & Wagnalls, 1952.

Baumgartner, Apollinaris W. *Catholic Journalism: A Study of Its Development in the United States, 1789-1930.* New York: Columbia University Press, 1931.

Beasley, Maurine H. *The First Women Washington Correspondents.* Washington, D.C.: George Washington University, 1976.

Beasley and Richard B. Harlow. *Voices of Change: Southern Pulitzer Winners.* Lanham, Md.: University Press of America, 1979.

Beasley and Sheila Silver. *Women in Media: A Documentary Source Book.* Washington, D.C.: Women's Institute for Freedom of the Press, 1977.

Becker, Stephen. *Comic Art in America: A Social History of the Funnies, the Political Cartoons, Magazine Humor, Sporting Cartoons, and Animated Cartoons.* New York: Simon & Schuster, 1959.

Bent, Silas. *Newspaper Crusaders: A Neglected Story.* New York & London: Whittlesey House, McGraw-Hill, 1939.

Bessie, Simon Michael. *Jazz Journalism: The Story of the Tabloid Newspapers.* New York: Dutton, 1938.

Bleyer, Willard Grosvenor. *Main Currents in the History of American Journalism.* Boston: Houghton Mifflin, 1927.

Blum, Eleanor. *Basic Books in the Mass Media.* Urbana: University of Illinois Press, 1972.

Bremner, John B. *HTK: A Study in News Headlines.* Topeka, Kans.: Palindrome, 1972.

Brown, Charles H. *The Correspondents' War.* New York: Scribners, 1967.

Brucker, Herbert. *The Changing American Newspaper.* New York: Columbia University Press, 1937.

Carroll, Wallace. *Persuade or Perish.* Boston: Houghton Mifflin, 1948.

Cater, Douglass. *The Fourth Branch of Government.* Boston: Houghton Mifflin, 1959.

Chafee, Zechariah, Jr. *Free Speech in the United States.* Cambridge, Mass.: Harvard University Press, 1941.

Chafee. *Government and Mass Communications,* two volumes. Chicago: University of Chicago Press, 1947.

Commission on Freedom of the Press. *A Free and Responsible Press; A General Report on Mass Communication: Newspapers, Radio, Motion Pictures, Magazines, and Books.* Chicago: University of Chicago Press, 1947.

Conlin, Joseph R., ed. *The American Radical Press 1880-1960,* two volumes. Westport, Conn.: Greenwood Press, 1974.

Couperie, Pierre and others. *A History of the Comic Strip.* New York: Crown, 1968.

Cross, Harold L. *The People's Right to Know: Legal Access to Public Records and Proceedings.* New York: Columbia University Press, 1953.

Daniels, Jonathan. *They Will Be Heard: America's Crusading Newspaper Editors.* New York: McGraw-Hill, 1965.

Dennis, Everette E. and William Rivers. *Other Voices: The New Journalism in America.* San Francisco: Canfield, 1974.

Desmond, Robert W. *The Press and World Affairs.* New York: Appleton-Century, 1937.

Drewry, John E. *More Post Biographies.* Athens: University of Georgia Press, 1947.

Drewry. *Saturday Evening Post. Post Biographies of Famous Journalists.* Athens: University of Georgia Press, 1942.

Ellis, L. Ethan. *Newsprint: Producers, Publishers, Political Pressures.* New Brunswick, N.J.: Rutgers University Press, 1960.

Emery, Edwin. *History of the American Newspaper Publishers Association.* Minneapolis: University of Minnesota Press, 1950.

Emery, ed. *The Story of America as Reported by Its Newspapers, 1690-1965.* New York: Simon & Schuster, 1965.

Emery and Michael Emery. *The Press and America,* fifth edition. Englewood Cliffs, N.J.: Prentice-Hall, 1984.

Emery, Michael C., R. Smith Schuneman, and Edwin Emery, eds. *America's Front Page News, 1690-1970.* New York: Doubleday, 1970.

Ernst, Morris. *The First Freedom.* New York: Macmillan, 1946.

Farrar, Ronald T. and John D. Stevens, eds. *Mass Media and the National Experience.* New York: Harper & Row, 1971.

Filler, Louis. *Crusaders for American Liberalism.* New York: Harcourt, Brace, 1939.

Fisher, Charles. *The Columnists.* New York: Howell, Soskin, 1944.

Forcade, Thomas King. *Underground Press Anthology.* New York: Ace Books, 1972.

Forcey, Charles. *The Crossroads of Liberalism: Croly, Weyl, Lippmann, and the Progressive Era, 1900-1925.* New York: Oxford University Press, 1961.

Ford, Edwin H. and Edwin Emery, eds. *Highlights in the History of the American Press: A Book of Readings.* Minneapolis: University of Minnesota Press, 1954.

Gillmor, Donald M. *Free Press and Fair Trial.* Washington, D.C.: Public Affairs Press, 1966.

Glessing, Robert J. *The Underground Press in America.* Bloomington: Indiana University Press, 1970.

Gordon, George N. *The Communications Revolution: A History of Mass Media in the United States.* New York: Hastings House, 1977.

Gramling, Oliver. *AP: The Story of News.* New York: Farrar & Rinehart, 1940.

Greene, Laurence. *America Goes to Press: The News of Yesterday.* Indianapolis: Bobbs-Merrill, 1936.

Gregory, Winifred, ed. *American Newspapers, 1821-1936: A Union List of Files Available in the United States and Canada.* New York: Wilson, 1937.

Harrison, John M. and Harry H. Stein, eds. *Muckraking–Past, Present, and Future.* University Park: Pennsylvania State University Press, 1973.

Hausman, Linda Weiner. "Criticism of the Press in U.S. Periodicals, 1900-1939: An Annotated Bibliography." *Journalism Monographs,* 4 (August 1967).

Hess, Stephen and Milton Kaplan. *The Ungentlemanly Art: A History of American Political Cartoons.* New York: Macmillan, 1975.

Hocking, William E. *Freedom of the Press: A Framework of Principle.* Chicago: University of Chicago Press, 1947.

Hohenberg, John. *Foreign Correspondence: The Great Reporters and Their Times.* New York: Columbia University Press, 1964.

Hohenberg. *The Pulitzer Prizes: A History of the Awards in Books, Drama, Music, and Journalism Based on the Private Files over Six Decades.* New York: Columbia University Press, 1974.

Horn, Maurice and Richard E. Marschall, eds. *The World Encyclopedia of Cartoons,* two volumes. Detroit: Gale Research, 1980.

Hughes, Helen M. *News and the Human Interest Story.* Chicago: University of Chicago Press, 1940.

Jakes, John. *Great Women Reporters.* New York: Putnam's, 1969.

Johnson, Walter C. and Arthur T. Robb. *The South and Its Newspapers, 1903-1953: The Story of the Southern Newspaper Publishers Association and Its Part in the South's Economic Rebirth.* Chattanooga, Tenn.: Southern Newspaper Publishers Association, 1954.

Jones, Robert W. *Journalism in the United States.* New York: Dutton, 1947.

Knightley, Phillip. *The First Casualty: From the Crimea to Vietnam: The War Correspondent as Hero, Propagandist, and Myth Maker.* New York: Harcourt Brace Jovanovich, 1975.

Kobre, Sidney. *Development of American Journalism.* Dubuque, Iowa: Brown, 1969.

Leab, Daniel J. *A Union of Individuals: The Formation of the American Newspaper Guild 1933-1936.* New York: Columbia University Press, 1970.

Lee, Alfred McClung. *The Daily Newspaper in America: The Evolution of a Social Instrument.* New York: Macmillan, 1937.

Liston, Robert A. *The Right to Know: Censorship in America.* New York: Watts, 1973.

Lofton, John. *The Press as Guardian of the First Amendment.* Columbia: University of South Carolina Press, 1980.

Lyle, Jack, ed. *The Black American and the Press.* Los Angeles: Ward Ritchie, 1968.

Marbut, F. B. *News from the Capital: The Story of Washington Reporting.* Carbondale: Southern Illinois University Press, 1971.

Marty, Martin E. and others. *The Religious Press in America.* New York: Holt, Rinehart & Winston, 1963.

Marzolf, Marion. *Up from the Footnote: A History of Women Journalists.* New York: Hastings House, 1977.

Mathews, Joseph J. *Reporting the Wars.* Minneapolis: University of Minnesota Press, 1957.

McMurtrie, Douglas C. *A History of Printing in the United States.* New York: R. R. Bowker, 1936.

Moran, James. *Printing Presses: History and Development from the Fifteenth Century to Modern Times.* Berkeley: University of California Press, 1973.

Morris, Joe Alex. *Deadline Every Minute: The Story of the United Press.* Garden City: Doubleday, 1957.

Morris, Richard B. and Louis L. Snyder, eds. *A Treasury of Great Reporting.* New York: Simon & Schuster, 1962.

Mott, Frank Luther. *American Journalism: A History: 1690-1960,* third edition. New York: Macmillan, 1962.

Mott and Ralph D. Casey, eds. *Interpretations of Journalism: A Book of Readings.* New York: Crofts, 1937.

Murrell, William. *A History of American Graphic Humor, 1865-1938,* two volumes. New York: Macmillan, 1938.

Nelson, Harold L., ed. *Freedom of the Press from Hamilton to the Warren Court.* Indianapolis: Bobbs-Merrill, 1967.

Nelson and Dwight L. Teeter, Jr. *Law of Mass Communications: Freedom and Control of Print and Broadcast Media,* fourth edition. Mineola, N.Y.: Foundation Press, 1981.

Nevins, Allan. "American Journalism and Its Historical Treatment." *Journalism Quarterly,* 36 (Fall 1959): 411-422.

Nevins. *American Press Opinion, Washington to Coolidge.* Boston: Heath, 1928.

Nimmo, Dan. *The Political Persuaders: The Techniques of Modern Election Campaigns.* Englewood Cliffs, N.J.: Prentice-Hall, 1970.

Oak, Vishnu V. *The Negro Newspaper,* volume 1 of *The Negro Entrepreneur.* Yellow Springs, Ohio: Antioch Press, 1948.

Pickett, Calder M. *Voices of the Past: Key Documents in the History of American Journalism.* Columbus, Ohio: Grid, 1977.

Pitts, Alice Fox. *Read All About It! Fifty Years of ASNE.* Easton, Pa.: American Society of Newspaper Editors, 1974.

Pollard, James E. *The Presidents and the Press.* New York: Macmillan, 1947.

Presbrey, Frank. *The History and Development of Advertising.* Garden City: Doubleday, Doran, 1929.

Price, Warren C. *The Literature of Journalism: An Annotated Bibliography.* Minneapolis: University of Minnesota Press, 1959.

Price and Calder M. Pickett. *An Annotated Journalism Bibliography 1958-1968.* Minneapolis: University of Minnesota Press, 1970.

Ray, Royal H. "Economic Forces as Factors in Daily Newspaper Concentration." *Journalism Quarterly,* 29 (Winter 1952): 31-42.

Reilly, Sr. Mary Lona. *History of the Catholic Press Association, 1911-1968.* Metuchen, N.J.: Scarecrow Press, 1971.

Rivers, William L. *The Opinionmakers.* Boston: Beacon Press, 1965.

Rosewater, Victor. *History of Cooperative News-Gathering in the United States.* New York & London: Appleton, 1930.

Ross, Ishbel, *Ladies of the Press: The Story of Women in Journalism by an Insider.* New York & London: Harper, 1936.

Ross, Robert W. *So It Was True: The American Protestant Press and the Nazi Persecution of the Jews.* Minneapolis: University of Minnesota Press, 1980.

Rucker, Bryce W. *The First Freedom.* Carbondale: Southern Illinois University Press, 1968.

Rucker, ed. *Twentieth Century Reporting at Its Best.* Ames: Iowa State University Press, 1964.

Seldes, George. *Lords of the Press.* New York: Messner, 1938.

Sim, John C. *The Grass Roots Press: America's Community Newspapers.* Ames: Iowa State University Press, 1969.

Sloan, David. *The Pulitzer Prize Editorials: America's Best Editorial Writing, 1917-1979.* Ames: Iowa State University Press, 1980.

Smith, A. C. H., Elizabeth Immirzi, and Trevor Blackwell. *Paper Voices: The Popular Press and Social Change 1935-1965.* Totowa, N.J.: Rowman & Littlefield, 1975.

Snyder, Louis L., ed. *Masterpieces of War Reporting: The Great Moments of World War Two.* New York: Simon & Schuster, 1962.

Stein, M. L. *Under Fire: The Story of American War Correspondents.* New York: Messner, 1968.

Stevens, John D. and Hazel Dicken-Garcia. *Communication History.* Beverly Hills: Sage, 1980.

Stewart, Kenneth and John Tebbel. *Makers of Modern Journalism.* New York: Prentice-Hall, 1952.

Taft, William H. *Newspapers as Tools for Historians.* Columbia, Mo.: Lucas, 1970.

Tebbel, John W. *The Compact History of the American Newspaper.* New York: Hawthorn, 1969.

Tebbel. *The Media in America: A Social and Political History.* New York: Crowell, 1975.

Villard, Oswald Garrison. *The Disappearing Daily.* New York: Knopf, 1944.

Watson, Elmo Scott. *A History of Newspaper Syndicates in the United States, 1865-1935.* Chicago: Publishers' Auxiliary, 1936.

Waugh, Coulton. *The Comics.* New York: Macmillan, 1947.

Weinfeld, William. "The Growth of Daily Newspaper Chains in the United States: 1923, 1926-1935." *Journalism Quarterly,* 13 (December 1936): 357-380.

White, David M. *From Dogpatch to Slobbovia.* Boston: Beacon, 1964.

White, ed. *Pop Culture in America.* New York: Watts, 1970.

Winkler, Allan M. *The Politics of Propaganda: The Office of War Information 1942-1945.* New Haven, Conn.: Yale University Press, 1978.

Wittke, Carl. *The German-Language Press in America.* Lexington: University of Kentucky Press, 1957.

Wolseley, Roland E. *The Black Press, U.S.A.* Ames: Iowa State University Press, 1971.

Wood, James Playsted. *The Story of Advertising.* New York: Roland Press, 1958.

Contributors

Wanda A. Arceneaux ....*Louisiana State University*
S. M. W. Bass ....*University of Kansas*
James L. Baughman ....*University of Wisconsin, Madison*
Beverly M. Bethune ....*University of Georgia*
Stephen D. Bray ....*Kentfield, California*
Richard M. Brown ....*Chapel Hill, North Carolina*
Stuart James Bullion ....*Southern Illinois University*
Jean C. Chance ....*University of Florida*
Clifford G. Christians ....*University of Illinois*
Maurice R. Cullen, Jr. ....*Michigan State University*
Philip B. Dematteis ....*Columbia, South Carolina*
John De Mott ....*Memphis State University*
Elizabeth Brown Dickey ....*University of South Carolina*
George Everett ....*University of Tennessee*
Mark Fackler ....*Wheaton College*
Charles A. Fair ....*Sam Houston State University*
Ronald T. Farrar ....*University of Kentucky*
James S. Featherston ....*Louisiana State University*
Nickieann Fleener ....*University of Utah*
Jean Lange Folkerts ....*University of Texas at Austin*
Harry H. Griggs ....*University of Florida*
Terry Hynes ....*California State University, Fullerton*
Michael Kirkhorn ....*University of Kentucky*
Edmund B. Lambeth ....*University of Kentucky*
Alfred Lawrence Lorenz ....*Loyola University of New Orleans*
Steven D. Lyons ....*Louisiana State University*
Ronald S. Marmarelli ....*Central Michigan University*
J. James McElveen ....*Falls Church, Virginia*
Achal Mehra ....*University of Northern Colorado*
Jo R. Mengedoht ....*University of South Carolina*
Whitney R. Mundt ....*Louisiana State University*
James E. Murphy ....*Southern Illinois University*
Mel Piehl ....*Valparaiso University*
Nancy L. Roberts ....*University of Minnesota*
Marianne Salcetti ....*University of Iowa*
Jack Schnedler ....*Northwestern University*
Richard A. Schwarzlose ....*Northwestern University*
Charles C. Self ....*University of Alabama*
Mary Alice Sentman ....*University of North Carolina*
Caryl H. Sewell ....*Brookfield, Wisconsin*
Rosemarian V. Staudacher ....*Marquette University*
J. Douglas Tarpley ....*Evangel College*
Sally Taylor ....*Temple University*

Cumulative Index

Dictionary of Literary Biography, Volumes 1-29
Dictionary of Literary Biography Yearbook, 1980-1983
Dictionary of Literary Biography Documentary Series, Volumes 1-4

Cumulative Index

DLB before number: *Dictionary of Literary Biography*, Volumes 1-29
Y before number: *Dictionary of Literary Biography Yearbook*, 1980-1983
DS before number: *Dictionary of Literary Biography Documentary Series*, Volumes 1-4

A

Abbot, Willis J. 1863-1934..................................DLB29

Abbott, Jacob 1803-1879 ....DLB1

Abbott, Robert S. 1868-1940..............................DLB29

Abercrombie, Lascelles 1881-1938......................DLB19

Abse, Dannie 1923- DLB27

Adamic, Louis 1898-1951 ....DLB9

Adams, Douglas 1952- Y83

Adams, Franklin P. 1881-1960............................DLB29

Adams, Henry 1838-1918...................................DLB12

Adams, James Truslow 1878-1949......................DLB17

Ade, George 1866-1944...............................DLB11, 25

Adeler, Max (see Clark, Charles Heber)

AE 1869-1935...DLB19

Agassiz, Jean Louis Rodolphe 1807-1873.............DLB1

Agee, James 1909-1955 ....DLB2, 26

Aiken, Conrad 1889-1973 ....DLB9

Ainsworth, William Harrison 1805-1882.............DLB21

Akins, Zoë 1886-1958 ....DLB26

Albee, Edward 1928- DLB7

Alcott, Amos Bronson 1799-1888........................DLB1

Alcott, Louisa May 1832-1888.............................DLB1

Alcott, William Andrus 1798-1859.......................DLB1

Aldington, Richard 1892-1962............................DLB20

Aldis, Dorothy 1896-1966..................................DLB22

Aldiss, Brian W. 1925- DLB14

Alexander, James 1691-1756..............................DLB24

Algren, Nelson 1909-1981......................DLB9; Y81, 82

Alldritt, Keith 1935- DLB14

Allen, Hervey 1889-1949.....................................DLB9

Allen, Jay Presson 1922- DLB26

Josiah Allen's Wife (see Holly, Marietta)

Allott, Kenneth 1912-1973 ....DLB20

Allston, Washington 1779-1843 ....DLB1

Alsop, George 1636-post 1673 ....DLB24

Alvarez, A. 1929- DLB14

Ames, Mary Clemmer 1831-1884 ....DLB23

Amis, Kingsley 1922- DLB15, 27

Amis, Martin 1949- DLB14

Ammons, A. R. 1926- DLB5

Anderson, Margaret 1886-1973 ....DLB4

Anderson, Maxwell 1888-1959.............................DLB7

Anderson, Paul Y. 1893-1938 ....DLB29

Anderson, Poul 1926- DLB8

Anderson, Robert 1917- DLB7

Anderson, Sherwood 1876-1941..............DLB4, 9; DS1

Andrews, Charles M. 1863-1943 ....DLB17

Anhalt, Edward 1914- DLB26

Anthony, Piers 1934- DLB8

Archer, William 1856-1924 ....DLB10

Arden, John 1930- DLB13

Arensberg, Ann 1937- Y82

Arnow, Harriette Simpson 1908- DLB6

Arp, Bill (see Smith, Charles Henry)

Arthur, Timothy Shay 1809-1885........................DLB3

Asch, Nathan 1902-1964 ....DLB4, 28

Ashbery, John 1927- DLB5; Y81

Asher, Sandy 1942- Y83

Ashton, Winifred (see Dane, Clemence)

Asimov, Isaac 1920- DLB8

Atherton, Gertrude 1857-1948 ....DLB9

Auchincloss, Louis 1917- DLB2; Y80

Auden, W. H. 1907-1973 ....DLB10, 20

Austin, Mary 1868-1934 ....DLB9

Ayckbourn, Alan 1939- DLB13

B

Bacon, Delia 1811-1859..DLB1

D

H

I

J

N

O

P

Q

R

S

Cumulative Index

Cumulative Index

Y

Z